CW01467888

The Life of
CHARLES
HODGE

The Life of

CHARLES HODGE

A. A. Hodge

THE BANNER OF TRUTH TRUST

THE BANNER OF TRUTH TRUST
3 Murrayfield Road, Edinburgh EH12 6EL, UK
P.O. Box 621, Carlisle, PA 17013, USA

*

First published 1880
First Banner of Truth edition 2010

*

ISBN: 978 1 84871 090 0

*

Typeset in Adobe Garamond Pro 11/15 at
the Banner of Truth Trust, Edinburgh

Printed in the U.S.A. by
Versa Press, Inc.,
East Peoria, IL

CONTENTS

PREFACE

The family of the late Dr Charles Hodge have been assured, by those in whose judgment they have the most reason to confide, that a memoir of his life should be prepared. This was rendered probable by the fact that, although his life had been a quiet one, varied by few external events of general interest, yet it had been one of very remarkable literary activity, and of protracted and extended influence, involving an intimate association with many of the most interesting characters and events of the century. The totality of the phenomenon, including personality and achievement, was unquestionably very remarkable. It matters not whether the effect is to be attributed in the largest measure to natural, gracious, or providential endowments, the study of the causes combining to produce such an effect must be instructive. Behind every cause, whatever its nature, is the beneficent efficiency of God, and to him will be all the praise.

I undertook the work because I could secure the agency of none of those who would be more competent. That I am a son is an advantage, in so far as the relation secures special opportunities of information, and the strongest motives to diligence. It need, on the other hand, occasion no embarrassment, as I do not purpose to intrude upon others my opinions of or affection for my Father, but simply to gather and present materials through which he and his work may speak for themselves, and the opinions of the most competent among his contemporaries may be impartially reflected.

At the repeated and earnest solicitation of his children, my Father jotted down during the last year of his life some reminiscences of his childhood and youth, and of his early friends. These I have recorded in the first and second chapters of this Memoir, preserving his order and language in the first person, but interpolating additional matter of the same kind, culled from the reminiscences of my Father's only brother, the late Dr Hugh L. Hodge, of Philadelphia, dictated to his daughter-in-law, Mrs Harriet Woolsey Hodge, during the winters of 1870 and 1871. I have preferred rather to fuse the new material with that of my Father, than to keep them mechanically distinct, and have marked the words of my uncle as his only in a few instances, when the propriety of doing so will be evident.

The other sources from which these memorials are drawn are a diary kept during his residence in Germany, from March 1827 to May 1828, meagre notices of events and dates preserved in connection with his daily record of the weather, his published writings and his extant manuscripts, his own letters, preserved by his mother, brother, and friends, his correspondents, estimates of his character and services published during his life and since his decease, and especially the printed records of his Semi-centennial Celebration, 24 April 1872.

The state of his letters and papers is accurately represented by what he said in response to an application from a daughter of one of his oldest friends: 'Through my long life I have never destroyed and never preserved letters.' With much care many interesting relics have been recovered from the mass, while doubtless much just as valuable remains undiscovered.

I am particularly indebted to my Father's pupils in Ireland and Scotland, Prof. Robert Watts, D.D. of Belfast, and Mr Charles A. Salmond of Arbroath, and to Rev. Professor Benjamin B. Warfield, and the Rev. Drs Henry A. Boardman and Wm. M. Paxton, of America.

A. A. Hodge
Princeton, N.J.,
August 19, 1880

ILLUSTRATIONS

Endpapers and pictures of Miller Chapel and Charles
Hodge's House courtesy of Jonathan Watson.

NOTE: In what follows, unattributed footnotes are from the pen of Dr
A. A. Hodge, while those marked '[Ed.]' have been added to this Banner of
Truth edition, 2010.

I

AUTOBIOGRAPHY

WITH EXTRACTS FROM THE
REMINISCENCES OF HIS BROTHER

*Ancestry – Childhood – Mother – Brother – Teachers
and Companions*

DURING THE LAST YEARS of the seventeenth and the first of the eighteenth centuries, William Hodge, and Margaret, his wife, lived in the north of Ireland. They were the parents of four boys and two girls, of whom two died in early childhood and one, surviving to maturity, left no record. The father died January 4th, 1723, and the mother October 15th, 1730.

Soon after the death of their mother, the three remaining children, William, Andrew and Hugh, emigrated to America and settled in Philadelphia, where they became successful merchants and men of influence in the community. William had but one child, Mary, who in August, 1757, married Mr William West, from whom are descended the Wests, Conynghams and Fraziers of Philadelphia, and the Stewarts of Baltimore. Hugh, the youngest of the three brothers, had but one child, a son bearing his own name, who graduated in the College of New Jersey, in Princeton, in 1773, and took his master's degree in course. Soon afterwards he sailed for Europe, but the ship he sailed in was never heard of after leaving port.

His mother, Mrs Hannah Hodge, known for many years in the family as Aunt Hannah, was recognized in all the city as a mother in Israel. She was born in Philadelphia, January, 1721, the daughter of John Harkum, of English descent. Her mother, whose maiden name was Doz, was the child of a Protestant who fled from France on account of the revocation of the Edict of Nantes, 1685, and afterwards with other French Protestants, was principally instrumental in founding the First Presbyterian Church, then standing on Market Street above Second, of which the Rev. Jedidiah Andrews was pastor.

Although Hannah joined the church in 1736 or '37 she thought her true conversion occurred under the preaching of Whitefield, when her life became eminently consecrated to religious interests. When, in 1743, the Second Presbyterian was formed out of the converts of Whitefield, she was one of one hundred and sixty communicants originally enrolled. In 1745, she married Mr Hugh Hodge, who was a deacon in the Second Church from its foundation to the time of his death. They had a dry-goods store on the north side of Market Street above Second. Their house was the resort of clergymen and the centre of religious meetings. After her husband's death Mrs Hodge, although left independent, retained the business in order that she might not curtail her charities. Dr Ashbel Green, her pastor, afterwards President of Princeton College, entertained a sincere reverence for her, and concludes his memoir of her, printed in the *Panoplist*,[1] vol. 2, for the year ending June 1807, with a glowing eulogium of his friend. 'Solid sense, sterling integrity, sincere piety united with great humility, the love of truth and the abhorrence of hypocrisy were her chief characteristics. These gave her an influence among her Christian associates perhaps superior to that of any other individual.' Her house was the home of several old and infirm ladies, supported in

---

[1] *The Panoplist, or Christian Armoury*, was a monthly religious magazine edited by Jeremiah Evarts, published between between 1805 and 1820. Evarts (1781–1831) was a missionary and champion of the rights of American Indians. [Ed.]

great measure by her bounty; and here[1] also originated the weekly meeting for prayer and religious instruction observed still in the Second Church, and in most of the other Presbyterian Churches of the city. The house in which she lived was, by the will of her husband, left upon her decease to the Trustees of the College of New Jersey for the education of candidates for the ministry. This endowment has continued to fulfil the pious design of its founders up to the present time, yielding an income varying from eight to fifteen hundred dollars annually; thus constituting with a few others the foundations of a system of endowments which has since attained magnificent proportions.

Aunt Hannah died December 17th, 1805, when I was eight years old. I was present at her funeral, and was standing with my cousin, John Bayard, rather older than myself, near the open coffin. We began to cry. We thought that was the right thing to do. But his mother came up, and giving us a little shake, said in an authoritative whisper, 'Stop.' The discovery that we were making ourselves ridiculous instantly dried the fountain of tears. By such filaments the present generation is connected with the past.

Andrew Hodge, the second in order of age of the three immigrant brothers, born in Ireland, March 28th, 1711, was my grandfather. He soon became a successful merchant, and acquired considerable property. His wharf, and store, and city residence in which he spent his life, were on Water Street, to the south of what is now termed Delaware Avenue. His country seat was on Mead Lane, now Montgomery Avenue, and he possessed one of the only six carriages then in the city. He was active and influential in all the affairs of the Church and of the community, one of the

---

[1] 'The crowd being often so great as to fill, not only the parlour and kitchen, but even the back garden, close up against Christ Church ground, and much to the offence of our Episcopal brethren, who called them "Those conventicles held by Mrs Hodge".'

founders of and a liberal contributor to the Second Church, and a member of its board of Trustees to the day of his death. In 1739 he married Miss Jane McCulloch. Her brother Hugh was an elder in the Second Church, and a man of great goodness and influence, though remarkable for the great tenacity with which he held on to his own opinions. He never would consent to the assertion that the earth moves, maintaining that it was contrary alike to his own observation and to Bible authority, as Joshua commanded not the earth but the sun to stand still. His character is said to have been imbibed by our family, 'Oh! there is Uncle McCulloch' having become quite a saying among the descendants of his sister.

The religious excitement which attended the preaching of White-field in this country about the middle of the last century, gave rise to two parties in the Presbyterian Church. Those who approved of the revival were called New Lights, and those who stood aloof or opposed to it were called Old Lights. The pastor of the First Church, then the only Presbyterian Church in Philadelphia, together with a majority of the congregation were Old Lights, while a minority were on the other side. These latter were, at their own request, set off and organized into the Second Church, of which the celebrated Gilbert Tennent was the first pastor. Of this Andrew Hodge, Senior, was a Trustee, and his son-in-law, Col. John Bayard, and his brother-in-law, Mr Hugh McCulloch, were ruling elders. The Church edifice was erected on the corner of Third and Arch Streets. It was an oblong building. The shorter side on the east faced Third Street; the longer side was on Arch Street. The steeple was on the west end, and the pulpit was on the north side. Subsequently the steeple was taken down and the tower included in the auditorium, and the pews were turned round to face the pulpit, which was placed at the west end. The Church in after years was removed to Seventh Street, near Arch, where it remained during the pastorates of Rev. Drs Cuyler and Shields. The shifting of the population necessitating another removal, a lot was purchased at the corner of Twenty-first and Walnut, on which has been erected one of the most beautiful church-buildings in the city. My grandfather's pew in the original edifice on Third and Arch Streets was the front one in the middle aisle to the left hand of the preacher. The same pew, that is, the same in relative position, has remained in the family ever since. It is now held by the great-grandson of the original occupant, Dr H. Lenox Hodge, who is also a ruling elder in his ancestral Church.

These family details are of interest to those whom they concern. I wish, however, that those who come after me should know that their ancestors and kindred were Presbyterians and patriots.

Andrew Hodge and Jane McCulloch were the parents of fifteen children, eight of whom died in infancy or early life. Their eldest child, Margaret, married John Rubenheim Bayard, of Bohemia Manor, Maryland, afterwards a Colonel in the Revolutionary army. After the war he settled in Philadelphia, but during the latter part of his life resided in New Brunswick, New Jersey. His sons were James A., who married the daughter of the Rev. Dr Rodgers, New York; Andrew, a merchant, and president of the Commercial Bank, Philadelphia; Samuel, clerk of the Supreme Court of the United States, and a resident of Princeton, New Jersey; John M., who resided on the Millstone river, near to a village of the same name; and Nicholas, a physician, who settled in Savannah, Georgia. His daughters were Jane, who married Chief Justice Kirkpatrick, of New Brunswick, N.J.; Maria, who married Samuel Boyd, Esq., of New York; and Mrs Samuel Harrison Smith, of Washington, D.C.

Agnes, the second child of Andrew Hodge, Sr., married James Ashton, a twin-brother of her brother-in-law. Col. John R. Bayard, who was a surgeon in the revolutionary army, and was accidentally killed in Charleston, South Carolina. Their children were John

Hodge Bayard, who lived in Cumberland and died unmarried; Jane, whom I remember as a portly lady, dressed in the simple habit of a Quakeress, which the stricter Methodists of that period adopted; and James Ashton Bayard, Jr., born July 28, 1767. He practised law in Wilmington, Delaware, and in 1787 represented his district in the National House of Representatives. In 1804 he was chosen United States Senator, as successor to his father-in law, Governor Bassett, which position he retained until he was selected by President Madison as a Commissioner, together with Gallatin, Clay, and others, to negotiate a peace with Great Britain. His son, Richard H. Bayard, was United States Senator from 1836 to 1839, and again from 1841 to 1845. His second son, the third James Ashton Bayard in the direct line, was United States Senator for many years. And again the office has been continued in the third generation, in the person of the present Senator, Thomas F. Bayard.

A third daughter of Andrew Hodge, Sr., married a gentleman from the West Indies, by the name of Philips. She left an only child, a daughter, who died unmarried.

A fourth daughter, Mary, married Major Hodgdon, a commissary in the revolutionary army. She lived to a great age, and left many children.

The sons of Andrew Hodge, Sr., were John, a physician, who died at twenty-three years of age, and William, a merchant, who, residing abroad, was called by acquaintances on the Continent, 'the handsome American'. After the revolution he was employed in the secret service of his government and, falling under suspicion, was for a time confined in the Bastille, where he was well treated. He died when only thirty years old. Of James, the youngest son of Andrew, Sr., it is only known that he died unmarried. Andrew, Jr., graduated in Princeton College in the class of 1772, and married Ann Ledyard, half-sister of the traveller and author. He was a Captain in the Pennsylvania line during the revolution, and was present at the battle of Princeton, and used to boast that he had captured a cannon in 'Stockton's woods'. He lived to a great age, and left many children. I heard the old gentleman say that at the battle of Princeton a company from Delaware formed a little in advance of his own, broke and ran at the first fire of the British. Its Captain, who was rather corpulent, came puffing by crying, 'Run, Captain Hodge, run, Captain Hodge, we shall all be killed.' The only answer I could get to the question 'Did Captain Hodge run?' was a little laugh. He fell back, however, upon his treasure trove, 'the cannon in Stockton's woods'.

Hugh, the eighth child and fourth son of Andrew Hodge, Sr., was my father. He was born in Philadelphia, August 20, 1755, graduated in the College of New Jersey in 1773, and studied medicine under the eminent doctor Cadwalader. He was appointed Surgeon, February 7, 1776, in the third battalion of troops raised in the Province of Pennsylvania, in the service of the United Colonies. He was captured by the British, and held as a prisoner at Fort Washington, N.Y., but through the intervention of General Washington was liberated on parole. After engaging in mercantile pursuits with his brother Andrew, he returned to the practice of medicine, and soon secured an influential connection. The tradition of his fine person and attractive manners lingered among the latest survivors of his generation. He was a prominent actor in the terrible scenes occasioned by the memorable epidemics of yellow fever in 1793, and afterwards in 1795. And through the exposure incident to his labours on these occasions his constitution was impaired, and he died after protracted sufferings, July 14, 1798, at the early age of forty-three. His pastor, Dr Ashbel Green, said of him, in his eulogium, that 'as a husband, father, brother, friend and citizen, none surpassed him'.

His wife, my mother, was Mary Blanchard, of Boston. Her mother's name was Hunt, probably of English origin. Her father,

Joseph Blanchard, was a descendant of the French Huguenots. She was born in Boston in 1765, and passed her earliest years amidst the excitements preparatory to the rebellion of the Colonies against the authority of Great Britain. Of course her opportunities for education were comparatively few, but such as they were she employed them well, and early manifested a great taste for reading, often retiring from the fire-side circle to a cold room, in the depth of a Boston winter, and there enveloped in a blanket, read and committed to memory passages from Pope and Dryden, which she could repeat in after life. The physician of her family was the celebrated Dr Joseph Warren, afterwards Major-General Warren, who fell at Bunker Hill, one of the first of his country's martyrs. Her recollections of him were always very vivid, as she often sat on his lap listening to his enthusiastic discourse upon the exciting controversies of the day. She was the youngest of several children. The descendants of some of her brothers remain in Boston to the present time, while those of others are in the extreme southwest. Her brother Samuel married a niece of the Hon. Timothy Pickering, a Colonel in the revolutionary army, and afterward was Secretary of War, under Washington. Her favourite nephew, Francis Blanchard, was father of the first wife of the distinguished Mr Winthrop, of Boston. Her parents died when she was young, and her brothers and sisters, being for the most part married, she came to Philadelphia to reside with her brother, John Blanchard, about 1785, at twenty years of age, and was introduced to our family through letters to Maj. Hodgdon.

After a courtship protracted by the failure of his mercantile enterprises, she was married to my father in 1790, by the Rev. Dr Green, and went to housekeeping in the dwellinghouse on the west of the store-house, on Water street below Race, belonging to the estate of his father, Andrew Hodge, Sr., then recently deceased. On December 19th, their first child was born, a daughter, whom they named Elizabeth. She was a healthy and promising child, until in August, 1793, she was suddenly carried off by yellow fever. Their second child was Mary, born September 1st, 1792, and their third child was a little boy named Hugh, born August 24, 1794. When her little boy was about a year old, after many years of absence, my mother revisited her home in Boston, leaving her little ones in Philadelphia. Very shortly the little Mary sickened with measles, of which fact, of course, the mother was instantly informed. She immediately left Boston in the mail stage, and after travelling three days and three nights she arrived home to find that Mary was dead, and Hugh also was dying of the same disease. Thus was she left again childless. Their fourth child, Hugh Lenox Hodge, was born June 27, 1796, the year after the death of his little namesake brother. The family at this time, because of the supposed insalubrity of Water Street, removed to a house on the south side of Arch Street above Fourth, the third door from Christ Church burying-ground. Here at midnight, in the last moments of the 27th or the first moments of the 28th of December, 1797, I, the fifth and last child, was born. Aunt Hannah used to inquire for 'that strange named child, Charles', as it was a new name in the family. My father died the 14th of July the next year, leaving my mother a widow in very limited circumstances, with two infants respectively two years and six months of age.

It is no marvel that mothers are sacred in the eyes of their children. The debt they owe them is beyond all estimate. To our mother, my brother and myself, under God, owe absolutely everything. To us she devoted her life. For us she prayed, laboured and suffered. My grandfather's property yielded her for some years a comfortable income. But as it consisted principally of the Water (Arch) Street wharf, with its docks, and the warehouse and dwellings by which, on three sides, it was surrounded, its proceeds depended on the state of commerce. As the non-intercourse act and embargo which preceded the war of 1812, and the war itself, led to the suspension of commercial business, our mother's income was almost entirely cut off. This was at the time we were preparing for college. Instead of putting her children off her hands, and leaving them to provide for themselves, by sacrificing all she had, by the most self-denying economy, and by keeping boarders, she succeeded in securing for them the benefits of a collegiate and professional education, at her expense, and without loss of time. She lived long enough to see both her sons settled in life and heads of families.

It is a tradition in the family that in her youth she was distinguished for personal beauty. A gentleman from Boston, after age and illness had produced their inevitable effects, exclaimed, 'Can that be the beautiful Mary Blanchard, of Boston?' In the eyes of her children she continued beautiful to the end. Her large blue eyes never lost their light of intelligence and love.

Although thus devoted to the support and education of her children, she was always active in promoting the welfare of others. Her son Hugh has recorded his recollection of trudging by her side through the snow many squares to assist, with other ladies, in the distribution of soup and groceries to the destitute, either as donations, or at wholesale prices. She was one of the founders, and to the time of her death, an active promoter and Directress of the 'Female Association for the Relief of Widows and Single Women of reduced circumstances', which still continues, after eighty years, one of the most useful, as it was one of the earliest, of the many benevolent institutions of Philadelphia.

Having been an invalid for several years, early in April, 1832 she took a slight cold, which did not seem to be of any importance for two or three days. But this was unexpectedly followed by pulmonary congestion and slight delirium, so that she expired on the fourteenth of that month; too soon, alas, for me to see her alive, though I left Princeton in response to the first note of alarm. Her funeral services were conducted by her aged pastor, Dr Ashbel Green, who had married her, baptized her children, and delivered an eulogium over the grave of her husband.

My brother was far more than a brother to me. Although only eighteen months my senior, he assumed from the first the office of guardian. He always went first in the dark. I never slept out of his arms until I was eleven or twelve years old. I have now (1877) distinctly before my mind the room in which that crisis in my life occurred. I well recollect how quickly, after blowing out the candle, I jumped into bed, and threw the cover over my head. Having lived through that night, I afterwards got on very well. No professor in Princeton was ever able to bring up and educate a family of children on his salary. My brother, without waiting to be asked, always helped me through. He seemed to regard me as himself, and my children as his own. Although he rose to eminence as a practitioner and professor of medicine, he was revered principally for his goodness. His life-long friend, Dr Caspar Morris, said in a published letter that he 'regarded Dr Hugh L. Hodge as the best man he had ever known'. He left five sons, three of whom are ministers in the Presbyterian Church, one is a minister in the Episcopal Church, and the fifth is a Presbyterian Ruling Elder. This is due, I firmly believe, to their father's prayers, and to the influence of their excellent mother, a daughter of the late Mr John Aspinwall, of New York.

The first school to which I went was taught by an old lady in Arch Street. It was attended by a room full of little boys and girls. I afterwards went to a school in Fifth Street, opposite Independence Square, taught by Andrew Brown, a worthy elder of the Second Presbyterian Church. His specialties were writing and arithmetic. He was an adept in making quill-pens, and an expert in the use of them. His flourishes were wonderful. He must also have been a good teacher of arithmetic. At least I knew more of arithmetic then than I do now. Within a few months a thin folio copy-book, having my name in it, and dated 1807, was found among some old papers. This book is filled with solutions of questions in Barter, Profit and Loss, many of which would puzzle me to solve now. My next school was taught by an Irish gentleman named Taylor. He was a Swedenborgian. He lived in perpetual sunshine, always happy and always amiable. He took little interest in drilling his pupils in reading, writing and arithmetic. His favourite method of teaching was to get half a dozen boys around him before a large wall map of England, France, Italy, or some other country, pointing out its rivers, mountains, cities, and its ancient ruins; descanting on the elements of its population; the manners and customs of its people; its productions; its great men; mixing up geography, antiquities, history and statistics. He would linger around the battle-fields, describe the conflicts, taking part vehemently with one side against the other. He was an enthusiast, and infected his pupils with his spirit. He used to flatter them; dubbing them with the names and ranks of his heroes. My associates in this school have, as far as I know, all passed away. There were two Ralstons, two McCalls, two Reeds, James Hopkinson, John Brinton, and others [with whom the elder brother Hugh says, 'Charles, as his manner was, through his whole life, contracted intimate friendships.'] These now are all gone.

During my early boyhood in Philadelphia, my brother and myself went to a drawing-school kept in a room over Woodward's Book-store, on the corner of Chestnut and Third streets. Its master was an Englishman named Cox. He was a character. He lived in the southern part of the city by himself, in a house filled from garret to cellar with books and odds and ends of all things curious. While under his instruction I executed a landscape in water colours, which now hangs in my study, and which is considered to possess considerable merit. How the merit got there is the mystery. Those who know anything of the history of my one work of art, are aware that when painting in India ink, the teacher looked over my shoulder, and said, 'Charles, I think I could spit paint better than that.' They therefore find it hard to believe that the merit of my landscape is due to native talent on my part, and not to the intervention of my teacher.

Our early training was religious. Our mother was a Christian. She took us regularly to church, and carefully drilled us in the Westminster Catechism, which we recited on stated occasions to Dr Ashbel Green, our pastor. There has never been anything remarkable in my religious experience, unless it be that it began very early. I think that in my childhood I came nearer to conforming to the apostle's injunction, 'Pray without ceasing', than in any other period of my life. As far back as I can remember, I had the habit of thanking God for everything I received, and asking him for everything I wanted. If I lost a book, or any of my playthings, I prayed that I might find it. I prayed walking along the streets, in school and out of school, whether playing or studying. I did not do this in obedience to any prescribed rule. It seemed natural. I thought of God as an everywhere-present Being, full of kindness and love, who would not be offended if children talked to him. I knew he cared for sparrows. I was as cheerful and happy as the birds, and acted as they did. There was little more in my prayers and praises than in the worship rendered by the fowls of the air. This mild form of natural religion did not amount to much. It, however, saved me from profanity. I cannot recollect that I ever uttered a profane word, except once. It was when I was thirteen or fourteen years old. I was walking with my brother, and struck my foot against a stone, and said: 'D—n it.' My brother was shocked, and exclaimed: 'Why, Charles!!' I cannot tell why I said it. I was not hurt, neither was I angry. It seemed to me to be an effect without a cause. I felt like a very, very small Paul, when he said: 'It was not I who did it, but something dwelling in me.' I am thankful that no similar experience ever occurred to me.

In the early part of the year 1810 my brother and myself were sent to the classical Academy in Somerville, New Jersey. The village was on high ground, very healthy, and on the line of the 'Swift and Sure Mail Coach Line' between Philadelphia and New York, near the confluence of the Millstone and Raritan rivers, and between ten and twelve miles west of New Brunswick. The reason for my mother's preference for that school was not its celebrity, but its situation, only a few miles from the residence of Mr John M. Bayard, who, although only our first cousin, was old enough to exercise parental care over us. For the first six months we boarded in the family of Mr, afterwards Judge, Vandevere. His oldest daughter was then an infant a few months old. I was sometimes allowed to carry her about on a pillow. After leaving Somerville, I did not see her until after an interval of fifty years. She was then a tall, thin lady, the widow of the Hon. William Dayton, U.S. Senator and Minister to France. I could hardly believe my eyes.

I had another experience of the same kind. During my school days at Somerville, the reigning belle of that region was Miss Martina Ellmendorf. We boys used to collect around the church-door to see her in and out of her carriage. She subsequently married the Hon. Dr Condict of Morristown. Some forty years after leaving Somerville I dined at Dr Condict's, and said to him that as I had known his wife when a young lady, I should be very glad to be presented to her. He replied that she was very much of an invalid, and never left her room, but that after dinner he would introduce me. Her room was on the ground-floor; and when the door was opened, a tall, emaciated, mild and courteous lady, evidently not long for this world, rose before me. I could not help thinking that if identity could be preserved in spite of so entire a change of all that was outward, it might well be preserved between that aged believer (as she then was) and what she would be when she rose resplendent in the image of her Saviour.

During the remaining eighteen months of my stay in Somerville, I lived in the family of Doctor, better known as General, Stryker. The beautiful country about Somerville, on the Raritan and Millstone rivers, was in a great measure occupied by wealthy and refined Dutch families — the Ellmendorfs, Van Vacters, Van Esses, the Frelinghuysens, and many others. Mr John Frelinghuysen lived on the Raritan, a few miles up the river; his younger brother, Frederick, lived in the village of Millstone. He was the father of the present U.S. Senator, the Hon. F. T. Frelinghuysen. A third brother, the Hon. Theodore Frelinghuysen, so long the ornament of New Jersey, and General Stryker had married sisters. This led to his frequently visiting the family in which I lived. I thus became acquainted with him in my boyhood, an acquaintance which, in after life, ripened, on my part, into a revering friendship. I was one of those who were allowed to stand around his coffin, and gaze on his saintly countenance in the repose of death. His pronounced evangelical sentiments militated against his political success. The late Governor Seward was on intimate terms with Archbishop Hughes of New York, and called on him with the request that he would use his influence with the Romanists to induce them to vote the Whig ticket, when Clay and Frelinghuysen were candidates for the offices of President and Vice-President respectively. The Archbishop shook his head, and said: 'We could stand Mr Clay; but we cannot stand Frelinghuysen.' This was told me by a distinguished gentleman from New York. My informant was satisfied of the truth of the anecdote.

Mr Clay was also a praying man. The late Rev. Dr Edgar of Nashville, Tenn., told me that when traveling through Kentucky, he spent a night with Mr Clay at the house of a mutual friend. It was a cholera season. During the night Mr Clay was taken alarmingly ill. Dr Edgar was one of his attendants. In course of conversation Mr Clay, after expressing his faith, said that he never had introduced a measure into Congress, without first kneeling down and invoking the guidance and blessing of God.

I began the study of Latin when I went to Somerville. During the first year the academy was taught by the Rev. Mr Boyer, afterwards pastor of the Presbyterian Church in Columbia, Pennsylvania. When he went away, the school was under the care of the Rev. Mr Vredenburgh, pastor of the Dutch Church in the village. On one occasion the pulpit was filled by the Rev. Dr Livingston, long the patriarch of the Reformed Dutch Church in America. He was a patrician as well as a patriarch: tall and elegant in person, careful in his dress, a model of courtesy in manners, hair perfectly white and reaching down to his shoulders. I could not believe that Abraham was more venerable in his appearance. The only thing I recollect of his sermon is that he exhorted the people to commit to memory the fifteenth chapter of the First Epistle to the Corinthians. The exhortation took effect, for a few days after I heard Dr Stryker call upon his daughters to repeat that chapter, the doctor himself prompting and helping them through.

One summer Dr Livingston invited Dr Archibald Alexander to take a seat with him in his carriage for a few days' tour through New Jersey, to attend Bible Society meetings. Dr Alexander told me that Dr Livingston addressed every one he had the opportunity to speak to, on the subject of religion. Even the hostler, who came out to water the horses, was sure to receive some word of admonition or counsel. This was a gift which Dr Alexander appreciated, but did not possess. During the entire six weeks' journey I made with him through Virginia in 1816, I never, except once, heard him make such a personal address to any one. The exception did not amount to much. The stage had stopped for a few moments at

Charlestown in the valley, and the driver, standing by the pump, called out to a companion, whom he saw going towards an open church, 'Take care, don't go there, you may get converted.' Dr Alexander said to him, 'Do you think that would hurt him?' Yet, Dr Alexander, in the opinion of all who knew him, was second to no one in piety and zeal.

The only one of my school-mates at Somerville with whom I was associated in after life was the Rev. Peter Studdiford. During his whole ministerial life, he was pastor of the Presbyterian Church in Lambertville, New Jersey. That church rose under his care from a mere handful, to being one of the largest in the Synod. Dr Studdiford, was distinguished for learning, wisdom and goodness in the most comprehensive sense of that word.

In the early part of the year 1812 my brother and myself removed to Princeton. In order to make a home for us our mother had removed from Philadelphia and rented a small frame house in Witherspoon Street, which runs directly north, starting in front of the College. The house is still standing, next door to the old session-house, since the parochial school.

In order to aid in meeting her expenses mother received into her family as boarders several boys preparing for College, all of whom were either relations or connections. Our cousin, Alexander Hodgdon, of Philadelphia, Nicholas Bayard, son of our cousin, Dr Nicholas Bayard, of Savannah, Georgia, and two young Master Wards, stepsons of Dr Nicholas Bayard through his second marriage. These young men were the half-brothers of Jane and Margaret Bayard, the former of whom married the Rev. Dr Leighton Wilson, and spent seventeen years as a missionary with her distinguished husband in western Africa. After that protracted service she returned to this country in as perfect health as any of her contemporaries who had remained at home. A year or two after her return she said to me that she still hankered after Africa. Her sister

Margaret married the Rev. Dr Eckart, and went with him as a missionary to Ceylon, and remained there ten years, until her broken health compelled their return. There was no physician resident at their station and, as cholera often prevailed among the natives, Dr Eckart told me he always kept on hand a bottle containing a mixture of calomel and opium, and when called to a sufferer, uniformly administered a teaspoonful of the combined powder. If rejected, he repeated the dose. If retained, a cure almost always followed.

My brother entered the College in May 1812, sophomore half-advanced. I entered the Academy, then taught by the Rev. Mr Fyler, who was afterwards the head of a prosperous classical school in Trenton. The Princeton Academy then stood between the church and the house of the President of the College. It was during the same season that Princeton Theological Seminary was founded, and Dr Archibald Alexander was inaugurated its first Professor. That important service was performed in the old Presbyterian church, which occupied the site of the present First Church, August 12, 1812. I can well remember, then a boy of fourteen, lying at length on the rail of the gallery listening to the doctor's inaugural address and watching the ceremony of investiture.

One day, during the same summer, the school-room door being opened, Dr Alexander walked in. He found me stammering over a verse in the Greek Testament. The process seemed to amuse the old gentleman (just forty – old to a boy). He asked me what $\pi i \sigma \tau \iota \varsigma$ was derived from. I could not tell him. Mr Fyler apologized for me by saying I had been studying Greek only a month or six weeks. This occurrence was the first thread of the cord which bound me to Dr Alexander – a cord never broken. He never failed to notice me when I crossed his path. Frequently he would take me with him in his gig, when he went out into the country to preach. On one occasion he took me to Flemington, a court town fifteen or sixteen miles north of Princeton. I was astonished at the knowledge he displayed of the country through which we passed. He knew the character of the soil in every neighbourhood; the character of the people, whether of Dutch or English origin; the name of all the streams, where they rose and where they emptied. We were hospitably entertained, from Saturday to Monday, in the house of Mr Samuel S. Southard, then a rising young lawyer, afterwards United States Senator and Secretary of the Navy. In my young days, he and the Hon. Theodore Frelinghuysen were the two most popular men in New Jersey. Mr Southard was a handsome man, and very cordial in his manners. He had the happy tact of making every man he met feel that he was glad to see him, and really enjoyed his society. As he liked everybody, everybody liked him.

Some years afterward (in 1825) during a meeting of the Trustees of the College of New Jersey, Chief Justice Kirkpatrick was staying with me, and Mr Southard, then Secretary of the Navy, called to see him, and gave him a glowing account of the rapidity with which he had fitted out the frigate *Brandywine* to take Gen. Lafayette back to Europe. When he had finished the Chief Justice turned towards him and said, 'Now, Mr Southard, if any man should ask you which end of a ship goes first, could you tell him?' This was hardly fair in the old judge, as it is not expected that a Secretary of the Navy should be an expert in naval architecture.

2

AUTOBIOGRAPHY
(CONTINUED)

FROM HIS ENTERING THE COLLEGE OF NEW JERSEY,
SEPTEMBER 1812, TO HIS GRADUATION, SEPTEMBER 1815

Professor of Religion – Revival – Classmates and Friends

THE COLLEGE OF NEW JERSEY was founded in the middle of
the last century by Presbyterian ministers and laymen, and in
large part by those belonging to the New Light party, the especial
friends of revivals and earnest, evangelical piety. Their object, as
expressed in the public declarations of all the parties concerned
in its foundation, including Governor Belcher himself, was to
promote the cultivation of religion, and of a liberal education
in common, and especially to provide an educated ministry for
the colonies. It was founded in 1747, in Elizabeth, New Jersey;
removed in 1748 to Newark; and in 1756 permanently established at
Princeton, in buildings then recently erected for its use. For many
years the instruction was in the hands of the President, always
one of the most eminent ministers of the Presbyterian Church on
the continent, assisted by two, or, at most, three tutors, who were
young men, changing every few years. For the first fifty years there
were never more than two professors at a time, in addition to the
above, and often only one, and sometimes not one.

From the first it had been the design of the Trustees to provide
for the instruction of a Theological class. For this purpose the

Rev. John Blair, of Fagg's Manor, Pennsylvania, held the position of Professor of Theology, from 1767 to 1769, and the Rev. Henry Kollock, D.D., afterwards the eloquent preacher at Savannah, Georgia, held the position from 1803 to 1806. In the intervals this function devolved on the President at the time in office. After the resignation of Professor Kollock, an effort was made to raise a permanent endowment for the support of the Vice-President, who was also to be Professor of Theology. But in order to secure the location in Princeton of the first Theological Seminary of the Presbyterian Church, then in contemplation, the Trustees agreed that the College should withdraw from the work of theological instruction as a preparation for the ministerial profession. The Presidents, up to the accession of Dr Green, had been Jonathan Dickinson, Aaron Burr, Jonathan Edwards, Samuel Davies, Samuel Finley, John Witherspoon, and Samuel Stanhope Smith. I entered the Sophomore Class, September, 1812, a date which marks a crisis in the history of Princeton. The Theological Seminary had just been founded, and Dr Alexander, the first Professor, inaugurated August 12th, and Dr Ashbel Green, the pastor and friend of my parents, now (September 29th) entered upon the office of President of the College. The faculty that year consisted of Rev. Dr Ashbel Green, President; the Rev. Dr Slack, Vice President and Professor of Mathematics, Natural Philosophy and Chemistry; Rev. Philip Lindsley, Senior Tutor, and Mr J. Flavel Clark, afterwards pastor of the Presbyterian Church, Flemington, New Jersey, Junior Tutor.

I was examined for admission by Mr John Bergen, one of the retiring tutors. In 1842 I went to Philadelphia to attend a meeting of the General Assembly. As I got out of the cars, there was a tall gentleman walking on the platform, who stopped when he saw me, and looking down on me, said, 'I ought to know you. My name is Bergen.' 'A former tutor in Princeton College?' I asked. 'Yes', he replied. 'Then you examined me for admission into College,

Sophomore, 1812.' 'Well, I have never seen you since. What is your name?' 'Hodge.' 'Where do you live?' 'Princeton.' 'You don't tell me you are the Rev. Dr Hodge, of Princeton?' 'Yes, I am.' Turning on his heel, he exclaimed, 'Oh! Pshaw! I thought he was an old man.' The poor man felt that he had been defrauded.

In 1861 Dr Bergen and myself were again members of the General Assembly. In that year the celebrated Spring resolutions were passed. These resolutions called upon all Presbyterians, ministers and churches subject to the General Assembly to support the General Government in the civil war which had then commenced. The Northern and Southern Presbyterians then constituted one body. It was evidently proper to exhort the churches in the non-seceding states to support the government, for that was an acknowledged moral duty. But to address the same injunction to Southern Presbyterians, was to assume that their allegiance was primarily due to the General Government and not to their respective States; and that was to assume that the United States constituted a nation and not a confederacy; and that assumed a given interpretation of the constitution. As that was a political question, a large minority of the Assembly, as loyal as the majority, deemed that no Church-court had a right to decide it.

Dr Spring's resolutions, when first introduced, were promptly laid on the table by a decisive vote. But the next morning, there was such a burst of indignation from the secular press of Philadelphia, and such a shower of threatening telegrams fell upon the members, that the resolutions were taken up and ultimately passed. During the discussion. Dr Bergen was in great trouble. He came to me repeatedly, and asked, 'What shall I do? I am opposed to these resolutions, but if I vote against them, I can never go home.' I told him I was very sorry, but I could not help him. It was easy for me to act, as I had nothing to fear from giving a negative vote. When his name was called in taking the final vote, he rose and said, 'Mr

Moderator, I want to say no, but I must say yes.' That saved him. This was all the personal intercourse I ever had with Dr Bergen. I am, therefore, surprised at the glow of kindly feeling of which I am conscious whenever I hear his name mentioned.

Dr Green conducted the instruction in the Biblical Department, in Belles-Lettres, Moral Philosophy and Logic. We regularly had lessons in the Bible. On one occasion, while reciting on the Acts of the Apostles, Dr Green asked me: 'Was St Paul ever at Malta?' I replied: 'Yes, sir, he touched there on his voyage to Rome.' 'Pretty hard touch,' whispered Johns (the Rt. Rev. John Johns, Bishop of Virginia), who as usual was sitting next to me. Of course, the apostle's shipwreck on that island flashed on my memory; and of course I laughed, and of course I was reproved. That was the kind of trouble Johns was always getting me into. We were also required to commit the Shorter Catechism to memory in Latin. The Episcopal students were allowed to study their own catechism. As that is shorter than the Westminster, many Presbyterians passed themselves off for the time being as Episcopalians. The doctor, to be even with them, required all who took the Episcopal Catechism, to prepare also for examination the Thirty-nine Articles. We attended worship every Sabbath morning in the Chapel. Dr Green also lectured every Thursday evening in one of the College recitation rooms. These lectures were very instructive, and were attended by a crowded audience.

In the department of Belles-Lettres, we studied Blair's *Lectures in Moral Philosophy*, Witherspoon's *Lectures*, and in Logic, Andrew's *Logic* – a little book about as large as an Almanac, which we got through in four recitations. I am ashamed to say that this is the only book on Logic I ever read. Some years ago a very intelligent Catholic priest came to Princeton (to the village, not to the Seminary), to spend a few months in retirement and study. His faith in the fundamental doctrines of Romanism having been shaken, to avoid trouble, he came first to America, and then to Princeton, to seclude himself while engaged in investigating and settling the questions involved. I think I never saw such concentration and power as he exhibited for two or three months in examining the controversy between Protestants and Romanists. He never revealed his conclusion. I asked him many questions as to the method of instruction observed in Maynooth,[1] where he had been educated. I asked particularly what was the effect of the study of the so-called 'Moral Theology', designed to prepare a priest for the duties of a confessor. He answered, 'Entirely to destroy the moral sense.' That was precisely the answer I expected, which is no disparagement of moral philosophy as a science, but only of the methods at Maynooth. So it is no disparagement to logic as a science or an art, to say, that the excessive study how to reason often impairs the ability to reason. The best way to make a man a good carpenter is not to confine his attention to his tools, but to set him to work. So, as has often been said, the best way to make a logician is to set him to study Euclid, or, as any old student of Princeton Seminary would say, set him to study Turretin.[2]

Our instructor in Greek was the Rev. Philip Lindsley. He graduated at the College of New Jersey in 1804, in the class with the Hon. Theodore Frelinghuysen, the Hon. Joseph R. Ingersoll, and the Hon. Samuel L. Southard. Mr Southard continued his intimate friend through life. During our first term Mr Lindsley was senior tutor. In the spring of 1813 he was elected Professor of Languages; afterwards he was chosen Vice-President; and on the resignation of Dr Green, in 1822, he was elected President of the College. This office he declined on impulse. He disliked some of the Trustees very much; and when his election was announced to him, having

[1] Roman Catholic seminary near Dublin, founded in 1795. [Ed.]
[2] Francis Turretin (1623–87), Professor of Theology in Geneva. His *Institutio Theologiae Elencticae* was the textbook at Princeton Seminary. [Ed.]

them in his mind, he promptly declined. I called to see him the next morning, and found him walking up and down his study a good deal perturbed. He exclaimed: 'If Sam Southard (one of the Trustees) had been here, I would now be President of Princeton College.' He was also offered the Presidency of Dickinson College, Pennsylvania, of Transylvania University, Kentucky, and of several other educational institutions, and finally accepted that of the University of Tennessee, at Nashville, where he spent most of the remaining active part of his life. His works have been collected and published in two handsome octavo volumes under the editorship of the Rev. Dr Halsey of Chicago.

Prof. Lindsley was very popular with the students. He was rather above the medium size, erect and imposing in his carriage. He used to walk up and down the lecture-room, while hearing our recitations, with his book closed in his hands. He was very fond of paradox. He told our class that we would find that one of the best preparations for death was a thorough knowledge of the Greek grammar. This was his way of telling us that we ought to do our duty. It was a favourite idea of his that civilization reached its highest stage before the Deluge; that the arts and sciences have never since reached the development which they attained among the antediluvians. He was a very frequent attendant on the debating society held years ago every Friday evening, in the Seminary, under the presidency of professors. He was sure to take the wrong side; Popery against Protestantism; heresy against orthodoxy. He was very kind to me. I had a crooked tongue, and had been studying Greek only six months before entering the Sophomore class, while some of my class-mates had been teaching Greek two years before coming to College. But the professor did all he could for me, pushing me up as high as his conscience would permit. He and old Dr Slack succeeded at last in getting me up very near the top. On several occasions in after life, I experienced his kindness.

The last time I saw him was during the sessions of the General Assembly in Buffalo, in 1854. I have always cherished his memory with affectionate regard.

When I entered College the faculty consisted of the President, one professor and two tutors. Now it has a corps of twenty-eight or thirty instructors. The departments then filled by one professor are now distributed among eight.

Dr Green says, in his autobiography[1] that when he entered on his duties as President, 'The several members of the faculty before the expiration of the vacation met in my study, and at my instance we agreed to set apart a day of special prayer, in view of the duties before us. We prayed once together, and then the several members spent the day in private prayer.' This was the spirit in which his administration was begun and continued to the end. The religious culture of the students was always uppermost in his mind. He preached regularly in the chapel on Sunday morning, introduced the regular study of the Bible, and lectured every Tuesday evening. When Dr Miller came to Princeton, in the summer of 1813, he, with Dr Alexander and Dr Green, preached in succession in the chapel to the students of the College and Seminary, the latter at that time being very few in number. Dr Alexander soon began to preach regularly every Sunday evening, at first in the junior recitation room, the southern half of the basement of the Old Library building (now the Treasurer's Office), which is still standing. That room is to this day sacred in the eyes of the old students of the College. It was then, and for forty years afterwards, the birth-place of many souls. We were thus brought under the influence of a man who, as an 'experimental' preacher, was unequalled and unapproached. It was said of him, that while most other ministers preached about religion, he preached religion. He recognized the fact that

---

[1] *The Life of the Rev. Ashbel Green, D.D.*, written by himself and prepared for the press by the Rev. Joseph Jones, D.D.

the religious and moral elements of our nature are universal and indestructible; and that these elements, in Christian countries at least, are so developed that every man knows that there is a God on whom he is dependent, and to whom he is responsible; that he is a sinner and deserves to be punished; and that punishment is inevitable. He is therefore, all his life, through fear of death, subject to bondage (*Heb.* 2:15). No matter how reckless and hardened the wicked may become, they can never free themselves from their fetters; and, at times, the horror of great darkness falls upon them, and they wish they had never been born. Dr Alexander revealed such men to themselves; showed them how vain it was to struggle against the laws of nature; that conscience was their master, and could neither be silenced nor sophisticated [falsified]; that all their efforts to make themselves infidels were abortive; that no devotion to the world, that no degradation in vice can obliterate the conviction that those who commit sin are doomed to the second death; that however calm may be the surface, there is always the rumbling of an earthquake underneath – 'a fearful looking for of judgment, and fiery indignation, which shall devour the adversaries'. There was a noted man at this time in Princeton who said, 'He was sure Dr Alexander must have been very wicked in his youth, or he could not know so well how wicked men felt.'

In like manner he would detail the experience of those under the conviction of sin; show how such convictions often came to nothing; what was essential, and what incidental and variable in such experiences. He would take the serious inquirer by the hand, and tell him all about himself, leading him along from point to point, until the inquirer was left behind, and could do nothing but sit and weep. He knew that he was a sinner, that he needed salvation, that he could not save himself, but when told to come to Christ, he knew not what to do. Often, going to his room, he would fall on his knees and call on his Saviour, and ask, 'Is this coming?', or

'Is this coming?' He never could understand what it was until it was done. It was easy to tell him that faith is simply letting go all other confidences and falling trustfully into the Saviour's arms, but no one knows what seeing is until he sees, or what believing is until he believes.

So also more advanced Christians, whether doubting, tempted, despondmg or rejoicing, were all subject to the same self-revealing process, all edified and strengthened. Those were memorable days.

[Charles Hodge's brother, Dr Hugh L. Hodge, says: 'In the spring of 1813, the boys, our cousins, who had become our mother's boarders a year before, having either left town or removed their lodgings to the college building, Mrs Dr Bache, of Philadelphia, and her children, became inmates in our family. Dr William Bache, then deceased, was a grandson of the celebrated Benjamin Franklin. Mrs Bache, his widow, was the sister of Dr Caspar Wistar, Professor of Anatomy in the University of Pennsylvania, and President of the American Philosophical Society. His house had become the centre of the literary and scientific society of Philadelphia. He was in the habit of receiving his friends to a frugal entertainment every Saturday evening. To these re-unions, the most distinguished foreign visitors in the city brought introductions, and the most intellectual of the professional residents gathered. And they have been continued, with their essential characteristics unchanged, to the present time, in the reunions of what has ever since been known as the Wistar Club. Mrs Bache, a very superior and high-toned woman, had, previous to her marriage, kept house for her brother for several years, during which time, she with her friend Miss Eddy, afterwards, Mrs Dr Hosack of New York, had the great pleasure and advantage of attending these remarkable Saturday evening meetings. Her children, who now entered our family, were Catharine, the youngest, a girl then of seven or eight, Benjamin

Franklin, since the head of the Pharmaceutical Department of the United States Navy, Brooklyn, N.Y., and Sarah, the eldest, then a girl of fourteen years of age, well-grown, in blooming health, handsome, full of imagination, and exceedingly enthusiastic, unconscious of self and absorbed in whatever claimed her attention; a most agreeable companion. It was no wonder, therefore, that she soon won the love of my brother Charles, young as he was, an experience which, nine years afterwards, in 1822, resulted in their marriage.']

My brother Hugh graduated from College in the fall of 1814, one of the four to whom the first honour was assigned. The commencement of that year was marked by an event of great interest. It occurred towards the close of the war of 1812 with the British, and soon after the brilliant victories of Lundy's Lane and Chippewa. Major-General Winfield Scott, the hero of those battles, then Colonel and Brigadier-General Scott, having been severely wounded in one of his shoulders, was making slow journeys from the Lakes to his home, in Virginia. He arrived in Princeton after the exercises began, and, though weak and emaciated, he accepted an invitation to enter the Church and take a seat on the stage with the President and Trustees of the College. He was received with every possible demonstration of enthusiasm. The degrees having been conferred, Bloomfield McIlvaine, brother of Charles Pettit McIlvaine, afterwards the Protestant Episcopal Bishop of Ohio, delivered the valedictory. After having delivered the valedictory he had prepared to the President, Trustees, class-mates, and undergraduates, he suddenly turned to General Scott, and with astonishing facility of extemporaneous conception and expression, he delivered an eloquent and moving eulogium. The General afterwards confessed that he 'would not have been more taken by surprise if he had been suddenly attacked by a whole regiment of Britishers'. He attempted to rise more than once, and finally was forced, by his emotions and physical weakness, to remain quiescent. He afterwards confessed to my brother that 'few attentions had ever given him so much, and so lasting pleasure'.

[On January 13th, 1815, Charles Hodge and his friend, Kensey John Van Dyke, of the class below him, made a public confession of their faith in Christ by joining the Presbyterian Church of Princeton, of which the Rev. William C. Schenck was the pastor. The venerable Dr John Maclean, who survives his friends, says he well remembers the Saturday when he was startled in the street by Edward Allen rushing to him with the abrupt announcement that 'Hodge had enlisted' – for the war with Britain had not yet closed, and a sergeant with a drummer was in the village endeavouring to enlist recruits. 'Is it possible', he exclaimed, 'that Hodge has enlisted?' 'Yes, he has enlisted under the banner of King Jesus!' Dr Maclean thinks that this public stand taken by these young men, among the youngest in the College, contributed much to bring to a crisis[1] that wonderful revival of religion which signalized the first half of 1815, one of the most memorable in the whole history of the town.]

It came not with observation. There was only a gradual change in the spirit of the College, and state of mind of the students – a change from indifference to earnestness, from neglect or perfunctory performance of religious duties to frequent crowded and solemn attendance on all meetings for prayer and instruction. Personal religion, the salvation of the soul, became the absorbing subject of attention. 'The divine influence', said Dr Green, in his report to the Trustees, 'seemed to descend like the silent dew of heaven, and in about four weeks there were very few individuals in the College edifice who were not deeply impressed with a sense of the importance of spiritual and eternal things. There was scarcely a room; perhaps not one; which was not a place of earnest, secret devotion.'

[1] The same is asserted by Dr Green in his 'Report to the Trustees on the Revival'.

Hymns, then, as always, were very efficacious. Luther's hymns, at the time of the Reformation, were to the German nation what the trumpet and the bugle are to the army. 'Ein' feste Burg' is still the battle-song of the German soldier. There are some hymns which did good service in my young days which have since lost favour. ''Tis a point I long to know', 'Come, humble sinner, in whose breast', are now regarded as too hypothetical. 'I can but perish *if* I go.' There is no *if* in the case. However this may be in logic, it should be remembered that there is a faith which saves, which cannot recognize, much less avow itself. Many get to heaven who can only say, 'Lord, help my unbelief'; for that is a cry of faith.

HIS MOTHER TO HIS BROTHER HUGH

Princeton, Jan. 23, 1815.

My Dear Hugh: – The last fortnight has been productive of events that have excited much interest, rumours of which no doubt reached you; but as rumours are seldom correct, I feel desirous of giving you a plain statement. An attention to religious duties, you know, has ever been a leading feature in the character of Charles, which has gradually strengthened with his years. The services of the Sunday previous to the fast determined him to make a public profession of them on the approaching sacrament, to which he was urged by his friend Biggs, and joined by Van Dyke. On Wednesday evening, C—, D—, J— and B— supped at Folet's (tavern) and gambled to a late hour. The faculty had information of it, and were waiting their return. Folet, alarmed for his own interest, at three in the morning, refused them more lights, and sent to give notice to those who were already acquainted with the circumstances. The consequence was they were all dismissed on Friday. J— called to take leave of us, humbled to the dust with the sense of his misconduct, and his heart overflowing with gratitude to Dr Green for the admonitions and kindness with which the sentence had been given. On Saturday J— came again and requested to see me. He caught my hand on entering, and exclaimed that this was the happiest day of his life. 'What, sir, are you reinstated?' 'Oh, no, madam, that is of little moment indeed at present. Religion has complete possession of my mind. After a night of agony, under the deepest convictions of my guilt, the morning brought some ray of comfort. I sent for Biggs. He spake peace to my soul. I have been to Dr Green, who received me with the tenderness of a parent, pointed out my path, and encourages me to persevere by the assurance of future favour. To your dear Charles I am indebted for these impressions. In our walks last summer religion was often the theme, and though I felt nothing at the time, yet now they return forcibly upon the mind. I am permitted to stay some days longer, and have been in College conversing with my friends, I think, with some effect.'

The next day the sacrament was administered. Though it is said two or three students ridiculed those that had joined the Church, this is very doubtful. But on Monday a great change took place in College. A general seriousness was observed in the Refectory. The rooms of Biggs, Baker and others were filled with students soliciting information on the subject of religion, and getting books. In the evening, while the Whig Society held their meeting, twenty Clios [members of another student society] met in Allen's room to pray. On Tuesday the call for instruction was so general that Dr Green proposed to give a lecture to those who chose to attend. The Senior lecture-room was full, and there have been prayer-meetings every evening. Blatchford and others of the divinity students spend a great deal of time in College, and the youths apply to either or all the professors indiscriminately. Johns, McIlvaine, Armstrong, Newbold, Smith, Rodgers, Ogden, Stewart, Clarke, Henry of Albany, are among those most seriously impressed, Lyttleton and Benjamin among those more lightly touched. No doubt there is much sympathy in the business, and as they instinctively followed each other last winter in mischief, they are led in the same manner this season to good. But it is very probable that after the effervescence subsides, there will be a good number who will experience a radical change.

You may suppose it has been a period of considerable agitation with me. The important step Charles has taken occasions much solicitude. He was so young, I could have wished it had been deferred at least to the end of his College course. But you know his importunity, and when duty and feeling urged him forward, I could not throw a straw in the way. He has raised expectations which I fervently hope may be realized. On Thursday he spoke his speech on Conscience, *and did himself justice*.[1] Mr Davis and Henry, two divinity students of superior attainments and polished manners, pay him flattering attention. They no doubt count upon him as one of their number. This revival, as it is called, will no doubt reach the city with much exaggeration. I write, therefore, to give you a plain statement of facts, that you may answer explicitly if applied to for information. As I should be extremely sorry that any one should suppose the step Charles has taken was in consequence of a sudden impulse of feeling, you will be enabled to rectify any such error.

Your affectionate mother,
M. Hodge

CHARLES HODGE TO HIS BROTHER

Princeton, February, 1815.

My Dear Brother: – I would indeed be most inexcusable should I permit an opportunity, so direct and so long known as that which our dear John offers, to pass unimproved. I hardly know how to part from him, even for a week. I expect to meet with few in this world who will love me as ardently and constantly as he does. He, Biggs and Van Dyke, are the three in College to whom I feel most strongly

---

[1] This is the only instance to be found in her correspondence when she makes any such admission. She had a high conception of Charles' talents, but a very dissatisfied estimate of his diligence, ambition, or power of concentrated and sustained effort. Her tendency was to self-repression, and to the expectation of disappointment. His natural disposition was easy, and to the gratification of his tastes. Sense of duty and love for the cause of Christ were the springs of his subsequent life-long labours. But up to the day of her death, when he had been professor for ten years, the mother lamented that Charles would 'never do himself justice'.

attached, and from whom I shall hope not soon to be separated. I think it probable we shall all choose the same profession. Of this I am not certain. John, as you have probably heard already, is one of those who have so lately experienced the most desirable of changes. When gay and thoughtless, though also affectionate and kind, I loved him. How then shall I feel towards him when we hope to be enlisted under the same banner, to have the same end in life and the same hope in death. The step which your brother has taken, accompanied by dear Kinsey, you are already acquainted with. And why not my dearest brother too? Oh! that you, that Atkinson, that all, were here to see what has been done! for I cannot but think that all who see the present state of the College must also feel that this is indeed the harvest, the accepted time, the day of salvation. Oh! my brother! though it is only your little Toby who is writing to you, yet he loves you; he knows how many inestimable qualities you possess, and shudders at the thought of your wanting the one thing needful. You must not, you do not, at least I hope you will not, want it. I remember what you said of the 'pious physician'. I cannot tell you how it made me feel. I was rejoiced; for I knew that 'he that seeketh findeth', and that 'he that asketh receiveth'.

You have probably heard exaggerated accounts of the revival, as must be expected on such occasions. I believe that there are about thirty who are really changed. Almost all the College attend the prayer-meeting, which is held every evening at eight o'clock, in Newbold's room. Dr Green lectures to us in the senior recitation room every Tuesday evening, and Dr Alexander on Friday evenings. These meetings also are attended by almost all the students. If you were to see me kiss Richards, you must think that a great change had taken place.

There are a thousand things I would tell you, but I must refer you to *our* dear *brother* Johns. It being half-past twelve at night is a sufficient reason for my bidding you good-night.

Your Brother

There were one hundred and five students in the College during the winter of 1814–15, of whom twelve had been previously professors of religion, and were very useful in promoting that revival. Most of them were much older than the majority of their associates. Of this number were Daniel Baker, afterwards the celebrated evangelist;[1] Thomas J. Biggs, subsequently professor in the Lane Theological Seminary; Isaac W. Piatt, long pastor of the church in Bath, New York; Robert Steele, the life-long pastor of the church in Abington, Pennsylvania; John de Witt, life-long pastor of the church in Harrisburgh, Pennsylvania. Of the remaining ninety-three students then in College, fully one-half gave to their fellow-men, in their after life, every evidence of having become true believers during this revival. In the light of God, the number was probably greater. Among these were John Johns, afterwards Episcopal Bishop of Virginia; Charles P. McIlvaine, afterwards Episcopal Bishop of Ohio; James V. Henry, pastor of Presbyterian Church at Sing-Sing, N. Y.; Symmes C. Henry, pastor of a Church at Cranbury, N.J.; Ravaud K. Rodgers, pastor of a Church at Bound Brook, N.J.; William J. Armstrong, afterwards Secretary of the American Board of Commissioners for Foreign Missions; Benjamin Ogden, pastor of a Church at Pennington; John Maclean, afterwards President of the College of New Jersey; Charles C. Stewart, Missionary to the Sandwich Islands, and George H. Woodruff and John Rodney, afterwards Episcopal ministers;

---

[1] Young men are sometimes disposed to determine present duty by their anticipations of the future. Mr Baker told me that he expected to spend his life in preaching the gospel in the mountains of Virginia; and therefore would not need a thorough theological training. On this account he declined to enter the Theological Seminary. In less than a year after leaving College he was married and licensed, and entered on his work. The first thing we heard of him was that he was called to be the pastor of an important Church in Savannah; then he was called to Washington, where he had Senators and Congressmen for his hearers. He subsequently discovered that God had called him to be an itinerant, and as such, he was eminently successful.

Benjamin W. Richards, afterwards Mayor of Philadelphia, etc., etc. Bishop Johns, together with William James, Charles Stewart, and others, made his first profession of religion in the First Presbyterian Church, Princeton, July 7, 1815. He afterwards removed his connection to the Episcopal Church, attended by his family in New Castle, Delaware.

Many of my College associates subsequently rose to distinction. Judge Haines of Ohio; William Pennington, Governor of New Jersey, and Speaker of the House of Representatives in Congress; James McDowell, Governor of Virginia; Richard H. Bayard, U.S. Senator, and Minister to Belgium; Henry Carrington and John Blair Dabney of Virginia. These last were inseparables; room-mates, with all their books marked 'Carrington and Dabney'. Mr Dabney became a prominent lawyer, but in middle life took orders in the Episcopal Church. Philip R. Fendall[1] was one of the first honour men of our class, and Attorney of the District of Columbia. Persifer F. Smith became a general in the U.S. Army. He was a great favourite, and exuberant in humour. If you heard laughter in any part of the building, you might be sure that Smith was at the bottom of it. He was greatly distinguished in both the Florida and Mexican wars. After the Florida war he was driving in Philadelphia (his native city) with a party of friends, and the question came up, 'What was the cause of the great difficulty attending the war against the Seminoles?' One of the party turned to the General and said, 'Smith, you were there, what do you think was the cause of the trouble?' He replied, 'I do not know, but I reckon it was the Indians.' His constitution was undermined by malaria in Mexico, and he died in 1858, while in command of the post at Fort Leavenworth.

---

[1] One day a dozen of us were standing on the front steps of the College, and Fendall was exercising his wit on those around him, when one of the crowd said, 'Fendall, why don't you cut C—?' The prompt reply was, 'What is the use of cutting mush?' C. was so amiable that even that gash healed by the first intention.

John Johns, Bishop of Virginia, Charles P. McIlvaine, Bishop of Ohio, and John Maclean, President of the College of New Jersey, have been my intimate, life-long friends. Besides these there were a considerable number who have become judges, or members of congress, or distinguished as lawyers, physicians, or ministers of the gospel.

There were two of my college associates, who are enshrined in my memory as remarkable illustrations of the power of goodness, that is, of holiness; these were Charles B. Storrs and John Newbold. The former was the son of the Rev. Richard S. Storrs, of Longmeadow, Mass., and uncle of the distinguished Dr Richard S. Storrs, of Brooklyn, N.Y. I remember him principally, as a member of Whig Hall,[1] where everybody deferred to him. He was intelligent, cultivated, gentle, courteous, unassuming and eminently devout. It was his piety which made him what he was. It was the halo that surrounded him, and which secured for him the affectionate deference with which he was always treated. His health was delicate, and he left college before graduation. After studying theology at Andover, he removed to Ohio, and became president of the Western Reserve College. He died in the house of his brother, the Rev. Dr Richard S. Storrs, of Braintree, Mass., in 1833, at the early age of thirty-nine.

I never saw him after he left Princeton, and therefore was the more interested in the following tribute to his memory, taken from the *New York Times*, January 24th, 1878. 'Many of the old readers of the (Boston) *Herald* may remember the beautiful poem of Mr Whittier, to the late President of the Western Reserve College, Charles B. Storrs, a man of high culture and great intellectual powers. The late Judge Humphrey, of Hudson, Ohio, said Dr Storrs was the most eloquent man he ever heard. President Storrs was an out-and-out anti-slavery and temperance man. In his

---

[1] A permanent secret Literary Society of the College.

advocacy of these two great causes, he knew no such words as falter or compromise. Slavery and intemperance were wrong, and they must be put down. Dr Storrs of this city, a nephew of President Storrs, who inherits the intellectual force of his uncle, and is a man of rare culture, perhaps unequalled by any man in the American pulpit to-day, told me not long ago, 'that when his uncle, President Storrs, was sick unto death, and his mother was watching him with the greatest and tenderest care, anxious for his life, said to him, 'Your brother, the doctor, says, "You must take a little brandy," he turned his sparkling eyes to his sister, and in tones of voice almost silenced by the touch of death, said, in slow and measured words: "No; I cannot take it. I must be true to the principle." These were the last words he ever spoke, and his great soul went up to God, who gave it.'

John Newbold was a native of Philadelphia, and a member of the Episcopal Church. I do not remember to have ever known a man who was so absorbed in the things unseen and eternal. He seemed to take no interest in the things of this life, except so far as they were connected with duty, or with the interests of religion. His conversation was in heaven. No one went to him to talk pohtics, or to discuss the relative merits of their fellow-students. But if any were in darkness or trouble, they would go to him for instruction or consolation. He had far more influence than any other man in the Seminary (which he joined immediately after leaving college). If an irritating discussion at any time arose, as soon as Newbold entered the room there was a calm. Or if it happened, to any two of the students, as it did to Paul and Barnabas, that a 'sharp contention', arose between them, so that they 'parted asunder', he was sure to bring them together and fuse them into one by his love. He was tall and long-limbed, and rather awkward, though a thorough gentleman. His face was plain; and would have been homely, had it not been irradiated by the beauty of holiness. His heart was set on going as a missionary to Persia or India. As at that time there was no foreign missionary organization in this country connected with the Episcopal Church, he induced Dr Alexander to offer his services to the Church Missionary Society in England. He was, however, cut down by a rapid consumption, and died before entering the ministry. For a series of years, I acted on the purpose of not allowing his memory to die out in the Seminary. Therefore, once at least in three years (an academic generation with us) I held him up as an example; I wished to cause the students to see how much good can be done by simply being good.

[Here end the autobiographical notes. These, also, were the very last sentences that Dr Hodge ever wrote, with the exception of two or three short family letters. A fit and characteristic closing of the vast volume of writing which for fifty years had flowed from his pen.]

He graduated from college, September 1815. John Johns and Philip R. Fendall shared the first honour, and Charles Hodge and Alexander Wurtz shared the second; Charles Hodge delivered the valedictory oration.

3

FROM HIS GRADUATION FROM THE COLLEGE, SEPTEMBER 1815, TO HIS GRADUATION FROM THE THEOLOGICAL SEMINARY, SEPTEMBER 1819

Study in Philadelphia – Journeys to Silver Lake and Virginia – Seminary Life and Friends – Letters to Mother and Brother

HIS PREPARATION FOR COLLEGE, especially in the Greek language, had been imperfect, and the effort which had been required to raise him to the high position in the class which he occupied at the time of his graduation, had decidedly taxed his physical strength. His mother, therefore, required him to return to her home in Philadelphia, and spend there a year in general reading, and seeking the recuperation of his health, before he should commence his direct preparation for a profession. Of this year, very naturally, but few memorials remain. He spent the winter as proposed, in Philadelphia, following a course of general reading, but the pain and weakness in his chest became the cause of serious uneasiness. After the spring opened he spent several months with his cousin, Mrs Harrison Smith, at her husband's country seat, in the neighborhood of Washington city, D.C. He afterwards related that Mrs Smith made him drink, frequently, new milk mixed with honey, a prescription at once pleasant to his taste, and strengthening to his chest.

His cousin Jane, eldest daughter of Andrew Hodge, Jr., and Nancy Ledyard, had, some years previously, married Dr Robert H.

Rose, an intelligent Scotch gentleman of great cultivation and taste, who had become the owner of a large tract of land in Susquehanna county, near the north-eastern corner of Pennsylvania. In that day the country to the north of Easton, at the forks of the Delaware, was, with the exception of the Wyoming valley, for the most part a wilderness, broken only here and there by clearings and humble homesteads. But Dr Rose built on the banks of the beautiful Silver Lake a residence which, more than almost any other then existing in the Middle States, took the place and fulfilled the offices of a country residence of an English nobleman. It was built of wood, yet of large proportions, and adapted to the entertainment of many guests, thirty at a time often staying with him for days or weeks, as suited their convenience. A large library, fine pictures and works of art, beautiful conservatories and gardens, and the eminent social gifts of the host, made the place a centre of attraction, and an astonishing oasis of civilization in the 'back-woods'.

Early in July of this year, young Charles paid a visit to this hospitable house, making the journey from Philadelphia in company with his aunt, Mrs Nancy Hodge. From Silver Lake he wrote several letters to his mother, two of which remain, which are given to the reader partly because they are among the earliest traces that survive of the pen of Dr. Hodge, afterwards so prolific.

CHARLES HODGE TO HIS MOTHER

SILVER LAKE, July 11, 1816.

My Dear Mother:—You most probably will have heard of our safe arrival here, long before this reaches you. It was just after sundown on Sunday evening when we came in sight of the Lake. We were much less fatigued than you would expect by our four days of constant riding and, part of the time, of constant jolting. The thirty miles we came on horseback affected aunt more than all the rest of the journey. A considerable part of the road between this and the city is dreary enough; scarcely any thing to be seen but fields filled with old stumps, and, in places on fire last spring, whole woods of leafless and limbless trees. There are, however, some landscapes more beautiful and extensive than any I can remember ever to have seen. From a mountain near Easton there is a prospect as rich and widely extended as your imagination can well conceive. You see before you a fertile valley, through which the Lehigh and Delaware flow, and in which they meet. Easton is situated on the point of land formed by their junction, and beyond you perceive the long ridge of the Blue mountains, covered with the richest foliage. The whole of the ride from Tunckhannock, about thirty miles, is very delightful . . .

They are all very kind, and have every thing about them they could wish. The place fully answers my expectations, and will be delightful when the country is more cultivated . . . The lake proves an abundant source of amusement, and also of healthy exercise, as we often paddle about in the old canoe. We catch here the salmon trout, of which the Doctor is very proud, as he thinks they are to be found no where in the State but in his tract. He told me that if I turned out to be as clever a fellow as my brother Hugh, he should like to make a backwoodsman of me . . . I feel the want of my other pair of cloth pantaloons very much. Cousin and the Doctor have repeatedly asked me to spend the summer here, but my want of clothes, and the impossibility of getting them, if nothing else, would prevent it . . .

You would think it strange, perhaps, if I were to close my letter without saying a word about my health, but I have little to say on that subject. I eat here, I believe, in one day as much as I did in a week in the city. My breast is sometimes painful, but not often, and my back is well enough if I do not stoop much.

The good people here desire their love to you.

My dear mother's affectionate son,

C. Hodge

CHARLES HODGE TO HIS MOTHER

Silver Lake, July 27, 1816.

My Dearest Mother:—Partly from being pretty constantly employed during the past week, but principally, I fear, from my procrastinating disposition, it is Saturday morning (instead of Monday or Tuesday, as I intended) before I am seated to fulfil my promise of writing to you before our return. As there is now no flattering tomorrow for me to look forward to, it *must* be done to-day.

I feel, my dear mother, fully sensible that the present is one of the most important periods of my life, viewing it as one in which the choice of a profession is to be made. Having left us to act freely in this respect, you are aware of the one on which, even for some years past, I have been conditionally determined. It is the one, I know, in which, generally speaking, there is the least prospect of earthly happiness, since there are so many deprivations and inconveniences to which those who embrace it must submit, as they must be ever so much more at the disposition of others than of themselves. Yet I feel that it is the only one in which I could be happy, believing it to be the path of my duty.

Considering, therefore, my choice of a profession as made, the next most important points to determine are the proper time and place of preparation for its duties. And here, my dear mamma, I leave myself entirely at your disposal, not, however, without urging my own wishes, and endeavouring to convince you of their propriety.

Had I been permitted to act as my own dictator, my feelings would have led me, agreeably to the advice of friends as inexperienced as myself, to have entered the Seminary immediately after leaving College. From this improper step my mother saved me. Since that time, however, a year has passed, and I feel anxious to be engaged in serious study, fearing that if kept back for another year, the time will be even worse than lost. For I believe it impossible for any young man whose principal business it is to pursue an object as indefinite as general information, to make his progress in any measure co-equal to the value of his time. For you know that it is necessary for the powers of the mind to be more or less concentrated in order to produce effects. The acquisition of this kind of knowledge must be the gradual and secondary work of a whole life, rather than the main object of any particular period. Besides general reading as a business must be injurious, as it has a tendency to render the mind incapable of attention to severer and less interesting studies. But should you consider that another year thus spent is absolutely necessary, do you think the present the most proper time? Would it not be better to wait until after the three or four years of professional studies, when the mind will be more matured, the habits of study and attention more firmly fixed, the stock of information increased, and the capacity for improvement in every way enlarged? For my own part, I am convinced that the benefit of a year devoted to reading at that period would be nearly quadruple that of an equal period at the present. You remember that Dr Alexander told us that if I were to spend a fourth year in reading under his (or their) direction, my progress would be greater than during all the other three together.

With respect to the most advantageous place for the prosecution of my studies, I think, my dear mother, you cannot hesitate between, on the one hand, a place in which I can enjoy the tuition of men of talents and information, whose time and attention are devoted to the improvement of their pupils, with the advantage of good libraries, of the company of persons of my own age engaged in the same pursuits, of being in a class, of constant recitations and lectures, and especially the advantage of a debating society attended by the professors of College and Seminary — and on the other hand, a place in which I must be under a private gentleman who is almost entirely occupied with other concerns, and in which I shall be destitute of nearly all the above-mentioned advantages.

I trust you cannot suppose that I am influenced in what I say by a childish fondness for Princeton. I am far from being sanguine in my expectations of happiness there. The College filled with strangers will not be the source of pleasure it was when it contained so many of my dear and affectionate friends, and I know that my situation must be far less pleasant in many other respects than it was when you were there.

I am ever, my dear mother, your affectionate

CHARLES

During the month of October of this year, young Charles had the great pleasure and advantage of accompanying Dr Alexander in a tour through Virginia, among the scenes of the Doctor's earlier ministry. It was accomplished chiefly in stages and on horseback. It extended over a line of about 600 miles from Philadelphia and back again; from Philadelphia to Baltimore; thence to Harper's Ferry, where the Potomac breaks through the Blue ridge; thence up the great valley thirty miles wide, reaching from the heart of Pennsylvania to the heart of Carolina and Tennessee, to Lexington, in Rockbridge county, where Dr Alexander was born and educated; thence back to Staunton, and through Rockfish Gap, by Monticello and Charlottesville, and thence to Fredericksburg, where they attended the sessions of the Synod of Virginia; and thence to Washington, Baltimore, and home.

Our father used in after years to recount to his children, with great interest, the scenes of that memorable journey, and the happiness of that blessed companionship. He told of the remarkable evidence given of the fervent and universal affection entertained for Dr Alexander, and the enthusiasm of his reception. Of how often when under the excitement of his cordial greeting, the Doctor, shut up to the alternatives of laughing or crying, would be shaken with a nervous laugh, while shaking hands by the half-hour, and with hundreds of old friends. Of how the inspiration of the old scenes and of the familiar faces lifted the Doctor to his original elevation of extemporaneous and dramatic eloquence, from which he had declined since he had formed the habit of reading his sermons, as a city pastor in Philadelphia. Especially he referred with unabated wonder to two sermons preached by the doctor on this journey. Once, when he preached on the sacrifice of Isaac by his father Abram, he so minutely described and enacted the scene, that the entire audience were thrilled and rent as though they were actually present at the impending tragedy. Again, when he preached on the judgment of the quick and dead by the Son of Man, he so keenly apprehended the event as real, and so graphically described it, that at the crisis, when the trumpet sounded, and the great white throne began to descend, the entire congregation, by one impulse, rose, and bent to the windows, that they might see Him, and take their places among the multitudes thronging to meet Him.

But one letter pertaining to this journey remains.

CHARLES HODGE TO HIS MOTHER

STAUNTON, VA., Oct. 10, 1816.

My Dear Mother:—I am now upwards of three hundred miles distant from you, and from almost all those who feel an interest in me. It often makes me feel melancholy to look on the map and see the very spot where my friends are, and then reflect what a space there is between us. I can in every hour of the day guess where you all are situated, and what you are most probably doing ; but you can only think of me as somewhere or other far from you, engaged in scenes which your imagination cannot call before you. I expect therefore that you are oftener in my thoughts than I am in yours, at least I can better bring you all before me from being acquainted with the places you constantly frequent.

The first opportunity I had of writing was on Friday evening after a fatiguing ride from Baltimore to Fredericktown, the hurried letter which I suppose you received a week ago. This last mentioned place we left between two and three o'clock on Saturday morning, when the moon, being full, shone with such brightness, that we could almost fancy it was mid-day. We rode eight miles to a place called the Trap, where we breakfasted just at day-break, when we had only ten miles to ride before we reached Harper's Ferry. During this time we had frequently beautiful views of the mountains, and could generally trace the course of the Potomac by the fog which rises in the morning, and which enveloping the foot of the Ridge, leaves only the summit visible, resting apparently on the clouds . . . After passing the Ferry and finding the stage was not ready, we hastened up the hill on the point formed by the junction of the Potomac and Shenandoah, to Jefferson's rock, and kneeling on that (for we were afraid to stand) we enjoyed the most beautifully grand prospect my eyes had ever witnessed or my imagination had ever painted. I shall not attempt to give you a description of the place, but only say that I think Jefferson less extravagant in saying that a sight of it is worthy a voyage across the Atlantic, than I did before I had seen it myself. When I return I will endeavour to give you some idea of it . . . We arrived at Winchester just at dark; the Doctor perceiving the Presbyterian Church was open, we put our baggage in the tavern and went up towards it. On our way we met Mr Hill, the Doctor's friend and the minister of the place, who insisted on the Doctor's preaching, although he had risen that day at two o'clock, and had ridden fifty miles over one of the worst roads in the Union. Here I met my old class-mate, Baker, who took me home with him, where I was treated very kindly by all of them (there were no less than half a dozen young ladies there). The next day being Sunday, and their communion season, Dr Alexander preached in the morning on the text, 'Ought not Christ to have suffered these things?' He was as usual most excellent and affecting. We left Winchester about three o'clock Monday morning, by moonlight . . . and our next stopping-place was Woodstock, the county-town of Shenandoah, and this being their court-day, the whole place was filled with the oddest looking, old-fashioned German men and women I ever saw. The Doctor enjoyed the scene very much, and was constantly telling me not to laugh, while his own mouth was wide open . . . We slept that night at New Market, and before three the next morning we were in the stage. It was exceedingly cold until the sun rose; we rode forty-five miles, and arrived at Staunton about four in the afternoon. Here we spent Wednesday and Thursday at Dr Waddel's, Mrs Alexander's brother, who is quite a young man. I received here all the kindness and hospitality which I could expect or wish for even in Virginia. A Mr McDowell, a friend of the Doctor, was so kind as to lend us each a horse; so on Friday morning we left Staunton for Lexington on horseback, and arrived there between five and six. This ride of thirty-five miles fatigued us more than all the rest of our journey together. I feel much better this morning, but my limbs yet ache a good deal. We are to visit the Natural Bridge on Monday, which is about fifteen miles from this. Then we are to return to Staunton, and on Monday week we are to leave Staunton with the two Misses Waddell. They will drop me at Charlottesville for a day to visit Monticello. They intend to stop at the Doctor's brother-in-law where I am to rejoin them on Wednesday evening. We shall then proceed to Fredericksburgh, get there on Friday, and, the Synod meeting there, we shall stay until the beginning of the next week, for the Doctor to see his old friends who will be there. We shall then take the steamboat for Washington, then the stage to Baltimore; then the steamboat to where my dear mother and brother now are.

I have been very happy during this jaunt (except when I felt uneasy about the state of my funds, which has sometimes even kept me from sleeping.) I have met with a great deal of kindness, and of course like the people very much. The Doctor is *the man of men*, talks a great deal about the country as we pass along, and tells me anecdotes of himself suggested by the sight of places where he used to be. I have much less pain in my breast than I had before I left home. I expect to return quite well.

I remain, dear mother,

Your son, C. H.

ENTERED THE SEMINARY

On November 9th, 1816, Charles Hodge was matriculated as a student in the Princeton Theological Seminary. This institution was founded in 1812. Dr Archibald Alexander was the first professor, and sole instructor, until the accession of the Rev. Samuel Miller, D.D., December 3rd, 1813. At first there were neither public buildings nor libraries. The houses of the professors were used as places for recitation and worship. The main Seminary edifice, supplying apartments for dormitories, library and public meetings, and recitations, and for the residence of the steward, and the refectory, was opened for use in the autumn of 1817, when only the two lower stories were finished. Charles Hodge was the first student who ever preached in the new Oratory, that sacred room with which his person and voice has been associated for sixty-one years. The residence so long occupied by Dr Alexander, was built early in 1819. The corresponding house at the other end of the main Seminary building, occupied by Dr Hodge for fifty-three years, was built during the latter part of 1824. 'The matriculations of students were in 1812, nine; in 1813, sixteen; in 1814, fifteen; in 1815, twenty-two; in 1816, twenty-six; in 1817, twenty-three.'

As the theological character and life-work of Dr Hodge was determined by the discipline he received in this Seminary, and especially as he always affirmed that he was moulded more by the character and instructions of Dr Archibald Alexander than by all other external influences combined, I will quote at length the information given by the biographer of Dr Alexander, as to the characteristics of the first professors, and as to their methods of instruction during the first years of the Institution.

'All Dr Alexander's life long he was free to acknowledge that his training, however laborious, had lacked much of the vigour and method of the schools. Theology had, indeed, been the study of his life. During his residence in Philadelphia he had gathered about him the great masters of Latin theology, whose works appeared in Holland, Switzerland, Germany, and France, in the sixteenth and seventeenth centuries. A rare occasion of adding to his stock of Dutch theology was afforded by the sale of a library belonging to a learned minister from Holland, the Rev. Mr Von Harlinger, of Somerset. These Reformed divines he regarded as having pushed theological investigation to its greatest length, and compacted its conclusions into the most symmetrical method. He once said to the writer, that on a perplexed subject he preferred Latin to English reading, not only because of the complete and ingenious nomen-clature which had grown up in the dialectic schools of the church, but because the little effort required for getting the sense kept his attention concentrated.

'His penchant for metaphysical investigation urged him, from an early date, to make himself acquainted with the philosophies of the periods, from which each system took its tincture, and without which it is impossible to survey the several schemes from a just point of view. Thus he perused, and generally in their sources, not only the peripatetic and scholastic writers, but the treatises of Descartes, Leibnitz, Wolff, and Voetius. And there was no subject on which he discoursed with more pleasure and success than upon the exposition and comparison of these ingenious, though now exploded, systems. He made himself famil-iar with the Christian Fathers, both Greek and Latin, and perused them at intervals during forty years. He did not confine himself to writers on one side. Through long years he was wont to seek with patience the best works in defence of popery; the argumentative dissertations of the extreme Lutherans and Dutch Remonstrants, as well as the Fratres Poloni, and other champions of Socinianism. It need scarcely be added that he was familiar with English theology, as treated both by authors of the Established Church, and by the great nonconformist divines. His recent travels in New England, and the prevailing excitement caused by the speculations of Hopkins and Emmons, served to keep him observant in regard to the phases of opinion in the American churches. As it respects his own conclusions, he has left on record the statement that on his return from New England, and during his residence in Philadelphia, his views, which had been somewhat modified by eastern suggestions, began to fix themselves more definitely in the direction of the common Westminster theology.

'Although called primarily to be a teacher of theology, in its stricter acceptation, he was led both by strong native tastes and by convictions of reason, to give first attention to the criticism and interpretation of the original Scriptures. With the Greek, as has been intimated, he was sufficiently familiar to be a competent instructor, but Hebrew literature was in its infancy in America. The works of Gesenius were as yet unknown, and the learned labours of Gibbs and Stuart had not been given to the world. Even in New England the vowel points were for a time held in suspicion, and those who desired to penetrate their mysteries were fain to seek often the different and rare volumes of Buxtorf, Leusden, and Opitius. Conscious of his own imperfect knowledge, he modestly, but indefatigably, set about the work of inculcation. For a number of years, and with increased ability, he worked this field, until relieved by the services of a beloved pupil, the Reverend Charles Hodge. Criticism and hermeneutics was a department which had great charms for him, and by extensive reading, compiling and original investigation, he prepared to furnish a system of instruction, which for years he delivered as lectures, a number of which still remain among his papers. To this he added copious instructions in Biblical Archaeology, on which he prepared numerous discourses, and which remained under his control for many years. No man looked more reverently upon the typical Christology of the Levitical law; and none of his pupils can forget the awe with which he approached the recesses of the expiatory system, or the felicitous use which he made of the altar and the propitiatory, in his more purely theological exposition of the atonement.

'Deeply persuaded that many theological errors have their origin in a bias derived from false metaphysics, he set about the methodizing of his thoughts upon mental philosophy. The German philosophy was yet unknown among us, and he was never led to travel the transcendental, or high "*a priori* road", but treated mental phenomena on the inductive method, as the objects of a cautious generalization. While he uniformly recommended the perusal of Locke, it was, as he often declared, not so much for the value of his particular conclusions, as for the spirit of his investigation; the calmness, patience and transparent honesty of that truly great man. He likewise expressed great favour for Reid, Beattie, Buffier, Campbell and Stewart, with whose general methods, as well as their views of intuitive truths and constitutional principles of reason, he was in agreement, while he dissented from many of their definitions, distinctions and tenets.

'From these topics he turned to the closely allied domain of Natural Religion. While he was far from being a rationalist, he was never satisfied with the tactics of those reasoners who, under the pretext of exalting revelation, dismiss, with contempt, all arguments derived from the light of nature. He rendered due homage, therefore, to the labours of such writers as Nieuwentyt, the younger Turretin, and Paley, and spent much time in considering and unfolding, with nice discrimination, the various schemes of argument for the Being and Perfections of God, and the necessity and antecedent probability of a revelation. Connected closely with this was the discussion of Ethical Philosophy, in which he taught, from the outset, the same doctrines which have been given to the world in a posthumous work.

'The anxieties belonging to an attempt to lay down the great lines of a method for teaching the whole system of revealed truth, to those who were to be the ministers of the Church, were just and burdensome. As compared with those later methods which grew out of continued experience with successive classes, they were probably more extemporaneous and colloquial; there was more use of existing manuals, and less adventure of original expedients. Dr Alexander, herein concurring with Chalmers, conceived that theology was best taught by a wise union of the text book with the free lecture. Finding no work in English which entirely met his demands, he placed in the hands of his pupils the *Institutions* of Francis Turretin. It would be very unjust to suppose that the young men were charged with the tenets of Turretin, to the injury of their mental independence. Dr Alexander often dissented from the learned Genevan, and always endeavoured to cultivate in his students the spirit and habits of original investigation. He very laboriously engaged in making such brief aids, in the way of syllabus and compendium, as might furnish to the student a manageable key to the whole classification. He prepared extensive and minute questions, going into all the ramifications of theology. He assigned subjects for original dissertations, which were publicly read and commented on by both professors and students; a near approach to the acts held in the old university schools, under the scholastic moderator. To this were added the debates of a theological society, meeting every Friday evening, always on some important topic, and always closed by the full and highly animated remarks of the professor.

'The division of his department into Didactic and Polemic Theology, which the Plan of the institution made imperative, gave the professor an opportunity to go over all the leading doctrines in the way of defence against the objections of errorists, heretics and infidels. In doing this he brought to bear his remarkable stores of recondite reading. He gave the biography of eminent opponents, clear analyses of their systems, and refutations of their reasons. What might be considered by some an inordinate length of time was devoted to the cardinal differences, such as the controversy with Deists, Arians, Socinians, Pelagians, Arminians, Papists and Universalists; all being made to revolve around the Calvinistic system, which, upon sincere conviction, he had adopted.'

Dr Samuel Miller was elected Professor of Ecclesiastical History and Church Government in 1813. After his accession, the entire instruction of the Seminary was divided between Dr Alexander and himself. 'He brought with him a high reputation, as a preacher and author, and a Christian gentleman. His name was widely known from his *Retrospect of the Eighteenth Century*, and more recently from his defence of Presbytery against the attacks of Doctors Hobart and Bowden.'

Hugh Hodge, in referring to his brother Charles's Seminary life, remarks that 'now he began to discover considerable facility in acquiring knowledge, although he was not much of a student.' This judgment must be understood, in view of the fact, that Hugh was eighteen months the elder, that he matured much more rapidly than his brother, and that he was himself beyond all his associates distinguished for the strictness of his method, the extent of his patience and power of self-denial, and the absoluteness of his devotion to his duty. The correspondence of Charles with his mother shows that, during his Seminary course, he attained to the habits of an earnest and successful student. He boarded and lodged at Mrs Bache's during the first year of his Seminary course. As soon as the public building was ready for use, in the fall of 1817, he took up his abode in it. During his junior year, he had for his room-mate Thomas Jacob Biggs, afterwards Professor in Lane Seminary, Cincinnati. During the middle year, John Johns, afterwards Bishop of the Episcopal Church in Virginia; and during the senior year, Thomas Scudder Wickes, afterwards a pastor in the state of New York. With all of these brethren Mr Hodge formed intimate friend-ships, cherished by him with warm affection all their lives. But the mutual love of Charles Hodge and John Johns was singular, and, in the experience of either of them, had no rival of its kind. It burned brighter and brighter for sixty years on earth, till now, after the briefest separation, Episcopalian and Presbyterian brother are together forever.

His most intimate friends among his classmates in the Seminary, were Johns, McIlvaine and William Nevins, They were an exceed-ingly joyous and playful company. Dr Hodge afterwards, writing of Dr Miller, said, 'Our class, one of the earliest, tried his patience a good deal. We were not bad, but boyish. One particularly, after-wards one of the most distinguished and useful ministers of our church, the late Dr William Nevins of Baltimore, was so full of fun and wit, that he kept us in a constant titter. The good Doctor wore out his lead-pencil in thumping the desk to make us behave, but he was never irritated. He made allowance for us boys, knowing that we loved and reverenced him.'

He often told us how Nevins' seasons of playfulness were fol-lowed by reaction and depression, and of his spending a large part of the night with him, seeking to restore the cheerfulness of his faith and hope.

Also, how after he became assistant teacher, he was once called upon to minister to the conscience of the eccentric but highly talented George Bush, who was overwhelmed with fear of the desertion of God, because he had killed a mouse.

LETTERS TO HIS MOTHER

PRINCETON, Jan. 11th, 1817.

My Dear Mother:—I am not quite so lazy here as I am when at home. Yesterday morning I rose with the prayer bell, and I have now been up more than an hour, and have seated myself to write before eight o'clock.

Our ride from the city here was very pleasant, as the roads are good, and the weather, especially in the morning, was very agreeable. Elizabeth found a young lady, formerly a school-mate of hers, in the stage coming on to Princeton, so that she had not to depend on poor me for the pleasures of conversation. For my part I never was more sensible of the superiority of the talents of ladies for talking than they made me.

Your son, C. H.

PRINCETON, Feb. 21st, 1817.

My Dear Mother:—We, the theological students, have entered upon the attempt of learning singing with considerable spirit. We have formed ourselves into a society, to be called The Musical Association of Princeton; have a constitution drawn, and no less than five officers, President, Vice-President, two Choristers, and Secretary. Biggs is our Secretary. Eaton, an excellent singer from the eastward, is President. We are to meet once a week, alternately on Monday and Wednesday evening. Ladies are to attend and enjoy the privilege of members on invitation. I hope it may succeed and be useful in improving us all in the important as well as pleasing art of singing. Dr Alexander is very warmly in favour of it, and the ladies of his family are as zealous in the cause as we can be.

Your son, C. H.

PRINCETON, June 24th, 1817.

My Dear Mamma:—Here I am once more in our little study fixed for another session. May the blessing of heaven rest with me here, as the kindness of providence has followed me during my absence, and may the richest mercies be multiplied to you, my dear mother and brother.

My love to Cousin Susan.

Yours, C. Hodge

Princeton, July 4th, 1817.

My Dear Mother:—Caroline wishes to stay and hear Mr Larned, who is to preach for us next Sabbath in the Hall. I hope they will conclude to remain, as I wish Miss C. to admire Princeton more than merely passing through would lead her to do. The better known, the more beloved—happy the person or the place of which this is true. And I believe, as it regards most people, it may be said with strict propriety of this little favoured spot. I am very glad you can perceive an improvement in my writing. I feared it was too small to be noticed. I write my copy regularly.

Your son, C. H.

Princeton, July 15, 1817.

Dear Mamma:—The Sabbath the Miss Bayards were here, Larned[1] preached, as was expected, his last sermon. The Hall was quite crowded, there being a considerable number of strangers present, and curiosity or a regard for the preacher enabled many of the inhabitants of town to overcome their reluctance to attend our church. They were, however, amply repaid, for Larned preached with a degree of eloquence which few could equal. The ladies bore, by their tears, testimony to his superior powers, and many of his fellow-students, who felt as though they were never to hear him again, were not much less affected than the ladies themselves. He has gone to New York to be ordained, and then intends to spend six or seven weeks with his friends. It is probable he will visit most of the Atlantic towns between this and Savannah as an agent for collecting funds for the Seminary.

---

[1] A prodigy of early eloquence, whose name is often mentioned with those of Whitefield and Summerfield; he shone brightly for a few years, and then closed his career in New Orleans.

This is the plan, should Dr Romeyn decline going. From Savannah he proceeds to New Orleans, there to remain and labour for the establishment of a church in that spiritual wilderness.

Your son, C. H.

PRINCETON, Dec. 13, 1817.

Dear Mother:—We are very much pressed in our studies, so that I begin to feel as Hugh used to do, at seeing so much more before me than I can accomplish. But it is not in my nature to worry myself much about what I cannot help, and it is surely best to do as much as you can and let the rest go. I shall arrive at this conclusion and make a practical use of it much sooner than he (Hugh) has done, though he says he has at length attained it. What is dearly bought is highly valued. I trust, therefore, he will take care not to lose the power of looking at what he cannot accomplish or attain, without feeling too great dissatisfaction with himself.

Dr Alexander recommended to us this morning at recitation nearly thirty different works, giving such a character of each as to excite a strong desire to read them, which must be done next week or left undone, for we then pass on to a new subject, on which we may expect a similar supply. One great thing, however, we learn — that is, where information is to be found when we shall be more at leisure to attend to these copious sources. And another benefit is, that to be constantly occupied is to be happy, provided you are convinced that the occupation is important in itself, and proper for you. Accordingly I never was in better spirits than I have been in, all this session. Up before sunrise, and not to bed ever much before twelve. But four evenings in the week we are occupied until nine, before we can get to study.

Susan Beattie (whom perhaps you may remember), the only daughter of Col. Beattie,[1] died on Tuesday morning, between sixteen and seventeen years old. I do not remember ever to have been more

---

[1] Father of the venerable and universally beloved Rev, Charles C. Beattie, D.D., LL.D., of Steubenville, Ohio.

shocked than I was when I heard of her death. Scarcely eight days before, I saw her apparently enjoying the most vigorous health. Her hold on life appeared firmer than that of any of her companions, and the prospect of length of days was to few more flattering. She was one of the pall-bearers for Susan Bayard, and now they lie mouldering together in mournful contiguity in the house of silence, where the intercourse of friendship never can be known.

Your son, C. H.

Princeton, March 22, 1818.

Dear Mother:—My duties are so numerous and constant that there is not an hour in the day in which I feel at liberty to attend to what is foreign to my present pursuits. I am happy that such is the case, being persuaded that it is necessary *for me* to be pressed forward, in order to do all I am able to accomplish. It has the effect also of making my time pass by on eagle's wings. I often think of Mr Bayard's telling me that as we grow old, our years, like the circumference of an inverted tea-cup, become less and less. I should feel old indeed if I judged of my age by this criterion, and young indeed if I judged by what I have done. Rapidly as our days and years are flying on, how difficult is it to realize that they are hastening to a close. In looking forward to the end of life, it appears no nearer now than it did five or six years ago; yet it is more than probable that half of my race is already run, and perhaps much more than half. Would that I could act accordingly !

Your son, C. H.

Princeton, April 2, 1818.

My Dear Mother:—My dear brother's letter gave me more pleasure than I ever before received from anything of the kind — perhaps much more than he experienced himself, as constitutionally he is not as much affected by these things as I am. To be crowned at the close of a hard-fought course is the highest gratification pertaining to this world, and to see a brother crowned is even sweeter still.

It has made me *proud* of him., though I think I never was more grateful for any blessing than for his success. To be thankful for the past, and to trust (yet with diligence) for the future, comprises no small part of our present duty. When the more important race of life is run, may my dear brother then receive an applauding welcome, and a crown of glory which fadeth not away!

Your son, C. H.

Hugh had graduated with the highest honours from the medical department of the University of Pennsylvania, and in order to secure the means for perfecting his professional education in Europe, he sailed as surgeon of the merchant ship *Julius Caesar* from New York for Calcutta, September 8th, 1818.

PRINCETON, Sept. 10, 1818,

My Dear Mother:—Every circumstance appears to conspire to render the prospect before our dear treasure pleasant and flattering. The gentlemen he goes with are, I expect, more than usually estimable. The Captain has a high character for amiability as a man and skill as an officer. And the ship is new, strong, swift, and handsome. We have indeed much reason for gratitude for the present and the past, and should therefore with cheerful confidence commend to God the keeping of the gift He Himself at first bestowed, and has thus far so graciously enriched and preserved.

When at Rockaway, as I had never seen nor heard the sea, as soon as we got there, though quite dark, I went out alone to go down to the beach, where the roaring was really dreadful, and not being able to see the water, and being quite alone, surrounded by the gloom of darkness, I felt chilled almost with a kind of horror of the ocean, and could not bear the thought of my brother ever venturing on its bosom. But when the sun had in the morning gilded the expanse, the awful was changed into the beautiful and sublime, and I wished myself at sea.

Your affectionate son, C. H.

I have found among his papers a small roll inscribed, 'Correspondence of C. H. and S. B., 1817 and 1818.' These are the remains of an exchange of letters he kept up with his future wife from the first of his Seminary life until their marriage. As a fair specimen of this remarkable love-letter writing, I record the following, written from Princeton, in 1818, day and month not given.

My Dear Sarah:—Our intercourse for some time past has been, as far as it is carried on by writing, not only very irregular, but very trifling. What can be the reason of this? Does a note of more than half a dozen lines require an effort which our feelings are inadequate to produce? Or are we really so constantly employed that a fortnight affords no half-hour on which affection might seize to devote to an occupation it considers and constitutes delightful?

But this is not the worst of it. Where, my dear Sarah, is our religion? Why have we banished it from our conversation and our writing? Can you recollect for weeks its being the subject of either? This change I know is to be attributed in a great measure, and perhaps entirely, to myself. I have never been enabled in all I have said to you to meet the difficulties you so constantly feel. Perhaps it would be right, therefore, not to attempt it again, but to commend you simply to the grace of God and to the teachings of His Spirit. But I think there is one thing which has not sufficiently engaged your attention, and which is of great practical importance. That is, that faith itself is the very first duty God requires us to perform, without which it is impossible to please Him in any thing. All attempts therefore which men so frequently make to obey before they believe, is proceeding in a way directly the reverse of what God has prescribed. All our ability to obey is obtained by faith. Nothing else will purify the heart. It is by faith that we become united to Christ, in whom all our strength resides. He then that wishes to attain to holiness will be disappointed after all his efforts, unless he begins by believing. It is to this single point then that our first and our constant efforts are to be directed. It is but 'looking unto Jesus', as dear Armstrong told us yesterday.

Until this act be performed we are struggling in our own strength, we are warring at our own charges; but as soon as we believe the battle becomes the Lord's, then all His attributes are engaged to subdue our sins and secure our salvation. And, my dear Sarah, the reason why persons truly pious make so little progress and meet with so many discomfitures is because they do not carry on the conflict in the right way. They endeavour to subdue their corruptions by arguing with themselves and bringing up motives to holiness, instead of using faith. That is, instead of throwing all upon Christ and pleading at the moment His promise to deliver us from sin. If we appeal to Him with confidence, He will never fail to appear in our behalf. And this is the course, my Sarah, I would recommend to you. Use Christ as though He were your own; employ His strength, His merit, and His grace in all your trials. This is the way to honour Him. Fear not that He will be offended at the liberty.

PRINCETON, —, 1818.

With regard to the subject of the first part of your last note, my dear Sarah, I have thought that a view presented some time since by Dr Alexander would be of use to you. In speaking of the justice of God in the punishment of sin, he observed that it was the foundation of the whole plan of redemption; for had there not been some absolute necessity, arising from the nature of God, that sin should be punished, how can we suppose that He would make the infinite sacrifice of His Son, rather than permit it to pass with impunity. Besides, as God is not only Holy, but *Holiness itself,* and as sin is the direct opposite of holiness, it follows from the nature of things that God must be opposed to sin, and of course to any being whose moral character it constitutes. But he to whom God is opposed cannot dwell with Him, and would not if he could; for the soul polluted by sin would find the purity of God more insufferable than the torments of hell. But not to dwell with God is by necessity to be miserable. And as sin is rebellion, self-destruction, and an attempt to destroy the peace and happiness of the universe, can God be unjust to confine its perpetrators, that they may not make His holy creation miserable, or to punish them for their malicious opposition to all that is good. Thus you see, my dear Sarah, that sin and misery are inseparably united from the nature of things, as well as from the holy decree of God. Pray for light, for that wisdom which comes down from heaven; and for your encouragement hear Him say, 'If any man lack wisdom, let him ask of God, who giveth liberally and upbraideth not.' There is more to be learned by prayer than by study. Beware, however, how you procrastinate and where you rest. Remember that every foundation is sandy *save one*—that is, Christ. Blessed be the Lord forever that there is one. To Him, my love, go. Go now, stay not, till by the use of means you make yourself better. This is not the purpose for which they were intended. Wait not till your heart becomes penitent and humble, but go with a proud heart for Him to change. This is the blessing you want. Then go as you are, since He alone can give you what you need.

Our mother always attributed her religious life to the instrumentality of her young lover and husband. On Aug. 4th, 1820, she writes:

I love to feel myself bound to you by indissoluble ties that not even the grave can change — to feel that after being cherished and guided by you through time, I shall, through your instrumentality, stand by you purified before the throne of our Heavenly Father when time shall be no more. Can any conception comprehend the ecstasy of such a moment, or any earthly happiness equal it? Am I guilty of detracting from the true source and first cause of all happiness when I suppose that even in heaven it may be augmented by the reflection that a beloved partner was the means of our attaining it?

About the middle of October he attended the meeting of the Presbytery of Philadelphia, held in Reading, about seventy miles north-west from the city, and passed his examination preparatory to licensure. He then went from Reading through Easton and Wilkesbarre to Silver Lake, from which he wrote to his mother:

SILVER LAKE, Oct. 26, 1818.

Dear Mother:—I met with a kind reception from the Doctor and Cousin Jane. Every thing is very delightful in this fairy place. The Doctor has made several considerable improvements since I was here before, and he bids fair soon to raise his country seat to a full equality with the villas of foreign lands.

Your son, CHARLES

JOHN JOHNS TO CHARLES HODGE

NEW CASTLE, Nov. 2, 1818.

Dear Charles:—I missed the pleasure of seeing Larned and Brecken-ridge. Not expecting any of my friends on that day, I had gone out of town . . .

I do hope most sincerely, my dear brother, that you have been recruited by your jaunt to the Lake. I feel more apprehensive for you now I must be separated from you, than when I could be constantly with you. I add another expostulation to the many already given that you commence this session with a determination to be more attentive to your health than to your studies. Friends, duty, usefulness demand this of you. Go see Sarah as often as you please, if nothing else will keep you out of your room, and tell her you are following my prescription. Guinea Lane (now Witherspoon street) is more salubrious than Silver Lake to some constitutions.

Although I have not roamed much since I saw you, yet I have studied but little. *Turretin De Vocatione, Witherspoon's* Treatise on *Regeneration, Doddridge's* Series of Sermons on the same subject, *Leland's* View of Deistical Writers, and a few reviews, and several biographical sketches connected with church history, comprise my labours.

I have attended a good many societies here, and several out in the country. In these last I have been prevailed upon to exhort, and have found more freedom than I ever expected on such occasions. When my own heart is affected and the people seem attentive, it is the most delightful thing, and I was going to say the easiest thing, in the world to talk to a few who have assembled to worship; but, dear Charles, it is heavy work, inexpressibly heavy, when views are dark and the affections languid. Very little experience on a contracted scale has taught me what I had often heard before, that nothing but sincere, deep and ardent piety will do for a minister of the gospel. I trust that I sincerely feel its necessity in a greater degree than heretofore, and hope that this conviction is the precursor of greater communications of grace and strength than I have hitherto enjoyed.

Dear Charles, write soon.   J. J.

CHARLES HODGE TO HIS MOTHER

PRINCETON, Jan. 11, 1819.

My Dear Mother:—Johns communicated to us the death of our brother Newbold. Dr Alexander, speaking of the event before the Seminary, said: 'As to John Newbold, I always thought that man, since I first knew him, one of the very best men I ever saw. I never knew a youth in whose piety I had greater confidence. It was not only genuine, but he possessed the deepest sentiments of piety. He had an intellect of the first order, and though the impediment in his utterance might have prevented his being popular as a speaker, yet he had a mind capable of the deepest and clearest investigation.' The Doctor then gave some particulars of his life and prospects. Such a testimony from such a man is a better legacy to friends than the richest bequests of princes.

PRINCETON, Feb. 1, 1819.

My Dear Mother:—The third and last year of my continuance at the Seminary is so rapidly passing by, that I cannot prevent myself from frequently looking forward to its close, and asking the question — 'Where am I to go?' or 'What am I to do?' And it is almost time that an answer to this question was prepared. For it is of so great importance that it would be wrong to defer it so long that the decision should at last be made without much deliberation. Unless I am greatly mistaken in my own heart, I have scarcely a wish on the subject save that the path I pursue may be the path of duty. Under Him, whose I am by particular obligations, I feel at the disposal of you and Dr Alexander; and should you agree in marking out the same course, I trust I should tread it with cheerful feet. It is of great importance to have some definite object placed before us to engage our minds and interest our feelings. Something at once great and good, on which we can dwell with complacency, to which we can feel consecrated, and for which we might be constantly preparing. I have often congratulated Nevins and McIlvaine on their possessing this enviable advantage, but now their prospect is as indistinct as my own.[1]

I hope to see my good brother Johns before a great while. I wish you would send me by him a little bag of *gingerbread* to eat after our long society evenings. You may smile at this coming from a *man* — but Johns will tell you it is worth being laughed at to gain so substantial a good.

PRINCETON, Feb. 10, 1819.

My Dear Mother:—I do not feel very impatient or anxious about the course I am to pursue on leaving the Seminary, except that it will be necessary to decide before the meeting of the General Assembly, in case it should be thought expedient for me to take a mission either through the Western or Southern States. This is the plan which Davis urges. He intends to travel in the character of a missionary over almost all the Union, and is quite anxious I should join him. Without my knowing it, he mentioned it to Dr Alexander, who said it would be an excellent thing for me, especially should my health need establishing. But this is all his doing. For myself I have scarcely thought of it for a moment, and at present have no more plan than

[1] The mission to South America to which these brethren had been designated had been abandoned because of the state of that country.

I had a year ago. I laughingly told the Doctor he must dispose of me before a great while. He asked if I would be willing to go where he would send me. I said 'Yes.' 'Take care,' says he; 'I may shock you when I come to tell you what to do.' But I am not afraid of him. The dear little man has been unwell two or three times this session, and as he won't take exercise, he is in danger of becoming quite enfeebled.

PRINCETON, N.J., March 31, 1819.

Dear Mother:—They have at last commenced the house for Dr Alexander. It is to be built on the Seminary grounds, having its front fourteen feet nearer to the road than the front of the main building. It is to be of brick, which will be very ugly, unless they intend painting it white. The *dear little man* will then be so near the Seminary, I am afraid, he will never take the least exercise. Walking from his study to recitation, under a pretty heavy burden of clothes, is now nearly all he makes out to accomplish.

PRINCETON, April 21, 1819.

My Dear Mother:—The close of session brings with it an additional burden of duties. During the last week mine has come upon me all at once, for it has happened that several extra exercises have devolved upon me at the same time. I have now to prepare for a difficult discussion by Friday evening, which will keep me diligent until it is over. I suspect that I shall always have stimulus enough of this kind to make me undertake as much as my strength is able to accomplish. My character for diligence is better than for any thing else, I am afraid. One of my fellow-students, who is quite fond of me, said the other day I must be a fool if I did not know a great deal, for I study so much. This is a difficult alternative to choose between—folly and great knowledge.

It became more and more evident that Dr Alexander must be relieved from some portion of his onerous duties, and that the faculty must eventually be enlarged by the addition of a third professor for the Department of Biblical Literature and Exegesis. The Doctor's preference was to train one of his own students for the position. He had, in the first instance, made overtures to this end to Mr John Johns, who, having graduated from the College of New Jersey with the first honour in 1815, had afterwards spent two years in the Theological Seminary, exhibiting the same high qualities as a scholar and Christian. But Mr Johns, one of whose parents was a Presbyterian and the other an Episcopalian, was at that time debating the question of the denomination to which he should ultimately attach himself. He in the end, with the advice of Dr James P. Wilson, pastor of the First Presbyterian Church, Philadelphia, and assent of Drs Alexander and Miller, decided to enter the ministry of the Protestant Episcopal Church, of which eventually he became so bright an ornament. The reason, on the part of the two Princeton Professors, for their part of the decision, was that, in their opinion, Mr Johns, as providentially situated, and as characterized by his decided evangelical and Calvinistic sentiments, could do more good in the direction determined on than in the other.[1]

[1] Bishop Johns was brought up in the bosom of a pious and highly cultivated family. His father, Judge Johns, was Chancellor of the State of Delaware. In his native town, Newcastle, Delaware, there were two churches, the one Episcopal, of which the Rev. Mr Clay was rector, and the other Presbyterian. Each of these ministers had an additional country parish; and they so arranged it that they never officiated in the town the same part of the day on Sunday. Hence it was that the same congregation went in the morning to the one church, and in the afternoon to the other. In Chancellor Johns' family, some of the children were Presbyterians, and others Episcopalians. Under these circumstances, it was not surprising that the bishop, in the early part of his preparatory course, was undecided as to the Church in which he should minister. The late Rev. Dr James P. Wilson, an eminent Presbyterian minister, before he embraced the ministry, was a distinguished lawyer, and an intimate friend of Judge Johns. It was under his advice that the bishop decided to enter the ministry of the Episcopal Church. 'This decision', says Rev. Dr Hodge, 'although neither of us at the time knew anything about it, determined my whole course in life. When Dr

In the morning of May 6th, 1819, young Charles Hodge, then approaching the end of his Seminary course, happened to call upon Dr Alexander in the study in the wing of the small wooden house on Mercer Street, first door east of the Episcopal Church-yard, which the Doctor occupied before his entrance upon his permanent residence. After the business which brought him had been transacted, Dr Alexander, without preparation, suddenly said: 'How would you like to be a professor in the Seminary?' Our father often in after years told us that this question overwhelmed him with surprise and confusion. The thought had never entered his imagination before. The Doctor, without waiting for an answer, said: 'Of course I have no power to determine such a result. It will depend upon the judgment of the General Assembly. Say nothing now, but think upon it. My plan for you, at present, is simply that you spend the next winter in Philadelphia learning to read the Hebrew language with points with some competent instructor.' A week afterwards Mr Hodge wrote to his mother as follows:

PRINCETON, May 13, 1819.

My Dear Mother:—The subject of my last letter has occupied my mind a good deal, though I have not come to any very definite determination. Did the duties of the contemplated office require

---

Archibald Alexander was appointed professor in the Seminary at Princeton, he had under his care the departments of didactic, polemic and pastoral theology, together with instruction in Hebrew. He soon found that this was too burdensome, and therefore determined to select some young man on whom he might devolve the Hebrew department. He selected Johns. When he decided to enter the Episcopal Church, he took up with me. Johns was always first — first everywhere, and first in everything. His success was largely due to his conscientious determination always to do his best. He was always thoroughly prepared for every exercise in college and in the seminary. He would be able, day after day, when in the seminary, to give what Turretin, our text-book, calls the state of the question; that is, the precise point at hand, then all the arguments in its support in their order, all the objections and answers to them, through the whole thirty or forty pages, without the professor saying a word.' — *Communicated by the Rev. Prof. Joseph Packard, D.D. Alexandria, Va.*

me to give up the prospect of preaching altogether, I think I should not hesitate in declining it; for I believe that preaching the gospel is a privilege superior to any other intrusted to men. But this is not necessary, for our professors preach now nearly as much as the stated pastors of congregations. This being the case, I think the comparative usefulness of a teacher in such an institution as this, and that of the generality of ministers, will not admit of much doubt. It is evident that the moral influence of Drs Alexander and Miller on the character of the Church is almost inconceivable; for they in a measure impart their own spirit to each of their pupils, who bear it hence to spread it through the lesser spheres of which they may become the centres. The very fact, therefore, of a man being pious in this situation makes him the means of incalculable good. It seems to me that the heart more than the head of an instructor in a religious seminary qualifies or unfits him for his station. This is a very serious aspect in which I have been led to look at this subject, and which renders it so responsible that I sometimes fear to undertake it.

With respect to my competency for the duties of the situation, I believe it will depend more on diligence than on natural talent. My attention will not, as you appear to suppose, be confined to the study of languages, and therefore no talent I may possess can lie unemployed, but will doubtless be put to its utmost strength. It will, however, be of great advantage to me that it will be necessary to become in some measure familiar with the dead languages; for I am convinced that they are as essential to a student as tools are to workmen of a different kind. I know I could have made a better choice (for the situation) than our dear professors have made, but the risk in this respect belongs to them. I feel myself too much disposed to look on the bright side of every thing I contemplate. Perhaps I may be corrected of this error before I am grey-headed.

As the event of this plan is and must for some time continue to be uncertain, every thing does not depend on my present determination. I do not think I have any right to dispose of myself, as I am not my own; but my duty is confined to the single point of trying to find out what the will of God regarding me is. I know no better way of learning this than by waiting the event — that is, to take the preparatory measures Dr Alexander proposed for the ensuing year, and then to consider it my duty to proceed, should the way be opened, and if it be closed, consider it an indication that my path lies in some other direction.

Your son, C. HODGE.

EXTRACT FROM THE MINUTES OF THE PROCEEDINGS OF
THE DIRECTORS OF PRINCETON THEOLOGICAL SEMINARY,
SEPT. 27, 1819.

The members of the committee who attended the examinations were highly gratified, both with the manner in which the examination was conducted, and with the manner in which the students acquitted themselves. The committee, therefore, recommend that a full certificate of their having passed through a complete course of theological education, agreeably to the plan of the Seminary, be given to the following young gentlemen, viz.: George S. Boardman, Remembrance Chamberlain, Samuel S. Davis, John Goldsmith, Charles Hodge, William Nevins, and Aaron D. Lane.

These Diplomas or Certificates of having passed through the entire Seminary course were publicly distributed to these young men the next day, September 28, 1819.

4

FROM HIS GRADUATION FROM THE SEMINARY, SEPTEMBER 27, 1819, TO HIS ELECTION AS PROFESSOR, MAY 24, 1822

Correspondence with Dr Alexander, and with His Mother and Brother – Visit to New Haven, Boston and Andover – His Licensure, Teaching in the Seminary, and Preaching at Lambertville and Ewing

HAVING GRADUATED FROM THE SEMINARY, Mr Hodge, in accordance with the plan suggested by Dr Alexander, now returned to his mother's house in Philadelphia, with the intention of spending the winter in the study of Hebrew, as written with points, with which Dr Alexander himself was not familiar. Mr Hodge improved this opportunity with the utmost diligence under the valuable tuition of the Rev. Joseph Banks, D.D., Professor in the Theological Seminary of the Associate (now United) Presbyterian Church – then situated in Philadelphia – and pastor of the Associate Presbyterian Church in that city. Dr Banks had the reputation of being not only a sound theologian, but also one of the most eminent Hebrew scholars at that day in America. Mr Hodge also, during this winter, widened his education by attending upon lectures on anatomy and physiology, delivered in connection with the medical department of the University. With all matters connected with human physiology, therapeutics, and the practice of medicine, he always continued to take a deep interest, and possessed, for a layman, an unusual knowledge.

In the meantime he was licensed to preach by the Presbytery of Philadelphia, at their meeting in Pittsgrove, N.J., October 21st, 1819; and from that time for several years, was pretty constantly occupied every Sabbath day in preaching.

The Minutes of that Presbytery disclose the following facts concerning his connection with it.

October 21, 1817, Charles Hodge was received as a candidate. All the College studies, a Latin Exegesis on the question 'An Spiritus sit Deus?', and a Presbyterial exercise on 2 Peter, 1:10, were assigned to Mr Hodge as parts of trial to be exhibited at the next fall meeting.

Reading, Pennsylvania, October 21, 1818. The above parts of trial were presented and sustained.

Pittsgrove, N. J., October 19, 1819. Lecture on Psalm 53 was sustained. Certificate was received from Professors in Theological Seminary, stating that he had, in a regular and creditable manner, completed the course of study prescribed by the plan of said Seminary. Examinations on Natural and Revealed Theology and Church History were sustained.

October 20, 1819, Charles Hodge and Samuel Cornish (coloured) were licensed on the same day.

June 27, 1820, Charles Hodge was dismissed to the care of the Presbytery of New Brunswick.

MR HODGE TO DR A. ALEXANDER

PHILADELPHIA, December 16, 1819.

Dear Sir:—Your kindness to me has been so great and so uniform that I now feel as though I pecuharly belonged to you, and (though you may not be very anxious to acknowledge your property) this feeling constrains me to tell you the little I have done since I left your more immediate care. I was licensed on the 20th of October. Since then I have preached every Sabbath, and usually twice, and have now to preach regularly at the Falls of the Schuylkill in the morning and at the Arsenal in the afternoon of each Sabbath. As October was my vacation, I did nothing as to studying during that month. But early in November I commenced attending Dr Banks, and recite to him five days in the week. Finding the points required so much attention, I was obliged to devote myself to them almost exclusively for four or five weeks, and therefore did little else than go through the grammar and read the first four chapters of Genesis during that period. Since then I have commenced reading the Psalms and studying Greek, and now recite alternately the Greek and Hebrew. I have not been able to read a great deal since I came to town. Two of the volumes of Home's Introduction, Lowth's Lectures, and three hundred pages in Glassius, together with one or two smaller works, include all I have yet had time to get through with. Your books have been of the greatest assistance to me, Opitius and Bythner especially.

Dr Banks is very much what you said he was. He will talk all day on any thing connected with Hebrew. It is quite amusing to see his zeal on the subject, especially for the points and accents, to the last of which he has devoted years of study, and which he estimates rather, I suspect, from the labour they cost him than from their real utility, which, however, may still be great. He is very anxious to show me the 'curiosities' of this system of the accentuation, which he thinks does every thing, regulating the rhetorical and grammatical construction, pointing out the ellipsis, indicating the emotions, etc.

Will you be so kind as in some way to let me know whether you approve of the plan I am pursuing, and what books you wish me to read after I finish this volume of Glassius. I am sensible that I am asking you to add to the debt of kindness I already owe you, and which, although I can never repay you, it will be the pleasure of my life to feel and acknowledge. What Greek Lexicon had I better obtain — Schrevelius being the only one I have? Please remember me most affectionately to Mrs Alexander and the boys. Tell little Jeanette she must not forget me.

And now, sir, may I ask you sometimes to pray for me? This is a favour of which I am utterly unworthy, but which I greatly need. You must excuse my asking so much. You do not know, sir, how much I owe you, and no one can know; but I hope God will reward you openly, I am yours,

C. Hodge

DR A. ALEXANDER TO MR HODGE

Princeton, Dec. 22, 1819.

My Dear Sir:—Yours of the 16th instant I have received, and the only thing in it which I dislike is the anxiety which you discover that you may not be troublesome by the length of your letter. There is not the least occasion for any apprehension of this sort. The mere reading of letters is never burdensome, and I have wished and expected a communication from you for some time.

That I take a lively interest in your welfare and usefulness I need not tell you, and of course I wish to know what you are doing, and what progress you are making in your Biblical studies. The information communicated in your letter on this subject is very gratifying to me. I entirely approve the plan which you are pursuing, except, perhaps, that the Greek recitations might be dispensed with, and the whole of your recitations with Dr Banks for this winter might profitably be in the Hebrew. Although I have not the least confidence in this whole system of punctuation, and especially of accentuation, yet I am satisfied that you should acquire an accurate knowledge of the whole system; and as this winter may be the only opportunity of enjoying the advantages of Dr Banks' instructions, my opinion is that it should be improved in reference to this object. Not that I would have you neglect the Greek, but I do not perceive the great advantage of your reciting on it, as there are no 'curiosities' in that language which you may not learn at home. In answer to your inquiry respecting a proper Greek Lexicon to be purchased, I would say that for the N.T., Schleusner should be preferred; but if you mean for classical Greek,

Morell is, I suppose, the best. Hereafter you must have *Suiceri Thesaurus Ecc., Suidas* and *Hesychius.* I learn that Schleusner has published a new and improved edition of Bird's *Thesaurus* of the LXX. That will be valuable; also Trommius' *Concordance.* But there is no advantage in accumulating too many books at once.

Mr Wisner left with me some volumes of *De Moor,* purchased for you, and with his consent I presume on yours to retain all except the first three, until you have read them. It so happened that these first volumes were already in my possession. You will find the head *De Scriptura* well worth perusal.

It is my plan that you should spend the next summer at this place, but it is not sufficiently matured to give details. Keep this, however, in mind.

I send you the second volume of *Glassius* with *De Moor.* The third is the most interesting, but you must read the second first. Read *Kennicott's* Dissertation, *De Rossi's* Prolegomena to Various Readings, Wettstein's and Griesbach's Prolegomena, etc.

Yours affectionately,

A. Alexander.

After his licensure, Mr Hodge was appointed by the Presbytery to missionary work. He had appointments every Sabbath morning at the 'Falls' of the Schuylkill, and later at Cohocksink, and on the afternoons at the Arsenal. In connection with a record of these services he kept the only religious diary of his life. Some specimens of this are here given.

On *Wednesday evening, October 20th, 1819,* I preached my trial sermon at Pittsgrove, before the Philadelphia Presbytery. Though the Lord had kindly afforded me solemn feelings in view of my entrance on the ministry, yet I found my heart but little engaged during the time of service. The circumstances in which I was placed gave rise to feelings of anxiety which prevented my weak principle of grace from being exercised as it should have been. My text was Rom. 8:1. The succeeding morning, October 21st, I was licensed to preach the gospel of Jesus Christ. Oh! that I may ever look upon this high vocation with the same feelings with which the Apostle Paul ever regarded it, and may the Lord Jesus work within me all the good pleasure of his will, making me such a minister as He would have me to be.

Sabbath, October 24th, 1819.—The preceding evening I rode out to Frankford and enjoyed sweet intercourse with my dear brother Biggs. The prospect of preaching on the ensuing day kept my mind serious, and gave to our conversation more of the religious character than usual. In the morning I preached on the 53rd Psalm. I enjoyed the service myself far more than I did when preaching before Presbytery, and the people appeared quite serious and attentive. Whether, however, the least good was accomplished must be left to the revelations of the great day. My prayer is for humility and zeal. The afternoon in Brother Thomas Biggs' room. In the evening he preached from Gal. 5:6.

Sabbath, October 31st, 1819, was spent in Woodbury. I went down the preceding evening, and was kindly entertained at Judge Caldwell's. In the morning I preached from John 3:36. Many of the people appeared attentive and serious. I know not what good was done. For myself, I did not enjoy the services as much as usual. I dined with Mr White, and did not introduce religious conversation. May God pity my weakness, and enable me to be more faithful hereafter. In the evening I preached from the 53rd Psalm. The audience was large and very attentive. The Lord granted me more feeling and ease than I had enjoyed in the morning. The fear of man, and the desire of applause, God in great mercy has hitherto kept from greatly disturbing me, especially in the pulpit. I feel myself entirely dependent on His sovereign grace for the continuance and increase of this great mercy. Were He to let me alone, I should indeed become dreadfully corrupt in practice as well as in heart. Bless the Lord, O my soul.

Sabbath, Nov. 7th, 1819.—The preceding day I rode up to Abington with Mr Steele. Here I had the pleasure of seeing several times good Mrs Tennant, and had the privilege of praying by her bedside, and of witnessing the composure and peace of one who had the hope of the gospel. Oh, precious Saviour, grant to my soul and the souls of all my friends the powerful supports of Thy grace in the hour of death . . .

Sabbath, Nov. 21, 1819.—This day I entered on my duties as missionary. Oh, Thou source of all good, grant me the continued aid of Thy grace, that with purity of motive and singleness of object I may zealously and faithfully discharge my responsible duties. Do bless me, O my God. I rode out in the morning to the Falls with Gerard R., and was very much pleased and surprised by his religious turn of mind, and the interest he took in the institutions of piety. I preached from the 53rd Psalm to a small but respectable audience. In the afternoon I rode out to the Arsenal, and spoke from the parable of the Great Supper, Luke 14:15. This was a pleasant season. I hope the Lord was there. Oh, incline that people to hear and obey the invitations of Thy gospel.

The evening Bro. Davis and myself spent in our room in delightful intercourse. The Lord blessed us. We prayed together before we separated, as on the succeeding day he expects to sail for Charleston. Good and powerful God attend and bless him abundantly in Jesus Christ.

Nov. 28th, 1819.—Sabbath morning I rode out to the Falls with Gerard R., and there preached from John 3:36. The congregation was not very large, and my feelings were cold. I dined with Mr Thomson, who accompanied me in the afternoon to the Arsenal, where I preached from Rom. 8:1 with somewhat more pleasure to myself than in the morning.

During this sacred day I have experienced very little spiritual enjoyment; my heart has been too far from God, and worldly thoughts have too much occupied my mind. This I suspect has arisen from my conduct during the past week. It is impossible to gain and lose at pleasure spirituality of mind. It must be cultivated constantly. Let not, my soul, the end of the week you now have entered find you still at such a distance from God. Oh, Holy Spirit, return unto Thy rest!

Deign to make my bosom Thine abode — and O attend my feeble preaching by Thy almighty energy, for Jesus' sake . . .

Sabbath, Dec. 26, 1819.—During the preceding week I had preached for Dr Janeway in his new session room. As this was the first time I had preached in the city (excepting once for Bro. Platt), I felt much too anxious to acquit myself well, and was disappointed. The evening was unusually rainy, and there were consequently few persons present. Among them, however, was my dear brother, who had just returned from Calcutta. This made me feel less at ease than I might otherwise have done. But the chief cause of my not enjoying the service was doubtless my pride. I felt almost depressed under the apprehension that I should never become even a moderately acceptable preacher. I would give the world were my desire of honouring Christ and of saving souls so strong that I should be indifferent to what related merely to myself. Oh, cast me not off from Thy presence; take not Thy Holy Spirit from me. Oh, grant to my brother unfeigned piety. Would to God I might be made a blessing to his soul.

Sabbath, Feb. 13, 1820.—This day my regular ministrations at Cohocksink were commenced. The audience not very numerous, but serious. The children of the Sabbath School form an important part of my charge. It is often quite unknown at how early an age God commences a work of grace in the heart, and it may happen that many children have utterly lost that impression through the carelessness of their parents and teachers. May I be taught of God that I may be able to teach others also. It is only the heart that has been deeply exercised in divine things which can enable us to preach experimentally to others. Piety is the life of a minister . . .

Sabbath, May 14, 1820.—I preached my last sermon this morning to the people of Cohocksink. In the afternoon at the Arsenal my text was, 'Lay hold on eternal life.' This was an interesting season. The presence of a considerable number of young men gave a cast to my train of thought which interested my own feelings, and fixed in a great measure the attention of my hearers. I have yet once more to preach to that people, and may it prove as a seal to all the rest. I have almost uniformly found that when I have commenced a service under a little depression of spirits, it has proved more than usually pleasant.

APPOINTMENT AS TEACHER IN THE SEMINARY

In their Report to the Board of Directors, May 15th, 1820, the Professors say: 'The Professors respectfully represent to the Board that in their opinion the interests of the Seminary require a distinct teacher of the original languages of the Scripture. The Professor, who has attended to this branch of instruction, finds that it interferes with the performance of duties which more properly belong to his office; and that he cannot, consistently with his health, devote to it that degree of attention which its importance demands.'

The above Report was committed to Drs Romeyn, Neill and Rodgers; to whom were subsequently added Drs Woodhull, Rice and McDowell and Mr Lewis. At a meeting of the Board in Philadelphia, May 25th, that Committee made the following report, which was adopted: 'That although the suggestion of the Professors on the subject of appointing a teacher of the original languages appears to be important, yet the state of the funds renders it inexpedient for this Board to endeavour to carry it into effect at present. Resolved that an extract of this minute, together with that part of the Professors' report, which relates to this subject, be laid before the General Assembly.'

On the next day, May 26th, the General Assembly, while approving the report of the Board of Directors, resolved 'That the Professors be authorized to employ an assistant teacher of the original languages of Scripture, until the meeting of the next General Assembly. Provided a suitable person can be obtained at a salary consistent with the funds of the Seminary; and provided also that such salary does not exceed the sum of four hundred dollars.'

This authority having been obtained, the Professors appointed Mr Hodge, who came into Princeton on horseback to prepare for his work, in the latter part of June.

MR HODGE TO HIS MOTHER

Princeton, June 22nd, 1820.

My Dear Mother:—I suspect the heat of yesterday made you regret my having commenced so long a ride. But I suffered less than I expected. I got to Frankford before seven, and stayed for breakfast. Mr Biggs then rode with me about nine miles. When we reached Holmesburgh, which is four miles from Frankford, I found the sun so excessively hot, that we stopped at a store, and I bought a great sheet of paste-board, and cutting a hole in it large enough to admit my hat, pinned it on. This effectually preserved my head and most of my body from the direct rays of the sun. I was quite amused to see the people along the road stop, lay down their work, and stare after me as long as I was in sight. Some laughed right out. And as for Bristol, I thought that I never should have got through it. I had courage enough, however, to be looked at and laughed at, rather than be made sick by the heat. By riding slowly, and stopping frequently, I arrived here, but little fatigued, about eight o'clock.

Your affectionate son,
Charles Hodge

He now boarded in the family of his paternal friend, Dr Alexander, and had his study and bed-room in that wing of the old residence of the Doctor, which had been used as a study, and in which he was first abruptly informed of the Doctor's plans concerning him. He at this time also began to suffer from that obscure and painful affection of the nerves of his right thigh which afterwards so greatly modified his habits of life.

Extract from Records of Presbytery of New Brunswick. July 5th, 1820: 'Mr Charles Hodge was received as a licentiate from the

Presbytery of Philadelphia, by certificate. He was appointed the supply of the Church in New Brunswick, and the united Churches of Georgetown and Lambertville a number of Sabbaths during the year.'

MR HODGE TO HIS BROTHER

PRINCETON, July 10, 1820.

My Dear Brother:—My situation here is as pleasant as even my fondest wishes had desired. I have a pleasant room at the upper end of town, and board with Dr Alexander's family. This I find a very advantageous arrangement, as the intercourse I enjoy with the Doctor cannot fail of being very profitable. I take a good deal of exercise, think my horse the best in the world, and am very well. The rheumatism in my limb, I think, continues pretty much as it was. I feel it most in my knee; it seems to be brought on pretty uniformly, by fatigue. Excepting a slight weakness, however, it is still as serviceable as the other.

Your affectionate brother,
C. H.

MR HODGE TO HIS MOTHER

PRINCETON, September 18th, 1820.

My Dear Mother:—On Saturday I rode to Bristol, and preached yesterday twice in their Episcopal Church. They have been without a pastor for some years, and though the population of the town is so considerable, they have only casual preaching. They are so liberal in their sentiments, that they seldom stop to inquire to what denomination a man belongs; if he is willing to preach, they are willing to hear.

I am very well: my riding so much gives me a colour, which has led to many congratulations as to the state of my health. My limb was, I think, a good deal better, but I believe I walked too much with it of late, which has occasioned a return of the pain. I intend to be more careful on this point, and continue diligent in observing the Doctor's [his brother Hugh's] directions.

VISIT TO BOSTON

In October of this year his friend, Mr Benjamin Wisner, afterwards the eloquent preacher and distinguished Secretary of the American Board of Commissioners for Foreign Missions, was invited to preach as a candidate before the Old South Church of Boston. Mr Wisner and Mr Hodge made a plan of riding there together, and after remaining in that attractive city three weeks, of returning in the same manner, including a visit to New Haven and Yale College on the way. They effected the journey in Mr Hodge's old-fashioned two-wheeled gig, on springs shaped like the letter C, a form of conveyance now utterly extinct. They were drawn by his small bay horse, of Canadian extraction, of whose fine qualities he often subsequently boasted. The two letters to his mother, subjoined, contain all the information now remaining, as to this visit, which produced a decided impression on himself.

Boston, Monday, October 9, 1820.

My Dear Mother:—I presume you are by this time anxious to learn something of your traveller. I should have written to you on the way, had you not told me you could wait until we reached Boston. We came within five or six miles of the town on Friday evening, but did not proceed, as it was then quite dark, and both our horse and ourselves were fatigued by a long day's ride. It would, indeed, hardly have been safe to have entered a strange city in the dark and without a guide. It was about eight o'clock on Saturday morning when we first saw the distant spires of Boston, and the lofty dome of the State House. The view excited a variety of pleasing and serious emotions. After changing our dress we called upon Mr (deacon) Cutler, the gentleman whom Wisner had seen in Princeton. We were soon introduced to Mr Salisbury, the Lieutenant Governor, Mr Welsh, and to several other gentlemen, who all received us with the utmost kindness. I had met with Mr Dwight, (son of the late President), at New Haven, and he had *made* me promise to consider his house as my home while I remained in Boston. As the weather had detained Mr Dwight from home longer than he had expected, it was my wish to have either remained at the public house, or to have gone with Wisner to the house of the widow of the late pastor, as a boarder. But finding that either of these plans would have wounded the hospitable feelings of these good people, I was obliged to remain with Mr Cutler until Mr Dwight returns. There is no danger of our not receiving kindness and attention enough. The danger is entirely on the other side.

I have been very agreeably disappointed in the general appearance of Boston. I have, to be sure, as yet seen only the southern section of the town, which is much the most pleasant. The green they call their Common, and the hill on which the State House stands exceeds anything I have ever seen. As Saturday was so clear, the gentlemen who were with us thought it best to improve the opportunity by going to the top of the State House. On reaching this elevated point our eyes rested on what is thought the finest prospect in America. Boston, Charlestown and Cambridge were all below us; the harbor, with its many islands, and the broad ocean full in view, altogether forms a combination of the beautiful and grand, which makes the Bostonians willing to enter into a competition with the admirers of the Bay of Naples.

Wisner preached twice yesterday for the Old South people. As far as I can judge, the impression has been universally favourable. I preached morning and afternoon in the Park Street Church, which is Mr Dwight' s charge.

The kindest providence has presided over our journey. We met with no accident, alarm, or difficulty. Our little horse came as briskly into Boston as he did out of Princeton. We spent two days and a half at New Haven. Dr Miller's letter secured us every attention we could wish. We were there, as usual, soon obliged to leave the tavern, and stay with Mr Taylor,[1] a young minister, who is the pride of the southern part of Connecticut. We found this one of the most improving incidents in our journey, as this young man (about thirty), who possesses uncommonly fine talents, differs very considerably in his theoretical opinions from the Princeton gentlemen. He kept us pretty constantly in an animated though temperate discussion of our differences. We have been delighted with the general aspect of things, and with the face of the country in New England, particularly in Connecticut.

I am well, excepting my limb, which, however, is considerably better than it was. I will write again before we leave Boston.

Your loving son, C. H.

The people of the Old South Church were delighted with, and eventually called Mr Wisner to be their pastor. But they required him, according to their custom, to preach as a probationer four Sabbaths. Therefore Mr Hodge left his friend, and came on to meet the duties of a new session in Princeton, bringing Mr John Maclean, afterwards President of Princeton College, in the vacant seat in his gig.

NEAR BOSTON, October 25th, 1820.

My Dear Mother:—If praising New England will do you any good, you shall have enough of it when I get home. I have now left Boston. Mr Wisner has remained. It was his intention when he came here, to have spent only three Sabbaths, but he has found the universal custom of the country requires that he should stay at least four weeks, which custom he has the more willingly submitted to, as his cold prevented his preaching more than once on the second Sabbath he

[1] Nathaniel W. Taylor, D.D., afterwards Professor of Theology in Yale College, and author of the modification of New England Theology, called 'Taylorism', against which the polemic guns of the *Princeton Review* were trained for forty years.

was in Boston. You know it was our intention to return by way of Albany, but we had heard so much of the extreme hilliness of the country, we were almost afraid to attempt it. The necessity of making the experiment being removed by the detention of Mr Wisner, I determined to take the direct road home, which will save me nearly a week. Happily Mr Maclean, tutor in Princeton College, was in Boston and anxious to return, and has therefore taken the vacant seat in the gig.

Of the first thirteen days we spent in Boston, only two were fair; it rained and blew from the *East* almost incessantly. The good people here did all they could to apologize for the weather, assuring us that such a season had never before been known. But that did not mend the matter. The great inconvenience we felt was that we were prevented from visiting the adjacent places, as Salem, Cambridge, Andover, etc. The Lieutenant Governor kindly offered to take us over to Cambridge and introduce us to the President of the University. But the weather prevented, until Monday last, when we rode over and were introduced to Dr Kirkland and several of the professors. I handed the Doctor Mr Astley's letter, and young as we were he kindly attended us over all their spacious building. The compliment of his personal attendance we no doubt owed to the presence of his Honour, the Lieutenant Governor. Dr Kirkland seems to be one of the happiest men in the world, always disposed to say pleasant things, and is entirely free from anything which would indicate that he believes, what those around him believe, that he is a great man.

I had the pleasure of spending a tantalizing hour with Mr Everett. I had intended, after the first visit was paid, to make an effort to see him frequently. But the weather, by preventing our first visit from being made in season, broke in upon this plan. I regret this very much, for I am satisfied that it would have been of essential service to have seen more of this extraordinary young man.

Several circumstances besides the state of the weather, induced us to postpone our visit to Andover until Friday last, particularly the absence of all the professors, except Dr Woods. I considered that the missing of Professor Stuart would frustrate the primary object of my visit. You may judge, then, how much I was rejoiced to hear, about an hour after we reached Andover, that he had just returned. We spent the evening with him, and returned the next day to Boston, as our arrangements made necessary. On Monday afternoon, however, I went up again and remained with him until this morning (Wednesday). I think Stuart is the most interesting man I have seen in New England. He is kind, sociable, condescending and communicative; free from all formality, he becomes your friend at once. His talents are of the first order, and no man in the country has made any progress comparable to his in the department of Biblical literature. He has done me great good, has marked out my road, and told me the right path, and enlarged my views as to the extent and importance of the study, more than I could have conceived it possible. He told me he had lost at least three years by taking a wrong course at first. I am persuaded that it would be the best thing I could do to spend a year with such a man. But it is impossible. I will write to him, however, and see him as often as I can.

The Doctor [his brother Hugh] wants to know whether I think the people here more intelligent and better informed than they are with us. I do, most decidedly, and the ladies beyond comparison. They are hospitable, and as attentive to strangers as they well can be. It is true, we came under peculiarly favourable circumstances, and therefore, perhaps, have been the more struck with the propriety of calling Boston the clergyman's paradise. Mr Wisner, of course, is just now the object of much interest, and through him I have received much of kindness and attention. We are now thirteen miles out of Boston, on the road to New Haven.

Your affectionate son,
CHARLES HODGE

In New Haven, Mr Hodge called again on Mr Taylor, and with his fellow traveller, Mr Maclean, reached Princeton again without serious misadventure.

MR HODGE TO HIS BROTHER

PRINCETON, Nov. 21st, 1820.

My Dear Brother:— . . . This, considering my six recitations, is doing very well. I wish to apprize you that all the indignation you may feel for my being thus oppressed, is due to me, as I have had the sole direction of the whole business, excepting that the Doctor (Alexander) was kind enough to prevent my going further. But you need not be uneasy. Most of my duties of this class are of such a nature, that I can get through them with very little study, while at the same time I might spend a week on each to great advantage. Thus I shall be able to accommodate my exertions to my strength. I never knew, until I undertook it, that hearing a class of twenty or thirty students recite is one of the most fatiguing things in the world. The unbroken attention you are obliged to pay for an hour and a half together, and the necessity of talking a good deal, withal, is more tiresome than any one who has not felt it would imagine. There is another thing which adds to the exertion, which is, that these students are men well informed and not easily satisfied, and not likely to let a mistake pass unobserved. I feel this difficulty a good deal in Greek, as almost all the students have been studying the language for years, and some of them have taught it, but in Hebrew I have more the advantage of them. There is one thing greatly in my favour, that I have not got your modesty to bother me.

Both you and Mamma seem to have taken up the idea that I am in a forlorn situation here, and I can't tell why. I feel as independent as a king, and will contrive some way to keep myself warm. If Dr Alexander spent so many winters in this dear study, I suspect you will find a good many more people to envy than to pity me for now possessing it. And without jesting, it is much the most pleasant and convenient situation I could have had in town.

Your affectionate brother,

C. H.

Princeton, March 9, 1821.

My Dear Brother:—We had the pleasure, last evening, of hearing Mr Ward.[1] If you have heard him you know he has little of the graces of elocution wherewith to adorn his discourse, but he has what is far more important even for an orator, a heart alive to the importance of the object for which he pleads. After describing the difficulties they had met in India twenty years ago, he told us how all in a great measure had been surmounted. The British government and their subjects are now in their favour. The schools connected with Serampore alone contain eight thousand children. One thousand of the natives have been baptized, and as a profession of religion there involves a living martyrdom, we may hope they are sincere converts. But what is above and beyond all is that they have given the Bible to hundreds of millions in twenty-five different languages. This is a good beyond all estimate. I never felt the importance and grandeur of missionary labours as I did last evening. I could not help looking round on the congregation and asking myself, 'What are these people living for?' Granting that each should attain his most elevated object, what would it all amount to? Then looking at these men in India, giving the Bible to so many millions, which I *know* can never be in vain, I see them opening a perennial fountain, which, when they are dead for ages, will still afford eternal life to millions. Should we die, which of our works would we wish to follow us? Which would mark our path or our grave with a ray of light? 'Cut it down, why cumbereth it the ground?' is a sentence we have reason to dread.

Mr Ward closed his discourse by urging all to join in advancing the cause for which Christ had poured out his soul unto death. Who so loved us that he died for us. And now, my dear Brother, do you not feel the force of this appeal. Is there nothing in you which makes you wish to make some return for such love as this? 'He that is not for me is against me.' *Can you bear that?* Oh, my Brother, do think of this.

Your loving brother, C. H.

---

[1] The distinguished Baptist missionary, Rev. William Ward, connected long and intimately with Carey and Marshman, at Serampore, near Calcutta.

PRINCETON, March 25th, 1821.

My Dear Brother:—I do not think you have any reason to fear that my system will be injured by too much excitement. I suffer more pain for not feeling enough, than from the reverse. Though I have not the least expectation of ever seeing India or any other foreign country, in the high character of a missionary, I still feel they are the most favoured men in the world.

Saturday was a laborious day to me. I spent it in procuring and setting out trees in front of Dr Alexander's house. We planted four tulip poplars, an elm, two ash, a hickory, and two dogwood. They are beautiful specimens. Should the tulip trees live they will be splendid, for it is the handsomest tree in America.

Your loving brother, C. H.

MR HODGE TO HIS MOTHER

PRINCETON, April 11, 1821.

My Dear Mother: —I have agreed, should I remain here next summer, to supply pretty constantly the congregation near New Hope, (since Lambertville, N. J.), which is about twenty miles from this. The situation of the congregation is critical and interesting, and the prospect of doing good there is very encouraging. I was reluctant to consent to be away from Princeton every Sabbath, and thought it would take up too much of my time. But both Dr Miller and Dr Alexander urged it as conducive, both to my health by exercise, and to my improvement by diversity of occupation. They will both assist me. So I shall have, in the three months, not more than eight or ten sermons to preach.

Your son, CHARLES.

MR HODGE TO HIS BROTHER

PRINCETON, April 21st, 1821.

My Dear Brother:—I heard the other day from Wisner, in Boston. He mentions a most painful circumstance respecting Mr Everett,[1] which

---

[1] Edward Everett, then a Unitarian minister, afterwards U.S. Senator, &c.

must have wounded his feelings very much. I will first copy Wisner's words. 'When Mr Keene was here, Prof. Everett went to the theatre. As he entered one of the boxes a student of the college, who was in the same box, lifted up both hands and said, loud enough to be heard all over the house, 'Let us pray.' The whole audience were looking at and talking about the reverend Professor till the curtain rose. The first act is finished, the curtain drops; a man in the pit, standing up and looking at the Professor, says aloud, 'Life is the time to serve the Lord.' It is said that some others of the clergy had concluded to go, but the reception the reverend Professor met with induced them to abandon their resolution.' This shows how deeply rooted are the modes of thinking among common people, and how essential consistency of character is to respectability. It is probable Everett will be more injured in the estimation of the people of New England by this casual occurrence, than anything which has happened to him. There is quite as much wickedness as wit in the conduct of the student, perhaps rather more, but a great deal of both.

Your affectionate brother, C. H.

The General Assembly, May, 1821, passed the following resolution: 'That the Assembly approve of the employing of Mr Charles Hodge, by the professors, as a teacher of the original languages of Scripture in the Seminary; and that the professors be authorized to employ him for the same purpose, or such other person as they judge proper, and that not more than four hundred dollars be allowed said teacher, per annum, for his services.'

The Presbytery of New Brunswick, April 25th, 1821, appointed him stated supply, at Georgetown (Lambertville) for one half of his time, during the ensuing six months. This service he performed regularly, and with such success that an efficient Church was organized there soon after he ceased to supply them. He also introduced to that congregation his friend and former school-mate, Rev. Peter Studdiford, D.D., who, with his excellent son, the Rev. P. A. Studdiford. D.D., have been to the present time the only pastors of the large and flourishing Church into which it has grown. The Presbytery, in the fall of 1821, appointed Mr Hodge stated supply of Trenton First Church, now known as Ewing.

EXTRACT FROM RECORDS OF PRESBYTERY, SEPT. 27, 1821

'Mr Charles Hodge, a licentiate under the care of this Presbytery, made an application for ordination, as he had engaged to supply the Trenton First Church the principal part of the winter term. Presbytery having considered his application, and his standing in the Seminary as a teacher of the Original Languages of Scripture, determined to proceed to his ordination at a convenient time, and accordingly assigned him 1 Cor. 1:21 as a subject for a sermon, and directed him to prepare for the examination requisite on such an occasion.' Mr Peter O. Studdiford, at the same time, made a similar application, the action on which was postponed for a time.

Newark, October 16th, 1821.—Presbytery met in intervals of Synod. 'Mr Wm. J. Armstrong, a Licentiate of the Presbytery of Jersey, having received a call from the Trenton City Church, was received by the Presbytery of New Brunswick.

'Whereupon it was *Resolved*, That Presbytery will hold an adjourned meeting at Trenton, on the last Tuesday of November next, for the purpose of ordaining and installing Mr Armstrong pastor of the congregation of Trenton,' and also, 'Presbytery agreed to proceed to the ordination of Mr Studdiford, also to the ordination of Mr Charles Hodge at the time of Mr Armstrong's ordination and installation at Trenton: viz., on the last Tuesday of November next.'

'The Rev. Dr Miller was appointed to preside at the ordination of Messrs. Armstrong, Hodge and Studdiford; Mr Woodhull to preach the sermon; Mr Cooley to give the charge to the newly ordained ministers and to Mr Armstrong as installed pastor of the congregation of Trenton; and Mr Brown the charge to the people.

'*Trenton, November 27th, 1821.*—Messrs. Wm. J. Armstrong and Charles Hodge were examined on their experimental acquaintance with religion, on Theology, Natural and Moral Philosophy, on Church Government and the Sacraments, and their examinations on these subjects were sustained. Mr Hodge delivered a discourse from 1 Cor. 1:21, and Mr Studdiford a discourse from Isaiah 45:22, which were sustained as the concluding parts of trial for ordination.

'*November 28th, 1821.* The arrangements made for the ordination services were carried out, the Rev. Mr Cornfort giving the charge to the people *vice* Mr Brown, detained by sickness in his family.'

MR HODGE TO HIS BROTHER

Princeton, Sept. 12, 1821,

My Dear Brother:—With regard to your prospects, my dear Brother, I have never thought them gloomy. I feel assured that whatever difficulties may attend the commencement of your course, it will, if you are spared, be successful. I feel this confidence because we see God does connect, in His providence, success with diligence and virtue. Not that we do not daily do enough to forfeit His favour, but for the good of the world, and for the encouragement of excellence, He has made virtuous exertion as much the cause of success, as any secondary cause is connected with its appropriate result. I saw the remark the other day that no one is ever great without having struggled with difficulties, and I believe it is still more generally true that few men are good who are not forced to it by affliction. If our difficulties make us both greater and better than we otherwise should have been, even our self-love would not have the arrangement altered.

Your brother, C. H.

MR HODGE TO HIS MOTHER

Princeton, Dec. 19, 1821.

My Dear Mother:—I hope the Doctor is well and in good spirits. I wish I could give him a portion of my hopes and happiness. I am

becoming daily more pleased with present duties and future prospects. Indeed, were I permitted to mould my own lot, I do not think
I could devise a plan of life more suited to my desires, than the one
Providence appears opening before me. Whether this is to continue,
and I am to remain in my present situation, I cannot tell, and I hope
to be cheerfully resigned to whatever Heaven may determine. But
I am getting so fond of what I have to do, and of what I see to do,
that if it be decided that this is not the place designed for me, it will
be a painful resignation of enjoyments and hopes.

Your son, C. H,

MR HODGE TO HIS BROTHER

PRINCETON, Jan. 1st, 1822.

My Dear Brother:— . . . A circumstance of rather more interest was,
that on Sunday last I was called to administer, for the first time, the
ordinance of Baptism, and, what does not happen every day, was
required to give my own name in full to the little stranger. It was the
child of one of the Elders of Trenton First Church (called Ewing),
where I frequently preach.

Your brother, C. H.

Mr Hodge had organized a society among the students, designed
to promote the investigation and discussion of questions connected
with the department of Biblical Criticism and Introduction. The
professors attended, but Mr Hodge conducted the work, and
directed the students in their special preparations on particular
themes. On this subject he wrote to his mother.

MR HODGE TO HIS MOTHER

PRINCETON, Jan. 19, 1822.

My Dear Mother:—I suppose you remember my mentioning that I
was obliged to prepare a dissertation to read before our new society

on its first meeting. This was done more than a fortnight since. The Professors and most of the Seminary were present. The following day Dr Miller suggested a thing to me which I heard with a good deal of surprise, but which he urged by considerations, the force of which I was obliged to admit. He said he hoped and expected in the spring some permanent arrangement would be made respecting the vacant professorship. That, although from my situation the attention of many of the members of the Church had been fixed on myself, yet that to the great mass of the Church I was a stranger. That in a matter of so much importance, it would be unpleasant for them to act without some knowledge of the person to whom so much would be officially entrusted. That, whatever they might hear from my friends, they would still be acting in the dark as it respected themselves. To remove this difficulty he wished the dissertation just mentioned should be published, and circulated among the clergy, as far as was thought expedient. Of course my feelings revolted from this very strongly, as from something unseemly. Since then Dr Alexander has spoken to me on the subject, and thinks it ought to be done, and that it can be done at the request of the Society, without any impropriety or indelicacy. Whether it *will* be done, I do not know. Sure I am that my own feelings would say no. Though from the peculiarity of the case, and the novelty of the subject, my judgment would, perhaps, be brought to acquiesce, were my opinion of the piece higher than it is.

This is a question to be left to my parental Professors. I am willing to follow their advice, even with hesitating steps.[1]

Your son, C. H.

---

[1] It was published, and a copy lies before me, with the title, A DISSERTATION ON THE IMPORTANCE OF BIBLICAL LITERATURE, BY CHARLES HODGE, A.M. TEACHER OF ORIGINAL LANGUAGES OF SCRIPTURE, IN THE THEOLOGICAL SEMINARY OF THE PRESBYTERIAN CHURCH AT PRINCETON. TRENTON. PRINTED BY GEORGE SHERMAN, 1822. And this is the *first publication* of Charles Hodge.

MR HODGE TO HIS MOTHER

PRINCETON, Feb. 21, 1822.

My Dear Mother:—I have just returned from the Seminary, and from the bed-side of one of our most promising students, who has just breathed his last. He was taken on Friday with a violent inflammation of the bowels, which made such rapid progress, that on Sunday his life was despaired of. On Tuesday morning, the doctor was considerably encouraged, but he soon grew worse, and this morning, about 10 o'clock, he died. You may suppose such an event would make a very deep impression on the minds of his fellow-students. He was in all respects one of the most interesting and promising of their number. He was about twenty-two years old, and remarkably healthy, and about a week since, was, perhaps, the very last who would have been selected as likely to find an early grave. As Mr Turner, (James Blythe Turner, from Kentucky) was the first who has died among the students, and was very much beloved, the dispensation is more sensibly felt.

I am very glad the first death I have ever witnessed was a happy one. Both of the professors were present, and his bed was surrounded by his brethren, whom he requested to sing for him, the hymn beginning with the words: 'How firm a foundation, ye saints of the Lord.' I never witnessed a scene better calculated to impress the mind with the importance and value of religion. It is, indeed, the 'one thing', and the only thing which can afford the least consolation in so trying an hour. I was also much impressed with the conviction of the truth and of the essential importance of some of the leading doctrines of the Bible, particularly that we are saved by faith, and only for the sake of what Christ has done and suffered for us. Mr Turner said over and over that the only foundation of his hope was 'the atoning righteousness of the Redeemer'. When he felt he had an interest in that, he was happy. I believe I was never more convinced that any thing which took that doctrine from the Bible, left no resting-place behind.

His particular friends are very much exhausted with watching and excitement, Breckinridge (Rev. John Breckinridge, afterwards

Professor) especially looks very badly. He was for some time Turner's room-mate.

Your son, C. H.

PRINCETON, April 2, 1822.

My Dear Mother:—I have not yet determined where nor how my vacation is to be spent. Should Providence decide I am to remain at Princeton, I would wish to devote the vacation to the study of German, and it has suggested itself to my mind it might be well to go and spend five or six weeks at Bethlehem or Nazareth (Pennsylvania). If there were an intelligent clergyman with whom I could stay, it might be of some advantage; but to hear the language as spoken by some plain country people would be of little service. If I go, the Doctor (Alexander) would let James go with me.

As the time of the session of the General Assembly approaches, I feel somewhat desirous of having the question of the permanency of my continuance here determined, simply to be freed from the unsettled feeling incident to a state of suspense. It is a question, however, which has never given me any disquietude. It is one indeed which involves consequences of greater importance than I am able to estimate, but the fact that it is one beyond my determination, the decision of which I can in no way influence, seems to remove from me in some measure the burden of responsibility. Should it ever be affirmatively made, however, that burden will then be mine; and it is great indeed.

Your son, C. H.

PRINCETON, April 10, 1822.

My Dear Mother:—I have been somewhat peculiarly situated in my official duties since entering the ministry. It became necessary for me on Saturday last to baptize a man by immersion (in Howell's Pond, a five minutes walk from the church, on the Trenton side, while acting as pastor for the Ewing, or Trenton first church), as his conscience would not allow him, though a Presbyterian, to receive the ordinance in any other way. My good Princeton friends, though they considered it as a matter of necessity, seemed very reluctant that I should run the risk to health by going at this season into the water. But it seems that no evil has resulted from it. The day was very mild, and all the circumstances of the case as pleasant as they could be. There were a great many persons present, but all belonged to the congregation, which is one remarkable for its respectability. It was a serious service, and all present seemed to feel it so.

Your son, C. H.

PRINCETON, April 19, 1822.

My Dear Mother:—Mr Summerfield preached for us here yesterday morning, and I had the pleasure of dining with him yesterday at Mr Bayard's. His sermon was excellent. Much better than I expected. His action was also excellent, but he is by no means as eloquent as I had supposed. He has very little power over his audience excepting to produce a pleasing excitement. He could not overwhelm them as Larned could, and he seemed to have but little talent at the pathetic. My judgment approved of him and his discourse more than I expected; but my feelings were much less interested.

Your son, C. H.

In answer to a letter from Dr Alexander, not preserved, Mr Hodge wrote:

PRINCETON, May 6, 1822.

My Dear Sir:—I would say then, in the first place, that if I know my own heart, I wish God's will may be done. If He plainly leads me on to the result we have so long contemplated, I confess the fondest wishes of my heart will be accomplished. But at the same time I believe that I would rather be homeless and penniless through life than in any way whatever enter such an office unsent of God. I have felt so much on this subject that I have never felt at liberty even to pray for the attainment of this object except in the most guarded manner. When this day three years ago, and in this place, you first mentioned this subject to me, the suggestion took me utterly by surprise. The plan you then proposed seemed to me so important, fraught with so many advantages to myself (upon any result), whose ultimate success depended so entirely upon the ordering of Providence, that I could not doubt that it was my duty to accede to it. Since that period my path has been very narrow. There has not occurred a single opening which was calculated either to tempt me aside or to give me a moment's anxiety as to the course I ought to pursue. Hitherto, therefore, has the Lord led me. Whether He will lead me any longer in this direction, I know not. With regard to the Professorship itself, I think now as I have always thought that it is decidedly the most eligible situation for improvement, for satisfaction, and for usefulness, which our church affords, and that as far as my feelings are concerned, I would prefer being here with the smaller salary, to any other situation with the largest, that the country affords. Should, therefore, my salary even be continued as it is at present ($400) I should not think it a sufficient reason for retiring from my present situation, unless accompanied with some further intimations that such was the will of Providence.

Though I have been greatly disappointed in the progress I have made in my studies, and the benefit I have derived from my many advantages, yet I am so sensible of the value of the privileges connected with my situation, that I esteem myself most highly favoured. You need never fear I shall regret the time I have spent in Princeton, and will you let me say it gives me a pleasure to be near you and your family, that money cannot purchase.

I now beg you to pray for me, that God would so order events that He may be honoured, and that by His Spirit I may be fitted for His pleasure. This request I make most earnestly.

With filial reverence, C. H.

5

FROM HIS ELECTION AS PROFESSOR, MAY 1822, TO HIS DEPARTURE FOR EUROPE, OCTOBER 1826

*His Election as Professor – Marriage – Birth and Baptism of Children
– Studies and Commencement of the* Biblical Repertory *–
Resolution to Go to Europe*

THE BOARD OF DIRECTORS, at their meeting, held in Philadelphia, May 17, 1822, reported to the General Assembly as follows: 'The Board with pleasure inform the Assembly that the First and Third (senior and junior) classes now in the Seminary, have each resolved to aid in founding a Professorship of Oriental and Biblical Literature. To effect this object, the students of the First class have bound themselves to raise and pay, if practicable, in five years, the sums which they have respectively subscribed, amounting in the whole to $7,000. And the students of the Third class have on similar conditions individually bound themselves in sums amounting collectively to about $4,000.'

May 21st, '*Resolved*, That it be recommended to the General Assembly, that they elect a Professor of Oriental and Biblical Literature in the Theological Seminary, with a salary of $1,000 per annum, provided that for three years the present funds of the Assembly be responsible for not more than $400, the sum now given to the assistant teacher of the Original Languages of Scripture, and that the residue be procured by subscription.'

On the same day the General Assembly resolved, 'That, agreeably to the above recommendation, a Professor of Oriental and

Biblical Literature be elected, and that the election be the order of the day for Friday next, at twelve o'clock.'

Friday noon, May 24th, 1822. 'It being the order of the day for twelve o'clock, an election was held for a Professor of Oriental and Biblical Literature. The ballots being taken were committed to Messrs. John F. Clark, Cox and Gilbert to count the vote and report the result to the Assembly.'

'The committee to which the votes for a Professor had been committed, reported, and the Rev. Charles Hodge was declared duly elected Professor of Oriental and Biblical Literature.'

At the meeting of the Board in Princeton, September 23rd, 1822, 'The Board were officially informed, by the Stated Clerk of the General Assembly, that that body had elected the Rev. Charles Hodge Professor of Oriental and Biblical Literature in this Seminary; and the Board being also informed that Mr Hodge has accepted the appointment, resolved that Dr Blatchford, Dr McAuley, and Mr Lewis be a committee to direct the order of exercises at the inauguration which is to take place to-morrow at 11 o'clock, A.M.'

Soon afterwards, 'The committee appointed to make arrangements for the inauguration of the Professor made the following report, which was adopted:

1st. Procession to be formed at 11 o'clock, A.M., at the Seminary in the following order: (1) Students of the Seminary. (2) Such clergy as may be present. (3) The Professors. (4) The Directors. The procession to enter the Church in the reverse order, to be conducted under the direction of a committee of one from each class of the students, consisting of Messrs. Breckinridge, Stanford and Myers.'

2nd. Hymn and introductory prayer, by the President.

3rd. Formula to be read and subscribed, by the Professor.

4th. Induction to the chair, by the President.

5th. Inaugural address, by the Professor.

6th. Charge, by Dr McAuley.

7th. Concluding prayer, by Dr Blatchford.

8th. Concluding hymn and benediction, by the first Vice-
President.'

Tuesday, September 24th, 1822. 'The Board attended to the inauguration of the Rev. Charles Hodge as Professor of Oriental and
Biblical Literature. The exercises were conducted agreeably to the
plan reported yesterday by the committee of arrangements.'

The original time-stained copy of this inaugural address the
compiler of this biography has now in his hands. The first sentences reveal the thought and animus of the entire discourse, and
constitute a divinely significant omen for the professional life now
opening.

'The moral qualifications of an Interpreter of Scripture may all
be included in Piety; which embraces humility, candour, and those
views and feelings which can only result from the inward operation
of the Holy Spirit.'

*'It is the object of this discourse to illustrate the importance of Piety
in the Interpretation of Scripture.'*

HIS MARRIAGE

In the meantime, on the 17th of June, he was married to Miss
Sarah Bache, who has already been introduced to the reader in the
second chapter, at Cheltenham, a country seat near Philadelphia,
belonging to a mutual friend, Judge M. McKane, Mrs Bache having deceased in 1820. The ceremony was performed by the Right
Rev. Bishop William White, the first American Protestant Bishop.
Dr White had been the pastor of the bride's family for several generations, and had married her father, William Bache, to Catherine
Wistar, in 1797.

Uniform tradition represents Charles Hodge and Sarah Bache
as being at that time an uncommonly handsome couple. He was

slender, of average height, very youthful-looking, with light brown hair, curling over a finely formed head, a light complexion and rosy cheeks, illumed by the light of blue eyes, and of a mouth in which benevolence and firmness, intelligence and humour were so subtly mingled as to elude the efforts of the best painters to represent it. She was of the full standard height for women, of symmetrical form, dark auburn hair, large blue-grey eyes, of that rare complexion in which the tender pink penetrates the delicate white, as in the interior enamelling of tropical sea shells.

She was endowed with the gifts, and characterized with the temperament, of a musician and an artist, full of imagination and enthusiasm, intensely affectionate and self-sacrificing within the circle of kindred, and at the same time thrilled by the widest and most delicate sympathies with all varieties of character and experience. These natural qualities had already been consecrated by religion, and through all her life they became more and more spiritualized and sanctified.

They came almost immediately to Princeton, and took boarding in the family of Colonel Erkuries Beatty, the father of their life-long friend, Rev. Charles Beatty, D.D., LL.D., of Steubenville, Ohio. Here they received great kindness, and remained until the spring of 1823, when they went to house-keeping in the house occupying the eastern corner of Witherspoon and Main Streets, immediately opposite the centre of Nassau Hall.

Here they remained eighteen months, until, on January 1st, 1825, they took possession of their permanent home, built by them on the Seminary ground – the square brick house at the west end of the main Seminary building. In this house Mr Hodge lived all his remaining life, here all his children, except the eldest, were born, and here he did his life-work and died. All the beautiful trees which adorn the grounds around this house he planted with his own hands.

MR HODGE TO HIS MOTHER

Princeton, June 24, 1822.

My Dear Mother:—We have been received with every possible kind attention by every body in Princeton, and it has given me the greatest satisfaction to witness the evident cordiality Sarah has been met with by all her old friends. Our circumstances at Mr Beatty's are very comfortable, and every thing promises well.

We go to Dr Alexander's to-day and to Dr Miller's to-morrow. It is well we came here a week before the session commences, for it will not be possible to get ready for study for some time. My room is yet in confusion, having no book-case and no table. In a short time, however, I expect to settle down to all the sober duties of my office and relations. Our Brother, the Doctor, was all-important to us. He performed his part so well on the day on which Sarah saw her friends, that I was completely relieved. It makes me happy to see Sarah cheerful and contented. She is now singing in my ears, so that I scarcely know what I am writing. I begin to fear that many of the fond schemes I had formed will never come to much. As to studying where Sarah is, it will be out of the question, unless there be some way of charming her tongue to rest which I have not as yet discovered.

Your son, C.H.

But things soon permanently adjusted themselves. The wife became occupied with household and family cares, and the husband, of all industrious students, became remarkable for his tolerance of interruption. His study was the home of his wife, and the gathering place of the entire family, and the highway of the children between the outside world and the other apartments of the house. While some of his children remained too small to unfasten the latch themselves, he had left it unfastened, so that even the least of us might come and go as we pleased.

During the first four years of his married life, the period covered by this chapter, two children, a boy and a girl, were born to him.

His constant letters to his mother and brother, and other intimate friends, were filled with notices of these children, and with the evidences of his absorbing, as well as tender, interest in them. This characteristic of his correspondence is far more than ordinary in its degree, and his consciousness of that fact becomes evident. To his brother he writes:

> People say I am a little foolish, and I think it quite likely. But I have a good excuse. With every desire that you may be as foolish, as happy, and a thousand times better than your brother,
>
> I am yours, C.H.

The whole family correspondence of this period is suffused by the glow of his rich and full happiness, having their springs in his religion, his family, and his beloved work.

PRINCETON, Dec. 25, 1825.

My Dear Mother:—Your dear little Mary Elizabeth was baptized this afternoon in the Oratory by Dr Alexander. Notwithstanding the rain, the place of service was so near we found it easy to take our dear little treasure out to be consecrated to God in this delightful ordinance. I never appreciated so highly before the privilege of thus giving to God what is dearest to us on earth. We feel now as though she were not our own, but something lent to be cultivated and prepared through our agency for heaven. To be instrumental in thus training up one of the children of the Lord to be presented before Him without spot or blemish, is so delightful and honourable a task, that we cannot help hoping that He who has made the prospect of the duty so pleasant, will aid us in its performance. There is, too, so much ground to hope that our efforts will not be in vain that we can address ourselves to the duty with all possible cheerfulness. The application of the pure element of water is not only designed to *represent* the purifying influence of the Spirit upon the heart, but it seems to be the appointed pledge on the part of God, that if we sincerely devote our children *to* Him, and faithfully endeavour to bring them up *for* Him, He will bestow upon them the blessings signified by the ordinance, and contained in that gracious covenant to which it is attached. Hence the ordinance is represented as so important in the Scriptures. He that believeth *and is baptized* shall be saved. It certainly never was designed to be an empty form. And as it imposes the most solemn obligations, so it contains abundant encouragement to fulfil them. Our dear little children we have promised to educate for heaven, and as God shall enable us, we mean to perform our vows. To this every thing must be made secondary. To gain this world is not what we have promised to aim at. It must therefore never be the direct and primary object of pursuit. I have lately, in reading Bonaparte's Russian Campaign, and the Life of Sheridan, been very much struck with the truth of the remark how little they really enjoy the world to whom the world is every thing. Bonaparte says the happiest part of his life was when he was a poor lieutenant. And Sheridan said the happiest part of his life was the short time he spent in a cottage. There is nothing lost, therefore, even as regards the present world, by seeking *first* the kingdom of God; that is, by making it the primary object of pursuit, seeing that godliness has the promise of the life that now is, and of that which is to come. We feel, therefore, determined, if God shall render us faithful to our purposes, to bring up your dear little grandchildren, as we are sure you would have us do, with the one object supremely in view of fitting them for heaven. I have great confidence in the effect of religious truth upon the infant mind. Children are so susceptible, their associations are so strong and lasting, that it does not seem strange that the effect of early education should so frequently be felt through life. And if we add to this God's peculiar promises to those who endeavour to bring up a child in the way in which he should go, we shall see that there is abundant reason to hope that exertions properly directed will be crowned with success.

Your affectionate son, C.H.

STUDIES AND COMMENCEMENT
OF THE *BIBLICAL REPERTORY*

During these years the weakness and pain of his right limb occasioned a good deal of inconvenience and apprehension, and at times he submitted to painful remedial applications. Nevertheless these were years of intense study. There remain in manuscript traces of elaborate discipline in Hebrew, Syriac and Arabic, and exegetical lectures on Romans and Corinthians, and dissertations on the origin of language, the general principles of Hermeneutics, etc. He preached before the Seminary every third Sabbath, and very frequently in the neighbouring churches. Writing to his brother, November, 1822, he says: 'I am incessantly busy, having six recitations a week, and a lecture to write besides.' December, 1822, he writes: 'I am studying German again: having a teacher in the house I hope to make more progress than I did before. We find Mr Jadownisky a pleasant and intelligent young man.' In November 1823, he writes: 'We have an unusually large accession to our numbers, and have commenced business under very promising circumstances. I have more writing to do than I should, and really believe that I shall find it essential to carry on the study of six languages this winter. I look forward to a pretty severe term, for I must keep before my students or they will find it out.'

In the beginning of 1825, he founded the *Biblical Repertory*, with which he was connected as real editor, with the exception of the period of his absence in Europe, for forty-three years. This Quarterly appeared at first under the title, '*Biblical Repertory, a Collection of Tracts in Biblical Literature*, Ἐρευνᾶτε τὰς γραφάς [Search the Scriptures]', consisting of reprints and translations, and making no pretensions to originality. The translations were furnished principally by the editor, and by the Rev. Robert Patton, then Professor of Greek in the College of New Jersey, and by James W. and Joseph Addison Alexander. It continued in this form for four years, until after Mr Hodge's return from Europe, when the new series began with January 1829, under the title *Biblical Repertory, a Journal of Biblical Literature and Theological Science*, to be conducted by an 'association of gentlemen', of which, however, Professor Hodge was always the working and directing member, in every sense the actual editor. In 1830 the title became *Biblical Repertory and Theological Review*, and finally, in 1837, *Biblical Repertory and Princeton Review*. Among the contents of the first four volumes the only translations which I can certainly identify as the work of Dr Hodge are 'History of Theology in the Eighteenth Century', by Dr Augustus Tholuck; and the 'Life of Kant', by Prof Stapfer, of Paris. These are both contained in the volume for 1828.

During his absence in Europe, from November 1826, to November 1828, Prof. Robert Patton took charge of the *Repertory* in place of the editor.

RESOLUTION TO GO TO EUROPE

During the year 1826, as his knowledge increased, his standard of the attainments necessary for a professor in his department was elevated in a more rapid ratio, and proportionably the sense of his own deficiencies became more intense. He felt the need, at the same time, of uninterrupted leisure for carrying on private study, and of access to the most learned and able teachers of Biblical Science that were to be found.

MR HODGE TO HIS BROTHER

PRINCETON, August 29, 1826.

My Dear Brother:—You will perhaps think me beside myself before you are done reading this letter, but I am about to speak the words of soberness and truth. I want to leave you all for two years! wife and children, mother and brother. I have long felt the very serious disadvantage under which I labour in filling a most conspicuous and important station to which I feel incompetent. My education, for which I owe my mother innumerable thanks, has been, notwithstanding her disinterested and strenuous efforts, by the force of circumstances, very defective. You remember I never opened a Greek Grammar until I came to Princeton in the spring of 1812. In the fall of that year I entered College, joining a class in which all its members had been studying the language from one to two years. The Sophomore year we studied Greek several times a week. During the Junior and Senior years, only once a fortnight. The year subsequent to my leaving College I did nothing at it. During my three years in the Seminary, my time was occupied with other concerns. This has been my Greek course. What a preparation for a Professor! Since I returned to the Seminary I have had continually so many recitations that almost my whole attention has been confined to the single point of preparing and hearing them. Little opportunity has been afforded for the prosecution of the important branches connected with my department. I feel constantly the most painful sense of unfitness for my work, and the conviction that with nothing more than fragments of time at command, I can make little progress. My plan, therefore, is to apply to the Board of Directors for permission to spend two years in Europe. If they will permit my salary to go on, it is all I can ask. I can rent my house for a sum sufficient to employ an assistant to take my place in the Seminary. All the Seminary will lose is the difference between my instructions and those of my substitute, which will be little indeed; and it will, on the other hand, gain all that will accrue from my having so much time for improvement, and from the increase of reputation, which is something where people are influenced by externals. By spending half my time at Göttingen and half at Paris, I shall be able to get possession of both the German and French, which will be an incidental advantage of no inconsiderable value. You may suppose I do not think of this course lightly. I feel the sacrifice I make, or rather should make, if this plan should be executed. But with me my improvement should be paramount to all other conditions, and I hope I should be found equal to the exile.

Mr Patton has been to Europe and taken much the same course, and has given me very definite information as to the expense, and I think I can accomplish my wishes without sinking money or running into debt.

This is all, however, *between ourselves*, and it depends upon a great many circumstances I cannot foresee, and which with every thing else I cheerfully leave to the directions of Providence. Sarah, of course, wishes very much (*should I go*) to accompany me, and Mr Patton tells me we could live cheaper there than we can do here – that a thousand at Gottingen would support us comfortably. But then it would take five hundred to go, and as much to return. Sarah would be without friends and without society. We could not afford to travel, and I should feel so much encumbered and so anxious in case of sickness, that I cannot help thinking the balance preponderates on the side of her remaining at home. Dr Alexander, who approves heartily of the plan as far as the Seminary is concerned, thinks that I should take my family; and then when he contemplates the difficulties attending such a course, he *questions* the prudence of the scheme. He thinks I could not command myself to remain six months without my family. Perhaps not.

Your affectionate brother, C.H.

At the meeting of the Board of Directors in Princeton, September 25, 1826, the following communication was received from the two senior professors of the Seminary:

The undersigned beg leave to lay before the Board of Directors the following representation. Their junior colleague, the Rev. Mr Hodge, although he has, ever since his appointment to the office of Professor, discharged its duties in a manner which reflects equal honour on his attainments, his capacity, his diligence and his fidelity, has been for a considerable time past under a deep impression that he needed further advantages of leisurely study, particularly in some of the higher departments of Biblical criticism, and the auxiliary branches of knowledge. These advantages he is persuaded he can never hope fully to enjoy, unless he shall be enabled to retire for a time from the discharge of his duties in the Seminary, and to obtain access to those richly furnished libraries and those eminently skilled and profound masters of Oriental Literature of whose assistance he cannot avail himself in his present situation.

For the attainment of these advantages it is his earnest desire that he may be permitted to suspend the discharge of his official duties in the Seminary for eighteen months or two years for the purpose of visiting Europe and pursuing certain select branches of study, with the peculiar aids which the best institutions in that quarter of the globe can alone furnish. He has no doubt that the benefits likely to accrue from such a step would be of great importance to himself, and would add in no small degree to his capacity for serving the interests of the Institution under the care of your venerable Board.

The undersigned would respectfully state that after bestowing on this plan the most serious and mature consideration in their power, they certainly concur in these views of their colleague, and would unite, as far as would be proper, the expression of their wishes with his, that it may be carried into effect.

In contemplating this subject they cannot overlook the fact that several of the most enlightened and important institutions of our country have adopted a measure of this kind, and in some instances entirely at their own expense; nor can it be doubted that an impression of the utility and importance of making this provision for the improvement of public instruction is daily becoming more deep and extensive.

The undersigned would also take the liberty of suggesting, in case the Directors should think proper to accede to the wishes of Mr Hodge, whether he might not unite with a short residence in Europe, for his own improvement, an agency to solicit monies and books for the use of the Seminary. They cannot, indeed, indulge very large expectations of the probable avails of such an agency, yet they entertain no doubt that quite enough would result from it to reward and justify the effort.

They have only to add that Mr Hodge, in case the Board should be pleased to think favourably of his plan, does not expect them to incur any additional expense whatever in giving their consent to the proposed enterprise. All that he asks is that his salary may be continued during his absence. He is ready and willing to provide at his own expense a reputable substitute to carry on his department of instruction in the Seminary, and one whose services he has no doubt will prove entirely acceptable.

A. ALEXANDER
SAMUEL MILLER

PRINCETON, Sept. 25, 1826

The Board gave their consent to the plan on the conditions above offered. Mr John W. Nevin, a member of the class just graduating, was appointed the substitute for Mr Hodge during his absence, and he fulfilled the office for the following two years with eminent ability. He has been since known over both continents as the founder of the Mercersburg school of Theology.

Mr Hodge placed his family in the care of his mother and brother, in Philadelphia, and sailed from New York for Le Havre, October 1826.

6

FROM HIS DEPARTURE FOR EUROPE, OCTOBER 1826, TO HIS RETURN TO PRINCETON, SEPTEMBER 1828

Letters to His Wife, Mother and Dr Alexander relating to His Voyage and Residence in Paris – His Journal Kept during His Residence in Halle and Berlin – Letters from Drs Alexander and Miller – His Own Letters relating to His Visit to Switzerland and Return Home, via Paris, London, and Liverpool

PROF. HODGE SAILED DIRECT FROM NEW YORK on the packet ship *Edward Quesnel*, for Le Havre, early in October. The first letter which remains is addressed to his mother from Rouen.

ROUEN, October 28, 1826

My Dear Mother:—Your kind letter, which I received before leaving Princeton, has often been the subject of my grateful remembrance, especially when reperused. Every day that I live I feel more deeply the extent of my obligations to you, for every day I become more sensible of the value of the education which your disinterested exertions secured your children, and of the restraints and counsels which kept our youthful feet 'from the paths of the destroyer'. It is one of my daily subjects of thankfulness that God has given us such a mother. May He, my beloved parent, richly reward you for all your sacrifices, and give you the satisfaction of seeing your children answering your expectations, and above all things the inexpressible happiness of finding them at His right hand in peace.

Your loving son, CHARLES

He writes to Dr Alexander from Paris:

PARIS, November 2, 1826

My Dear Sir:—There is no person beyond my own family of whom I think as frequently, or with as much affection, now that I am a stranger in a strange land, as yourself; and there is no person excepting my mother to whom I feel so deeply obligated. From my boyhood I have experienced your paternal kindness, and shall cherish as long as I live the recollection of your goodness, and of the many blessings which through you God has mercifully granted me.

It is now a week since we arrived at Havre. Our passage was rather longer than usual, as we were at sea twenty-five days. The greater part of the time the weather was unpleasant, and the voyage much more boisterous than I expected at this season of the year. We, however, escaped every accident, and, indeed, were never in circumstances to excite any apprehension. I found the sea delightful when the weather was fine, but very much the reverse when we were driven to the cabin by rain and storms. It requires no little strength to withstand the disposition to listless idleness which seems to take possession of every one on shipboard. If I may judge by my own experience the sea is no place for study. The only thing of much interest I saw at Havre was the port itself, which is entirely formed of piers, projecting a considerable distance into the sea, between which the water flows at high tide into the docks, where it is confined by large gates, which are closed as soon as the tide begins to fall. Here the shipping is kept floating, although the canal which leads to the docks is at low water perfectly dry. Hence, it is only at high tide that vessels can go either in or out. This is a great inconvenience, for it obliged us to beat on and off the harbour from eight in the morning until five in the evening. The moment the ship touched the dock, a police officer in military dress came on board and demanded our passports. As I and several others had none, we were obliged to appear before the American Consul, and produce evidence of our being citizens of the United States. The Consul gave us a certificate to that effect, upon which the police granted us a passport to proceed to Paris. Our baggage was subjected to the same ceremony. This form was carried through with a good deal of politeness by the officers, who frequently begged our pardon, and asked permission very humbly to do what we had no power to prevent.

The moment you set your foot on land you see you are in the old world. The houses are antiquated in their appearance in the extreme. The streets are narrow, destitute of side-walks and dirty. The people are poorly dressed, clattering along on wooden shoes, none of the women (at least the poorer ones) wearing bonnets, but in place of them a singular kind of cap. You soon see also, that the land is France. We had not walked far before we heard the violin, and discovered singing and dancing going on one side of the way, while on the other people were praying on their knees at the door of a chapel. There is a very ancient and fine-looking church at Havre. On entering it I was very much struck with finding nearly two hundred boys in companies of about fifty each, reciting their prayers or other religious lessons to the priests. I have never in any Sabbath-school, nor in any Protestant church in our own country heard children recite so well. They appeared to have got their tasks perfectly, and repeated them with wonderful volubility. The priest appeared to take a great deal of pains in instructing them, explaining and enforcing what had been recited. The necessity of the sacraments was in one case the subject of the teacher's remarks. I found the same thing in Rouen when I went to the great cathedral after the service in the Protestant church was over. It is no wonder that the Catholic religion takes so firm a hold of its votaries, since it is so faithfully instilled into the minds of the young. I fear that in this respect Protestants are not as assiduous.

I expected as soon as I got into the country to lose sight of the striking indications of a foreign land which were so obvious in town. But in this I was disappointed. Every thing strikes a stranger as novel. He sees women working in the fields, asses harnessed with immense wooden saddles and almost hid by the immense baskets appended to either side, ploughs furnished with wheels; the whole country destitute of any enclosure, fields of grass or grain and vineyards all mingled together and coming down to the road-side without the slightest fence to protect them. The cattle I saw feeding were generally tied by the horns to a tree, or to a movable stake fixed in the ground. If this was not the case, they were watched. I frequently saw a woman with two or three cows tied by the horns, which she attended from one part of the field to another. Flocks of sheep were always attended by a shepherd and his dog, neither of them very romantic-looking. The cottages looked ancient, were thatched, and green with moss. The people appeared healthy and happy, but their habitations very destitute of what we should consider comfort. The country from Havre to Rouen is very far superior in beauty to any I have ever seen. I had no conception of the effect of long-continued cultivation on the general aspect of the country. The fields of grass were as smooth as lawns, and the fields intended for grain were like *Dr Miller's garden.* Our country is too new to enter into a comparison with this in any species of beauty which does not come at once from the hands of the great Creator. But our country people are far superior in their appearance to the same class here. Not in their personal appearance, for the population of France, as far as I have had an opportunity of observing, look more healthy, and consequently handsomer than ours, but in their appearance of comfort, independence and cultivation.

There are two views on the banks of the Seine which struck me as the perfection of the beautiful. The one is near the village of Cordbec, the other is at the entrance into Rouen, the city as seen from a high hill just on the edge of the town. I presume the latter is one of the finest in France, as it is the subject of a Panorama Mr Eastburn saw exhibited in London. I entered Rouen with greater interest than I should almost any other place in France, because of the many interesting historical events with which it is associated. Of its eighty thousand inhabitants, only twelve hundred are now Protestant. I had the pleasure of attending their worship on Sabbath, which is so similar to our own, that I felt myself quite at home. There were not more than two or three hundred persons present, sitting principally upon chairs, before a plain pulpit. The preacher appeared to be about thirty-five years old, and was fervent and simple in his manner. His sermon was nearly an hour long, and was listened to with commendable attention. I went up to the pastor after the service, and asked him whether he could speak English. To my great gratification he answered in the affirmative. He told me the extent of his charge, and that the venerable church in which they worshipped was formerly a Catholic chapel, given to the Protestants at the time of the Revolution. He also informed me that there were several British subjects in Rouen, principally Scotch weavers, who assemble every Sabbath afternoon to hear a sermon read by some English gentleman. On this Sabbath there happened to be a clergyman of the Church of England in town, who preached and performed the service. I felt rejoiced to hear the praise of God in a foreign land in my own language, and could not help contrasting the beautiful simplicity of the service, both morning and afternoon, with the service which I had witnessed in the early part of the day in the great Cathedral. This is said to be the finest Gothic structure in France, and certainly to an eye accustomed to the church in Princeton it is sufficiently imposing. I saw it first late in the evening, and on entering its 'long-drawn aisles', lighted only here and there by a dim lamp which scarcely revealed the lofty roof, I did not wonder that such places were trod with awe. In the morning I found at least fifty priests and other religious officers engaged in chanting the service, and about two hundred persons, principally poor, kneeling or sitting in different parts of the building. No one appeared attending to what was going on, or at least few. This building is said to have been founded by William the Conqueror. One of the towers is two hundred and thirty-six feet high, and another much higher was destroyed a few years ago by lightning. The painted windows are very striking to one who has never seen any thing of the kind. The statue of Joan of Arc stands in the centre of the town. There is nothing very striking in it, except that it marks the spot on which the heroine met her melancholy fate.

After leaving Rouen the vineyards became very frequent. They appeared to be composed of currant bushes rather than grape vines, which are only two or three feet high. The grapes were all gathered and the leaves burned. The gardens here, however, look much more green than they do with us at this season. We have lettuce every day for dinner, and I have eaten strawberries which were very fine. They cultivate a species called the Alpine, which continues in bearing until frost. There has yet been no cold weather, but the sun has scarcely been visible since I arrived, and the rain, though not heavy, is almost constant. We did not reach Paris until nine or ten o'clock at night, so that I lost the pleasure of a distant view of this great city. We entered by a very broad, fine street, passing the garden of the Tuileries, the Place Vendôme (ornamented with the column made of the cannon taken by Napoleon at Austerlitz), and several of the finest buildings of the city. It is to this circumstance that I refer the strong impression I received of the grandeur of this celebrated metropolis on first entering it, which has been rather weakened than increased by viewing other and less imposing parts of it. The streets are generally narrow, excessively muddy, destitute of sidewalks, and constantly crowded with all kinds of vehicles. I have taken a rapid review of the Louvre, which contains a gallery of paintings one thousand three hundred feet in length, of the Tuileries, of the Luxemburg, of the king's library, and of some other objects of interest. I attended the celebration of mass in the king's chapel on the first of the month. This chapel is a tastefully ornamented room in the Palace, surrounded on the inside by a gallery supported by large stone pillars. I unfortunately took a stand which prevented my having a view of his most Christian Majesty and the Royal family. The officiating bishop was dressed in a splendid robe of gold cloth, and several of his attendants were almost as richly adorned. The middle aisle was filled with the royal guard. The music was said to be very fine. It made no impression on me, much less, at least, than I have experienced from hearing the simplest melody. There was nothing in the whole service which appeared to me at all adapted to make any man either wiser or better. To-morrow is the regular day for a great festival (the king's birthday,

I believe), on which it is customary to distribute wine and provisions to the multitude, to illuminate the garden of the Tuileries, to exhibit fire-works, etc. But as to-morrow happens to be a fast-day, all this is put off to the Sabbath!

I hope you will be kind enough to write to me. Letters from home are more precious than gold. Remember me most affectionately to Mrs Alexander and every member of your family. I beg of you, my dear father, not to forget me in your prayers, for I greatly need them. I need hardly request you to present Dr Miller the assurance of my affectionate and grateful remembrance.

Yours with respect and affection,

C. Hodge

LIFE IN PARIS

He remained at Paris from the 1st of November to the 15th of February, studying French, and Arabic and Syriac with De Sacy. He settled in a handsomely furnished room near the Pont Neuf, in the Place Dauphine, at the apex of the Island, formed by the Seine, in the heart of the city. He boarded in the family of a Mr Oberlin, one of the librarians of the King's Library, living on the opposite side of the thoroughfare to his lodging-room. All his associations were with the Oberlin family, who spoke only French, and with a number of agreeable fellow-boarders, consisting of two barons, one doctor in philosophy, and one captain in the army, who were Swedes, together with a young Englishman, son of Sir Henry Parnell, M.P.

MR HODGE TO HIS WIFE

Paris, Nov. 20, 1826

Dear Sarah:—Young Parnell made his appearance among us this morning for the first time. He is a handsome, amiable-looking youth of about twenty. He asked me, immediately after our introduction, whether I came to Paris with a view of studying the French language. I answered, 'Partly so, but principally with a view to Biblical studies.' 'Ah!' said he, 'they are the most delightful in the world. I wish I could devote my whole life to them.' I said, 'You are a citizen of a free country, and can do as you like.' He answered, 'Yes; but as I happen to be the oldest son, my father wishes me to enter political life. I still hope, however, the Lord will open my way to the ministry.' You may suppose that I felt somewhat surprised and greatly pleased.[1]

PARIS, Dec. 21, 1826

My Dear Sarah:—I went on Monday evening to Professor Stapfer's – a gentleman who has been very kind and very useful to me. I had the pleasure of meeting there Benjamin Constant, with whose name you must be familiar. He is one of the most distinguished liberals of the Chamber of Deputies, and is a man of extensive influence. He reminded me very much of Timothy Pickering in his appearance, although a younger man. There were two Protestant clergymen there. One of them was the younger Monod,[2] a very evangelical man, who has undertaken the Herculean task of translating Scott's *Commentary* into French.

I wrote to Mr Robinson (Rev. Dr Edward Robinson), of Andover, now in Germany, to ascertain which university offered the greatest advantages, and the expenses of living, etc. I have received a very full and satisfactory answer from him. He tells me that for the purposes for which I have come hither there is no comparison between any other university at present and Halle. That the advice of every person he consulted directed him to that place, and the result of his own observation, after spending six weeks in Göttingen, and then proceeding to Halle, confirmed him in the correctness of all he had previously

[1] John Vesey Parnell, 2nd Baron Congleton (1805–83), became a prominent member of the Plymouth Brethren, among whom he undertook missionary work. [Ed.]
[2] Adolphe Monod (1802–56), who became the foremost Protestant preacher of nineteenth-century France. [Ed.]

heard. There is one very important consideration, that one of its leading theological professors (Tholuck) is a very pious man, the like of which is not to be found elsewhere. Halle, like all old European cities, has narrow, gloomy, and dirty streets. The society, however, he says, is good, and the facilities for study very great. I had, before I received his letter, heard enough to determine me that Göttingen was not the place for me. Eichhorn is superannuated; Staudlin is dead; Planck is in ruins under the epilepsy, so that, as far as theology and Biblical literature is concerned, it is almost despoiled. With regard to expenses, Robinson says that Halle is cheaper than Göttingen, though at the latter a student need not spend more than three hundred or two hundred and fifty dollars per year. With respect to Halle he says: 'I find all my expenses here, exclusive of clothes, books, and travelling, and including instruction, lectures, etc., amount to about five rix-dollars[1] per week, i.e., three dollars and seventy-five cents of our money, which is at the rate of less than two hundred dollars per annum.' After making all allowance, it is certainly *very, very* cheap. I pay my Arabic teacher alone almost as much for three lessons a week, *i.e.*, I have to pay five francs or one dollar per lesson. Paris, therefore, is not the cheapest place in the world. Mr Robinson informs me that the spring lectures commence about the middle of April. Unless I am there at least two months before that time, I shall be utterly unable to enjoy the benefit of the course. I have, therefore, made up my mind to leave this about the beginning of February.

PARIS, Dec. 28, 1826

My Dear Sarah:—I would follow your plan of writing something every day, if I were not in the habit of spending all my days in the same manner. I rise about eight, at which hour I have my French teacher to attend on Tuesday, Thursday and Saturday. On other days he comes at two o'clock. I read and study until half past ten, when

---

[1] From Dutch *rijksdaalder*, a silver coin current in several European countries. [Ed.]

I go to breakfast, which takes rather more than an hour, including delays. I then return to my room, and remain until half past three, when I go three times in the week to my Arabic teacher. At five I go to dinner, and remain at Mr Oberlin's generally to seven or later. The evening is almost always spent at home reading and studying until twelve, when I go to bed. When I go out it is generally from ten to two.

Paris, Jan. 10th, 1827

My Dear Sarah:—I went as I told you I expected to do, to see the king dine on the first of this month. We passed through several of the apartments of the palace, which were very splendidly furnished, especially his chamber of audience, which is hung with crimson velvet and ornamented with gold. The dining-room is very long and narrow. One end was crowded with ladies in their court-dresses, the opposite end was occupied by musicians and singers. Around the table, which was in the shape of a horse-shoe, the principal officers of the king were standing, old Talleyrand among the rest. His Majesty sat in the centre, the Dauphin on his right, and the Dauphiness on the left. The former looked like a very good-natured man, but his wife always appears out of humour. The little Duchess de Berry sat next to the Dauphin, and as usual seemed full of gaiety and good spirits. She is as much liked by the French as the Dauphiness is disliked. Although royalty always sinks upon a close inspection, yet I am very glad I went. How it is that the million can by choice consent to exalt one like themselves so much above them, I cannot conceive.

My young friend Parnell has entered the army. This step was much against his will, but the Duke of Gloucester had, as a great favour, offered his father a commission for him in the guards, which he accepted, and then sent to his son for his consent. He is one of the most faultless young men I have ever seen. This, however, is only negative praise, though amounting to a great deal. His simple, humble, devotional piety is his great characteristic. When he is gone I shall lose the principal source of my enjoyment in Paris.

PARIS, Feb. 12th, 1827

My Dear Sarah:—I am now preparing for my departure from Paris, which I expect to leave on Thursday or Friday, the 15th or 16th.

I preached yesterday for the fourth time for Mr Wilkes, the English preacher in Paris, who has been so unwell that he has not been able to preach for more than a month. I had the honour of having among my hearers Gen. Lafayette's family; that is, half a dozen of his daughters and grand-daughters. I was very much pleased with them when I saw them a few evenings since at the General's. His grand-daughters are very unaffected, pleasing girls, and some of them are quite pretty. The old gentleman looked remarkably well, and is as kind and polite as possible. I left my letter and card on the third ineffectual call, and received soon after a very kind note from him. I met there Baron Humboldt, and was introduced to him. He is not a striking, but a pleasant-looking man, very affable, and has a fine forehead. He kindly offered me letters of introduction to Germany, to any of his correspondents I might desire. An offer I was not slow to accept.

Your affectionate husband, C. H.

A former occasion of his preaching at the Rev. Mr Wilkes's service, is noticed in the Journal kept by Dr Thomas Guthrie, then a young man studying in Paris:

Jan 21. I then set off for Mark Wilkes's service, which is held in a part of the Oratoire. The preacher was a Mr Hodge, an American professor, who had come to Europe for the purpose of studying the Oriental languages. He intended to do so in Germany, but was at present studying French in Paris, as a medium of communication with the Germans. He was a young-like, intelligent, fair, good-looking, thin and rather little man, (Guthrie was six feet two inches); and gave us a capital sermon from the 19th verse of the fifth chapter of 1 John. The singing was very beautiful. The English sounded most sweetly and pleasantly to my ear. It brought vividly before my mind the memories of my native land; while the smallness of the numbers, the upper room in which we were met, the irreligious and idolatrous country in which we were maintaining the pious worship of God, reminded me of the infant state of the Christian Church.

Mr Hodge writes to Dr Alexander:

PARIS, Jan. 29, 1827

My Dear Sir:—From the time at which the winter course in the German universities commenced, it was impossible for me to derive any advantages from the public instructions had I proceeded according to my original plan. I therefore thought it most advisable to spend a few months here in studying Arabic, and in gaining as much knowledge of the French as would enable me to prosecute my journey without suffering all the inconveniences of being completely deaf and dumb. The advantages for the study of the Oriental languages here are very considerable, especially for those who wish to cultivate them for the sake of their own literature, or for commercial purposes. De Sacy lectures three times every week on Arabic, and three times on the Persic. His method does not differ from the ordinary manner of hearing a recitation with us. His class, which does not consist of more than seven or eight, read the Koran on one day, and a part of his Chrestomathy[1] on the other. He does little more than explain the force of the words, and any difficulties which may occur in the grammatical form or construction. He is very particular and very attentive, devoting upwards of two hours to each exercise. Besides this Professor Caussin de Perceval lectures on the Arabic grammar three times a week. De Sacy also lectures on Persian, Quatremere on Hebrew. His course, however, is purely elementary, at least at this season, and he has only two or three hearers. Lectures are delivered upon almost all the Eastern languages; Sanskrit, Chinese, Bengalee, Hindoostanee, etc. All these, as well as the instructions in the sciences, law, and medicine, are public and gratuitous. There is a great difference between the lecture-rooms of the Professor of Chemistry

[1] An anthology of choice or literary passages, used by students in learning a foreign language [Ed.]

and the Professor of Hebrew. The latter having two and the former two thousand hearers. The establishments connected with the medical profession, the schools and hospitals are upon a most munificent scale; indeed nothing can be more liberal than all the arrangements of the government connected with the great literary and scientific institutions of the metropolis.

I have attended the meetings of the Asiatic Society, which consists of forty or fifty near-sighted Orientalists, of whom De Sacy is the President. It was at first amusing and surprising to see every man with the paper or book he wished to read almost in immediate contact with his face. The worthy President is as remarkable for the shortness of his sight as for the depth of his knowledge. This is not a comforting account for Addison, who has commenced already paying the penalty for this species of learning. The proceedings of this Society, having no connection with the Biblical subjects, are not to me very interesting.

I have also attended the meeting of the Institute, which consists of the most distinguished literary and scientific men of Paris, having La Place for their President. At these meetings some paper is read by one of the members, and afterwards discussed. Arrangements are made for the accommodation of strangers and others not connected with the Society, of whom a considerable number are usually present.

I have made up my mind to go to Halle instead of Göttingen. Mr Robinson informs me that more attention is paid to Biblical literature at Halle than at any other university. It has also the great advantage of having Tholuck within its walls, who is as much distinguished for piety as for his learning. I have seen a little work of his on the Theology of the Ancient Persians, which states in the title-page that the materials were derived from Arabic, Persic and Turkish manuscripts, in the Royal Library of Berlin. As Tholuck is at present not more than eight or nine and twenty, he must have published that work when he was about twenty-four or five! This is a wonder to me. I have also seen a treatise of his to show that Christ is the central sun and key of the Old Testament. His work on the Romans, I was told by Profesor Stapfer here, was the best that has been published. He has also written a work which has produced a great impression, on the doctrine of Redemption. One of the leading Professors of Berlin also, Neander, is orthodox on all the great points.

Yours with filial respect and affection,

C.H.

LEAVES PARIS FOR HALLE

He left Paris on the 15th of February, 1827, at 5 o'clock, p.m., and travelled by diligence[1] during the coldest weather of that entire winter, through Chalons, Metz, Mayence, Frankfort and Leipzig to Halle, passing the Rhine on the ice. He arrived at Halle, Wednesday morning, February 28th, at 2 o'clock.

The same day he wrote to his wife.

My Dear Sarah:—Halle is, beyond dispute, the dirtiest, ugliest, gloomiest town of its size I ever saw. It is a great relief to find two Americans here who welcome a countryman with sincere pleasure. Mr Robinson I think you saw in Princeton. He is reserved and cold, but at the same time he appears to be really kind, and puts himself to more trouble to be of service than many whose feelings lead them to a more warm and cordial expression of good-will. He is one of those men, I suspect, who slowly and surely make their way to your confidence, which they seldom show to be misplaced. I anticipate, therefore, much solid advantage from being associated with him. I have taken a room next to his in a house which belongs to and is in part occupied by Gesenius. Mr Cunningham, from Boston, is in the same house. He is a handsome young man, apparently very amiable and quite prepossessing. We breakfast and tea separately in our own rooms, and dine together at half-past twelve at a public house. The rest of the day is taken up in studying and attending lectures, which is the best manner of attaining this exceedingly difficult language.

---

[1] Diligence: a French or continental stagecoach. [Ed.]

The day after his arrival he was introduced to Gesenius, Niemeyer, Tholuck and Jacob. The day of this introduction he wrote to his mother,

Halle, March 1, 1827.

Dear Mother:—I have seen two of the most celebrated Professors, and have experienced very sensibly how a man sinks into his proper size when seen face to face. When viewed from the other side of the Atlantic, these men seemed something out of the ordinary course of things, but here, whatever their minds may be, their bodies are made of very vulgar clay. I have never been so disappointed in my life as in the appearance of Gesenius, who is the first Hebrew scholar probably in the world. He is not more than forty years old, *frivolous*, and, what is a wonder here, rather foppish in his appearance. He has a silly laugh for every thing he says, and is in short the last man I should have selected from ten thousand as a distinguished philologist. He is, however, affable, polite and kind in his manners. Although you cannot force yourself to respect him, you feel at ease and pleased in his society. All physiognomy and craniology fail, I think, in reference to such men, for his talents and erudition are unquestionable. I heard him lecture this afternoon, and though by no means imposing even in the desk, he appears to more advantage than in his own study. Tholuck, who is only twenty-nine or thirty, is a very remarkable man. He is a wonder in this part of Germany for being pious, and his countenance is expressive and pleasing. He speaks a multitude of languages, and English among the rest. The German Professors study in complete *dishabille*. It is a great pity that the literary men of this country should be kept so perfectly distinct as to have none of the advantages which the intercourse with society gives. Tholuck, however, has travelled considerably, and, when out of his study, exhibits a very different appearance.

When he had been a little more than three months in Halle, in a letter to Dr Alexander, Mr Hodge corrected the statement of his first impression of Gesenius given above, and gives an account of his own occupations: 'Of the critics, Gesenius appears by far the ablest, and is, perhaps, doing the most harm, although he confines himself to the Old Testament, and appears to give himself no manner of concern about any doctrinal subject, and to take no interest in any discussion not purely of a critical character. He says a book is genuine or not, without caring in the least whether it pleases one party or the other. And this increases his influence as it gives him the appearance of impartiality. The first impression which his manner and appearance make, as I mentioned in one of my first letters from Halle, is by no means favourable. But in the lecture-room it is very different. He is so clear and animated, and so perfectly master of his subject, that I do not wonder at his being so popular. His lectures on Job this summer are attended by more than three hundred students, who fill the room almost to suffocation. I attend this course – four times a week – and his lecture on Syriac – twice a week – Reisig on the more difficult points of Greek grammar – five times a week; and Tholuck's Introduction to Theology – twice a week. My reason for attending the latter is principally to gain an acquaintance with the theological literature; as his object is not merely to give a systematic arrangement of the subjects, and point out the way in which they should be studied, but also to give the character of the most important works belonging to each department. I have private lessons in Syriac three times a week, and German still every day.'

He was at once admitted to the intimacy of Tholuck, and formed a personal friendship, which on both sides remained unabated to the end of their long lives. Not long before his own death, in 1877, Tholuck sent his friend with warm expressions of love, a photographic likeness of himself, which was cherished by his friend with great tenderness for the short year he survived him.

On the 11th of March, 1827, Mr Hodge wrote to his wife:

My Dearest Sarah:—I have by this time become quite reconciled to Halle. The weather has been of late so fine, that every thing looks more pleasant. I have not seen much of any of the Professors here excepting Tholuck, with whom I walk three or four times a week for an hour or two together. He has been also kind enough to call two or three times and read German with me. Being a young man and a pious one, and being very fond of exercising himself in English, which is one of the fifteen languages he understands, he puts us entirely on a level with himself, and is very instructive. I look at him frequently with wonder. Not older than I, he is the author of some of the best Biblical works in Germany, and has a fund of knowledge which few men attain at the end of the longest life. The great superiority of German learning (and the superiority is great) arises not from the mode of instruction in the universities, but from the excellence of their primary schools. A boy is so well grounded in Greek and Latin that he has no trouble with these languages. As these are the great instruments of learning in all departments, they have nothing to do but to apply them.

Your affectionate husband, C. H.

FROM MR HODGE'S JOURNAL

March 4th, Sabbath. The evening was spent at Prof. Tholuck's, with Mr Robinson and Mr Cunningham. Our conversation was principally on the doctrines of religion. Tholuck said he thought the doctrine of depravity was the most important doctrine of the gospel, and that he did not believe a Pelagian could be a Christian. Justification, he explains after the manner of the old Lutherans, as founded on the imputed righteousness of Christ. He does not believe in the personal efficiency of the human soul, and, therefore, thinks that all acts come from God; when good, both as to their *substance and quality;* when evil, the quality is from the sinner himself.

In prophecy and types he is also of the same opinion, holding to the *double sense*. He asked me if I did not find myself unsettled in reading the exegetical works of the modern German school. I answered, no, at which he seemed surprised, and asked what views I entertained about prophecy. I told him I considered the Prophets under the guidance of the Holy Spirit, and that they often wrote what they themselves did not understand, and when intending to describe their own circumstances, or events immediately at hand, really did describe the circumstances of Christ and his church, etc., etc., etc. He exclaimed, Oh, if you are upon that ground Neology never can touch you.

He gave us a very interesting account of the state of religion in Berlin, which he described as very flourishing. He mentioned particularly a Prussian Baron, whose eminent piety first brought him (Tholuck) to reflection and seriousness. The thought which constantly struck him when contemplating the character of this good man was – Can all this be the effect of natural disposition? Is it not the result of divine influence? Neander, he also represented as a model of Christian excellence.

March 6th, Tuesday. This morning I called on Prof. Tholuck, agreeably to appointment, and walked a mile or two out of town with him. Our conversation was principally upon biblical and doctrinal subjects. In their university studies, he told me, they generally commenced by giving a course of *Encyclopædia,* which pointed out the several departments of Theology, the method of studying them, and the books of most importance under each. They give the Einleitung or Introduction to the Scriptures, which includes an account of the criticism, authenticity, contents, etc., of the sacred volume. Then Exegesis, and then a Philosophical view and systematic arrangement of the doctrines.

He talked a great deal about the philosophical opinions of the present German Literati. Kant's system is universally abandoned.

Fichte, who followed him, is also forgotten. Schelling has shared the same fate. The reigning philosopher of the day is Hegel. Schleiermacher has a system of his own. The present systems are all Pantheistic. Hegel and Schleiermacher both deny the personality of the Deity and the individuality of the soul of man. The universal principle with them is God, and, according to Hegel, the world itself is the *Realität* of the Deity, and all it contains, the different races of men, and the animals in their various orders, are all modes of existence of this one universal principle. This, at least, is the idea I got from Tholuck's description. For I do not pretend to understand a system which its author says is comprehended only by two theologians in Germany; and which, as Gesenius very properly remarked to Mr Robinson, was thereby proved to be not worth understanding. Even the Biblical Theologians of Germany are so led away by the speculative spirit, so characteristic of its inhabitants, that it seems impossible they should be restrained within the bounds of sober and important truth, except by the influence of religion on their hearts. Tholuck, himself, who has much of this philosophizing spirit, considers matter as only a different modification of spirit, the essence of both being the same. I understood him to say that Neander was of the same opinion.

March 7th. This morning, at 9, I attended Wegscheider's lecture upon the Acts of the Apostles, and then Gesenius on Ecclesiastical History. I have as yet been by no means favourably impressed with this oral method of instruction. The only advantages I can perceive attending it, are that information is conveyed to a greater number than would take the trouble to take it out of books, and that *viva voce* communication is perhaps more spirited and impressive. I called, with Mr Robinson, upon Wegscheider, and found him in his study surrounded with books. He is rather a dull, heavy man, in his appearance and manner of lecturing. But he was very affable and agreeable in his manners, and appears frank and kind.

March 8th. This morning, at 11 o'clock I called upon Prof. Tholuck, and walked with him until one. He said it was evident that vital religion was very much increasing in Germany, and he thought that the pantheistic philosophy of the day was doing good inasmuch as it led men to entertain a 'deep religious feeling', and showed them the insufficiency of the neological systems. Schleiermacher, especially, he thought was made an instrument of great usefulness, partly without designing it, or in a way which he did not contemplate. His authority stands so high that the respect which he manifests for the Bible, and the reverence with which he speaks of Jesus Christ, has great influence. He has thus been the means of awakening the attention to religion of many young men, and of some of great eminence, as Neander, who after renouncing Judaism, was for some time a disciple of Rousseau. Tholuck, himself, attributes much of his religious feeling to Schleiermacher's influence. About 4 o'clock Tholuck called for me to walk with him, and, although much fatigued by the morning excursion, I could not deny myself the pleasure. His conversation was principally on practical religion.

Saturday, March 10th. This morning I had for the first time the pleasure of hearing Tholuck. He was upon the first part of the 5th chapter of Malachi. It was pleasant to hear at least one of the celebrated Professors of the University giving a religious cast to his exposition of Scripture. After his lecture, I walked with him until dinner time. He said he did not always approve of the manner of interpretation adopted by the Tübingen Professors, and that he thought that Storr especially was often very unnatural. In the afternoon Tholuck was kind enough to call and read with me, or rather for me, a part of Olshausen, on the secondary sense of SS [Sacred Scripture]. He professed himself an adherent to the grammatical historical method of interpretation, but said this would bring out the secondary sense.

Monday, March 12th. Spent mostly at home alone, pursuing the dull task of learning German. Heard Wegscheider in the morning and Gesenius in the afternoon.

Tuesday, March 13th. In conversation with my German teacher, who is a pious young man, I learnt that the number of pious students here is not so great as I had been led to expect. He said there were not more than twenty of the seven hundred theological students; a much larger number, however, are more or less orthodox. At Tübingen, he said, there was no pious professor in the university, although much piety in the town. At 11 o'clock I walked with Tholuck. He said he thought the number of pious students here was greater than my teacher had admitted. But that it was impossible to say. He was disposed to think that very few of those not religious were orthodox – that in Germany there is such an indefinite variety of opinion that men do not admit of classification. Many profess to be supernaturalists, merely because they believe in miracles. He said the works in general belonging to the department of periodical literature were superficial. *Bertholdt's*, though neological, was the best, except a Catholic one published in Vienna. Tholuck spoke in terms of great admiration of Martyn, and said he was so delighted with his memoirs that he had determined to translate them, but was anticipated. He has himself long cherished a strong desire to consecrate himself to the missionary work. But Providence has as yet closed the way. He spoke feelingly of the peculiar difficulties which most of the present pious learned men have to contend with. Having most of them been previously neologists, they found their old sceptical doubts, particularly with regard to the Old Testament, continually to harass them.

Wednesday, March 14th. I have, this evening, had the pleasure of conversing for two or three hours with Tholuck in my own room. Our conversation was principally on the philosophical systems of Germany. He said that many Christian theologians were inclined to many of the principles of the Pantheistic philosophers – that they could not conceive how God could create out of nothing – and therefore admit that the material universe and the soul of man are of the divine essence. But they differ from the Pantheists in being persuaded of the personality of the Deity, and the individuality of the human soul, believing that it is the highest exercise of divine power to confer this personal individuality upon his creatures.

Schleiermacher would not admit the appellation of Pantheist, which he says is a nickname, and belongs to the materialistic Pantheists, while he is himself what would be commonly understood by the term. Tholuck said that of English philosophers Reid and Hume were most esteemed, Stewart less, and Locke not at all. It seemed to me a great misfortune that philosophy is mixed up with religion in this country, for it gives so abstruse and mystical a character to the explanations of important truths that there is little reason to be surprised that the term Mystics has been applied to the advocates of piety. Thus, for instance, they make faith to be the development of the life of God in the soul – that is – the divine essence everywhere diffused and the universal agent unfolding itself in the heart. Tholuck read several passages for me from Schleiermacher's *Dogmatik*, but they seemed to me to darken counsel by words without wisdom, Tholuck surprised me by saying that since his twentieth year he had seldom been able to secure more than three or four hours a day for study.

Thursday, March 115th. Tholuck called at eleven for me to walk with him. He said he thought the Rabbinical dialect more important for the illustration of the New Testament than any other whatever, and, therefore, more useful to the Biblical student than either Arabic or Syriac. Arabic was of little use except to make use of the 'helps' in reading the Old Testament. He said he had been very much struck with the coincidence between the manner of expression and argument in the Rabbinical writers and those of the New Testament. In the evening, together with Mr Cunningham, I drank tea with Prof. von Jacob, who is an old gentleman, author of some works of distinction on political economy. His daughter is also an authoress, and remarkable for her knowledge of language.

Tuesday, March 20th. Walked with Tholuck at eleven. We were led at first to talk on the possibility of a Christian's falling from grace, which led to the doctrine of the freedom of the will. Tholuck said he agreed entirely with the doctrine of Edwards, on that subject. He told me that Schleiermacher, who belongs to the Reformed Church, was strenuous in his defence of some of its peculiar doctrines, maintaining that they alone were consistent. He told me also that there was more vitality among the Reformed than among the Lutherans. Basle, Bremen, Bonn and —, the four places in which religion is in the most flourishing state, were principally settled by the Reformed. At Berlin, also, where there is so much religion, the Reformed are numerous. In the evening, I drank tea with Robinson, Tholuck, etc. Tholuck was in fine spirits, and surprised me by his familiar acquaintance with the poetry and lighter works of his own country. Scarcely a book was mentioned from which he could not at once repeat numerous passages.

Thursday, March 22d. This morning I again had the pleasure of walking with Tholuck. He finds a great deal of difficulty, he says, in reconciling the doctrine of the final perdition of all men who die in unbelief to his feelings, and seems disposed to adopt the opinion, that there will be, hereafter, other offers of mercy to the souls of men. The passage in Peter, referring to Christ's preaching to the spirits in prison, he interprets as teaching a descent into the abodes of departed souls, and the offer of salvation, to those who had either not received or rejected them when on earth. He says, that some evangelical men, in Germany, hold something similar to the old doctrine of the Limbus Patrum. Wegscheider maintains strenuously, that Paul taught the doctrine of predestination just as the Calvinists hold it, and urges this as a proof of the little dependence we can place on that Apostle.

Saturday, March 24th. This morning I took my last walk with Tholuck. He is just leaving town for the vacation. He told me he had much to endure from the many unfounded reports which the enemies of piety were constantly spreading, respecting the few of that character here. He is much worried at what the Germans call *Kleinstadtigkeit,* that is, little-cityism, a most expressive word, which prevails in Halle. As all the other professors are far from orthodox, he is regarded as a strange being, and subject of suspicion and tale-bearing.

March 30th. Yesterday at dinner, I made the acquaintance of our countryman, Rev. B. Kurtz. This evening I spent in his company. He informed me that in St Petersburg he had received one thousand rubles from the Empress, and experienced considerable attention from distinguished personages. He spoke favourably of the state of religion among the Lutherans in the sea provinces of Prussia. Among the Greeks, as far as he could judge from the service of their churches, there was very little piety. The service was in Slavonic, which the people do not understand. At Königsberg, he also found a great deal of piety, and in Berlin, as much as is to be met with in Philadelphia or New York. The Royal family paid him great attention, and contributed handsomely to the funds of the Seminary for which he is soliciting. In Copenhagen, he was also received graciously by the King and Queen.

April 1st. Sabbath. I had the pleasure of hearing Mr Kurtz preach a real evangelical sermon on Ephesians 3:19. May God of His infinite mercy bless brother Kurtz for having praised His Son, and representing love for Him to be the one thing needful, without which, with all eloquence and all learning, we should be only as a tinkling cymbal.

April 3rd. Mr Kurtz says he has met a great many pious Prussian officers. That in Berlin, in one company, he saw twelve of this character. That the aides of the Crown Prince, and almost all the Governors and Governesses in the Royal family, are of this character. The Moravians at Herrnhut retain, he says, their evangelical character.

Sabbath, April 8th. This morning I attended the Reformed Church, and heard Herr Rinecker, who is considered the best preacher in Halle. In the afternoon, I witnessed the interesting service, attending the confirmation of from fifty to one hundred children. They came to the church in a procession preceded by the pastor, and attended with music. As soon as they entered the building the organ commenced playing, and an appropriate hymn was sung. The minister then took his stand at the altar, and the children stood up around him. After a short address he commenced a catechetical exercise, which continued for about half an hour. Another hymn was sung; the organ was accompanied by four trumpets. This is the first time I have heard this kind of music in a church. The effect upon my feelings was very strong and very pleasing. The preacher, Superintendent Tiemann then commenced his sermon from Proverbs, 'My son, give me thy heart.' His discourse appeared to me very good, recognizing the leading doctrines of the gospel, and delivered with a great deal of animation. His audience was frequently in tears. In his prayers for the dear children, whom he was about to receive into full fellowship in the church, he prayed for every blessing a Christian heart could desire. After leaving the pulpit he again addressed the children, who read aloud the Apostles' Creed, and audibly before the congregation professed their faith. After this, they approached the pastor four or five at a time, and kneeled before him. He, in the name of the ever blessed Trinity, blessed them, and recognized them as members of the church, taking each one by the hand, and placing his hand upon their heads successively, as he addressed to them a short exhortation. The impression which this whole service made upon my mind was very pleasant. And I could not help feeling that however little authority there may be for confirmation, as of divine appointment, that some service of the kind might properly be introduced into our churches. It would have at least this good effect, that baptized persons would then be brought more under the discipline of the church, and the nature of their connection with it would be rendered more definite. I could not help feeling also, from the impression made upon the children and the audience, that few occasions would, humanly speaking, offer better opportunities of doing good to the souls of all present. (This, I bear testimony, was Dr Hodge's opinion, often expressed to the end of his life.) God grant that this little flock of lambs which has been gathered into the fold today on earth, may be recognized by the Good Shepherd, as a part of that little flock to whom it is the Father's good pleasure to give the kingdom.

Wednesday, April 11th. This morning I went with Robinson and Mr Müller[1] to visit Merseburg and the battlefield of Rossbach. We set off at five o'clock, and the day proving remarkably fine, we had a very pleasant ride. Merseburg is a pleasantly situated town of about nine thousand inhabitants, and about half an hour beyond it lies the field upon which Frederick the Great, in 1757, defeated the French. A simple monument is raised on a small mound in the middle of the extensive plain. The inscription states that the monument was erected by the 3rd corps of the Prussian army after the battle of Leipzig in 1813, the previous monument having been removed or destroyed by the French. From the foot of this monument we counted between forty and fifty villages, which were all distinctly visible from the spot. From Rossbach, we rode over the country to Lützen. Here we had the pleasure of visiting the simple

---

[1] The Rev. George Müller (1805–98), of Bristol, England, who was Mr Hodge's German teacher in Halle.

monument erected on the spot where the body of Gustavus Adol-phus was found, after the sanguinary battle of Lützen, 1632. This monument is nothing more than a large granite stone, on which the name of the fallen hero, and the date of his death are cut. Stone seats are placed around for the convenience of visitors. Here one of the greatest generals and monarchs of his age fell. Here Charles XII of Sweden stood. Here Napoleon fought and conquered almost for the last time. The great battle between the French and the Al-lies, in 1813, occurred on the opposite side of the town. But Lützen itself was afterwards occupied by the French, and the Allies filled the surrounding country.

Friday, April 13th. This being Good Friday, I attended the serv-ice of the Lutheran church this morning. The Lord's Supper was administered after the ordinary exercises. The three pastors of the church proceeded to the altar, on which was a small silver image of our blessed Saviour, and several large wax candles, very like the altars seen in Catholic chapels. The officiating clergyman read an explanation of the sacred supper, and an exhortation to the people, and then turned to the altar, and in a solemn voice chanted the consecrating service. The two other clergymen first received the communion from his hands kneeling; then one of them took his stand at one end of the altar, while the officiating clergyman stood at the other. One took the bread and the other the cup. The people then approached, three or four at a time, and kneeling before the first suffered him to place the consecrated wafer in their mouths; they then rose and, proceeding to the second clergyman, in the same way received the wine at his hands. In neither case were they allowed to touch the element with their hands. I should have thought myself in a Catholic chapel, were it not for the sound of the German language instead of the Latin. Very few of the Lutheran clergy retain their belief in the doctrine of consubstantiation, and yet the customs and ceremonies which arose out of it, are almost all preserved. I felt like a stranger here, and longed for the time when again, in the simple Scriptural manner of our church, I could partake of the memorials of our dying Saviour's love.

Wednesday, April 18th. This day has been observed as the Jubilee of Niemeyer, the Chancellor of the University, who has now completed the fiftieth year of his academical life. We called with all the rest of the world to present our felicitations to the old gentleman this morning. His rooms, which are spacious, were crowded with strangers, and ornamented with the numerous presents which had flowed in upon him at this season. Here we met among many other strangers, Schleiermacher and Bishop Eylert, from Berlin, Bishop Westermeyer, from Magdeburg, Tittmann from Leipzig, etc. etc. At eleven o'clock the company met in the Hall of the University. Professor Schultz read a Latin address; after which, the Curator of the University, presented Niemeyer with a beautiful porcelain vase in the name of the King. Bishop Eylert made a long discourse in German. Tittmann and his colleague from Leipzig each spoke in Latin. The pro-rector then exhibited the marble bust of Niemeyer, which the University had caused to be made as an expression of their esteem. He received also a porcelain vase, presented by his numerous pupils of past days, and a silver civic crown from the city of Halle, to which he was a great benefactor during the last war.

Gnadau, Saturday, April 28th. This morning at eight o'clock I left Halle with the intention of making a short tour before the lectures commenced. The whole of this part of the country is a great plain. The land is generally fertile, and the villages frequent and miserably built, and the people poorly clad. Gnadau is a settlement of the Moravians, the congregation including only two hundred members. The village is remarkably neat, and the people superior in appearance to those of the neighbourhood. In the evening, at seven o'clock, I went to the Prayer Hall, where the brethren assemble for their evening worship, and heard only singing. In the morning at half-past eight, I went again, and heard the Liturgy read and sung. At ten o'clock was the regular preaching. The preacher chose for his text the passage of St John which describes our Saviour as the Good Shepherd. Like all the sermons I have heard in Germany, this sermon was hortatory, instead of doctrinal, and unlike most it was pious and animated. From all I could see and hear, I should judge that the spirit of pure and simple piety is preserved in a high degree among these people, and the superior comfort and intelligence of the inhabitants was very striking.

Monday, April 30th. This morning early I rode over to Gloetke, a small village about five miles distant, and spent a very pleasant day with the pastor, Westermeyer. This is a pious and intelligent young man, son of the Bishop of Magdeburg. He was brought to an entire change in his views and feelings during a six months' residence in England and Scotland.

Magdeburg, Tuesday, May 1st. As this city, with the exception of the Cathedral and a few small houses, was utterly destroyed by the Austrian general Tilly, 1631, it is comparatively modern, and therefore agreeable. It is situated on the Elbe, has numerous manufactures, and contains about 33,000 inhabitants. The fortifications of this place are said to be among the most formidable in Germany, and the garrison at present between two and three thousand men.

In the evening I called upon Bishop Westermeyer, and was very kindly received.

Wednesday, May 2nd. I visited this morning the celebrated Cathedral. The *tout-ensemble* of this building, either externally or internally, is not striking, and will not admit of comparison with that of Rouen. But it contains many most interesting monuments and works of art. Near the altar is interred the Emperor Otho I, who died AD 973. His tomb is now covered with a plain marble slab without an inscription; the silver railing by which it was surrounded was taken away by Tilly. His wife's tomb, an English Princess, is striking from the ancient figures which are sculptured upon it. I was shown the helmet, commander's staff and gloves of mail of Tilly, which were secured after his defeat near Leipzig, and deposited here by Gustavus Adolphus. The pulpit was a most beautiful piece of 17th century workmanship, made of alabaster and profusely ornamented with figures relating to Scripture history. Among the various tombs which are shown to the stranger, there was none to me so striking as that of the Archbishop Ernest, erected in 1497. It is entirely of bronze, and covered with figures for the most part emblematic. A figure of the Archbishop in his robes lies upon the top; his countenance is remarkably fine. The whole monument, although so old, appears fresh and new . . . I drank tea to-day with Bishop Westermeyer, and was impressed very much with the free and friendly manner in which he treated me. They all had so much to ask about America that I learned but little about Germany. Through the influence of the good Bishop, I obtained permission from the Commander to ascend the tower of the Cathedral, a thing which on military grounds is permitted to few. The ascent is by 240 stone steps, and the view is very extensive.

In the evening I called on the pastor Storig, who, I understand, is almost the only orthodox minister in Magdeburg. Here again the warm-hearted kindness of the Germans was manifested. The pastor and his family were particularly desirous of learning the character of the Presbyterians in America, whom they appeared to regard very much as we do the Covenanters or the Puritans. He told me he agreed with the younger Westermeyer, who, I find, is looked upon as something out of the ordinary course, since he is what we should call faithful and pious. On Thursday, May 3rd, I left Magdeburg, and reached Leipzig the evening of the next day.

Saturday, May 5th. I walked out this morning to see the appearance of Leipzig during the great fair, which attracts people from so many different and distant places. The streets were thronged with a very heterogeneous crowd, Greeks and Jews, Hungarians, Frenchmen, etc., etc. All the streets which were wide enough for the purpose, were lined with booths in which every variety of article was exposed for sale. The most numerous class of merchants appear to be Jews. Their signs written in German and Hebrew are everywhere to be seen. They almost all wear their beards, and the better sort are clothed in a silk frock-coat reaching down to their feet, and bound round their waist with a girdle. The poorer class have a similar dress of cotton and woollen, and many of them seem miserably destitute. The Greeks were dressed in a loose frock of green cloth reaching to the knees, the sleeves large and open except at the wrist. Their appearance was tasteful. The Hungarians had large loose coats of wool, of its natural colour, reaching to the feet. I spent a considerable part of the day in the museum, which contains all the literary publications of this part of the country and some from France and England.

Sabbath, May 6th. This morning I went to the St Thomas Church at half-past seven, when the service commenced. The church was crowded, the singing continued for nearly an hour, when the superintendent, Tzchirner, ascended the pulpit and preached a very interesting sermon, as far as I could understand. The Lord's Supper was afterwards administered with more ceremony than I had yet seen it in a Lutheran Church. The Consecration Service was as usual chanted, one minister standing at the altar, and the other immediately behind him. Two little boys clothed in black frocks and white scarfs stood on each side of the altar. I observed that the ministers and their attendants bowed not only when the words 'Jesus Christ' occurred, but when he repeated the phrases 'This is my body', 'This is the New Testament in my blood.' When the communicants received the wafer, it was placed in their mouths, and the little boys held a blue napkin spread out beneath to prevent the least particle falling to the ground. The same precaution was observed when the wine was administered.

Monday, May 7th. This morning I called on Professor Hahn, to whom I had a letter. He is a man of about thirty-five, I should suppose, rather small and by no means imposing in his appearance. He received me with great kindness, and offered to call with me upon any of the other Professors whom I wished to see. We accordingly called on Professor Linden, who has the superintendence of the Pedagogium. He as well as Prof Hahn are Christians, as pious men are emphatically called here. In the afternoon, I went with Messrs. Robinson and Cunningham to the garden, in which there is a simple monument to Prince Poniatowsky, erected near the spot on which he lost his life, in attempting to cross the Saale.

Tuesday, May 8th. This morning Prof. Hahn called, and accompanied us to Prof. Tzchirner's. This gentleman is the continuator of Schröckh's *Ecclesiastical History*, and author of the *Analecta* and some other works. He is now engaged in writing the history of the fall of Paganism. He is also distinguished as the great anti-Catholic champion. He is a very polite and agreeable man, considerably advanced in life. In his sentiments, I am told, he agrees more with the English and American Unitarians than with the German Rationalists.

I also had the pleasure of seeing Prof. Winzer and Prof. Beck, who is quite old, but very amiable and kind in his manners, Rosenmüller was the only other one of the Leipzig literati whom I had the pleasure of calling upon. He is a tall, great-headed man, has an impediment in his utterance, and does not impress a stranger so agreeably as some other of the gentlemen mentioned.

This evening I returned to Halle.

May 12th. I have had the pleasure of seeing Tholuck several times since my return. He seems much benefited by his journey, and has had, he says, his heart warmed in Berlin, and has heard many circumstances of an encouraging character, relative to the progress of vital piety in Germany.

May 20th. Having since this day week dined in company with Tholuck every day, and expecting to continue this agreeable and profitable arrangement, I have already increased my acquaintance with the character and opinions of persons whom I have no opportunity of seeing personally, and I hope to do so still more.

Tholuck says, that Professor Hengstenberg of Berlin was formerly of Bonn, and a very warm and decided rationalist. Although now not more than twenty-five years old, he was already so distinguished that professorships in several departments were in his offer, Greek, Oriental Languages, Philosophy and Theology. He determined, however, to leave Bonn, and left behind him a strong and open declaration of his principles. Shortly after, he was led to attend a religious service among the Moravians. The discourse made such an impression on his mind, that his confidence in the truth of his own opinions was very much shaken. He betook himself to the simple study of the Bible, and at last came out a firm and practical believer in the great truths of the Gospel. He is now Professor of Oriental Languages at Berlin, and exceedingly bold. In one of his first lectures he said: 'It matters not whether we make a god out of stone, or out of our own understanding, it is still a false god; there is but one living God, the God of the Bible.' This declaration was received with hissing and scraping by a large part of the students, by which he was little intimidated. He often asserts that it is only the heart which doubts.

Olshausen, the pious professor in Königsberg, is also a young man not more than two or three and thirty. He too was formerly a Rationalist, but when his heart was once touched his opinions changed of course. Tholuck told me he used to think he was one of the last persons likely to be converted. He was continually exhorting him (Tholuck) to beware of Pietism and Mysticism, and reproaching him with being a Herrnhutter. Shortly after one of these conversations, Olshausen thought he would see for himself what Moravianism was, and so read the *Life of Zinzendorf*. On Tholuck's next visit he was surprised to see him dejected and sad, and asked him if he were not well. 'Yes,' he answered, 'but my dear Tholuck, I have been railing at you as a Herrnhutter, but I knew not what it meant, and *that* book (*Life of Count Z.*), showed that I did not know what I am myself.' He is now one of the warmest and most decided Christians in Germany.

May 26. I have within a few days had the pleasure of several interviews with the Rev. Mr McCall, who has been for six years a missionary among the Jews in Poland. He appears to be a warm and sincere Christian, entertaining most of the opinions relative to the Jews which their peculiar friends generally hold respecting their restoration and future exalted state in the church on earth, etc. He says that the Jews are very willing to hear, so much so that there is no necessity to seek them; they come in crowds to the house in which they know the missionary is to be found. They are exceedingly ignorant; when best educated their learning being confined to the Talmud. The Scriptures have little authority with them. They have a common saying which illustrates their sentiments on this point, viz.: 'The Scriptures are water, the Mishna wine, the Gemara spiced wine.' The Pentateuch and historical books they can generally understand, but the Prophets few of them can translate. They are complete Pharisees in all their opinions and customs, and are generally sincere in their faith. There is a class among them calling themselves German Jews, who are generally infidels. Another sect, which is of recent origin, but which has taken the old name Hasidim, pretend to peculiar sanctity. Their rabbis are infallible, work miracles, give absolution, etc. The Jews are miserably filthy and offensive when not raised much above the ordinary level by wealth. They are, however, more moral than either the Catholics or Protestants of Poland. Little has been effected among them as yet, except the production of a general spirit of inquiry, and the diminution of their prejudice against Christians. Very few of them can be induced to engage in agriculture. They prefer merchandise in its various forms.

Among the Catholics, who are exceedingly degraded and superstitious, there have recently been several conversions. That of a young priest has excited a great deal of attention. Mr McCall speaks of him as likely to become a second Luther. The Grand Duke Constantine is very favourable to missions and adverse to the Catholics. Mr McCall, when passing through Berlin, was sent for by the Crown Prince,[1] who was very inquisitive about the mission, and expressed his approbation and interest in its success. It is interesting in a country where the King is head of church and state, and has such uncontrolled sway, to know the character of those who are likely to influence the religion of Germany. As illustrative of the character of the Crown Prince it is worth while to mention some things which he said to Mr McCall. He expressed his deep regret that so large a portion of the clergy had renounced the pure 'Bible faith', and preached such 'stupid stuff' as the Rationalists do in its place. He was rejoiced, he said, that there were several in Berlin who now preached the true doctrines. He spoke of the state of the English Church, where, he said, they retained the doctrines, but had not much of the living power of the gospel. God grant that he in whose hands so much power may one day be lodged may use it for his glory.

Halle, June 20th. Tholuck surprised me very much this evening by the account which he gave of the prevalence of Rationalism in Germany from 1790 to 1815 or '17. During this period, with the exception of the Tübingen theologians, there was scarcely a voice

[1] Frederick William IV, elder brother of the present Emperor of Germany [Kaiser Wilhelm I, d. 1888].

raised against the prevailing system of Deism. He had himself lived to his fifteenth or sixteenth year without having seen any person who believed in the Bible, excepting *one boy*, in the school to which he went! In this school the Deistical system alone was taught: and this was almost universal. Of the old men, who belonged to the preceding generation, some few remained who still held to the old system, but in town and country, among professors and pastors, the Rationalistic opinions were so dominant, that with few exceptions no one had courage to support the contrary doctrines. Professor Harms of Kiel (blessed be his memory!) was the first to break this dreadful stillness. Upon the occasion of the tercentennial celebration of the Reformation of Luther, he published the theses of that great man, and added many of his own against Rationalism. He was overwhelmed with abuse. No less than eighty pamphlets of all kinds in German and Latin were directed against him. But from this time the advocates of the truth began to multiply, and its progress has been constant, and in some departments rapid ever since.

August. I have recently had the pleasure of seeing two pious preachers from the neighbourhood of Elberfeld, Messrs. Sanders and Krummacher. The account which they give of the state of religion in that region is very encouraging. In a small party, however, the doctrine of predestination has been carried out into practical antinomianism. These people feel themselves above the gospel and all its ordinances, and when they condescend to enter a church it is easy to see from their listless, careless, assured manner, that they think the doctrines which they hear are only fit for babes.

Monday, August 27th. This morning I left Halle with Dr Tholuck and Mr Ehlers for Dresden. Our ride to Leipzig was pleasant, and enlivened by the debates of these gentlemen on philosophical points. Tholuck maintained that what *actually* is, is all that is *possible*. That the world cannot possibly be other than it is. He bases this opinion on the attributes of God. He urges the idea that attributes and essence are the same in the divine Being. That beauty, holiness, knowledge are in God essential, that is, that God is essential beauty, holiness and knowledge, etc., and that all the beauty, holiness and knowledge in the universe is not only derived from God, but *is* the beauty, holiness, etc., of God, so that God is not only the most perfect Being, but *is* all that is good or beautiful in the universe. He makes the conscience of man and all his moral and religious powers the essence of God. For God cannot be only the partaker of good, but must be all that is good. In answer to my objection that we cannot conceive of beauty as an essence or *sein* (*esse*), any more than of proportion as an essence, Tholuck replied, that proportion was an essence, so that the proportion or relation of four to eight, and of eight to sixteen is an *essence, sein*. Proximity is also an essence, a *sein*, etc. Tholuck appeals strongly to Augustine in support of his ideas on this subject, particularly to his *Confessions*. One very important principle of Tholuck's whole system seems to be entirely false. He appears to make what the Germans call *Anschauung,* the test of all truth respecting invisible things, that is, the ability of forming a distinct image of the subject before the mind. This they call intuition, and when they cannot have such an *Anschauung* of any subject they cannot feel its truth. But, as I said to Tholuck, it is utterly impossible to form such a *bild,* or image of the soul, or of God, or of any spiritual subject. But he maintained that all clear ideas of these subjects assume this form, and that this is the test of the correctness of these ideas.

We reached Dresden, Tuesday evening, August 28th, and put up at the *Golden Anchor* tavern. The next morning I visited the gallery of paintings, which is the object of most interest among the curiosities of this city. This famous collection, thought to be the finest in modern Europe, is by no means so imposing in its arrangement as that of the Louvre. With regard to the pieces themselves, I am not able to give any judgment. I was much disappointed. Many of the paintings which are extolled as masterpieces produced very little impression upon me. The *Night* of Correggio belongs to this class. I can conceive that an artist can take pleasure in discovering the beauties of the proper distribution of light, which proceeds from the infant Saviour, but this is as little adapted to the untutored eye as the intricate harmony of sound to the untutored ear. The figures in this piece have no individual beauty. The same confession I am obliged to make with regard to most of the productions of Rubens. The colouring is indeed surprising, but the effect, for me, seldom, either strong or pleasing. The *Madonna* of Raphael is an exception. This was as much above, as the others were below my expectations. The infant here is wonderful; the expression of the eye belongs to no human infant, but we may well imagine such an expression in the case of our Saviour. The Virgin is the ideal of human purity and beauty; what the human frame may be when this corruption has put on incorruption, and this mortal is clothed with immortality. The *Magdalen* of Correggio, also, is a beautiful picture, and many others which at first produced little impression. I found it far more interesting, after repeated visits to the gallery. But on every visit I was attracted and held bound by Raphael's *Madonna*.

On Thursday morning I called with Tholuck and Ehlers upon the pastor Stephani, a man of about forty-five, of very friendly and open manners, plain and blunt in all he says. He is a warm Lutheran, reads the works of the Reformer by day and night, and unfortunately insists as much upon the peculiar tenets of his church as upon the points essential to godliness. He is, however, a great blessing to Dresden, and has served to keep alive a spirit of piety among the common people. He was educated in Halle about twenty years ago, and related many circumstances to show how utterly to all appearance religion and orthodoxy had died out. No one ever thought of preaching on the leading truths of the gospel, and some went so far as to propose to introduce a new Bible, which should contain more interesting histories than those relating to the Jews, and a purer system of morals.

This evening we drank tea with Mr Zahn, a pious young man who is director of a seminary for the education of country schoolmasters. At 9 o'clock all his pupils were collected in the lecture room for prayers. After singing a few verses Tholuck read and expounded the words, from our Saviour's last address to his disciples, 'In this world ye shall have tribulation,' etc. He made this a test of Christian character in a very happy manner. 'If', said he, 'the world satisfies us; if in the society and pleasures of the world we find no deficiency, nothing that gives pain, that leaves our most urgent wants unsatisfied, we are not the disciples of Christ. But if we are constantly longing for the joys that flow from His presence, then we have part in His promise, "I will give unto you eternal life."'

Saturday, September 1st. We left Dresden on an excursion of a few days in the interesting country further up the Elbe, called the Saxon Switzerland. Mr Zahn accompanied us a few hours distance to our dining-place. He and Tholuck, in a long argument against Ehlers and myself, maintained that every thing in nature had *Bewusstsein*, consciousness, a sense of life – trees, stones, everything that exists. The arguments for this opinion were mostly drawn from general pantheistic principles. For although these gentlemen abhor Pantheism, they have, as far as their philosophy is concerned, many principles in common with it. About 10 o'clock we passed the Elbe at Pillnitz, the country residence of the King of Saxony. The grounds are simple and neat; the palace is simply a row of low buildings, occupying three sides of a hollow square, facing inwards. We dined at Lohmen, a village situated at the foot of the first mountain. After dinner we rode about an hour up the mountain, and then commenced our tour on foot under the direction of a guide. We descended, by a flight of narrow stairs, partly cut in the rock, and partly made of wood, into a deep valley, or rather cleft, which intersects the mountain in various directions. It is sometimes twenty or thirty yards wide, and at others only a few feet, the rocks rising on either side, in most instances perpendicularly, two, four, or six hundred feet. Huge masses of rock have fallen into this cleft, and where it is narrow, have been stopped in their course, and remain jammed between the sides. After a while we began to ascend at an opening where the ascent is gradual and easy. Poor Tholuck began to walk too soon after dinner, and hence was exceedingly unwell and could enjoy nothing. The ascent brought us to the summit on the bank of the Elbe; here the rocks rise perpendicular to the bed of the river, eight hundred feet high. From this point the view is very extensive and very peculiar. On the right you look over a large plain gradually rising toward the horizon, over which immense piles of rock are scattered. Some of these, as the Königstein and the Lilienstein, are miles in circumference, and rise perpendicularly for twelve hundred feet. On the left we look over a vast number of these rocky prominences, which stand as the skeletons of mountains, from which all the softer parts have been washed away. The prominence on which we stood is called the Bastey. A bridge of wood is built over some of these caverns, which gave us access to part of the mountain which was formerly the resort of thieves, and afterwards the place of refuge of the inhabitants in times of war. Evident indications that this wild region was once inhabited are still visible—such as flights of stairs cut out of the rocks, the remains of walls by which the breaches of the natural bulwarks were closed, etc., etc.

Tholuck, being too unwell to proceed, went by a nearer way to the rendezvous of the carriage, and I proceeded with the guide for an hour or two through the customary pathway along the mountain. Early in the evening we reached a bathing establishment, with an excellent public house, romantically situated just without the small town of Schandau, on the banks of the Elbe. Here we had a quiet Sabbath, September 2nd. On our return we passed through Pirna and Königstein. Near the former place we visited a very extensive hospital and asylum for insane persons. The physician kindly went over the establishment with us, and showed us the means of amusement and cure they had devised for their patients. The latter are various bathing establishments, chairs, and beds, which can be set in rapid rotary motion, the quickness and duration of the motion being proportioned to the state of the patient. Near this is Königstein, the celebrated fortification, built upon the rock above mentioned. It has, I believe, never been subdued by force. It contains a well said to be seven hundred feet deep, cut through the rock. We reached Dresden again on the afternoon of Monday, September 3rd.

September 4th, Dresden. This morning we spent about an hour with Dr Neander. He is rather an old-looking man for thirty-five, has much of the Jewish countenance, and his manners, though peculiar and awkward, are exceedingly kind. The poor man has studied himself almost to death. He is so weak, and his nerves so much shattered, that he is not allowed to walk out alone. There is perhaps a constitutional weakness of nerves about him, as his sisters are very peculiar. The one who is travelling with him came hurrying home the other day in a great fright, lest some one should murder her brother in her absence. Neander is beyond competition the first man in his department in Germany, and is as much distinguished for his piety.

Yet his opinions are peculiar and arbitrary. He believes in miracles, and yet gives himself the greatest trouble to explain away the gift of tongues. I heard him at length endeavour to interpret the passage in Acts as a mere natural occurrence – but very unsatisfactorily. He said the various classes there mentioned spoke for the most part the same language, that the number spoken did not exceed four, and these the Apostles might have learned in the ordinary way. The λαλεῖν γλώσσαις mentioned in Corinthians, he explains of 'ecstatic speaking', as Plutarch says the priestess of Apollo 'spoke with tongues'. I am told Neander is a Sabellian and Patripassian, but I know not. It is pleasant to see that talent in Germany, at least in the learned professions, has fair scope. Neander's father was a Jew, who trafficked in old clothes. Twesten's was a lamp-lighter. Tholuck's a silversmith.

I had the honour of dining twice with Twesten, who is a hale, healthy-looking man. He belongs to the orthodox party, and has the character of being more variously learned than most of his literary brethren – not only in the various branches of Theology, but in Philosophy, and the natural sciences, medicine, law, etc., etc. He seems to have the principle that a man to be properly cultivated should submit his mind to the influence of all kinds of knowledge. He goes to the theatre from a sense of duty to cultivate his taste. He has published the first volume of a system of Theology, which, as far as its philosophy is concerned, is like that of Schleiermacher, from whom, however, he of course differs in many important points. He has got free from the chains of Pantheism, the fragments of which hang around many otherwise orthodox professors of the present day. He makes the world, however, a living being, if I understand Tholuck correctly.

I had also the pleasure of meeting Prof. Ritter, of Berlin, who is more of a gentleman than most of the German Doctors in externals. He has lately published a system of Logic, directed against the Half-Kantians and Pantheists. What his own opinions are I do not know, and suspect that it is not easy, from his books, for a common man to discover. He says that every earnest and deep thinker has always acknowledged that the human race has a general personality distinct from that of the several individuals, i.e., the *personalität der Menschheit*, distinct from that *der Menschen*.

September 10th. I left Dresden in the Post for Leipzig, where I remained three or four days, and had the pleasure of seeing much of Prof. Hahn, whose kindness I have much reason to remember with gratitude. I heard him lecture on the 15th chapter of 1st Corinthians. His manner was feeble, but what he said was clear and to the point. Hermann I heard read on Hesiod. His lecture was in Latin, and his manner very hesitating, a fault, I am told, which he has as much when speaking German as Latin. I called also on the preacher Wolf, and had about an hour's conversation with him. Dr Heinroth, who has written several works in favour of orthodox Christianity, is a small, active, familiar man, speaking loud and bold on every subject. His views are his own, and as he expresses his ideas on Christian doctrines in philosophical language, it is not always easy for the uninitiated to understand what he means.

I left Leipzig on the evening of the 14th, in order to reach Weimar on the morning of Saturday, the 15th. After spending an hour or two in walking through the town, and particularly through the Park, I rode over to Jena. Jena lies in a hollow, surrounded by abrupt and high hills. On one of these the Prussian army was encamped when it was so totally defeated by Napoleon in 1806. The pass through which he led his army and drew his cannon is so steep and difficult, that an unencumbered man finds it no easy task to make his way. In Jena I heard two miserably cold antichristian sermons: the one delivered in the University Church, was by a young man without a trace of Christian character in his discourse, and was intended for the students, of whom I saw only one present. I have nowhere else been so strongly impressed with the total absence of religion. I am told that the students boast of the fact that they have nothing of fanaticism among them. Fighting duels seems to be as common here as ever. A few weeks since, a young man, the only son of a widow, was killed. I have been in Halle seven months without hearing a word said on the subject. Yet one of the students lately said that they occurred almost every day or two. Jena, however, has always been particularly famous in this respect, and here the method of fighting is more dangerous than in the other universities, as thrusting is the fashion and not 'slashing'. In Göttingen also, according to the statement of one of its students, duelling is still exceedingly common. The students are divided into innumerable Landsmannschaften, which are not formed merely for the different states, but for every neighbourhood of the same state. Those from the same district band together, and have to maintain their own honour. If one be insulted, accidentally touched while passing in the street, or the like, he or some other of his company must fight the offender, or some one belonging to his clan. And so it goes on, often half a dozen such affairs in a week.

I had a letter from Dr Tholuck to Dr Baumgarten Crusius, and from Gesenius to Dr Hofmann. The former I found buried in his books, although it was afternoon. He had not yet made his toilet, which with a German Professor, whose studying habiliments are rather peculiar, is essential to his appearance in public. This good and famous man was driving his studies without, to the best of my observation, even the encumbrance of a pair of pantaloons. As, however, he is one of the most learned theologians of his day, and withal received me so kindly, I should not discourse on such particulars. He is now engaged in printing three works – the one is a *Dogmengeschichte* [history of dogma]; another a Biblical Theology; and the other I have forgotten. He was kind enough to introduce me to Prof. Schott, Editor of the New Testament, etc. He is an old man, and rather peculiar in his manners. With Dr Hofmann I supped on Monday evening, and was very much pleased with him and his family. He is distinguished as an Orientalist. Reads Arabic, Syriac, Hebrew, Sanskrit, etc., etc. His Syriac Grammar, which is just leaving the press, will be far the most full and extensive yet published.

I left Jena on Tuesday, September 18th, for Halle, where I remained until October 10th, engaged principally in writing. It was vacation ; my friends were absent. I supped one evening with Gesenius, in company with Reisig, the two Professors Niemeyer, Professors Meyer, Jacob and Friedländer. Such loud talking and laughing would seldom be heard among an equal number of English literati. Reisig is a complete *Bursche* [boy, lad], loud and indelicate, but apparently good-natured.

LETTER FROM THOLUCK RECEIVED BY MR HODGE WHILE STILL IN HALLE

RADENSLEBEN, Near Ruppin, Sept. 22, 1827

My Dear Beloved Brother in the Lord: — I am sitting in a stately castle; opposite me are the dovecotes and gardens, and the great highway; in the room near me my beloved friend, Hengstenberg; round about me the articles for the Church journal. The sky is cloudy, the air is heavy, but my heart is light and dwells upon a far distant land, and a beloved brother in another part of the world, whom God has given to me. You, dear brother! You have become so dear to me that I can scarce express to you my love. But were our bond not secure in God, it would be in vain; and had we not been directed to each other, in the spiritually dead Halle, our bond would not have become so firm on God. Therefore I am sincerely thankful to gloomy Halle . . . I reached Berlin about 8 o'clock in the evening. On the second day I met by appointment Justice Focke, a very intimate friend of mine, who said much to me regarding you, and is very proud of you. On the third day I dined with the Patriarch (Baron Kottwitz), in a great company. O what vivifying power springs from such Christian fellowship. Hengstenberg was not in Berlin, but at his parents-in-law, upon a country estate 40 miles from Berlin. On the fourth day of my presence in the city, a coach suddenly made its appearance, and bore me in the country to visit him. Here I have been for eight days.

My dear friend, how are you passing your time in Halle? Does it pass pleasantly or drag upon your hands? Pray leave behind the gloomy place, and hasten to friendly Berlin.

Now with sincere love, I commend you to God, and to the protection of His grace.

Your faithful, A. Tholuck

FROM THE JOURNAL

On Wednesday evening, October 10th, I left Halle, after a residence of seven months, probably forever. A thought which makes one sad, however little interest the object may have in itself, which is seen for the last time. I reached Wittenberg about six o'clock the next morning. I first visited the Seminary which is intended for the more practical part of the preparation of students of theology for their office. At present there are about twenty-five students, of whom a considerable portion are considered really pious. The old Prof. Schleusner, whom I wished very much to see, was not in town. Prof. Heubner I heard lecture on the history of Jacob and Joseph. This exercise was altogether practical, and his remarks were characterized by a spirit of genuine and devout piety.

After the lecture, I had the pleasure of attending him, in a walk around the town, in company with the Chevalier Bunsen, the Prussian ambassador in Rome, who also has the reputation of being a Christian. He is at least very zealous against the rationalists. We spent the evening at Dr Heubner's, the conversation turning on the King's new liturgy, to which the clergy of Wittenberg are warmly opposed; more, I believe, from the source from which it comes, than from its contents.

I visited, in the course of the day, the church in which Luther used to preach, and in which Luther and Melanchthon lie buried. A simple iron or bronze plate marks the spot where these great men are awaiting the resurrection of the just. An original likeness of each hangs on the wall over their graves. These likenesses, which are in themselves fine pictures, are said to be remarkably true. The Church is also ornamented with bronze figures of the Electors of Saxony of that period. In walking down the main street I was struck with the following inscription on one of the houses, *Hier wohnte, lehrte und starb Melanchthon.* 'Here Melanchthon lived, taught, and died.' The house in which Luther lived was formerly a cloister, and is now occupied by the Seminary. His chamber, however, is left undisturbed, as he occupied it ; the same stove, the same table of solid oak, and the same window chair, which three hundred years ago supported the cumbrous weight of the bold Reformer. The walls are covered with a thousand names of insignificant persons – distinguished from the number, the cipher of Peter the Great is preserved from a fate, to which the others seem with little remorse relinquished, by being covered by a pane of glass.

BERLIN

On Friday, the 12th of October, I arrived at Berlin and put up in the Stadt Rome, under the Linden [*Unter den Linden,* the main thoroughfare of Berlin]. The first impression which Berlin makes on a stranger is very imposing. The streets are broad, the houses large and well built, and the avenue lined with a four-fold row of trees is certainly the finest street I have yet seen in Europe. On Saturday, the 13th, I went early to see Tholuck, who was on a visit to Berlin. I found him wrapt up in his *schlafrock* [dressing gown], hard at work. His reception was extremely affectionate. We walked together about the town and through the Tiergarten, which is a great forest before the Brandenburg Gate. In the evening he took me to the house of Otto von Gerlach. Here I met with a number of Christians; the Landgerichtsrath Focke; Kammergerichtsrath le Coq; the Count von der Reke; several military officers, and others. Tholuck read and expounded a passage of Scripture; we prayed and sang a couple of hymns. The rest of the evening was spent in religious conversation. My heart was rejoiced at the prospect of having such a place of religious communion accessible every week.

[In order to introduce to the reader this remarkable circle of Christian men with which it was the happiness of Mr Hodge to be associated during his residence in Berlin, and with some of whom he corresponded for many years, I will give a short account of the brothers von Gerlach, drawn chiefly from Tholuck's biographical notice of Otto von Gerlach in Herzog's *Encyclopaedia*. There were four brothers von Gerlach, born in the following order: William, a lawyer; Ernest Ludwig, statesman; Leopold, a soldier, and Otto, a clergyman. They sprang of a noble family; one of the few which followed the Brandenburg family when they went into the Reformed Church, the members of which had, for a hundred years, served the king in office. The friends of Mr Hodge were Ludwig and Otto. Of the latter, Tholuck says that, 'in 1820, after studying law, he came to Berlin, entering a circle in which Christian life existed in freshest bloom. It was the beautiful time of first love, when a number of young men of rank, principally of the military and legal professions, some of them returned from the wars of liberty, drew together in loving friendship in Christ. Under the impressions made on him in this beautiful society, his early love for the gospel was strengthened, and after much conflict he gave up the prospects of ambition, and entered again the academic career. In 1828 he became *Privatdozent* [a university teacher qualified for but not holding a professorship] in the University of Berlin. In 1834 he became pastor of the Church of St Elizabeth, built by the king, in the suburbs of Berlin. Here he was indefatigable in preaching and all kinds of pastoral labours. *He was the Wesley of Berlin*. Translated the lives of Wesley and Baxter. Founded the Berlin Foreign Missionary Society. All the methods of promoting worship and religious life, which have since been adopted, found in this man a previous example.' He reached the very highest positions possible in his profession. Councillor of the Consistory, Court Preacher and Honorary Professor Ordinarius. He died Oct. 24th, 1849.

Ludwig von Gerlach, the elder brother, was born nearly three years earlier than Mr Hodge. He fought through the wars against Napoleon, and afterwards entered the judiciary service of his country. He founded the *Kreuz-Zeitung*, the organ of the High-Church party. In 1865 he became Privy-Councillor of the Supreme Court of Justice of the province of Magdeburg.

The *Life of Hengstenberg*, by Dr Bachman, frequently details these gatherings of devoted Christians, mentioning the same names that recur so frequently in Professor Hodge's Journal – Hollweg, Lancizolle, the Gerlachs, the Chancellor le Coq, the adjutants of the Crown Prince von Roeder, Count v. d. Grobcn, von Senfft, the Oberpräsidentin von Schonberg and Caroline Focke, the Theologians Neander, Tholuck, Strauss, Couard, Lisco, and the preachers Ritter, O. von Gerlach, Lindl, Gossner and others. It was a wide-embracing bond of friendship in the Lord, of men and women of the most different ages, rank and conditions in life, in the midst of which the Patriarch Baron von Kottwitz moved pre-eminent. – Sec. 1,193.

Much light is thrown upon the society with which Prof. Hodge was brought in contact, by the description given in this work of the great revival of piety against Rationalism which had several years before sprung up in Germany, i.e., in 1823. The most varied elements of rank and culture, of church connection and of Christian tendency found themselves thrown together in these awakened circles. But the feeling of inmost union held all together; in faith and love they knew they were one. In every corner of Germany and Switzerland, wheresoever a little believing company came together, a living witness for evangelical truth arose. The remarkable move in the Catholic Church of South Germany, emanating from Boos and Gossner, drew thither more than one traveller from Berlin; young men of the Kottwitz circle, von Lancizolle, Hollweg and others, made the journey to Bavaria, and there knit together the most intimate relations, and received the impulse to an eternal progress. It was thus, as Tholuck expresses it, 'that beautiful primitive time of first love, when the consciousness of that which unites the Church of Christ far outweighed the consciousness of that which divides it.' Confessional differences constituted no barrier to the communion in love and work for the kingdom of God; in the joy and custom of what is common, the idea of a union of believers out of all churches could arise. One hears with the same edification the Reformed Theremin and Couard, the Lutheran Janicke and Strauss, the preachers of the Brother Communion [the Moravians], with the Catholic Lindl and Gossner;[1] one embraces in the same love the believing brethren in the Catholic Church, with the Reformed Swiss and Lutheran zealots in Silesia. Not to what confession one and another belongs, is the question; it is enough to know themselves one, and to confess faith in the name that is given to men, one Salvation. A Catholic ecclesiastic commended to a Protestant pastor for directions, a humble person, taking it for granted that he was to receive the Lutheran communion. Many Catholics were active members of the Bible Society.

Full twenty different devotional hours could be enumerated during twenty years in Berlin, (p. 192) daily on Sunday and week-days. Sometimes in many parts of the city, and without by the Hamburg gate, &c., at an appointed evening hour larger or smaller circles might be found gathered about their leader. And it seems to be regarded as a healthful life that in none of these assemblies any sectarian tendency, a disposition to degrade the public worship of God, was manifested. Had any worshipper been disposed to

---

[1] Gossner joined the Evangelical Church in 1826.

this, he was immediately set right, and confuted out of the Word of God.

At the same time the so-called pietism of the revival times is clearly distinguished from the old pietism, in that the latter set itself in opposition to the Church, in which, with all its lifelessness, the foundation, the pure doctrine of the Word of God, remained untouched; the new pietism developed itself in opposition, not to the Church itself, but against the rationalistic corruption of doctrine in the Church. The pietism of the revival times had not, like the old, orthodoxy as its opposite, but it carried orthodoxy in its bosom. It was easy, therefore, for it to proceed by appointed churchly paths. Only when the Church placed itself in opposition to the newly awakened life, did this enter upon a separate existence. Fortunately, in Berlin, the churchly connections were never entirely broken, hence the possibility and security of a decided Church development later, was secured.

In 1823 the evangelical party constituted a great people, increasing from year to year. In many pulpits of Berlin, the witness for Christ, the only Saviour, had again become clear as a power which filled the deserted churches anew. Theremin at the Dom, Bishop Anders, of the Brother Communion, Couard at St George's, Loffler at the Gertraude Church, Frederick Strauss in his double office of Dom and Court preacher and Professor in the University, brought multitudes under the influence of the truth. From the whole city multitudes came together who had an ear for the Word of God; and many also who had hitherto stood aloof were aroused to ask after the way of life. Couard's preaching was particularly crowded, so that there was not standing room in the ample church (Vol. i. pp. 187, etc.).

If any discrepancy between this account and that which Prof. Hodge gives in his Journal is perceived the reader will consider (i) the difference of the means and standards of estimate of the

German Professor and the American stranger; (ii) the difference between the times described by each, i.e., between 1823 and 1827–8 – and (iii) The difference between Halle and Berlin.

JOURNAL RESUMED

On Sunday, the 14th, I went to hear Schleiermacher, not knowing of any more evangelical preacher who had service in the morning. The sermon was peculiar. The words were biblical, but the whole tenor so general, the ideas so vague and indefinite, that it was impossible for me to understand exactly what he meant. His text was, Thou shalt love the Lord thy God with all thy heart, etc. This is the first and great commandment. This, he remarked, was the highest end of our existence, to come to this full love of the Supreme Being – that this end can be attained only through Jesus Christ, whom he called the source of all truth, and the truth itself. The difference between this law as presented in the Old Testament and as it stands in the New, is this, that in the Old Testament it was part of a law, a coercive, external command, while in the New it is the spontaneous result of a renovated nature. It is no longer a law, but the voluntary bent of the heart; and to bring about this spontaneous tendency of the soul to God is the great work of Christ. This is what I took to be the drift of his discourse. In the afternoon I went with Tholuck to see the good patriarchal Baron Kottwitz, who has been so long and actively engaged in the service of the Redeemer. In the evening I attended a religious service at the Baron's, and heard a very warm, pious sermon from the Moravian Bishop Anders, who is to sail for America in a few days. Here I met a large circle of religious friends, partly the same I had met the evening before. Among others a very interesting man, Prof. Hollweg, the present Rector of the University.

Saturday evening, October 20th, I attended the same meeting that I did a week ago. Tholuck had left town a day or two before for Halle. The services were conducted by a young candidate of Theology.

On Sunday I heard Marheineke, a warm advocate of Hegel's philosophy. His sermon was dry and general. In the afternoon, in the same Church, I heard an evangelical discourse from the junior Pastor, delivered with a good deal of animation and feeling.

On the 23rd Neander began his lectures to a crowded audience, on the Epistles to the Corinthians.[1] His manner is clear and simple, and the wonderful compass of his historical knowledge enables him to bring many very interesting and striking illustrations of the passages he wishes to explain.

December 16th. Since my last date I have attended regularly the lectures of Neander, and part of the time those of Hengstenberg[2]

---

[1] A MSS. report of these lectures, fully written out by Prof. Hodge, is in existence.

[2] Extract from the *Life of Hengstenberg*, by Dr I. Bachman, Gutersloh, 1876–9, vol. 2, p. 30. (1879): Particularly pleasant to Hengstenberg was his acquaintance with Professor Hodge, of Princeton, in America, who, after he had spent the summer of 1827 at Halle, in intimate association with Tholuck, came, in the winter of the same year, to Berlin, and here, as also Monod, industriously attended upon Hengstenberg in his lectures and at his house. Even at their first meeting he had much pleased Hengstenberg, particularly because of his 'simplicity, modesty and sincerity', and at the end of the Semester, April 27, 1828, he thus expresses himself: 'I was, in those days, much with Hodge, whose departure grieves me much, and to-day I took a long walk with him. He told me much that was delightful of America, of the great Christian earnestness which prevails there, the great moderation in conduct, the consistency in denying the world; and he himself is the best evidence of the truth of what he says.' But in the following letter he speaks of both these foreign friends: 'I have now, for the first time, heard much of the beautiful activity which the French preacher, Monod, has exercised here. For instance: Hodge and Monod sit together at the lecture ; a student looks into Hodge's note-book, which is written in English, and asks him whether he is an Englishman. No, says Hodge, an American. That caused the student, who supposed that all Americans must be copper-coloured, such astonishment, that he uttered an oath. Monod reproves him with earnest words for the misuse of the name of God. The student receives the reproof thankfully, Monod goes home with him after lecture, and talks with him of salvation in Christ. He finds a receptive heart, and the acquaintance is continued until he came to full decision. – Monod is at table with Ancillon, and hears that a little French physician, a Catholic, is studying here, who

and Böckh. Mr Monod, of Paris, came early last month to reside in the same house with me, which I have found very agreeable. Some time since he gave me a very interesting account of the religious exercises of the daughter of Baron Cuvier on her deathbed. She had been some years pious, a state to which she was suddenly brought after a long season of thoughtfulness; awaking, as one of her friends expressed it, one morning, without well knowing how or why, in peace with God. She was on the eve of being married when taken ill. As she approached the hour of her dissolution her faith became more and more triumphant, so that she was the astonishment and admiration of all who saw or heard her. Her physicians, ignorant of the gospel and of its effects, looked on in silent wonder. Her poor father, whose name is famed through the civilized world, was often seen kneeling for a half an hour together in prayer, by her bedside. God grant that he and others by this event may be brought to the knowledge of the truth as it is in Jesus.

The death of the Baron de Staël, who was one of the leading men among the pious Protestants of France, is an event, humanly speaking, to be deeply regretted. His last hours also were such as to evince the power of the gospel, and to leave the most pleasant conviction on the minds of his surviving friends, that he had entered into his rest.

I have heard several evangelical preachers since coming to Berlin, particularly Strauss and Lisco. The former is court preacher, and much of an orator; the latter is remarkably simple and faithful.

The French Protestant Church here, once so flourishing, is now in a very low state. There are nominally 5,000 persons belonging

---

has an earnest disposition. This is motive enough for him to visit him. He finds in him absolute ignorance of the doctrine of salvation, but a very receptive spirit, and it was not long before he was united with him in the Lord. Yesterday he was with Hodge. Such activity cannot fail to give offence. There are about Hodge and Monod the most wonderful and wildest stories in circulation.'

to their several congregations, and they have funds to the amount of $500,000, but the congregation on a Sabbath does not generally exceed twenty or thirty persons.

I drank tea, the other evening, with the Lieutenant Senfft. Prof. Hollweg, the Rector of the University, who is a very interesting man, apparently about thirty-five years old, gave us an account of the recent revival of religion in Pomerania. A young officer of Hussars, who was for some time in service in Berlin, was brought to the knowledge of the truth. He resigned his commission in the army and retired to his estate in Pomerania. Here he found the clergy and people alike sunk in the deepest indifference to vital religion. He began his work in his own family. God blessed his efforts. His brothers, who had hitherto lived at variance, were reconciled to each other, in being reconciled to God. His father also was converted. He and his brothers now began to assemble the peasants on their estates for religious instruction and worship. The clergy, of course, opposed them violently, and appealed to the Government. But the Word of God produced a most powerful effect. Multitudes were awakened. In one house belonging to these gentlemen 600 persons, regarded as truly pious, are in the habit of meeting to worship God. The Government issued an order to the military to disperse all such assemblies. But the colonel refused, and appealed to the military commander of the Province, the Crown Prince, who forbade any such step being taken. A commission was now appointed to examine the nature of this religious excitement, all the members of which, with the exception of Prof. Heubner of Wittenberg, were Rationalists. Their report was unfavourable. But Heubner made such a representation to the king that all persecution from the side of those in authority has been prevented. This is not the first instance I have been informed of in which the king and members of his family have shielded true Christians from the oppressions of the civil and ecclesiastical authorities. Unfortunately the writings of two famous mystical writers, Gichtel and Jacob Boehme, fell into the hands of two of these young noblemen, and gave them a complete mystical cast. They have ceased all their efforts to do good, contemn all their former active course, and place all religion in mystical union with God, and private contemplation.

This morning I attended worship at the Duke of Cumberland's. His Chaplain appears to be an amiable young man of the High Church orthodox order, but a very cold, uninteresting preacher.

December 24th. This morning I went with Justice Focke to the Erziehungshaus. It contains about fifty boys, from seven to fourteen years of age, all of whom have been already convicted of some crime. They are placed here for reformation and education. The institution has been in operation about three years, in which time thirty pupils have been regularly dismissed, of twenty-seven of whom the directors have the most favourable accounts. After the children had sung a hymn they were examined by the teacher respecting the object and the observance of Christmas, and then more generally on the history of our Saviour, giving all the leading prophecies of Him in the Old Testament, and then showing their fulfilment in Jesus of Nazareth. Since I have been in Europe I have witnessed no scene with such pure and decided pleasure.

On the 23rd I attended, for the first time, the Lord's Supper in the Lutheran Church. It was administered by the Pastor, Lisco, at 7 o'clock in the morning. The communicants proceeded into the confessional, where, after a very feeling address, the Pastor repeated a general confession of sins, and called upon those present to say whether they confessed themselves sinners in the sight of God, trusted in Jesus Christ for pardon, and had the purpose of leading a holy life. On receiving an affirmative answer, he pronounced the usual form of absolution. We then returned into the Church, and the sacrament was administered in the usual way. I have recently been more than ever, I think, affected by the sense of the indescribable excellence of our adorable Saviour, His character has appeared in a purity and beauty which my blind eyes have been long in discovering. O that I could see more of this loveliness every day, and be more transformed into his image.

December 27th. I took tea this afternoon with Lieutenant von Senfft. He gave us a very interesting account of a revival of religion in a village in Silesia. A young man, a miller, came from that village to Berlin for employment, and was providentially directed to a pious man, in whose family he lived some time. On his return he related to his father that the man with whom he had lived used to read and pray in his family. The father immediately declared his purpose to do the same. The neighbours came in from time to time to hear the Scriptures, Some mocked and others prayed. The result, as Lieut. von Senfft witnessed, was about thirty persons, of all ages, in this village were converted to the Lord, and were living in the faith and love of the gospel. From this village the fire spread to others.

In the evening all our usual circle of friends assembled at Justice Focke's to meet Tholuck, who had just arrived. It was a great pleasure to meet the dear man once more after so long a separation. The evening was spent chiefly in religious conversation. Returning home, I walked with Ludwig von Gerlach, a man who has excited more love and respect in me than almost any other I have seen here. He took this opportunity of speaking to me very seriously respecting my political principles, not so much in their political as their Christian aspect. I was surprised to find how much that was unchristian mingled in all my *feelings* on this subject. With this dear man I cannot agree in his opinions, yet I felt that he was much more a free-man in his heart (with all his strong ideas of the divine right of kings) than I.

This night thirty years ago I was born. Thirty years of love and mercy. Thirty years of sin. Thirty years and nothing done. Oh my God, from my soul I pray thee, grant me thy Holy Spirit that if permitted yet longer to live, it may be to more purpose, – that my time may be better improved in working out my own salvation and the salvation of my fellow-men. Bless, O God, my dear, precious mother, who, thirty years ago, first rejoiced over me. That thou hast so long spared her to me I thank and bless Thee. Still spare her, O Lord, and grant that every succeeding day she may be more and more filled with thy Holy Spirit, and more richly crowned with thy tender mercies.

December 28th. Today I dined with Tholuck at Justice Focke's. They both made me a present of a devotional book on the occasion of my birthday. The Lord bless these dear friends for being the means of quickening me in the life of godliness. The love of the Saviour is of all bonds the purest and the strongest. Tholuck drank tea with me and Mr Monod. In answer to a question of the latter, he spoke very much in favour of always reading with the pen in hand. He said that for the period of two months in the year 1820, he recorded every important idea which occurred to his own mind – everything interesting he heard in conversation, or in reading. The records of these two months he finds still valuable.

EXTRACTS FROM LETTERS OF DRS ALEXANDER AND MILLER TO MR HODGE WHILE STUDYING IN GERMANY

Their affection and care for him is rendered very evident by their long and frequent letters; and their prayerful anxiety for the preservation of his personal orthodoxy and spirituality under the special exposures of his life in Germany is interesting, especially in view of the fact which his after-life rendered so conspicuous, that their prayers in this behalf were fully answered.

Dr Miller writes, July 21st, 1827:

You have no doubt been informed that we are going on in Princeton, as to the Seminary, very much as heretofore; but with respect to the College and the congregation by no means favourably. The number of students in the College is about eighty, and when the present Senior Class shall leave us, the number, I think, will fall below fifty. Nor do I perceive any prospect of a better state of things. On the contrary, I am afraid the Institution has not reached the lowest point of depression. The multiplication of Colleges all around us; the zeal, enterprise, and ostentatious publications of their officers, and the incessant importunity of their begging for funds, seem to be gradually taking away from us all our human resources and hopes. Some of the members of the Board of Trustees, however, are still sanguine that the College will retrieve its affairs before long

We all long to see you, and shall be glad of your return at the earliest possible hour that your plans will admit. I do not believe, my dear colleague, that you appreciate as you ought your importance and acceptance in our Institution. I know that your mind was often much oppressed by a sense of your own want of adequate qualification, and I was willing and even desirous that you should visit Europe if it were for nothing else than to get cured of this inordinate and morbid impression. But pray come back as soon as you can consistently with the substantial execution of your main purpose. We greatly desire and need your presence.

Again Dr Miller writes, Jan. 29, 1828:

You will probably learn by letters which will have reached you before this, that the winter session in our Seminary opened with a larger accession than we expected. We have matriculated thirty-eight new students. Four more have returned whom we expected never to have seen again, and who had been absent for some time. So that our whole accession may be estimated at forty-two, which makes our whole number at present one hundred and nine – something like fifteen more than we had the previous session. Our College goes on feebly. The present number of the students is about sixty-five or sixty-six, and rather on the decline than on the increase. I am afraid it will be reduced to extremity before long, and that some crisis in its affairs is not very distant. What that may be, whether for the better or the worse, I can scarcely conjecture.

Dr Alexander wrote:

PRINCETON, March 24th, 1827

My Dear Sir: – . . . I hope while you are separated from your earthly friends, you will take care to keep the communication with heaven open! Remember that you breathe a poisoned atmosphere. If you lose the lively and deep impression of divine truth – if you fall into skepticism or even into coldness, you will lose more than you gain from all the German professors and libraries. May the Lord preserve you from error and from all evil. You may depend upon any aid which my feeble prayers can afford. Write as often as you can. Do not be afraid of troubling me.

Affectionately, yours.

And again, Dr Alexander writes:

PRINCETON, July 27, 1827

. . . I suppose that before I write again you will have left Halle, but of this you must give me early notice . . . The air which you breathe in Germany will either have a deleterious effect on your moral constitution, or else by the strength of faith required to resist its effects your spiritual health will be confirmed. I pray God to keep you from the poison of *Neology!* I wish you to come home enriched with Biblical learning, but abhorring German philosophy and theology. I have been paying some attention to Kant's philosophy, but it confounds and astonishes me.

Again Dr. Alexander writes :

Princeton, Aug. 16, 1827

I feel anxious to hear from you, to know how you are, and what progress you make in the literature of Germany. You must come home loaded with riches. Much will be expected of you. But I know how little can be acquired by man in the course of a whole life-time – and when I think that you have the disadvantage of having the language to acquire and the multiplicity of objects to which your attention must be turned, I confess that my hope of any great success is not sanguine. But it will be worthwhile to have gone to Germany to know that there is but little worth going for. It will at any rate place you on a level with the other *travelled* literati of this country. But whatever you may gain of literature and knowledge of the world, I hope and pray that you may not lose any thing of the love of the truth and spirituality of mind. On many accounts we miss you very much . . . For many weeks Dr Miller was sick, and then the whole charge of the Seminary was on me. I wish now to begin in good earnest to prepare for another world. I think before very many years you will be senior Professor in this Institution, and I am afraid you will see trouble. But sufficient to the day is the evil thereof. Let tomorrow take care of itself.

I remain affectionately yours,
A. Alexander

On October 30, 1827, Dr. Alexander writes:

I rejoice to learn that you live in an infected atmosphere, without being yourself infected. May God preserve you.

Again Dr Alexander writes:

Princeton, May 14, 1828

I mentioned to you that Dr Henry intended his library for our Seminary. But the entire matter became subject to the disposition of his father, and under the influence of *certain persons* he has been induced to give another direction to the bequest. At least there remains no doubt but the books will be transferred to the Allegheny Seminary. The matter was laid by him before the Directors in a letter, but they referred the whole question to him again, to dispose of as he thought best. The idea which the old gentleman seems to entertain is that we have books enough, and that his son's library is not needed here. *Inter nos* this new Seminary will affect us here more than all the rest put together. It is received by many as the last stronghold of orthodoxy, and the most secure deposit for funds intended to support the truth; and at this time I have little doubt that Dr Green and others of our staunch friends feel a deeper interest in that Institution than in this. These are merely my own conjectures. After all, we shall be forced to look to New England for students.

Your little family we see very often, and they are as well in health as they can be. April was a month of storms, and Mrs Hodge experienced some inconvenience from coming so early, but she seems to bear everything patiently, and is cheerful.

Make haste and come home. There will be much for you to do. The two crazy old men that are here need some one who has vigour of nerves to put his shoulder under the burden. In truth, however, we do not expect your aid until the fall, so make the best of your visit to Britain. You were very specially remembered in the public prayers offered up here during the late meeting.

I remain affectionately yours, A. ALEXANDER

JOURNAL RESUMED

[From this time Mr Hodge, having obtained a ticket from Baron Humboldt to attend his lectures on physical science, regularly kept full notes of those lectures as long as he continued in Berlin.]

December 29. This evening I heard Tholuck lecture at Otto von Gerlach's. This was the most Christian, heartfelt exhortation I have heard for a long time. He spoke principally from the words, 'Quench not the Spirit.'

Dec. 30, Sunday. This morning heard Strauss preach a New Year's sermon. As usual, it was evangelical, but his manner is too violent. Lieut. Senfft walked home with me. He is one of the most brotherly Christians I have seen. Prince William, the king's second son [the present Emperor, Wilhelm I] with an income of 36,000 thalers, which is very small for his expenses, gives 6,000 to the poor. He is remarkably correct in his conduct. He wished very much some years ago to marry a young princess to whom his father objected as not *vornehm* [aristocratic] enough for a king's son. The matter was committed to the faculties of law, etc., in the universities, but the king at last decided positively in the negative, and poor Prince William had to give up the lady. This is hard.

Berlin deserves the name which French Christians have given it, viz.: *La Ville de St Jean.* Of the propriety of the name I had a proof this evening at the Lady Schönberg's, in the affectionate manner in which the Christians here act towards each other, and towards strangers whom they regard as such. The two adjutants of the crown prince and their wives were there. Major von Röder (one of these gentlemen) is fondling even in his manners. 'Kiss me,' he said to Count Graben, his brother officer, who was passing him. Which request was complied with without hesitation and without remark. There is something delightful in the exhibition of the gospel in these military men; such a warmth and openness of feeling; such an entire absence of stiffness or presumption. The whole company seemed as if they were of one heart. The Graf Schepin was another of these Christian officers. Gossner lectured in his usual extempore manner on the 13th chapter of Mark. Speaking of Christ's coming, he said, 'Are you so ready that you could see the world destroyed as calmly as a child looks at his falling house of cards?' The peculiar prominence of the Saviour, common to the preaching and prayers of the Germans, is very marked in the case of Gossner. I have heard him pray several times exclusively to the

Saviour. Not praying in the name of Christ, but simply to Christ. The manner of address too, is such as would appear very strange in English; as *O, du kleines Kind.*

I was told this evening by Judge Focke, that in all the great revivals of religion which have occurred in Germany of late, the same bodily exercises which excited so much attention in the south and west of our country have been present to a greater or less degree. In Pomerania, cases of what were called demoniacal possession occurred. A young woman was often thrown into the greatest bodily agitation, rolling over and over, and her mind subsequently thrown into a state resembling the heathen ecstasy, in which she would prophesy (in what sense of that word I know not). These were only transient seasons; for the rest she appeared to be a true, humble Christian. These extra ordinary appearances soon ceased. It is certainly remarkable that on both sides of the Atlantic, seasons of religious excitement should be attended by such similar outward disturbances. I suppose it was to cases of this kind that Tholuck referred the other evening, when speaking on the passage 'Quench not the Spirit', he said, 'We should be careful not off-hand to condemn as fanaticism anything of an extraordinary character, which attended unusual outpourings of the Spirit.'

December 31st. I spent this evening with Tholuck, in company with others, at Neander's. Neander had just been reading a review of Bishop Hobart's sermons in the *Christian Observer.* He was much surprised to find such high-church principles in America, which he thought little accordant with the spirit of freedom. He said he was going *Catholisch.* Tholuck said that it was singular that from England three works should at this period make their way to the Continent, all tending to promote the Catholic cause; Lingard's *History,* already translated into German, French and Italian; Dallas's *History of the Jesuits,* also translated; and Cobbet's *History of the Reformation in England,* this last, particularly as translated by

Catholics, is a matter of offence to the Protestants here. Neander said, he thought Hug's *Introduction to the New Testament*, although the best, was very imperfect in its historical part. The accommodation theory, he said, had been given up by all Rationalists of any consequence. This led to a conversation on the doctrine of Inspiration. Neander was disposed to recognize the infallibility of the Apostles in all doctrinal points, but not in their manner of proving them. Thus it was certain that Christ was God, but all Paul's arguments in support of the doctrine from the Old Testament are not of force, as in the first chapter of Hebrews.

To this succeeded a long discussion on the doctrine of Predestination. All were opposed to it. Calvin, Neander said, makes God the author of sin, and this he considered the dangerous tendency of the doctrine. He admitted that those who represent the cause of a sinner's rejection of the gospel as lying in himself, avoided the dangerous practical tendency of the doctrine. He acknowledged freely that it is entirely of grace, that men are brought to faith and salvation. But it lies with every man, either to accept or reject this grace. This he considered to be involved in the idea of man's efficiency and freedom, *selbstbestimmung* [self-determination]. Tholuck remarked that the two extremes were Pelagianism, and the making God the author of sin. Truth lies in the midst. To this I believe all freely assented, predestinarians and anti-predestinarians.

Neander maintained that it was clearly to be inferred from the Scriptures that those who have no offer of the gospel in this world will have it in the world to come. This follows necessarily, he said, out of the principles contained in the Bible. As to others nothing can be distinctly affirmed. He thought that the passage in which our Saviour says, 'The sin against the Holy Ghost shall not be forgiven either in this world or in the world to come', implied that other sins might be forgiven, or that sinners might be brought to faith in Christ after death. In both these points Tholuck concurred. In coming away, Neander shook me very affectionately by the hand, and said to Tholuck, 'Tell our friend Hodge, that though we dispute with him, we belong to the same Lord, and are one in heart.'

Read at evening prayer with Monod the 90th Psalm.

So closed another year of sins and mercies. To Jesus Christ, God over all and blessed forever, may my life be consecrated. His kingdom come, His will be done. Amen. *Charles Hodge.*

January 2nd, 1828. I spent this evening at Professor Hollweg's, Rector of the University, with Tholuck, the Gerlachs and others. Tholuck asked which was the better way when working among the heathen, or Christians sunk in error, as the members of the eastern churches, to preach publicly against the reigning doctrines, and come out as reformers and form a distinct sect, or to confine attention alone to the heart, and let all abuses alone, to be cast aside by those whose hearts are changed. Prof. Hollweg was for the latter. Tholuck seemed more inclined to the former. It seemed to me that neither pointed out the exact course. The truth and all the truth should be preached as by Paul with like wisdom and faithfulness, and each truth in proportion to its importance; regeneration and atonement above all. The men of our day are too feeble. They speak too softly to the people. They are not like the prophets and apostles.

The Christians here seem inclined to think it is against the spirit of the gospel for women to be authors!

Saturday, 5th. This evening I went with Mr Robinson to Otto von Gerlach's. A discourse from Zinzendorf was read.

Monday 7th. Called with Mr Robinson upon Neander, and found the dear little man in a very talkative humour. He is very inquisitive about the United States, and seems afraid of the increase of the Catholics among us.

Thursday, 10th. Drank tea this evening with Hengstenberg. He remarked, that Gesenius scarcely in any one point differs in his views of the Old Testament from De Wette. He has only carried further out what De Wette had said in fewer words. Jahn, he thinks, on the testimony of Heubner, was a Christian, and did not defend the authenticity of the various parts of the Old Testament, because he was a Catholic. This led to a conversation on Jahn's view of the original state of man. Hengstenberg maintained that our first parents were in many respects children; they had indeed the image of God, but undeveloped and *unbewüsst* [unsuspected]. I objected to this the light in which they are presented in the Old Testament, and especially the position of Adam as our federal representative. This led to a long conversation on the point of representation. Hengstenberg said, he would willingly admit it as a fact if it was taught in Scripture. But he thought it was not, or at least not clearly, and that if it were, it left us just as we were without it, as it is impossible to conceive how we are made sinners in this way. He admits hereditary original sin – not as an evil or sickness, but as a sin – but how to reconcile it with the attributes of God he cannot answer. This is the mystery; the fact he admits.

Sunday, 13th. Heard, this morning, Theremin preach a very plain, excellent sermon on the barren fig-tree. In the evening I attended the meeting at the Frau von Schönberg's, the company much the same as before. Gossner lectured on the 12th chapter of Acts. His remarks on the efficacy of prayer, and the influence of afflictions in driving us to pray, were very excellent. His Roman Catholic peculiarities are striking. He addressed both his prayers from beginning to end to the Saviour; and as the last verse of the hymn which was sung spoke of the hand of the Saviour leading His people, he addressed this hand for some time, *O du liebe Hand*, O thou dear hand, which was nailed on the cross for us. His warm piety, his experience, his sufferings make him an interesting man.

Ludwig von Gerlach came home with me and remained until 2 o'clock. As usual we got into a religious political debate, for politics with him rests on religion. The result of our conversation was for me very interesting, as I have clearer views of his ideas of the foundations of government. He had previously spoken of the authority of kings as analogous in its basis to that of fathers. But tonight he made it rest solely or mainly on the right of property. He said, We have only to think of a man with considerable property, servants, tenants, etc.; whose property is constantly increasing, until he becomes a prince. Two hundred years ago the King of Prussia, as Graf von Nürnberg was not so rich as an English lord. But by marriages, by gifts, by purchases, by conquests, his *property* has increased to its present size. He and all kings are *ground own-ers*; all others are tenants under him. But their rights are as sacred as his, and his rights may, as has occurred in England particularly, continually decrease – he and his tenants may, from time to time, as circumstances require, make new contracts. If the king disregards the rights of the tenants to a certain degree, they have a right to exclude him and call the next heir, from whom they may exact a promise of respecting their rights – as, for instance, when James II. of England was excluded and the Orange family succeeded, it was upon the condition that they and their successors should remain Protestant.

It is with states as with individuals, property may be increased in an unjust, as well as in a just manner; but as in the case of the individual, the title of property, though bad at first, became sanc-tioned by time, by contracts, etc.; so it is with kings. All this he forced me to admit, and I feared that I was completely foiled in the argument. My resort was this – having obtained the concession that the king's authority is founded on property, and not on the parental relation, which is entirely a different thing, I put him *first* to historically proving that kings were the real proprietors of all the *ground* in their respective kingdoms, and here my great inferiority in historical and legal knowledge put me to a great disadvantage. I therefore asked *secondly*, on what rested the right of property itself? What was its moral ground? He answered, 'God's command', but he conceded that the ultimate ground was *expediency* in its best sense, i.e., a tendency to promote the good of society. Then, I claimed, when this right interfered with this object, it ceased to exist. This principle he recognized. It is recognized in every community. When the private right of property vesting in an individual comes evidently into conflict with this object, his right is sacrificed to the public good, e.g., the sacrifice of private property in cutting new streets and roads, and in time of war. Having fixed this principle, we agree that, admitting this right of property in kings, it could be justly invalidated on the same grounds on which the private right of property may be invalidated. So far we agreed. Now it is for me to prove that the immense accumulation of property in the hands of kings, as proprietors of whole countries, is inconsistent with the well being of society, the best interests of man. When the enjoyment of another's right of property is inconsistent with the enjoyment of my right of property, one or the other must yield. In the case of nuisances, when the right of property of one interferes with the right of property of many, there is no doubt which must yield. But *a fortiori*, when the right of property of one interferes with or endangers not merely the rights of property of millions, but their moral and religious improvement, their best interests in this world, and their hopes (more or less) in the next – the case is clear enough – what is to be done. He is a noble fellow. Though grieved with my obstinacy, he gave me two kisses when he went, (one, however, less than usual). Happily he does not wear mustachios.

Wednesday, 16. This evening I drank tea with Major von Röder, his two brothers, and several others. The Major is a very affectionate, free and easy man. His heart seems always full of pious feeling. He talks of the Saviour as one talks of a friend. The difference between the free German manifestation of feeling, and our reserve, is very striking. Röder had three brothers killed in the last war, and he himself was shot through the side of his head, which has destroyed the hearing of one ear and the sight of one eye without disfiguring him in the least. Yesterday and to-day the thermometer is about one degree above zero of Fahrenheit.

Friday, January 18. Thermometer still about zero. This evening the Lieutenant von Senfft drank tea with me. He read some letters which he had received lately from friends. One from an officer, whom he described as a rough and imperfectly educated man, who, having been brought to the knowledge of the Saviour in Berlin, is now working with great effect in the place in which he is stationed. All these were dead before, but at present several of his brother officers have been converted, and many of the citizens come to him to talk about their souls, and the children flock to him for tracts and religious books. *Er muss viel beten* [He must pray much], said Senfft. He related also that six or seven of his personal friends had been awakened from their indifference in the first instance by Schleiermacher. Monod related a conversation he had this afternoon with Mr Ancillon, one of the Councillors of State. He spoke very severely against devotional meetings, and thought that all religious meetings out of the Church should be forbidden. His reason was that those assembled could talk of politics. Happily for Prussia, the king has much more liberal and Christian views than many of his ministers. Senfft, speaking of the king, praised his economy very much. He is far from spending his income, and is constantly laying up money, although he gives liberally whenever called upon. He allows his unmarried sons 36,000, his married sons 80,000, and the Crown Prince 120,000 thalers per year.

Sunday, 20th. I heard this morning a very indifferent sermon from the Probst Neander (not the professor). In the evening I was at Neander's. He is very much interested in the state of the Church in America, and wishes very much that the Church and State could be separated here. On this subject there was much conversation this evening, for his liberal views are not shared by all his friends.

Thursday, 24. This afternoon I attended a meeting of the Royal Academy of Sciences. Schleiermacher read a short paper on 'Kings being authors', Humboldt, on 'The Analogy of Language', and a translation of an Eastern mythological poem. The astronomer Enke read an account of his progress in forming certain astronomical tables. It was strange to see the old Duke of Cumberland, the Crown Prince, and several other members of tlie Royal family at such a meeting.

Friday, February 1. I called this morning upon the ex-minister Bekedorf. This gentleman, while in the government, had the charge of the primary schools and the Seminaries for teachers. Since his passing over to the Catholic Church he has vacated his station, but continues the superintendence of the journal devoted to the school system. He was exceedingly polite in communicating information on this subject, and promised to send me his work, in which the whole system is explained. He said his first grand object was to get proper teachers, and for this purpose at least one main seminary for teachers is established in each of the ten Prussian provinces. These are intended for the preparation of teachers for all schools below the gymnasia (which are under another system) excepting those of the very lowest order, in which merely the most indispensable branches are taught. The preparation of teachers he considered the main object. The support of the teachers came from the people, not from the government. Every man, whether he had children or not, was assessed according to his property, and all then had the right to send their children to the school, and the civil authorities had the right to force reluctant or negligent parents to send their children. The same plan is carried out in all parts of the kingdom among Protestants, Catholics, and Jews. All must send their children to school.

Monday Evening, February 4th. I was at Professor Hollweg's. There were several Professors of the University and their wives present, and Ritter, the great geologist and physical-geographer, among the number. I was very glad to have an opportunity of seeing this interesting man. He is mild and humble, with a remarkably intelligent face. I was always under the impression that he was rather of the free-thinking school, as so many devoted to his branch of science are. But to my delight I learned that he was a Christian. Strauss, the popular Court Preacher, was also there; a man of astonishing vivacity. The subject of the connection between Church and State was introduced. On this subject his opinions are ultramontanist. He makes the king the *ordinarius* of the whole Church – the supreme bishop. Against this the whole company exclaimed – Baron Bunsen, the Count von Gräber, Major von Röder, Senfft, Le Coq, Hollweg. This I thought was a good sign. They appeared almost as much shocked as I was to hear Strauss declare his conviction, that if the State withdrew its support from the Church in this country, it would fall entirely. After a hundred years, there might be some traces of Christianity left, but that would be all!!

Tuesday, 5th. This evening I attended a meeting at Strauss's. There were about fifteen or eighteen students, *privatim-docentes*, etc., present, with Baron Bunsen and Count Gräber. One of the students read a translation of one of the discourses of Macarius. On this there was considerable conversation, displaying on the part of the young men a considerable acquaintance with this and other Fathers. The subject of conversation was then stated – whether the *justitia vitae* [righteousness of life] of a Christian was really or only figuratively a *sacrificium* [sacrifice]; on this point there was a warm debate pro and con., for above an hour: the whole a mere logomachy. This gave me occasion to remark the effect on their minds of the universal attention to philosophy required of the students in Germany. They were acute and discriminating, but amazingly deficient in plain, healthy good sense. A second question was started. 'In what sense can public worship be called a sacrifice? In the same, or in a different sense from that in which the *justitia vitae* is so called?' Here again the opinions were various. Bunsen, though a layman, has occupied himself much with the subject of Liturgies, and has got the notion that the *Opferidee* [offering idea] should be the reigning idea in Christian worship. In this there is nothing of a papistical sense; he means merely a presentation of ourselves before God, as a living sacrifice consecrated to his glory. But the abuse of this term lies so near, that most present objected to its being employed. I was particularly delighted to hear Gräber, in his soldier's uniform, cry out against the idea that men could give anything to God. 'I have', said he, 'nothing but my sinful, hateful self to give. Shall I call that an offering, when the Bible calls Christ an offering? To apply the same term to things so infinitely different, is too much.' His good sense and warm Christian feeling made him see more clearly and express more forcibly the true merits of the case, than all the speculating theologians present.

Sunday, February 10th, 1828. This evening Otto von Gerlach came to see me. His conversation is always instructive. He spoke a good deal of the Jews, and of the efforts made for their conversion. Of all those with whom he had anything to do, he found only one in whom he has entire confidence. The numerous instances of disappointed hopes exceed almost belief. They turn out badly after the longest probation; they make the most enormous demands; have the idea that they are the lords of the world; that all exists only for them. In short they are here as they are with us in America. The *good* king, much to the scandal of all classes, today gave a ball at mid-day, during Church time, and is said to have requested his sons to give a mask-ball next Sunday. This is something quite unusual here. The king appears to have few resources in himself, takes little interest in the government, and therefore turns to the theatre and to balls to fill up his head and heart. A. von H— said he was '*l'homme le plus ennuyé et le plus ennuyant dans le mond*' [the most bored and most boring man in the world]. Otto von Gerlach thought the measures of the minister Hardenberg, for the liberty of the peasants, most unjust. In many cases, where they were tenants on leases of six years, the rule that by giving up one-half of the land to the proprietor, they should receive the other in fee-simple, was applied. The peasants themselves, he says, regard the king as making them *pure* peasants. The liberal party, which had its fall in 1819, was unfriendly to the rights of cities and communes, and confined its views to making the general government liberal, while it endeavoured to stretch governmental authority over the most minute arrangements, allowing no town to elect its own officers. The Anti-liberal party opposed this, and by its success prevented Prussia being brought into the state in which France is at present, where the mayor and officers of every city, commune, department, and province, is appointed by the central government. In Bavaria, Würtemburg, and other places, where constitutions have been given, the people are in reality less free than before, as the central governments meddle with everything. This almost everywhere in Germany is far more the case than it was one hundred years ago, except in the kingdom of Saxony, and in Mecklenburg, where the old regulations are preserved. Gerlach gave several instances of the evil of the central government meddling with everything. The ministry ordered at one time that mathematics should be introduced into all schools in the kingdom, and made the *Bildungsprincip*. After a few years another general order came directing that all the schools should be newly organized, and conducted on a different principle, and so it changes. In one province an order was issued that all houses must stand fifty feet apart, and they actually tore down houses to prevent their standing too near together.

Wednesday, 27th. This evening I drank tea with Hengstenberg. I was surprised to hear him and other gentlemen present say that the idea usually entertained of the learning of the German clergy generally was erroneous; that he was sure the majority could not read the Greek Testament. This he ascribed to the influence of Rationalism, as formerly the reverse was the case. Almost every preacher was in the habit of taking the original Scriptures in the pulpit and commenting on them more or less in every discourse.

March 2nd, 1828. To-day I attended the disputation of my good friend, Otto von Gerlach. His Theses were in a true evangelical spirit, and were not attacked by his opponents with much force. His opponents were the *privat-docent* Pelt, and Drs Wegner and Schneckenburger. The accession of Otto von Gerlach to the University may be considered as a very favourable circumstance for the cause of truth in Berlin.

Wednesday, March 12th, This evening the Herrn von Bülow and von — , from Pomerania, drank tea with me, in company with the Gerlachs, Focke, Le Coq, &c. These two gentlemen come from the very midst of the revival which is still continuing in that country. It commenced in 1820–1, by the agency of two brothers of von Bülow. After various struggles with the ministers and civil authorities, in which this gentleman was often fined, and the *gens d'armes* were sent to scatter the people who assembled in his house, the work appeared to subside. But it has now broken out anew. Eight hundred often assemble in his mansion; these he regards as true Christians. Much that is disorderly and much that is very remarkable has occurred – visions, prophetic powers, possessions, etc. – as might have been expected among a people so little cultivated, and in a state of so much excitement. With these two gentlemen I was exceedingly pleased. They had the same fervent freshness of feeling which men active in revivals most commonly have with us. Before the evening was over, they proposed singing and prayer. As the clergy in Pomerania are peculiarly opposed to every thing like vital piety, these, and other young men, have taken upon themselves the office of preaching, and stand in a very uneasy relation to the Church, their sentiments on Church discipline, on the nature of the Church, and the rights of members agreeing very much with those of the Puritans.

Friday, 14th. I dined to-day with these gentlemen at Justice Focke's. A servant, with whom they were previously acquainted, came from Potsdam to see them, and these noblemen kissed and hugged him as though he had been their equal and brother. In the evening I called for a few moments, with Lieutenant von Senfft on the Gräfin von Gräben. She is a most interesting, lovely woman, full of ardent feelings of piety, and with much more vivacity than is common among German ladies.

Saturday, 15th. Had a long conversation with Otto von Gerlach about our form of Church Government. Here all the ecclesiastical affairs are under the direction of the consistorium and the ministerium. Each province has its consistorium; the members appointed by the king, of equal numbers of clergymen and laymen. There are many merely nominal members, as the title of Consistorial Rath is often given as a mere matter of honour. The consistorium has very little power. It has the duty of examining candidates and watching over the doctrines preached. The executive government of the several circles, of which there are generally two in each province, has the right of patronage, i.e., exercises the king's patronage within their limits, which extends to about one-half the congregations. The other half receive their pastors, some by the appointment of the magistrates of towns, others by that of the landholder; a very few have the right of choosing their own pastors. The power of the Minister of Ecclesiastical Affairs, and of his council, extends over the whole kingdom, and is very great. Otto von Gerlach relates several instances of the interference of the government in the most harmless affairs, as in the case of his own brother, who was several times molested for having a prayer-meeting in his house. And the candidate Meinhof told me of his being called to account for having talked and prayed with a man who called to see him under considerable religious excitement.

[Under date of March 20th, Mr Hodge writes to his wife, 'I shall soon be left alone here. That is, my house companions, Mr Robinson and Mr Monod, are going in a few days, the former to Halle, the latter to Paris. You will be surprised to hear that the sober Mr Robinson has fallen in love. I received a note, a day or two ago, written by him (as his modesty prevented a personal communication) with the official information that the Fraülein von Jacob had consented to accompany him to America as his wife. I have spoken to you, I believe, of this lady and her family before in my letters. *Robinson has done well.* The lady is agreeable and very accomplished, speaking several languages, and acquainted with the literature of most European nations.']

Sunday, March 23rd. I heard Lisco preach this morning on the Fall of Peter. The Church was so full that it was impossible to get a seat. Last Sunday Mr Robinson could not get in at all, not even open the doors. It is a good indication that those ministers who preach the gospel faithfully have their churches overflowing. In the evening I drank tea with Lisco, met the Moravian minister, Mr Semler, and von Senfft. The conversation at first turned on the late order of the Ministerium, requiring every student, who is to be examined, to produce a certificate of regular attendance upon Church and the Lord's Supper. The students, with the approbation of the faculty, petitioned against this. The Ministerium returned a very severe, harsh answer, viz.—that such inexperienced youth ought not to have the presumption to think they could change the opinion of Ministers, etc., etc. This the students received in the mildest possible manner, and said they would endeavour to show the Ministerium that they did not need such external inducements to make them do their duty. In consequence of the active part which one of the students took in the petition, his *licentia conscionandi* has been refused him. This whole affair has excited great attention. The Christians, as well as the liberals, are exceedingly opposed to the order of the Ministerium. Schleiermacher, who belongs to the latter description, refuses to give certificates to those who attend his Church or Communion table, and he tells them to say to the Consistorium, that he will not act according to the requirements of the Government in this respect. The whole thing will, I suspect, fall through.

Mr Couard complained of the operation of censure [censorship] in reference to printing the tracts of the Tract Society. He said it was so hard to satisfy those in authority that a tract did not lead to *separatismus*, a thing as much dreaded as a revolution in politics. Mr Semler said that in an article he wrote for the newspaper on establishments for the poor, he remarked that 'nothing could be done until the education of the poor was put on a Christian basis'. The word 'Christian' was struck out, and 'moral' inserted, because the Ministerium had forbidden any thing to appear which might bring before the public the 'religious movement' of the day. Lindner, a Professor at Leipzig, was displaced from his office as teacher of religion in one of the largest schools there, because in explaining the passage that a man must love Christ more than father, mother, etc., his remarks tended to diminish the respect of children for their parents, and therefore had a revolutionary tendency. Prof. Lindner is an excellent man. This is equal to the solicitude of the pastors of Geneva, who requested Mr Monod to erase from his sermon the expression, that 'if a man hate not his father', etc. I have been pained to hear from Monod that the state of morals, even in the

Protestant Cantons of Switzerland, is exceedingly corrupt, and particularly in Berne and Lucerne, Geneva forms a striking exception. The Swiss battalion in Berlin from Neufchâtel is said to be the most corrupt of any in the Prussian guards, if not of the whole army. Monod says it is the same with the Swiss officers in Paris. Mr Semler mentioned that the battalion in the Tyrol has been the means of the greatest good in that country. The soldiers serve eight years, and during that time they have a constant course of religious instruction.

It is said that the Ministerium wish to send Prof. Hengstenberg to Bonn, or force him to relinquish the *Kirchen-Zeitung*. It seems as if a storm was brewing. The Ministerium censured the Theological Faculty respecting the petition of the students, and particularly Neander. The Hegelians are working strongly against the Evangelical party. Marheineke had the amazing presumption to say to Neander in a meeting of the Senatus Academicus, 'Thou ignorant man (p. 149). You are unworthy that I should answer you.' 'Happily', replied Neander, 'You are not my judge.' When some person present exclaimed at Marheineke's conduct, asking how he could call one of the most learned men in Germany an ignoramus, he answered, 'He knows nothing of Philosophy', i.e., Hegel's system.

Wednesday, March 26th. Das Hohe Ministerium are much dissatisfied with the *Evangelische Kirchen-Zeitung*, and have given Hengstenberg to understand that he must either give it up or be removed to another University. He preferred the latter. Whether their threat will be executed remains to be seen. They warned him that if he appealed to the Crown Prince, who they know is favourable to the *Zeitung*, he would be lost, so says Ancillon. In Weimar a tract society has been suppressed, and the distributor punished with a fine of 20 Florins. The state of things throughout the Herzogthum Weimar must be deplorable. The superintendent, Pröhr, in writing for a person to fill an important vacancy in the Church, told his correspondent to select a rationalist, and added 'but do let him be of good morals'.

Sunday, March 30th. I was, this evening, at Madame Schönberg's for the last time, as she is about to leave Berlin for a while. The company was larger than usual. Gossner preached in his peculiar way from *Matt.* 27:1. He said, as the enemies of Christ rose early to plot His death, should not Christians rise early to take counsel with the Holy Spirit, how they may serve, love, and honour Him? As they bound the Saviour with cords, so should we bind Him with faith, love and hope, to our souls. As Judas betrayed his Master for gold, he begged us to think how often we had sold Christ, His presence, His communion, for the sinful enjoyments of this world; and that ill-gotten wealth could do us no good; that one day we would be glad to throw it away. Judas's repentance not being joined with faith availed him nothing, etc. Prof. Lancizolle, who was present, gave me an interesting account of the course of instruction for confirmation which he had received from von Ancillon, then a pastor in the French Church. He said it was not until the last week that he was told there was such a book as the Scriptures. All the previous instruction was about sun, moon, stars and all other points than those relating to the doctrines of the Gospel. It is in this way that the good effects of the method of instruction are lost.

March 31st. There was a review to-day of the whole Guard in garrison in Berlin. The King conducted the review, attended by all the higher officers, his sons, etc. Through the kindness of Lieutenant von Senfft I obtained an excellent place on the Zeughaus for viewing this display of the flower of the Prussian army. There were 10,000 men, cuirassiers, lancers, dragoons, infantry, horse and foot artillery. The Prussians think their own army the finest in the world, and I should think it ought to be, from the amount of attention devoted to it.

April 1st. I dined to-day at Madame Schönberg's in company with the Graf Lippe, his wife and daughter, a Polish Hauptman Gauratcki, and another Graf [count], whose name I do not know. This Graf Lippe is from Cleves. His lady takes a great interest in missions, inquired of the state of religion in America, and spoke of Mrs Judson's letters, etc. Almost everywhere the indications of the spread of religion among all ranks in this place, are to be seen. Strauss said, some days since, that it was seldom he had an hour to himself before night, since he was so constantly occupied by persons calling to see him to converse on the state of their souls and ask his counsels.

Friday, April 4th. This was Good Friday. I attended Church in the morning and went to the communion. Lisco preached, as usual, with much simplicity and feeling. It gave me pleasure to find by my side, at the communion table, the dear Neander; for whose character I have conceived the greatest reverence.

Sunday, 6th. In the morning I was at Church; in the evening with Neander. He showed me several passages from the letters of Jacobi, in which he speaks of the folly and extremity to which the German philosophers permit themselves to be led away in their speculations. He expressed the greatest abhorrence of the spirit at present prevailing among this class of men; this making themselves God, or reducing God to an idea (*Begriff*) – so that Hegel says that *Nichts ist die allerhöchste Realität* [nothing is the supreme reality]. I asked Neander if he did not think that something of the spirit or principles of the Pantheistical system had passed over into the evangelical writings of the present day in Germany, and said that the idea that *alles Sein ist das Sein Gottes* [all being is the being of God] seemed to me of this character. He said, 'By no means – all that was meant by that phrase is that God is the only real independent substance, and that all other existences are grounded in a mysterious way in Him.' This, he said, was contained in the idea of the omnipresence of God, and in the declaration of Paul that

'in Him we live, and move, and have our being' – and that ἐξ ὁυ
και δἰ ὁυ [of him and through him] are all things. The ἐξ ὁυ, he
said, means something more than merely efficient cause. I asked
him, then, in what relation our efficiency stood to that of God?
He replied, that in all good we were merely the organs of God, and
that sin only broke off this relation, I said, this coincided with the
idea of the older theologians as to the *concursus Dei* [divine concur-
rence] in all our acts. He replied, 'Yes, I think they were perfectly
right on this point.'

In coming away, the dear man pressed my hand very kindly, and
said, 'I think we can agree.' He seems to think that if he debates
with any one, or differs from him, he does him a wrong, and is
uneasy until the feeling of perfect peace is restored.

A few days before this I had a conversation with the Gerlachs
on the *Personalität der Menschheit* [personality of humanity]. They
maintained that the race of man was a whole, as a tree is a whole.
No one stands for himself; so that the race is not a collection of
individuals as an army is, but of the constituent parts of one great
whole. It is on this idea they explain the idea of original sin. The
whole race was then in Adam, as completely and as really as an oak
is in an acorn. It was not Adam as an individual, but Adam as the
human race who sinned. To the question, 'Are we conscious of having personally participated in the sin of Adam?' they replied, 'That
very question is founded on a false view. It is not *I*, as an individual,
that there sinned; it is not a matter for my consciousness, but for
the consciousness of the *Menschheit* (humanity).'

Thursday, April 8th. This evening the Lieutenant von Senfft
called for me, and we went to drink tea with the Geheimrath and
Professor Schmalz. There is here a large family of daughters, who,
with their mother, are pious. There were two or three other gentlemen present. Otto von Gerlach, who is much of a musician, took
his seat at the piano, and the company sang various parts of an

oratorio by Gans, the death of Christ, which is always performed here on *Charfreitag* [Good Friday] – also parts of Handel's *Messiah* and of his *Judas Maccabeus*. They sang, also, one piece from an old German composer, Bach, whose works have long been neglected, but which they say are equal to almost any of the best German compositions.

Friday, April 11th. This morning I rode out in company with Messrs. Amory and Cunningham, to see the prison, at Spandau. The Inspector went round with us and showed us everything. There are here five hundred prisoners, of whom ninety are females. The greater part of these are employed in the manufacture of cotton and wool in various shapes. Those condemned to hard labour turn the great wheel which sets the machinery in motion. The prisoners are neatly dressed. There are thirty-six cells for solitary confinement, for the punishment of offences committed within the prison. A young man is considered ruined when once sent to prison in this part of Germany, the corrupting influence is so great. The number of crimes since 1806 have increased amazingly. Four thousand persons are arrested every year in Berlin alone, and of these seventy-five per cent, are condemned. The greater part of the female prisoners are in for life, for murdering their infant children. The proportion of murderers is astonishing. The Inspector said that his confidential prisoners were all murderers, whose sentences had for some reason been exchanged from death to imprisonment for life. He said he found they were uniformly less hardened and depraved than the thieves who came back upon them half a dozen times. There is a Chaplain for the prison who preaches every Sunday, and visits the prisoners twice in the week. They are also supplied with Bibles,

Sunday, 13th. I heard Lisco this morning preach from the words, 'I am the light of the world.' In the evening I was at Neander's. Dr Julius, a gentleman from Hamburg, was there. He has been some time in England, examining their prisons, and is about publishing a work on this subject. Neander, as usual, found occasion to speak of the danger arising from the spread of Hegel's philosophy, which, by making the *Begriff* [concept, idea] God, deifies man. He showed me a remarkable passage in Jacobi's work on religion, in which the Prophecy of Lichtenstein is quoted. This predicts that the world will become so refined that it will be as much unfashionable to believe in God as in a spectre, and that men will go still further, and make themselves, and God, and the universe, but a spectre. This, he says, is wonderfully accomplished by Hegel's system, which makes God but an idea – nullity the origin of everything – and the universe a mere phantom. Neander thinks that Schleiermacher's change of opinion, as exhibited in the difference between his *Reden über die Religion* and his *Dogmatik*, has arisen from his approaching nearer to Christianity – the main point of difference is that in the latter he appears to admit the personal existence of the soul after death. He spoke also of the wonderful contrast between the practical common sense of the English, and the speculative spirit of the Germans, and he again referred to the passage in Jacobi, in which he says, that the Germans must always have a golden calf to go before them, and an Aaron to offer sacrifice – but that they are always willing to see the calf destroyed and reduced to powder, provided this be not done by a Moses, but by another Aaron, who will make them another calf. Thus is it with their philosophical systems. The system of Hegel has become a matter of ridicule in the little, low papers which appear here in Berlin. One man is made to ask his neighbour, *Weisst du wohl dass du gar nicht existirst? – Wie so denn? – Weil alles was ist, ist vernünftig; du bist unvernünftig; daher existirst du nicht* [Do you know that you do not exist? – How so? – Everything that exists is reasonable. You are unreasonable. Therefore you do not exist].

Tuesday, 15th. I went on Saturday last, with Messrs Amory and Cunningham, to visit the Gewerbs Institut, an establishment for the education of artists and mechanics, similar, though on a much larger scale, to the Franklin Institute in Philadelphia. Lectures are delivered on Chemistry and the various branches of natural philosophy, and the students have regular instruction in drawing, modelling, etc. They also work in the preparation of all kinds of machinery and make casts, original and copied. The institution is furnished with models of the best English, French, and American machines. There is a young American here employed by the Prussian Government to erect and superintend various spinning and weaving machines. He was raised in the Brandywine factories, near Baltimore, and seems to give great satisfaction. The American machines have displaced the English, and every year there is a complaint that one expensive machine is rendered useless by the Yankees inventing a better. A spinning machine, established in Spandau, a year since thought to be the best possible, is put into the background by one just received by the Government; the production of the latter to the former being as eleven to five.

Wednesday, 16th. Spent the evening with Justice Focke, and Ludwig and Otto von Gerlach. John 10 —

Saturday, 19th. Visited Potsdam in company with Messrs Amory, Cunningham, and Mr Lowell, an intelligent and interesting young man from Boston. The day was fine and our ride agreeable, although the country is remarkably uninteresting until you reach the neighbourhood of Potsdam, where the dull, barren, sandy wastes are rendered somewhat susceptible of cultivation by the numerous lakes of the Havel. When we entered Potsdam the cavalry regiment of the Guard were parading with their fine music in the garden of the palace. We went first to visit the palace of *Sans Souci* and its grounds. The latter are beautifully laid out and ornamented. Before the time of Frederick the whole was a barren waste of sand. *Sans Souci* stands on the top of a hillock, the south side of which is covered its whole length with hot-houses, from top to bottom. The palace was built after the Seven Years' War, and is only one storey high. It consists of the main building, and two wings separated at some distance from it, and one of them on much lower ground. The east wing contains the picture gallery. The Hall is splendid, made entirely of Italian marble. The pictures are of the Flemish and Italian schools. These are twenty-seven by Rubens, all horrible. The most celebrated are a Vertumnus and Pomona, by L. da Vinci; a Sleeping Venus, by Titian; two or three by Raphael, the most distinguished being an *Ecce Homo*, which is by far the most affecting picture in the whole collection.

In the palace of *Sans Souci* itself there is nothing very interesting, excepting the rooms of Frederick as he left them. Voltaire's room, his bed and table, are still *in statu quo*. It made me almost sick to look around me. For of all men who ever lived he most excites my bad feelings.

From this we walked through the gardens to the new palace – another piece of Frederick's enormous extravagance – it is conjectured to have cost 11,000,000 Prussian dollars. Nobody ever used it. It is the Versailles of Prussia. In returning, we stopped at the Church where Frederick and his father are buried. Under the pulpit there is a recess in which their coffins lie on a marble floor. To stand near the ashes of a man who had acted so conspicuous a part during his life, and contrast the gloomy little receptacle of his body with his gorgeous palaces was well adapted to produce a deep impression of the emptiness of worldly glory.

Tuesday, April 29th. I visited, with Justice Focke and a few other friends, the Kunst Cabinet in the palace. The collection is neither very large nor remarkable. The king has caused to be prepared a wax figure of Frederick I which is said to be a most striking likeness. The face is formed after a cast taken immediately after death. The clothing is such as he wore, and the sword is the one which hung by his side during the Seven Years' War. The insignia of the various orders, and the hat worn by Napoleon and taken at the Battle of Waterloo, are here preserved.

In the evening some of my friends came to drink tea with me and bid me farewell for ever in this world, humanly speaking. Otto von Gerlach sang a hymn and his brother Ludwig prayed before we separated. They were kind enough to present me with a German *Stamm-Buch*, i.e., a book in which friends inscribe their names under the date of their birth, together with some sentence or verse expressive of kind feeling or important truth. That written by Neander is beautiful. I happened the other day to be sitting in his study, when the messenger handed this book to him, then altogether unknown by me. Neander quietly and rapidly wrote his sentence (in Greek) and returned it to the messenger without remark.

16th January
Let us stand fast in the liberty in which Christ has made us free; whom alone to serve is a glory and a joy; and let us not become slaves of men or of any other creature. To rejoice in the Lord, to be nothing in one's self; in the Lord all things.

A. Neander

Wednesday 30th. I remained at home. Justice Focke, Tippleskirch, G. von der Recke, and Cunningham, came to see me in the course of the day. I left Berlin, taking my last farewell of von Senfft and Dorfs at the Post-office. I did not expect to have my heart so interested by a stay of six months in any place. The kindness, the Christian love, the warm-hearted conduct of those with whom I have passed this winter so happily, will remain deeply impressed on my heart as long as I live. When I bid my friends farewell I cried like a child. Neander's farewell I shall never forget.

May 1st. I arrived in Halle about 12 o'clock. The evening I spent with Mr Robinson at the Staaträthin von Jacob's.

Tholuck had gone to Rome for a season, and Mr Hodge saw his friend no more. A little while before, while Mr Hodge was at Berlin, Tholuck, on the eve of his departure for Rome, addressed him the following letter. (The original in English).

HALLE, April, 1828.

My Dear Hodge:— You will have been greatly astonished as many have at my resolution to spend this year in Rome. There is certainly a number of circumstances that make it a scrupulous matter, but the opportunity was so very favourable, and some accidents encouraged it so much, that I could not resist any longer. A pious Professor will supply my place this year, and according to all probability remain my colleague. This is the most important fruit of the plan with respect to Halle.

As to my state here, I must thank God that, since my complaints have lessened, I feel like new-born. I feel, of course, the burden of a lonely, friendless life. I feel particularly the tediousness of continual dogmatical researches and disputations, which are so very seldom interrupted by other occupations and distractions ; but being more delivered than I was when you were here from the constant aggression, I can find access to the throne of grace, and can be satisfied with God's ways . . .

I am sure that I shall not only enjoy much at Rome, but that I shall be of use also as well to Bunsen as to the congregation. I shall draw much profit myself, I hope, from being employed practically in the gospel . . .

I cannot express what I feel at the idea of my not seeing you again. You have been sent to me through God's mercy as a messenger of glad tidings, as a comforter in cheerless hours, as an elder brother to show me the simple way to heaven. I owe you very much, or more properly I have reason to be most thankful to God for what He has bestowed upon me by your means. And never! never! on this side of the grave shall I see you again. My eyes run with tears! Dear friend, do not forget me; do not forget to pray for me . . .

I am in Christ Jesus our Lord,
Yours most cordially, A. THOLUCK

Remember me most cordially to our dear Monod.

Again he wrote from near Rome, at the time that Mr Hodge was on the eve of embarking from Liverpool, and believing that he was already at home, Tholuck addressed the letter to Princeton. (The original in English.)

FRASCATI, July 30, 1828.

My Dear and Beloved Friend and Brother in Christ:—You are now, I am sure, safely brought to your dear home, and sit cheerfully smiling among wife and children, thankful for all the great mercies of our Lord. And here I sit, too, among dear children (although not my own) in happy Italy, thankful for the mercies of my Lord, where I can rest a little from all the afflictions and tribulations of past years . . . I found myself well, better than in Halle, and soon became delighted with the enjoyments which the family circle of Bunsen and he himself offered to me. He has six amiable children, a most respectable wife, and him I found a thorough and sincere follower of Christ. My pastoral duty also gave me much pleasure, having an audience before me in which the simple gospel tidings met with a ready reception. Since the first of July (the heat in Rome getting more and more intense), we removed to the country, where I now reside with the family in a beautiful villa surrounded with the Sabinian and Albanian mountains, having Mons Soracte in the face, and in a distance at the right side the *aeterna Roma*, at the left the borders of the sea. One day passes swiftly away after the others, under useful and edifying conversation. The morning begins with family prayer and hymns sung by the boys. The day closes again with singing hymns. Neither philosophical nor critical doubts trouble the mind where it daily experiences the sweet comfort of Christian communion. Like a dreary waste my life in Halle lies behind me. I was sick all the days I lived there – sick in body and sick in mind. Oh! what patience have you then had with me! I hope you would find me now another man.

But blessed be my Saviour who sent you then to my great consolation and comfort. You see then, dear Hodge, that I may justly call this, my present abode, a place of rest. When the disciples returned from their missionary tour, the Saviour told them: ἀναπαύεσθε ὀλίγον [rest a while]. This I do now, but only ὀλίγον [a while]. By no means I shall protract this absence from Halle.

Much is hoped from Bunsen's future career. He is decided to leave soon his present situation and to occupy an important one in the ecclesiastical department of the Ministerium. He now studies Hebrew very hard. I read the Psalms with him. He is a little too averse to Republican States, and consequently to your happy country.

Believe me, my dear brother.

Your true friend in Christ,
A. Tholuck

ON HIS WAY HOME, VIA GERMANY, SWITZERLAND, FRANCE, AND ENGLAND

Journal. – On the morning of the *3rd May*, I left Halle for Göttingen. I dined at Eisleben, where Luther was born. The room in which this event occurred is a schoolroom. In another apartment are preserved many relics of the Reformer; such as his table, desk, letters, etc. The country from Halle to Nordhausen is much more varied than any part of North Germany I had yet seen. From Heiligenstadt to Göttingen, the first part of the road is very interesting, hilly and abounding in trees. I arrived in Göttingen about eleven, and stopped at the crown tavern. In the morning Mr Wm. Amory called to see me. We walked together round the town, and found the public promenade very pleasant. Göttingen itself has little to recommend it in externals. In the afternoon we visited the museum and attended the lecture of Blumenbach. It is impossible to give any idea of the manner of this extraordinary man. One would suppose he was desirous of showing the capability of the human face of assuming queer forms. He talks with as much unconcern as in his study. We called to see him the next morning. He received us very kindly, showed us his collection of skulls, and begged us to try and get him from America various articles he yet needs to complete his collection. He spoke very favourably of many Americans he had known. Although about eighty years of age, he has all the vivacity and interest in all persons, and things he has anything to do with, as though he were in the prime of youth. I called on Prof Lücke with the letter of Dr Neander. He appears to be about thirty-five, an amiable and friendly man. He was kind enough to call on me at four o'clock and take me to see several of the other theological professors. We first called on the elder Planck, a man apparently between seventy and eighty. He had such an asthmatic affection that it appeared difficult for him to converse. We then called on Prof. Pott, a man of about fifty. He talked chiefly about books, and the great library, the pride and pillar of the university. We called also upon Prof. Hemsen. The decided manner in which he came out in the late difficulties, respecting the missionary society, has gained him the confidence of all Christians. He and Lücke both spoke very warmly against the Berlin philosophical school. Lücke appears to be a great friend of Schleiermacher, although reckoned as belonging to the orthodox party, and not a little abused by the opposers of the present struggle for life in Germany. He said that he had little difficulty in this place; that the professors treat him kindly, and his auditorium is well filled.

On the evening of May 6th, I drank tea with the two Messrs Amory, and met several professors and teachers of the university. I had a long talk with Prof. Reiche on Mysticisms. He is a most decided Rationalist, yet without that bitter hatred to the truth and its advocates which so strongly characterizes most of his school. It is as clear as day that the most intolerant and bitter spirit rankles in the bosom of many who have made the greatest advances in the *Aufklärung* [Enlightenment] of the times. I visited the library and

saw Prof. Beneke, to whom Prof. Patton had given me a letter. He
spoke of Patton with affection, and it is pleasant to find how universally the Americans, who have been to Göttingen, are remembered
with respect and affection. I called also to see Prof. Ewald, whom
I regard as one of the most remarkable men I have seen in Europe.
He is about twenty-four, looks much younger, is modest in his
manner even to bashfulness, although confident even to arrogance,
in his writings. He has more hearers than any other Professor who
reads on theological subjects. He expressed his hope of being soon
able to find time to write a Syriac Grammar. Hoffman, he says, has
made no new step, has been diligent, but that is all. He regrets the
opinions of Vater, Eichhorn, etc., on the Pentateuch; makes it with
the exception of Deuteronomy very old. Job he sets between seven
and eight hundred years BC. The present prologue is, he thinks,
spurious. The latter part of Isaiah he rejects.

We went afterwards to meet Mrs Goeschen, a lady whom I had
met nearly a year ago at her son-in-law, Westermeier's. We drank
tea with Blumenbach. Mrs Goeschen and family were there. The
old gentleman talked a great deal of our Indians, for whom he
seemed to have a great liking. His wife is mother general of the
Americans, whom she praised to the skies. The last thing she said
to me was, 'Send us plenty of Americans.' Prof. Hemsen was kind
enough to come and sit half an hour with me this afternoon. He
gave no very encouraging account of the prospect of doing much
good to students at present. No missionary-society, after all, had
been formed. No prayer-meetings were allowed. All that had been
gained in the late struggle was that a missions *stunde* [hour] was
held, in which the missionary journals were read. He presented me
in the name of Prof. Pott with the first part of the commentary on
Corinthians, an attention on the part of Dr Pott I had no ground
to expect. I supped at Prof. Lücke's, but was obliged to come away
early, in order to meet the stage passing from Hanover to Cassel.

The 8th and 9th of May, I passed in Cassel. The new part of this city is very beautiful. The old part is not remarkable. The gardens and walks round the town are the finest I have seen in Germany. At 5 o'clock I left Cassel. The country from this to the Rhine is generally varied, and fertile, and beautiful. The dominions of the Elector of Hesse-Cassel are marked by a degree of poverty I cannot account for. The villages are the most miserable, and the people more ragged-looking than any I had elsewhere seen in Germany. The aspect of things change for the better as soon as you enter the possessions of Prussia. As soon as the Wupperthal (the valley of the Wupper, a short but copious stream entering the Rhine on the eastern side, about fifty miles below Cologne) commences, a scene is opened which could not have been expected in Germany. The poverty which everywhere else characterizes the peasantry, here disappears. Well-built houses, tasteful gardens, and a general appearance of refinement and comfort everywhere meet the eye. The entire valley, of which Elberfeld is the centre, is almost a continual village, filled with manufactories of every kind, so that the traveller feels as if he were suddenly transported to England. Elberfeld contains about twenty-two thousand inhabitants, and is probably the richest place of its size in Germany.

These Rhine provinces of Prussia have much that is peculiar and interesting in their ecclesiastical arrangements. They formerly had, under a Catholic Prince, their own Presbyterian form of Government. This, however, has been much weakened since they were brought under the dominion of Prussia. Each Circle has its Presbyterium, consisting of the pastors and one or two elders for each congregation, and each Province has its Synod. But the actual government of the Church is taken, for the most part, out of the hands of the Presbyteria and Synods, and given to the Consistoria, as elsewhere in Prussia. The Consistoria examine candidates, and alone can depose a pastor, and that only by reporting to the

Ministerium in Berlin, from whom the act of deposition must proceed. The changes which have recently occurred, have principally been brought about through the influence of the clergy. The Rationalists in this part of the country are said to be favourable to the Consistorial form of ecclesiastical administration, as it brings them more in connection with the state, and gives them more worldly power. The congregations, however, have retained the right of electing their own pastors, and hopes are entertained that the powers and rights of the Presbyteries will be restored.

I heard the pastor Krummacher preach in the morning. The Church was large and crowded. The people seemed mostly of the poorer class, although, I am told, that the richer part of the population are remarkably regular in their attendance on Church. The sermon was peculiar. The subject was the rainbow, which he made, first a sacrament, and then considered as a type of the Church. The points of resemblance were five; origin, colour, form, position, and —. This was carried through with a good deal of taste and talent, but the whole discourse wanted that authority and power which belong alone to truths obviously contained in the Word of God. I called to see the Pastor Wichelhaus, to whom I had a letter. He received me kindly, and gave me the information concerning the ecclesiastical government of these provinces I have recorded above. He also informed me that in the Wupperthal, during the prevalence of infidelity all over Germany, orthodoxy still retained its place, and the spirit of piety, although for a time depressed, never lost its hold on the people. All the preachers in this neighbourhood are considered orthodox and pious. In the present state of lively religious feeling here, there are two dangers which struck me as threatening to disturb the beauty of this part of God's vineyard. The first is a tendency among some few of the preachers to antinomian principles. The other is the extravagant allegorical interpretation of the Old Testament. In the evening I visited the Superintendent Snecklager, where I met four or five other preachers from the neighbourhood, and a Mr le Grand from Basle.

Tuesday, May 13th. I left Elberfeld at six o'clock for Düsseldorf, distant about fifteen miles. It contains about sixteen thousand inhabitants, a majority of whom are Catholics. The country in this neighbourhood is perfectly flat on both sides of the Rhine, and continues so until Bonn. In the afternoon I walked out to Düsselthal, the institution of Count von der Recke. This was originally a cloister, surrounded by a brick wall, and including thirty-six acres of land. There are now a large dwelling-house, a brewery, oil and flour mills, a long house, including carpenter's and smith's shops, etc. The Count has now eighty boys and fifty girls, all poor protestant children, with the exception of two Jewish children. He told me that all his long-continued efforts to do something good for the Jews had proved ineffectual. They had all proved themselves to be actuated by such selfish and worldly motives that he was unable to say that he regarded one of all those under his care from the commencement of the institution a sincere Christian. The amazing pride they always manifested made it exceedingly difficult to get along with them. Simon, he said, had given him more trouble than words could well express. He complained of the extravagant ideas entertained by the English Christians as to the dignity and future destiny of the Jews, and said he could not find in the Bible that they were destined to be the rulers of the world. The Jewish inmates left in mass when he made it plain that the attraction he offered them was religious instruction and not worldly gain. The Count has the entire expense of the support of the institution on his own hands. Voluntary contributions from Christian friends amount to very little – and the product of the labour of those engaged in the various industries is far from being sufficient. I asked him what he thought of the plan of the American Jewish Society. He said he thought they were engaged in an utterly hopeless effort.

On the 14th, at four o'clock in the morning, I left Düsseldorf for Cologne, where I arrived at nine o'clock. It contains sixty thousand inhabitants, chiefly Catholic, twelve thousand beggars, and twenty-seven churches. The Cathedral, commenced in AD 1248, but never finished, is the most beautiful specimen of Gothic architecture in Germany. It contains the bodies of the wise men of the East, and the staff of Peter. St Peter's church contains the famous picture of the Crucifixion of Peter, by Rubens, and some remarkable painted windows. In another church are preserved the bones of the eleven thousand virgins. This is a hot-bed of Catholic superstitions.

I left Cologne at two o'clock, and arrived at Bonn at six. Here the mountains commence and the beautiful scenery on the banks of the Rhine. I soon met Mr Woolsey, who continued with me three days in Bonn, and went with me by steamboat to Coblenz. I have got to love him ten times more than ever.[1] I called on Prof. Nitzsch, to whom I had a letter from Neander. He is a middle-aged man, rather melancholy-looking. I also called on Prof. Sack, a very agreeable and affable man, and apparently a friend of piety and the truth. I heard Schlegel lecture, and was disappointed in his appearance and manner. Freytag lives a mile or two out of town, and therefore I did not see him. The University of Bonn is not more than ten years old. Yet it has nearly one thousand students, of whom from three to four hundred are studying theology, about two-thirds being Catholic. The Elector's palace and its beautiful grounds have been appropriated to the service of the University.

(Here the Journal ends.)

---

[1] President Theodore D. Woolsey said at Dr Hodge's Semi-Centennial Commemoration, April 24th, 1872: 'Some years after (I had known him in Princeton Seminary) I was in Bonn, and he coming into Germany, I think in 1828, stopped in Bonn. I saw him, and went up the river with him to enjoy his society. Then he spoke to me (I may say – if permitted to speak of myself – that I was in darkness) – he spoke to me words of cheer, of comfort, of strength. I do not remember the words, but I remember the impression, and that impression will go with me through life.'

PROF. HODGE TO HIS WIFE

Surisee, May 28th, 1828.

My Beloved Sarah:—I have seen the Alps! If now I never see any thing great or beautiful in nature, I am content. I felt that as soon as I saw you, I could fall at your feet and beg you to forgive my beholding such a spectacle without you, my love. You were dearer to me in that moment than ever. I left Basel about one o'clock with a young English gentleman for Lucerne. We rode about fifteen miles and arrived at the foot of a mountain. As the road was steep and difficult, we commenced walking up the mountain in company with two Swiss gentlemen. We ascended leisurely for about two hours before we reached the top. I was walking slowly with my hands behind me, and my eyes on the ground, expecting nothing, when one of the Swiss gentlemen said with infinite indifference – 'Voilà les Alpes.' I raised my eyes – and around me in a grand amphitheatre, high up against the heavens, were the Alps! It was some moments before the false and indefinite conceptions of my life were overcome by the glorious reality. The declining sun shed on the immense mass of mingled snow and forests the brightness of the evening clouds. This was the first moment of my life in which I felt overwhelmed. Every thing I had ever previously seen seemed absolutely nothing. The natural bridge in Virginia had surprised me; the Rhine had delighted me – but the first sudden view of the Alps was overwhelming. This was a moment that can never return; the Alps can never be seen again by surprise, and in ignorance of their real appearance.

Berne, June 2nd. I am now writing in Berne. After having completed a short tour among the mountains, we reached Lucerne about twelve on the 28th of May. We took a hasty dinner and set out for Mount Righi, after having procured mountain shoes and walking poles. We crossed Lake Lucerne, and then commenced the ascent for three hours. The sun was shining for the first hour, which, with the difficulty of the way, made it by far the most severe task I had ever undertaken. We were obliged to lie down every ten minutes. After the first hour the ascent was not so severe. There was a shower of rain, and enough of cold wind. After three hours and a half, we had accomplished the task. It was so cloudy and so late that we could see little from the summit, which is 5,550 feet above the sea. We went flattering ourselves with being repaid by beholding the rising sun. But we were again disappointed. There was so dense a fog that nothing could be seen. About 7 o'clock it began to clear – and then the sight was splendid. From this point you overlook the varied surface of the north of Switzerland. To the right and on the left you have a view of the long, unbroken chain of lofty Alps. Of these we could see but little, yet we were amply repaid by the grandeur of the prospect to the right, and the ever-varying forms of the clouds as they drove over the plain below. We descended to the lake on the other side of the mountain. The lake of Lucerne deserves all the praise which has been lavished upon it for romantic scenery, and almost every spot on its vast borders is rich in associations with the heroic memories of the deliverance of Switzerland. At Stanze my English companion gave out. We took a carriage to Sachseln, where we slept. The next morning we rode to Lungeren, and then, partly on horseback and partly on foot, crossed the Brünig and dined at Brienz. We were rowed over this beautiful lake in three hours, and on the evening of the 29th reached Unterseen [Interlaken], which lies on a plain between the lakes of Brienz and Thun. The next morning I set out alone with the guide for Lauterbrunnen, distant about a three hours' walk. This is one of the most beautiful valleys in Switzerland, closed by the Jungfrau, one of the loftiest mountains. It is also famous for the waterfall of the Staubbach, which falls nearly perpendicularly 925 feet. I rode up the Wengern Alp, which separates Lauterbrunnen from Grindelwald, on a mule, in four hours. On the top we enjoyed two cloudless hours of surpassing grandeur. We were within musket shot of the immense masses of rocks of the Jungfrau and Eiger, which rose from our level between 6,000 and 7,000 feet. This near view of these immense mountains of ice, rock and snow is as overpowering as the first distant view of their grandeur. We saw and heard at least twenty avalanches. It was like a long-continued thunder-storm, so rapidly did one falling mass succeed to another. The mountain we passed had still so much snow that the mule could proceed no further. I therefore commenced the descent on the opposite side on foot. In four hours we reached Grindelwald, having made a detour to get to one of its famous glaciers. What will my wife and mother say to my lameness – walking nearly twenty miles and riding ten in one day? But with heartfelt gratitude I may say it has not injured me in the least. Saturday was so disagreeable that I had to relinquish plans – and so, returning to Unterseen, a walk of five hours, and dismissing there my guide, I made the best of my way to Berne.

Yours, etc., etc., CHARLES HODGE

PROF. HODGE TO HIS MOTHER

LONDON, June 28th, 1828

My Dear Mother:— From Geneva I made an excursion of three days to the valley of Chamouny to see its celebrated glaciers and to get a view of Mont Blanc. Having seen in the Canton of Berne scenery of the same kind, the impression was by no means so strong as when things at once novel and sublime strike the sight. I crossed the celebrated sea of ice, an enterprise of much more difficulty than I expected, and attended by a degree of danger that, had I been aware of it, would have deterred me from the attempt. The ice changes from month to month in these immense glaciers, so that you are never secure in finding it in a good state, unless your guide has passed at that particular place within a few weeks. These glaciers are immense bodies of snow and ice, and will fill up the elevated valleys of the mountains. The one called the Sea of Ice is eighteen leagues long, and from one to three miles broad. The surface is as irregular as the ocean. What may be called the waves are ten, twenty, or fifty feet high. The difficulty consists in getting up and down these waves, and over the chasms which run in all directions, and are often slightly covered with snow. With a careful guide, however, accidents are exceedingly rare.

Those which do occur are generally the result of the folly of young men who disregard the advice of their conductors. The guides in these mountains are regulated just as pilots are in the difficult harbours of maritime nations. They are examined, must receive certificates, and are responsible for the safety of all whom they conduct. I found the excursion of this day – walking nine hours under circumstances which required great muscular effort – too much for my limb. Otherwise I was scarcely fatigued at all. Were it not for that weakness, I should think myself equal to any amount of bodily fatigue.

From Geneva to Paris the country is not peculiarly interesting. At Paris I felt myself almost at home. I dined one day with ten Americans – Dr J. R. Clark, Dr Hopkinson, Dr Ralston, Dr Cunningham, Mr Chauncey.

I left Paris for London with the dear good Mr Chauncey, and am now settled with him in good, comfortable lodgings.

Your son, C.H.

PROF. HODGE TO HIS WIFE

LONDON, 27th, 1828

My Dearest Sarah:— As Mr Chauncey had been by Calais and Dover, he preferred the route by Dieppe and Brighton. We spent one day in Rouen to view the old churches, etc. After a ride of six hours we found ourselves in Dieppe. Our passage over the Channel was not pleasant – but in twelve hours after leaving Dieppe we were standing on the chalky shores of old England. You may suppose it was with a swelling heart I trod upon the soil of the mother country, which, with all her faults, is the most wonderful and admirable the world has ever seen . . . St Paul's church is much the most sublime and striking of any I have seen when viewed from under its immense dome. We attended last evening the House of Commons. You are aware that they sit in a room very much like a Methodist meeting-house – that the members wear their hats and lounge about as they please. I heard about twenty speak in the course of three hours, and never heard so much poor speaking in my life. I have never attended Congress, and therefore can make no comparison; but I am sure our General Assembly does not offer a sight of twenty such dull people.

Your own husband, C.H.

LONDON, July 5th, 1828

My Dear Sarah:— A few evenings ago I attended the debates in the House of Lords, and heard the Duke of Wellington, the Marquis of Bute, Lord Calthorpe, and several other members speak. All most miserable speakers, excepting the Duke, who can say what he wants in a plain, sensible manner. The whole assembly is far from imposing, and the members almost as negligent as those of the Commons, lounging about and talking to each other. Lord Calthorpe is a very pious, excellent man, and therefore I heard him with pleasure, although he is a very poor speaker.

Your own husband, C.H.

Mr Hodge visited the usual sights in London, and heard Dr Wardlaw of Edinburgh preach twice. He was kindly entertained over Sabbath at the house of Mr Roberts, about five miles out of the city. He and Mr Chauncey spent the 12th, 13th, and 14th of July in Cambridge, and heard Charles Simeon preach, with great delight, and visited Professor Lee, to whom he was introduced by a letter of Tholuck's. But as it was vacation the majority of the professors were absent. Returning to London, he went to Oxford and visited the Colleges, but all the gentlemen to whom he bore letters were absent, enjoying their vacation. He then visited Blenheim, the seat of the Duke of Marlborough, and Warwick, the seat of the Earl of Warwick, and went thence to Liverpool. On the twenty-second he left Liverpool for a rapid visit to Edinburgh, of which not a single line of record survives. On the 1st of August he sailed from Liverpool, in the *Caledonia*, for New York. He reached his home, in Princeton, about the 18th of September, 1828, WHERE THERE WAS JOY. Then was the first abiding image of his

father, and of Drs Alexander, Miller, and Maclean, who gathered to
the greeting, fixed in the mind of the collector and recorder of these
memoirs. From this point journals and domestic letters cease to be
copious, and personal recollections begin to yield their contributions
to the history which remains to be traced.

7

FROM HIS RETURN TO HOME AND WORK IN PRINCETON, SEPTEMBER 1828, TO HIS TRANSFERENCE TO THE CHAIR OF SYSTEMATIC THEOLOGY, MAY 1840

Work as Professor and Preacher – Correspondence with German Friends – Children, Family Relations, and Recreations – Correspondence with Brother – Death of Mother – Politics – Lameness – His Department of Instruction Reinforced by Mr Hubbard and Prof. J. A. Alexander – Gathering of Professors and Friends in Study – The BIBLICAL REPERTORY AND PRINCETON REVIEW *– Its History and Estimate of Its Character and Influence – The Qualifications and Success of Dr Hodge as an Editor and Reviewer, His Associates and Principal Contributors – His Commentary on Romans – His Constitutional History of the Presbyterian Church of the United States*

THE ELEVEN YEARS, the record of which is assigned to this chapter, were years of critical significance in the history of the American Presbyterian Church, as well as those in which passed the crisis of Professor Hodge's life. During this period the conflict of elements in the church flamed into open controversy, and the great division into its Old and New School branches was consummated. Dr Hodge's part in this ecclesiastical convulsion was so important that it will be reserved for a chapter by itself. This same period was marked in the history of Professor Hodge as the one in which, through protracted confinement and acute physical suffering, he achieved his reputation as a scholar, teacher, writer, and pre-eminently as an effective controversialist and church leader.

He returned from Europe comparatively an unknown young man, and he entered upon his new professorship of Didactic theology in 1840, with very much the same general reputation he enjoyed to the end of his life.

He opened the session of 1828–9, with the Introductory lecture, in which he endeavoured to impress upon the minds of the students 'the practical truths which the circumstances of foreign states and countries had deeply impressed upon his own'. These were: *First*, the great importance of civil and religious liberty, as illustrated by the effect of our institutions in elevating the intelligence and character of all classes of the people, and in setting religion and the church free from the trammels of the State. *Second*, the training of youth in knowledge and religion. In this respect he declared the institutions of Germany to be greatly in advance of those of the United States. He sketched the system of public instruction, through all the grades of schools, throughout the Kingdom of Prussia, with special reference to religious teaching and its results. 'But the most interesting feature of the whole system is that religion is as regularly and as systematically taught as any other subject. Each class of schools has its regular text-books on this subject; and in all, the history and leading principles, both in doctrines and morals, of the Scriptures are inculcated. The nature of this instruction depends of course very much on the individual character of the man to whom it is committed, and it is too often the case that it embraces little more than the leading facts and moral principles of the Bible. Still even this is of immense advantage. So thoroughly is this system carried through in Prussia, that I never met a boy selling matches in the street (and I made several experiments of the kind) who could not answer any common question on the historical parts of the Old and New Testaments.'

'The German system provides for education of Protestants, Catholics and Jews alike, and where it is possible, by separate schools. Is it not possible in this country to have the Christian religion taught in the common schools? The selection of teachers and the course of instruction depends on the commissioners of the several districts. If public opinion once be brought to decide for the measure, it can be accomplished. The various sects are uniting not only to distribute the Bible, but also to circulate doctrinal tracts. May they not be induced to unite in the preparation of religious school-books in which the historical facts and essential doctrines, in which all evangelical denominations agree, may be taught and inculcated? If such books could receive the sanction of the ruling bodies of the various sects among us, there would be no difficulty in their being generally introduced.' The *Third* head was the intimate connection between speculative opinion and moral character. The correspondence between opinion and character is strikingly observable in the various religious parties in Germany. The leading parties are the Orthodox, the Rationalists, and the Pantheists. 'Wherever you find vital piety – that is, penitence and a devotional spirit – there you find the doctrines of the fall, of depravity, of regeneration, of atonement, and of the deity of Jesus Christ. I never saw or heard of a single individual who exhibited a spirit of piety who rejected any one of these doctrines. Holiness is essential to the correct knowledge of divine things and the great security from error.'

'If these be so, brethren, "keep your hearts with all diligence"; beware of any course of study which has a tendency to harden your hearts and deaden the delicate sensibility of the soul to moral truth and beauty. Lean not on your own understanding, and keep as you would your hold on heaven your reverence for Jesus Christ.'

Mr Hodge now devoted himself with renewed enthusiasm and with untiring diligence to his studies and class instructions. His professorship covered all the ground now distributed between the professorships of 'Oriental and Old Testament Literature', of 'New Testament Literature and Biblical Greek', and of the 'Instructor in Hebrew', etc. Until his lameness, he met two classes every day, teaching and lecturing on the Hebrew language, literature, and exegesis in the mornings, and on the New Testament literature and exegesis every afternoon. He prepared also extensive courses of lectures on Biblical criticism, hermeneutics, special introduction, sacred geography, and the exegesis of several books of both Testaments. He delivered to the junior class exegetical lectures on Paul's Epistles, an exercise which he continued without interruption to the end of his life, a period of fifty years. At this time, also, until incapacitated by lameness in the summer of 1833, he preached in his turn in the village church, and afterwards in the Seminary Oratory, and the various Churches of the neighbouring cities and surrounding country.

His preaching at this time was more fresh and animated than it was in his later life. He engaged in the work with genuine enthusiasm, and was heard with universal interest and profit by intelligent audiences. He uniformly wrote and read the entire sermon. In style they had the well-known characteristics of all that proceeded from him; clearness, comprehensiveness, and vigour. He read naturally and simply, at times perhaps too quietly, but with his strong and inflammable emotional nature ready to burst forth at any moment as a boiling spring, or as a volcano, flashing light as well as sending forth streams of passionate feeling. None of the sermons preached at that period are extant. The tradition, however, yet remains of certain occasions when his feelings were powerfully wrought upon, and when, leaving his manuscript, he for a while melted or thrilled his audience by the tenderness or the passion of his appeals. Such an occasion was the funeral of Edward, second son of the venerable Dr Samuel Miller, in the autumn of 1832, when Mr Hodge preached in the old Church which preceded the present first Church of Princeton. Dr S. Irenæus Prime writes me, 'My first sight of your illustrious and now glorified father was in the

pulpit in Princeton, in the autumn of 1832, when he preached the
sermon at the funeral of Dr Miller's son, Edward. The tenderness,
simplicity and beauty of the discourse filled me with wonder and
with love, and awakened a new train of thought in connection with
the science of religious education. In my mind theology had not
been associated so much with the writings of John as with those
of Paul; but suddenly I saw both these men of the Bible blended
and reproduced in the teacher and preacher who stood before
me.' The compiler of these memoirs, then a child in the gallery,
can still vividly recall the wave of emotion which swept over the
whole audience, when the preacher lifted himself and addressed to
the college students, filling the gallery on his right hand with the
voice and the countenance of a herald from the eternal world, the
message sent to them by Edward Miller just before he died – 'Tell
them to stop; they are mad!'

An instance of the same kind, though much more remarkable,
occurred when he was called to deliver the funeral oration on the
occasion of the death of his intimate friend, Rev. Dr Albert B.
Dod, the brilliant Professor of Mathematics in Princeton College,
in November 1845. Dr Hodge had spent days and nights at the
bedside of his dying yet triumphant friend. His whole soul was in
the highest state of spiritual exaltation. An account of this address
and the effect it produced is given by Dr Paxton in the closing
chapter of this volume.

HIS CORRESPONDENCE WITH GERMAN FRIENDS

During these years he kept up a very active and general correspondence with his personal friends, and with the leaders in the
Church's work alike in England and on the European continent
and in America. Of his own letters not many except those written to his brother can now be recalled. But several of the letters
from his beloved German friends are given because of the intrinsic

interest attached to the names of the writers, and because they beautifully illustrate the warmth of personal love which it was a characteristic gift of Dr Hodge to attract in all communities and during his whole life.

PROFESSOR HODGE TO PROFESSOR THOLUCK

PRINCETON, October 12th, 1828

My Dearest Tholuck:—You can hardly conceive of the pleasure I experienced when my little boy came into my study two days since, and said, 'Father, here are two letters for you from over the wide sea.' A single glance was enough to assure me that one was from that dear friend to whose kindness and affection I am so much indebted. The many happy and instructive hours I have spent in your society, will be the subject of delightful recollection to the close of life. I look back to my sojourn in Germany with feelings of unmingled pleasure, so far as the recollection of misimproved advantages will permit. I love the German character, as exhibited in Christians, quite as much as though I were myself a German, and cannot pass a German immigrant in the street without feelings of interest I experience for no other people. You beg me to inform you 'of my affairs'. This maybe done in a few words. After taking a tour from Düsseldorf up the Rhine, I went to Heidelberg, thence to Basle; spent two or three weeks in travelling in Switzerland; passed a few days in Geneva, and proceeded thence to Paris. I reached England about the 20th of June; delivered most of your letters. I visited Cambridge, and was kindly received by Professor Lee, whom I found determined to write down all your German neologists. In Oxford I missed both of the gentlemen to whom your letters were addressed. I sailed from Liverpool on the 2nd of August, and arrived in New York on the 8th of September. To my inexpressible joy, on reaching Princeton the following day, I found my wife and children in perfect health and surrounded with every blessing.

Dear Tholuck, you can hardly think how happy I now am. My lovely children (for they are *very* lovely), are hanging on my knees all the time, and my dear wife – I will not talk about – you must come and see her! Our seminary is prospering, and is furnished with its ordinary number of students. The spirit of piety has not declined among them, and perhaps more of a disposition to embark in foreign missions was manifested during the last term than usual. My venerated colleagues, Drs Alexander and Miller, you would love very much. They are the lights of our church, and their memories will long be blessed when they are gathered to their rest.

The American Board of Missions met last week in Philadelphia. Their report was very interesting, and their income last year was 108,000 dollars, and the information received from their various stations encouraging. I will endeavour to send a printed copy of their report to Berlin by the first opportunity. The History of Theology in the 18th Century has been printed. It would, I presume, be much too expensive to you if we should send it to you at Rome. I will, therefore, forward it to Halle for you. I am very much distressed to hear of the state of mind of poor Krummacher. It was nearly as bad before I left Berlin, but I cannot help regarding it as mainly the effect of disease, and consequently hope to learn, that with returning health, his faith and hope have been restored. I am very much surprised to hear what you mentioned of Otto von Gerlach. I wish he would come to this country. He would, I am persuaded, find a wide field for the exercise of his talents. Should a kind Providence ever send any one of the dear friends I love so sincerely, to these distant shores, I should be overjoyed to meet them – my house and heart stand ever open to them. I should have written to you sooner, had I not thought it better to write by the way of Leghorn; but opportunities for that port occurring so seldom, I hasten to take advantage of the first packet for Le Havre. I thank you most cordially for your dear letter. Do write to me as often as your time will permit. Tell me whatever of interest occurs in your section of the kingdom of God. Let me know of important theological works which you think I ought to send for. I obtain books now regularly from the Buch-handlung des Waisenhauses in Halle, and shall therefore be able to procure whatever works you may recommend to me.

Give my best respects to Herr Bunsen, who, I rejoice to hear, is likely to attain a station of so much usefulness, as a seat in the Ministerium.

And now my dearest friend accept the assurance of my warmest and most grateful affection. Do not forget me – may love to our common Saviour bind our hearts in perpetual union.

Your brother in Christ, C. Hodge

LETTER TO PROF. HODGE, FROM PROF. A. THOLUCK

Rome, Feb. 27th, 1829

My Dear Brother in the Lord:—The distance that separates Princeton from Rome is such, and the waves that roll between my dear brother and myself are so numerous, that I really despaired of our ever being able to stretch our hands to each other beyond the ocean. However, you have received from the hands of your little darling the lines of your poor German pilgrim in Rome, and Sir Thomas, the '*maestro di casa*' of the Prussian ambassador, has put in my hands the unexpected news which I have received from the dearest friend I possess in your part of the world. You can scarcely imagine, my dear Hodge, the delight and the eagerness with which I broke the seal of your message. So delighted was I, that scarcely any letter from my country excited in me the same degree of eagerness. All the sweet and quiet evenings, spent in the floor room of the Ulrichs Strasse, and the little green spot out of the Galgthor, all the delicious enjoyments of the Kuhstall and Tharand, all the solemn hours passed in the fellowship of the Berlin brethren stood at once before my eyes. Earthly and spiritual enjoyments, earthly and spiritual cares have linked our hearts together, and space and time shall never separate what God has united.

You enjoy again all the delights and the sweetness of a Christian family-life, and your days will pass on quietly to the end. To me new scenes of life have appeared, and are opening again before my eyes, but for me the spot of undisturbed tranquillity lies forever beyond, in that life, from which none has ever returned, but He who will lead there all troubled souls, and myself among them, as I trust in God. The days of my residence in Rome are running fast to an end. Before German spring begins, I shall find myself once more at the solemn gateway of the Galg-Strasse. The time spent in Rome has been for me a time full of various enjoyments and various engagements; and, although the sting in my flesh has made many an hour gloomy, I must still and will ever praise the Lord for the great mercies he has shown me during the past year. I shall leave Rome with my bodily vigour partly recruited, and with faith and hope still more increased. I have good reason to hope that the spiritual condition of Halle will improve. Although hindered by various intrigues the appointment of Guericke as *extraordinarius* is almost sure, and very lately Prof. Ullmann has been called there to the professorship of Niemeyer. He will probably become a more sincere fellow-labourer than Thilo, although there is about him a good deal of fear and timidity of men. A little flock of faithful students is still remaining in Halle, and under God's blessing will increase. The Berlin Church journal (*Kirchenzeitung*) is becoming more and more a standard for the faithful in Germany. The persecutions Hengstenberg has suffered on its account evince it the more a work agreeable to the Lord of the Church, and dangerous to its adversary, the foul fiend. The communications which it contains from America, have been a stimulus to many others as well as myself to fresh exertions. They are truly delightful. Pray send to me at Halle some more of your publications.

I cannot help mentioning again our dear little Krummacher. I understand that the mist which involved his mind is disappearing. His spirit was terribly excited by the grand subject of predestination, which his uncle had enforced upon his mind, and which was so violently combated at Berlin, and this has now come to be apprehended by him as by his whole family as a truth.

I send this letter to Le Havre by the kindness of Dr Jarvis, an

Episcopalian from Boston, who saw you in Paris. He intends to spend the summer of 1830 at Halle. Our dear Robinson has not yet reached Rome, and I do not know whether I am still to expect him. Pray dear friend write to me very soon and send to me whatever you think interesting. In the bonds of Christian fellowship, and with a greeting to your esteemed, though to me unknown, wife.

Yours sincerely and faithfully,

A. Tholuck

PROF. HODGE TO PROFESSOR THOLUCK

Princeton, February 28th, 1829

My Dear Friend and Brother:—I wrote to you some months since, directing, as you requested, to the care of the Prussian Legation, Rome. I write now to Halle, in the expectation that this letter will find you there by the first or middle of April. My affection for you remaining undiminished, I am very desirous to hear from you and learn the state of your health, and the character of your present prospects. I trust that your long absence in so delightful a country, and under such favourable circumstances, has been the means of restoring your spirits and preparing you anew for the arduous duties of your station. Let me know how things look in Halle. What progress the cause of truth is making there and elsewhere in Germany? I feel a deep interest in all that concerns your important section of the Church, and cannot but hope that the time is coming when she will arise in new splendour from the ruins of her lamentable fall.

With us there is little of much interest which you will not learn from the American journals. Although I feel as deeply as ever the great advantages which our ecclesiastical liberty confers upon us, and think that we have great reason to rejoice in the general prevalence of truth and piety in most sections of our country, I am now aware to a greater degree than formerly of the evils which attend even the best system. Our worldly men are more worldly even than yours. Religion being no concern of the state, they do not even pay it the formal regard which in your country it receives as a part of one general secular establishment. Everything depends with us on public opinion, and this will, in the main, be right as long as vital piety be prevalent to the extent it is at present. Revivals of religion continue in every section of the country, particularly to the North and East, and greater exertions are now made than ever before for the propagation of the Gospel, both at home and abroad, and for the diffusion of knowledge.

My Berlin friends have never written to me. I wrote a few weeks after reaching home to Ludwig von Gerlach, but have as yet received no answer. I long to hear from them, but fear to trouble them with my letters. I am very desirous to be kept informed of the progress of theological literature in Germany, and for this purpose have ordered several of your periodicals – the *Tubingen Zeit-Schrift*, that by Umbreit, Lucke, etc., the *Evangelische Kirchen-Zeitung*, and several others, but they come very slowly. July 1828 is the last number that I have received of the Berlin journal. Please speak to Mr Funke (the manager of the Buch-handlung), and beg him to forward the periodicals as rapidly and as regularly as possible. Please order for us, from time to time, any book which you may think important for us to have, to the amount of from 50 to 100 Prussian dollars annually. You know the kind of books I want, valuable works on the language, literature and exegesis of the Old and New Testaments.

As I presume so far on the bond of Christian fellowship which binds us together as to make such demands on your goodness, cannot you find something for me to do for you? Are none of your friends ever coming to our side of the Atlantic? I should be delighted to have it in my power to manifest my gratitude towards Germany, by showing kindness to any German. I wrote a letter of introduction for Rev. Edmund D. Griffin, of the Episcopal Church, to you about a week since. He is the son of an eminent lawyer in New York, and a young man, I understand, of amiable character. I do not know him personally, and therefore cannot say whether he belongs to the High-church or the Evangelical party of the Episcopal church. My dear Brother in Jesus Christ do not forget me. Write to me often.

Give my best love to Dr Guericke, and to all my Berlin friends. May the best of Heaven's blessings always attend you.

Your friend and brother in Christ,

C. HODGE

PRINCETON, June 8th, 1829

My Dear Friend:—I received some weeks since your second letter from Rome, written on the eve of your departure for Halle. Some time before your letter was received, I had written and directed to you at Halle, under the expectation that you would be there in March or April. I greatly rejoice at the renewed health and spirits with which you return to your usual duties, and cannot but hope that Providence will render you a great blessing to the section of the church in which he has called you to labour. The accounts which I have incidentally received regarding the progress of the Redeemer's cause in Germany, are very encouraging, and make me regret that my means of intercourse with you are not more frequent and more direct. You are the only one of my German friends who has written to me.

I have just returned from Philadelphia, where I have been for the last two weeks attending the meeting of our General Assembly. We had a large and interesting meeting, and have much reason to rejoice in the progress of the cause of Christ in our country. We received several very excellent letters from the French Protestant churches, with whom we have opened a correspondence, which bids fair to be mutually useful. I will endeavour to send you a copy of our minutes, and of the reports of our several religious and benevolent societies. They will serve to exhibit to you more of the activity of 'the hands and feet' of the church, and arouse you, who constitute the head and heart, to do your work in unison. I had the pleasure of seeing our good friend Bishop Andres in Philadelphia. This was his first visit to that city. He had been shut up in Bethlehem, and has, I fear, not received the most favourable impression of his new residence. He complained much of the heat of the climate and of the difficulty of adapting himself to it. I hope he may make me a visit in Princeton, it would give me the greatest pleasure to be kind to a real German.

Please write to me soon and often. My heart yearns toward you with all its first affection, and I cannot bear to think that my dear friends abroad have so soon forgotten me. I heard lately from dear Monod, who is labouring faithfully and successfully at St Quintin, and a little while after received from the Stadtrath Semler a beautiful little picture of Lisco's church, and a short note. I wish you would thank him for me, should you have an opportunity, though I hope soon to write to him myself. Give my best love to all my friends – both the von Gerlachs, Le Coq, Focke, von Senfft, Hengstenberg, Guericke, etc. I often think of them with great affection. The intelligence which you gave me of Krummacher's return, did not surprise, though it greatly rejoiced me. He will, I hope, come out from the fiery trial, by which he has been tried, as gold doubly purified.

May God our Saviour bless and keep you my dear friend and brother, and enable us both to run, with joy, the race which has been set before us.

Yours, with much affection and esteem, C. HODGE

LETTER FROM PRESIDENT LUDWIG VON GERLACH TO MR HODGE

BERLIN, July 14th, 1829

To Mr Hodge:—How ungrateful must I have seemed to you, my friend dearly beloved in the Lord, in that I have left unanswered until today your letter of the 28th of last September – a letter so friendly and gracious! I ask you, nevertheless, to believe that I, like yourself, hold fast the common interest which faith in Christ and His love has awakened in us, and that I constantly and thoughtfully recollect the blessings which God has bestowed upon me through the instrumentality of His children in America, and especially through an acquaintance with the American churches, and particularly through yourself, since you have shown me the living image of that which written and printed descriptions but imperfectly represent. I feel so deeply in myself and most German Christians the lack of determination and completeness which are to be found in both theory and practice among the followers of Christ in England and America; and I know so well that whatever profoundness of thought and feeling may exist in Germany is but a poor substitute for these effectual operations of the Holy Spirit. These latter qualities of the German character may very easily entice and lead us not to God, but into the abysms of Pantheism. For this reason communion with the Lord's people beyond the sea is a necessity. If, notwithstanding, I have left your letter so long unanswered, I must plead in excuse the press of affairs and business which my stay in Berlin brings with it. Not every moment is fitted for converse with so true and dear a friend. We await rather a time when heart and soul are fresh and free from business cares and outside impressions, and while thus waiting, month after month passes away. I am not even now able to write to you because the proper mood is come, but to-day is an important epoch and turning-point in my life, and I do not wish to carry over into the new period the debt of love which your letter of the 28th of September has laid upon me, although I repay it poorly and unsatisfactorily with these rapid lines, and your undeserved friendship and love will make me ever your debtor.

To-day is my wedding-day. Let me but look into your house in Princeton at the joy of seeing once more your loved wife and children 'all loveliness and promise to a father's eye', and then you will feel with me what I experience to-day, especially when you recall that it is, as you know, my second marriage. My life has not been, as you once said of your own, 'like a silver stream'. It has overflowed with sorrows. The mercy of the Lord meets me once more with consolation and joy, but my heart has not yet recovered from its wounds, and longs to be free from sin and death, to rest in Him who alone hath everlasting joy and life. My bride is the cousin and dear friend of my late wife, and in this way first became dear to me. Gossner is to perform the ceremony. Day after to-morrow we leave for Halle, where I have been appointed Landgerichts-director, President of an inferior court of justice; and there I hope to enjoy Tholuck's companionship. You will learn from the accompanying letters of Otto von Focke, together with much beside, that during last May we suffered a sore affliction in the loss through death of our dear friend Le Coq, with whom we were so often together. The peace and tranquillity of mind which characterized him lasted through many sorrows to the end, and his death awakened the heart of his brother, whom you also know, and moved him to give himself up wholly unto the Lord.

The little time which remains for me to stay is almost gone. Let me beg you once more to pardon my long silence, and to rest assured of my warmest brotherly affection. As Cato always said, 'Praeterea censeo Carthaginem esse delendam',[1] so I say to you, and would like to say the same to all Christians in America, among others to Dr Alfred Post, in New York. Be on your guard against materialistic politics and the false liberalism of the infidel French and English of the last century – Voltaire, Gibbon, Rousseau, etc., etc. Compare not only your doctrines, but also *your feelings*, with those of the blessed Lord, of St Paul, and of the saints of former times, on the one hand, and with those of the liberals of our own time on the other; but compare thoroughly and candidly, without prejudices, as before the all-seeing eye of the Holy One, and shudder if you disagree with the former and agree with the latter. Alas! that Satan should always prefer to build chapels close beside the churches of God!

Yours forever, L<small>UDWIG</small> <small>VON</small> G<small>ERLACH</small>

My warmest regards for Mrs Hodge, my half-countrywoman.

LETTER FROM JUSTICE OTTO FOCKE

B<small>ERLIN</small>, July 29, 1829

My Dearest, Dearest Brother:—Oh! that I could express by words, my dearest friend, how I love you, and how my heart longs to see you

---

[1] Cato the Elder used to end every speech before the Roman Senate with the same sentence, 'Also, I believe that Carthage must be destroyed.' Ludwig von Gerlach seems to have held a similar attitude towards political liberalism, as seen in the infidel leaders of the eighteenth-century Enlightenment, and to have suspected that American democracy was tainted with the same dangerous ideas. [Ed.]

again in this life! But that is the blessing of the bond of Christian love, that, although far separated by land and sea, the hearts are and remain united in tender and firm love and in prayer. God bless likewise our bond of love; and as I never will forget my dearest and loveliest friend Hodge, you may sometimes remember Berlin, and pray for the friends you have in this city. Your friendly letter to von Gerlach has rejoiced us very much, and I hope that you will continue to communicate to us from time to time news of your welfare.

My friends have probably written to you that one of our dear brethren, the soft and lovely Adolph Le Coq, walks no more amongst us. He was the best of the Christian friends here at Berlin, and therefore God hastened to bring him in peace. Oh, that we may see ourselves with him before the throne of God. What a joy to be united there with all friends in unseparated connection. There shall be no more leaving nor separations by land or by sea. Yes, there shall I see you again, and see your beloved wife and dear children.

We had the last winter, also, some very dear friends from America here amongst us, the dear Post and Woolsey, but they were no Hodge.

That beloved word, 'America', has been a great deal more in my mind and heart since I met such dear friends from there, and know that they are safe at home again. Alas, that the world is so large, and friends so widely scattered. Prof. Tholuck was here during Whitsunday and stayed with me. Remember him often in your prayers, that the Lord may give him faith, the most steadfast and happy, and also aid him with firmness and decision in his course of life. He is now engaged to a young lady in Halle. May the Lord bestow his blessings on this bond. He remembers you constantly with much love.

Our circle of Christian friends, through the removal of the beloved Ludwig von Gerlach to Halle, and of Prof. Hochweg to Bonn, and through the death of the blessed Le Coq, has suffered a very painful loss, and there is great need that the Lord raise up new brothers. Alas ! that there are so few Christians, and that even among Christians themselves, there is so little firmness and decision. The Lord has visited Europe with severe trials and heavy calamities, with earthquakes, floods, violent storms, diseases, etc., but the majority of the people heed neither the voice of love nor wrath.

The times appear to me to indicate more and more that the coming of the Lord is near at hand. Therefore we will take courage and await Him with watching and praying. Yes, He will surely come, and we will pray, 'come soon!' Now, farewell, God bless you and your dear wife and children, with His everlasting blessing. Let us receive good tidings from you very soon, and write also some lines to me.

Farewell, and remember your faithful and obedient brother in the Lord,

OTTO VON FOCKE

LETTER FROM PROF. A. THOLUCK

HALLE, March 30, 1830

My Dear Friend Hodge:—I sent you a letter last summer, some time in August. Did it not reach you ? It was my heartfelt expression, but I have received no answer to it. I have been quite well during the past winter, and have been able to do a great deal of work, but my wife[1] is very sickly the greater part of the time. In no way can I keep her with me very long; yet the Lord's will be mine. Our beloved Guericke, who enjoyed the happiest of marriages, has suddenly lost his wife in child-birth. He is so afflicted thereby that he is thinking of resigning his professorship, and becoming a pastor. We have experienced much in many ways during the last few months. The King has now appointed an able committee to investigate the teaching of Profs. Gesenius and Wegscheider,[2] but no further results will be reached. On the whole I have not been able to agree with Von Gerlach's action – he is the author of the article in the *Kirchenzeitung*. The excitement is still going on here. I know not whether the cause is really advanced by it. Yet there was a warmer and a firmer bond of love between some thirty students last winter than ever before.

---

[1] He had married since his return to Halle from Rome, in the summer of 1829.

[2] Ludwig von Gerlach had accused these professors of infidelity and profanity and recommended the intervention of the civil power. [Ed.]

We had also established a missionary society, the regulations of which I enclose with this letter. I besought you urgently in my last letter to prove your friendship toward me by sending a contribution to the *Literary Advertiser.* I will now limit still further my wish expressed at that time, and ask you only for the notice and critical opinion of the most current work in America for or against predestination, together with a historical review of its advocates and opponents. I beg you not to refuse me this friendly service. I shall soon expect its execution.

> In the Lord our Saviour, yours ever the same, A. THOLUCK

PROF. HODGE TO PROFESSOR THOLUCK

PRINCETON, February 9th, 1831

My Dearest Tholuck:—How often and how affectionately my thoughts and heart have been turned towards you since I last wrote, it would be difficult for me to state. It is seldom, I believe, that a day passes without your image presenting itself in some form or another before my mind. I commune with you in your writings, where I trace those same features which were so familiarly exhibited during our personal intercourse. Or I hold intercourse with your spirit through the recollections of the past. Rejoice over the remembrance of your friendship, and in the prospect of meeting you *Jenseits* [hereafter] in a purer world. I have sympathized with you much in your trials in Halle. The more, because you could not, as you mention in your letter, fully approve of the course of your own friends. It is difficult for a stranger to enter understandingly into all the circumstances which should modify the application of general principles to particular cases, in a distant land. To us the principle on which our dear friend von Gerlach seems to have proceeded, that the members of a church should, while they continue such, conform to its standards, seems self-evident. And in such a country as ours, its application is easy. But how it is possible, *rebus sic stantibus* [with things as they are], to do the same with you, it is not for me to judge. My feelings, however, side with von Gerlach and Hengstenberg in this business, and force me to dissent from the course the venerated Neander would have the friends of religion in Germany to pursue. I rejoice much in the spirit of your communication to the *Evang. Zeitung*, respecting the nature of your relation to the Rationalism of Halle. You will excuse my saying, that the drift of some passages of your discourse on the Relation of Revelation to Reason, published in your *Anzeiger*, made me fear that we differed considerably on this point, and that you were less impressed with the radical difference between the two systems, Rationalism and Faith in God's word, than we Positive men could have wished. The spirit of your communication to the *Kirchen-Zeitung* has removed in a great measure this apprehension, and made me feel that we all are of one mind on this subject. I regret that I do not receive the *Anzeiger* and other periodicals more regularly and frequently. Nothing later than May, 1830, has come to hand.

The wonderful changes that have occurred in the political state of Europe since you wrote, are full of interest for the Christian. I fear troublous times are at hand for your poor Prussians; with Poland convulsed on the east, and intoxicated France on the west, it seems scarcely possible that peace can long be maintained. Will you not be tempted to seek an asylum on our peaceful shores, far from the struggles of the dying systems of feudal Europe? I have profited much from the lessons of Ludwig von Gerlach, and though I rejoice in the progress of liberty as much as ever, am rather cautious to see that what is *just*, as well as what is desirable, should be kept in view. I have not the purpose of writing on politics to you. The state of things in our country, politically, is not without its clouds. I do not apprehend any serious convulsions, but our present rulers take such a view of our relation to the dependent Indian tribes on our borders, that I very much fear our national character will be deeply stained by their disregard of solemn treaties. The religious state of the country is as favourable as in years past. The number of extensive revivals in various quarters is considerable. For particulars I must refer to the *New York Observer*. The progress of the Temperance Reformation has been astonishing. No one could have imagined that such a result could have been produced by the simple proposition, that men should agree never to use ardent spirits except as a medicine. The consumption of this destructive article has, by the exertions of temperance societies, been diminished perhaps one-half.

I thank you for the books which you ordered in my name at the Waisenhaus. I wish to receive the most important of your theological works, that I may be kept going, so to speak, with the German mind. We have not received the 2nd part of the 2nd volume of Neander's *Ecclesiastical History*. Will you order for me a copy of Freytag's edition of Golius; of Schlegel's *Philosophische Vorlesungen*, delivered in Dresden; of the Greek Testament, Scholz; of Draseke's sermons, and whatever good and new works you choose within moderate limits.

Give my best love to Guericke. How severe has been his loss, and how shameful the treatment he has received! I did intend writing to our friend Ludwig von Gerlach this afternoon, but am prevented by company. Assure him of my continued and warm affection. Dear Friend, do write to me. I long to hear from you. Do not punish me for my silence. Write at once on the spur of the moment. You have a home in America whenever you choose to come and claim it. I saw Mrs Robinson last October in Boston. I was much delighted with meeting her again. She appeared well and happy, and takes just and philosophic views of things in this country. The *Richtung* [outlook, drift] of the people is so different from hers, that she can hardly feel herself at home yet, particularly at Andover. I want to send you a set of the *Biblical Repertory* published here in Princeton.

Love to all dear German friends.
Yours, affectionately, C. Hodge

Princeton, April 6th, 1833

My Dear Friend:—In commending to your kind and affectionate reception Mr J. A. Alexander, I feel as though I were commending my second self to you, if you will understand this expression as intended to convey, in the strongest terms, the interest which I feel in his welfare, and that I will rejoice as much over kindness shown to him, as if I experienced it in person. Mr Alexander is my associate in the department of Biblical Instruction in our Seminary. He is more of a scholar, especially in your favourite field of Oriental languages, than any American within my knowledge, who has visited Europe. He is an amiable and excellent man, and what is of more importance, and of greater interest to you, he is a Christian. I feel assured, therefore, you will receive him for his own sake as well as mine, with open arms, and facilitate in every way you can his improvement and happiness. I wish it were possible for him to spend the winter with you, as I have no doubt it would be of great service to him, and a great pleasure to you. His plans are not yet definitely fixed, and you may greatly aid him in making the most advantageous disposition of himself during his stay in Germany. Will you be good enough to facilitate his access to your scholars and libraries, and do for him as you did for me, which includes all kindness. That neither time nor distance has either weakened or changed my feelings for you, I hope your own heart will lead you readily to believe. You are as bad a correspondent as I am. I wish you would reform in this respect, and I will promise to follow your example.

Yours, affectionately, C. HODGE.

LUDWIG VON GERLACH TO PROFESSOR HODGE

HALLE, Whitsunday, 1833

My Beloved Friend and Brother in Christ:—From this subject in regard to which I have ventured to presume a perfect unity of feeling between your Christian fellow-countrymen and myself, I will now pass to another, which by its close relation to the fate of the kingdom of God, affected me not less than the former. In regard to this I cannot presume upon such a unity with you and your fellow-countrymen. I mean the shock of Christendom through Liberalism since July 1830. It is true you remarked in a letter to Tholuck, Feb. 1831, 'That you have profited so much by my lessons, that though rejoicing in the progress of liberty as much as ever, you are rather cautious to see that what is *just* as well as what is *desirable* should be kept in view.' But when the 'just' and the 'desirable' become placed near each other, as two different things with a like meaning, then indeed does this seem far different from the

lesson which Christ the Lord taught us, 'Seek ye first the kingdom of
God and His righteousness (which comprehends all that is 'just') and
all these things (the desirable) shall be ADDED unto you.' Few things
in my life have so long and so deeply affected me as the existence of
Liberalism and its relation to the Church of Christ and to our age. If
therefore, as I hope, the brotherly love which you entertained for me in
Berlin, and have preserved on the other side of the ocean by letter, still
dwells in your heart, then you will see nothing more than a desire for
brotherly communication when I ask you to read what I have written
since the July revolution in the *Evangelical Church Journal* upon this
subject, and also in regard to Church power, authority, freedom, etc.,
etc. It has surely reached you, and may I ask you to express yourself
to me freely thereon. Should Christians be at variance on such grand
and fundamental questions ? Is it not a disgrace to the Church, that
it becomes divided into two heads by political ideas, while in the 16th
and 17th centuries religious doctrines divided the political world? Is it
not a shame that the earnest Christians of North America and Scotland
should be under the same yoke with the Roman Catholic O'Connell,
and the deistical and atheistical French liberals?

O, that the Lord would gather together the sheep of His fold! That we
who bear the name of Christ were at all points of like mind and heart!
What victories we could win under the banner of our Heavenly King!
. . . With the most sincere brotherly love, yours most truly,

Finished Jan. 23, 1833.   LUDWIG VON GERLACH

FROM OTTO VON GERLACH[1]

BERLIN, Feb. 28, 1834.

My Dear Friend:—Three years have already flown by since I received
your friendly letter, and during all this time I have left it unanswered.
Meanwhile, I have heard with many heartfelt sympathies of your great
bodily affliction which you have, however, if not altogether, yet in
good part overlooked for the sake of your calling. May the Lord soon

[1] 'The Wesley of Berlin'.

restore you to health, and prepare you anew both in body and mind for the responsible position you hold. It has given me much joy to receive through Mr Alexander[1] news from Princeton and America. I am of the opinion that the school of Prof. Stuart, to judge from his new 'Commentary on the Epistle to the Romans', will become the source of many heretical opinions, the beginning of which lies in his teaching concerning original sin, and of the Son of God, the eternal Sonship of Christ. I think it an excellent thing that opposition to this departure from the true doctrine is already taken at Princeton. Moreover, I deem it a happy result that more life and animation infuse themselves into the English and American literature through the influence of German theology. In England, where one finds so many treasures of books, and where Christian life especially prevails, things in the realm of theological learning are at a greater standstill than ever before. With us, thanks be to God, prospects have greatly brightened since you were here. In Pomerania, where at that time the first great revival had occurred, the number of orthodox ministers has more than ordinarily increased. In one region there were seven of them in immediate neighbourhood, and among them there is much genuine sympathy and much fellowship in the service of the Lord. The Bishop Ritschl has constantly been becoming more determined in his avowal of the Gospel. He is a blessing to the whole province, favouring everywhere the installation of Evangelical ministers and the removal of the incapable and vicious.

The number of believing ministers here in Berlin has increased. You are aware that the Methodist Minister Gossner, whom we have so often heard together, has become a disciple of Jänicke. His Church is crowded at all times, and his labours among the lower orders are especially rich in blessings. I am constantly forming the acquaintance of persons who have been brought into the Church through him. The Rev. Mr Kuntze, who was in London assistant to Dr Steinkopf when you were here, is also preaching now; and for the past year. Rev. Mr Arndt, a pupil of Strauss, has been labouring with churches constantly filled, and his labour results in many blessings. Further, no one of our believing

---

[1] Professor Joseph Addison Alexander.

pastors has been called away by death, and everywhere the number of
their hearers has increased rather than diminished. Our missionary society is in a very prosperous condition, that is, when considered from a
German and not from an American or English point of view. Its revenue
in comparison with the past has increased threefold in the last six years,
and it now has thirty missionary posts. These have of course in many
places to contest vigorously with the authorities, but these engagements
have almost always resulted successfully, and they have brought about
and increased brotherly relations. Last fall, the first five missionaries
were sent from here to South Africa. Since they were detained by
storms a long while on the Isle of Wight, the latest information we have
of them is of their being on the Atlantic Ocean. The number of ministerial associations (*Predigervereine*) has greatly increased in Germany.
In Silesia, in Prussia-Poland and in Prussia proper they are in part quite
numerously attended. The persecutions on the other hand on the part
of the Consistories have only begun here and there.

Thus only recently a society in Königsberg, which was under the
direction of Dr Ashansens, was suppressed by order of the King,
because (a striking circumstance which calls to mind the ἐνέκοψεν ἡμᾶς
ὁ Σατανας ['Satan hindered us', *1 Thess.* 2:18]) two of the ministers had
become crazy for the adjournment of the convention. How effective
Tholuck's sermons are at present in Halle you will hear through Mr
Alexander. An old school-friend of mine, together with his wife, has
lately been brought to Christ through one of them. The Christian work
is progressing in Prussia as in several other of the German lands. Many
active ministers of the gospel have made themselves conspicuous in
the kingdom of Hanover, which a few years ago was apparently dead.
In Göttingen my dear friend Julius Müller has become the university
chaplain; he is a profound and righteous man, who has written an article
against Hegel's philosophy in the *Studien und Kritiken*. He also deliv-
ers lectures on exegesis and practical theology. Lücke, as you know, is
there also. He is, however, at present, so feeble and undetermined, that
I would not be surprised to hear that he accomplishes little. In several
of the cities of Hanover, where lately the Christian cause was entirely

dead, there are now active ministers of the cross of Christ. Especially is the condition of the free-city Bremen encouraging. Five ministers are labouring there with great earnestness and effect. They are aiding each other in their work, and a struggle between light and darkness, which is highly interesting, has begun there. In Hamburg the rising generation give promise of quite a number of ministers; while the old people are for the most part worldly and inclined to universalism. The most discouraging outlook, however, is in middle Germany. In Leipzig and Jena scepticism is prevalent, and particularly in the province of Saxony matters have of late become rather worse than better. You will not be surprised when I state that the liberal constitution which that unfortunate land has received, increases still more this sad condition. In Hesse affairs are becoming now somewhat more encouraging.

At Cassel there are several evangelists, and also a clergyman. In Marburg, Kling, the editor of *Flatt's Lectures*, has recently become professor of theology. The worthy Harless has now become professor extraordinary at Erlangen, and from him we look for a thorough commentary on the epistle to the Ephesians, in a short time. Only in Tübingen does the future seem dark. The old school of Storr, Flatt, etc., is now completely supplanted by the followers of Schleiermacher, as Baur, Hegel, Strauss and others. Steudel has very few hearers. This is not to be wondered at, for that old school had become too indogmatical and too partial to exegesis, and their successors were becoming even shallower.

At present the Prussian lands are enjoying in general the richest blessings, and the others are beginning to rise from their wretchedness. But in the otherwise so greatly blessed Wurtemburg, the cause of Christ seems to be greatly in danger on account of the many sects prevailing there. In our university here in Berlin things appear in many respects far otherwise than they did six years ago. Since the evangelical *Kirchenzeitung* of 1830, Neander has laboured in much closer connection with Schleiermacher, and withdraws still further from Hengstenberg. One notices this especially in the students, among whom since that time it appears to me that the Christian life has been sadly lacking in decision. On the other hand, since that time, Hengstenberg has had many hearers, and it is especially pleasing that so many thoroughly energetic disciples of Christ have attached themselves to him and to me. You have probably learned ere this that Dr Schleiermacher died on the 12th of February of this year. Up to the eighth day before his death he had been in excellent health, and had read with me for three hours daily. Everything is now in great commotion over the important question as to who is to become his successor. The great majority as far as shown by open manifestation are for Twesten – particularly so is Neander and his followers, together with all the partisans of Schleiermacher. On the other hand the theological faculty (to which Neander at present does not belong) has come forward with a request to the *Minister* to call Olshausen; a step which has caused great surprise. Should the latter be called I would be more than ordinarily rejoiced, for notwithstanding a peculiar weakness of his, I regard Olshausen as one of the best thinkers and most determined men among our University theologians. His commentary has already had a second publication in two volumes. It is widely circulated and accomplishes much good. Twesten, on the other hand, agrees almost altogether with Schleiermacher, and is said to be a worldly-minded, fickle man, who visits the theatre, indulges in high living and neglects in this manner the proprieties of his vocation.

After this much of public news, let me say a few words about our friends here and in other places. Frau von Schönberg, at whose house you often met with us, has dwelt for the last three years in Stettin, where her husband is the Ober-president of Pomerania. Her quiet, devout disposition and her energetic love have accomplished even more there than they did here, where she laboured in a more retired position. She is helping greatly the advancement of the cause of Christ. Count Groben is still in his former position. It was only last week that he lost his only and very amiable daughter, yet he will be greatly strengthened in the Lord by this calamity. Our old friend Senfft has been married for four years, and already has three children. He has an excellent, truly Christian wife, and gives evidence of being happily married. He heartily returns your greeting, and thinks of you often with tender love. Focke has been in very poor health for three years, so that we have often indeed believed that God wished to call him out of this, to him, oppressive life. However, he is now recovering again by degrees, and we hope yet longer to keep him with us. The old venerable Baron Kottwitz is still living, now in his 77th year. The king has often of late shown him confidence in a noteworthy way, and he has thereby brought it about that four new churches have lately been built in our densely populated suburbs. I am to become pastor of one of them in a few months, but will also continue to lecture in the university.

The great gap that was made by the death of our beloved friend Le Coq, is still at all times painfully present to me. You will be able to imagine in some degree how sad his loss was to us. What a lovely image of our Lord shone in his heart! How one could turn to him at all times, and ever find the same honest, loving, friendly heart, the same desire for the advancement of the kingdom of God. Hengstenberg has been married also for some time, and although 'considerably under thirty', yet is even now the Dean of the theological faculty. The third volume of his *Christologie* will appear soon. After which he is purposing to write either a great work on the authenticity of the Pentateuch, or a popular commentary on the Psalms. I advise him, by all means, to undertake the former of these in the first instance, since I deem a critical examination of the Pentateuch as the most important work for a Professor of the Old Testament. My own studies draw me more and more from the peculiar German kind of scholarship. I am inclined too much to action, too greatly adapted to church work. Hence I cannot bury myself so to speak, among my books, as is necessary for a German scholar. Yet I have chosen for myself a subject which sooner or later will prove of greater importance, if God gives me time and strength, viz., a history of Christian Church government in connection with a dogmatic exposition of the doctrine of the Church.

I have been engaged for three years on a practical edition of the Bible, which is to contain the Lutheran text, with short explanatory remarks. The printing of the New Testament will begin this summer. For the future I am purposing to found near my parish a small Minister's Seminary, similar to that of Wittenberg, but 'non salarié par l'étât' [not funded by the state] – but upon the American principle of disconnection between church and state. You have perhaps seen my plans in regard to these things (much talked about between us in 1827 and '28) in Tholuck's *Literary Advertiser*, of 1832, where the article upon 'The Re-arrangement of the Church Government in the Evangelical Church' was written by me. You have no doubt also seen the long article by me, which appeared in the September number of the *Evangelical Church Journal*, for last year, entitled, 'Concerning the cultivation of the relations between Church and State in the Lutheran and Reformed Churches'. In regard to this, your acquaintance has been a great advantage to me; for without it I could scarcely have become acquainted with North America in general, or interested myself in any degree in it. I have requested Mr Alexander to send me the most important historical works on North American Church history. You promised me this six years ago, but I have received nothing. May I ask you to assist him with your advice, since you understand me and my needs.

Now I must conclude, my dear friend, ever present to me in my thoughts. Keep for me across the ocean your sincere love until we see each other in the future, where we may embrace without sin in the society of the blessed. O! may no one of all those who are mentioned in this letter be left behind. 'May each one who has such hope within him, purify himself even as he is pure', and unceasingly seek for the jewel of a heavenly calling. With the request for a few lines, as opportunity may offer,

I remain in sincere love, your friend and brother,

OTTO VON GERLACH

CORRESPONDENCE WITH HIS BROTHER
CHILDREN, FAMILY RELATIONS AND RECREATIONS

During all these years he exchanged weekly letters with his brother. He had never known a sister nor any other brother. They were only eighteen months apart in age, and in childhood and youth had been all in all to each other. They were one in principles, opinions and interests, temporal and spiritual. Their differences of character and position were precisely such as to cause them to be mutually attracted to and dependent upon each other. In this correspondence Dr Charles Hodge's whole life, inward and outward, personal and family, lies embalmed. Through this channel, for fifty-three years, from his settlement in Princeton in 1820, to his brother's death in 1873, he poured out without reserve all the contents of his mind and heart. The whole is a singular monument of that brother's nobility. The Philadelphia brother was the elder, with much more of the instinct and habit of the anxious care taker than was proportioned to the difference of age. He was of the more cautious disposition, and of the more deliberate and cooler judgment. He was a skilful and experienced physician. He lived in a great city, lately the seat of government of the United States, and, at the time of which we write, the ecclesiastical metropolis of the Presbyterian Church in America. After his practice was established, and he had entered upon his professorship in the medical department of the University of Pennsylvania, he became the richer of the two. Thus it came to pass, that in all things he was his brother's counsellor, supporter and comforter. Before the days of railroads, telegrams and express agencies, he was the unwearied agent for the execution of a ceaseless stream of commissions. No matter who else was the family physician, every detail of morbid symptom of every member of the Princeton family was narrated to him, and his advice sought, and often his personal presence asked for and obtained. When the children multiplied, and expenses with them, when the theological professor's salary failed to be paid for months, and the Editor of the *Repertory* was pressed for money to pay its bills, for which the returns from subscription were at first entirely inadequate, the Philadelphia brother, with inexhaustible generosity, came to the rescue by loans and absolute gifts.

It was during these years, from February, 1830, to December, 1840, that Professor Hodge's six youngest children were born. The letters, like an echoing gallery, repeat the voices of those days, and bring back into the present, not only the words but the very flush, and tone, and gesture by which his love for and delight in these little ones is expressed. They are full of their doings and sayings and of the father's joy and pride and hope on their account. They were at every age and at all times allowed free access to him. If they were sick, he nursed them. If they were well, he played with them. If he were busy, they played about him. His study had two doors, one opening outward towards the Seminary for the convenience of the students, and a second one opening inward into the main hall of the home. Hence his study was always the family thoroughfare, through which the children, boys and girls, young and old, and after them the grandchildren, went in and out for work and play. When he was too lame to open the door, and afterwards when he was too busy to be interrupted by that action, he took the latch from the doors, and caused them to swing in obedience to gentle springs, so that the least child might toddle in at will unhindered. He prayed for us all at family prayers, and singly, and taught us to pray at his knees with such soul-felt tenderness, that however bad we were our hearts all melted to his touch. During later years he always caused his family to repeat after him at morning worship the Apostles' Creed, and a formula, of his own composition, professing personal consecration to the Father, and to the Son, and to the Holy Ghost. But that which makes those days sacred in the retrospect of his children is the person and character of the father himself as discovered in the privacy of his home, all radiant as that was with love, with unwavering faith, and with unclouded hope.

His musical tastes and talents were not remarkable, yet he loved good music, and especially singing, which appealed to the religious affections. His older children remember him before his lameness walking up and down his study singing devotional hymns. Finding that his second son, while an infant on the knee, discovered special susceptibility to music, he revived his own flute-playing, which he had practised when a theological student. Afterwards he got a violin for his boy, and the grave professor and commentator himself used it until he had acquired quite a respectable skill.

Partly because of his lameness, and partly because of his taste, he always kept a single horse or pair from 1832 until his death. Partly to provide for their support, and partly for his own recreation, he purchased, November 1830, six acres of ground, immediately adjoining the Seminary property to the westward. To these he subsequently added by purchase, two acres in the spring of 1832. He cultivated these lots for more than a quarter of a century, with great interest and success. He manured and limed and drained them in the most advanced methods. He raised the best crops, of the finest quality and largest quantity in proportion to his ground, known in the neighbourhood. Successes of this kind pleased him very much, and the only boasting his most intimate friends ever in all his life knew him to express by word or look, came from him coloured with a boy's enthusiasm in view of such achievements as these effected through the instrumentality of his hired man. Especially was this the case when on some occasion he exhibited to a farmer or other competent judge some highbred calf or colt he had raised. He intelligently appreciated and heartily delighted in all the points which exhibited and proved their perfection of type and style, and their physical excellence in general. To the end of his life he delighted in fine horses, and would listen with animated interest to the conversation of gentlemen who also happened to be connoisseurs in horse lore, and were describing the perfections of some celebrated horse, or narrating his achievements on the road or course.

DEATH OF HIS MOTHER

In April, 1832, his beloved mother died after a brief illness, so unexpectedly that her youngest son, although he used all diligence, was unable to reach her bedside until after her departure. As soon as he returned to Princeton after her funeral, he wrote to his brother:

I was much mistaken in thinking I should have little comparatively to call dear mother to mind. Almost everything, I find, is in some way associated with her. So many articles of clothing of the children, so many of their books and playthings, and so many of my own clothes bear marks of her care, that she is constantly recalled to our recollection. The loveliness of the children now gives a mournful pleasure, as I know that the eyes which would have looked on it with so much delight, are now closed. But constant recollection of the mercy of God to her and to us, the thought of how much everything has been ordered as she would have wished, soothes and satisfies me. I feel very much for you, my dear brother. Great as I feel my own loss to be, I know yours is greater. You have a daily and sensible void in your circle of duties and enjoyments. But as you have more to mourn for, you have more to console you. You were the chief earthly stay and comfort of our dear parent, and most of the happiness of this world which she enjoyed came through you. You too had the inexpressible satisfaction of being with her to the last; of seeing and receiving the evidences of her confidence in her Redeemer, and the assurances of her love. So dear brother you have every consolation of which such an affliction can admit.

Your loving brother, C.H.

In July and August of that year, the Asiatic Cholera prevailed in this part of America for the first time. Its character and the condition of its progress appeared mysterious; its virulence baffled the skill of the physicians, and its ravages were dreadful. Four citizens of Princeton fell victims to it that season, and quite a number of the labourers on the canal and stragglers from the road came into the village hospital to die. Mr Hodge was very active in ascertaining from the most competent sources the proper treatment of the disease, and in visiting the patients in person, and in making arrangements for their comfort. Every case and its treatment was made a subject of consultation with his brother. The son as well as the brother of a physician, and having in early manhood attended lectures on anatomy and physiology, he always took the greatest interest in reading upon and discussing medical questions, and in cases of necessity, was himself capable of acting the part of a respectable practitioner.

POLITICS

He was always an attentive and interested witness of political events, and entertained and expressed the most decided opinions. He was trained by his family in the opinions of the old Federalist party of Washington, Hamilton and Madison, and he held them tenaciously as principles to the end of his life. He had a poor opinion of President Jackson, and of the Locofoco party [a radical faction of the Democratic party], and was a warm advocate of the protective tariff, and of the United States Bank. He always adhered to the old Whig party until its death; then in 1857 voted for Fremont, the first Republican candidate for the Presidency, and continued to be a decided Republican as long as he lived.

He writes to his brother, October 1st, 1831:

My Dear Brother:—The commencement passed off much in the usual manner. As I seldom attend on such occasions I cannot speak of it from personal knowledge. Mr Dallas' oration on the preceding afternoon was better than that of Forsyth the year before, but still very deficient in solid worth. The only production of this kind which seems to have given much satisfaction generally was that of Mr Wirt. He, it seems, is the anti-masonic candidate for president. I wish he could succeed. But this splitting up the anti-Jackson men into Calhoun, Clay and Wirt factions will only secure their own defeat, and burden the country with the present miserable incumbent for another term. The apathy of the people in respect to his misconduct is of serious omen for the future. The missionaries in Georgia are probably, through his desertion, by this time condemned to the penitentiary for four years! Verily, I think I could in such a case join a rebellion, with a clear conscience, as I am sure I could with a full heart. But not a voice is raised on the subject. The dreadful excitement on the negro question will absorb all interest in the South for a time. I heard to-day that fresh murders had been committed, and that one planter had called up four of his slaves, and caused them to be shot without the pretence of a trial, and that it was feared a dreadful massacre of the blacks might yet occur. The papers state that tortures are resorted to to extort confessions; that the suspected are flogged to make them confess and disclose. This is a most deplorable state of things, and will serve to exasperate the feelings of the South against the North, although it be more than ever unreasonable.

Your brother, C.H.

March 10, 1832

The decision of the Supreme Court has filled all hearts here with gratitude and joy. The memory of these judges will be cherished as long as good men live in America. It is the most important decision, taking all things into view, which that court ever made. Jackson men here, at least the best of them, say they will stand by the Court in preference to their master, and I hope there will be enough equally well principled to cause it to be the course of policy to execute the laws.

Your brother, C.H.

December 15, 1832

My Dear Brother:—I rejoice with you over the President's proclamation – it is excellent, worthy of Washington in doctrine and spirit. I presume it was written by Taney, the Attorney General, who is a Federalist. Livingston took different ground, I remember in his speech on nullification in the Senate from that assumed in the Proclamation. He differed from Webster, especially where Webster and Jackson coincide. That is as to the origin of the Government. Webster and the Proclamation saying that it was formed by the people of all the states as a whole. Livingston maintaining that it was a compact between the several states as such. I conclude, therefore, that he is not the author of this paper. Besides its whole spirit is too elevated. It is a striking proof of Jackson's imbecility that he can put his name with so much composure to documents which differ so entirely in doctrine as the Veto Message and the Proclamation. I should feel still more rejoiced at the character of the latter if I thought the old gentleman really understood it, or knew what he said. I should not be surprised to find that when called to act on the principles just avowed, he should allow Amos Kendall to prepare a proclamation worthy of the most atrocious Jacobin, and sign it without remorse, or even the consciousness of his folly. Still what we have is a great good, for which we should be thankful. And if the President be true to his text, I would be for voting him a statue and for evoking the spirit of Phidias[1] to make it.

Your brother, C.H.

January 23, 1833

My Dear Brother:—We should all be very thankful that God has led Jackson to do his duty in the present crisis so promptly and ably. I like the Proclamation, however, better than the Message, though the latter will do. The true policy now for the Nullifiers is to secede from the Union (i.e., according to their own principles). Their laws and ordinance rendered the collection of the revenue under the existing laws of the Government out of the question. Jackson proposes to alter those so as to secure the revenue, and render nugatory all that Carolina has done. If they go no further they are ridiculous. Besides standing on the ground of nullification they stand alone. The whole South as well as West and North pronounce that a heresy – but the advocates of the right of secession are ten to one to those who advocate nullification. As soon as they assume the position of seceders, they have the opinion and sympathy of a large portion of the South in their favour. If Virginia holds the right of secession how can she either aid or allow the exercise of that right being denied to a sister state? Beside the *casus* contemplated in the ordinance has so

[1] One of the greatest sculptors of classical Greece (c. 480–430 BC). [Ed.]

nearly arrived should the President's suggestions be acted upon, that it would be folly in them to think of hesitating for a moment. This seems to me so clearly the policy of these disorganizers that I much fear they will pursue it, and then, unless God in mercy prevents, we shall have hard times.

Your brother, C.H.

January 28th, 1834

My Dear Brother:—Nothing, I think, has yet appeared comparable to Binney's speech, except Webster's short expose of his views. Gold coin drops from his lips whenever he opens his mouth. He is still among the statesmen *facile primus* [easily first].

Your brother, C.H.

August 1st, 1837

My Dear Brother:—Is it true that Maryland is going with the Administration?!! It is beyond all comprehension, and affords another proof of the ascendancy of the rabble. If we could have a Republic with the right of suffrage restricted to householders, who can read and write, and have been at least ten years in the country, we could get along grandly. But a democracy with universal suffrage will soon be worse than an aristocracy with Queen Victoria at the head. I feel such an interest in that youthful sovereign, that I could acknowledge her authority with far more complacency than that of Martin Van Buren.

Your affectionate brother, C.H,

January 9th, 1834

My Dear Brother:—I have been reading Major Downing's Life and Letters. It is a most excellent and useful book! not merely for excellent humour and point, but for a complete exhibition of the whole nature, machinery and chicanery of American politics. It is grand. There are a multitude of letters which I never saw in the papers, and some of the best of the Portland, or real Major's production. Of the New York Major there are only two or three given by way of appendix.

Your brother, C.H.

August 17th, 1837.

My Dear Brother:—It seems that, notwithstanding all the country has suffered, the elections are going in favour of Van Buren, almost as much as ever. I do not believe we can stand it much longer. We must get rid of universal suffrage or we shall go to ruin.

Your brother, C.H.

June 7th, 1839

My Dear Brother:—The little Queen has my hearty approbation! Which she will no doubt appreciate duly. Sir Robert Peel has made a great mistake as far as I can see. He moved too soon. He ought not to have displaced the ministry until his road was clear, but having done it, to be frightened back by these ladies of the bed-chamber appears ridiculous.

Your affectionate brother, C.H.

Although heartily and conscientiously an American patriot, maintaining that the United States is a Nation, and loving it and admiring its institutions as more excellent than those of any other, he was ever proud of his part in the inheritance of Anglo-Saxon traditions and glories. Great Britain was loved and honoured as the Mother-country, and her history and prestige were sacred to him. Above all was he a life-long admirer of the Duke of Wellington, and the history of all of his campaigns and battles was known to him in all its various versions and critical details.

LAMENESS

The portion of his life allotted to this chapter was for the greater part a long scene of severe physical suffering and confinement. His affliction was an obscure affection of the thigh of the right leg; as to the nature and proper treatment of which different opinions were given by different physicians; and the views of the same physicians wavered with the changing aspects of the case. The final judgment was that it was an inflammation of the thigh-joint, which was arrested by entire rest and depleting treatment in its earlier stages, after which the cold douche and gradual exercise restored the tone and usefulness of the limb.

He had suffered much pain, and undergone treatment for the same trouble in the earliest years of his professorship. During his residence of two years in Europe, he was almost entirely relieved from any inconvenience from this source, so that he was able to climb over the ascents and the glaciers of the Alps for days. A result which Mr Hodge attributed to the salubrity of the climate. After he came home, for the first four years, he suffered only as he was limited in his powers of locomotion, by the weakness and tenderness of that leg. But in the spring of 1833, he was commissioned to canvass the Presbyterian Churches of the city of New York, for the purpose of collecting money for the erection of the new chapel for Princeton Seminary. He made several visits to the city, and spent many days in going over its vast distances on foot. The result was a violent and permanent aggravation of his disease. The pain became severe, the distress occasioned by walking unbearable, and the limb shrank in size. He returned home, and was put almost at once upon his back, and subjected to a most violent system of counter-irritants. While in Philadelphia consulting several eminent physicians, Dr Archibald Alexander wrote to him from Princeton:

PRINCETON, August 18th, 1838.
My Dear Sir:—I hope you will not suffer your mind to be disturbed about Seminary affairs. It is in every way for the interest of the institution that you should take the most effectual measures for the restoration of your health. Make this for the present your only object.

Composure of mind is one of the best medicines in all diseases. 'Be careful for nothing.' Roll all your burdens on the Lord. He knows best how to dispose of you, and what afflictions are necessary. We shall, I trust, get along very comfortably here. The students, when I was attacked, wished to have a suspension of all exercises for a week or two, but it was judged inexpedient. Several, however, have gone home, and will not return this session.

Yours, affectionately, A. ALEXANDER

When Mr Hodge came back he was put flat upon his back upon a hard palliasse, resting upon a narrow couch, moving on rollers. The policy of absolute rest was tried in the first instance, his body was perfectly and rigidly horizontal, and his right leg fixed immovably in a wooden splint. For months he was kept in that position, night and day, without change, until at last it was only gradually, and interrupted by many turns of faintness and dizziness, that he could be accustomed again to assume a sitting or standing position. In January 1834, the methods of cure began to be so far ameliorated that his limb was released from the wooden splint, which was replaced by a splint made of straps of steel, more elastic and capable of being easily carried while he was in a vertical position, and of being put on or off as occasion required. While reclining horizontally, by far the greater part of the time upon his couch, he now began to move somewhat about upon crutches. In June 1834, he tried sea-bathing at Old Point Comfort, the site of Fortress Monroe, Virginia. During August of the same year he tried the same agency with little effect at Cape May, New Jersey. On his return he was again almost entirely confined to the house, and by far the greater part of the time to a horizontal position. He slept by himself in the back parlour, where after so many years he died. His couch occupied during the day, from September, 1833, precisely the same position in his study as that subsequently occupied by his chair until the time of his death, a period of forty-five years. The chair in which all his students and surviving friends remember to have seen him either sitting or reclining was given to him by his brother, November 1839, and was thenceforward used by him exclusively as long as he lived. Indeed he did not leave it until about the end of his last sickness. He said pathetically a few days before he died, 'This chair and I for forty years have been growing to each other very closely.' This fact is a striking and characteristic illustration of his constitutional trait of conservatism – forty-five years reclining and sitting, reading, writing, praying and talking in one spot of one room. During all these years also he omitted on no single morning, when at home, to record the direction of the wind, and the state of the thermometer, and of the sky. He likewise, until almost his last years, resisted all the efforts made by a younger generation to induce him to have his clothes made elsewhere than at the same old shop which he had patronized from the first, through all its succession of occupants. There was no element of his nature inclined to new measures, any more than to new doctrines.

During this time, from the early autumn of 1833 to 1836, he was most heroically treated with violent counter-irritants. His hip, and thigh, and knee were over and over again blistered, cupped, rubbed with tartar emetic and iodine; treated with issues, and setons, and the moxa, i.e., burnt with actual fire from the hip to the knee. All this he bore, not only with bravery and resignation, but with habitual cheerfulness, and continued without serious interruption, constantly engaged in his studies and writing. In the fall of 1834, his distinguished friend. Professor Joseph Henry, brought his battery to Mr Hodge's study and applied galvanism to his limb, without any known effect. In the spring of 1838, he believed that he had made no progress toward recovery, and becoming impatient of the old methods, he urgently pressed upon his physicians the propriety of his trying either the hot springs of Baden in Germany, or those of Virginia. After much discussion and many plans, he settled down to trying the effect first of warm baths, and then in October 1838, of the cold douche upon his lame hip and thigh, in his own home. With the use of the latter, the tone and strength of the limb gradually returned, and he slowly increased his exercise, and laid aside first one crutch and then the other, and finally settled down upon the support of a cane which he used until the end of his life.

All this time of languishing pain and confinement, his general health was preserved almost in perfection. He not only was well, but he appeared to others unusually fresh and youthful. This is to be attributed to the strength of his constitution – the placidity and sunny cheerfulness of his disposition, his Christian faith, and his remarkable temperance in food, and regularity of habit. Few men have ever been known who possessed a more complete control over their appetites, and although his emotions were always strong, and on occasion uncontrollable, he was characterized to a remarkable degree by the faculty and habit of throwing off from his mind all painful or disagreeable subjects. On December 3rd, 1834, he writes to his brother, 'I have not walked across the room without a crutch for a year and a half.' He has marked as a note attached to his daily record of the weather, under date of July 16th, 1842, 'Preached in Elizabethtown for the first time since 1833'; that is, this was the first instance of his preaching in that time. Again, under the date of September 18th, 1842, 'Preached in the Chapel for the first time.' And on the 19th of June, 1843, 'Walked to town (the village) for the first time in ten years.'

During the worst of this time, the latter part of 1833 and the first of 1834, he employed at his own expense, with the assistance of a friend or two, of whom the sainted Dr Miller was the principal, the Rev. Austin O. Hubbard, of the last graduating class, as an assistant. Mr Hubbard relieved him of the Hebrew, while Mr Hodge continued to lecture on Introduction and Exegesis. Mr Joseph Addison Alexander was appointed assistant in his department, and entered upon its duties immediately upon his return from Europe in May, 1834 – declined his election of Adjunct Professor of Oriental and Biblical Literature in 1835, and accepted it, and was formally installed in 1838.

From the summer of 1833 to the 22nd of February 1836, with a trifling exception, in June 1834, Dr Hodge met his classes in his own house, sometimes in the study and sometimes in the back parlour. The rooms being crowded up to the edge of his couch with settees during class time, while during the intervals the settees were pushed together to the walls.

Meantime, it was evident that he was conducting his studies and using his pen under the most serious physical embarrassments. From 1833 to 1840 inclusive, he wrote twenty-eight articles for the *Repertory*, besides reading and editing all the rest. While at the worst, lying perfectly horizontal, and at times, at least, with his right leg in a splint, he wrote his reviews of Stuart on the Romans, and of Barnes on the Romans, his two articles on the *Act and Testimony*, which shook the Church, and shaped its history, and his own commentary on the Romans.

He learned then to write upon a board covered with leather held upon his breast by his left arm. This plan he practised exclusively until 1853, when he was with some difficulty induced by his wife to substitute for the board the table, which in the wood-cut of the study is represented as standing at the side of the chair. His later articles, commentaries and his *Systematic Theology* were written sitting at that table. While confined to his couch his books were placed in part in a revolving case, and stood in every available place on stands and chairs by his side, while, of course, at that time he fell back constantly upon the assistance of members of his family, to get his books and place them in convenient positions, and to read to him while he copied or translated passages for quotation.

THE GATHERINGS IN THE STUDY

The fact of his long confinement, and the further fact that he was in age and general qualities the central man, the common bond of intercourse and action among the Princeton Professors of that day, caused his study to be for many years the meeting place and intellectual exchange of both Institutions. Here during all these years the faculty of the Seminary held all its meetings. Here the Association of gentlemen which conducted the *Repertory* met for the reading and criticism of articles, and for the discussion and decision of the policy of the *Review*. Here all debates and consultations of general interest were held, and here literary strangers, visitors to either Institution, were brought to meet the gentlemen of the town.

Here almost every night for long years came Professors Dod and Maclean, and frequently Professors James W. Alexander, Joseph Henry, and the older Professors, A. Alexander, and Samuel Miller, President Carnahan, and frequently when visiting the town, Professors Vethake[1] and Torrey, and Dr John W. Yeomans. Thus at least in the eyes of the young sons, gleaming out from the corners, from the shadows of which they looked on with breathless interest, this study became the scene of the most wonderful debates, and discourse on the highest themes of philosophy, science, literature, theology, morals and politics. When Professor Dod was here alone, the time was also improved by playing chess, at which he was a distinguished master. Mr Hodge at that time attained to such skill in this intellectual game, that he held his own respectably, not only with his habitual antagonist, Professor Dod, but also upon occasion even with Professor Henry Vethake of the University of Pennsylvania, one of the most distinguished chess players of the United States.

[1] Henry Vethake (1790–1866), of Dutch Reformed stock, taught mathematics and political economy at various institutions, becoming the eighth Provost of the University of Pennsylvania. [Ed.]

PROF. HODGE TO HIS BROTHER

August 2nd, 1836

My Dear Brother:—I am glad you were in season to welcome your fourth son into the world. There is no reason for turning up your nasal member at boys. They are not to be despised. Happy is the man who has his quiver full of them, he shall talk with his enemy in the gate. If he turns out to be a good man, that is better, because a harder and a rarer thing than a good woman. Train him up in the right way, and leave the result to God.

Your affectionate brother, C.H.

January 11th, 1838

My Dear Brother:—I have had Dr Sweet[1] to see me! What a fall was there, my countrymen! I, the son, the brother, the husband(?), the father, it may be, of a doctor, harbouring a quack, illiterate and presumptuous. I suppose you will cut my acquaintance *instanter*. You must at least admire my courage in telling you. Send me a dose of prussic acid. Yesterday afternoon when I came from recitation I found a plain, respectable old gentleman, about sixty, sitting in my study waiting my return. He handed me a letter from a clerical friend, begging to introduce Dr Sweet, who, he assured me, had been effecting a multitude of marvellous cures in his neighbourhood, and entreating me not to allow the fear of quackery to induce me to decline his services. Here then was the man himself, of whom I had heard so much, who had been recommended to me by lawyers, bishops, merchants, ministers, sent without any agency or preconcert of my own. Was this not Providential? Would it not be a foolhardy rejection of a chance of relief to turn my back upon his offers of assistance? I confess I thought so, and felt quite moved. On conversing with him I found he was ignorant to a wonder. He informed me that the sciatic nerve was the round ligament; that the doctors were in a manner unaccountable to him, unable to discover a dislocation, when he

---

[1] One of a family of bonesetters and healers, the Sweets of Rhode Island, credited with many remarkable cures. [Ed.]

could see it in a moment. His whole language was that of an illiterate man. On the other hand there was much to inspire confidence. In the first place he was plain and serious, just such a man, they say, as General Harrison, whom you tried to make President of the United States. In the second place, his grandfather and his father had been bone-setters before him; he himself has done nothing else for more more than forty years. If there is anything in a hereditary gift, or if practice makes perfect, he surely might challenge confidence in his own calling. In the third place, admitting one-half of his vaunted cures to be imaginary, there remains a multitude of cases which cannot be questioned. I know of several on the best human testimony. Young — is one; Mr — of Rahway, is another, who had been for years under Stevens & Mott, and could hardly walk on crutches, who was dancing in a ball-room within a month after Sweet took hold of him. He is sent for all over the United States. He went not long ago to Kentucky, to see a Mr —, who had not walked in ten years. In a week he was walking about, and in three weeks he was riding on horse-back, and carrying on like a young man. For this cure he received five hundred dollars, and is to receive a like sum if the cure proves permanent. This last story is his own. He certainly has a wonderful memory, for he went into details, the most minute, about cases which I had heard of from other sources. Well, do you blame me now? Only the other day he cured (he says) at Mount Holly a young man whom Randolph had kept twenty-three months in a splint. He was walking about the streets when he (Sweet) left him. This is one of the cases my clerical friend referred to.

When he examined my limb, he pronounced immediately that the hip was out of joint and the knee also!! This was really too much. However he convinced me that my diseased limb is nearly an inch longer than the other. At least I did my best to make the measurement accurate. He was not unduly urgent for me to submit to his operation. He said it would not last more than ten minutes, nor give more pain than drawing a tooth; that it would require very little force, nor more than half his strength; that I could immediately walk about the house without crutches, and in a week or two walk as well as ever; that he never persisted in an operation when a patient complained or fainted! but used all possible gentleness. Even Sarah began now to give way, and urged that I should let him begin, and make him stop when the pain became severe. But I refused, and manfully held fast to my integrity. So after he had sat here four hours and a half, I paid him $5 for the expense of coming at the request of my friend, and dismissed him, saying, that as soon as I was convinced that my hip was out of joint I would send for him. Now if you do not glorify me at a great rate for this, I will send for him right off. For I am by no means sure that I have not acted like a big fool. He may be entirely mistaken in his absurd talk about dislocations, and yet, like those famous shampooers of the East, have a knack of cracking a man's spine, neck and limbs, greatly to his edification. I maintain I have performed a great action. Whether a wise or foolish one you must judge.

Your brother, C.H.

January 16th, 1838.
I feel unsettled and dissatisfied about myself, and you must not be surprised if (should we all live till spring) I should enter on some desperate enterprise. I have of late suffered more pain than usual, particularly at night. What gradual change there is in my limb is for the worse, I am sure, though I cannot trace its progress. I am also impressed with the belief that this limb is longer than the other. I have repeatedly had it measured since I first mentioned the fact, and always with the same result.

The idea that is now haunting me is the possibility of getting to some hot mineral baths. I should greatly prefer those in Virginia, could I get to them. But how to travel so far is the question, and the accommodations for bathing, I am told, are very poor. I have thought that by getting a dearborn wagon [a light four-wheeled coach] on easy springs, and large enough to hold my mattress, I might lie down and ride even over the rough roads, for the one hundred and fifty miles from Richmond. Were I rich I would venture on going to Baden, though I have no desire to cross the ocean again. By going first to London, then to Rotterdam, and then up the Rhine, I could reach those springs with little or no land carriage.

Your brother, C.H.

His brother, while with characteristic generosity offering him pecuniary assistance to execute his desire of visiting the hot springs of Baden, expressed his want of confidence in the proposed remedy, and in the virtue of natural mineral waters in general. Hence the following philippic[1] against doctors in reply.

January 29, 1838.

My Dear Brother:—I am going to write a philippic against doctors, founded on your last letter. If the public have no confidence in the profession you have to thank yourselves for it. You not only call yourselves pretenders, vain boasters, etc., etc., but make assertions which shock the common sense of mankind. For example, you say that hot water is hot water whether it be in Germany, Virginia or Princeton. This of course means that the hot natural mineral baths have no greater remedial powers than artificial hot baths. Now this, I maintain, is contrary to reason, to testimony and to experience, i.e. it is opposed to all the kinds and degrees of evidence that can by possibility apply to the case. It is contrary to reason that different things should have precisely the same effects, and hot water is a different thing from hot sulphureous water impregnated with iron, magnesia, and other matters. Secondly, a hot bath is a very different thing from those natural bathing places where the patient imbibes, exhales, inhales, absorbs and drinks down, for what I know, the fumes of these medicated waters hour after hour. Your assertion is contrary to the testimony of all classes of men. Dr Johnson says, that though he cannot explain it, it is still the fact that one grain of iron in the natural mineral waters produces a greater tonic effect than one

[1] A discourse full of invective. [Ed.]

hundred grains administered as an artificial preparation. Besides this kind of testimony there is that of those who, having tried the artificial baths to no effect, have been essentially benefited by the use of the natural ones. And finally as to experience, those baths have been frequented, in some cases for six hundred years, by hundreds and thousands of people. Are all mankind crazy? Might all these people as well have stayed at home, and sat down in a tub of hot water? Is a medical fact (the most slippery thing in nature, I admit) utterly incapable of being established even by the experience of thousands of years and of thousands of individuals?

I know your answer to all this – 'Charles wants to go, and he *will* prove it reasonable.' But I have no fancy for the journey nor for the isolation from friends and home comforts. I should rejoice to be able to believe that all the advantages of these springs could be obtained at home. As to the French douches, you forget I tried them all one summer to no purpose. The idea of comparing such matters with one of nature's steaming caldrons, in which the patient lies for hours at a time beneath a vaulted roof, inhaling sulphureous fumes, while his body soaks in hot medicated waters, is like comparing a trickle of tepid water to a thundering cataract. So much for the philippic, in which there is so much good nature, I fear it will be but a *brutum fulmen* [an empty charge]. You must consider it as written in great wrath.

Your affectionate brother, C.H.

He, however, submitted to try first the hot and then the cold douche at home, and afterwards rapidly and permanently improved.

June 5th, 1838

My Dear Brother:—We have had a visit of two or three days from the Rev. Samuel Hodge, of Tennessee, an humble, pious and sensible old gentleman. His grandfather came from the North of Ireland, and settled in North Carolina. He says the name is quite common in Carolina and Georgia, and he is inclined to think from the similar

physique, that all who bear it are of one origin. 'They are characteristically large men, with light complexions, friendly, *yet ready to
fight.*'

Your affectionate brother, C.H.

When writing his *Constitutional History of the Presbyterian
Church in the United States,* he consulted his brother as to the best
sources of information upon the subject of nervous epidemics, etc.
This he sought by way of preparation for discussing the history of
the physical phenomena accompanying the revival of religion in
Kentucky in the early years of this century.[1]

August 15, 1839

My Dear Brother:—You seem to think I meant to penetrate very far
into the labyrinth, of medico-metaphysical speculations about nervous diseases. You need not be apprehensive on that score. A single
page will probably embrace all that I have to say, but to write that
page, I should like to read a volume or two. A page will contain a
good many assertions, and I should like very much to be able to
make them on good authority. The phenomena of fainting, convulsions, jerking, etc., which have in all ages attended strong and general
religious excitements, I am persuaded are nothing but one form of
an *infectious* nervous disease, generated by strong impressions on
the imagination and lively emotions. If so they have nothing to do,
properly speaking, with religion, and instead of being encouraged or
tolerated, as they almost always have been by good men to the great
injury of religion, they ought by all means to be guarded against and
suppressed as much as epilepsy or hysterics.

Your brother, C.H.

October 10, 1839

My Dear Brother:—I was greatly concerned to hear of the suspension
of your banks. It must be a death-blow to the Whig party, as it will

---

[1] See Thomas Cleland, 'Bodily Effects of Religious Excitement', in *Princeton versus
the New Divinity*, Edinburgh: Banner of Truth, 2001. [Ed.]

turn popular clamour against all banks and their advocates. There was great joy in Washington when the news reached there, beyond all doubt. The sub-treasury is now inevitable, and we shall have all the loco-focos¹ dipping their straws into the molasses hogsheads of the people's money, and smacking their lips at a great rate. This is not the worst of it. I cannot see how the banks can retain their charters. If these are withdrawn, what a revolution of property must take place. How many hundreds, who depend on bank dividends, will have no income, until they can get their money back and reinvested, should the banks prove ultimately able to pay their stockholders. However, the Lord reigns.

With regard to your physico-theological investigation, I fear I can give you little assistance. You are beyond my depth. I do not know of any speculation on the subject, and I suspect we all know just nothing. We can only reason from analogy. A plant is a plant the moment the seed begins to sprout. It has all that is essential to its nature, not only as a plant, but as a plant of a certain genus or species. It has its own specific *vis formativa* [formative force], if that is anything more than an infidel expression for the divine energy. Still it has its own character from the beginning. So with regard to every animal. I should suppose it must be granted that it has its specific character from the commencement of its organization. If this is so, why must it not be allowed that the human being is a human being from the beginning? There is no greater difference between the new born infant and the embryo, than between the infant and a full-grown man. I should say, therefore, that the moment life begins, it is the life of a human creature, having all the essential attributes of such a being. And life begins when development or growth begins. The human soul, as I understand the matter, has no separate existence (in this world) from the body, nor the body from the soul.

If I can hear of anything on this subject, I will let you know. Do write to me and let me hear how the world wags.

Your affectionate brother, C.H.

¹ See p. 247. [Ed.]

October 15, 1839

My Dear Brother:—I am happy to hear of your professional success, and hope you may meet with many such instances to make up for your sleepless nights and laborious days.

I feel very much concerned about the poor Bank of the United States,[1] not only, and, as I fear, not chiefly because of the distress which her misfortune must occasion, but I am mortified as a Whig, as a Philadelphian, as an American. It is a shame, no doubt, to blame Mr Biddle and the Bank for measures, which, before the issue was known, were almost universally regarded as wise and salutary. Still his reputation must suffer, as there can be no doubt that the present result has proceeded mainly from his measures. The general causes, of which you Philadelphians speak, will account for the general pressure on the money market, but not for the peculiar pressure upon the United States Bank. You may remember that Mr Biddle, in his last letter to Mr Adams, said, that instead of restricting its operations during the suspension of '37, the Bank greatly enlarged them; that it advanced freely to planters and banks on the pledge of cotton, and he boasted, and with great reason, that he had thus saved the country millions, and had enabled it to pay honourably its debt to England; and now, he added, the bank should resume its appropriate sphere as a Bank. Unfortunately, however, the Bank was not able to get out of its mercantile business. It was still obliged to deal largely in cotton. Whether this arose from the premature resumption of *specie* payments, or from hope of gain, it is acknowledged that the Bank did deal immensely in cotton. It subjected itself, therefore, not only to banking, but also to mercantile risks, and now that cotton has come down, the Bank suffers. I have seen these things said over and over, and long ago in the English papers, and Mr Biddle censured for making the Bank a great trading concern. Add to all this, the large investments which the Bank has made in other banks, in railroads, etc., etc., thus locking up its capital, and I think there is no great mystery in the result. I sincerely hope she may weather the storm,

[1] The Bank's charter was removed in 1836 and it subsequently went bankrupt.[Ed.]

though it be at a great loss. Some of the newspapers are perfectly atrocious in their abuse. The *Journal of Commerce* calls it a broken concern mercantilely and morally, exhorts all the Philadelphia banks to throw out its paper as bankrupt rubbish, or they will all sink with it, etc., etc., and points with exultation to its stock at 70.

This is rather a strange letter for me to write. It is written before breakfast, while waiting for the lazy part of the family, and therefore may be a little crusty.

Your affectionate brother, C.H.

THE BIBLICAL REPERTORY AND PRINCETON REVIEW

Its History and Estimate of Its Character and Influence. Dr Hodge's Qualifications and Success as an Editor and Reviewer, His Associate Editors, and Principal Contributors

As has been above noticed, Mr Hodge began, in January 1825, the publication of a quarterly journal under the title of the *Biblical Repertory. A Collection of Tracts in Biblical Literature.* The design of this publication was 'to assist ministers and laymen in the criticism and interpretation of the Bible'. It had been occupied for the first four years almost exclusively with reprints and translations of the essays of European scholars. Prof. Robert B. Patton had acted as editor during Mr Hodge's absence in Europe. The translations had been prepared for the most part by President James Marsh, then of Hampden Sidney, Virginia, Drs James W. and Joseph Addison Alexander, and by Professor Patton and Mr Hodge. In January 1829, the entire plan and management of the journal was changed, and the 'New Series' of Volumes date from that year. It was thenceforward entitled *The Biblical Repertory and Theological Review.* Its object is declared in a long Advertisement to be, 1st, to furnish Christian readers with 'facilities for a right understanding of the divine oracles'; 2nd, 'to bring under strict, impartial review the philosophy and literature of the time, and show their influence, whether for good or evil, on biblical interpretation, systematic theology, and practical religion, in doing which it will be necessary to correct and expose the error of founding religious doctrines on isolated passages, and partial views of Bible truth, or forcing the Scriptures to a meaning which shall accord with philosophical theories'; 3rd, 'To notice and exhibit the dangers of the particular form of error prevailing in the period'; 4th, 'To present the history of religious doctrine and opinion, to notice the revival of old and exploded doctrines, and their effects on vital religion'; 5th, 'To consider the influence of different principles of ecclesiastical polity on piety, morals, literature and civil institutions'; 6th, 'To observe and sustain the various enterprises of Christian benevolence, especially the vast and growing interest of Sabbath-schools'; 7th, 'Such attention as the limits of the work will admit, will be bestowed on the important interests of general knowledge, and select literary information will be given in every number'; 8th, 'The work is not designed to be controversial in its character, but to state temperately and mildly, yet firmly and fearlessly, Bible truth in its whole extent.' This commendatory advertisement is signed by the following leading ministers of the day: Ashbel Green, Samuel Miller, Archibald Alexander, John H. Rice, Ezra Fisk, Ezra Styles Ely, Francis Herron, Thomas Cleland, Samuel H. Cox, Thomas H. Skinner, James Hoge, Henry B. Weed, William Nevins, Joseph Sanford, Thomas J. Biggs, Samuel L. Graham, Luther Halsey. Thus some of the strongest and most prominent partisans of each of the two Schools into which the Presbyterian Church divided in 1831 were in 1829 united in laying the foundations of the *Biblical Repertory*, destined to take so decided a part in the coming conflict.

The new Review henceforth instead of bearing the name of a single man, was edited by an 'Association of Gentlemen in Princeton'. These were Rev. Drs Archibald Alexander and Samuel Miller, the Rev. Mr Hodge of the Seminary, and President Carnahan, and

Professors Maclean and Dod, of the College. The Rev. James W. Alexander, then of Trenton, New Jersey, and Mr Joseph Addison Alexander, then of the College, and afterwards of the Seminary, were from the beginning copious and most important contributors to the *Review*, and they soon began to take a leading position in its editorial management. In 1837 the title was changed to *Biblical Repertory and Princeton Review*. In January, 1840, the *Literary and Theological Review* of New York, hitherto edited by the Rev. Mr Pigeon, in the interests of the old orthodoxy, was merged into the *Biblical Repertory and Princeton Review*.

Although conducted by an association of gentlemen from 1829 to 1855, Mr Hodge was the actual working editor during the greater part of the time, to whom fell the correspondence, the procuring of contributions, and in the first instance, their examination. In 1856 he again put his name on the title page as sole editor, which position of unrelieved labour and unshared responsibility he maintained until the end of the year 1868. Then he was fortunate enough to secure the consent of Rev. Lyman H. Atwater, D.D., of Princeton College, to act as his colleague in the Editorship. Dr Atwater had abundantly proved his pre-eminent fitness for this great office, by the ability and steadfast orthodoxy of his contributions to the *Review* for many past years. And henceforth, although Dr Hodge's name continued to appear on the title page as senior Editor, and he continued to share in its direction and to contribute to its pages, Dr Atwater discharged the major part of the work. After the reunion of the two branches of the Presbyterian Church, the *Biblical Repertory and Princeton Review* was in 1872 combined with the *American Presbyterian Review* of New York, with the title of *Presbyterian Quarterly and Princeton Review*, under the editorial management of Rev. Dr L. H. Atwater, and Rev. Dr H. B. Smith. And in the latter end of 1877 it was sold to the present editor of the new *Princeton Review*, a transfer for which Dr Hodge was in no degree responsible. He was the founder of the *Review*, and he continued in connection with it as sole or joint editor from January 1825 to December 1871, a period of forty-six years. Of the management of the *Review* by an 'Association of Gentlemen', which continued from 1829 to 1856, Dr Hodge writes in his 'Retrospect of the History of the Princeton Review' published in the Index Volume in 1868:

> The Association above-mentioned was not defined within very strict limits, nor was it controlled by any special terms of agreement. It consisted of the more frequent contributors to the pages of the journal, who were willing to assume the responsibility before the public of its character and contents. It included the Professors of the Theological Seminary, and some of the officers of the College. Although the labouring oar was still in one pair of hands, it was of importance that the work had the sanction of a number of gentlemen who had the confidence of the public; and it was a real advantage that all contributions touching delicate or difficult questions were read and canvassed by the Association before being committed to the press.

The most eminent and frequent contributors were Dr Samuel Miller, Drs Archibald, James W. and Joseph Addison Alexander, Profs. Dod, Maclean, Stephen Alexander, J. H. McIlvaine, Wm. H. Green, James Moffatt, Lyman H. Atwater and John Forsyth; the Hon. Chief Justice Lowrie, the Hon. Stephen Colwell, of Pennsylvania, and Samuel Tyler, of Washington. Dr Samuel Miller contributed between 1830 and 1842 twenty-five articles; Dr Archibald Alexander in all seventy-seven articles; Dr Joseph Addison Alexander, ninety-three; Dr James W. Alexander, one hundred; Dr Lyman H. Atwater contributed from 1840 to 1868 sixty-six articles; and Dr Hodge in all contributed one hundred and forty-two articles, averaging with his proportion of the literary notices, at least five thousand octavo pages, or ten ordinary octavo volumes. These articles of Dr Hodge were in the form both of essays and of reviews, didactic and controversial, and they ranged over a wide circle of subjects, including besides theology and biblical criticism, discussions in metaphysics and psychology, in personal, ecclesiastical and political ethics, and in all the range of ecclesiastical polity, constitutional and administrative, theoretical and practical, springing from the passing events of the time.

The grand characteristics of these reviews are knowledge, clearness and faith. These, in the degree and combination in which they existed in Dr Hodge, gave them the qualities of breadth, independence, moderation, conservatism, clearness of thought and style and eminent conviction. His religion was a personal experience. The most close and critical observer never in any moment of his living or dying hours saw in him the least symptom of doubt. That Christ is what he is set forth in the Scriptures to be, and that the Bible is the infallible Word of God, were facts inseparable from his personal consciousness. The logical force and habit of his mind made him see and grasp all things in their relations. All that he saw to be logically involved in a vital truth by which he lived, was to him part of that truth. Thus he experienced the whole Calvinistic system, and would defend it at all cost as the truth of God, from loyalty to Christ, and love for human souls. The whole was a matter of conscience and of life and death. Hence, also, he was apt sometimes, as his critics have successfully pointed out, to go beyond the warrant of historical fact, in asserting that the Church had everywhere and always held as he held as to secondary matters. Hence, also, he saw all truths in their relations. Defect at the circumference threatened heresy at the centre, and defective theistic conceptions of men of science in the various spheres of nature threatened atheism, and were to be met and vanquished at the time and place of their birth, before they had gathered strength, or extended their pernicious influence. Hence, also, from his logic, came the symmetrical form into which his essays were arranged, like an army skilfully set for battle; and from his faith came that momentum and penetrating force of absolute conviction which rendered the serried ranks of the attacking army irresistible. Hence he was transparently disinterested and essentially impersonal. He fought only in obedience to the Master, for the honour of Christ and the salvation of souls. It was God's cause, and all personal share in it was swallowed up in that awful fact, always and perfectly realized. He cherished inimical feelings to no man, or class of men, except in as far as he thought he saw they were opposing God's truth, and were thus knowingly or ignorantly dishonouring Christ and imperilling souls.

Only once in all his life did he strike out with an angry, personal intent, and that was in the article entitled '*The Princeton Review and Cousin's Philosophy*', April, 1856. The occasion was that Caleb S. Henry, D.D., after waiting seventeen years, had attacked Dr Hodge's friend, Albert B. Dod, eleven years in his grave, for an article on Transcendentalism published in 1839. He did strike in wrath the man who tore open the grave of his friend. But with regard to all other opponents, he had no other thought or feeling than that involved in the reverent defence of the ark of God. If others praised him, he rejoiced in their love, and thanked God, to whom only praise belongs, and from whom alone all graces come. If others angrily scourged him in their attacks or replies, then, after the first sentence in which he detected the flavour of the hostile animus, he closed the page, and refusing even to hear what had been said, he banished the whole thing from his mind.

He certainly missed much improving discipline, which his antagonists had laboriously prepared for his good. There probably was never another warrior of equal extent of experience who sat so habitually in placid unconsciousness of the missiles of the enemy, whether from the ambush or the open battle, whether the pistol or rifle of the newspaper, or the siege-guns of the great reviews.

The same qualities caused him to be both conservative and moderate. He was conservative because the truth he held was not the discovery of the progressive reason of man, but the very Word of God once delivered to the saints, and therefore authoritative and irreformable; and because reverence for that Word repressed in him all ambition for distinction as the discoverer of new opinions, or as the improver of the faith of the Church. The consistency with which, under all changes of times and party-combinations, he for fifty years maintained without shadow of change absolutely the same principles was very remarkable, and without any parallel in this age. He held precisely the same doctrines in his age as in the early controversies of his youth, and the same principles as to the relation of government to moral and religious questions, and as to temperance and slavery after the war as he did years before. He was always moderate also, because his loyalty to the Master made party spirit impossible, and because the amount of his knowledge and force of his logic caused him to see things in all their relations in all directions, by the aid of the sidelights as well as by the aid of those shining in the line of his direct vision.

Of the fact of his moderation, his whole controversial history is an illustration. Dr Ward, the editor of the *Independent*, notices this trait in an editorial on occasion of Dr Hodge's semi-centennial celebration, April 1872. The form and spirit of his *Systematic Theology* abundantly and conspicuously show it when compared with the representatives of the extreme parties of the Reformed Churches, as Beza and Gomarus, on the one hand, and Amyraldus and Placaeus, on the other. The same is shown by his position as to the questions of slavery, temperance and Romish baptism. At first he opposed the ultra-Old-School men in 1836 who were bent on the division of the Church, because the New School brethren were too bad to live with. Again, he opposed the same men and their successors in 1866 and 1868, who would precipitate the re-union of the two branches, because the same New School brethren were too good to live without. 'As early as 1855, some of our southern friends who had taken extreme ground as to the policy of boards, raised a further question as to the prerogatives of the Church respecting matters that had secular relations and bearing. Dr Hodge, in the Review, earnestly opposed the extreme action carried by a small majority at Indianapolis. A harmonious understanding, however, seemed to have been reached, after the warm, though courteous, debate at Rochester in 1860. But when the Church in 1861 (the Spring Resolution) apparently leaned over to the opposite extreme, he still adhered to the principles of the Rochester action. No articles from his pen have attracted more general attention or called forth more praise and censure than those on the state of the country and affiliated subjects. During the excitement of the times, the radical friends of the North and the ultra friends of the South criticized him with unmeasured severity; but the Church and the country appears to be gradually returning to his moderate position.' Thus the rock in the sea by maintaining through all tempests an unchanged position, at once opposes and measures the oscillations of the changing tides and of the restless waves.

He possessed in perfection that kind of bravery which, while perfectly consistent with humility, love of approbation, and love of ease, yet makes it easy for a soldier to do his duty regardless of opposing odds and of consequences. It is an historical fact that he quietly took the personal responsibility of the Princeton side of all the controversies for the forty years of the most momentous controversies ever known to the American Church. He just as often stood up in defence of his opinions in the face of opposing majorities as with their support. He alternately opposed both sides, and often stood almost alone, as before the General Assembly in Philadelphia in 1861. The press of the city, the mob in the street, the majority in the Assembly, the constituencies at home, were all violently excited at the futile opposition made to their wishes. Many men were swept off their feet by excited feeling, and many more were intimidated. One confessed to Dr Hodge: 'I am opposed to these resolutions, but if I vote against them, I can never go home.' But then, as under all other circumstances, for fifty years Dr Hodge stood fast where the Master put him. Not one of his debates or controversies was ever prompted by ambition, or by any inspiration of the mere *gaudia certaminis* [joy of battle], but in every instance he spoke by way of obedience as the servant and soldier of Jesus Christ. 'Here I stand, and cannot do otherwise. God be my help. Amen.'

Of the general character and conduct of the *Review*, Dr Hodge himself wrote in his 'Retrospect of the History of the *Princeton Review*', in the Index Volume, 1868:

> The conductors of the *Princeton Review*, however, were Presbyterians. They firmly believed that the system of doctrine contained in the Westminster Confession of Faith, the system of the Reformed Church and of Augustinians in all ages, is the truth of God revealed for His glory and the salvation of men. They believed that the upholding that system in its integrity, bearing witness to it as the truth of God, and its extension through the world, was the great duty of all those who had experienced its power. They believed also that the organization of the Presbyterian Church, its form of government and discipline, was more conformed than any other to the Scriptural model, and the best adapted for preserving the purity and developing the life of the Church. It was, therefore, the vindication of that system of truth and of the principles of that ecclesiastical polity, the conductors of this Journal, from first to last, had constantly in view. In this world life is a constant struggle against the causes of death. Liberty is maintained only by unsleeping vigilance against the aggressions of power; virtue is of necessity in constant antagonism to vice, and truth to error. That a Journal consecrated to the support of truth should be controversial is a matter of course; it is a law of its existence, the condition of its usefulness. The Bible is the most controversial of books. It is a protest against sin and error from beginning to end. To object to controversy,

therefore, is to object to what is in this world the necessary condition of life. It is, consequently, no just ground of reproach to this Journal that it has been engaged in controversy during the whole course of its existence. If it has always contended for the true and the right, and done this with due humility and charity, it has fulfilled its destiny. That it has often failed – at least in spirit and manner – may, and we fear must, be conceded. All such failures are to the surviving conductors matters of regret; but they can honestly say they have ever laboured to support the truth of God and to promote the interests of His kingdom to the best of their understanding and ability . . .

It is with unfeigned and humble gratitude to God that the conductors of the *Biblical Repertory and Princeton Review* can look over the comparatively long period of its existence with the conviction that from first to last it has been devoted to the vindication of that system of doctrine contained in our standards, and which, as all Presbyterians believe, is taught in the Word of God. No article opposed to that system has ever appeared in its pages. It has been the honest endeavour of the conductors to exhibit and defend the doctrines of our standards under the abiding conviction that they are the doctrines of the Word of God. They have advanced no new theories, and have never aimed at originality. Whether it be a ground of reproach or of approbation, it is believed to be true that an original idea in theology is not to be found in the pages of the *Biblical Repertory and Princeton Review* from the beginning until now. The phrase 'Princeton Theology', therefore, is without distinctive meaning.

The following interesting testimonies as to the character and conduct of this *Review* is furnished by independent and competent witnesses. The *British Quarterly Review*, in an article on the American Press, January 1871, says:

The *Princeton Review* is the oldest Quarterly in the United States. It was established in 1825 by Charles Hodge, the well-known commentator on the Epistle to the Romans, a Professor in Princeton Theological Seminary. It is beyond all question the greatest purely theological

Review that has ever been published in the English tongue, and has waged war in defence of the Westminster standards for a period of forty years, with a polemic vigour and unity of design without any parallel in the history of religious journalism. If we were called to name any living writer who, to Calvin's exegetical tact, unites a large measure of Calvin's grasp of mind and transcendent clearness in the department of systematic theology, we should point to this Princeton Professor. He possesses, to use the words of an English critic, the power of seizing and retaining with a rare vigour and tenacity the great doctrinal turning-points in a controversy, while he is able to expose with triumphant dexterity the various subterfuges under which it has been brought to elude them. His articles furnish a remarkably full and exact repository of historic and polemic theology. The great characteristic of his mind is the polemic element; accordingly we find him in collision with Moses Stuart, of Andover, in 1833, and with Albert Barnes in 1835, on the doctrine of imputation; with Prof. Park, in 1851, on 'The Theology of the Intellect and the Theology of the Feelings'; with Dr Nevin, of the *Mercersburg Review,* in 1848, on the subject of the 'Mystical Presence'; with Prof. Schaff, in 1854, on the doctrine of historical development; and with Horace Bushnell in 1866 on vicarious sacrifice. In fact, a historical duel has been going on between Andover and Princeton for over forty years, the leading controversialists of Andover being Stuart, Park, Edward Beecher, Baird and Fisher, and those of Princeton Hodge, the Alexanders and Atwater. The articles in the *Princeton Review* on science, philosophy, literature and history have generally displayed large culture and research. The review of Cousin's Philosophy, in 1839, by Professor Dod, was one of the most remarkable papers that appeared on the subject in America, and was afterward reprinted separately on both sides of the Atlantic.

Prof. James Macgregor, D.D., of the New College, Edinburgh, in an article in the British and Foreign Evangelical Review for July 1874, on 'Dr Charles Hodge and the Princeton School', says:

In thus speaking of Dr Alexander we are not led away from Dr Hodge. The two men are only two parts of one whole. We might set the matter thus: – Alexander was the Socrates of the Princeton School, and Hodge has proved to be its Plato and Aristotle. The two between them have been the leading power in eliciting a school of Christian thought, which more and more manifestly, is destined to be the dominant thought of Christian America.

The Princeton school has been markedly Biblical in its thinking. Dr Archibald Alexander was all his life-long an enthusiast in biblical studies, especially in relation to hermeneutics and criticism. His son, Joseph Addison, author of the learned commentaries on Isaiah and the Psalms, who was reckoned a prodigy of linguistic erudition, devoted his whole life to the study and exposition of Scripture. The *Princeton Review* was at first, for some years a *Biblical Repertory*, directly devoted to the expiscation [examination] of questions regarding Holy Writ. Dr Hodge, the now acknowledged Coryphaeus of the school, had been twenty years Professor of Biblical Theology before he became Professor of Systematic Theology. The influence of this biblical culture appears not only in his production of commentaries on the Romans and Corinthians, but appears most clearly and fully of all in his great work now completed of Systematic Theology.

The manner of the Princeton School has been peculiar. Controversy is perhaps not a good test of Christian character. The proverbial *odium theologicum* [theological hatred] may be really creditable to the theologians as a class, because evincing the glowing earnestness of their convictions. Still we cannot close our eyes to the fact that controversy brings about surprising revelations of natural character. Some men, heretofore supposed to be simply saints, will betray a frailness in the fibre of their manhood. Other men will evince a firm fibre of manhood, either by sweet and uncomplaining acceptance of defeat, or by magnanimous forbearance and kindness towards those over whom they have got the upper hand. This greatness of nature has been exhibited in remarkable measure from first to last by the Princeton school in general, and by Dr Hodge in particular. They have in their controversies been earnest, eloquent, warm, even passionate; but so far as we know, they have invariably spoken as true Christian gentlemen, who in relation to adversaries make due allowance for the fact that – speaking *more Americano* [in American style] – 'there's a good deal of human nature in man'. They have shown themselves to be manly men of the heroic type.

Dr Charles P. Krauth, the great theologian of the Lutheran Church, testified at Dr Hodge's semi-centennial celebration in 1872, 'that he (Dr Hodge) had always treated the doctrines of Churches and parties differing from his own with candour, love of truth, and perfect fairness'.

Dr Irenaeus Prime, of the *New York Observer*, said at Dr Hodge's semi-centennial, April 1872, 'I think, and I have had connection with the Press for thirty years – I think Dr Hodge the ablest reviewer in the world. Any one who has carefully studied the *Princeton Review* for the last thirty years will bear witness when I testify to the trenchant power with which he has defended the truth, and put forth the peculiar views which have made that *Review* a power in the Church and in the world.'

And in an editorial in the *N.Y. Observer*, the week after Dr Hodge's death, June 27th, 1878, Dr Prime says:

The *Princeton Review* in his hands was an army with banners. It did not array itself on the side of the Church, or of any party in the Church. It was the organ of his opinions. And they were set forth with no dogmatic stubbornness, but with such Christian meekness and deference to the Divine Word, that they carried weight with them as if his was the flagship of the fleet, iron-clad, that sailed in with victory on its prow. We recall a case in which the General Assembly, after one of the ablest debates ever held on its floor, came to a decision on an important ecclesiastical question (Romish Baptism) with almost entire unanimity. Dr Hodge reviewed the decision in the *Princeton Review* with such masterly power, as to set back the opinions of the Church, and hold it on the other side to this day. And to us this power of his appears the more wonderful, as we believed then, and do now, that he was wrong, and the Assembly was right.

The editor of the life of Dr Lyman Beecher says, with reference to the article of Rev. Prof. Albert B. Dod, July 1837, on 'Beecher's Views in Theology', that 'the *Princeton Review* was the most powerful organ in the land' (*Autobiography, etc., of Lyman Beecher by his Son*, vol. 2, p. 402).

Mr Hodge, whom henceforth we will style by his title of doctor of divinity, which was conferred upon him in 1834 by Rutgers College, New Brunswick, N.J., contributed to the *Review*, during the eleven years now under review, from January 1829 to April 1840, thirty-six articles as follows:

1829: Introductory Lecture; Public Education; Reply to Dr Moses Stuart's Examination of the Review of the American Education Society.

1830: Reply to Dr Moses Stuart's Postscript to his Letter to the Editors of the *Biblical Repertory;* Regeneration and the Manner of its Occurrence; Review of an Article in the *Christian Spectator* on Imputation.

1831: Sunday Mails; Sprague's *Lectures to Young People;* Doctrine of Imputation; Remarks on Dr Cox's Communication.

1832: Hengstenberg on Daniel; The New Divinity Tried.

1833: Suggestions to Theological Students; Stuart on the Romans.

1834: Lachmann's New Testament; The Act and Testimony.

1835: The Act and Testimony; Barnes on the Epistle to the Romans; The General Assembly; Narrative of Reed and Matheson.

1836: Rückert's Commentary on Romans; Slavery; The General Assembly.

1837: Voluntary Societies and Ecclesiastical Organizations; Bloomfield's Greek Testament; The General Assembly.

1838: Oxford Tracts; The State of the Church; The General Assembly; West India Emancipation.

1839: Clapp's Defence of the Doctrine of the New England Churches; The General Assembly; Dr Dana's Letters; Testimonies on the Doctrine of Imputation.

1840: January. Latest Forms of Infidelity.

The most important of these articles may be classified as follows for the purpose of a brief notice :

1. *Those relating to the controversy with Professor Moses Stuart as to the American Education Society.* Dr Hodge, in his 'Retrospect of the History of the *Princeton Review*, 1871', says on this subject:

> The first controversy on which the *Repertory* took an active part was the Education Question. In 1829 the General Assembly had reorganized the Board of Education, and called upon the churches to sustain it in providing for the expenses of candidates for the ministry in their preparatory studies. At the same time the American Education Society, a voluntary society having its origin in New England, and its chief seat of operations in Boston, Mass., offered to grant its aid to all suitable candidates for the sacred office in any part of the United States. Branch societies were organized in different parts of the country, and a large number of Presbyterian churches contributed to its funds in preference to the treasury of our own Board. In the July number of the volume for 1829, the late Dr Carnahan, President of the College of New Jersey, published an article on 'The General Assembly's Board of Education and the American Education Society', in which the objections to the plan of the American Society were briefly and clearly stated. This called forth a long communication from Professor Stuart of Andover, in reply. Professor Stuart's article was printed at length in our October number, with a rejoinder from the conductor (Dr H.) of this *Review*. A separate edition of Professor Stuart's article, with a postscript of sixteen pages, being published, that postscript was reviewed in our number for January 1830. This ended the discussion as

far as this journal was concerned. In this controversy, the general question of ecclesiastical boards and voluntary societies was not brought under discussion. The simple point was the wisdom, propriety and safety of the plan adopted by the American Society. That society not only required its beneficiaries to make a quarterly report, detailing how the amount they had received had been expended, and what each had received from other sources, but regarded its contributions as loans. All the candidates under their care were required to give their notes for the sums received, payable in one, two and three years after the close of their preparatory studies, with interest after the same had become due. All the candidates for the ministry were thus placed in the relation of debtors to the society, and must enter on their work burdened by this load of pecuniary obligation.

To this it was objected, 1. That the whole plan proceeded on a wrong principle. It assumed that the candidates had no right to the aid afforded; that it was a pure gratuity, which the donors, if they pleased, were authorized to demand should be refunded. This placed the candidates in the position of 'charity scholars'. Being so regarded by their patrons, they were so regarded by their associates and by themselves. This was an injustice and an injury. This journal took the ground, 'that whenever a man devotes his whole time and talents to the service of any community, *at its request*, it is obligatory on that community to provide for his support.' The recognition of this principle changes the whole status of the candidate. He ceases to be regarded as an object of charity. All ground for the minute inspection into his receipts and expenditures is done away with. He is regarded as a man receiving no more than he is entitled to, and for which he renders a full return. This principle, it was contended, was scriptural, lying at the foundation of the institutions and commands of the Bible. It was, moreover, evidently just and reasonable, and was acted on by all civilized governments in the education of young men designed for the public service, especially in the navy and army.

2. It was objected to the plan of the American Society that it was unjust to bring young men into the ministry burdened with debt.

The salaries of young ministers are very seldom more than sufficient for their support, and in the majority of cases utterly inadequate for that end. If, in addition to providing for their necessities under these circumstances, they had to pay the money advanced for their education, they could not fail to be painfully embarrassed and harassed. To be in debt is to be in a state of depressing anxiety.

3. The Scriptures say: 'The borrower is servant to the lender.' If the plan of the American Society had been fully carried out, the great body of the younger ministry in the Congregational and Presbyterian Churches would have been in this state of bondage to that society. Every one knows that virtually and effectively the power of such societies is in the hands of the executive committee. Thus, some half dozen men, with no official relation to our church, would have this controlling power over our ministers. This was evidently intolerable. The objection was not that the power had been abused, but that it existed. It was a power of dictating to a large proportion of the pious youth of the country in what academy, college or theological seminary they shall pursue their studies. It is the power of deciding under what theological influences our future ministers are to be formed. It is the power of holding and influencing these ministers as bondmen when they come out into the Church.

4. This society was, in a great measure, independent of public opinion; first, because it elected its own members; and, secondly, because its income, so far as derived from the payment of the notes given by the beneficiaries, was not derived from the churches.

The General Assembly's plan was not subject to these objections: 1. Because the Assembly did not elect its own members, but was renewed every year by the Presbyteries. 2. Because its Board was not the creditor of those aided by its funds. 3. Because the candidates for the ministry were not under its control."

2. *Two of these articles, that on 'The General Assembly, 1836', and another in the January number of the volume for 1837, relate to the respective advantages of voluntary societies and ecclesiastical boards.*

Of this Dr Hodge said in his 'Retrospect', etc.:

Much greater interest attached to the controversy respecting the conduct of the work of missions, foreign and domestic. The General Assembly in 1828 reorganized its Board of Domestic Missions. The American Home Missionary Society was at that time in operation, and rapidly increasing in influence. At first, it seemed to be hoped that the two organizations might operate harmoniously over the same field. The General Assembly, as did Dr Green and Dr Philips and other leading friends of the Assembly's Board, expressed their cordial willingness that all Presbyterians should be left to their un-biased choice as to which organization they should support. But it was soon found that in the existing state of the Church, harmoni-ous action was impossible. There were so many interests at stake; so many causes of alienation between what became known as the Old and New School parties, that the Assembly's Board, under the control of the one, and the American Society, under the control of the other, came into constant and painful collision. This of necessity gave rise to serious conflicts in the General Assembly. The friends of the American Society took the ground that the Assembly had no right to conduct the work of missions; that it was incompetent for that purpose; that voluntary associations were more trustworthy, more efficient and more healthful ; that two organizations for the same purpose were not only unnecessary, but injurious. They endeavoured, therefore, in every way, to embarrass the Assembly's Board. In the Assembly of 1836, they nominated as members of that Board men known to be hostile to its very existence, and secured one hundred and twenty-five votes in their favour. In the same Assembly they suc-ceeded in preventing the Assembly establishing a Board of Foreign Missions. One of the reasons most strenuously urged against the appointment of such a Board, was that the Assembly had no right to conduct such operations. On this point, Dr James Hoge, one of the wisest and most moderate ministers of our church, said: 'As the subject has been proposed in other forms, I have always objected. But the question is now brought before us in a new form, and is to be decided on the naked ground of the power and rights of the Assembly to conduct missions. And on this ground I cannot abandon it while I love the faith and order of the Presbyterian Church.' He further said that, if the majority pursued the course which they did actually take, 'it would convulse the church to the very centre'. And so it did. The action of the Assembly of 1836 in reference to matters of doctrine and to the Boards of the Church, was the proximate cause of the disruption which occurred in the following year.

The question of Voluntary Societies was not an isolated one. Its decision did not turn upon the point, which mode of conducting benevolent operations was in itself to be preferred. It was far more comprehensive. The friends of the Assembly's Board not only contended that the Assembly had the right to conduct the work of Missions, Foreign and Domestic, but that it was highly expedient that that work should be under the constituted authorities of the Church; that the selection, sending forth, and locating ministers, was properly an ecclesiastical function, and that it was to the last degree unreasonable and dangerous that that work should be committed to a society meeting annually for a few hours, composed of all who chose to subscribe to its funds, (which was the fact with the American Home Missionary Society), and to a large degree controlled by Congregationalists, hostile on principle to our polity, if not to our doctrines. Besides the objections founded on principle, there were others not less cogent founded on the action of the American Home Missionary Society. It was regarded as a great party engine, devoting, apparently, its immense influence to revolutionizing the Church. It sent out men educated in New England, holding sentiments condemned not only by Old School Presbyterians, but by the Woods, Tylers, Nettletons, of New England, and by such men as Drs Richards, Fisher and Griffin of our own church. Its friends and beneficiaries voted *en masse* in the General Assembly against the condemnation of those sentiments, and in favour of allowing men never ordained as elders, sitting and voting in our highest judicatories. It is no wonder, therefore, that this controversy excited so much feeling.

Throughout the struggle this journal sided uniformly and earnestly with the friends of the Assembly's Boards.

3. A third class of articles are those on 'Imputation', 'Regeneration, and the Manner of its Occurrence', and 'The New Divinity Tried', which, together with his *Commentary on the Romans*, first established Dr Hodge's reputation as a theologian. Of these articles he says in his 'Retrospect', etc., 1871:

As early in the history of this *Journal* as 1830, Dr Archibald Alexander published two articles, one on 'The Early History of Pelagianism', the other on 'The Doctrine of the Church on Original Sin',[1] and, in 1832, another on 'The Articles of the Synod of Dort'. To the first of these the *Christian Spectator* for June 1830, published a critique, over the signature of 'A Protestant' (Prof Stuart), which was reviewed (by Dr Hodge) in our October number for the same year. The discussion was continued in the *Spectator*, in the number for March 1831, which contained two articles in reply to our review; one from 'Protestant', and the other from the editors, continued and completed in the June number. Of these articles this journal contained a review published in October of the same year (on 'The Doctrine of Imputation' by Dr Hodge). See also the article entitled 'Testimonies on the Doctrine of Imputation', 1839, of which twenty-four pages are filled with quotations from the Protestant Confessions and Theologians, in support of that doctrine. The same subject was discussed in review of Professor Stuart's Commentary on the Epistle to the Romans, 1833, and of Mr Barnes' Commentary on the same Epistle, 1835, and incidentally in several other communications in subsequent years.

At the same time the doctrine of Regeneration was under discussion. It was maintained, by some prominent theologians among us, that regeneration was the sinner's own act; that it consisted in his making for himself 'a new heart'. What that was, was differently explained. According to some it was loving God; according to others, it was the

---

[1] These two articles, together with 'The New Divinity Tried', have been reprinted in *Princeton versus the New Divinity*, Edinburgh: Banner of Truth, 2001. [Ed.]

purpose to seek happiness in God instead of in the world; according to others, it was the purpose to seek the happiness of the universe. According to all the new views, man was active in regeneration. The idea of passivity, as it was called, was held up to ridicule. The old doctrine, common to all Christian Churches, that regeneration is the act of God; that man is the subject, and not the agent of the change; and that it consists in the quickening of the soul, or imparting to it a new principle of life, a new disposition, or, in the old scholastic language, 'a new habit of grace', was vindicated in the article on 'Regeneration, and the Manner of its Occurrence' (by Dr Hodge).[1] To this article Dr Samuel H. Cox replied at length in our number for October 1831, which number contained our answer (by Dr Hodge) to his 'Remarks'.

4. *In 1835 he began to write a series of annual articles in review of the action of each successive General Assembly*, in which he furnished a brief recapitulation and analysis of the proceedings, and discussed the doctrinal and ecclesiastical principles involved. He contributed each of the articles of this series from 1835 to 1867 inclusive, with the exception probably of 1841. They contained a summary of the arguments used by the prominent speakers on each side of disputed questions; they are to this day of great historical value, affording information not elsewhere accessible. He says of them himself:

It is not the object of these accounts of the proceedings of the Assembly to give the minutes of that body, or to record all the motions and debates, but simply to select the topics of most importance, and to give the best view we can of the arguments on either side. We make no pretensions to indifference or neutrality. The arguments of those from whom we differ, we try to give with perfect fairness, as far as possible, in the language of the reports given by their friends. But we do not undertake to argue the case for them. This we could not do honestly or satisfactorily. On the other hand,

---

[1] This article also appears in *Princeton versus the New Divinity*. [Ed.]

we endeavour to make the best argument we can in favour of the measures we approve, using all the speeches of the supporters of those measures, and putting down anything which may happen to occur to ourselves.

Hence it has come to pass that they contain an exposition of his views of all the fundamental principles underlying the constitution of the Church, and its administration, and of the practical application of these principles to the various historical conditions experienced by the American Presbyterian Church during that long period. These, together with a series of articles upon the 'Idea of the Church' and its various attributes, which appeared from 1845 to 1856, are the source from which the important posthumous work on 'Church Polity' has been compiled by one of his best pupils, the Rev. William Durant.

5. *His reviews of the Commentaries on the Epistle to the Romans of Stuart, 1833; of Barnes, 1835; of Rückert, 1836.* For Professor Stuart, Professor Hodge felt and expressed the strongest admiration and gratitude.

We have, therefore, long been in the habit of regarding Prof. Stuart as one of the greatest benefactors of the Church in our country, because he has been the principal means of turning the attention of the rising generation of ministers to this method (philological and exegetical) of studying the Bible. This we doubt not is the great service of his life: a service for which the whole church owes him gratitude and honour, and which will be remembered when present differences and difficulties are all forgotten. We do him, therefore, unfeigned homage as the great American reformer of biblical study; as the introducer of a new era, and the most efficient opponent of metaphysical theology. Alas, that he should have himself fallen on that very enchanted ground from which it was the business and glory of his life to withcall [recall?] his younger brethren.

Mr Hodge's criticisms are directed to the exposure of Prof. Stuart's false and inconsistent metaphysical theology, as far as that was involved in his interpretation of the Epistle to the Romans.

> We have now surely seen enough to convince the reader of two things: First, that the doctrine of imputation is not touched either by Prof. Stuart's exegesis or metaphysics. It is precisely where it was before; and, second, that his whole exposition of Rom. 5:12–19 is so inconsistent with itself that it cannot possibly be correct. In reading this portion of his commentary we have been reminded of a remark of Lord Erskine in reference to one of Burke's efforts in the House of Commons: 'It is a sad failure; but Burke could bear it.'

Dr William Cunningham, in *The Reformers and the Theology of the Reformation*, speaks in the highest terms of this article.[1]

With reference to Mr Barnes' book, Mr Hodge asserted that 'he had plucked his pear before it was ripe'. That it gave evidence of prejudice and crudity of opinion, and was transparently inconsistent in the various statements of doctrines it contained, was the product of a perverting controversial animus.

> We beg our readers to bear in mind that our review is not of an aggressive character. The book, which we have been examining, contains a violent, and, as we think, gratuitous attack upon some of the more important doctrines of the church. If there be, therefore, an offensive and defensive attitude in relation to this subject, we certainly are in the latter. Had Mr Barnes adhered to his design and given, according to his own views, 'the real meaning of the epistle without any regard to any existing theological system', what a different book would he have produced! So far, however, from his having no regard to any system, the system of doctrines contained in the standards of the Presbyterian Church seems to have been constantly before his mind. Instead of simply stating and defending his own

---

[1] See *The Reformers and the Theology of the Reformation* (1862; repr. London: Banner of Truth, 1967), p. 394. [Ed.]

views, he frequently and at length attacks those of the Confession of Faith. He goes out of his way repeatedly for this very purpose; introducing these topics where the passage on which he comments gives not even a plausible pretext for so doing.

6. There remain *a number of important articles*, the consideration of which, for various reasons, we must defer to a subsequent chapter. The articles on the 'Act and Testimony', October 1834, and January 1835, and on the 'State of the Church', 1838, will be considered in connection with the 'Disruption of the Presbyterian Church', under the next chapter. The article on 'Slavery' will be considered in connection with that on 'Abolitionism', under the date of the latter article, 1844. The article on 'The Oxford Tracts' belongs to a class of articles on the Church appearing from 1845 to 1856.

COMMENTARY ON ROMANS

It was during the period embraced in this chapter that Dr Hodge published his first books. His *Commentary on the Romans* was written during the darkest days of his confinement, the winter of 1834 and '35, while stretched horizontally on a couch, and his right limb often bound in a steel-splint. It was published by Grigg & Elliott in Philadelphia, but soon afterwards passed into the hands of William S. Martien. A cheaper and abridged edition for the use of Bible-classes was published in 1836. A new edition revised and in a great measure re-written was published in 1864.

Every good commentary on such texts as that of Paul's Epistle to the Romans must possess in greater or less degree two distinct qualities. It must show evidence of scholarship and exegetical tact and skill in the interpretation in detail of the words and sentences constituting the original text. It must also discover a comprehension of the subject discussed, and of the design of the writer and the scope of the ideas which constitute the subject-matter of the treatise commented on. It is self-evident that in Dr Hodge's *Commentary* the latter of the two characteristics predominates. He has done his best honestly to get at what the words and sentences mean. But he has written in a prevailingly doctrinal interest. And in expounding that doctrine he is as clear as a crystal in the sunlight. He gives an analysis of the epistle as a whole. He gives the contents of each chapter; an analysis of each logical subdivision of the apostle's argument; then a commentary, or exegetical discussion of each clause and verse; and then he presents a minute statement of all the doctrines taught in the section, and closes with a series of remarks illustrative and practical. The church at that time was convulsed with the controversies growing out of the intrusion into a community deriving its Presbyterianism from Scotland and the Westminster Assembly, of the new anthropology of the New England School. These 'improvements' were rather negative than positive, and involved a rejection of the consensus of the Reformed Churches as to the imputation of the guilt of Adam's sin to his descendants, as to original sin, as to inability, and as to the part of God in man's regeneration. From early in 1830 the *Biblical Repertory* had been engaged in an active controversy with the champions of the New Theology on these points. Dr Stuart and Mr Barnes published Commentaries on Romans in which the new doctrines were brought into association with the Word of God. Dr Hodge wrote his Commentary under these moral and ecclesiastical conditions, and he has striven to defend the ancient faith of the Reformation by a faithful appeal to exegesis, on the side which that faith presents to the hostile lines of what were then known as the 'improvements' in theology imported from New England.

In his new edition published in 1864, he again reviewed his whole work, and restated and defended his interpretation with the added light of Meyer and other German commentators, and with additional notice of the realistic theories which lie over against the truth on the side opposite to those New England theories against which, in his first edition, his energies were chiefly directed.

While writing his original *Commentary*, because confined to his couch. Dr Hodge communicated with Dr A. Alexander by an interchange of notes. Although they were all designed for a temporary purpose, and no effort was made to preserve any of them, it happens that a few of these waifs have drifted into the hands of the compiler. They are given because they illustrate the relations of the two men, and because they prove, what has sometimes been denied, that Dr Hodge never departed from the theology of his beloved teacher.

DR A. ALEXANDER TO DR HODGE

My Dear Sir:—I have read over with some care the whole of these sheets. I am truly thankful that you have been enabled to write so much in the diseased state of your body, and I sincerely rejoice that God has helped you so thoroughly to expound this difficult and important portion of divine revelation. In the main, I am deeply persuaded that you have brought to view the doctrines which the Holy Ghost intended to reveal by the pen of Paul. In a few minor points I hesitate as to the correctness of your interpretation. It seems to me that there is less clearness and lucid order in your exposition of the fourth chapter than of any other, as far as you have gone. Indeed, this part is more involved and intricate than any other. I think your exposition of the latter part of the fifth chapter is admirable. It exhibits the truth with a lustre that cannot easily be resisted. I cannot easily express how much good will probably result from the publication of this exposition. The language of the whole is characterized by simplicity and conciseness, and needs no improvement.

The parts entitled 'Doctrines' and 'Remarks', especially the latter, might be advantageously amplified. There are too many parentheses. Often the sentence would be more perspicuous by leaving out the dashes and parentheses.

Some method must be invented to prevent the *Commentary* from being encumbered with the references. Consult James and Addison on this point. The text of each chapter had better be placed at the beginning of the Commentary.

When your exposition depends on a criticism of the original words, it will be best to subjoin a critical note at the bottom of the page; but let the text of your Commentary be pure English. By this means it will be studied by all intelligent Presbyterians, and will become a *hand-book* for teachers of Sunday Schools and Bible Classes.

I entreat you to go on with the work as speedily as you can. I am anxious to have it in general circulation. It ought to be so continued as to make an 8vo. volume of 500 pages.

I assure you I have not for a long time read anything with so much interest as these sheets.

I am affectionately yours, A. ALEXANDER

DR HODGE TO DR A. ALEXANDER

My Dear Sir:—Few things in my life have given me more pleasure than the approbation which you expressed of the part of the *Commentary on the Romans*, which you were kind enough to look over. I trust, too, that I shall derive great good from having the prospect of usefulness presented as something attainable.

I will endeavour to profit by all your suggestions. I feared that the *Commentary* on the fourth chapter would not be satisfactory to others, as it is not to myself. I find great difficulty often where there seems to be the least. Though I would not make the remark as an apology for my failure in this case, yet there seem to be many passages in which the sacred writers, who wrote as men, are obscure and confused in themselves. In many cases of apparent confusion there is a real principle of logical arrangement which it requires only a little attention to discover and exhibit. But in others there seems to be no such principle any more than there is in the 119th Psalm. This remark, I know, very rarely applies to the writings of Paul, and certainly not to the former part, at least, of the fourth chapter.

I now send you the Commentary on chapters vi. and vii. As a great part of the paper is written upon only on one side, it appears much longer than it really is. In looking over the *Commentary* on the early part of the sixth chapter, which I think peculiarly difficult, I feel a good deal dissatisfied. It has to myself the appearance of being written during the actual process of studying out the meaning of the passage, and might, perhaps, be improved as to clearness by being written over again.

I feel grateful to you for taking the trouble to read my manuscript. You can hardly know how much peace of mind your *imprimatur*, my revered Father, gives me.

Very respectfully,
C. Hodge

DR A. ALEXANDER TO DR HODGE

My Dear Sir:—I have cursorily read your manuscript on the sixth and seventh chapters of the Romans. As before, I think you have done best on the most difficult and disputed part. The opinion which I have formed of the exposition of the two chapters bears a near analogy to the opinion which I have already expressed on the fourth and fifth. I do not think of anything that could improve the seventh. It comes up fully to my ideas of the apostle's meaning; and I have no objection to make to the exegesis of the sixth, but it is not so luminous as the exegesis of the seventh. The only thing which I would like to have added is a few observations on the meaning of the phrase 'buried with him in baptism', to show that it does not necessarily relate to immersion. Readers will expect something of this kind.

If you live to execute this work, you may be contented to say, if it should be the will of God, 'Now lettest thou thy servant depart in peace, etc.' I do believe that it will do more to confirm the orthodox faith of our church than any book which has been published for a century. I must still exhort you, therefore, to labour at it as much and as fast as you can. Some measures ought to be taken to have the printing commenced by the beginning of winter.

Yours affectionately, A.A.

My Dear Sir:—The eighth chapter of Romans is, at the same time, one of the most precious and difficult portions of Scripture.

Forty years ago I was led to study the first part of it from hearing an Arminian preacher expound it very ingeniously on Arminian principles. For some time I hesitated whether his exposition was not correct, but after studying it intensely, as I travelled on my mission, I came ultimately to the same views of its meaning as those which you have given in your *Commentary*. And all subsequent examinations have confirmed the opinions then adopted. But I can scarcely designate a portion of Scripture in which all the expressions are so susceptible of a double meaning.

On the very 'vexed passage' about 'the creature being subject to vanity' you have also given my opinion exactly. Dr J. P. Wilson, Dr Green, and, I believe. Dr Miller, held that by κτίσις [creature] the body should be understood. 'The redemption of our body' they considered as expository of the whole passage. Perhaps you ought to notice this interpretation, though I doubt whether it can be found in any respectable commentator.

The only passage in which I have any difficulty in adopting your explanation relates to the 'witness of the Spirit', which you seem to consider of the nature of the direct suggestion of a truth to the mind. Now this would partake of the nature of inspiration, and lays a foundation for enthusiasm. My opinion is that the witness is indirect by the illumination of the mind through the word, thus filling it with love and peace, and these graces, in present, conscious exercise, are 'the witness of the Spirit'. Please to re-examine the comment on this passage.

I am gratified exceedingly, and thankful to God, that you have been enabled to go forward so expeditiously in this work. My opinion of its value increases with the perusal of every new portion. As soon as you have reached the twelfth chapter you ought to prepare a prospectus and subscription paper. It will not be necessary for you to run any risk in the publication. A sufficient number of subscribers can soon be obtained to authorize the publication of a large edition. It will possess an incalculable advantage over Stuart's and other learned works, as it can be read by the plain, intelligent Christian, who knows nothing of the original.

Please let me have the ninth chapter as soon as it is completed. This will be easy after you have surmounted the difficulties of the eighth, except verse 3rd,

I am affectionately yours, A. A.

DR HODGE TO DR A. ALEXANDER

My Dear Sir:—I send, agreeably to your request, the *Commentary* on the ninth chapter, and a few verses of the tenth.

I cannot tell you how much your approbation cheers and encourages me, and especially the coincidence of the *Commentary* with your own views of the apostle's meaning. Fashioned as I have been by your hands, you can indeed hardly be surprised at finding your own opinions more or less correctly reflected from anything which I may write.

I find, on reverting to the passage, that what is said of the 'witness of the Spirit' is inaccurately expressed. I did not intend to intimate that the Spirit conveyed any new truth to the mind, but rather produced a new feeling. As when he 'sheds abroad the love of God in the heart', he produces an intimate persuasion that the soul is the object of divine favour. And when he bears witness to the truth he produces a like persuasion that the gospel is of God. In the case referred to in the eighth chapter, I suppose Paul meant to say that the Spirit produced the conviction that God regards us as His children. All these cases seemed to me to be analogous. All that I meant to say was what I understood our Confession to say when it refers our full persuasion and assurance of the truth 'to the inward work of the Holy Spirit, bearing witness by and with the word in our hearts'. This seemed to me something different from the mere judgment of the mind on the evidence afforded by the nature of its feelings to the fact of the divine favour. It appeared to me that the apostle, if the σύν in συμμαρτυρεῖ [he bears witness with] is to be urged, meant to distinguish between the evidence which consists in filial feelings towards God and the persuasion of the divine favour which the Spirit sweetly insinuates into the mind when those feelings are in exercise.

I should be glad to know whether you still think my views, as thus explained, incorrect. For, if you do, the *Commentary* can easily be still further modified so as to express the idea more generally, and consequently in a way less liable to objection.

Should Providence permit me to get to the end of the ninth chapter, I have thought it would be best to turn back to the beginning. The plan of the work has been so much enlarged as I advanced that the *Commentary* on the first three or four chapters must be re-written in order to make the work uniform. When the *Commentary* on the first eleven chapters is completed the printing might commence at any time; the residue could, Providence permitting, be got ready before it was required.

With filial respect and affection.

Yours, C. HODGE

Early in 1841 this *Commentary* was published in France. The translation was made by the Rev. Adolphe Monod of Montauban, at the instance of the venerable Professor V. A. Stapfer,[1] who had made Mr Hodge's acquaintance in Paris in 1826, and had subsequently corresponded with him. The means to meet the expense of the enterprise were collected through the agency of Rev. Robert Baird, D.D., the eminent agent in Europe of the Foreign Evangelical Society. In his preface Dr Monod said:

I am authorized to say that Mr Stapfer attaches the highest value to the *Commentary* of Dr Hodge, and that of all the works which have in our day been devoted to the Epistle to the Romans, there is none which appears to him, upon the whole, superior, nor perhaps equal to this.

[1] See pp. 120, 126. [Ed.]

It possesses qualities that are among the most valuable that can be desired in such a work, and which we have seldom found elsewhere so combined and carried to such extent. A pure and vigorous spirit; a simple and precise style; an intelligent and clear exegesis; a constant care to dwell upon those points which embarrass the reader of the Bible; a profound examination of all the great questions; substantial observations; solid and well-drawn inferences. When we add that there is evident in every part a spirit which is jealous for the divine doctrine and the divine glory, a soul deeply pious and ripe in the experience of the Christian life; in fine, an unction of mingled sweetness and gravity, which would almost lead one to conjecture that our *Commentary* was painfully written upon a bed of suffering, – our readers will understand the continued interest with which we have read the work from beginning to end.

Dr Hodge belongs to the religious opinion known in America by the name of the 'Old School'. His doctrine is precisely that of our own churches, and it is exhibited in the *Commentary* with remarkable distinctness and vigour. If we may venture the inquiry, we would ask as to this point whether the matter is not rather more precise and formal in Dr H.'s exposition, than in the Bible itself. We have learned from this Holy Book to have some dread of formulas that are too straitened, and of what Felix Neff, with his usual originality calls 'squared doctrines'. Happy are the authors who know how to preserve the proportions and balance which the Holy Spirit has observed in the development of the various topics of divine revelation.

The editor of the *London Patriot*, in a notice of Barnes' *Notes on the Romans*, naïvely remarks:

Mr Barnes acknowledges his obligations to Calvin, Doddridge, Macknight, Rosenmüller, Tholuck, and Flatt. We regret that he does not appear to have seen Dr Hodge's admirable *Exposition* of this Epistle, which would have been of more use for his purpose than all the rest.

HIS CONSTITUTIONAL HISTORY OF THE PRESBYTERIAN CHURCH IN THE UNITED STATES

In the early part of 1839, he published the first volume of his *Constitutional History of the Presbyterian Church in the United States*, and the second volume in the early part of 1840. This was for him the least natural, and most laborious work he ever undertook.

DR HODGE TO HIS BROTHER

Princeton, Oct. 12, 1838.

My Dear Brother:—I have before now read volumes to feel authorized to make one assertion. I want to state in few words what were the constituent materials and peculiar views of our church at the beginning, and to do this requires a good deal of previous reading. I am not the man for such business. My lameness is more in my way now than it ever has been, as I have to depend on others to make search for old things in my behalf.

Your brother, C.H.

The design and character of this work is stated in his preface to the first volume, March 1839.

During the past summer, the Rev. Dr Hoge, of Ohio wrote to one of his friends in Philadelphia stating that a work was greatly needed, which should give a distinct account of the present controversies in our Church. He conceived that in order to the proper exhibition of the subject, the documentary history of the formation of the first Presbytery, of the Adopting Act, of the great Schism, of the union of the two Synods, and of the formation of our present constitution, should be clearly presented to the public. The gentleman to whom this letter was addressed submitted it to a meeting of clergymen and laymen, who all concurred in the opinion that such a work ought to be prepared, and united in requesting the undersigned to undertake the task. The plan was afterwards enlarged, and the writer was led to undertake a general review of the History of the Presbyterian Church in the United States. The design of this work is to exhibit the true character of our Church; to show on what principles it was founded and governed; in other words, to exhibit historically its constitution, both as to doctrine and order. He has, therefore, ventured to call the work *A Constitutional History of the Presbyterian Church in the United States*. His readers will not expect more than this title promises.

Recent events have led to various speculations on the origin and constitution of our Church. It has been said that we owe our ecclesiastical existence to Congregationalists; that the condition of ministerial communion among us was assent to the essential doctrines of the Gospel; and that the Presbyterian form of government which our fathers adopted was of a very mitigated character . . . The writer was, hence, led to inquire what foundation was laid for a Presbyterian Church in the character of the early settlers of our country . . . The next subject of investigation was the actual character of our Church before the year 1729, as far as it can be learned from its history and records. The third chapter contains the review of our history from 1729 to 1741. As the act by which the Westminster Confession of Faith was adopted by the Synod as their standard of doctrine, was passed in 1729, this seemed to be the proper place to exhibit in full the testimony furnished by the records, not only as to the true interpretation of the act, but as to the condition of ministerial communion in the Presbyterian Church.

It is intended in a second volume to continue the history from 1741 to 1789. This will require an exhibition of the causes of the great schism, an investigation of the doctrinal and constitutional questions involved in that controversy, and of the principle on which the Church was settled at the time of the union of the two Synods.

It is believed that in the execution of this work Dr Hodge fully proved that the founders of our Church in the United States intended to plant a true Presbyterian Church, a genuine daughter of the Church of Scotland, and that the terms of ministerial communion among us have been from the beginning, and by the constitution of the Church continue to be, the real belief and honest profession that 'the system of Doctrine taught in the Holy Scriptures', is the one contained in the Westminster Confession of Faith and Catechisms.

The following letters of Dr A. Alexander to Dr Hodge, and of Dr Hodge to Dr Henry A. Boardman, on the subject of disputed points falling within the period embraced by this History will explain themselves.

DR A. ALEXANDER TO DR HODGE

My Dear Sir:—I do not know whether you expect any fuller exposition of opinion from me after making your explanations. The truth is, it is a matter in which I have no right to interfere otherwise than by expressing my opinion. I have no responsibility in the matter; but yours is great. You are writing a history which will probably connect your name with the orthodox Presbyterian name as long as it lasts; and you are not at liberty to depart one iota from what appears to you to be a correct statement of facts, and correct judgment on them. If other persons take a different view of either that is no reason you should change anything in deference to them.

I must, however, in candour declare that my own opinion, as expressed in a former note, remains unchanged. I object to the rule of the Synod on ground which applies to them just as it does to our Synods, namely, that the examination of candidates, with a view to ordination, is properly a Presbyterial and not a Synodical act. I admit that the Synod, as then constituted, might, after consulting Presbyteries, determine what should be required of candidates, and on what they should be examined, and might have censured the New Brunswick Presbytery for disobeying such rules; but it was, in my judgment, improper for them to take upon themselves to make the examination. On this principle, as the protestants argued on the occasion, they might usurp all the prerogatives and powers of the Presbyteries, and thus render them useless bodies. I never received the doctrine 'that a Synod is merely a larger Presbytery', and may do whatever Presbyteries can. Their business is to see that Presbyteries do their duty, and to attend to concerns which relate to the whole body.

The year on which I was Moderator of the General Assembly this principle was largely discussed, and in the first instance decided in favour of the rights of Presbyteries; but the Kentucky Synod came forward with great zeal and power, and had a different opinion pronounced next year. To this decision I never gave my assent, and I believe that more than one half of the ministers then were of like mind.

And I must remain of the opinion that when the schism took place, any attempt at a regular course of discipline would have been perfectly futile and unwise. They might, and ought to have separated with less heat and violence than was manifest, but it is evident to me that a separation had become necessary.

The subject of disciplining an organized body is an extremely difficult thing. The General Assembly of the Church of Scotland, under the influence of the high-church principles of Dr Robertson, undertook to discipline a Presbytery for resisting the exercise of patronage, and when it came to the punishment they selected one man out of the Presbytery and deposed him, not because he was worse than the rest, or a prime leader, but for other reasons. This very man laid the foundations of the relief Presbytery (now Synod). All that the majority could have done would have been to suspend the whole Presbytery, which was the same (in effect?) as what took place.

Yours, etc., A. ALEXANDER

DR HODGE TO DR HENRY A. BOARDMAN

PRINCETON, Jan. 1st, 1840

My Dear Sir: . . . As to the *History*, all my feelings are in favour of your Board publishing it. It would be effectually done without putting my friends, Dr Mitchell and others, to any trouble; and I shall be gratified in doing something for the Board. My judgment, however, is decidedly against the plan. As I must bear the responsibility, I must feel perfectly free to write as my judgment and conscience dictate. I know I should feel trammelled and uneasy if I was always thinking that what I wrote was to come out with the sanction of the Board. I have little doubt that the *History* will give more or less offence to a great many of our friends. I mean that kind of offence which men feel when they see a different view of any subject than their own presented. For example, the next chapter, which relates to the Whitefieldian revival, I suppose will be considered by many as very objectionable. This will be but a small matter if *I only* say what is disliked; but if your Board were to say it, it might be very offensive to many of our own friends. So of the 5th chapter, relating to the Schism, I am sure that many of our good old people will think it dreadful. I had received the impression that all the Old side were irreligious, unworthy men, and that all the New side were excellent and fervently pious. This impression, among the older ministers who received the tradition-ary accounts of that period, is so strong as to take something of the character of the original party feeling. Dr Alexander, after reading the manuscript, wrote me a long letter, telling me what he had heard about the character of the two parties when he was a young man, and how strong his feelings still were upon the subject, and his conviction that the Old side were a great deal worse and the New side a great deal better than I had represented them. This letter gave me, in one view, a great deal of uneasiness. I know that documents and books retain and transmit a very imperfect view of the spirit of any age, and therefore felt that my representation might be very far from the truth. But, at the same time, I must go by those documents, and to take the traditionary representations of those who had conversed with the actors in those scenes, and who had all the feelings of the conflict, would make a perfectly one-sided history.

I answered the Doctor's letter, stating how I viewed the matter, to which he replied that he would not have me alter anything out of deference to anybody – that he had no responsibility, but that mine was very great. I do not mean to give you the idea that the Doctor thought the *History* very wicked, or that he would object to my publishing it; but I do not believe at all that he would take the responsibility of publishing it, or of sanctioning such a representation as I have given of the violence and disorders of the zealous men of that day. It would require the gift of prophecy for me to be able to state what will be the character of the last volume, should I live to write it. I no more knew beforehand what the character of the present volume was to be than a stranger did. I indeed question very much whether I shall have courage to undertake the labour of bringing down the *History* to the present time. It may be too soon to write the history of the last ten years.

   All my friends here whom I have had the opportunity of consulting agree with me that your Board ought not to undertake the publication. If any one chooses to attack and abuse me, what harm is it? But to have your Board hauled up and abused is a very different affair. You have a very difficult and delicate task to perform, and will get abuse enough I doubt not. I think you ought, at least for a while, to confine yourselves to books of known character, and by no means to publish too many.

Yours very truly, C.H.

The *Constitutional History of the Presbyterian Church in the United States of America* was accordingly published by William S. Martien in 1839 and 1840. But it was subsequently copyrighted and published by the Presbyterian Board of Publication in 1851.

8

THE DISRUPTION OF THE PRESBYTERIAN CHURCH (1834–1838)

*The Historical Conditions out of which the Conflict Sprang –
The Several Parties in the Church – The True Position of the
'Princeton' or Conservative 'Party' – Dr Hodge's Own Statement
of the Principles on Which He and His Associates Acted – The Thorough Agreement of All the Princeton Men as to Principles and Measures – Misconceptions Corrected – Dr Hodge's Relation to the 'Act
and Testimony' – His Letters to His Brother and to Dr Boardman*

WE ARE CONCERNED HERE with the history of this great struggle only so far as this is necessary to the understanding of the part taken by Dr Hodge at that time. He was a young man, with no influence resulting from past experience or achievement in church affairs, and for the greater part of the time involved in the struggle excluded from church courts and confined to his room and to his couch by physical pain and weakness. Nevertheless, he was the most active member of the 'association of gentlemen' who edited the *Repertory*, and the author of the articles which attracted the chief attention and were the objects of the most hostile criticism by the strong party men on both sides.

The Presbyterian Church in America was founded by Scotch and Scotch-Irish immigrants. The Congregational Churches of New England were founded by English Independents. They originally agreed in doctrine, but were radically different in their principles of organization and polity, their traditions, and their tendencies. The English Independents settled the New England colonies during the first half of the 17th century, the Scotch and Scotch-Irish immigrants settled New Jersey and Eastern Pennsylvania and Delaware in the last of the 17th and the first of the 18th centuries. Subsequently, for the most part, the Presbyterians moved westward and southward through Pennsylvania, the Valley of Virginia and the Valley of the Ohio, while the teeming population of New England moved westward through the State of New York, northern Ohio and the Valley of the great lakes.

The two streams mingled in northern Ohio and western New York, and the exigencies of church extension in the new settlements led to the 'Plan of Union' contracted between the General Assembly and the Congregational Association of Connecticut in 1801. This plan was designed to promote harmony and to combine the heterogeneous elements of the population in the new settlements in aggressive church extension. It proposed to effect this end not by forming a new and compromising form of church government, but by providing for the practical working together in the same congregations of ministers and people belonging to both denominations. Congregational ministers were to be pastors of Presbyterian churches, and Presbyterian ministers pastors of Congregational churches, and Presbyterian and Congregational communicants were to combine in one church, appointing a standing committee instead of a session to govern them and represent them in the Presbyterian ecclesiastical courts. The effect of this was at the same time to stop almost absolutely the multiplication of Congregational churches, and rapidly to extend the area of the Presbyterian church by the multiplication of Presbyteries and Synods, composed largely of imperfectly organized churches.

In the meantime the American Education Society, in Boston, and the American Home Missionary Society, in New York, sprang into the most active exercise of their functions, equally within the spheres of the Presbyterian and the Congregational churches. They were both purely voluntary societies, subject to no ecclesiastical control, their officers elected and their action directed by self-perpetuated 'Executive Committees'. Their funds were drawn from the New England churches, and their affairs were controlled, in the larger part, by Congregationalists. New England, at this time, had in great part ceased to afford a field for home missionary effort, but on the contrary was full of energetic young men pressing into the ministry and ready to be educated and marshalled and supported in the field by the great voluntary societies above mentioned. These young men, of course, were educated as Congregationalists, and were imbued with the religious and theological sentiments at that time prevalent in New England.

These sentiments may be classified as follows: (1) The old Calvinism identical with the original and constitutional orthodoxy of the Presbyterian church. (2) That variation of Calvinism styled Hopkinsianism, which, while maintaining the essentials of Calvinism, denied the imputation of Adam's sin, the absolute inability of the sinner to repent, and a definite atonement. This type of doctrine, prevalent among Congregationalists, while foreign to the traditions, and uncongenial to the native Presbyterians, was yet never regarded as so far injurious as to be a bar to ministerial communion. (3) The heresies associated at that time with the School of New Haven, which were far more radical, imperilling, if not destroying, the church doctrines of original sin, and vicarious atonement, etc., and which were abhorred and resisted by the larger and sounder masses of Congregationalists, as well as by Presbyterians.

Thus it is evident that an immense and effective machinery was in operation for the rapid destruction of the integrity of the Presbyterian church, alike in its organic form and in the system of doctrines professed and taught. New England was the fountain; young New England missionaries the stream bearing with them Congregational church polity and New England theology;

the American Education and the American Home Missionary Societies the powerful engines; and the Presbyterian church the depository into which these foreign and revolutionizing streams were poured.

These were, in general, the unquestionable historical conditions of that epoch. It is evident that, without involving any one's fault on either side, sooner or later these conditions must precipitate a struggle for existence, and that the 'fittest' must survive. Either Presbyterianism in America and Congregationalism outside of New England must alike perish, issuing in some better third form, or in ecclesiastical chaos, or they must separate and each recover its constitutional integrity. Sooner or later the time must come when the true Presbyterians must fight for the existence of their inherited system and save it by constitutional means if they can, by revolution if they must. The Old School party among the Presbyterians of that day did fight for all Presbyterians of all time, New as well as Old, and for pure Congregationalism as well. The event has vindicated them beyond question as to their general purpose.

In a very few years after the disruption the New School Presbyterians followed the same course. They, in like manner, abrogated the 'Plan of Union', formed and exclusively patronized their own ecclesiastical boards, except in the department of foreign missions, and came into the Re-union in 1870 as thoroughly organized on exclusive Presbyterian principles as the other party, and tolerating in their terms of Ministerial Communion no variations from the old orthodoxy, more extreme than that falling under the Hopkinsian or Edwardean variety, above referred to, which none of the sober-minded among the Old School had ever deliberately regarded as putting a man beyond the pale. At the same time the Congregational church emerges over the whole north-western country, as homogeneous as in New England itself. Yet there is absolutely no evidence that the same result would have been attained if the denominational consciousness of the two rival parties had not been aroused and intensified by the conflict and division of 1837–8.

On the other hand, this same result, while it vindicates the general position and aim of the Old School party in the disruption period, vindicates specifically the peculiar position of the Princeton wing of that party. The subsequent course of the New School, as a separate denomination, clearly proves that in all essentials the majority of them were sound Presbyterians, alike in principles of order and in doctrine, the recognition of which fact in those days distinguished the 'Princeton' or 'Middle' party. There were in those days four parties in the church: (1) Those congregations and groups of con-gregations which were imperfectly organized, and those ministers and people who maintained the extreme type of error they styled 'Taylorism'. These occasioned all the trouble. Without them all the other parties could have coalesced together in a sufficiently homo-geneous Presbyterian church. (2) The New School party as a body. These were in themselves sound Presbyterians, although somewhat tinged with the Hopkinsian quality of theology. Their peculiarity arose from the fact that from position, antecedents and associations they were disposed to prevent the discipline of those whose opinions departed further from the type of normal Presbyterianism than their own, and to oppose the abrogation of the 'Plan of Union', and the reorganization, by force of ecclesiastical authority, of the churches formed upon it; and to keep the church open to the operation of the Voluntary Societies, to the exclusion of those under ecclesiasti-cal control. (3) The 'Princeton Party' or 'Middle Men'. (4) The Old School party in Pennsylvania and part of the South, who, under the leadership of Drs Green, R. J. Breckinridge, George Junkin and others, were convinced that the crisis was imminent, that the evils were so great as to be intolerable, and who, therefore, pressed urgently the prosecution of heresy, and demanded peremptorily either the speedy abatement of these evils or the division of the church.

The Princeton or Middle party was wholly Old School, adhering in principle and affection to the original normal type of doctrine and church polity. Of this there never was any doubt on either side. They desired to have the 'Plan of Union' abrogated; to have the churches organized on that basis reorganized or cut off by constitutional ecclesiastical authority; to have all ministers holding and teaching the graver errors then known as 'Taylorism' tried and excluded from office; to have new measures discouraged; and denominational Boards of Education, and of Missions, Home and Foreign, substituted in the place of the Voluntary Societies, which were really the organs of the Congregational churches. Hence, as Dr Hodge said, their 'feelings were always, and their judgment generally, in harmony with their Old School brethren and their measures of reform.' But, on the other hand, they did not wish to see the church divided either by the voluntary departure of the extreme Old School wing, which for a long time appeared imminent, or by the forcible exclusion of the great body of the New School, which the Old School leaders at least appeared to desire.

The Princeton men protested against some of the Old School measures, as, for instance, that Hopkinsian peculiarities, which should be tolerated, were indiscriminately confused with Taylorite errors, which must be excluded; that some of the measures were unconstitutional and injurious, as the procedure by the Synod of Philadelphia to try the appeal of Dr Junkin in the trial of Mr Barnes while the records of the inferior court were absent; and the use of the 'Act and Testimony' as a test of loyalty to Presbyterianism. They believed the measures pursued by the party men would divide the church, whereas the exigency for such a violent expedient had not arrived. The New School for several years had held sway in the General Assembly, interrupted only in 1845, and regained in 1846. If they had constituted the majority in the Assembly of 1847 the worst apprehension of the Princeton men would have been realized by the secession of the most determined of the Old School party without the succession and without the property, and the Presbyterian church would have been left predominantly New School, with a helpless Old School minority. When the Old School party found themselves in power in the General Assembly of 1837, the 'Princeton Men', as represented by Dr Archibald Alexander, voted for the abrogation of the 'Plan of Union', for the establishment of ecclesiastical boards, and for the excision of the Synod of Western Reserve. They regretted the peremptory excision of the three Synods in western New York yet passively acquiesced in the measure as one of 'substantial justice', but would have preferred the plan offered by Dr Cuyler, which summoned those Synods to purify themselves, and suspended their right to representation in the General Assembly upon their obedience. The 'Princeton Men' regretted exceedingly the secession of the 'New School' division of the church in 1848, but rejoiced in the assurance that neither they nor the Old School majority were responsible for that division, which they (the Princeton men) had always feared and had tried so loyally to prevent.

Dr Hodge says himself in his 'Retrospect of the History of the *Princeton Review*', 1871,

> In all the controversies culminating in the division of the church in 1837–8, the conductors of this *Review* were in entire sympathy with the Old School party. They sided with them as to the right, and under existing circumstances the duty, of the church to conduct the work of education and foreign and domestic missions by ecclesiastical boards instead of voluntary independent societies. They agreed with that party on all doctrinal questions in dispute; and as to the obligation to enforce conformity to our Confession of Faith on the part of ministers and teachers of theology under our jurisdiction. They were so unfortunate, however, as to differ from many, and apparently from a majority of their Old School brethren, as to the wisdom of the measures adopted for securing a common object. In our number

for January 1837, it is said: 'Our position we feel to be difficult and delicate. On the one hand, we respect and love the great mass of our Old School brethren; we believe them to constitute the bone and sinew of the Presbyterian church; we agree with them in doctrine; we sympathize with them in their disapprobation and distrust of the spirit and conduct of the leaders of the opposite party; and we harmonize with them in all the great leading principles of ecclesiastical policy, though we differ from a portion of them, how large or how small that portion may be we cannot tell, as to the wisdom and propriety of some particular measures. They have the right to cherish and express their opinions, and to endeavour to enforce them on others by argument and persuasion, and so have we. They, we verily believe, have no selfish end in view. We are knowingly operating, under stress of conscience, against all our own interests, so far as they are not involved in the interests of the Church of God.'

The FIRST point of difference related to the *Act and Testimony*, and the measures therewith connected.

Such departures from the standards of the church in matters of doctrine and order; such diversity of opinion as to ecclesiastical boards and voluntary societies; such alienation of feeling and agitating controversy had for years so disturbed the peace and impaired the efficiency of the church as to produce a state of things which on all sides was thought to be intolerable. With the view to reform these evils, and secure the peace and purity of the church, a meeting of ministers and elders was held in Philadelphia, May 26, 1834. At that meeting it was determined to issue an Act and Testimony, setting forth the evils under which the church was labouring, and proposing means of redress. This document was originally signed by thirty-seven ministers and twenty-seven elders. It was sent forth among the churches, and all the friends of sound doctrine and of Presbyterian order were exhorted to sign it. 'We recommend,' say the original signers, 'all ministers, elders, Church-sessions, Presbyteries and Synods, who approve of this Act and Testimony, to give their public adherence thereto, in such manner as they shall prefer, and communicate their names, and when a church court, a copy of their adhering act.' It was further recommended 'that on the second Thursday of May, 1835, a Convention be held in the city of Pittsburgh (where the General Assembly was to meet), to be composed of two delegates, a minister and ruling elder from each Presbytery, or from the minority of any Presbytery, who may concur in the sentiments of the Act and Testimony, to deliberate and consult on the present state of the church, and to adopt such measures as may be best suited to restore her prostrated standards.'

Many Old School men, as zealous as any others, could not sign this document. They did not object to it as a testimony against false doctrine; nor as a means for arousing the attention of the church; nor as designed to concentrate the energies of its sounder members for the reform of existing evils; but, 1. Because it contained assertions as to matter of fact, and expressions of opinion (not, however, as to matters of doctrine) in which they could not conscientiously concur. 2. Because it operated as a new, unauthorized and invidious test of orthodoxy and fidelity. Those who did not sign it were looked upon as timid and recreant. The editor of the *Presbyterian* (Aug. 21, 1834) said, 'We verily believe that every orthodox minister and elder, who refuses his signature under existing circumstances, will throw his weight into the opposite scale, and strengthen the hopes and confirm the confidence of those who aim to revolutionize the church.' 3. Because its obvious tendency, and as the event proved, its actual effect, was to divide, instead of uniting, the friends of orthodoxy and order. The document was never signed by a moiety of the Old School body. 4. Because the issuing a document of this kind, calling for the signatures of all sound men, who, by their delegates, were to meet in convention and prepare for further action, was an extra-constitutional and revolutionary measure, which many good and true men could not approve. They believed that when evils exist in any organized community, civil or ecclesiastical, redress should be sought in the regular exercise of the constitution and laws, unless the evils be such as justify revolution. 5. From the natural tendency of the measures adopted, and from the open avowal of some of the leaders in this movement, it was believed that if the party represented by the Act and Testimony did not gain ascendancy in the church, the result would be secession and schism. There were, however, many who believed that secession, under the circumstances, would be a violation of principles and a breach of trust. They, therefore, stood aloof and abstained from taking part in measures of which, as it seemed to them, schism was the natural consequence, if not the intention. They held that so long as the standards of the church were unaltered, and its ministers were not called upon to profess what they did not believe, or prevented preaching what they believed to be true, or required to do what their conscience condemned, to withdraw from the church was the crime of schism, which the Scriptures so expressly forbid. Moreover, they regarded the funds, the institutions and the influence of the church as a trust committed to their care, which they were not authorized to throw up or to leave in the hands of those whom they regarded as likely to abuse or pervert it. To abandon the church whenever an adverse majority gained ascendancy for a time in its administration, would lead to never-ending divisions and incalculable evils. Many of the signers of the Act and Testimony disclaimed any intention to secede from the church; but others, among whom was the venerable Dr Green, openly declared that such was their purpose. Happily, the matter was not brought to that issue. The reform of the church was effected without that sacrifice. Candid men, we think, will admit that the above-mentioned reasons are sufficient to justify the course of those who dissented from the Act and Testimony movement. Their conduct, at least, can be accounted for on other grounds than those of faint-heartedness or unfaithfulness.

The SECOND point on which the Old School men were divided, was the proper grounds of ecclesiastical discipline. Our ministers and elders are required to adopt the Confession of Faith, as containing the system of doctrine taught in the Holy Scriptures. No doctrine, therefore, inconsistent with the integrity of that system is the proper ground of discipline. It is not enough that the doctrine be erroneous, or that it be dangerous in its tendency; if it be not subversive of one or more of the constituent elements of the reformed faith, it is not incompatible with the honest adoption of our Confession. It cannot be denied that ever since the Reformation more or less diversity in the statement and explanation of the doctrines of Calvinism has prevailed in the reformed churches. It is equally notorious that for fifty or sixty years such diversities have existed and been tolerated in our own church; nay, that they still exist and are avowed by Old School men. If a man holds that all mankind, since the fall of Adam, and in consequence of his sin, are born in a state of condemnation and sin, whether he accounts for that fact on the ground of immediate or mediate imputation, or on the realistic theory, he was regarded as within the integrity of the system. If he admitted the sinner's inability, it was not considered as a proper ground of discipline that he regarded that inability as moral, instead of natural as well as moral. If he taught that the work of Christ was a real satisfaction to the justice of God, it was not made a breaking point whether he said it was designed exclusively for the elect, or for all mankind, etc., etc.

We do not say that the diversities above referred to are unimportant. We regard many of them as of great importance. All we say is that they have existed and been tolerated in the purest Calvinistic churches our own among the rest.

But within the last forty years other doctrines came to be avowed. Men came to teach that mankind are not born in a state of sin and condemnation; that no man is chargeable with either guilt or sin until he deliberately violates the known law of God; that sinners have plenary ability to do all God requires of them; that regeneration is the sinner's own act; that God cannot certainly control the acts of free agents so as to prevent all sin, or the present amount of sin in a moral system; that the work of Christ is no proper satisfaction to divine justice, but simply symbolic or didactic, designed to produce a moral impression on intelligent agents; that justification is not judicial, but involves a setting aside of the law, as when the Executive remits the penalty incurred by a criminal. The doctrines of this latter class were regarded as entirely inconsistent with the 'system of doctrine' taught in our Confession of Faith. In the General Assembly (O.S.) of 1868 a protest was presented against the adoption of the plan of union then before the churches, urging as an argument against the union the alleged fact that such doctrines were tolerated in the other branch of the Presbyterian church. The majority of the Assembly, in their answer to that protest, denied that allegation. They pronounced it to be incredible, on the ground that such doctrines were so obviously subversive of our whole system, that no church professing to be Calvinistic could tolerate them within their borders.

When in 1830, and the years immediately following, church discipline was invoked to arrest the progress of error, the Presbytery of Philadelphia included among the doctrines to be condemned those belonging to the first as well as those belonging to the second of the classes above mentioned. This was objected to by a large class of Old School men, and by the conductors of this *Review*, among their number, 1. Because, if the errors in question do not affect the integrity of the system, they were not the proper grounds of discipline. One of these doctrines was 'that faith is an act and not a principle'. But surely a man may hold this opinion and yet be a Calvinist. The immediate imputation of Adam's sin we regard as a very important doctrine; not so much on its own account as on account of the principle of representative accountability on which it is founded, which principle runs through the Bible, and is involved in the vital doctrines of atonement and justification. Nevertheless, it is notorious that the doctrine of immediate imputation has not been considered by our church as essential to the integrity of the Calvinistic system.

2. It was considered unreasonable and unfair to condemn one man for errors which had been, and continued to be tolerated in others.

3. This course was deemed unwise because it could not fail to embarrass the administration of discipline and to divide the friends of truth and order in the church. It was impossible that they could be brought with unanimity to concur in sustaining charges so heterogeneous, embracing doctrinal statements with which only a small

minority of the church could agree. We are constrained to say, with
great respect for the Presbytery of Philadelphia, that the censures
which that body pronounced in 1830 on the sermon entitled 'The Way
of Salvation', contained doctrinal principles which we do not know
a single minister in the Presbyterian church who is willing to adopt.
It makes the penal character of the sufferings of Christ to depend
on their nature and intensity, and not on the design for which they
were inflicted. We think that any candid man will admit that those
who disapproved of such a judicial judgment did not deserve, on that
account, to be deemed lacking in fidelity or zeal for the truth.

We do not wish to intimate that the books on which the Presbytery,
and afterwards the Synod of Philadelphia, founded their judicial
action did not contain errors which called for the exercise of discipline. We believe they did contain propositions which, according
to the unanimous judgment of the Assembly of 1868, any minister
should be required to retract as the condition of his remaining in
connection with the Presbyterian church. The complaint is that matters were included in the charges which even the friends of sound
doctrine could not regard as proper grounds of discipline.

The THIRD point about which Old Schoolmen differed was the
wisdom of some of the acts of the Assembly of 1837. When that
Assembly met, it was found that the Old School had a decided
and determined majority. The opportunity had occurred to rectify
some of the abuses which had so long and so justly been matters of
complaint. It was not to be expected or desired that the opportunity
should be lost. The abuse which was more immediately under the
control of the Assembly was the admission of Congregationalists as
constituent members of our church courts. This was as obviously
unreasonable and unconstitutional as the admission of British subjects to sit as members of our State or National Legislature. To put an
end to this abuse, the Assembly adopted the following report of their
committee: 'In regard to the relation between the Presbyterian and
Congregational churches, the committee recommend the adoption
of the following resolutions:

1. That between these two branches of the American church there ought, in the judgment of this Assembly, to be maintained sentiments of mutual respect and esteem, and for that purpose no reasonable effort should be omitted to preserve a perfectly good understanding between these two branches of the Church of Christ.

2. That it is expedient to continue the plan of friendly intercourse between this church and the Congregational churches as it now exists.

3. But as the 'Plan of Union' adopted for the new settlements in 1801 was originally an unconstitutional act on the part of that Assembly, – these important standing rules having never been submitted to the Presbyteries – and as they are totally destitute of authority, as proceeding from the General Association of Connecticut, which is invested with no power to legislate in such cases, and especially to enact laws to regulate churches not within its limits; and as much confusion and irregularity has arisen from this unnatural and unconstitutional system of union, therefore, it is resolved that the Act of the Assembly of 1801, entitled a 'Plan of Union' be, and the same is hereby abrogated.

These resolutions were carried by a vote of 143 yeas to 110 nays. Dr Archibald Alexander, and all the other delegates from the Presbytery of New Brunswick, voted for their adoption.

The question then arose, How was the above resolution to be carried into effect? In other words. How was the Congregational element to be eliminated from our body? Three methods were proposed. First: To cite the judicatories, charged with this and other irregularities, to appear at the bar of the next Assembly. This was actually adopted, but afterwards abandoned as likely to be cumbersome and interminable.

The second method was that proposed by the Rev. Dr Cuyler, the substance of which was a direction to the judicatories embracing Congregational churches to require them to become Presbyterially organized, or to withdraw from our connection; and refusing to such judicatories the privilege of being represented in the General

Assembly until this elimination of Congregationalism had been effected. The consideration of these resolutions was postponed to await the report of a committee, consisting of five members, from either side of the house, to consider the question of the amicable separation of the church. That committee reported that they unanimously agreed, 1st, That in the present state of the church such a separation was desirable. 2nd, They agreed as to the terms on which it should be effected; but 3rd, They disagreed as to the time when it should be accomplished, and as to the legal succession. The committee representing the majority insisted that the separation should be accomplished at once, during the sessions of that Assembly; the committee on the part of the minority insisted that it should be deferred for a year, by a reference of the matter to the Presbyteries.

On the failure of this attempt, the Assembly, instead of taking up the resolutions of Dr Cuyler, proceeded to effect the separation from Congregationalism by its own authority. This was done by what are called the 'Abscinding Acts'. It was resolved, first, 'That by the operation of the abrogation of the Plan of Union of 1801 the Synod of the Western Reserve is, and hereby is declared to be, no longer a part of the Presbyterian church in the United States of America.'

And subsequently it was resolved, 'That in consequence of the abrogation by this Assembly of the Plan of Union of 1801 between it and the General Association of Connecticut, as utterly unconstitutional, and therefore null and void from the beginning, the Synods of Utica, Geneva and Genesee, which were formed and attached to this body under and in execution of the said Plan of Union be, and are hereby declared to be, out of the ecclesiastical connection of the Presbyterian Church of the United States of America, and that they are not in form or in fact an integral portion of said church.'

It was stated on the floor of the Assembly that less than one in four of the churches in the Synod of the Western Reserve was Presbyterian. We do not see how any one can censure the Assembly for refusing to recognize that Synod as a Presbyterian body when three-fourths of the churches of which it was composed were Congregational. Dr

Alexander, who had voted for the abrogation of the Plan of Union, felt free, therefore, to vote for the disowning of the Synod of the Western Reserve as a constituent part of the Presbyterian Church. For the resolution disowning the three Synods in Western New York he could not vote.

The grounds on which the majority of the conductors of this *Review* dissented from the Act of the Assembly disowning the three Synods of Utica, Geneva and Genesee were: 1st, That it was not a legitimate consequence of the abrogation of the Plan of Union that those Synods, with all their Presbyteries and churches, were out of connection with the Presbyterian Church in the United States, and neither in form nor in fact an integral part of that church. Even if originally formed on the Plan of Union, if they had become, and so far as they had become, Presbyterian in their organization, and had been duly recognized, they were entitled to be regarded and treated as Presbyterian churches and judicatories. This is all the constitution required. This the Assembly itself admitted, as it promised to recognize any of the constituent churches or judicatories of those Synods, as soon as they reported themselves as constitutionally organized. But if Presbyterial organization entitled them to recognition it was a valid reason why they should not be disowned.

2. The presence of a few Congregationalists in a church court did not destroy its character nor afford a reasonable ground for refusing to recognize it as in connection with the church. Committee men (i.e. Congregationalists) have been allowed to sit as members of the General Assembly; and so were the delegates from the several Associations in New England. If their presence rendered the Assemblies in which they sat unconstitutional bodies, then all the acts of those bodies were null and void, and we have lost our legal succession.

It is to be remembered that the excision of the Synods in question was not an act of discipline; it was not founded on the prevalence of error in doctrine, or of 'new measures'. This the Assembly expressly disclaims. In answer to the protest of the commissioners from those Synods it is said, 'There is no judicial process instituted.' 'Without impeaching the character or standing of the brethren composing those Synods, this Assembly, by a legislative act, merely declares them, in consequence of the abrogation of the Plan of Union of 1801, no longer a constituent part of the General Assembly of the Presbyterian church in the United States.'

The objection to this action is, that the presence of a small minority of Congregationalists in a church court did not so vitiate its character as to justify its being disowned.

3. There were Presbyteries within the bounds of the Synods of Albany and New Jersey composed in part of Congregational churches, and yet the General Assembly did not disown either those Synods or the delinquent Presbyteries. This was an admission that the presence of Congregational members did not destroy the character of those bodies as Presbyterian organizations.

4. The action of the Assembly in disowning the Synods of Western New York was not necessary to secure the reform of the church. That end would have been attained by the due operation of the abrogation of the Plan of Union. The legitimate effects of that abrogation were: 1st, To prevent the reception of any new churches formed upon that plan. 2nd, To render it obligatory on all the Presbyteries to require the churches within their bounds to adopt an organization in accordance with our constitution, and to refuse to allow the representatives of Congregational churches to sit and act as elders. 3rd, To justify, and it may be to render it obligatory on future General Assemblies to refuse to allow Presbyteries continuing their connection with Congregationalism to be represented in those bodies. This would have effectually accomplished the reform contemplated by the abrogation of the Plan of Union of 1801. After having allowed for more than thirty years this union of Congregationalists and Presbyterians in our church courts, all that the Assembly had the right to do was to require that such union should forthwith and thenceforth cease. This was the ground taken by Dr Alexander and the majority of the conductors of this *Review* in 1837, and on which the few of their number who still survive (in 1870) still stand. What, however, was

regarded as very lukewarm Old-Schoolism in 1837 has now come to be looked upon as obsolete and narrow-minded. The Assembly of 1869, by a vote nearly unanimous, not only admitted (the abrogation of the Plan of Union notwithstanding) that Presbyteries do not forfeit their connection with the Presbyterian Church, although they include Congregational churches, but authorized, as far as it could do so, their being represented in the General Assembly for at least five years to come.

It was suspected and has been since charged that the gentlemen at Princeton were not perfectly at one with regard to the various questions which emerged during the contest, and that Dr Hodge was responsible for separating them from the more extreme Old School leaders. It is, however, certain that they were cordially agreed on all points as far as any men of independent minds could be on so wide a range of subjects. If there was any difference it was that Dr Hodge was more urgently impelled to speak out his whole mind, while others at times counselled reticence for prudential reasons. That they were at one is certain: – from the public action of Dr Miller in the General Assembly of 1836, where he voted to sustain the appeal of Mr Barnes, and then to condemn the errors contained in his book; and the public action of Dr Alexander in the Assembly of 1837, where he voted to abrogate the Plan of Union and to exscind the Synod of Western Reserve, but voted against the exscision of the three Synods of Western New York; from the uniform assertions of Dr Hodge to the end of his life, confirmed by the assertions of Dr James W. Alexander, one of the actors in the scenes, in his *Memoirs of his Father*, p. 480, and by the assertion of Rev. Dr Samuel Miller, Jr., in his *Memoirs of his Father*, p. 271; from the fact that the article entitled 'The Present State and Prospects of the Presbyterian Church' (*Bib. Rep.*, Jan. 1835,) is claimed alike by the representatives of Dr A. Alexander and Dr Miller, and was certainly written by one of them. This article is, *at least*, as decidedly and offensively opposed to the extreme action of the Old School leaders as anything written by Dr Hodge.

The only point as to which it is known that the conductors of the *Repertory* differed among themselves was with reference to the action of the Assembly of 1837 in exscinding the three Synods of Western New York. They habitually met in Dr Hodge's study to discuss every article of importance. With regard to this difference of opinion, Dr. Hodge has left a clear statement, drawn up at the time.

> *Note in Dr H.'s Journal* – July 19, 1837.—The conductors of the *Repertory* met a second time to decide on the article on the Assembly. Drs Miller and Breckinridge approved of the action of the Assembly respecting the three (New York) Synods *in toto*. Prof. McLean and Dr A. Alexander thought it might be justified, although not on the grounds upon which the Assembly placed it, and would have preferred Dr Cuyler's plan (this plan was stated above). Professors James W. Alexander, Dod and Hodge disapproved the Assembly's action, and would have preferred Dr Cuyler's plan, and they wished this idea to be expressed in the *Repertory*. It was decided to leave out that portion of the article (written by Dr Hodge) containing this expression, leaving it, as it was supposed, undecided how the conductors viewed the matter. To this course all ultimately assented, except Dr Hodge. He objected on the ground that the impression it would make, as it now stands, would be that the conductors decidedly sustained the measure in question. Dr Alexander, Prof. Dod, and ultimately Prof. J. W. Alexander thought that such an inference could not be fairly drawn from the language employed. The disapproval of the action of the Assembly in relation to the third Presbytery of Philadelphia was sustained by all the conductors, except Dr Breckinridge. Profs. J. W. Alexander, Dod and Hodge were afterwards strongly in favour of inserting a note of explanation.

With reference to these questions Dr Hodge wrote the following letters to his brother:

DR HODGE TO HIS BROTHER

Nov. 21, 1834

My Dear Brother:—As to church matters, I know not what to think, and you would find yourself in chaos were you to attempt an analysis. The Act and Testimony is doing what was from the first apprehended – splitting the Old School portion of the church. How far this will go it is hard to say. The Philadelphia men, Dr Green, etc., etc., are driving matters to an extremity, and if they succeed we shall be ruined for the next ten or twenty years. That is if by their ultraism a portion of the Old School party is broken off, it will leave the remainder completely in the power of the New School men and give them the command of our Seminaries, Boards and Education and Missions, &c., &c. I still hope this consummation will be avoided. It was to guard against it, and to warn the Old School party of the evil and danger of thus splitting the church that the article on the Act and Testimony in the *Repertory* was written. It has had the effect of making whole classes of signers declare that they do not wish nor look for a schism in the church. But on the other hand, the obvious tendency of the measure and the avowed design of some of its authors are to that result. That article has given prodigious offence to the Philadelphia men. The Synod passed a vote which amounts to a formal declaration of want of confidence in the Seminary. They propose transferring their patronage to Pittsburgh, or to found a new institution. I do not believe this will hurt anybody but themselves. No person here regrets as yet the publication of our article. We all think it will do good on the whole. As far as I know, the Synod of Philadelphia is the only one in the whole church which is what we call ultra. It is the only one, I am persuaded, which would have entertained for a moment the proposition about a new seminary on the grounds then urged, and therefore I feel a strong hope that they will find themselves in so small a minority as to be induced to keep quiet.

Your brother,
CHARLES HODGE

PRINCETON, June 11, 1837

My Dear Brother:—I have at once to prepare a history of the doings of this momentous Assembly, in which the New School have experienced a Waterloo defeat. Their only recourse is now to the law, which I suspect will give them small consolation. I think substantial justice has been done, though there may, in some cases have been some informality in the mode of doing it. I have little doubt the public sentiment of the church and of other denominations will sustain the proceedings of the Assembly as soon as they are fairly understood. The simple truth is, that the church has tolerated the Congregationalized portion of the body until its very existence was in danger, and it has aroused and shaken them off. I presume that the New School will form themselves into an American Presbyterian Church, and we shall have two denominations. I am very sorry the Assembly dissolved the third Presbytery of Philadelphia, and that in an unconstitutional manner. It looks badly, and was done by a very small vote.

Your brother, C.H.

PRINCETON, July 26, 1837

My Dear Brother:—Dod seems to have produced a great commotion among the gentlemen of the Old School party in Philadelphia. They sent a message up to entreat and expostulate, besides a multitude of letters filled with lamentations and prophecies of coming evil. These letters were, some of them, from very moderate men, such as Mr —, &c., &c. I presume Dod stated clearly enough how the matter stood to the few persons he spoke to, but the accounts were doubtless greatly magnified as they diffused themselves abroad. I do not believe that what I wished to do would have done any harm or have given any offence. The fact is that we are all agreed as to all the principles involved in the questions before the Assembly, and agreed also as to their application, except as to one case (the case of the three Synods of Western New York). With regard to this some were satisfied, and some were not (*i.e.* by the action of the Assembly). The *Repertory*, speaking the language of all the conductors, could not say anything which a portion of us could not assent to. My difficulty was that I believed the article, as altered by the majority of the conductors, did, at least impliedly, express approbation of the act of the Assembly in reference to the three Synods. I had no right to say that it should not do so, but I certainly had a right to say that the majority should not make me say so. I therefore insisted on stating in a note that some of the conductors, meaning Dod, J. W. Alexander and myself, felt that we had not as yet a sufficient knowledge of the facts in the case to enable us to see the propriety of this measure. This was resisted with great earnestness by some one or two as likely to do great harm. It was, however, a point which I could not yield, and which those who agreed with me were also unwilling to give up, The note was finally thrown into a form by J. W. Alexander, to which Breckinridge assented, and to which I agreed, though with a good deal of reluctance. It is less explicit than I wished it, and yet may be understood to mean more than even I wanted to express, and it now speaks the language of the whole and not of a part. After saying in the text that the summary plan of exclusion was undoubtedly constitutional in its application to all those Synods which could be clearly proved to be irregularly organized, we add in a note, that as the facts in regard to the three Synods in New York are in a constant process of disclosure, the full discussion of this question is deferred to a future occasion.

I had two reasons for assenting to this. The first was that all I wished was to satisfy my conscience, and not to be made to say what I did not believe. This note answers this purpose by saying that though satisfied as to the principles, we must wait for more facts before we can say anything as to their application. My second reason was, that I really believe, or rather expect that facts will soon be brought forward which will show the substantial justice of the action of the Assembly. How far this evidence was before the Assembly I do not know, and therefore cannot say, how far they acted in the dark. But if substantial justice has been done, that is the main point. I never had such a time in my life. On the one hand my own views of duty and propriety and even expediency were clear and unwavering. On the other hand the opinion of almost all my friends, and the vehement expostulations, appeals, and forebodings of a good many of them. Dr Alexander did just what he ought to have done. He said he could not see the grounds of my scruples, and thought the thing inexpedient, but gave his cheerful assent to my saying in the note just what I pleased. You may depend upon it, it is very hard for a man to act upon his own opinion, when opposed not only to the opinion of those he has been accustomed to reverence, but to the ardent expostulations and dreadful forebodings of others. I believed, to be sure, it was all nonsense; that no such terrible consequences would follow. However, I feel thankful the thing is arranged without producing a breach, and that I have still a good conscience. Dod and Maclean both think that the note, as it now stands, is a great deal worse for the Old School than what I wanted to say. You will wonder when you see it, how little a matter has kindled such a flame. The *Repertory* will not be made a party concern, I am persuaded. Its conductors would rather see it die.

Your affectionate brother, C.H.

It was inevitable, under all the conditions of the case that the excited leaders of the Old School majority in these conflicts should have been annoyed by the independent position of the 'Princeton gentlemen' and those who agreed with them. This annoyance naturally led to hard thoughts and derogatory language. No one at any time doubted their doctrinal soundness, but the entire class of men, wherever resident, was called the 'Princeton Party' to belittle it. They were characterized as 'moderates', 'trembling brethren', 'compromisers'. They were suspected of want of courage, if not of a supreme regard to their supposed temporal interests. Some New School men held them as weakly succumbing to the will of the Old School majority when, after protesting against the earlier steps in the controversy, they afterwards consented to the abrogation of the Plan of Union and the excision of the Synods. Some of the Old School charitably excused them on the ground that as secluded professors they were necessarily less perfectly informed as to the actual condition of affairs than active pastors.[1]

However natural these derogatory representations were at the time, they were absurdly untrue. The accuracy and wide extent of their knowledge of the state of the church, and the wisdom of their judgment has been vindicated abundantly by the events which, after thirty years, led to reunion. That they were right in voting to abrogate the Plan of Union and establish denominational Boards has been established by the action of the New School Assembly itself while a separate denomination. That they were right in resisting the confusing of the lesser with the graver doctrinal errors, and in believing that the latter were not prevalent among the majority of those acting in the New School party, has been demonstrated in reunion and its consequences. That they were eminently brave and disinterested is abundantly proved by the very fact complained of, that instead of sheltering themselves in the mass of either conflicting army, they chose to expose themselves to the conspicuous and unsupported position of independent soldiers, following reason and conscience without regard to the pleasure or displeasure of men. That they were not inconsistent with their past convictions or pledges when they finally consented to the abrogation of the Plan of Union and the excision of the Synod of Western Reserve has been shown plainly above.

[1] The Presbytery of Newton, of the Synod of New Jersey, appointed a committee, February 1835, 'to confer, by letter or otherwise, with the Professors of the Theo. Sem. in Princeton' with regard to their stand against the Act and Testimony. And in the autumn of 1836 'a company of gentlemen were designated by a large and respectable number of the Old School to proceed in a noiseless and unobserved manner to wait on the Professors at their homes, to reason and remonstrate with them, if possible, to concur with their brethren in the public actions of the church.' These gentlemen met in the study of Dr Hodge. Their appeals were respectfully heard, but little effect was ever attributed to them.

Dr E. H. Gillett, in his account of these events, (vol. 2, p. 496) sneeringly says: 'The *Princeton Review* of July of that year (1836) still pleaded for union . . . Only a few weeks after the *Review* had denounced division, New Brunswick Presbytery (to which all the Professors belonged) unanimously declared themselves unable to see any prospect of good in the continued union of the discordant parts of the church.'

This innuendo is borrowed from 'A Plea for Voluntary Societies, and a Defence of the Decisions of the General Assembly of 1836 against the Strictures of the Princeton Reviewers, New York, 1837', in which the conductors of the *Repertory* are charged with insincerity because their Presbytery so soon made a deliverance inconsistent with the spirit and professed aim of their article, and made it by a vote reported to be unanimous. This might have been a natural suspicion in the excitements of 1837, but it is an inexcusable insinuation as coming from Dr E. H. Gillett, the professed historian of the Presbyterian Church in 1864. The explanation was in his hand in an article in the *Repertory* for January 1837, reviewing 'The Plea for Voluntary Societies', aforesaid: 'Of the eight ministers resident in Princeton only one of them was present at that meeting of their Presbytery, or knew anything of the resolutions until after they were passed . . . But we have still further to remark, that the only one of their number ('Association of Gentlemen in Princeton') who was present when these resolutions were adopted exerted all his influence to have them reduced to the standard which he and his friends had already adopted.'

Out of the attitude assumed by the conductors of the *Repertory* towards the Act and Testimony there sprang a personal misunderstanding. In the month of May 1834, in the height of his physical affliction, Dr Hodge stayed for a few days with his friend, Professor Dod, at the house of his brother, in Philadelphia. While there Dr R. J. Breckinridge, the author of the Act and Testimony, with whom he was on terms of intimate friendship, called to see him, and consulted him on the subject of the character of the document he was preparing. From this it came to be currently rumoured that Dr Hodge was one of the authors of the Act and Testimony, and hence much painful surprise was felt by many when his articles appeared in the *Repertory* in October 1834, and January 1835, vigorously criticizing that document, and opposing the use to which it was applied by its friends. In his 'Plain Statement' in the *Presbyterian*, April 16, 1835, Dr R. J. Breckinridge affirms 'That Dr Hodge dictated, with the aid of the manuscript put into his hands by me, and drawn in part from Dr Miller's letters, then recently published, the very words and letters now found under the head of 'Errors' in the Act and Testimony . . . And so far from his making any general objections, such as he has since reiterated, I left him, confidently hoping that he would favour, if not actually sign, the Act and Testimony.' It was a question of 'impression' and 'hopes', which must always depend largely upon subjective conditions of opinion and feeling and temperament. Under all the circumstances, it is not wonderful that Dr Breckinridge should have misunderstood Dr Hodge. But that he did entirely misunderstand him, and hence that this 'Plain Statement' misrepresents him, is absolutely certain.

Dr Hodge, in his address to the 'Christian Public', in the *Presbyterian*, April 30, 1835, says:

> The facts of the case, to the best of my recollection and belief, are briefly these: During my short stay in Philadelphia, in May last, I received a note from a friend that he would call upon me in company with Dr. R. J. Breckinridge on important business, but without any more special reference to the object of his visit. At the hour appointed they came. The first annunciation of their special object was in nearly these words: 'Brother Hodge, we want you to draw up a statement of the doctrinal errors prevailing in the Presbyterian Church.' I answered that this was work for a month; that I was incompetent

to the task, it being out of my line, and that I was to leave town the next morning for the sea-shore. I was, of course, at this time entirely ignorant of the purpose for which the statement was wanted. In order to make known this purpose, and that I might understand precisely what was desired of me, Mr Breckinridge stated that there had been a meeting on the preceding evening of the minority of the General Assembly, and of some other gentlemen, at which he was appointed the chairman of a committee to draft an address to the churches. This address he then read, and said he wished to introduce into it a statement of the prevailing errors, and that it was in preparation of this statement he desired my assistance. This led to a conversation especially as to the class of errors which it would be proper to notice. In this conversation Professor Maclean, Mr Breckinridge, his friend and myself, all took part. It was agreed that the statement ought to be confined to errors of the more important kind. After this Mr Breckinridge took his pen and with the aid of his notes previously made, wrote down the several specifications in the form which, after mutual consultation, was thought to be the best. In this point there was generally a coincidence of views: as to one of the articles, however, that respecting imputation, Mr Breckinridge differed from his friends, and wrote it down as it now stands, in opposition to their judgment. This was the whole of my agency in the business. It was not only unsolicited on my part, but was entirely unexpected; it was performed as an office of friendship, and it was neither different nor greater than I both could and would, under similar circumstances, perform at the present moment, and with my present views and feelings respecting the Act and Testimony.

To the best of my recollection, there was but one other prominent topic of remark, and that was the article respecting Elective Affinity bodies. To this I strongly objected on the grounds afterwards urged in the *Biblical Repertory*.

Professor, now ex-President Maclean, wrote to the *Presbyterian*, April 17, 1835:

In the *Presbyterian* of last week allusion is made by the Rev. R. J. Breckinridge that I was present at the interview which took place between him and Rev. Professor Hodge, on the subject of the Act and Testimony. I feel constrained to let the readers of the *Presbyterian* know that my impression with regard to the views then entertained and expressed by Professor Hodge, differs entirely from Dr Breckinridge's. Both Professor Hodge and myself expressed our apprehension that the measures suggested were to say the least of doubtful tendency, and that they might be productive of serious difficulties . . . I recollect that after Mr Breckinridge had expressed his determination to have the document under discussion sent forth, by the minority of the last Assembly and their friends, as an official paper declarative of their views and course of action, Professor Hodge observed that if it were a settled point that the Act and Testimony was to be issued, it was important that the statement should be limited to serious and important errors, and that particular care should be used in specifying these errors, so that the same errors should not be presented in different forms, and that those clearly related should be classed with each other.

Mr Breckinridge then avowed that his object in reading the paper to Professor Hodge was to get his aid in doing this very thing. Prof. Hodge consented to aid him, not, as I understood the matter, that he would, upon these alterations being made, be willing to give his countenance to the measures proposed, but merely because he wished the Act and Testimony to be as free as possible from objection, and because he felt a disposition to aid a friend, as far as he could do it conscientiously.

Yours, John Maclean.

Also on the same day Professor Albert B. Dod wrote to the *Presbyterian*:

During the time that Dr Hodge was in Philadelphia last spring, I lodged at the same house with him. In the evening of the same day on which the Rev. R. J. Breckinridge called upon Dr Hodge to consult him in relation to the Act and Testimony, I had much conversation with him on the subject of this interview, and of the character and probable effects of the instrument. The opinions and views which he then expressed were substantially the same with those that have since been published in the *Biblical Repertory*. I cannot be mistaken in my recollection of the nature of his remarks, as they had a decided influence in forming my own views of the Act and Testimony, and in leading me to decline, before leaving Philadelphia, to affix my signature to it.

In consequence of the 'Exscinding Acts' passed by the General Assembly of 1837, the stated clerk, in making up the roll of the members of the Assembly of 1838, omitted the names of all the delegates from the Presbyteries comprised in the exscinded synods. Motions to recognize them were declared by the Moderator, Rev. Dr David Elliott, to be out of order until after the Assembly was duly constituted by the making out of the roll. Mr John P. Cleveland, of the Presbytery of Detroit, then read a paper, of the nature of a protest and declaration of the necessity of revolutionary methods. In spite of being called to order by the constitutionally presiding officer, he nominated Dr Beman to the chair. Dr Beman took his station in the aisle of the church, and put the motion whereby Drs E. Mason, and E. W. Gilbert were proposed for clerks, and Dr S. Fisher for Moderator. These gentlemen, with their sympathizers, then withdrew to the First Presbyterian Church, where they formed the New School Assembly.

The trustees of the General Assembly had been incorporated under a charter from the Legislature of Pennsylvania, approved March 28, 1799. The funds entrusted to their care had been raised in by far the largest part by the adherents of the Old School party, and fully four-fifths belonged to Princeton Theological Seminary. The New School Assembly, on the assumption that they carried the legal succession, necessarily chose new trustees in the place of those of the existing body adhering to the other party. Just as necessarily the existing members of the Board of Trustees, holding that the other Assembly carried the true succession, refused to recognize the new appointments of the new Assembly. Hence the New School applicants brought suit for the establishment of their rights as trustees, and hence for the legal settlement of the question of succession from the historical line of General Assemblies, before the Supreme Court of Pennsylvania.

The trial was brought in the first instance before Judge Rogers at *Nisi Prius*[1] and a special jury, March 4, 1839. Under the ruling of the judge the jury brought in a verdict in favour of the New School trustees and Assembly. The Old School trustees appealed to the Supreme Court in Banc[2] for a new trial, when the case was heard and decided by all the supreme judges together. On May 8th, 1839, Chief Justice Gibson, read a judgment in which all the judges except Judge Rogers concurred, which reversed the finding of the lower court. They affirm that 'the apparent injustice of the (exscinding) measures arises from the contemplation of it as a judicial sentence pronounced against parties who were never cited nor heard; which it evidently was not. Even as a legislative act, it may have been a hard one, though certainly constitutional and strictly just. We hold that the Assembly which met in the First Presbyterian Church was not the legitimate successor of the Assembly of 1837; and that the defendants (Old School trustees,) are not guilty of the usurpation with which they are charged.'

This bare statement of facts is sufficient to explain the following letters:

[1] A court of *nisi prius* is a court that tries questions of fact before a judge and, in some cases, a jury. The term ordinarily applies to the trial level court as opposed to a higher court that entertains appeals without a jury. [Ed.]

[2] *En banc, in banc, in banco* or *in bank* is a French term (meaning 'on a bench') used to refer to the hearing of a legal case where all judges of a court will hear the case (an entire 'bench'), rather than a panel of them. [Ed.]

DR HODGE TO HIS BROTHER

PRINCETON, N. J., March 27, 1839

My Dear Brother:—As you may well suppose, the decision of the protracted law-suit against us has taken us altogether by surprise. No one here considered such a result as more than possible. We thought it probable the jury would not agree, and should not have been astonished at an unfavourable verdict. But that the Judge should be against us, and that with bitterness, never appeared as even possible. All our friends, legal and clerical, had perfect confidence in our ultimate success up to the moment when the Judge pronounced his opinion. Our opinion of the justice of our cause, of course, remains unchanged. Whatever errors may have been committed in 1837, the assumption that the New School Assembly, organized in 1838, was regularly organized appears perfectly preposterous, and therefore the Judge's decision is a mystery. I have long taken pains to find out what disinterested and intelligent persons thought on this subject, and I have never seen or heard of one who expressed a doubt upon it.

I regard the decision as a very great calamity, and as a very severe judgment of God, and bow to it accordingly. I firmly believe the New School party, as a party, to be the promoters of error and disorder; that the interests of religion are deeply involved and greatly endangered by the weight of power and influence which this decision will give them. God will doubtless bring good out of evil, as he will make the success of the Unitarians in New England, and the Hicksites in the Middle States, ultimately a blessing. His bringing good out of evil is his great prerogative, but the evil still remains evil.

I have very great fears as to the result to the Old School party. If they had cohesion enough to hang together, and act together with vigour, they might soon recover from this blow. But there are so many geographical and sectional causes of disunion that I am very much afraid that if once deprived of the bond of a common and venerated name, and of common property, we shall be split into insignificant fragments. We are, in the eye of the law, a secession from our own church; the New England men have succeeded in getting that church to themselves.

A re-union appears out of the question ; and I can hardly conceive of any arrangement by which the Seminary can be preserved should the decision of Judge Rogers be confirmed by the Judges *in banc*. I trust our leaders in Philadelphia will be preserved from rashness and imprudence and all evil speaking. A dark cloud is hanging over us, and our ways seem to be hedged up. It is very painful to think of Princeton Seminary going to ruin; for it must go to ruin in the hands of New School men. They have a Seminary in New York, and cannot possibly supply both with students. Still, the Lord reigns, and He will do all things well.

Your brother, C. Hodge.

DR HODGE TO DR HENRY A. BOARDMAN

Princeton, Feb. 28, 1839

My Dear Sir:— . . . The important crisis in our church's history is just at hand. Its importance constantly rises in my view. The funds and institutions, though matters not to be slighted, are but a portion of the great interests at stake, and to have these interests committed to twelve men, taken up at random, is a very serious matter. It seems to be one of God's purposes in this dispensation to make us feel that we are completely in His hands. The decision of a jury in such matters is very little different from the casting of the lot; and I should feel nearly as I feel now if the great question at issue were to be decided on Monday by the throwing of dice. I hope this will make us all feel disposed to wait upon God, and earnestly to plead with Him to plead our cause and sustain the right. And should the cause be decided in our favour I trust there will not be one word of exultation uttered from any quarter.

Princeton, March 28, 1839

My Dear Sir:— . . . I hope soon to get through with my revision of the *Commentary on the Romans* to prepare it for translation into

French, and will then go at my *History*. Perhaps it is now more important than ever that the work should be done, if, as I hope may be the case, it will tend to increase the respect and affection of Presbyterians for the church of their fathers. We shall need now every bond to keep us together; we must increase in mutual love and zeal for the truth, and for the order of our church, and for its real usefulness. The danger is that if we lose our old name and standing and common property we shall break into little fragments and cease to have much power to do good.

I hope God may guide by his wisdom the brethren who are now to decide on our course. The interests at stake are far too momentous to be abandoned while there is any prospect of saving them. Taylorism never received such a mighty impulse as when Judge Rogers pronounced the New School Assembly the true General Assembly of the Presbyterian Church, and if that judgment is confirmed I shall think God has sore judgments in store for our land. This unexpected blow, after all our confident hopes, I trust will make us humble and lead us to submit to God without murmuring at Him or complaining of one another or of the opposite party.

If the Old School could hang together now and do their duty we should, with God's blessing, soon recover from this severe stroke. Let me hear soon what has been determined upon; and if the cause goes to the Judges *in banc*, when it is likely to be heard.

Yours affectionately, C. Hodge.

Princeton, April 13, 1839

My Dear Sir:—I want to say a few things to you about the present position and prospects of our church, in which, I presume, you and I will not differ much.

There can be no doubt that the present is one of the most trying periods in our whole history. It will try not only the principles but the graces of the church. And our future prospects depend, under God, very much upon the manner in which we shall now act. The great object is to produce unanimity; to prevent any such diversity in counsels or measures as shall cause a division in our own ranks. You do not appear to fear this as much as I do. I have heard, however, so many and such discordant expressions of confident opinions and purposes that I shall regard it as a special indication of God's power if the Old School party are led to act harmoniously and to keep their ranks unbroken. This can be effected in no other way than by humility and mutual concessions. No one man, and no few men, ought to attempt to decide what course the church should pursue in this emergency. We should remember that we are brethren, and that no one has a right to dictate to others, but that subjection to our brethren in the Lord is part of our ordination vows. As this is the case, I think we ought to keep ourselves uncommitted and unpledged until the meeting of the Assembly. It is impossible to know till then what the church generally will think right, and the way ought to be left open for it to take that course which the great body of the brethren shall deem to be right. It is on this account that I regret to see our papers, the *Presbyterian* and *Watchman*, pronounce so confidently what the party will or will not do; and the latter even denouncing beforehand any who should advocate union with the opposite party even for an hour. I doubt not there will be found a large portion of sound Old School men who, on the supposition of an ultimate decision against us, will be in favour of a temporary union of the two parties with a view to such a separation as shall prevent litigation and secure our property and legal standing. We have heard here that Messrs Alexander Henry, Bevan, Newkirk, Chauncey, Kane, Bayard, are all in favour of this course. Mr Musgrave is in favour of it; and I was told that a clergyman who was among his friends in Western Pennsylvania, when the news of the decision arrived, said that was the general feeling there. It will be found, also, I suspect, the general feeling in New York. Now, what a spectacle shall we exhibit if we go to denouncing each other; if difference of opinion as to the best means of attaining the same end be made a breaking point among us.

My own opinion is that this plan will be found impracticable. It obviously cannot be done at all unless there is a general unanimity in favour of it. Of this I have very little expectation; and therefore think that those who would prefer it ought by all means to give way to their brethren. Even if a considerable minority were opposed, it could not be urged. Still, I think it unfortunate that it should be decided and given out beforehand, that we can and will in no case and for no purpose go back. This is the very position that the New School papers are driving us by taunts and insults to take. We are playing into their hands, therefore, by joining in this cry that the Old School cannot go back. They do not want us back; they ought to feel that they are not quite secure from such visitation.

A second plan is to stand aloof and claim to be the true church. This is beset with difficulties. We shall be seceders in the eye of the law, in Pennsylvania at least, and all titles to church property will be unsettled. In the second place, it will give rise, in all probability, to protracted litigation in all parts of the country, to the great scandal of the church and injury to religion ; and it will be voluntarily throwing in the hands of the friends of error and disorder immense advantages.

A third plan is a legal compromise. This seems to me so obviously necessary and desirable for both parties that I do not believe the mass of the New School could be brought by their leaders to oppose it. There may be legal difficulties in the way which I cannot appreciate. It has occurred to me, however, that it might be effected by some such plan as this: According to our present charter, the General Assembly has two rights in relation to the Board of Trustees – first, to appoint its members; and second, to control the application of the funds. Why may not the charter be so altered as to confer these rights on the two Assemblies? Let each have nine trustees in the Board, and each be authorized to direct the application of the funds, which, according to mutual agreement, shall be recognized as belonging to each. Such a contract could not be broken when once made, and our funds would be entirely under our own control. Neither party would then be in the position of seceders, and all litigation would be prevented throughout the country. The more I have thought of this plan the more does it appear to be practicable and desirable. I wish you would consult Mr Chauncey and others on the subject. I have mentioned it to several brethren, who seem to think it would be wise. Among others, I talked with Dr Nott about it, who was here yesterday, and who went from here to Philadelphia. The Doctor, I suspect, feels that the Philadelphia brethren have not as much confidence in him as he feels he deserves. But I am convinced that his aims are right, and that he could be of immense service to the church in adjusting our present difficulties to the satisfaction of all parties, if they would but confide in him.

We, of course, are looking forward with great anxiety to the result of the argument next week.

Yours truly,

C. HODGE

9

FROM THE CHANGE OF HIS PROFESSORSHIP, MAY 1840, TO THE DEATH OF DR ARCHIBALD ALEXANDER, OCTOBER 1851

His Transfer to the Chair of Systematic Theology – His Method and Success in Teaching – THE WAY OF LIFE – Letters from Dr A. Alexander, Bishop Johns, Ludwig and Otto von Gerlach – His Articles in the PRINCETON REVIEW – Slavery – Sustentation – Romish Baptism – Letters to His Brother, and from Drs Biggs and Johns – Friendship and Correspondence with Dr William Cunningham – Death of Professor Albert B. Dod – Marriage and Departure of His Children – Death of His Wife – Disturbed Health – Death of His Senior Colleagues

AT THE SUGGESTION OF DR A. ALEXANDER and the Board of Directors, the General Assembly, in May 1840, made a readjustment of the chairs in the Seminary, in view of the advancing age of the Senior Professor. Dr Alexander's title continued thenceforth till his death Professor of Pastoral and Polemic Theology. Dr Hodge was transferred to the chair formerly occupied by his venerable teacher, Dr A. Alexander, and his title was made Professor of Exegetical and Didactic Theology. And Dr J. A. Alexander became full and sole Professor of Oriental and Biblical Literature. At the death of Dr Alexander, Polemic Theology was added to the title of Prof. Hodge. In the meantime he retained to the day of his death his exegetical lectures to the Junior Class on the Pauline Epistles. While Dr Addison Alexander took, besides the Old Testament, the historical books, and the entire literature of the New Testament.

Charles Hodge aged 49.

Miller Chapel, built 1834, remodelled 1874. Charles Hodge gave his 'historical sermon' at the reopening in 1874 (see pp. 585–97).

Miller Chapel, interior.

This change, which was one of the capital and most advantageous turning points of Dr Hodge's life, was not only not sought by him, but regarded at first with decided aversion.

DR HODGE TO HIS BROTHER

PRINCETON, May 11, 1840

My Dear Brother:—How did you hear so soon of my being made Dr Alexander's adjunct? The thing is not done yet, nor is it likely to be done in a hurry. It must pass the Assembly unanimously, or lie over for a year. That no one should object to it I should consider well nigh miraculous. I have felt it to be my duty to be perfectly quiet, and to make no intimation of my own wishes on the subject. For two reasons – First, because I do not think my wishes ought to have anything to do with the business. I ought to be willing to do just what the church bids me. The second reason is, that I would not presume to put my wishes in opposition to those of Dr Alexander. I think he ought, so far as I am concerned, to be allowed to do just as he pleases. To you, however, I may say in confidence, that I would give five thousand dollars, if I had them, to be let off. The new arrangement knocks all my plans in the head, and will increase my official labours for years to come fourfold. You must not say this to anybody, because, having given my consent to be disposed of as they see fit, it would be unfair to raise any obstacle, either directly or indirectly. I live in great hopes that it will fall through without any agency of mine. And then I shall have a clear conscience as well as a merry heart.

Your affectionate brother, C.H.

This feeling is remarkable in consideration of the fact that, from our point of view, his natural qualifications for the attainment of eminent excellence and usefulness in the new chair were far greater than any he possessed for the attainment of the same rank in the old one. Yet, it was surely not the least of the many singularly favourable providential adjustments of the conditions of his life that he should have been required, by official duty, to exercise himself for twenty years in a department of theological study to which his natural tastes did not dispose him. Thus, in a way in which for him it was alone possible, he was led to make acquisitions in the original languages of Scripture and in the science and practice of Biblical exegesis, which are professedly the basis of systematic theology, and yet are the qualifications in which the vast majority of speculative theologians have been more or less deficient. Consequently, it is confidently believed that very few of the eminent authors of our classical theological literature have equalled the subject of this memoir in the consistency in which they carried out their common principle of making the faithful and natural interpretation of the inspired Word the basis of all doctrinal induction, and in the scriptural form and spirit, as well as substance, of their systematic writings.

For the first eight or nine years of his work in the new department Dr Hodge's method was such that he was enabled to accomplish the best results of his life in class instruction. Dr Alexander continued to read his former theological lectures to the classes until Dr Hodge had his course prepared. The first lectures the latter wrote were those on the Church, which were delivered during the winter of 1845–6. The first lectures forming parts of the theological course proper were written on the topics of the 'Will' and the 'Second Advent', and were read to the class the same year. In the meantime he met both the Middle and Senior Classes twice a week each, Tuesday and Thursday, or Wednesday and Friday afternoons respectively. Before the first meeting of either class for the week the Professor assigned a topic and a corresponding section of Turretin's *Institutes of Theology* in Latin for previous study. When they met the hour was occupied by a thorough discussion of this subject in the form of question and answer. In this form of discipline his chief excellence as a teacher was brought into play.

He questioned with consummate skill, forcing the pupil to do his own thinking, drawing him irresistibly to the conviction of the truth, or overturning his false positions with an inevitable *reductio ad absurdum*. As the truth was thus evolved, or as the Professor finally amended the result in his own words, the students eagerly wrought to fix the whole in their note books. At the same time the Professor gave them a list of questions on the topic, numbering from twenty-five to forty, answers to which, written out in full, were to be read to him at the meeting of the class nine days afterwards. These answers were elaborated out of materials drawn from Turretin, and the notes taken in the class-room, and from any other source rendered accessible by the Seminary library. The highest enthusiasm was excited, and the most earnest diligence. The students built up to a degree their own systems of theology, and were vigorously exercised in criticism, construction and expression. Many carried away from the Seminary from two to six quarto volumes of manuscript filled with the results of this exercise, which, having afforded them the most profitable discipline in the past, continued to supply them with digested and arranged material for preaching which lasted during several of the early years of their ministry.

About 1847–8 he began to lecture, at first in connection with the questions and answers written by the pupils, and afterwards without them. For years, although he re-wrote his lectures several times, he was harassed with the inevitable experience of lecturers, in having his lectures systematically taken down by stenographers, and subsequently copied from hand to hand and given back to him verbally at recitation. Long afterwards, for the few years that he taught after his *Systematic Theology* was published, his teaching became much more satisfactory to himself, when he used his work as his text-book and devoted the entire time allotted to his class in the old effective exercise of drill by questions and answers.

THE WAY OF LIFE

In 1841 the American Sunday School Union published his *The Way of Life*. This is a duodecimo of 380 pages, in which his design is to set clearly before the minds of educated youth the great truths involved in the Gospel method of human salvation. The book is eminently luminous; its characteristic attribute is light suffused with love. The doctrines of Evangelical Protestantism are clearly and fully stated, yet in non-technical language, and with such simplicity and self-evidencing power that the compiler of these memoirs has constantly advised his theological students to read *The Way of Life* on the subjects of 'Conviction of Sin', 'Faith', 'Justification', 'The Sacraments and Profession of Religion', and 'Holy Living' in connection with the discussion of the same topics in the *Systematic Theology*. It is so richly and definitely theological that Dr Archibald Alexander, after reading the manuscript, while expressing his cordial approbation of it, declared his conviction that the Publishing Committee of the Sunday School Union, consisting of the representatives of all evangelical denominations, could not agree in giving it their *imprimatur*. Yet, in fact, no suspicion even was manifested, except by the representative of our then freshly antagonized New School brethren, and his apprehensions were easily set at rest, and the book was adopted unanimously. It was immediately reprinted by the London Religious Tract Society, and was subsequently translated into Hindustani. Thirty-five thousand copies have been circulated in America, and the author's heart has been often filled with grateful joy from information of its having been, in many specific instances, owned of God in the conversion and edification of souls, alike in America and in Europe and in Asia.

His own account of it is thus given in the Preface:

It is one of the clearest principles of divine revelation that holiness is the fruit of truth; and it is one of the plainest inferences from that principle that the exhibition of the truth is the best means of promoting holiness. Christians regard the Word of God as the only infallible teacher of those truths which relate to the salvation of men. But are the Scriptures really a revelation from God? If they are, what doctrines do they teach? And what influence should those doctrines exert on our heart and life?

The Publishing Committee of the American Sunday School Union have long felt the want of a book which should give a plain answer to these questions, and be suitable to place in the hands of intelligent and educated young persons, either to arouse their attention or to guide their steps in the WAY OF LIFE.

The *New England Puritan* (March 1842) said of it:

We know not where the evidence of the divine origin of the Scriptures is presented in a way so well adapted to take effect upon the mind. It wins while it convinces. Here, in our opinion, is the sterling excellency of Dr Hodge. While his mind is endowed with such clearness that it can throw a blaze of light upon any given subject, his heart is impregnated with such benevolence towards his fellow-men that almost every one who comes within the sphere of its attraction becomes a willing convert to his opinions. While he convinces the judgment, he carries captive the will.

But the evidence of the divine origin of the Scriptures is not the best part of the volume. The author was most at home on the doctrines, and there he is *primus inter pares*. No one, we think, can read the volume under consideration from the 53rd to the 245th page – almost two-thirds of the whole work – without coming to the conclusion that nowhere else within the same compass, out of the Sacred Record, can he find so much to instruct and to satisfy his mind and to edify his heart. The chapter on Justification especially pleased us.

Yet, it is true that the expositions of Baptism and the Lord's Supper, of the Nature and Necessity of the Public Profession of Religion and of Holy Living are as exquisitely executed and as precious as any other parts of the work.

DR ALEXANDER TO DR HODGE

May 11, 1841

I have read the greater part of your manuscript and find nothing from which I feel disposed to dissent. Indeed, your views of the subjects treated correspond very exactly with those which I entertain.

On the subject of faith, while there is a substantial agreement, there may be some slight shades of difference. For example, I make no difference between a saving and a justifying faith. I think that you make a difference with Dr Owen.

The chapters are entirely too long. It is of much importance that in such a work the chapters should be of moderate length. The first chapter ought undoubtedly to be divided into three. But even where the same subject is continued, it is better to have it divided. I find that in my own reading I am often turning to see how many pages remain before the termination of the chapter.

As you have written the book for the Sunday School Union, it is useless to offer any remarks on that subject, otherwise I would strongly recommend the Board of Publication. It struck me as doubtful whether the S.S. Union could publish all that you have written without offence to some of their friends. For, to say nothing of Arminians who patronize that Institution, there are few of the New School ministers who believe in the imputation of Christ's active obedience, which is made prominent in your book. I would not have you, on any account, to alter a word for that reason, which would be disloyal to the truth. This is the great defect of the Institution, that they cannot teach the whole truth, but only that part of it in which all their patrons are agreed.

Yours, etc., A. Alexander

BISHOP JOHNS TO DR HODGE

Baltimore, Feb. 15, 1842

If I were to write to you, my dear Charles, as often and as much as I muse about you, you would have to complain of the tax upon your time and your purse. Fortunately for you, my musings end where they begin, in my own mind and heart, and whilst they afford me no small amount of pleasure, inflict nothing upon you. If you desire to know how it comes to pass that they insist on expression now, understand that you alone are answerable for it. I have been reading your book, and it is not in me to refrain from communicating the proud satisfaction with which I have perused it. Will you believe it? – I was silly enough to feel all the while as if I had a hand in it myself, and my enjoyment was increased by a fiction, which I had no disposition to resist, that I was somehow honourably concerned in the production. One thing, however, is certain, I shall use it as freely as if it were all my own, and shall find it serviceable to myself in a way in which it cannot be a help to its author. I have sent it out into my congregation with an unqualified endorsement, and hope soon to find it in every family under my care. I am sure it will be received with as much favour by the evangelical portion of our communion as among your own people, and do great good where, perhaps, you little anticipated it.

The fifth chapter I read with peculiar satisfaction. It is so simple, so clear, so scriptural, I do not see how any one who bows to the authority of the Word can except to a single sentence, or how a sinner, conscious of his own guilt, can fail to acquiesce in it as indeed the Way of Life. The succession of arguments is stated conclusively, and the biblical illustrations are most happily set forth and applied . . .

The passage from page 184 to the bottom of page 186 strikes me as the best of all the good things in the book. It has furnished me with a new form of presenting the subject to such as seek salvation, and I hope to be able to employ it for the guidance and relief of anxious minds.

I admire the calm dignity with which you have written from the beginning to the end, yet with quite as much earnestness as is necessary to rouse and retain the interest of the reader.
On the whole, those who *don't know* you personally will form a very *good* opinion of you from this book, and to those who *do*, it will *disclose* nothing to disturb such impression.

Now let me write a little about the Doctor (Hugh Hodge). I suppose you know he has had my dear wife under his care ever since I was with you in September last . . . Hugh received me with a brother's interest, and has rendered us such services, and in such a spirit, that, apart from early and long cherished affection, he has bound me to himself by the strongest obligations.

Truly your brother, J. JOHNS

The publication of *The Way of Life* was the occasion of his receiving from his old friend, Ludwig von Gerlach, then President-Justice of the province of Magdeburg, the following letter:

LUDWIG VON GERLACH TO DR HODGE

MAGDEBURG, August 8, 1847

My Dear Sir:—By these lines a friend wishes to be recalled to your memory, who twenty years ago was connected with you in Christian fellowship, and who has never met you since that time, nor expects to meet you on this side of eternity. It is your tract *The Way of Life* which has led me to call on you by this probably unexpected letter; for during an official journey through the province of my jurisdiction, I have read this work; and my feeling of union with you in faith and profession of the great fundamental truths of religion has, by this reading, become so strong and so lively, that I cannot forbear to express it, and to thank you for the spiritual blessing you have conferred on me by this book. These feelings are the more powerful on my mind on account of the difference of my present tendency from that of your tract. For this very minor difference is shedding a brighter light on the essential unity, which our blessed Saviour, by His grace, His word, and His Spirit, has established between us; and which, I trust, He will maintain through time and eternity. The development of Germany, in a religious and in a political respect, makes the Christians of our country to long after catholicity, and perhaps after the essential truth of what you would call 'sacramental religion'. It is not the way of salvation, which is now the prominent subject of our minds, but rather the high articles of the Divine Majesty, which occupied so much the primitive Church, and about which there was no difference of opinion between the contending parties of the 16th century. Being surrounded by Atheists and Pantheists, we strive to establish a consciousness of the essential unity of all Christians, Romanists not excepted; and the great fact of the *whole* Church being the body of Christ is foremost in our minds. It will not do with us to take it for granted that the Bible – the 'sacred volume', as the English-speaking Christians call it – is a whole (*ein Ganzes*) without inquiring how it came to be such, for the New Testament no where exhibits the idea of the New Testament as a book. And we cannot suppose, as you perhaps are entitled to do, that our inquiries are standing vis-à-vis of this book, and examining it as a whole. They oblige us to take higher ground, and to develop the ideas of authority and of inspiration, etc., in order to establish on firm ground the, for us, all important doctrine of the Church. But all this shall only give you an idea of the feelings with which I have thankfully perused your excellent tract, which exhibits in a very clear way and with great force those blessed doctrines, which constitute the true Way of Life, and in which it is delightful for me to think that you on that, and I on this side of the ocean so heartily coincide. God grant that this coincidence be a pledge that we shall be united for ever before the throne of grace.

You know that my brother Otto is now *Hof-prediger* [court chaplain] of our king. I am president of the court of justice of this province. During the summer of 1844 I was in England, Scotland and Ireland, chiefly to study the law-institutions of those countries. But even this voyage has not prevented you, as you see, your being troubled by the very bad English of this letter, since I have very little occasion of speaking this language.

I remain, through the Lord's grace, your very *thankful*,

VON GERLACH

P.S.—I do not know if you are reading the *Evangelische Kirchenzeitung*. If you do you will find in the papers of June 1847, an article on the 'Indivisibility of the Church', from my pen, which may give you some idea of the questions – very important ones I trust – now occupying our German minds.

The chapter of your tract on baptism and the Lord's Supper is the only one from which I must dissent on any essential point. Your doctrine of the sacraments, as it seems to me, does not quite do justice to the 'objective content and import' of these ordinances, but subjects them too much to the state of mind of the recipient, whom they are destined to justify and to sanctify. It is not clear to me, how, according to your doctrine, you can avoid rejecting pedobaptism. I hold the sacraments to be in their nature, the actual means, not only signs and seals of grace; though the grace, by man's sin may be converted into [a] curse.

DR OTTO VON GERLACH TO DR HODGE

Paris, July 27, 1842

My Dear Friend:—A long time has again elapsed since I last wrote to you. Meanwhile I have passed four months in England, 'the country of your forefathers', as you remarked when leaving Berlin. When there I was upon point of following my inmost desire and visiting North America, and again, as I can truthfully say, seeing you my friend, who has become so dear to me.

The bearer of this letter is your fellow-countryman, Mr Prentiss,[1] from the State of Maine. He is one of the worthiest and most estimable Americans I have ever met. He is acquainted with all the particulars concerning my journey in England and will relate them to you.

While in London I had many thoughts of you, and I also purchased your *Way of Life*. In fourteen days I hope to be in Berlin again. I am residing there now in very great activity, which also yearly increases. Our king has not only introduced a general tolerance, but he will also elevate the standard of the established Church, in order that it

---

[1] George Prentiss (1816–1903). See *Elizabeth Prentiss: More Love to Thee* (Edinburgh: Banner of Truth, 2006). Prentiss studied in Germany and became acquainted with Tholuck, Hengstenberg, Neander and others of Hodge's German friends. [Ed.]

may manifest its own wants. Advisory synods have already arisen in a greater part of the land. It is untrue that he wishes to introduce the English Episcopal Church, as is urged against him especially in France. He has, indeed, a liking for certain of its institutions, but not, however, for the organization as a whole. Moreover, generally speaking, he will not introduce anything into the Church by virtue of his kingly authority, but only upon decision of the Church itself. That the bishopric in Jerusalem should point toward this is therefore false. I disapprove of some things in this organization so much that I can only regard the present situation of our Church on the whole as most highly gratifying and rich in blessings – for which all Christians, who, like myself, are not English Episcopalians, and do not wish to become so, ought to thank God. On the whole I hope that the Christian life will progress, as indeed the sorrowful condition of our great cities especially causes terror. In this respect we can now learn much in England, for it is truly wonderful how many churches have arisen there.

Indeed, if Puseyism should be more widely spread, a terrible crisis might threaten the English Church, and I believe that this tendency, although in a more moderate form, is spreading considerably. Theological learning is lacking very greatly in English evangelical works, and therefore the people cannot withstand the evidently ignorant, but yet more influential and important men of the Puseyite sect. I spent several days at Oxford in dispute with Dr Pusey. He is a very poor, weak man. How much would I have to say to you in regard to all this. Yet I must draw my letter to a close.

Pray let me hear from you again as occasion may present itself.

In sincere love I remain, as ever,

Your friend,
OTTO VON GERLACH

Though he subsequently received some letters from Tholuck, yet from this time his correspondence with his Christian German friends practically ceases. Time and distance, and occupation with new scenes and persons made active intercourse impossible. Yet the affection was immortal, and in his very last days the photographs of Ludwig von Gerlach, of Tholuck, and of Bishop Johns were around his desk and kept in constant recognition, while those of many friends of more recent acquisition were pushed aside for them.

HIS ARTICLES IN THE *PRINCETON REVIEW*

During this decade he wrote no book except *The Way of Life*. But his pen was more active than at any other period of his life in writing his lectures on the Church and on Theology, his articles in the *Princeton Review*, and innumerable letters in answer to applications made for his opinion, or aid to others in forming their opinions on all conceivable subjects.

His contributions to the *Princeton Review* during this period were:

1840 – Presbyterianism in Virginia; Dr Hill's American Presbyterianism; New Jersey College and President Davies; The General Assembly; Discourse on Religion by Mr Coit.

1841 – Bishop Doane and the Oxford Tracts (with Prof. J.A.A.).

1842 – The Theological Opinions of President Davies; Milman's History of Christianity; The General Assembly; Rule of Faith.

1843 – Rights of Ruling Elders; The General Assembly.

1844 – General Assembly of the Church of Scotland (with Prof. J.A.A.); Claims of the Free Church of Scotland; The General Assembly; Abolitionism.

1845 – Beman on the Atonement; Thornwell on the Apocrypha; Schaff's Protestantism; The General Assembly.

1846 – Theories of the Church; Is the Church of Rome a Part of the Visible Church? The General Assembly; Neil's Lectures on Biblical History; The Religious State of Germany; The late Dr John Breckinridge; The Life and Writings of Dr Richards.

1847 – Finney's *Lectures on Theology*; The Support of the Clergy; The General Assembly (with Dr Hope); Bushnell on Christian Nurture.

1848 – The Doctrine of the Reformed Church; The General Assembly; Dr Spring on the Power of the Pulpit (with Prof. J.A.A.).

1849 –The American Board, Special Report of the Prudential Committee; Bushnell's Discourses; The General Assembly; Emancipation.

1850 – The Memoir of Walter M. Lowrie; The General Assembly; Prof. Park's Sermon.

1851 – Civil Government; Remarks on the *Princeton Review*; The General Assembly; Prof Park and the *Princeton Review*.

The most important of these may be classified as follows:

SLAVERY

1. The articles 'On Slavery', April 1836, and 'On Emancipation as accomplished in the West Indies', October 1838, and 'On Abolitionism', October 1844, and 'On Emancipation as Proposed by Dr R. J. Breckinridge in Kentucky', October 1849, form an important class. The first and the last of these were included in a selection from his articles, and published in a volume in 1856, and again in 1879, under the title of *Essays and Reviews*, by Charles Hodge.

It was his most conspicuous and uniform characteristic, all his life, and in every region of thought, to make the inspired Word of God, and neither his intuitions, nor his sentiments, nor the opinions of mankind, the absolute rule of his thinking and of his convictions. Hence he was equally out of sympathy with the pro-slavery men who regarded the institution as divine and to be perpetuated as good in itself, and with the 'Abolitionists', who held the holding of slaves to be a sin in itself, to be in every case visited with Christian condemnation and ecclesiastical discipline. He was, on the other hand, in hearty sympathy with the many

Southern Christians who strove to follow the will of Christ under the providential conditions He had imposed upon them, and with the Colonization Society, and with the noble efforts of Dr R. J. Breckinridge and his coadjutors in the work of emancipation in Kentucky. This position he maintained, in all respects unchanged, to his dying day. His own explanation of his position on these delicate points is given in his 'Retrospect of the History of the *Princeton Review*', written in 1871:

> The conductors of this *Review* have always endeavoured to adhere faithfully to the principle that the Scriptures are the only infallible rule of faith and practice. Therefore, when any matter, either of doctrine or morals, came under discussion, the question with them was, 'What saith the Lord?' Nothing that the Bible pronounces true can be false; nothing that it declares to be false can be true; nothing is obligatory on the conscience but what it enjoins; nothing can be sin but what it condemns. If, therefore, the Scriptures under the Old Dispensation permitted men to hold slaves, and if the New Testament nowhere condemns slave-holding, but prescribes the relative duties of masters and slaves, then to pronounce slave-holding to be in itself sinful is contrary to the Scriptures. In like manner, if the Bible nowhere condemns the use of intoxicating liquors as a beverage, if our Lord himself drank wine, then to say that all use of intoxicating liquor as a beverage is sin, is only one of the many forms of the infidelity of benevolence. It is as much contrary to our allegiance to the Bible to make our own notions of right or wrong the rule of duty as to make our own reason the rule of faith.
>
> It is well known that both slavery and intemperance were matters of national importance, and awakened earnest and continued controversy. As to slavery, so far as the North was concerned, it was universally regarded as an evil, which ought in some way to be brought to an end. The difference of opinion related to the means by which that end was to be accomplished. The Abolitionists, so-called, maintained that all slave-holding, as inconsistent with the inalien-

able rights of man and with the law of love, is sinful; and, therefore, that immediate and universal emancipation was an imperative duty. Another necessary consequence of the assumption that 'slave-holding is a heinous crime against God and man', is that no slave-holder could properly be admitted to Christian fellowship. As the people of God, under the Old Dispensation, were allowed by law to purchase slaves, and to hold those of heathen origin in perpetual bondage; as slavery existed among the Romans, Greeks and Jews during the apostolic age; as neither Christ nor his apostles denounced slave-holding as a crime, nor taught that emancipation was an imperative and immediate duty; and as, beyond doubt, the apostles admitted slaveholders to the communion of the Christian Church, the conductors of this *Review*, from first to last, maintained that the doctrine that slave-holding is in itself a crime, is anti-scriptural, and subversive of the authority of the Word of God.

The principles maintained in the articles above named are, (1) That slavery is, as defined by Paley, 'An obligation to labour for the benefit of the master, without the contract or consent of the servant.' It involves the deprivation of personal liberty, obligation of service at the discretion of another, and the transferable character of the authority and claim of service of the master. (2) The slave, according to this definition, is the property of his master. But property is merely the right of possession and use. The rights therein involved differ according to the nature of the thing possessed. A man has the right of property in his wife, his children, in his houses and land, his cattle and servants. Property in a horse does not involve the right to treat it as a log of wood; and property in man does not involve the right to use him as a brute. He can be used only as a rational, moral and immortal creature can, according to divine law, be rightfully used. All the rights conceded to him by the Word of God must be faithfully regarded. (3) The master, therefore, is bound to provide for the intellectual and moral education of the slave. Every human being has the right to be taught to read the Word of God, and learn the way of salvation for himself. Secondly, the master is bound to respect the conjugal rights of his slaves; and this forbids the separation of husbands and wives. Thirdly, he is bound to respect their parental rights, and this prevents the separation of parents and their minor children. Fourthly, he is bound to give them a fair compensation for their labour, which supposes the right on the part of the slave to hold property. Any laws inconsistent with these principles are unscriptural and unjust, and ought to be immediately abrogated. (4) The consequences of acting on these principles would be the speedy and peaceful abrogation of slavery, the gradual elevation of the slaves to all the rights of free citizens. This is the ground taken in the article of 1836. In the conclusion of that article it is said: ' It may be objected that if the slaves are allowed so to improve as to become free men, the next step in their progress is that they will become citizens. We admit that it is so. The feudal serf first became a tenant, then a proprietor invested with political power. This is the natural progress of political society, and it should be allowed freely to expand itself, or it will work its own destruction.'

The great popular mistake on this subject – a mistake which produced incalculable evil – was confounding slaveholding with slave laws. Because a despotic monarch may make unjust and cruel laws, in order to keep his people in a state of degradation, that his power may be secured and rendered permanent, it does not follow that an absolute monarchy is 'a heinous crime in the sight of God and man'. In like manner, because the laws of a slave-holding State may be unscriptural and wicked, it does not follow that slave-holding is itself sinful.

2. The articles on the 'Rule of Faith,' 'Beman on the Atonement', 'Bushnell on Christian Culture', and 'Professor Park's Sermon, entitled *The Theology of the Intellect and That of the Feelings*', all of them attracted general attention, and built up his reputation as a sound theologian and an effective controversialist. They were all reprinted in America and Great Britain in the volumes entitled *Princeton Essays* and *Essays and Reviews*. The article in review of Beman on the Atonement was published in Scotland under the title, *The Orthodox Doctrine regarding the Atonement vindicated by Charles*

Hodge, D.D., etc., with a Recommendatory Preface by the Rev. Dr Cunningham, Prof. McCrie, and Drs Candlish and Symington.

In the *Free Church Magazine*, 1846, there is a notice of that volume by Dr W. M. Hetherington, as follows:

> It would be difficult to mention another treatise of the same size in which so much useful information will be found, both in regard to the nature and to the extent of the Atonement. Dr Hodge is already most favourably known in this country by some theological works as remarkable for the profound learning they indicate as for the dignified simplicity with which themes of sacred learning are discussed in them. One prevailing feature of his writings is the evidence they constantly supply that his orthodoxy is not merely a passive impression, but the attainment of a mind vigorously exercised in the search of truth . . . This treatise gives a lucid summary of the most important points bearing on present controversies respecting the Atonement, is written in a strain of calm power and dignity, and successfully combats the sophistries through which so many authors attempt to refute the old and orthodox doctrine, not by fair arguments against it, but by an utter caricature of the doctrine itself.

3. His article on the 'Claims of the Free Church of Scotland' was written in the spring of 1844, just after the first two visits of Dr William Cunningham to his house. It was regarded by that eminent Free-churchman himself as a faithful exposition of the principles of that body, and as an efficient plea for its moral and material support. Upon his return to Scotland Dr Cunningham read copious extracts from this article, in connection with his report to the General Assembly. The moderator, Dr Gordon, in thanking Dr Cunningham and his colleagues in the commission said among other things:

> I think he (Dr C.) has produced in the extracts which he has read from the living American divine, who, of all others of whom I have read, I do most honour and esteem, evidence that the feeling which

he (Dr C.) has awakened by the simple exposition of our principles is already working for good in America itself.

4. His article on 'Civil Government' and the transcendently important principles he held as to the relation of the Church to the State, and of the State to the Christian Religion, will be more appropriately discussed when we come to his articles on the state of the country and of the Church, written during the civil war.

5. His article on the 'Theories of the Church', and that on the 'Rights of Ruling Elders', form part of a series covering the entire department of ecclesiology, which, although written and delivered as lectures to his Seminary classes during the decade embraced in this chapter, were nevertheless, for the most part, not published until ten years afterwards, when they led to considerable discussion and to the exhibition of much diversity of opinion.

SUSTENTATION

6. The article on the 'Support of the Clergy', July 1847, was a review of 'An Earnest Appeal' to the Free Church of Scotland on the subject of 'Economics', by Thomas Chalmers, D.D. At the same time Dr Hodge made his sermon as Moderator at the opening of the General Assembly at Richmond, an earnest appeal to the American Church in behalf of the great principles fought for by Dr Chalmers in Scotland, and subsequently by Dr McCosh and Dr Jacobus by means of the 'Sustentation Scheme' in America. Dr Hodge is thus proved to have been the first and the most persistent advocate of this most necessary reform in our ecclesiastical administration. Nineteen years afterwards, in an article on 'The Sustentation Fund', January 1866, he reiterates this plea with increased force of argument and intensity of conviction. He defines a 'Sustentation Fund' to be, 'A sum raised by annual contributions to carry out the two principles, first, that every minister of the gospel, devoted to his work, is entitled, by the command of

Christ, to a competent support; and secondly, that the obligation to furnish that support rests upon the Church as a whole. That is, that the Church, in her organic unity, is bound to provide an adequate support for every man whom she ordains to the ministry, and who is qualified and willing to devote himself to her service. The soundness of these principles we have endeavoured to establish.' These principles he always held to be not only true, but of the greatest practical importance, and that their practical execution was especially demanded by the conditions of the American Presbyterian Church. He sympathized with all his heart with the gallant struggle to carry those principles into action by Dr Jacobus and the Sustentation Committee, and he lamented the failure of that enterprise as a great ecclesiastical disaster.

7. In his articles on the General Assembly, the most important subjects of permanent interest discussed were the 'Validity of the Baptism of the Roman Catholic Church', the 'Quorum', and 'Elder Questions', and the 'Marriage of a Man with the Sister of his Deceased Wife'. The 'Quorum' and 'Elder Questions' will fall properly under the consideration of his articles on the Church and its officers, which is reserved for a future page. As to the marriage of a man with the sister of his deceased wife, he argued, both on the floor of the Assemblies of 1842 and 1847, and in his articles on the Assembly for 1842, 1843 and 1847, that such marriages are forbidden in Scripture, and therefore unlawful for Christians, to be forbidden and made the occasion of discipline by the church courts; but, on the other hand, that they are not invalid, and that the parties to them should not be separated and might, after a period of suspension, be restored to the communion of the church.

ROMISH BAPTISM

The General Assembly which met at Cincinnati, Ohio, May 1845, suddenly fulminated by a vote of one hundred and sixty-nine to eight, *non liquet*[1] eight, the new and anti-Protestant doctrine that baptism administered by a Roman Catholic priest was not Christian Baptism. Dr Hodge always lamented this as a great blunder, as well as an untrue decision of injurious consequence. In his article on 'The General Assembly' for that year, and in his article, 'Is the Church of Rome part of the visible Church?', published April 1846, he vigorously combated that decision. He held that the papacy – the institution, not the person – is anti-Christ,[2] and that the order and teaching of the Romish Church is in many respects corrupted and overlaid by false and soul-destroying abuses and errors. Yet he held and believed that he proved (1) that the great body of people constituting the Roman Catholic Church do profess the essentials of the true Christian religion, whereby many of them bear the image of Christ, and are participants of His salvation. (2) Hence that that community, however corrupt, is a part of the visible Church on earth, the field with the wheat mixed with tares. (3) That the essentials as to 'matter' and 'form' of Christian Baptism are observed by the Catholic Priest, when he administers that sacrament. (4) And hence it was to be recognized by all loyal to the great Head of the whole Church as Christian Baptism. (5) That the Reformers and great Protestant theologians had universally and uniformly held and practically recognized Romish Baptism to be Christian Baptism, irregular and deformed by superstitions, but still valid. (6) That this truly Protestant position had been held by the great body of the Protestant Churches to the present time.

He was the author of the Answer[3] to the invitation addressed by Pius IX, in his Encyclical to all Protestants 'to return to the one only fold', on the occasion of the Ecumenical Council of the

---

[1] 'It is not clear'; In law, a *non liquet* is a situation where there is no applicable law. [Ed.]

[2] *Systematic Theology*, vol. 3, pp. 812–23.

[3] Reprinted in the *Banner of Truth* magazine, 415, April 1998, pp. 22–5. [Ed.]

Vatican, held in Rome, 1869–70. This response, signed officially by Drs M. W. Jacobus and P. H. Fowler, the Moderators of the two General Assemblies of 1869, was certainly surpassed as to lofty dignity, knowledge, charity, steadfast and ecumenical orthodoxy, and power by none, and equalled by very few of the many answers on that occasion addressed by Protestants to the Head of the Catholic world.

On the occasion of writing this address to the Pope he received the following letter from Dr William Adams, now President of Union Theological Seminary, New York:

DR WILLIAM ADAMS TO DR HODGE

NEW YORK, June 17th, 1869

My Dear Dr Hodge:—I have received from Dr Musgrave the manuscript of your reply to the Pope. It is *admirable every way*. I see not how it could be improved. You were right in judging that objurgation was impertinent to the occasion. Every thing is put in the simple, pointed, dignified manner becoming a Christian scholar and theologian.

You may be sure that you have done an excellent service in consenting to prepare this paper. It will do good at home, in other churches besides that of Rome, and I beg you to accept my sincere thanks as one of the Nominating Committee . . .

With cordial esteem,

Your friend and brother,
WILLIAM ADAMS

In August 1872, he was asked by letter his opinion as to the propriety of granting tracts of land along a railroad for the purpose of building Roman Catholic churches. He answered:

Others say that inasmuch as the Roman Catholic Church teaches truth enough to save the souls of men (of which I have no doubt); inasmuch as it proclaims the divine authority of the Scriptures, the obligation of the decalogue, and the retributions of eternity; and inasmuch as it calls upon men to worship God the Father, Son and Spirit, it is unspeakably better than no church at all. And, therefore, when the choice is between that and none, it is wise and right to encourage the establishment of churches under the control of Catholic priests. For myself, I take this view. The principle cannot be carried out that no church is to be encouraged which teaches error.[1]

He closes his argument in the *Princeton Review*, April 1846:

It is said we give up too much to the Papists if we admit Romanists to be in the church. To this we answer – Every false position is a weak position. The cause of truth suffers in no way more than from identifying it with error, which is always done when its friends advocate it on false principles. When one says we favour intemperance unless we say that the use of intoxicating liquors is sinful; another, that we favour slavery unless we say slave-holding is a sin; and a third, that we favour Popery unless we say the Church of Rome is no church, they all, as it seems to us, make the same mistake and greatly injure the cause in which they are engaged. They give the adversary an advantage over them, and they fail to enlist the strength of their own side. It is a great mistake to suppose that Popery is aided by admitting what truth it does include. What gives it its power, what constitutes its peculiarly dangerous character, is that it is not pure infidelity, it is not the entire rejection of the gospel, but truth surrounded by enticing and destructive error.

There is no more characteristic passage to be found in his whole writings. And in these opinions he agreed with all his brethren in Princeton, with the Reformers, the great theologians of the past and the Scotch theologians of today.

MODERATOR OF THE GENERAL ASSEMBLY

He was a member for the first time of the General Assembly of 1842, having been hitherto prevented from attending by his

---

[1] *Presbyterian*, August 10th, 1872.

lameness. He was again sent as a delegate to the General Assembly which met in the 10th Presbyterian Church, Philadelphia, May 1846, when he was elected Moderator. He attended as a commissioner the next Assembly in Richmond, May 1847, and opened its sessions with a sermon in which he advocated the erection of a Board of Sustentation for the more uniform and systematic support of the clergy.

HIS LETTERS TO HIS BROTHER

His letters to his brother during this period, from 1840 to 1851, continued frequent and regular, and were filled with all the details of family life. All he thinks and feels, all his anxieties with respect to his children or the church or the country, all the symptoms of the children's successive sicknesses, all the events which marked the stages of their mental or physical growth are minutely recorded.

PRINCETON, March 13, 1840

My Dear Brother:—My remark about my horrible poverty, in my last, was not intended as a hint. When very bad off, I shall go beyond hinting. It is true, I had not a cent in the world, nor have had for some time. But then here is the Bank; and what is a Bank worth but to let people overdraw? Ours is good-natured enough to let us suck out fives and tens through a straw; a check for a hundred or two they might endorse, 'No Funds!' – but they would hardly insult a gentleman for five dollars. Still, this is ugly business, and I feel much better since I received your hundred dollars, for which, therefore, I am much obliged to you. I will give you an order on my publisher for payment. You surely need not open your eyes at a poor author; for when was an author otherwise than poor, unless he wrote novels.

Your affectionate brother, C.H.

PRINCETON, April 28, 1840

M— (a daughter visiting her uncle) tells me that you laughed much at my sending her *two* dollars. I can remember the time, old fellow, when the sight of two dollars would have made you laugh with a very different emotion. You do not know what it is to be a Presbyterian Abbé, with seven children. Only think of seven mouths, seven pair of feet, seven empty heads, and worse than all seven pairs of knees and elbows. Don't take this for a begging letter; for Friday is the first of May, when I expect to be as rich as Croesus for a week.

Your brother, C.H.

PRINCETON, June 18, 1841

My Dear Brother:—The conduct of the House of Representatives, in Washington, is enough to put one out of conceit with Republicanism. The Southern members act like a set of big boys, and the Northern ones are just as foolish. The fuss they make about the right of petition is just as unreasonable as the commotion about abolition. It has always, however, been so. Commotion, noise, nonsense, and at times violence are the price of liberty, and on the whole are better than the stagnation of despotism. Wise is the *beau ideal* of Southern gasconade [boasting].

Your brother, C.H.

PRINCETON, Sept. 17, 1841

My Dear Brother:—I thank you for sending the papers at this unprecedented crisis in our affairs. It seems to me there can be but one opinion either as to the President's conduct, or as to the duty of the Whigs. Mr Ewing's letter contains irresistible evidence of its truth, and is confirmed by all kinds of collateral evidence. Assuming the truth of its statements, Mr Tyler is not only a weak, but a dishonourable and dishonest man. Now that this humiliating fact has been disclosed, people begin to look at his past history. And the singular fact, which had escaped notice, that not one of the Virginia delegates at the Harrisburg Convention voted for his nomination to the Vice-Presidency shows that they knew more about him than others did. Still, it is probable that it was not until his head was turned by his being made President that his principles were found to be too weak to stand the temptations of that exalted station. Dr Benjamin Rice told me that he remembers when he (Tyler) became Governor of Virginia, people lifted up their hands and said 'Think of John Tyler being Governor of Virginia!' His messages, especially the first veto, show him to be a man of inferior mind, and his conduct to his Cabinet and his party show him to be mean and dishonest.

It seems to me that if the Whigs would only act on moral instead of party principles, it would be a great blessing to the country and the best course for themselves. Let them give the President a fair hearing and every opportunity of clearing himself from the overwhelming charges of Mr Ewing. If he can do it, then all is well. If he cannot, then let them say to him, 'We are done with you. Not one of our party will accept or retain office under you. We will do what we can for the country, but we will not condescend to serve under you.' If the other party would pick him out of the gutter let them do it. But I do not believe they would. On the contrary, I believe he would be forced to resign in less than six months.

Thinking that this is the plain course of duty, I feel greatly mortified at the conduct of Mr Webster. I am glad he retains his place for the time being, but his reasons for doing so condemn him. His saying that there was no sufficient reason for the resignation of the Cabinet, and by implication that his colleagues did wrong in giving up their places, shows that his state of mind on the whole subject is entirely different from that of his friends. I have sufficient confidence in the moral feelings of the community to be confident that if Mr Webster joins himself with Tyler he will sink with him. The load of infamy which attaches to the latter is enough to weigh down all that associate themselves with his fortunes. I cannot have any respect for any man who accepts a place in the new Cabinet; and shall be astonished if Mr Legare or Judge Maclean accept their appointments.

As to the charge against Mr Ewing, of revealing Cabinet secrets, it seems to me to be entirely unfounded. The obligation to secrecy cannot extend to all cases. It is limited by the nature of the object for which that secrecy is enjoined. If a President should be plotting treason, his Cabinet are bound to disclose it. And if it is necessary to the vindication of the character of a Minister to relate what passed in the Cabinet, I am not sure that he has not a right to do it. But Mr Ewing does not need the advantage of either of these grounds of defence. Mr Tyler commissioned him and Mr Webster to communicate his views to Mr Sergeant, and to Mr Berrien and others. Mr Ewing, therefore, has revealed no secret; the main facts were communicated by the President's message. This seems to be a full vindication, without resorting to the example of the President himself, through whom Cabinet secrets are said to have found their way to *Bennett's Herald!* Taking it altogether, the whole affair is the most extraordinary event in our history, and the issue, I fear, depends very much on Webster. If he separates himself from the Whigs, who will and ought to repudiate the President, on him will rest the responsibility of the schism in the Whig party. And the result will probably be defeat to them with certain disappointment and disgrace to him.

Here is a letter of real politics, which, when connected with morals and the character and interests of the country, is a subject second only to religion in importance.

Your brother, C.H.

PRINCETON, Dec. 15, 1844

My Dear Brother:—You ask me for a dish of politics. I could only give you a plate of picked bones. The Whig party seems to have made a great mistake; either they have not patriotism enough to give up personal objects for the general good, or, what is probably the case, they have not been able to identify themselves with the masses. In this country the Democratic party must always be the strongest, and it is only on extraordinary occasions, and for a short period, that the Whig, the Conservative, the Federal, or by whatever name the mass of the intelligence and property of the country may be called, can get the upper hand. Such an occasion occurred in 1840. The fruits of that triumph were lost mainly by the treachery of Tyler, partly by the passion and selfishness of the Whigs. I am afraid, when they found that Tyler was unfaithful, they determined to make his administration as unpopular and as disastrous as possible. If the country, at the end of his term, is prosperous, there will be no crying necessity for a change of policy, and for Mr Clay; but if everything is going to ruin, as under Van Buren, then a change will be demanded. I fear this is the ground of their opposition to the Tariff, which passed by a bare majority, and especially of their refusal to adopt the exchequer bill of Tyler (i.e., of Webster). It seems evident that an addition of $15,000,000 to our currency, in the form of paper of equal value in all parts of the country, would be an inestimable benefit. But the Whigs refuse, and by doing so will break their own heads.

Your brother, C.H.

PRINCETON, March 26, 1844
My Dear Brother:—The papers make a great stir about Texas. I cannot believe it is possible to get two-thirds of the Senate to vote for the annexation. Should such a thing happen, it would be a great crime and a great calamity; but I think the North ought to submit. We have agreed that any treaty made by two-thirds of the Senate shall be the law of the land, and we ought to abide by the contract. After the annexation of Louisiana and Florida, the constitutional question must be considered fixed. The cases are not alike; but they are not essentially different.

I rejoice greatly that O'Connell has been convicted. If the law and justice would fully sustain the sentence, I think it would be a great good to give him a life estate in Australia.

Your affectionate brother,
CHARLES HODGE

PRINCETON, April 4, 1844
My Dear Brother:—There is, financially speaking, always a shallow spot with me during the month of April. If my salary is paid, I can generally get over it; if it is not, I am very apt to stick fast. As not the half of the salary due the 1st of February last has been paid, I am in

the latter predicament just now. I must either submit to the mortifi-cation of begging time – etc., or to that of borrowing from you. The latter, though something, is much the less trial of the two.

I have yet to learn the art of paying without being paid. All this is a prelude to my saying that I wish you to lend me a couple of hundred dollars, or one, if convenient. If you have it not on hand, say so. For it is not a case of necessity, but of feeling. I must pay certain calls which have already come in; but I can, on an emergency, get the money from the Bank, but that I, of course, do not like.

Your brother, C.H.

PRINCETON, April 22nd, 1844

My Dear Brother:—I told you some time ago, in reply to what you said about Mr Barnes' pamphlet – 'The Position of the Evangelical Party in the Episcopal Church' – that, judging from the extracts which I had seen, I disapproved of its whole design and tendency. Since then I have read it, and my first impression has been confirmed. I wrote a notice, of a few pages length, of it in the *Repertory*, which has the full concurrence of all the gentlemen here, and which I hope you will read. That notice, I am sorry to say, has given immeasurable offence to the ultra-Presbyterians of Philadelphia, and if you see the *Presbyterian* you will see two columns and a half of a reply to it. I am very sorry for this, as it evinces a very unnatural state of mind in the Philadelphia brethren. What the notice says they would all have said six months ago. And if a man whose feelings are so strongly Presbyte-rian as Dr Miller approves of it, it is very plain that it is only a morbid state of mind that leads to this outcry. Mr Hope, poor fellow, has, as he writes me, been almost persecuted to death for it already.

Your brother, C.H.

PRINCETON, May 28, 1844

My Dear Brother:—I have just been reading Bishop Hughes' smart, but not very prelatical letter to the Mayor of New York. He confounds two very different things: opposition to foreigners, as foreigners, governing the country, and opposition to Papists, as Papists. It is true that most of these objectionable foreigners are Papists, but the opposition to them is as foreigners. It is also true that they are mostly Irish, but the opposition is not to them as Irish. I think this whole struggle will do good, and that a majority of all parties will soon unite in calling for an alteration of our naturalization laws. Bishop Hughes artfully represents the American party as leagued to deny liberty of conscience, and to infringe on the rights of a particular class of citizens. But what right have the paupers of Europe to be citizens of America? We must take care of ourselves, or we shall have all our affairs under the control of the mob of foreigners who swarm our cities.

We are all well as usual; nearly through the pangs of house-cleaning. It is with difficulty I have kept the invasion of tubs and buckets out of the study.

Your affectionate brother, C.H.

Princeton, June 20, 1844

My Dear Brother:—We returned day before yesterday from the North, having had a very pleasant journey of two weeks and five days. We went first to Newburgh, where we spent Saturday, Sunday and part of Monday. Thence to Netherwood (the residence of James Lenox, Esq.,), where I remained till Wednesday, when I went to Poughkeepsie to attend the Synod (Dutch Reformed), as a delegate from the General Assembly, leaving Sarah, who was in bed with a sick head-ache. At the close of the week I returned to Netherwood and remained until Tuesday, and then, agreeably to an invitation from the Rosevelts, took Sarah to Poughkeepsie and spent that day there.

The country up the North river greatly exceeded our expectations, and Sarah was greatly delighted. Newburgh has a beautiful situation, and the views in the neighborhood are extensive and picturesque in a high degree. Mr Lenox's situation, Netherwood, is very delightful and very highly improved. He is a man of very uncommon taste. His brother-in-law has a cottage on his place; another brother-in-law,

Mr Sheefe, owns the next seat up the river, and Mr Sheefe's mother the one above that. The four families are so near and so united as to form a compact society for themselves. Poughkeepsie also surpassed our expectations. The view from College Hill is one of the finest in all that region of country.

It is impossible that people could be kinder than we found them everywhere, at Newburgh, Netherwood, Poughkeepsie, Albany and New Haven.

Your brother, C.H.

PRINCETON, Dec. 16, 1844

My Dear Brother:—I believe that we have not exchanged lamentations over the result of the election. I feel more for Mr Clay than for the country. For I presume the general policy of the Government will be substantially the same under Mr Polk. Mr Clay, however, has finally lost the great object of his natural ambition, and lost it by the votes of foreigners and Catholics, aliens and enemies really of the country. In New York, the silly Abolitionists decided the State, and that again decided the country. The course which Tyler and Calhoun have been pursuing is so extreme that I hope it will lead to a split in their own ranks and induce the Northern and Western Democrats to unite in putting them effectually down.

Your affectionate brother, C.H.

PRINCETON, April 17, 1846

My Dear Brother:—I felt really alarmed at the speech of John Quincy Adams in the House, declaring his opinion not only that our title to Oregon was good to 54.40, but that we ought not to compromise on 49.[1] Now, as he and every President since Jefferson has offered that compromise, it does appear to me a piece of pure wickedness to refuse to accept that offer now; to refuse to accede to our own terms,

---

[1] Hodge feared that extending the border of Oregon to 54° 40′ N., the Alaska boundary, would inevitably lead to war with Great Britain whose claims in the region would be encroached on. [Ed.]

and that with the certainty that war must be the consequence of such refusal. Great Britain has not the power to give up the country beyond 49. The public sentiment of the nation and of the world would be so against it that it could not be done, any more than we could give up the country south of the Columbia, which England has offered over and over as the boundary. I greatly fear that, unless Providence over-rule the folly of our rulers, we are destined to the miseries of a wicked war.

Your affectionate brother, C.H.

Princeton, Dec. 25, 1846

My Dear Brother:—Give the love and gratulations appropriate to this season from all our circle to all yours. We are getting to be pretty old men, though we do not know it, and, I suppose, really enjoy life in the consciousness of useful and conscious exertion more than when we were younger. The kinds and sources of pleasure change as we advance in life, but the maturer are always of the higher grade, and therefore few men would be willing to go back and live life over again; they would rather live onward and continue to grow in knowledge and in the power to do good. It is a great thing to be content to be less than others, provided we do our best. Self-depreciation is a more amiable, but scarcely a less hurtful failing than self-exaltation, or rather self-glorification.

Your brother C.H.

Princeton, Dec. 29, 1847.

My Dear Brother:—It is true, I am fifty years old, and that the meridian of life is past. The years that remain must be few and less fitted for exertion or usefulness. On the review of such a period, a painful feeling of having accomplished so little, of having acquired so much less than we see we might and ought to have done, is, perhaps, stronger even than the feeling of gratitude for all the goodness and forbearance of God. I feel that almost all the usefulness of my life is to be crowded into the coming ten years, should I live so long. If I am to accomplish anything it must be within that period, and yet how much reason is there to fear that, should they be granted, they will slip by much as any preceding ten years have done.

Your affectionate brother, C.H.

FROM PROFESSOR BIGGS TO DR HODGE

CINCINNATI, Jan. 7, 1847

My Dear Doctor Charles:—You had almost forgotten, I suppose, that the little man whom you first knew in the blue frock coat in Nassau Hall is still among the living. Once in a while I hear something of your own dear self, and then I feel a stirring up of things of bygone days – such as watching from the window of No. 18 your movement down the campus, cross the road and down the lane, to the white house with the little white fence in front, opposite to which lived the far-famed Sam Plum. Charley, d'ye mind the days we spent in the white house together? (Mrs Bache's). Oh! ho! what times have passed o'er us since then! But, indeed, they have been times of mercy, such as my most sanguine hopes could not have imagined. Here I am an old man, grey-headed, with nose spectacle bestrid, and a house full of men and women children! What is still more wonderful, I am just about as fit for service as ever . . .

I preach in the vicinity of my old stamping grounds, Lane Seminary, where I have as part of my audience some of the students from the Seminary, with several others from the families belonging to the Seminary Church. This looks a little like bearding the lion in his own den. It is rather amusing as I pass out on Sabbath morning from the city to meet Dr Beecher coming in to supply the '1st Orthodox Congregational Society of Cincinnati', and sometimes Prof. Stowe.

You remember our old redoubtable Vice-President Slack! I have the felicity of seeing his ex-ship quite often. He has what he calls his Gothic mansion on one of the most elevated points about our city, very conspicuous indeed, most romantically difficult of access. He is pretty much after the old stamp, except as time has corrugated his squatty face. He sojourns on the heights in elevated retirement. He is a good old man, nevertheless, and loves to recount his Princeton glories. Our old friend, Wm. M. Atkinson, spent a few days with us recently. We had quite a refreshing time of it. He is a huge body of divinity, beats me some twenty or thirty pounds.

Your affectionate brother,
Thos. J. Biggs

Bishop Johns wrote to 'Charley' about the same time:

Biggs—Thomas J.!! What would I not give to have you both here at once! But I suppose that is out of the question.

And again, in April of the next year, he writes:

I received a full and affectionate letter from Biggs. I am afraid he will not live long. This sudden revival of early feeling is ominous.

FRIENDSHIP AND CORRESPONDENCE
WITH DR WILLIAM CUNNINGHAM

In December 1843, Dr Hodge formed one of the most signal friendships of his life. The Rev. William Cunningham, D.D., afterwards Principal of the New College, Edinburgh, visited America at the head of a delegation of the Free Church of Scotland. He was then thirty-eight years of age, at the fullness of all his powers, recognized everywhere as beyond question the greatest logician, polemic and theologian among the leaders of the second heroic age of the Church of Christ in Scotland. He always recognized Charles Hodge, then just forty-six years old, as occupying precisely that position in the American Presbyterian Church of this age. The meeting and the rapid friendship generated between two men having so much in common, meeting for the first time and for a brief season, was very beautiful to witness and very memorable. A Princeton witness of that first meeting, quoted by Dr Rainy in his life of Cunningham, wrote at the time:

You know Brother Hodge is one of the most reserved of men, nor is a first acquaintance with him generally very assuring or attractive to strangers. But I remarked with what warmth and cordiality he met Dr Cunningham, as if he had met an old friend from whom he had been long separated. And it was so with Cunningham, too. The two greatest theologians of the age were at once friends and brothers. They seemed at once to read and know each the other's great and noble mind.

After Dr Cunningham's lamented death, just eighteen years afterwards, Dr Hodge wrote as follows:

He was twice (it was really three times) at Princeton, and on both occasions made my house his home. He was a man you knew well as soon as you knew him at all. He revealed himself at once, and secured at once the confidence and love of those in whom he felt confidence. I do not recollect of ever having met any one to whom I was so much drawn, and for whom I entertained so high a respect and so warm a regard as I did for him, on such a short acquaintance . . . His visit was one of those sunny spots on which, whenever I look back on my life, my eyes rest with delight.

Dr Cunningham wrote to his wife at this time:

As I have not much public business till next week I have come out to spend a few days in Princeton. I have had great pleasure in the society of the theological professors here, who are all men eminent for their talents and learning, and are known in Britain by their writings. I am staying with Dr Hodge, a very admirable and interesting man, whose wife is a great grand-daughter of Dr Franklin.

The compiler of these Memoirs was repeatedly assured in Scotland that his father's pre-eminent position in the respect and confidence of the Scotch Presbyterian Churches dates from the period of Dr Cunningham's return from his visit to America, and that it was characteristic of Dr C. to give free expression to his high estimate of him as a man and a theologian. Dr Rainy affirms in his *Life of William Cunningham D.D.*, p. 462, that the great Scotchman 'felt for Dr Hodge, of Princeton, a very great regard as a man, and in his theological opinions generally a greater confidence than in those of any (other) divine now living'.

I can well remember those memorable days, the pleased excitement of our father, as he lay back upon his easy chair listening to Dr Cunningham as he strode gesticulating through the study with his long arms laying down the principles and narrating the story of the great Free-Church Exodus, or when our father walked with him in the larger parlour, or once or twice, when the February sun shone clear in the paths around the house, laying down the principles and narrating the story of the great controversies, as to slavery, New England theology and voluntary societies, in which his own part had been not insignificant.

DR HODGE TO DR CUNNINGHAM

PRINCETON, March 21st, 1844

. . . Dr Burns preached a delightful sermon in our chapel last evening. I believe we are all disposed to let him abuse us and our domestic institutions as much as he pleases, if he will only preach the gospel ? as purely and spiritually as he did last night.

I cherish the recollections of your visit with great pleasure and feel an interest in your success and welfare which is constantly increasing as my knowledge of you and your cause increases.

I should be much gratified to hear from you at any time. As Dr Miller has insisted on your going to his house when you again visit Princeton, I feel at liberty to beg that you will send to me any of your brethren who may join your deputation, should they come thus far south. With great affection and respect,

Your friend and brother,
CHARLES HODGE

PRINCETON, March 30, 1844

My Dear Sir:—We have had 500 extra copies of the article on 'The Claims of the Free Church' struck off. I send you a copy by this mail.

If, after reading it, you think it likely to be useful, I will place at your disposal any portion of the 500 you wish. I can send them to Mr Carter in New York, to abide your order.

I was greatly interested in the copies of the *Witness* which you left with me. I think he has most effectually answered the *Record*, and I regret that we were misled into saying what we did in our January number by the last named paper. Professor A. Alexander wishes me to subscribe to the *Witness*, and begs me to inquire of you how payment for it can most conveniently be made. Is there anybody in this country authorized to receive payment on its behalf, and who would order it for him?

I should be very glad to hear from you and learn how you get along among the 'Yankees'. I do not use the word in Mrs Hodge's sense of the term. I know if they get their eyes open they will put us Old School Presbyterians to shame. I sincerely hope they may.

The whole family join in the assurance of kind remembrance.

Affectionately and respectfully,

C. Hodge

DR CUNNINGHAM TO DR HODGE

Boston, 9th April, 1844

My Dear Sir:—I have received your two letters, and am much obliged to you for the accompanying papers. I am grieved to be under the necessity of informing you that, in consequence of letters which I received from Scotland by the last steamer, urging me most strenuously to be present at our own General Assembly, I have felt it to be my duty to resolve on leaving this country on the 1st of May, and that, of course, I must leave Dr Burns to go to Canada alone, and Mr Lewis and Mr Chalmers to attend your General Assembly. I greatly fear that I shall not be able to visit Princeton again. I intend to visit New Haven or Hartford on Sabbath next, Albany on the 21st, then make a run to Niagara, get to New York on Saturday the 27th, and leave it for Boston on the 29th. So far as my own personal feelings and inclinations are concerned I would have been most happy to have spent two months more in this country, where I have been received with so much kindness and seen so much to interest and to gratify. I felt quite dull the other day after having taken my berth in the steamer, although I was going home. I will not soon forget the kindness I have received and the gratification I have experienced; and the time I have spent in your society at Princeton will always occupy a prominent place in my recollection of America.

I will henceforth consider myself entitled to call you my friend, and will be most happy to have occasional correspondence with you. I will consider it my duty to begin this correspondence and write to you soon after reaching home. I have read with great pleasure your article for the *Repertory*, and would like very much to see it circulated for the benefit of our cause. I would like very much to have a parcel of the articles addressed to me at Albany, to the care of Dr Sprague, and I would like to have some of them to take home with me, as I am sure they will be read with great interest by my brethren. I fear that in other respects I must request you to take the trouble of disposing of them in the way you yourself may think best fitted to promote the object in view, except I would like a small parcel of them addressed to Mr Chalmers, care of the Rev. Mr Blagden, Old South Church, Boston.

The cause has been taken up cordially here by the Congregationalists and the Baptists. I don't know what may be the result in a pecuniary point of view, but as I have not heard of any very large subscriptions from individuals, I fear the sum total will not come to a great deal.

Give kindest regards to Mrs Hodge and all the members of your family, to Dr Miller, to Dr Alexander and his sons, and believe me, my dear sir,

Very sincerely yours,
WM. CUNNINGHAM

In order that the allusions to the Abolitionists in this correspondence may be understood, it must be recollected that Dr

Hodge, and the great mass of the American Christians with whom Dr Cunningham came in contact, were not pro-slavery men, but held, as Dr R. J. Breckinridge told Dr Cunningham in a letter, dated November 1844: '(1) That slavery is a great evil, and ought to be somehow and sometime brought to an end. (2) That it is not a sin, in the proper sense of the word, and, therefore, cannot be a proper ground of expulsion from the Church.' 'On the other hand,' says Dr Rainy, in his *Life of Wm. Cunningham,* p. 221, 'some of the American Abolitionists ('technically so called,' as Dr Breckinridge says), seeing some likelihood of troubled waters, came across to fish in them. That party included, as is very well known, a number of persons who were not particular in their choice of weapons. They vilified the Free Church as associating with slave-holders for the sake of pecuniary gain, and raised the cry of "Send back the money." As their antecedents became known and their methods of warfare observed, they lost their influence and vanished again.'

DR CUNNINGHAM TO DR HODGE

Edinburgh, 15th of July, 1844

My Dear Sir:—I arrived safely in Edinburgh on the 16th of May and found my wife and children in the enjoyment of good health, and the affairs of the Free Church in a very flourishing condition. We have had a very interesting and gratifying meeting of the Assembly. We are now delivered wholly from the unpleasant contentions with unchristian men, in which we had been so long engaged, and are, I think I may say, devoting ourselves with united energy and zeal to the improvement of the important facilities for the promotion of true religion, with which in providence we are favoured.

I regretted that I had not an opportunity of revising the *Witness'* report of the statement I made about my visit to America. Reporting here is not nearly so perfect as in London, and the report of what I said is neither very accurate nor complete.

I succeeded in preventing our Assembly from doing anything on the subject of slavery, except appointing a committee to consider it, and I shall do what I can to get them to do as little as possible. I suppose I must submit to being branded by the Abolitionists as having been corrupted by the money and hospitality of slave-holders.

I most earnestly wish, however, that the churches of the United States could be stirred up to do something more than they have been doing of late years in regard to slavery, at least to the extent of seeking the abolition of what all condemn, such as the prohibition of instruction and the separation of families, for, although we generally profess here to hold anti-slavery principles, I believe that it is these atrocious slave laws and their immediate practical results that chiefly excite our indignation, not only against those who practise them, but against all who may be supposed to connive at or tolerate them. I would fain hope that the proceedings of the Methodist Conference in regard to Bishop Andrews, which I have just read in the *Presbyterian*, indicate a growing sense of the necessity of the churches bestirring themselves in this matter. Dr Burns has, since his return, been lecturing in different parts of the country upon his visit to America, and upon the whole has not, I understand, been guilty of any very great indiscretion. He has usually introduced the subject of slavery, and told some stories of church members being sold, the husband separated from the wife, and the mother from her children. I will continue to do what I can to preserve peace, as I am satisfied that nothing we can do will have any beneficial effect, and because I cannot see that there rests upon us any obligation to testify upon the subject irrespective of a testimony being likely to do good.

By the kindness of a friend I have got the use of a very comfortable and beautifully situated country house, nine miles to the south of Edinburgh, where I expect to have three months of uninterrupted study to prepare for the labours of our Theological Seminary in November. I would fain hope that the decisive votes in your Assembly will put an end to your contentions about the Elder question, and leave you at leisure to prosecute the important objects you have taken up in regard to churches and schools. Just before leaving America I received a few copies from home of a book for young people, called *Witnesses for the Truth*, and I sent one to Mrs Hodge through Mr Carter, which I hope she has received.

The Duke of Sutherland has yielded to the force of public opinion and gives us sites, and the Duke of Buccleuch, under the pretence that he thought the Lord's Supper would be desecrated by being administered in the public road, offered to the people of Canonbie permission to meet in a field on the occasion of the communion, which was last Lord's Day. We think he will scarcely venture to drive them back to the road again.[1]

No part of my statement gave more satisfaction to the General Assembly than the extracts I read to them from your article.

W. C.

I would like very much to hear from you when you have a little leisure. Any thing addressed to me at Edinburgh will reach me. I will ever retain a grateful sense of the kindness I received from you, and a lively recollection of the pleasure I enjoyed in your society. Be so good as to present my kind remembrances to Mrs Hodge and the young people, to Dr Miller, to Dr Alexander and his sons, to Dr Carnahan, Rice and Maclean, and Messrs. Henry and Dod, and believe me to be sincerely and affectionately yours,

WM. CUNNINGHAM

DR HODGE TO DR CUNNINGHAM

PRINCETON, Sept. 13, 1844.

My Dear Sir:—All your Princeton friends were very happy to hear of your safe return to your native land and of the cordial welcome everywhere extended to you. We have rejoiced in the abundant manifestations of the divine favour granted to the Free Church during the past year, and in the inviting prospect of usefulness which is spread out before her.

---

[1] Landowners in many parts of Scotland at first refused to allow congregations of the Free Church to build or even to meet on their property. [Ed.]

Here there is little new or interesting. I am afraid that little will be done in behalf of the Free Church in virtue of the recommendation of our last Assembly. It was a mistake merely to pass resolutions expressing sympathy with your body and urging congregations which had not done anything to make a collection in aid of your funds. If a particular day had been appointed, and all the churches, without any distinction, whether they had done anything or not, called upon to make a collection on that day, I think something better might have come of it. However, you have a better dependence than the distant and feeble churches of America.

We shall be happy to make the arrangements which you suggest with regard to periodicals, etc.

We have all felt a good deal aggrieved by the articles in the *Witness* on American Slavery. It is very evident that they were not written by the editor of that paper; but we are surprised at his publishing them. They are unjust, inaccurate, injurious to the American churches, and of evil tendency in all respects. If the Abolitionists of Great Britain wish to do us any good, let them first define what slavery is, making due discrimination between slave-holding and the varying laws by which, in different countries, slave-holding is regulated. And then let them prove that slave-holding, not the slave laws of this or that State, but slave-holding, is contrary to the Word of God. It cannot do us any good to tell us that it is wrong to be cruel, to be unjust, to separate husbands and wives, parents and children, or to keep servants in ignorance. Our churches do not sanction any of these things, though our laws often do. Instead of really arguing the question, and affecting the conscience through the understanding, such men as the writers in the *Witness* take up reports of this or that case of cruelty, and hold it up as an indication of the character of whole classes of men in this country. They might, of course, as well cite passages from the reports of the commissioners on your mines to show the character of the Free Church of Scotland.

I know, my dear sir, how much superior you are to all such things, and I would not write thus to you if I did not know that you are well aware of the respect which we all have for your principles and conduct in reference to this subject. But I really feel concerned for the effect such articles are likely to produce. It is the want of sense, as much as the want of justice, manifested in such effusions and in the proceedings of some of your emancipation societies that tries our patience. I see Dr Burns is very desirous, in his anti-slavery speeches, to bring to his support 'his respected friend, Dr Cunningham', as much as possible; and to represent himself and you as standing on the same ground on this subject. In the estimation of good people here, there are few things less alike than Dr Burns and 'his respected friend', and it will require hard pulling to get them together. I hope you have seen in the *New York Observer* a notice of the article in the *Witness*. That notice is from the pen of Dr James W. Alexander, who lived many years in Virginia.

I hope you will often write to me, or to some of your friends in Princeton. We shall never forget the pleasure we derived from your visit. Will you present my regards to Dr Gordon, to whom I look up with the deepest respect. I once (1828) had the pleasure of hearing him preach, but had not the advantage of an introduction to him during my short visit to Scotland.

I see by the *Witness* that you are down on the Erastians with a heavy hand. They will think you have let your hair grow during your visit to America. All your friends here, including all the members of my family, unite in assurances of affection and respect.

Your friend and brother,
CHARLES HODGE

PRINCETON, Jan. 29th, 1845

My Dear Sir:— . . . I thank you sincerely for the number of the *North British Review* containing the article on the United States. All your friends in America feel under obligations to you for that manly defence, and all the more that they see you suffer for it. I notice with pain the pecking of the *Record*, which is noticeable only as revealing the animus of the editor. High-churchmen are accused of loving the

Church more than Christ or Christians, and the *Record* really seems to love aristocracy more than men. It can see no good, or rejoice in nothing good, where there are not kings and nobles. I have never noticed an expression of satisfaction at the evidence of the power of the Gospel in this country, but a uniform disposition to rejoice in all our infirmities and vices . . .

I rejoice to see that your New College meets with so much favour. We all cherish the recollection of your visit as something we can never let die out of our minds. I hope you will brighten the chain occasionally by letting us hear from you. Mrs Hodge and my children beg that you will not forget them . . .

Very sincerely your friend and brother,

CHARLES HODGE

DR CUNNINGHAM TO DR HODGE

EDINBURGH, 26th April, 1845

My Dear Sir:—I have to thank you for two letters, and to apologize for not answering them sooner. For the last six months I have been occupied very thoroughly with the duties of a first session in our Theological Seminary. I had made very little written preparation before the beginning of the session, as for nearly five months I have, besides other duties, to compose each week three lectures of fifty minutes each. The session, however, is now over, and we have a vacation of six months. I sent you lately two numbers of the *Witness* containing a report of a discussion in our Presbytery on 'American Slavery', which has, I think, put down 'Abolitionism' in its technical sense, so far as the Free Church is concerned . . .

I read with much interest the article on 'Abolitionism' in the *Repertory*. It contained some important truths, which, in this country, when judging of the American churches, we are far too apt to overlook. But I am not satisfied of the soundness of some of its principles. I cannot see how any human being can justly and validly lose his own personal, natural right to control his time and labour, unless the element either of his own consent or of penal infliction for a crime proven be brought in. I cannot but think that every man is entitled to escape from slavery if he can, an idea decidedly confirmed by the decisions of the Mosaic Law about runaway slaves, and as the master's right and the slave's obligation must be correlative, it would seem that the slave's right to run away disproves the master's right to retain him in slavery. But I have no doubt that where slavery exists and is established by law, individuals may innocently occupy the position of slave-holders, because in the actual circumstances in which the community and they themselves and the slaves are placed the greatest benefit which it may be in their power to confer may be to purchase a slave and to exercise to *some extent* the power which the law may give them over him. And it is very certain that no power on earth is entitled, in the face of Apostolic practice, to prescribe it as a law to the Church of Christ that they shall not admit slave-holders to ordinances or even to office in the Church. I think too much stress has been laid on both sides on a specific answer to the question 'Is slave-holding sinful?' With the views I entertain upon the subject I could answer this question either affirmatively or negatively, *cum distinctione* [with a distinction], according as it might be explained and applied. There is surely a class of cases which are intermediate between things indifferent and those which are in their own nature, and in all their circumstances, morally right or wrong.

The country is involved in a great excitement at present in consequence of Sir Robert Peel's resolution to endow permanently the College at Maynooth for the educating Popish priests. He adverted the other night in the House of Commons to the possibility of a war with the United States as a reason for reconciliating the Irish Papists. Let us hope and pray that the Lord may avert so fearful a calamity.

We have suffered a great loss in our Theological Seminary by the death of Dr Welsh, at the age of fifty-one. He was Professor of Church History, and a man very highly esteemed and respected among us. He had published the first volume of a church history, which, however, is by no means a fair specimen of what the work was to have been had he been spared to complete it. His death will probably lead to some remodelling of our arrangements in the Seminary, and it is not altogether unlikely that I may be appointed to succeed him; *not*, however, as Professor of Church History, but of Historical and Polemic Theology. Dr Chalmers continues to enjoy good health, though he does not now take much part in the management of the ordinary business of the church. His strength is failing a good deal, and he is very anxious now to retire from public life and active duties. He is not likely to continue to take the regular charge of a class in the Seminary for more than one or two years longer.

I am going to visit Sutherland for a fortnight before the Assembly. The Duke of Sutherland, as I anticipated when in America, was shamed into giving sites for our churches; but he resolved, since we had carried off the whole adult population, to try to bring back the young men to the establishment, and has refused to give us sites for Free Church schools. The people won't send their children to the establishment schools, and there are no others in that part of the country. As he made 24,000 pass a winter without churches, he has made their children pass two without school-houses. But he seems now to feel that he must yield on this point, too; and I expect to be able to report to the Assembly that the matter has been adjusted.

It will always give me the greatest pleasure to hear from you. I will write again (D.V.) after the Assembly. Give my kindest remembrance to Mrs Hodge and the members of your family, and to your colleagues, and believe me to be, my dear sir,

Sincerely and affectionately yours, Wm. Cunningham

DR HODGE TO DR CUNNINGHAM

Princeton, January, 1846

My Dear Sir:—If my negligence in writing to you entails on me the penalty of not hearing from you I am severely though justly punished. I beg you, however, not to let justice grow into severity and lead you to keep silence even after I have performed my epistolary duty. If writing is a disagreeable work to you, consider that reading is very agreeable to us.

Since I last wrote two things have occurred in our Church, the one a public and the other a more personal affair, which have been peculiarly interesting to me. The former is the decision of our General Assembly, pronouncing baptism as administered in the Romish Church to be invalid. This decision took us all very much by surprise. I think a decided majority of our ministers, over fifty years of age, are opposed to the decision, and a large proportion of our more intelligent laymen. All the brethren connected with the College and Theological Seminary are in opposition, and if the *Repertory* still reaches you, you may have noticed in the number for July, 1845, an argument against the decision . . . I beg you to let me know your own views and what you take to be the sentiment of your church as to the decision of our Assembly.

The other and more private event to which I alluded is the death of Mr Dod, Professor of Mathematics in our College. I suspect you hardly saw enough of him to get an insight into the man. He was one of the most highly gifted of our ministers; the best public debater, I think, in our church, and one of the best of our controversial writers.[1] I greatly relied upon him in all times of emergency. He died on the 20th of November, after a week's illness. His death-bed experience was very remarkable. He had for some years been so absorbed in literary and professional pursuits that he appeared less before the public as a minister and a religious man than his friends wished; and there was a latitude of remark and a freedom in speculation in which he was apt to indulge which produced an impression as to his Christian character which was not altogether favourable. His intimate friends, however, never doubted his piety, and when he came to die, which in his case was a slow process, continuing from Tuesday evening until Thursday afternoon, he evidenced a calm, intelligent, Scriptural faith, without any emotional excitement, which filled every one about him with surprise. He was just as completely Albert B. Dod, in all his

[1] An example of his controversial writing, *On Revivals of Religion* (1835), a review of Charles G. Finney's *Lectures on Revivals of Religion*, appears in *Princeton versus the New Divinity* (see pp. 262, 278). [Ed.]

intellectual and social peculiarities, in his cheerfulness, even playfulness, in his clear and strong discriminating sense, as when in perfect health. I had often known of men's dying in peace or in triumph, but to see a man dying cheerfully in the full possession of his intellect, in calm, unexcited confidence in Christ as his God and Saviour, was to me a perfectly novel sight. His death is the greatest loss I have ever sustained in the death of friends.

I learn by letter just received from the Rev. Thomas McCrie, of Edinburgh, that some friends there think of republishing the Review of Beman on the Atonement, published in the *Repertory*, for January, 1845. In my answer to his letter I ventured to suggest some reasons for thinking it better that the Review should appear without a name. You know a man can talk very 'big' when he is speaking behind a curtain, and in the name of a whole class of men – the Old School party for instance – when he would feel rather foolish if the curtain were suddenly drawn up, and only one little fellow seen standing there. This, however, is only a personal affair. I am willing you should do what you think is most likely to be useful. At all events, leave out the compliment to Dr Cox in the last paragraph, about his σοφία [wisdom] and γνῶσις [knowledge], which none but an American can understand.

Mrs Hodge and the whole family unite in begging you not to forget them. Your friends in America have a great hankering after you, and despite of the claims of the Free Church, would be glad to get you permanently among us. The good people in this country have such a notion of Lord Palmerston's pugnacity that they are all rejoicing at the return of Sir Robert Peel to power. Can a greater sin be imagined than England and America going to war about Oregon? I question whether Dr Chalmers even knows where Oregon is.

Your affectionate friend, CHARLES HODGE

DEATH OF PROFESSOR ALBERT B. DOD

On the 20th of November, 1845, the subject of this Memoir met one of the chief bereavements of his life. Professor Albert B. Dod had married his cousin, Miss Caroline S. Bayard and was, with the exception of his brother and Bishop Johns, the most intimate friend he ever had. As narrated above, Professor Dod spent several evenings every week in his friend's study, where he formed by far the most brilliant and inspiring of the remarkable set of conversationalists who met there constantly for the discussion of all questions of interest to educated men. Nine years after his death Dr Hodge wrote an account of him for Dr Sprague's *Annals*, affirming: 'I have not yet ceased to mourn his departure as a personal loss.' He describes him as:

> Rather above the ordinary standard in height, somewhat inclined to stoop; rather square-shouldered; but active and graceful in his movements and carriage. His head was unusually large; his forehead broad, but not high; his eyebrows massive and projecting; his eyes hazel, brilliant and deep-seated; his countenance intellectual and pleasing. His disposition was very cheerful and amiable, which rendered him with his extraordinary conversational powers, particularly agreeable as a companion. His reputation as a talker threatened at one time to eclipse his fame in higher departments. But this was only the sparkling of a really deep and rapidly moving stream.
>
> He had a taste for literature and the fine arts, and considerable fertility of imagination, and was, I think, disposed to estimate these gifts at a higher value than his more solid mental qualities. To me, it always appeared that his understanding, his power of clear and quick discernment, of analysis and lucid statement, and of logical deduction, was the leading power of his mind, to which his reputation and usefulness were mainly due.
>
> It was that gave him his success and power as a teacher. There was nothing that he could not make plain. He delighted in unfolding the rationale of all the processes of his department, and to elevate his pupils to the study of the philosophy of every subject which he taught. To this clearness and discrimination of mind is also to be referred his fondness for metaphysics, and his skill in the discussion of subjects connected with that department.

Those of his writings which excited general attention are on topics of this character. His mind was ever on the alert, and teeming with thought and suggestions. It was a common thing for him when he entered my study, to say: 'I was thinking, as I came along, of such and such a question', announcing some problem in mental or moral science. Indeed, I do not know that I ever was acquainted with a man, who so constantly suggested important topics of conversation, or kept the minds of his friends more on a stretch. His consciousness of power in debate, no doubt, contributed to the formation of this habit, for the pleasure of discussion was in his case so great, that he would often start paradoxical opinions, either for the sake of surprising his hearers, or exercising his skill in defending them. The talent to which I have referred, was conspicuously displayed in all public assemblies. Had his life been spared, I doubt not he would have established for himself the reputation of one of the ablest debaters in our church.

His best and most effective sermons are distinguished by the same character of mind. His voice was melodious and his delivery free and untrammelled by his notes, which were generally written out in full. Though his preaching in the latter years of his life was generally addressed more to the understanding than to the affections, yet he had great emotional power, and could, when roused himself, control in an uncommon degree the feelings of his audience.

I regarded him as one of the most gifted men of our church. His having chosen an academical, instead of a pastoral career, kept him in a measure aloof from our ecclesiastical courts, and turned his attention to science rather than to theology. But I have a strong conviction that he had in him rich stores of undeveloped resources (he was only 41), which, had it pleased God to prolong his life, would have rendered him one of the most eminent and useful ministers of our church.

As described above in Dr Hodge's letter to Dr Cunningham, Prof. Dod's death-bed experience was very remarkable. All his peculiar intellectual and social traits and habits were in full play to the last. When unexpectedly and instantly brought face to face with death, he took up every question of pressing personal interest and settled them in their order. First, his family, of wife and seven little children, unprovided for. These he committed to God in an act of absolute faith, which the heavenly Father has not disappointed. And this matter remained thus permanently disposed of. Then he took up the relation of his own soul to God.

As soon as the object of faith was presented to him in the free, full and explicit declarations of Scripture, he seized it with a clearness and strength which left no doubt in his own mind whether he had faith or not. As promise after promise was repeated to him, he said with emotion: 'I thank you for that,' 'God bless you for that.' 'I know myself to be nothing and less than nothing, and God all in all. And Christ precious. I know no other God but him.' The text was then repeated: 'Whosoever believeth that Jesus is the Son of God, is born of God.' 'Thank you for that,' he replied, and attempted to raise his friend's hand to his lips.

That friend was Dr Hodge, who remained with him all the long period of his death struggle, and who wrote an account of it which he read at the funeral, and which was subsequently printed in a pamphlet. It was at this funeral that Dr Hodge made one of his few but nevertheless intensely characteristic bursts of eloquence, described by Dr Paxton in the last chapter of this book.

MARRIAGE AND DEPARTURE OF HIS CHILDREN

Two years after this, in the late summer and autumn of 1847, Dr Hodge's immediate family began to have its first experience of the inevitable separations which await us all. Up to this time there had been no parting. Neither parent, nor either of the eight children had died. Their education also in school and college had been conducted together and at home. But now at once the eldest son went to India as a Missionary, and the eldest daughter went to Danville, Kentucky, as the wife of the Rev. Wm. M. Scott, Professor of Ancient Languages in Centre College, and afterwards Professor of Biblical Literature and Exegesis in the Theological Seminary at Chicago.

Such an experience makes an epoch in any family, leaving it changed forever. Our family was never completely regathered on earth again, for before the son returned from India, the Mother was making the beginnings of the home in heaven. The parting was the occasion of the utter pouring forth of the treasures of love of both parents' hearts. To us these are unspeakably precious, but they are too sacred to be given here. From this time for years our Father's letters to his brother had but one burden, his children and their welfare, and then the memory and the virtues and the love of their sainted Mother. He writes to his brother, September 14th, 1847:

> To marry a daughter I find to be a very different thing from marrying a son. It is a complete sacrifice of self to the good of your child, and it is right it should be so, but it is most peculiarly painful. How little we know of anything but by experience. Whoever sympathizes with parents on the marriage of a daughter? Men congratulate me, when I can hardly help feeling they do it in designed mockery. Still we had M— for two and twenty years, and that is a good deal, and though she is not now, and never again can be to us what she once was, she is still our precious child. I trust we shall be happy in her happiness.

His never failing friend, Bishop Johns, wrote to him, Richmond, April 17th, 1848:

> We rejoice with you in the intelligence of A.'s safe arrival and in his health and comfort in his new field. Distance, dear Charles, is a small consideration. To have a child so devoted and employed should overtop all else. And to have a daughter wedded to a faithful minister of the gospel, who will be her guide to heaven, as well as

her affectionate companion by the way, is a privilege with which the heart of a Christian parent may well be contented. Forget oceans and miles in your gratitude. All unite in most affectionate regards to you and yours. In the beginning yet of our friendship,

Yours truly. J. Johns.

Is not that beautiful? They were past fifty years old, and in the twenty-eighth year of their ministry, 'and in the beginning yet of their friendship'!

THE DEATH OF HIS WIFE

During the summer of 1849 Mrs Hodge had visited her daughter in Kentucky, and had returned in September, as her husband reported to his brother 'wonderfully well, fatter and stronger than before her journey, and in excellent spirits'. She became ill however later in the same month with a disease which, in the judgment of her physicians, while involving crises of imminent danger, yet upon the whole admitted a strong expectation of ultimate recovery. His beloved brother visited their home as frequently as possible during the first week of December, and contributed much to prolong life, and to sustain hope. The bereaved husband left this minute in his record book:

> On Tuesday, the 18th of December, in the afternoon, she sank so low that we feared she could not live until sundown. She was sweetly humble and resigned. I asked her, Do you love the Lord Jesus? She said: 'I hope so.' I asked, do you trust in him? 'Entirely.' Is he precious to you? 'Very.' She afterwards often answered the same questions by saying: 'Inexpressibly.' 'He is my all in all.' She expressed the greatest penitence and self-condemnation in view of herself and life, but the most peaceful confidence whenever she thought of the blessed Saviour . . . Afterwards, towards the end of that week and the beginning

of the next, she improved. During these days she frequently requested me to pray with her, and was never weary of the repetition of hymns, especially of the hymns 'How sweet the name of Jesus sounds', and 'Jesus, lover of my soul'. But Monday night, at another violent crisis in her complaint, she began to sink, and about half past four o'clock on Christmas morning she softly and sweetly fell asleep in Jesus. She evinced throughout the most perfect composure and resignation. She said she knew she was dying. Spoke of her children, said she could not see them now and added: 'I give them to God.' She responded in full appropriating faith to the promises of Scripture repeated in her hearing, and over and over again expressed her full and entire confidence in Christ, and her overwhelming sense of his value and of the love of God in the gift of his dear Son.

Her death was calm, peaceful and holy. She was full of humility, faith and grateful, admiring love to God. Her children, save the eldest, were all about her. They all were renewedly given by her to God, and around her sacred remains they all knelt in consecrating prayer to God.

She had lived with her husband, his joy and crown, twenty-seven years and a half. She had borne for him eight children, three daughters and five sons, all of whom, by God's singular mercy, lived to mature age, and have been gathered with their parents into the number of those who profess Christ.

The sorrowing husband caused this inscription to be graven on her tomb:

SARAH BACHE,
Wife of Rev. Charles Hodge,
Departed this life, December 25, 1849, aged 51 years.
An humble worshipper of Christ,
She lived in love and died in faith.
Truthful woman, delightful companion,
Ardent friend, devoted wife.
Self-sacrificing mother,

We lay you gently here, our best beloved,
to gather strength and beauty
for the coming of the Lord.

'A grain of wheat is not quickened except it die.'

This is indeed the outpouring of a bereaved husband's heart. But it is all true. And now, when, after twenty-nine years, we, their children, lay our father by our mother's side and read this inscription on her tomb, we all say 'Amen!'

BISHOP JOHNS WRITES TO HIM

WILLIAMSBURGH, March 19, 1850

My Dear Charles:—If all the letters which I have penned in thought had been forwarded you would know how much you have been in my mind. Yes, both sleeping and waking, I have been with you – not, indeed, as you now are; for it requires an effort to realize that your house is not as I always, except at my last brief visit, joyed to find it – but as enlivened and cheered by the presence of the blessed one who has from the first been so identified with us that it seems impossible for me to think of either of you without seeing both. I am so willing to allow the illusion which the happy association of many past years produces, that I can scarcely bring myself to the conviction that my dear Charles is bereaved, and alone in his desolate home, and that I am no more to receive the cordial greeting and gaze on the bright countenance of Sarah. That one sentence in your letter, 'since their blessed mother entered heaven', pressed for a while the truth upon my consciousness, and in my strong sympathies for my afflicted brother I found the experience of the time of my own like visitation very vividly renewed. Yes, dear Charles, they are together 'in heaven', and may we but be successful in training to a meetness for the same mansions the precious children they have left us, the hour is not far off when we shall rather think of their sainted mothers as there than encounter the struggle of leaving them on earth. My solicitude for the spiritual welfare of my children increases as my opportunities of being useful to them shorten, and this anxiety is, of course, more intense in the case of those who thus far have given no indications of the new birth into righteousness. Nothing seems so strongly to stir up my feelings in prayer as the effort to intercede for them with God. But a few days before the receipt of your letter I was, I think, more than usually engaged in this way with tenderness toward them, but I fear small faith and hope. Is my almost 'extremity' to prove 'God's opportunity'? How wistfully I wait for further intelligence! Oh, for more of that 'great faith in the baptismal dedication of children, and of that believing prayer', of which you speak! The confidence is authorized, and in exercise, how great the comfort !

I have written to my dear boy (in Princeton College) the overflowings of my heart for counsel. Should he be sufficiently interested to desire it, I have commended him to you as to a father, and it is to me cause of great thankfulness to know that he is so near one who will 'naturally care for his state', and truly show him the way of salvation.

Do let me hear from you, for I shall be anxious to learn something of the good work which I trust the Lord has begun in the College. How the tidings carry me back, as well they may, with gratitude and praise to the never-to-be-forgotten scenes of our own College course there. But for the gracious dispensation of those days, giving effect to parental instruction and example, what and where should *I* have been. Bless the Lord, O my soul!

I need not say, my dear Charles, that all here join me in love to you and yours.

J. JOHNS

After this many months were almost absorbed by this great sorrow. In every way he gave it full course, dwelling upon it in his imagination, and indulging unrestrained the physical expression of it. He wrote to his brother on the 12th of November, 1850, the anniversary of his (the brother's) marriage in New York:

This is the 12th of November. During my days of happiness the anniversary of my marriage generally passed without special notice; every day was as the day of our espousals. But now that day is invested with sacred interest. As you are still happy, and pressed forward with the full tide of life, you may let this day pass with scarcely more than a few ejaculations of thanks to God for his goodness. It is now one of my anniversaries. I know the history of my Sarah for this day twenty-two years ago, and can recall her appearance as she then was distinctly before me. The night before we spent in New Brunswick. In the morning we went to New York in the steamboat. We put up at Bunker's. I know the room we occupied. I know where Sarah sat at dinner, and what she ate. In the afternoon Miss Boyd came to aid her in dressing. I can see her as she sat by Margaret (his brother's bride) on the sofa in the evening, and how she smiled when I called her 'old Mrs Hodge'. It is thus I can recall her by associating her with particular times and places. The general recollection is painfully vague; these definite associations are poignantly vivid. And yet I assiduously cultivate them as part of the homage due her memory. No human being can tell, prior to experience, what it is to lose out of a family its head and heart, the source at once of its light and love.

In December 1850, his brother lost, by a rapid and uncontrollable disease, his third son, James Bayard, a beautiful and beloved Christian youth of seventeen years. After his return to Princeton from the funeral Dr Hodge wrote:

PRINCETON, Dec. 16, 1850

My Dear Brother:—You were kind in writing to me when God's hand had touched the apple of my eye, and you expressed what were no doubt wise and pious sentiments, but I felt you did not and could not understand the case, and that such counsels had but little power over a broken heart. I do not feel disposed, therefore, to say anything of the kind to you and sister Margaret.

There is no help in such afflictions but in God. He alone can reach the heart. Earthly friends speak only to the outward ear. Their sympathy, I know, by experience, is consoling and gratifying. It is viewed as a tribute to the departed, an acknowledgment of the greatness of our loss, and is therefore to be valued and cherished. That sympathy you have from a very large circle, and prayers constant, numerous and fervent are going up to God in your behalf, and in behalf of your dear children. It was never meant that we should not sorrow after the most cherished objects of our affection. Our duty is to take care that we 'sorrow after a godly sort', for 'the sorrow of the world', such sorrow as the world or worldly people have, 'worketh death'. Pious sorrow, that is, sorrow mingled with pious feeling, with resignation, confidence in God, hope in his mercy and love, is every way healthful to the soul; while melancholy is irreligious, and is a cancer to true peace and spiritual health. The great means of having our sorrow kept pure is to keep near to God, to feel assured of his love, that he orders all things well, and will make even our afflictions work out for us a far more exceeding and an eternal weight of glory.

Christ is our God. When we speak of keeping near to God, we mean God in Christ, and God as reconciled and made propitious to us by his blood. And Christ is near to us, and dwells in us, and shows us His love, and works all grace in us by the Holy Spirit. The doctrine of the Trinity is not a mere speculative doctrine, it is an essential part of the Christian's practical faith, the truth on which he daily lives. If, therefore, God will graciously give you and Margaret the Holy Ghost, He will thereby give you Himself, and open to you the infinite sources of peace and consolation that are to be found in Him. To give our grief this pious character, I think it must be expressed, not hidden or kept in one's own bosom. At least, it seems to me much more consistent with Christian feeling to give proper expression to our sorrow, and to talk of those whom God has taken to heaven, than to cast the pall of silence over all that concerns them.

I was, therefore, truly rejoiced to find that dear M. had the heart to talk freely of Bayard. As he cannot be forgotten, so he ought not to be remembered merely in silence. He and his death and his present blessedness can bear to be talked about among those who loved him and still long to manifest their affection for his memory.

I began this letter with the intention of saying nothing that could be considered like counsel, but I fear I have run into this mistake. We cannot tell how what we say will affect the exquisite sensibilities of a bereaved heart, and therefore must hope that what we write will be taken as an expression of love, though it may be, as such expressions often are, more or less painful.

Your affectionate brother,
CHARLES

DR HODGE TO HIS BROTHER

PRINCETON, May 28, 1850

My Dear Brother:—I am sorry to hear that your fears respecting Mrs Chauncey have proved so well founded. I feel for him, but there is no help but in God. If God comforts him he will be comforted, but vain are all human comforters. I will try to write to him, but my experience teaches me not how to write, but that letters of condolence, though not without their value, are powerless. I have received many and value them highly, not merely as expressions of kind feeling towards myself, but far more as evidence of regard for my blessed Sarah. Still, I have never read any of them a second time.

I feel also for you. I know how much you suffer from the loss of patients, not only from sympathy, but from a feeling of responsibility. You should remember, however, that it is appointed unto all men once to die, and that no degree of skill, and no assiduity of attention, can avert the shaft of death. You have great consolations, as well as great trials. How often are you the means of saving life! How often do patients and friends look up to you as their greatest benefactor! You cannot have this exquisite satisfaction without paying the tribute of occasional sorrow when all your efforts fail.

Your brother,
C.H.

DISTURBED HEALTH

During this period, and for some years later, Dr Hodge's health continued in an uncomfortable, though hardly in a precarious condition. In the summer of 1848 he met with an accident which proved to be the starting point of a long sequence of disturbances in his nervous and circulatory systems. His letter to his brother on the occasion will explain the case:

PRINCETON, July 14th, 1848 – Friday

My Dear Brother:—I had made my arrangements to preach on Sunday next at Netherwood (Mr Lenox's place), and therefore was to leave home last evening for New York, so as to be able to take the morning boat up the North river for to-day. They had tea at six o'clock that I might be ready for the cars. While we were all at table something was said to produce a laugh, just as I had my cup at my mouth, and some of the tea got into my larynx, producing a violent fit of coughing. I rose to leave the table, and took a step or two towards the door, and then I remember nothing until I saw the family around me in alarm raising me from the floor. They say I staggered to the wall, and fell, striking my head against the sofa. I remember nothing of the staggering or falling, or of the blow. The unconsciousness was only for a moment, for as they raised me to a sitting posture I spoke, and asked what had happened. I was aware I was coming out of unconsciousness, and had forgotten the antecedents. They told me I had choked, and then it all came back. They were all a good deal alarmed, and begged me not to leave home. The hack was at the door, and the whole occurrence seeming perfectly intelligible, the spasm of the larynx producing suffocation, and that momentary congestion, I determined to go, taking Wistar with me to New York for company. When, however, I got to the depot I felt unwell and determined to return.

We sent for Dr Schanck. He took the same view of the matter that I had done, and advised, what I had already ordered, a hot bath for the feet and cold water for the head. I thought he would have taken a little blood, and think it would have been better had he done so. I felt no inconvenience through the night, beyond a slight headache and a heaviness about the chest, inducing frequent sighing. I feel well this morning, except this little headache.

I am not free from concern about this dispensation, as I think it shows a great tenderness about the brain. I never could bear to have my head jarred, nor exposed to heat, especially in the back part of it. I am not certain, however, the difficulty is not in the chest, as I so frequently feel oppression there.

I am so well that I expect to leave home at noon, so as to take the night boat up the river. The Lord our Saviour reigns, and we are in his hands, and not a hair of our heads can perish without his notice.

Your brother,
CHARLES HODGE

Again he writes to his brother, as soon as he returns to Princeton, on Wednesday, the 19th of July:

My Dear Brother:—As Dr Schanck advised my going up the North river, I left home on Friday morning, and reached Hampton, five miles above Newburgh, about half-past nine that evening. I had a very pleasant journey, and the fresh evening air on the river I thought did me good. I reached Mr Lenox's the next morning about eight o'clock. My head has been gradually improving. On Saturday it ached constantly on the back or top, and I had a good deal of new nervous feeling – not giddiness but feeble *inervation* [nervous weakness], so that my step was unsteady, and at times I experienced the initial sensation of fainting. I kept quiet and did not attempt to preach on Sunday. Monday I felt better. I left Netherwood about noon yesterday, in the day boat, stayed last night in New York, and reached home at noon to-day. I find that writing a few short letters is as much as my head will bear.

I found your kind letter awaiting my return, and shall be careful to follow your directions.

Your brother, C.H.

The nervous disturbance occasioned by this accident was subsequently confirmed and aggravated by the severe and protracted emotional excitement he went through during the year, which followed the death of his wife. This effect was doubtless dependent upon the fullness of his habit of body, the constitutional changes, incident to his time of life, and the long confinement which had resulted from his lameness. For years he suffered from fullness and dizziness of the head, and constant restlessness. He was frequently bled and otherwise depleted, and necessarily lived far more in the open air than at any other period of his life. Consequently from 1848 to about 1855 or '56 was his least productive period, so much so that it then often seemed as if he might fail to gather the complete harvest of his previous labours. It was now that he formed the habit of seeking recreation and of amusing the hours of his necessary rest by a moderate reading of novels, and by playing backgammon, and in the summer season croquet on the lawn before his study windows.

DR HODGE TO HIS BROTHER

PRINCETON, Jan. 25, 1849

My Dear Brother:—Were it not for what you say I should feel a good deal concerned about my head. That there has been a great change since my attack last summer there is no doubt. And sometimes the disturbance and pain are so great that I can do nothing. Often, after three or four hours' work, I am obliged to put by everything and go into the open air. All this is new and strange for me. I have been relieved in a measure by observing that the pain was partly external at times – that is, the scalp on the top of my head is tender to the touch. It may all be neuralgia, but it unfits me for the labour I could once sustain.

Your brother,

C. H.

Princeton, June 18, 1851.

My Dear Brother:—This is my wedding day. This day, and not far from this hour, twenty-nine years ago, my blessed Sarah gave me her hand in pledge of life-long love and devotion. That pledge she sacredly redeemed. For twenty-seven years God spared us to each other, and no man had ever more reason than I have had to rejoice in the unwavering affection of a most superior woman. My feelings now are in some respects very different from what they were this time last year, but in others they remain unchanged. No day has intervened that I have not often and literally shed tears to her memory; no week has passed that I have not been twice or oftener to her grave. And yet I think of her now with less of that dreadful sense of bereavement which then oppressed my spirit. I turn my heart towards her with much of the same feeling with which a Romanist, who stops short of idolatry, looks up to his patron saint. No one can know, prior to experience, the mystery of those affections which are interwoven with the whole tissue of our lives, and whose objects God has exalted to heaven.

Your affectionate brother,
C. H.

DEATH OF HIS SENIOR COLLEAGUES

And now, within less than two years of one another, Dr Hodge's two senior Colleagues were removed, leaving him to occupy the position of senior professor, with its attendant dignity and responsibility for twenty-seven years. Dr Miller died January 7th, 1850, and Dr Alexander died October 22nd, 1851.

It is natural that every institution which has attained to a history should possess away back in its past, if not a heroic, at least a golden age, when the remote forefathers dwelt in a world of love and purity, not known to their degenerate sons. But the holy character and mutual love of the first three professors of Princeton Theological Seminary is not a myth, nor is it certified to us only by a dim tradition. Many of their contemporaries have left their written testimony, and many of us, their children and pupils, survive to testify of what we have known ourselves. For many years I witnessed, as a member of one of their families, their going in and out together, and since then I have had a wide experience of professors and of pastors, and I am certain, I have never seen any three who together approached these three in absolute singleness of mind, in simplicity and godly sincerity, in utter unselfishness and devotion to the common cause, each in honour preferring one another. Truth and candour was the atmosphere they breathed, loyalty, brave and sweet, was the spirit of their lives.

Dr Alexander bore testimony to Dr Miller, that he had 'never known a man more entirely free from vainglory, envy and jealousy'. His students regarded him as the most perfect illustration of the Christian graces they had ever seen. Dr Hodge often narrated that:

In the summer of 1819, Dr Alexander delivered to the then Senior class a lecture, which so impressed his pupils, that Dr William Nevins said to his classmates that it was a shame they should enjoy such instructions and do nothing to secure the same advantage for others. He, therefore, proposed that we should endeavour to found a scholarship, to be called 'The Scholarship of the Class of 1819'. To this the class assented, and a committee was appointed to inform the Professors of our purpose. When the committee waited on Dr Miller, Nevins with his characteristic naïve frankness told him the whole story, and dwelt on the enthusiasm cherished by the students for Dr Alexander. Dr Miller having heard him through, expressed his pleasure in view of what the class had done, and then lifted his hand and said, 'My young friend, I solemnly believe that Dr Alexander is the greatest man who walks the earth!' When we left the Doctor's study, Nevins said to his associates on the Committee, 'Well, if Dr Alexander be the greatest, Dr Miller is surely the holiest that walks the earth!' We were boys then; but this incident serves to show how Dr Miller was regarded by his pupils.

Dr Hodge also says of Dr Miller:

Some men are good in one respect and not in another. – Dr Miller was thoroughly good; good in every respect, because he was good in principle . . . The fact that for over thirty years he was intimately associated with colleagues to whom he never said an unkind word or exhibited an unkind feeling, is proof enough of his habitual self-control.

In the last year of his life Dr Miller wrote a letter to Dr Henry A. Boardman of Philadelphia, which ought never to be read except through tears. Its existence is a proof of the singular favour with which God regarded the *old* Princeton. We preserve it, and again and again we publish it as an inestimable record of God's goodness to our Fathers, and of the religious character of the heritage they have left us.

DR MILLER TO REV. H. A. BOARDMAN, D.D.

Princeton, Feb. 28, 1849

I thank you, my dear brother, for the kind expressions which you employ on the prospect of my retiring from office. I am, indeed, nearly worn out. Far advanced in my eightieth year, I have outlived all my relatives, and all my own expectations, and am compassed about with so many infirmities that I am persuaded a longer continuance in office would be in no respect just, either to the Seminary or myself. Yet, in looking forward to retirement from official labour, and especially to that day which is near at hand, when I must 'put off this tabernacle', I desire to bless God for the humble hope which I am permitted to entertain, that I have so good a home to go to, where there will be no more infirmity, and especially no more sin; but perfect union and conformity to Him who, though He was rich, for our sakes became poor, that we through His poverty might be rich. I desire to unite with you, my dear brother, in thanksgiving to the great Head of the Church, that our beloved Seminary has been made so useful to our Zion, by training so large a portion of the ministry under the same teachers; and I hope I have some sincere gratitude that I have been permitted to occupy a place, and take some humble part in this hallowed work. But I can truly say that the sentiment which most strongly and prominently occupies my mind is that of thankfulness that the Lord has been pleased to unite me with colleagues so wise, so faithful, so much superior to myself, and so eminently adapted to be a blessing to the Church. I consider it as one of the greatest blessings of my life to be united with such men, and pre-eminently with my senior colleague, whose wisdom, prudence, learning and peculiar piety have served as an aid and guide to myself, as well as to others. I desire to leave it on record, for the eye of intimate friendship, that in my own estimation my union with these beloved men has been the means of adding to my own respectability and my own usefulness far more than I could ever, humanly speaking, have attained, either alone or in association with almost any other men. I desire especially to feel thankful that I ever saw the face of my venerated senior colleague. He has been for thirty-six years, to me a counsellor, a guide, a prop and a stay, under God, to a degree which it would not be easy for me to estimate or acknowledge.

The union in our Faculty has been complete. And the solid basis of the whole has been a perfect agreement on the part of all of us in an honest subscription to our doctrinal formularies. There has been no discrepance – no pulling in different directions.

Hoping to see you in a few days, I am, my dear sir, your friend and brother in Christian bonds,

SAMUEL MILLER

In his article on the Memoir of Dr A. Alexander, in the January number of the *Princeton Review* for 1855, Dr Hodge says:

Having incidentally mentioned the name of Dr Miller, we may be permitted to pause and in a sentence pay our humble tribute to that sainted man. He could be appreciated only by those who knew him intimately, who saw him day by day, and year in and year out, in all circumstances suited to try and to reveal the true character. We have never heard any one who enjoyed such means of knowing him, speak of him otherwise than as one of the holiest of men. May the writer be further pardoned for obtruding himself for a moment, so far as to say, that during twenty-nine years of intimate official association with these two venerated men, he never saw the slightest discourtesy, unkindness nor acerbity manifested by the one towards the other; and that he never heard a disparaging remark from the one in reference to the other. Thank God, Princeton Seminary has a history! The past is safe. The memory of the two eminent men who were its first professors, and who gave it character, rest over it as a halo, and men will tread its halls for their sake with something of the feeling with which they visit the tombs of the good and the great.

That Dr Hodge was worthy by the endowments of Providence, and by the gifts of grace of his place in that circle of the first three professors, and to be associated with the colleagues he ardently loved and venerated, will be shown hereafter by the testimony of those surviving colleagues, who so long delighted in him as their friend and academic head.

The relation which Dr Hodge sustained to Dr Archibald Alexander has been plainly disclosed in the foregoing memoranda. He was noticed as a school-boy, and made a companion of rides and of distant journeys. He was chosen as an assistant, and for two years made an inmate of the family. He was chosen as a colleague, and habitually and intimately consulted and counselled in all the public and private interests of either. He was chosen to be his successor in the chair of Didactic Theology, And now, when the aged saint came to die, his disciple and successor was summoned (October 12th, 1851), to his side. Dr Alexander held out his hand and called him his son. In another interview he transferred to him the account book of the scholarships, and told him what he wished to be done in respect to them, and handed him a white bone walking-stick, carved and presented to him by one of the chiefs of the Sandwich

Islands, and said, 'You must hand this to your successor in office, that it may be handed down as a kind of symbol of orthodoxy.' When he dismissed him from the first interview he said, 'Now, my dear son, farewell.'

I saw my father when he returned from that interview, standing in his study in an agony of weeping, exclaiming, 'It is all past, the glory of our Seminary has departed.' At the funeral he walked with the sons, claiming to be a true son also.

DR HODGE TO HIS BROTHER

PRINCETON, Oct. 15, 1851

My Dear Brother:—We begin to be very much concerned about our dear venerated Doctor Alexander. Four weeks ago he was seized with a debilitating sickness, and although the violence of the attack has abated, his stomach seems to be giving out, his appetite is gone, so that food is unpleasant to him, and he is very feeble, should he live to April he will be eighty years old. Last week he drove out several times, and I thought he was getting well. On Sunday afternoon he sent for me. I found him lying on the sofa in his study, and when I came near to him he put out his hand and said, 'My dear son, I have a few things to say to you, to which I wish you to listen without making any reply.' He then went on to say 'that those around him thought he was improving, but his own strong persuasion was that his end was drawing nigh; that he was going just as Mr Samuel Bayard went, from utter failure of the stomach; that he had thought much on the subject and had arrived at the conclusion that it was best for him to leave the world now. He had done his work. After eighty he had never known a man to be useful, and he did not think it desirable for him to live and drag on a few years more a burden to himself and others.' He said, 'I wish you to know my views of my case now, and I want to speak to you while I have strength. I consider it one of my greatest blessings that I have been able to bring you forward, and now, my dear son, farewell. You will not see me again.' I was, as you may suppose, greatly humbled and affected by this address from the man to whom I owe so much. I sank on my knees by him and kissed his hand. He told me to pray. I did so for a few sentences. He said, with emphasis, 'Amen', and again giving me his hand said, 'Farewell.'

This is for your eye alone. Burn this letter. I should be deeply mortified that this record of the parental tenderness and partiality of the old gentleman should ever be seen. It is forty years next spring since I first, as a boy, attracted his notice. He has ever since acted to me as a father, and God has given me grace to love and revere him as a child would such a father. I believe I have never offended him, or hurt his feelings. I cannot prevent this solemn interview having a very strong impression upon my feelings as to the prospect of his recovery, though I know he is often disposed to take gloomy views.

Every thing is covered with gloom here now. It is a sad season of the year – the hour of desolation is drawing near again, – and the prospect of the patriarchal head of our Church and Seminary being taken away makes us feel very sad. The nearest circle to Dr Alexander is his family, the next the Seminary, the next his thousand living former pupils, and next the ministers and members of the Church. He is the centre of all, and the same feeling, decreasing of course according to its diffusion, pervades the whole.

Your brother,
CHARLES HODGE

10

FROM THE DEATH OF DR ARCHIBALD ALEXANDER, 1851, TO THE COMMENCEMENT OF THE CIVIL WAR, 1861

A Member of the Boards of the Church – Trustee of the College of New Jersey – Methods of Teaching – Second Marriage – Correspondence with His Brother, Politics – Dancing and Card-Playing – The Baptism of the Infants of Non-Professors – Commentaries – Articles in the PRINCETON REVIEW – Correspondence with Dr William Cunningham and Bishop Johns – The Death of Drs James W. and Joseph A. Alexander – Letter of Dr R. L. Dabney – Election of His Son, C. W. Hodge, as Professor of New Testament Literature, etc. – His Great Debate with Dr Thornwell in the General Assembly of 1861

D URING THESE YEARS Dr Hodge was active in the public counsels of the church. He became a member of the Board of Foreign Missions in 1846; and in 1868 he was elected President of that Board to succeed Dr Spring, and acted as such until the reconstruction of the Boards, consequent upon the Reunion of the Presbyterian Church in 1870. Dr Ellinwood writes, 'We regard your father as one of the very ablest and most earnest supporters of the cause of Foreign Missions we ever had in the Presbyterian Church.' He preached the sermon before the Board in the Church on University Place on Sabbath evening, May 7th, 1848, on Matthew 28:19, 20, on 'the teaching office of the Church'. It was afterwards published in the Report of that year, and was considered as a signal exposition of the fundamental principles on which Christian missions should be conducted. He was a member of the Board of Domestic Missions from about 1840 to 1870.

He also acted as a member of the Board of Education, from 1861, and as President of it from 1862 to the Reconstruction of the Board consequent on Reunion. He was made one of the Vice-Presidents of the Presbyterian Historical Society in May 1852, and a Trustee of Princeton College in the place of the Rev. Dr Samuel Miller, deceased in 1850.

TRUSTEE OF PRINCETON COLLEGE

His work as a Trustee in the College often taxed all the energies of his heart and will. Professor Lyman H. Atwater, D.D., writes of Dr Hodge that 'he took a foremost rank in the Board from the first, and wielded a commanding influence in its proceedings. His efforts were especially directed to filling vacancies in the professors' chairs with able incumbents and to increasing the corps of instructors as rapidly as funds for the purpose could be procured, and in maintaining a due proportion in the relative strength of the different departments, especially in maintaining the importance of the languages and the humanities in competition with the pressure of the physical sciences.'

His Co-trustee, Dr William M. Paxton writes,

Considering the fact of Dr Hodge's antecedents and associations, it is no wonder, that as a Trustee of the College for the long period of twenty-seven years, he should feel his whole life bound up in the interests of that institution. During the last twelve years, it has been my privilege to be associated with him as a member of that Board, and it was a pleasure to observe the fatherly – I might perhaps say the Patriarchal – interest he manifested in everything connected with the prosperity of the College. He understood its history, the questions of policy connected with its management, its dangers and the conditions of its prosperity as the younger members of the Board could not. Hence he was always listened to with the profoundest attention, and his judgment in many cases of difficulty had great weight in deciding the action of the Board. There were two points about which he manifested special solicitude. The 1st was *the maintenance of the religious character of the College*. It was founded for religious purposes. It was sustained by the prayers, activities and contributions of God's people as an institution for Christian education, and especially for the training of young men for the Christian Ministry. It has enjoyed throughout its history the blessing of God, in numerous and powerful revivals, and in the character and influence of the ministers and devout laymen educated in her halls. Dr Hodge frequently referred to these facts and insisted that they never should be lost sight of in the settlement of any question of policy. He urged it upon the Board that they should make the religious character of the College the first great aim of its administration.

He appeared to apprehend as a definite possibility the operation of causes by which this seat of learning might be perverted from the purpose to which it had been consecrated by so many prayers.

2nd. The other point which interested the mind of Dr Hodge was *the maintenance of a high grade of scholarship in the College*. He had a dread of a *little* as well as of an unsanctified learning. The completion of his own education in Germany furnished him with the standard of the higher culture attained in the European universities. Hence he was anxious to advance prudently, but as rapidly as possible the standard of learning in our colleges as a preparation for all the diversified enterprises of American life.

But he especially desired to provide a remedy for the deficient classical culture, which has hitherto been so painfully prevalent among the graduates of our Colleges, who seek to enter the learned professions. His own experience as a theological professor had discovered to him how many of the candidates for our ministry have great difficulty in reading the Greek of the New Testament and the simple Latin of Turretin's *Institutes*. I am glad to be able to express his views upon this subject, because it is one of the vital points connected with our present educational systems. If the furor for scientific courses and the study of the modern languages is to displace the study of the classics then we must look for a great change in the mental culture of the coming age. The purpose of education is to develop mental power. I believe that the experience of the past has shown that the best mental development is attained by the study of the classics and mathematics. Each of these studies has its peculiar influence, and it requires the balance of the two to produce the kind of development and culture in which grace, strength and efficiency are conjoined. We ought not to be too ready to forsake the methods of our fathers, for 'there were giants in those days'.

METHODS OF TEACHING

During these years Dr Hodge matured his methods of instruction. His exegetical exercises with the Junior classes continued throughout his life to be very much what they were before his change of professorship. Through successive years he accomplished the exposition of all the Pauline Epistles, except those to Timothy and Titus, but going most frequently over the doctrinal portions of Romans, 1 Corinthians, Galatians and Ephesians. An account of the main characteristics of his exegetical teaching will be given in a subsequent chapter by one of his ablest and most accomplished pupils. At the period at which the present chapter commences, his theological lectures were fully written out, and were habitually read by him in a quiet manner. From year to year they were rewritten, being thoroughly recast, and much enriched and extended, but his method of teaching for many years continued unchanged. The lecture was delivered on a topic on one day, and at another within the same week, the entire hour was devoted to his matchless cross-examination. He soon gave up in despair, his former most excellent method of requiring all to make up systems of theology for themselves in the form of written answers to questions covering the entire course, because by this time each student was possessed of a written copy of the lectures before they were read, and copied to the professor's questions answers in his own words. Hence often the method became irksome alike to him and to his classes, for they sat reading with their eyes for the most part the same sentences they heard read from the desk. He often proposed to print his lectures that he might use them as a text-book, but was restrained by the counsel of his most trusted advisors among the Directors of the Seminary, who feared that if these lectures were given to the public, they would in ceasing to be the peculiar attribute of this Seminary, cease also to attract students to its classes. But in his last years, when his *Systematic Theology* was the common property of the Church, and it was made the text-book in Princeton, as it was also in several other theological schools, he felt as if set free, and his power as a teacher greatly increased. His great skill as a teacher found its fullest play in the exercise of his gift for questioning, and by that means of compelling the student to think, and to refute himself if wrong, or to develop his own thought into completeness if right. He always maintained that the true method of teaching didactic theology, involves the use of the text-book, the living teacher, practice in writing, and an active drill in verbal questions and debates.

The following paper originating from some of his most intelligent students, and his own letter in response to a request to him by the Rev. Wm. S. Plumer, D.D., for suggestions as to the method of conducting the instruction of classes in his branch, will explain themselves in the light of what I have just said.

PRINCETON THEOL. SEM., Feb. 19, 1853.

PROF. CHARLES HODGE.

Dear Sir:—The different classes of the Seminary, in meetings held during the present week, resolved to request of you a Syllabus of your Lectures on Theology, to be printed for the use of the students;

and appointed committees to convey to you their request. We, the members of those committees, would respectfully submit the following as some of the reasons suggested as giving urgency and propriety to such requests.

1. From the amount of matter and the condensed form of your lectures, notes taken in the class-room afford a very inadequate and unsatisfactory guide in the prosecution of our studies in theology. Most of your students, satisfied of this, have been constrained to resort to the use of manuscript copies of your lectures.

2. These manuscript copies present to our minds several objectionable features. Copied by students, the manual labour is injurious to health and eyesight, and consumes important time that should be given to study and investigation. Transcribed by copyists, the expense places them beyond the reach of the great majority of the students. Besides, they are the occasion of various abuses. Professing to be exact copies, they lead to the neglect of investigation and of the study of collateral works, so important in itself and so often recommended by our Professor. Carried by students to different parts of the country, they tend, by their many errors, to create misapprehension as to the doctrines taught in this Seminary, a result which we, in common with our Professors, greatly deprecate.

3. A printed Syllabus, besides promoting original research and compelling more close and vigorous study, seems to us the proper corrective of such evils. Moreover, printed and not published, it can scarcely seem liable to objection, as the premature publication of a System of Theology; but even this objection seems to be met by the consideration that it would avert the danger of a surreptitious publication from imperfect copies already so widely circulated.

Such, sir, are some of the reasons which have induced this expression of a desire presented now with entire unanimity, and (we feel assured) entertained for years by the students and graduates of the Seminary.

Hoping that this communication may not fail of its end, and trusting that in presenting it we may not appear presumptuous, or as exceeding the propriety of our position,
We remain, with very great respect,

> Truly yours,
> JOHN E. DAVIDSON, JAMES M. PLATT – *1st Class.*
> THOMAS R. MARKHAM, E, D. JUNKIN – *2nd Class.*
> E. KEMPSHALL, P. A. STUDDIFORD – *3rd Class.*

DR HODGE TO REV. WILLIAM S. PLUMER, D.D.

> PRINCETON, N.J., July 25, 1854

Rev. and Dear Brother:—I sincerely rejoice that Providence has opened for you a field of labour so congenial to your tastes, and which promises so much for your future usefulness and comfort.

I fear I shall not be able to make any suggestions such as you refer to in your letter of the 20th inst., which will be of much value to you. It may be the best thing I can do simply to recite my experience, or the course which I pursued, when called to teach theology.

For some years after I was assigned to the theological chair, Dr Alexander continued to give his lectures, and I was simply the catechist. That is, I catechized the class on the several subjects without reference to the Doctor's lectures. He was often lecturing on one subject while I was examining upon another. The two courses of instruction were therefore independent of each other.

The method I adopted in preparing for these exercises was to read everything I could command on the subject in hand, making notes of each author. From these notes I prepared a logical analysis of the topic under consideration, and that analysis was my guide in examining the class. Of course all such examinations called for explanations and remarks as we went along.

When the whole department was thrown upon me I endeavoured to unite the advantages of the three methods of lectures, catechetical examination and writing. I lectured regularly on the whole course, spent the next day of meeting the class in questioning them on the subject of the preceding lecture, and gave out a list of questions in writing, to which I urged them to write answers *in extenso*. I still think this a good plan, if it could be carried out as it was here for several years. The practical difficulties which have gradually accumulated are these, which very much impair its value:

First, The students taking notes of the lectures have come, in a succession of years, to have almost complete copies of them. I am subjected, therefore, to the embarrassment of reading lectures, copies of which many members of the class hold in their hands. This I find a great bore. How the difficulty is to be avoided I do not know. It is the same in other Seminaries,

Secondly, The students, instead of writing answers to the questions given to them, after studying and reflecting for themselves, in most cases simply transcribe the copies of the lectures which are handed down to them by the preceding classes.

The result is that the interest in the lectures and in the written exercise has greatly decreased, while that in the oral questioning remains. For several years no one has come to the lecture who could help it; whereas the room is commonly crowded at the oral examinations. I am at a loss how to get over this difficulty.

The two defects of my system of instruction of which I am most sensible are, *first*, that the students are not rendered familiar with proof texts, so as to quote and recite them readily when called upon. I believe they have a real Scriptural foundation for their faith, but this they get rather by reading whole books of Scripture in their connection than by getting proof texts by heart.

The *second* deficiency I had in mind is the lack of information as to theological works. I frequently lecture on a subject, question the class, and give out written questions and mention no author whatever. It does not, somehow, come in my way, and when done, it is done of set purpose.

Your question as to what books I have found most useful I really know not how to answer. I have read, generally, everything I could on each topic, orthodox and heterodox, and got what good I could from each. Turretin's *Institutes* I regard as incomparably the best book as a whole on systematic theology, but on the subjects of the attributes of God, Trinity, sin, atonement, grace, etc., the books, you know, are endless, and I have no such estimate of particular treatises as to lead me to point them out as especially important. At least, you need nothing of the kind from me.

With sincere desire for your usefulness, success and happiness, I am, very truly, your friend,

CHARLES HODGE

HIS SECOND MARRIAGE

On the eighth of July, 1852, he contracted his second marriage with Mrs Mary Hunter Stockton, widow of the late Lieutenant Samuel Witham Stockton, of the United States Navy, and sister of Major General David Hunter and of Dr Lewis B. Hunter, of the United States Army and Navy. This noble Christian lady supported and brightened all his later life, and assiduously attended him with her tender ministrations until his eyes closed in death. She has been an admirable mother to his children, and head of his household, uniting the family and completing the education and training of its younger members in a manner their own mother would not have desired to excel. She survived him for twenty months, presiding in his place in the large family circle, preserving with us the traditions and associations sacred to his memory, the object of the affection and gratitude of all their children. Left by his death as a stricken deer, she had no desire to live. Through much pain, yet with unwavering faith, she went to rejoin him on the early morning of February 28th, 1880.

On the occasion of their marriage Dr Hodge wrote to his dearest friend, Bishop Johns:

DR HODGE TO BISHOP JOHNS

PRINCETON, August 27, 1852

My Dear Johns:—You would not have heard of my marriage from others before hearing of it from me had I known where to address you. It was only a month or two before the event that I could bring myself to inform my own children of my purpose. Other friends I intended to inform afterwards. I do not know that you remember Mary Hunter, the constant companion of Caroline Bayard (now Mrs Dod). I have known her by sight since she was fifteen years old. For the last six or seven years she was a sister to Sarah, and therefore to me. She was familiarly known and greatly loved by all my children, who were almost as much at home in her house as in my own. She has come into my family as an old friend, every heart already her own, and we all feel her presence as a token and assurance of God's favour.

I told her what kind of a man you were, and she said, 'Well, as I don't know him, I can't love him desperately yet; as soon as I see him I'll do my best.' Her best is very good, indeed; so you may be sure of an affectionate greeting from her, as well as from your old friend, when you pay your promised visit. Dear John, do not let that visit be only for a day. Old friendship deserves more than that, and remember I spent ten days with you in Richmond as meek as a mouse, never answering to all your sharp things out of deference to your wife. It will greatly add to our pleasure if Mrs Johns will come with you, and the girls also. Hope deferred, etc.

I have already made the acquaintance of Mr Peterkin, and have heard him preach. He has made an exceedingly pleasant impression on his church and on the community. Every one speaks well of him, and his people seem disposed to receive him with confidence and affection. There are some High-church persons among them who think he is below the mark in some things; but even they speak highly of him as a man and preacher.

Your affectionate friend,
CHARLES HODGE

CORRESPONDENCE WITH HIS BROTHER

During these years he continued to keep up his weekly correspondence with his brother. In the latter years of this period, from about 1856, his letters began sensibly to decrease in frequency and length, until some years before the death of his brother, in February 1873, they had ceased to be regular, and became occasional. The cause of this was, in part, increasing infirmity, resulting from advancing age on both sides, but especially the increasing defect of his brother's vision, which resulted in blindness so far entire as to prevent all reading or writing more than ten years before his decease. The following are given as specimens of this correspondence and of his political opinions:

PRINCETON, July 8, 1850

My Dear Brother:— . . . I hear you are a Fillmore man. That is better than going for Buchanan. I am for Fremont. Not for the man, but for the platform. I would not vote for my father if he endorsed the Cincinnati resolutions; and Fillmore has committed himself to worse nullification than South Carolina ever dreamt of. He has drawn a broader line between the North and South than was ever drawn before, and exalted the 300,000 slave-holders into an equivalent of the 20,000,000 of the free men, entitled to an equal share in the government of the country. I think the great danger to the country and to the cause of justice and good government is from the divisions and concessions of the North. If Ohio had done to Kentucky what Missouri has done to Kansas, the South would have risen as one man and redressed the grievance. And if the North had risen as one man and told the South that Kansas should have justice, we should have had no difficulty.

Your brother, C.H.

PRINCETON, Dec. 29, 1851

My Dear Brother:— . . . My view of the character of Louis Napoleon is not altered by recent events. He is a name and an instrument which able military men use for their own aggrandizement. The army in all ages has an *esprit de corps* which makes them a distinct class from the people, and when they are addressed as the elite of the nation, and invited by their official head to become the ruling power, it is rare indeed that they refuse. France seems to me like a great bear led about by a soldier and ridden by a monkey, – if it be not wrong to speak thus of rulers. What is to come of all this God only knows. The choice for Europe just now seems to be military despotism or socialistic anarchy, and, therefore, it is not wonderful that so many are willing to choose the former. Hungary seems to present the only prospect of rational liberty, because the Hungarians are a religious people, and their leaders are professed Christians. I am filled with admiration for Kossuth,[1] and cannot but hope that God means him to be a great instrument for good. So far from regretting his coming to this country, I think his visit to England and America is likely to prove a turning point in the history of the world. He appears to be chosen and fitted to impress certain truths, before indistinctly recognized, as living principles in the minds of the people, which must hereafter control public policy. I think his principle of non-intervention, and the right of all nations to prevent the violation of that principle, is so obviously true, and so beneficent, that it will command universal consent. In our case the question is not as to our right to intervene to prevent the aggression of Russia; nor as to our duty to do so if we can do it effectively, but simply as to our power. A protest would do little, a war not much more. We are too far off. But if by union with other nations we could so intervene as to make our intervention effectual, then I think the path, both of policy and duty, would be plain.

You affectionate brother, C.H.

Princeton, Feb. 16, 1852

My Dear Brother:— . . . I feel provoked at the way Z— talks of Kossuth. It is just as absurd and arrogant to call him a humbug, as it

---

[1] Lajos Kossuth (1802–94), Hungarian leader and champion of liberty. [Ed.]

would be to call Newton an idiot, or Raphael a dauber. Z— should remember other men have eyes and ears and sense as well as he. Kossuth is beyond question one of the greatest men of the age, whatever may be thought of his history or of his principles. And as to his principles, I do not believe there is one good and sensible man in a hundred who doubts their soundness. The great mistake is that people do not distinguish between the principles themselves and their application. It may be very unwise for us as a nation to interfere as he would have us do, but the right and duty to interfere in certain cases, when it can be done effectually and safely, is just as plain as that it is the right and duty of one man to interfere to prevent another man murdering his neighbour. There is in the February number of Dr Van Rensselaer's *Presbyterian Magazine* an article on 'Kossuth and his Mission' which I think takes the right ground.

As to Louis Napoleon,[1] I am not prophet enough to say what is to happen. He has on his side four of the six classes into which the French population is divided: the army, the priesthood, the peasantry (who are governed by the priesthood), and the capitalists or business men. These constitute the vast majority of the people, and by the instinct of self-preservation cling to despotism as the necessary condition of order. The only class against him is that of professional men (lawyers, doctors, politicians) and the mechanics or working men of the towns. It is so clear to me that liberty can exist only on the foundation of intelligence and religion, that I have no hope for France, where the intelligent part of the population have no religion and the religious part no intelligence. It seems, however, almost incredible that such a nation can submit to be so insulted, abused, and down-trodden by such a pretender as Louis Napoleon.

Your brother,
CHARLES HODGE

---

[1] Louis-Napoléon Bonaparte (1808–73), nephew of Napoléon Bonaparte, also known as Napoléon III, elected President of France, 1848, but seized supreme power in a coup d'état in 1851. [Ed.]

Princeton, April 14, 1852

My Dear Brother:—Six weeks does indeed seem a long period of non-intercourse between you and me. It did not use to be so. But circumstances, habits, and powers alter even when, as doubtless is true in our case, the affections remain unchanged. It is painful, how ever, that we should thus drift asunder as we grow older. I have been rejoiced several times to hear that you were and looked better than usual this winter, notwithstanding its length and severity.

You see from the papers that Senator Choate has been making a great speech in Trenton on the India rubber case. James Alexander told me that he met Chief Justice Green of Trenton the other day, who told him that Choate was a great Princeton man – that he thought the *Princeton Review* the greatest quarterly review in the country!!; and Princeton the great conservative influence, etc., etc. What do you think of that? I did not know that our rays penetrated so far into the hyperborean[1] regions.

Princeton, March 15, 1854

My Dear Brother:—On Sunday evening I went to Church for the first time in some months.[2] When near home I struck my foot against a stone and fell with great force on my lame limb. The jar was con-siderable, and has made the limb tender and painful, very much as it used to be. I rode out yesterday, but found the motion gave me the same kind of pain I used to suffer. I cannot now walk about the house without occasioning more pain than walking two miles occa-sioned before the fall. I am afraid the socket of the hip joint received a concussion which has made it irritable, though the blow and bruise were presumably below the knee.

I feel somewhat concerned lest this accident may throw me back to my former state of lameness, though I hope it may be only a temporary inconvenience. I am, however, for the present as lame as

---

[1] From the extreme north. [Ed.]

[2] Sabbath morning and afternoon he worshipped in the Seminary, Chapel and Oratory.

I was in '43. I propose keeping as quiet as possible for a while, and to use cold water and rubbing. Last night I pushed the hydropathic system to the extent of wrapping my limb in a wet towel and then in flannel. It did no harm that I could perceive. It made the limb red, the pores of the skin seemed dilated and raised, and a little rubbing was more effective than a good deal before.

I shall be really sorry to be again laid up. I trust this may not be. Dr Duff has again disappointed us. He is not to come for a month. This makes it doubtful whether we shall see him at all.

DANCING AND CARD-PLAYING

An old pupil, the Rev. Wm. C—, had consulted him on a case of discipline likely to come up on appeal to the General Assembly, involving the question of dancing and worldly amusements. As his former letter to the Rev. Mr C— had been misunderstood and hence misrepresented, Dr Hodge wrote again and very explicitly:

DR HODGE TO REV. WM. C—

PRINCETON, April 1st, 1853

Dear Sir:— . . . I very much regret that the matter is coming up. It is a very serious matter to transfer a local difficulty and agitation to the whole Church. If this controversy has done harm in your neighbourhood, it will do harm in a much larger theatre. There are the same elements of disagreement in the Assembly that exist in your Presbytery.

Again, it is very doubtful how the Assembly will decide. The question does not come up in the abstract, but in the concrete. It is not a principle to be decided, but a given case with all its circumstances. The Assembly is a very uncertain place for such discussions and decisions.

And once more, if I understand your letter, you are on very different ground from that which I meant to assume in my former letter to you, and from what would be sustained by the general sentiment of the Church in this part of the country. It is one thing to state general principles as to things indifferent and as to the power of the Church in reference to such matters, and a very different thing to decide upon the propriety or impropriety of indulging in such things. Dancing, card-playing and wine-drinking all belong to the same class. They are not in their essential nature sinful. But there may be a kind of dancing, a kind of card-playing and a kind of wine drinking in their nature evil; and when not evil in themselves it may be very wrong for professors of religion to indulge in them. They are all so associated with frivolity and worldliness that no minister or church member in this part of the country can countenance them in any form without injuring his influence and the cause of religion. I have never allowed my children to learn to dance, or to attend dances, or to be present where it was going on. I have directed them to leave the company and return home if it was unexpectedly introduced. But I understand that you have advocated the propriety of Church members dancing, and have even remained present where it was going on. This could not be done with impunity by any minister here any more than his playing cards or countenancing card-playing by his presence.

I think, therefore, if the case comes up before the Assembly, however irregular or unwise may have been the action of the session, the decision will not be in accordance with your wishes.

I hope you will excuse my expressing myself so plainly on this subject, but as my name has been mixed up in this business, and my former letter to you quoted in reference to it, it is proper that you should understand exactly how I regard the whole subject.

Very sincerely your friend,
C. HODGE

THE BAPTISM OF THE INFANT CHILDREN
OF NON-PROFESSORS

A fellow-citizen and friendly neighbour applied to him to baptize his children in a case in which neither parent was a communicating member of the church, at the time when the Rev. Benjamin H. Rice, D.D., was pastor of the congregation. He refused, and in the following letter fully stated his views of duty in such a case.

DR HODGE TO MR B—

PRINCETON, N. J., April 4, 1843

My Dear Sir:—Your request that I should baptize your children presented a question of duty which I felt to be so important that I have delayed longer than would otherwise have been excusable in giving you an answer. On the one hand, the desire that you and Mrs B— express, of having your children recognized as members of the Christian Church, is not only natural but worthy of respect. On the other hand, the obligations which parents assume in presenting their children for baptism are of the most serious nature. From the nature of the case, the parent professes faith in Christ; he professes to believe all the doctrines which Christ taught, especially all those which are particularly brought to view in that ordinance – viz.: the fallen state of man, his need of pardon and sanctification, the suitableness and sufficiency of the provision made in the gospel through the merit and Spirit of Christ for our salvation, and the right which Christ has to our confidence and obedience. Besides this, it results from the nature of the ordinance in question that the parent not only professes his faith in Christ, but promises to live in obedience to all his commands. This is included in professing himself to be a Christian; and the Bible as well as our own reason teaches that all who partake of the ordinances of the Christian Church do thereby profess to be Christians, just as those who offered a Jewish sacrifice in the temple professed the Jewish religion. While, therefore, the desire to have our children baptized is natural and proper, we ought to feel that the profession and promises that we of necessity make when we present them to God are so solemn and comprehensive that they cannot be properly made unless we are sincere in our faith, and determined, by the grace of God, to be faithful to our engagements. I make these remarks not only because I wish you to feel that you, as parents, would incur before God and his Church very serious responsibilities in having your children baptized, but also that no minister could, in this view of the case, conscientiously administer the ordinance unless the parents (or one of them) were prepared intelligently to make the profession and incur the responsibility which it necessarily involves.

What the minister is bound to consider as a profession entitling the parent to have his children baptized is, as you know, a question on which the ministers of our Church are much divided. I doubt not the majority take the same view of the case as Dr Rice. I feel, however, that I am precluded by a previous consideration from the right of deciding that question for myself, or at least acting on that decision. I do not stand in the relation of pastor to this people; Dr Rice does; he has been made the overseer of this flock; I have not. He, therefore, is responsible for the administration of the word and ordinances to this people, and other ministers have no right to interfere with his charge. I feel, therefore that I have no right to comply with your request. I am sure, therefore, you will readily excuse me, which you would do the more readily if you knew the pain it has given me to come to this decision.

I cannot conclude this letter without begging you and Mrs B— not to let this matter rest here. The benefits and blessings connected with infant baptism are so great that no parent has the right to debar his children from them. We are bound to give our children to God in the way which He has appointed, and to secure for them the blessings of that covenant which He has formed with His people. We are therefore bound, as we desire the salvation of our children, to do whatever on our part is necessary to secure for them, according to the rules of His church, the great benefit of being devoted to God by the ordinance of baptism.

May I ask you to show this letter to Mrs B—, for whom I entertain the sincerest respect, that she may see that I decline a compliance with your request only from a sense of duty, and that I consider this a question which neither she nor you can safely allow to rest as it now is.

Very sincerely your friend,

CHARLES HODGE

COMMENTARIES

In the early part of this decade, Dr Hodge, together with Dr Joseph Addison Alexander, formed a plan for the joint production of a critical Commentary of the whole New Testament, based on the Greek Text, in a series of volumes of an approximately uniform size.

Dr Hodge published his Commentary on Ephesians[1] in 1856, that on 1 Corinthians in 1857, and that on 2 Corinthians[2] in 1859.

ARTICLES IN THE PRINCETON REVIEW

Besides these volumes he wrote during this decade the following articles in the *Princeton Review*:

1852. The General Assembly.

1853. Idea of the Church; The General Assembly; Visibility of the Church.

1854. Beecher's Great Conflict; Dr Schaff's *Apostolic Church;* The Church of England on Presbyterian Orders; The Education Question; The General Assembly.

1855. Memoir of Dr Archibald Alexander; Bishop McIlvaine on the Church; Presbyterian Liturgies; The General Assembly.

1856. The *Church Review* on the Permanency of the Apostolic Office; The *Princeton Review* and Cousin's Philosophy; The General Assembly of 1856; The Church, Its Perpetuity.

---

[1] Reprinted London: Banner of Truth, 1964. [Ed.]

[2] *Commentaries on 1 and 2 Corinthians* reprinted as one volume, Edinburgh: Banner of Truth, 1974. [Ed.]

1857. Free Agency; The General Assembly; The American Bible Society and its New Standard; Inspiration.

1858. The Church; Membership of Infants; The General Assembly; Adoption of the Confession of Faith; The Revised Book of Discipline.

1859. The Unity of Mankind; Demission of the Ministry; The General Assembly; Sunday Laws.

1860. What is Christianity?; The First and Second Adam; The General Assembly; Presbyterianism.

This list of bare titles shows that he was now at the very summit of his life, making the most effective demonstration of his powers, and pouring forth the richest fruits of his labours as a student and thinker. The list is so rich in volume and variety that space is available only for a very cursory notice of those articles which possess special or most permanent significance.

1. The Articles on the annual General Assemblies contain matters of various and paramount interest. Dr Hodge was himself a member of the Assemblies of 1854 in Buffalo and of 1860 in Rochester, and took a prominent part in the debates of both of them. He has left in these articles forcible expression of his opinion on the following among other subjects.

i. In the General Assembly of 1853, there were two questions debated as to the Board of Domestic Missions, (a) The relation of the Board to the Presbyteries, and (b) Whether the Board is only a Missionary and not also a Sustentation organization. Dr Hodge maintained as to the *first* question, that the Board and not the Presbytery is to be judge in every case as to its own ability to grant the aid asked, and on the other hand the Presbytery and not the Board is the only judge in every case whether the particular church concerned deserves the aid sought. He also maintained as to the *second* question that it is anti-scriptural, inexpedient, and contrary to historical fact to hold that the Presbyterian Board of Home Missions is only a missionary organization, that on all these grounds it is proved to be also the organ of the church for sustaining weak churches, and that practically it is the prerogative of the Presbytery and not of the Board to decide whether the particular weak church deserves any longer to receive aid or not.

THE CONSTITUTIONALITY OF OUR CHURCH BOARDS

ii. In the Assemblies of 1854 and 1860, there were great debates on the question whether the Boards as then organized were consistent with the principles of New Testament Presbyterianism. Dr Thornwell and others argued the negative, and Dr Hodge and others the affirmative. The principles maintained on both sides are reported by Dr Hodge in his Article on 'Presbyterianism' in the *Princeton Review*, July 1860.

The theory, as propounded by Dr Thornwell in his first speech, was understood to embrace the following principles: (1) That the form of government for the church, and its modes of action, are prescribed in the Word of God, not merely as to its general principles, but in all its details, as completely as the system of faith or the moral law; and therefore everything for which we cannot produce a 'Thus saith the Lord' is unscriptural and unlawful. (2) Consequently the church has no more right to create a new office, organ, or organization for the exercise of her prerogatives or the execution of her prescribed work, than she has to create a new article of faith or to add a new command to the Decalogue. (3) That the church cannot delegate her powers. She must exercise them herself, and through officers and organs prescribed in the Scriptures. She has no more right to act by a vicar, than Congress has to delegate its legislative power, or a Christian to pray by proxy. (4) That all executive, legislative and judicial power in the Church is in the hands of the clergy, that is, of presbyters, who have the same ordination and office, although differing in functions. (5) That all power in the Church is joint and not several. That is, it can be exercised only by church courts, and not in any case by individual officers.

In opposition to this general scheme the 'Brother from Princeton' propounded the following general principles. (1) That all the attributes and prerogatives of the church arise from the indwelling of the Holy Spirit, and consequently where He dwells, there are those attributes and prerogatives. (2) That as the Spirit dwells not in the clergy only, but in the people of God, all power is in *sensu primo*, in the people. (3) That in the exercise of these prerogatives, the church is to be governed by principles laid down in the Word of God, which determine, within certain limits, her officers and modes of organization; but that beyond those prescribed principles and in fidelity to them, the church has a wide discretion in the choice of methods, organs and agencies. (4) That the fundamental principles of our Presbyterian system are first, the parity of our clergy; second, the right of the people to a substantive part in the government of the church; third, the unity of the church, in such sense that a small part is subject to a larger, and a larger to the whole.

If every thing relating to the government and action of the church is laid down in detail in the Word of God, so that it is unlawful to employ any organs or agencies not therein enjoined, then the Boards are clearly unlawful; if it is not so, the having them or not having them is a matter of expediency.

Dr Hodge proceeded to prove that their continuance was expedient, because they did not differ in principle, but only in the accident of numbers from Committees, and because they were in fact established, had worked well, and in some form not radically different from that in existence, they were practically essential to the work of a church so large and so circumstanced as our own. The Assembly of 1860, the last one in which the Northern and Southern Old School Church acted together, decided in favour of the ground advocated by Dr Hodge, by a majority of 234 to 56.

COMMISSIONS

iii. The question of the constitutional right of our ecclesiastical courts to appoint commissions to try and decide judicial cases was debated in the Assemblies of 1854 and 1855. It was argued against the right that no court, civil or ecclesiastical, can delegate its powers. Dr Hodge argued earnestly for the right, because:

> There is no delegation of powers involved in the appointment of a commission. A quorum of a Presbytery is the Presbytery; a quorum of a Synod is the Synod; and a quorum of the Assembly is the Assembly. In like manner, inasmuch as a commission must embrace at least a quorum of the appointing body, a commission is not of the nature of a committee with powers, but it is the appointing body itself, adjourned to meet at a certain time and place, for the transaction of a specific business – with the understanding expressed or implied that while the whole body may convene, certain members are required to attend . . . It is well known that our ecclesiastical courts have often appointed such bodies, and that the General Assembly of the Church of Scotland annually appoints a commission, to which all unfinished business is referred . . . It is therefore, a mere question of expediency. Something must be done to relieve the Assembly of the pressure of judicial business. The appointment of a commission is a long tried and approved method of relief, and we hope it will be ultimately adopted, not only by the Assembly, but by Synods and Presbyteries.

AMERICAN BIBLE SOCIETY

iv. In 1847 it had been brought to the notice of the Board of Managers of the American Bible Society that there existed a great number of 'discrepancies between our different editions of the English Bible; also between our editions and those issued by the British and Foreign Bible Society'. Hence the Board of Managers, in 1848, directed the Committee on Versions to collate copies of all the standard editions for the purpose of correcting the discrepancies alleged to exist, relating principally to 'orthography, capital letters, words in italics, and punctuation'. The Committee on Versions, however, transcended in practice these perfectly legitimate and wise directions of the Board of Managers, and made changes affecting the sense of the text, and especially sweeping changes in the headings of chapters, on the ground that they were no part of the inspired Word of God. This work of the committee was practically accepted by the Board, and large editions of the altered Bibles were printed and put in circulation. When this was realized by the Christian public, such general alarm and indignation was expressed that the Bible Society receded from their hastily and only-half-designedly assumed position, and peace and confidence was restored.

The General Assemblies of 1857 and '8 considered the matter. A strong condemnatory resolution, presented by Dr R. J. Breckinridge, was passed unanimously by the General Assembly of 1858. Dr Hodge argued with great energy on the same side, in his articles on 'The General Assembly' in the *Princeton Review* for July, 1857 and 1858, and on 'The American Bible Society and Its New Standard Edition of the English Version', July 1857. The principles upon which this earnest opposition was urged were (a) The Bible Society, as the agent of the Churches, is the mere publisher and not the editor of the version, with discretionary powers, (b) According to the sense of the contracting parties, the Bible Society was entrusted by the Churches with the duty of publishing the standard edition of King James' version, as printed in 1811, as then furnished with headings, marginal notes and references. The contract, therefore, to circulate the Scriptures, without notes or comments, must be understood to mean without any other notes or comments than those already incorporated in the standard editions of the English Bible.

In this sense it was understood and acquiesced in by all Protestant denominations. Thus, while the Board had the right and duty of ascertaining the standard, the assumption of the right to change it in any particular was unwarranted and most dangerous, and must be prevented from exercise at once, without regard to the character of the changes actually proposed; while 'the fact that these changes (actually made), in almost all instances, eliminated the evangelical element from these headings, tended greatly to increase dissatisfaction and alarm'.

SUBSCRIPTION TO THE CONFESSION

v. In the General Assembly of 1858, the Rev. Dr. R. J. Breck-inridge offered a resolution directing the Board of Publication to nominate men subsequently to be appointed to work under the direction of future Assemblies in preparing a Church Commentary on the whole Bible, adopting the standard King James version, in the sense of the constant faith of the Word of God, as that is briefly set forth in the standard of the Westminster Assembly. This was referred to the next Assembly, and finally abandoned.

Dr Hodge exposed the weakness of the scheme very freely. He argued (a) That it was unprecedented, and would be destructive of all liberty for any Church to provide an authoritative explanation of all the Scriptures in detail. (b) That the men do not exist who are competent for such a task. (c) That while the Confession of Faith is the rule controlling among us ministerial communion, it has never been made the rule for the interpretation of Scripture. (d) Even as to the Confession of Faith agreement is not perfect. 'We could not hold together a week if we made the adoption of all its professions a condition of ministerial communion.'

> Who is to tell us the Church's sense of the Confession? It is notorious that as to that point we are not agreed. In the second place, even as to the points in which the sense of the Confession is plain, there is want of entire concurrence in its reception, and what is the main point, there is no such thing as the sense of the Westminster Confession as to the true interpretation of thousands of passages of Scripture. The

standard is an imaginary one. What does the Confession teach of the dark sayings of Hosea, etc.?

These paragraphs made a great sensation, and the old-school newspapers generally condemned them as teaching the loose view that the standards were subscribed by the entrants to the ministry of the Presbyterian Church only for *substance of doctrine;* that is, in the sense of evangelical Christianity in general. Dr Hodge, therefore, published an article on the 'Adoption of the Confession of Faith', in the October number of the *Princeton Review*, of the same year, in which he defends what he said in July, and fully states his whole position on the subject of creed subscription. The difficulty with the statements just quoted is that they present only that one-half of the subject which was related to the question then in debate.

In the October article he maintains (a) That subscription binds in the sense of the *animus imponentis*[1] – i.e., not the mind of the moderator, or Presbytery ordaining the candidate, but the mind or intention of the whole denomination, (b) That to the question, 'What does the Presbyterian Church understand the candidate to profess when he "receives and adopts the Confession of Faith of this Church as containing the system of doctrine taught in the Holy Scriptures"?', three answers have been given. First, that 'system of doctrine' means 'substance of doctrine'. Second, that he who affirms it adopts every proposition contained in the Confession as part of his own faith. Each of these answers he discards for different reasons. Third, that the phrase 'system of doctrine' is to be intelligently and honestly taken in its fixed historical sense. It presupposes belief in all those truths which are common to all Christians, and those common to all evangelical Protestants, and embraces in addition all those special doctrines by which the Reformed or Calvinistic Churches are distinguished from the Lutherans and

[1] The intention of the party imposing the oath. [Ed.]

Arminians and other Protestants. This system is well known, and easily ascertainable; it is clearly taught in the Confession, and is professed by all who adopt this as the standard of their faith.

vi. The General Assembly of 1857 appointed a committee, of which Dr Thornwell was chairman and Dr Hodge a member, to revise the Book of Discipline. Dr Hodge attended to all the meetings of this committee, and wrote his views extensively as to the changes proposed, in an article published in the *Princeton Review*, entitled 'The Revised Book of Discipline', October 1858. He regarded the changes in general as wisely made, and objected only to the change in the affirmations made with regard to the relation of the baptized members of the Church to its discipline. He accepted the language adopted on that subject as susceptible of a good sense, but preferred the language of the old book. He referred the coldness with which the work of the committee was received to a strong aversion to change on the part of the Church, and expressed his belief that 'the time is not distant when a verdict will be rendered with great unanimity in favour of the majority of the alterations proposed by the Committee of Revision.'

RELIGIOUS EDUCATION AND THE RELATION OF THE STATE TO RELIGION

vii. The late admirable Dr Van Rensselaer, when Secretary of the Board of Education, attempted to introduce a permanent system of parochial and presbyterial schools and synodical academies. This was met by a violent opposition from two opposite quarters. First, Dr Thornwell and those who agreed with him that the Church's commission confines it to the preaching of the gospel, in the technical sense of that word, of course objected that the Church had no right to give secular education even to her own children. Secondly, The rationalistic and infidel supporters of a purely secular education opposed it as fanatical and as interfering with the system of State schools.

Dr Hodge earnestly advocated the system in his Articles on the 'General Assembly' for 1854 and 1856, and in an Article entitled the 'Education Question', July 1854. He there maintains with great force of conviction the following principles, (a) The absolute necessity of popular education. (b) That this education should be religious; that religion should be a regular part of the course of instruction in all our non-professional educational institutions. The new doctrine that secular education should be entirely separated from religion he declared to be *first* 'a virtual renunciation of allegiance to God, as destructive to society, and as certainly involving the final overthrow of the whole system of public education'; and *second*, absolutely impracticable, since true or false doctrines as to God and his relation to us and the world must go along with all knowledge; and *third*, destructive, because the attempt to exclude religion must tend to teach atheism either sceptical, virtual, or practical. (c) That the doctrine that our state schools must teach no religion, because the state has no religious character, he pronounces to be false as a fact, and absurd as an opinion. 'Christianity is the common and supreme law of the land from the necessity of the case, because it is the religion of those who constitute the country.' 'Our real statesmen, our highest judges, our chief magistrates and founders of government and the ornaments of our country, have with one voice and in various forms acknowledged that Christianity is the law of the land.' It is a matter of history, and a matter of fact as to the existing state of the law, of the institutions, customs, and convictions of the vast majority of the people. (d) That if the people are to be educated, the state must teach; if the state teaches at all, she must teach religion; if she teaches religion, it must under the past and present state of facts teach Protestant Christianity. (e) The responsibility of providing education for the people rests, co-ordinately upon parents, the state and the church. As to the right and obligation of the Church to teach, it evidently springs from its nature. It was originally commissioned 'to disciple all nations, baptizing them, teaching them'. This has from the beginning been the uniform faith and practice of the Church of all denominations and ages, and the more conspicuously in the periods of her greatest spiritual enlightenment and faithfulness. (f) 'That in the existing state of our country the Church can no more resign the work of education exclusively to the state, than the state can leave it exclusively to parents or the Church. The work cannot be accomplished, in the way she is bound to see it accomplished, without her efficient co-operation.' (g) 'That in the performance of this great duty, the Church cannot rely on the separate agency of her members, but is bound to act collectively, or in her organized capacity.'

In answer to a letter of inquiry addressed to him by the Rev. Morris Sutphen, D.D., of New York, Dr Hodge wrote the following letter on this subject, April 10th, 1869.

PRINCETON, N.J., April 10, 1869

My Dear Sir:—I am not aware that my views have undergone any change on the education question. I still believe that the Church is bound to see to it that all within her influence, especially her own children, have a religious education; to which end parish or church schools are indispensable. 2. What is the duty of Presbyterians is the duty of other denominations or churches. 3. That in such a heterogeneous and liberty-abusing population as we have in this country, church schools cannot reach the masses sufficiently, and therefore State schools are a necessity. 4. That church or denominational schools are entitled to a share of the school fund of the State, proportioned to the number of children they educate; the State having the right to see that its standard of secular education is come up to. And, to finish my creed, 5. I would let none but the educated in the schools established and approved by the State – vote.

I do not remember anything I have written on this subject. I had forgotten the address of 1847, to which you refer.

Your friend, etc., Charles Hodge

When a society was formed and memorials signed in order to move the Houses of Congress to send down the following clause to the States as an amendment to the Constitution of the United States: 'Humbly acknowledging Almighty God as the source of all authority and power in civil government, the Lord Jesus Christ as the Ruler among the nations, and His revealed will as of supreme authority, in order to constitute a Christian government, etc., etc.' – Dr Hodge, on every proper occasion, signified his approval, and publicly subscribed his name to the following sentence: 'We cordially approve of the object of the foregoing memorial, and desire to do all that we lawfully can to promote it.'

FREE AGENCY, INSPIRATION, ETC., ETC.

2. His Articles on 'Free Agency', 'Inspiration', 'the Church membership of infants' and 'Demission of the Ministry' are all in his most effective style of theological discussion, and have been repeated and expanded, but hardly excelled in the corresponding chapters of his *Systematic Theology*. Dr McGuffey, late professor of metaphysics in the University of Virginia, told the writer that he regarded the former of this list as a most clear and able exposition of its subject, and habitually referred his classes to it. It was written in the first instance as a lecture, and was as such the very first lecture he read to his classes, when commencing to lecture in the department of Didactic Theology.

In his article, 'Demission of the Ministry', he earnestly argued the right and the propriety of providing a way of honourable retreat for the many honest Christian men who have become ministers while destitute of the qualifications for usefulness and success.

The growing number of these nominal ministers out of office, and often completely secularized in character and reputation, and their frequent predominance in our church courts, is coming to be recognized as the greatest evil and danger in our American Presbyterianism.

PRESBYTERIAN LITURGIES

3. In the Article on 'Presbyterian Liturgies', July 1855, he expresses the following opinions, (1) That the use of Liturgies is neither a peculiarity nor a natural adjunct of Episcopacy. 'They were introduced into all Protestant Churches at the time of the Reformation, and in the greater number of them they continue to the present day.' (2) He exhibits the reasons which justified Presbyterians in resisting the imposition of the English Prayer Book, which have led in Scotland and America to the general disuse of Liturgies altogether. (3) He declares it to be his opinion that their total neglect has been injurious, especially in the imperfect and diverse manners in which the sacraments and the special rites of the church, such as marriage, ordination, burial, etc., are performed. (4) 'These two conditions being supposed, first that the book should be compiled and not written; and second, that its use should be optional – we are strongly of opinion, that it would answer a most important end.'

4. The article entitled, '*Princeton Review* and Cousin's Philosophy', April 1856, should be read by every one desiring to see all the sides of Dr Hodge's character. Professors Dod and James W. Alexander had together written the article on Transcendendalism in 1839. It attracted great admiration, and was several times reprinted by parties entirely disconnected with Princeton, both in New England and Great Britain. In 1856, Caleb S. Henry, D.D., the translator of the 'Lectures of Cousin on Locke', one of the works

reviewed in that article, in the preface to his *Elements of Psychology*, fills many pages with coarse vituperation, and imputation of the basest motives against the authors, one of whom, Dr Hodge's intimate friend, had been eleven years dead. Dr H. is often said to have been like the apostle John; if any one will read this vindication of the memory of his dead friend, they will nevertheless see that like his Saviour he knew how to address the 'fools and blind' and the 'generation of vipers'.

BISHOP McILVAINE ON THE CHURCH

5. In the April number of the *Review* for 1855 Dr Hodge had prepared a short article under the title of 'Bishop McIlvaine on the Church', to show that his old friend and classmate, although a decided Episcopalian, held the same evangelical and Protestant doctrine of the 'Church' as he himself had taught, and which many of his Old-school and New-school Presbyterian 'brethren in the ignorance of their reactionary zeal' denounced as too low-church, and as virtually giving away of everything to the Independents.

In May 1855, he delivered the first annual address before the Presbyterian Historical Society, in which he laid down the essential general principles of Presbyterian Church organization. In October of the same year the *Church Review and Register*, a high-church quarterly review of New Haven, reviewed that lecture, and set over against it an argument, purporting to come from the pen of Bishop McIlvaine, maintaining the permanency of the Apostolic office. In his January number of the *Princeton Review*, Dr Hodge answered and refuted this argument in an article entitled 'The *Church Review* on the Permanency of the Apostolic Office.' In April 1854, he published an article entitled 'The Church of England and Presbyterian Orders' in which he exhibits the historical argument of the Rev. William Goode, in support of the position that the founders and great theologians of the Church of England while maintaining the expediency or even the divine right of Episcopacy, had never considered it essential to the being of the Church.

The following interesting correspondence sprang up on the occasion of his response to Bishop McIlvaine's argument in favour of the perpetuity of the Apostolic office.

DR HODGE TO BISHOP McILVAINE

PRINCETON, Dec. 18, 1855

Dear Charles:—I address you in this affectionate college style not only because my heart dictates it, but also because I fear, if I did not do so now, I may not be able to do it at all. It may be that the January number of the *Princeton Review* may indispose you to recognize me as your old friend, though I hope not.

In May last I was called upon to deliver an address before the Presbyterian Historical Society on the question, 'What is Presbyterianism?',[1] a copy of which I send you. That address was made the subject of criticism in the *Church Review*, New Haven, Conn. The Reviewer, instead of discussing the argument in the address, republished *in extenso* [at full length] your sermon on the permanency of the Apostolic office; which he called upon me to examine. I have made the attempt to examine your argument, and have endeavoured to treat you as a friend and advocate of evangelical truth, while I treated your argument as a Presbyterian. I really and honestly think there is nothing in my review of your sermon which ought to lessen our personal friendship. But as things seem so differently when viewed from different positions, you may think otherwise. I should be exceedingly pained should this be the case, for much as I feel pained and aggrieved at the positions assumed in your sermon, I feel nothing but affection and respect towards you. Indeed I cannot but hope you will regard my review as I do, a mere act of self-defence. Granting all I say, you are untouched in your ministerial and even your episcopal standing. But granting what you say, I am no minister, and if a Christian, am in a state of rebellion against one who has a divine

[1] This is available on the Web from Google Books and other sources. [Ed.]

right to my submission to him as the bishop of New Jersey. It is not reasonable to expect that Presbyterians can silently submit to these claims of Episcopacy. So long as they emanated only from professed Anglicans or High-Church-men, I, for one, cared little about them. But when I found to my surprise that they had been advocated by one of your high character as an evangelical Christian, I felt bound, when specially by name called upon, to say what I have said in reference to the whole matter.

I hope you will feel toward me while reading my review, as I felt toward you after reading your sermon.

Affectionately your friend,
CHARLES HODGE

BISHOP McILVAINE TO DR HODGE

CINCINNATI, Dec. 22, 1855

My Dear Charles:—I have just received your kind and affectionate letter of the 18th, and am much obliged to you for such kind desire and pains to prevent any evil influence on our long established friendship from a review of my sermon, which I doubt not your sense of duty has prompted. And by the way, I a little suspect that a part of the *animus* [intention] of the re-print in the *Church Review* was to bring me into such relations with my Presbyterian brethren and friends as would wean me from my affectionate feelings towards all of them who love Christ as my brethren, and especially towards some of whom I have the superadded regard as dear friends.

I cannot say, my dear Charles, what I shall feel when I read the review, but believing you would aim only at the truth and not at *me*, I will hope and expect so to receive it, that *love* shall not be the sufferer, however other feelings may be. From what you say I infer that you have not understood my *mind* in the sermon, but have interpreted the bearing on non-Episcopal ministers and churches as I do not. I do not perceive that the sermon contains anything in advance of the usual low-church doctrine prevailing in our Church. It teaches *Apostolical Succession*, just as I understand real Presbyterians to teach it, namely, that *a certain part* of the authority committed to the Apostles was intended to continue in the ministry to the end of the world, and, has continued – such for example as the power of ordination. The difference between the Episcopalian and the Presbyterian being that the latter hold the descent to have been in the line of Presbyters, the former in the line of diocesan Bishops. The Apostolical succession is held in my opinion as much in one Church as the other – the difference between the so holding and high-churchmanship in both, being when it is not held in such a sense as to exclude by the inferences drawn from it all other ministers than its own from *validity and reality*, nor other Churches from being real Churches of Christ whatever it may think of their defective conformity to the *Apostolic* pattern. Such Apostolic succession is vastly removed from that of Romanism and Puseyism, which not only makes a ministry so descended, essential to the *being* of the Church, and essential to the *reality* of all sacraments, but makes the communication of *saving grace* essentially dependent on the sacraments of that succession – and thus it is the exclusive succession of the *gifts of the Spirit* as well as of a certain office.

My sermon was written in '39, some sixteen years ago. How far I should now enter into all its details I cannot say, for it is very long since I have given my mind to that line of subject. But when I preached it, as ever since, I considered it as a simple maintenance of an alleged fact, with a studied abstinence from all attack or reflection on other churches, and as leaving me at full liberty to believe in and acknowledge other churches as real churches, and their ministers as real ministers of Christ, often greatly blessed of the Spirit. I did not consider, nor do I now, Episcopal ordination essential to the *being* of the ministry or sacraments, any more than to the Church, though I do consider it essential to the full order and model of the primitive church. So you think of Presbyterian ordination.

While I thus vindicate the position of the sermon, I do not mean to intimate that under present feelings I should take such a track of thought again on a similar occasion. It is one thing to maintain certain doctrines, and another to give them a certain relative position. My mind is so *off* from the *externalism* of the Church, in the higher estimate of the invisible and eternal, so much more on the everlasting ties of the Church Catholic, than upon the temporary and distinctive (features ?) of the Church Episcopal, that I sometimes fear I am too much losing sight of the one in the mountain shadow of the other.

Farewell Charles. Let us be one in Christ. How soon the *seen and temporal* will have passed to us and the unseen and eternal be our all. *In Christ no condemnation*. It is faith not orders or ministers that place us in Christ. May that uniting grace abound in us more and more; then we shall have a place in the Father's house where all in Christ of whatever name or form of religion on earth shall be the one household of love and peace and holiness made perfect.

Yours very affectionately,
CHARLES P. McILVAINE

P.S.—I wish you would read my sermon on 'the Church of Christ in its essential being', the third in my volume *The Truth and Life*. As the volume was noticed in the *Princeton Review*, I suppose it is within your reach. I do not know how much you have seen of the sermon copied in the *Church Review*, as I do not know how much of it they copied – the merely argumentative part on Episcopacy, or more. I have therefore hunted up an old copy and send it, hoping you will read it enough to see that I preached on that occasion on something else than outward order. Please observe the note on page 15 and the lines marked on page 28.

DR HODGE TO BISHOP McILVAINE

PRINCETON, Dec. 29, 1855

My Dear Charles:—Your letter touched me so, I wished my review in Guinea. The *Church Review* said, 'We give the argument of the sermon, notes and all, without alteration. Even the italics are preserved.' I find they began with page 10 of the pamphlet and ended with page 27, omitting the introduction and conclusion. So far as the argument is concerned they gave all they professed to do, but as far as the impression of the sermon goes, it was of course one-sided.

I very much regret that it did not occur to me to omit all reference to you as author of the sermon and review it as an argument of the *Church Review*, as the Editor so fully and strongly adopted it. Still I hope no harm will be done. It has not in the least diminished my affection for you, nor my high estimate of your services in the cause of our common Master. I was taken by surprise to find that you had written in favour of the permanence of the Apostolic office, and had endeavoured to prove that bishops are the official successors of *the Apostles*, i.e. that they are Apostles. I knew that this is the *alpha* and *omega* of the Romish system, that no man could hold to the perpetuity of the Apostleship, in the ordinary sense of the term, without destroying the ground under his feet as a Protestant. I think so still. I think there is no hope for us, for you or for me, for Episcopalians or for Presbyterians, if the perpetuity of the Apostleship be conceded. I know that some have used that language, meaning that the office of ministry is perpetual, and others, as you have done, meaning that prelacy is perpetual. But this cannot help the matter. Let it once be granted that the Apostleship is permanent, then Rome can prove, what nine-tenths of Christians have always believed, viz: the Apostleship in its essential nature includes infallibility and supreme authority. If you have a perpetual Apostleship, you have according to the common judgment of Christendom an infallible Church.

You are therefore just as much interested as I am in proving that the Apostleship is not permanent. Dear Charles, I beg you to forgive me in advance if there is anything in my review which wounds your feelings. Of you I have spoken in the terms which you would expect. Of the arguments for the perpetuity of the Apostolic office, I have spoken as you would yourself speak of the divine right of the patriarchs and popes. I believe the argument for the latter is much stronger from Scripture than for the former, and I believe further that if the doctrines of your sermon can be established it is all over with Protestantism and Evangelical religion. You say beautifully and truly in your letter that you are far more interested in what is spiritual and internal than in what is external. This question, however, touches the very heart of the gospel, and therefore I am sure you will excuse the zeal with which I have written.

Your sermon on the 'Being of the Church', I have not only read, but made the subject of review, and the occasion of setting myself right with some of my Presbyterian brethren, who thought that the articles which I had printed on the Idea of the Church were unsound because they made too little of the external Church. I hope you will receive the copy of my address sent with my former letter, for it will enable you to understand the ground I occupy.

With all my old confidence and affection.

Very truly yours, Charles Hodge

LECTURES AND ARTICLES ON THE CHURCH AND ELDERSHIP

6. In 1845 and '6, in consequence of the declining health of his venerable colleague, Dr Miller, Dr Hodge began to prepare his lectures on the nature and constitution and officers of the Christian Church. Some of the most important of these were published as articles, from time to time, in the *Princeton Review*. His whole mind on these subjects has been fully set forth in the articles on the General Assemblies of different years, on the 'Rights of Ruling Elders', 1843; 'Theories of the Church', 1846; 'Idea of the Church', and 'Visibility of the Church', 1853; 'The Church, Its Perpetuity', 1856; and 'Presbyterianism', 1860. These articles attracted a vast deal of attention and hostile criticism both in this country and Scotland, with respect to the positions assumed on two points. These are, *first*, as to the extent and minuteness of the binding directions for church organization and government set down in the Word of God and *second*, as to the nature of the office of Ruling Elder.

As to the *first* point, he taught the following principles: 1st, The Church of Christ, to which all the promises of Scripture belong is, in its essential nature, not a visible organized society of men, but the whole body of the elect, who exist either in heaven or on earth, or who are to come into existence in the future. 2nd, That the visible church which exists as an organized society on earth is not a different body from the above, but is the same body as far as at any part of the world's history its members may be recognized as such by one another. And that the marks by which the members of this body are to be recognized, and on the ground of which they and their children are to be presumed to be members, and treated as such by all other Christians, are competent knowledge and credible profession of the true faith, and a corresponding life. 3rd, That it is the duty of all communities of such mutually recognized members of the true spiritual church to form organized societies, with constitutions, officers, laws and sacraments. 4, That the New Testament does not prescribe in detail any precise form of church organization, nor can any existing ecclesiastical organization claim divine authority for the particular form or elements of its constitution. 5th, But the New Testament does teach by precept and example certain general principles of church organization, and these are universally and perpetually binding on all Christian communities *jure divino* [by divine right]. These are: (1) 'The right of the people to take part in the government of the church. Hence the divine right of the office of Ruling Elders, who appear in all church courts as representatives of the people. (2) The appointment and perpetual continuance of Presbyters as ministers of the Word and sacraments, with authority to rule, teach and ordain, as the highest permanent officers of the Church. (3) The unity of the Church, or the subjection of a smaller to a larger part, and of a larger part to the whole' (*The Presbyterian*, April 21, 1855). That within the limits of these principles Christ had left his Church free to do His work under the guidance of His providence and Spirit, in the manner found to be most effective under the changing conditions of time and place.

The *second* point of his doctrine which was criticized related to the nature of the office of Ruling Elders. He taught in this respect (1) That Christ committed the government of the Church to the people or communicants themselves, in connection with the Presbyters or preachers and pastors. (2) That the people generally exercised their power through representatives chosen by themselves, and that these 'representatives of the people' are our Ruling Elders. (3) This view of the office establishes it as *jure divino*, and exalts its honour and usefulness. (4) That it is everywhere asserted and assumed in our standards and in those of the Mother Church of Scotland. (5) That the rival theory of the nature of the office, which made the ministers and elders one order, is subversive of Presbyterianism. It provides for no representation of the lay element. The right of a minister to preach and rule is inherent in his office. In all ages of the world the clergy have formed a class by themselves. The rival view is latent Episcopacy, making one presbyter the permanent president over his colleagues of the session, endowed with the supreme power of administering the sacraments. Our form of government groups elders and deacons together, provides for the ordination of the minister by the laying on of hands of the Presbytery, and on the other hand directs that a single minister shall set apart an elder or deacon indifferently to either office, by the proposition of a list of questions, by the vote of the people to be represented, and by prayer.

These views, as they were gradually unfolded, were, doubtless, misapprehended by many, and were certainly violently attacked and misrepresented in the newspapers and some of the church courts of that time. It would, however, seem that they have been substantially accepted as sound by the church at large, from the overwhelming vote on his side on occasion of his great debate with Dr Thornwell on the Boards of the Church, in the General Assembly, in Rochester, 1860; from the publication and continued circulation by the Presbyterian Board of Publication of his address on 'What is Presbyterianism?' of 1855, and its republication with emphatic approbation by the strictest Presbyterians of Scotland; and from the reception recently given to the volume on 'Church Polity'.

DR HODGE TO DR JOHN HALL

PRINCETON, June 20, 1851

My Dear Sir:—I do not know that I can point you to the law in the book which contemplates just such a case as that presented in your letter, but I think the principles which regulate it are perfectly plain.

An elder is a representative of the people of some particular congregation, selected and appointed by them to act in their behalf in some judicatory of the church. He can act as such representative only when duly elected for that purpose. He has no power over any congregation except in virtue of their delegation of it to him. If he is divested of it by resignation, deposition, or dismission, he cannot resume it again any more than a Governor of a State could resume his office, after resignation or dismissal. If Governor Fort should resign his office to go to England and become a subject of Queen Victoria, not even a Philadelphia lawyer would have the face to maintain he could on his return (before his term would have expired) resume the chair again.

The sense in which the office of ruling elder is said to be perpetual is, that after the church has once ascertained to her satisfaction that a man possesses the requisite gifts for that office, and has solemnly testified to that fact by his ordination, there is no need of ever repeating that service. The man is declared to belong to the class of elders, i.e., of those to whom the Spirit has given the gift of ruling, and from whom any congregation may select their rulers. The reason why this public sanction to the possession of the necessary gift is required, is because the whole church is one. A congregational church may select whom it pleases for deacons or elders, because their functions do not extend beyond the limits of the congregation. But with us an elder in a particular church may be a member of Presbytery, Synod or General Assembly, rule over the whole church, and therefore the whole has the right to prescribe the qualifications for the office, and the mode in which their possession in any case shall be ascertained and authenticated; and when this has once been done, the church is satisficd, thc man is always an elder; any congregation may call him to exercise that office over them. But he cannot exercise it without such call, any more than a minister can act as pastor of a given congregation without a call. If you were to resign your present post, turn Episcopalian, and then come back to Trenton, who would say you could without re-election have a right to resume your office? I suspect if your head was not so full of law[1] before the gospel had a chance to enter it, you never could have had any doubt upon such a case. You see the advantage of having only one profession. You men of two trainings always see double.

Your friend,
Charles Hodge

DR HODGE TO H. A. BOARDMAN

Princeton, April 13, 1855

My Dear Sir:—The only objections which I ever heard against the doctrine of the Church as presented in the *Repertory* are: 1. That it left the visible church without authority, its organization being altogether discretionary, so that we had no *Jus divinum* ground for any part of our system. In other words, that we held Stillingfleet's doctrine, 'Government [is] of God, [but] the form of man.' This was the idea presented in —'s published letter; this is the objection I heard from — here, and from other quarters. And Professor Green has just told me that this was the only form in which he had ever heard the objection. To this, therefore, I directed my explanation, and showed that our doctrine as to the nature of the Church did not suppose its organization to be undetermined or indifferent, and that for myself

---

[1] Dr Hall was in the first instance trained for the bar.

I fully believed that the discretion of the Church as to its organization was limited to details, the essential principles relating to it being preceptively enjoyed. I did not go further because I was not aware that the objection went further, and because there is not the least shadow of ground for the objection in any other form.

In my lectures I endeavoured to prove: 1. That there is no form of church organization laid down in Scripture as essential to the being of the Church – against Papists and the High-Church party of England. 2. There is no plan of church organization prescribed in all its details, so as to leave the church no discretion in the matter – against the Seceders and Brownists and some High-Church Presbyterians. 3. That there are certain principles relating to the organization of the church which were obligatory as matters of divine precept, as, e.g. (1) The right of the people to take part in the government of the church, and hence the divine right of the office of ruling elders as the representatives of the people. (2) The appointment of Presbyters as rulers, teachers and ordainers, as the highest permanent office in the church – against the claims of prelacy, asserting the parity of the ministry. (3) That the church is one, and therefore each part is subject to the larger part and to the whole. Hence the right of review and control, the right of appeal and the authority of church courts as laid down in the Westminster Confession. This is against the Brownists and Independents and Congregationalists.

It would have been very easy to include this statement in the article just published ('Bishop McIlvaine on the Church') had I been aware of the nature of the objections made to the former articles. This only shows the impropriety of attacking a man in the dark, making general charges of error without letting him know what the errors are. These principles, however, have been so often and in so many ways presented in the *Repertory*, and some of them in the pamphlet signed 'Geneva', which you had such a hand in getting printed, that I cannot feel called on to assert them anew. I do not think it would be becoming in me to come out with them now. It seems like answering publicly charges unnecessarily as they have never been publicly made.

2. The only other objection is the one referring to the relation of infants to the church, which I hope has been sufficiently met. Thanking you for your kindness in this whole matter, I am

Affectionately yours,
CHARLES HODGE

P.S. – Since writing the above letter, it has occurred to me that the accompanying paper might be printed as a note to the paragraph on p. 355, in the event of the republication of the article.

I perhaps know less about the state of feeling on this subject than others. I have heard of objections from various quarters, but on the other hand I have received such strong expressions of approbation of the articles from many unexpected sources, that I have not been led to suppose that there were any extensive misgivings on the subject. If there are it might be well to reprint the article in the last number as a pamphlet with the note.

TO THE SAME

PRINCETON, April 20, 1858

My Dear Sir:—I see the *Presbyterian* contains your note and my answer. I think I am done now. I have said all I have to say, and those who are not satisfied must seek satisfaction from other sources . . . It is humiliating to find that doctrines and views which are presented in almost every system of Protestant theology and in every work against Popery should through sheer ignorance, and a kind of instinct of High-Churchism – the working of what Bunyan calls 'the Pope in the belly' – be denied by Presbyterians – and they think they are thereby serving the truth!

Your friend, CHARLES HODGE

CORRESPONDENCE OF DR WILLIAM CUNNINGHAM

In the *Witness*, of Edinburgh, February 29th, 1860, in the absence and without the knowledge of the editor, an article appeared entitled the 'True Idea of the Church', in which J. A.

Wylie expresses his contempt for the articles on the church by Charles Hodge, republished in Scotland, with a preface by Dr William Hanna.

The same paper, on the 3rd of March, contained a letter from Principal William Cunningham.

To the Editor of the *Witness*.

Edinburgh, 29th Feb., 1860

Dear Sir:—I hope you will allow me to record in your columns a protest against the style and tone exhibited in an article in to-day's *Witness*, with reference to Dr Hodge, of Princeton. Most people, I presume, are aware that he is one of the ablest and most influential expounders and defenders of Calvinism in the present day, and admirably accomplished in almost every department of theological literature. There is no living man entitled to treat him in the very peculiar style in which the author of the article referred to has thought proper to indulge. When he alleges that Dr Hodge 'wanders in darkness, and never for five minutes on end keeps clear of contradiction', that 'in his pamphlet the contradictions are more numerous than the pages', etc., etc., he is propounding what is simply absurd – so absurd, indeed, as to be incredible. I indicate no opinion as to the subject of controversy which the article discusses.

I remain yours truly,
Wm. Cunningham

In his letter dated Edinburgh July, 1844, a part of which has been already given, Dr Cunningham had said:

I received the pamphlet on the Eldership, and am much obliged to you for it. I have never been able to make up my mind fully as to the precise grounds on which the office and functions of the ruling elder ought to be maintained and defended. For some time before I went to America I had come to lean pretty strongly to the view that all ecclesiastical office-bearers were presbyters, and that there were sufficiently clear indications in Scripture that there were two distinct classes of those presbyters, viz. ministers and ruling elders; though not insensible to the difficulty attaching to this theory from the consideration that it fairly implies that wherever presbyters or bishops are spoken of in Scripture ruling elders are included. I have been a good deal shaken in my attachment to this theory by the views I have heard from you, but I have not yet been able to abandon it entirely. If I am spared till next summer I must examine it with more care.

DR CUNNINGHAM TO DR HODGE

EDINBURGH, Oct. 16, 1852

My Dear Dr Hodge:— . . . I have noticed with much interest what you have been doing and suffering of late years in domestic, official and literary matters. The removal of your two venerable colleagues was well fitted to produce solemn reflection, and must have occasioned to you no little anxiety. I am glad to think that the arrangements ultimately made in the Seminary in consequence of Dr Miller's death, were such as you approved and desired, and I would fain hope that those which have resulted from Dr Alexander's death may turn out equally satisfactory.

We have been much interested in and pleased with the way in which you have been fighting the battles of the faith against Drs Bushnell and Park. It seems to be still as necessary now as ever to be contending for the great truths, that the Bible is fitted and intended to be a rule of faith, and that it really means what it says; for it is really at bottom against these fundamental principles, these *principia theologica,* that the views of Bushnell and Park are directed. I have been a good deal struck of late with the importance of giving prominence in the training of candidates for the ministry, especially under the head of the History of Dogma, to the illustration of the fairness and rationality of the process by which the right use of the Bible has produced, and of course still sanctions, the substance of the common orthodox formula employed in the statement of the fundamental doctrines of Christian theology. This appears to me of much importance for guarding young men against some of the influences which are in this present day most apt to mislead them.

We continue to enjoy in the Free church a large measure of outward prosperity, and we are improving, I think, to some extent, the opportunities of usefulness which the Lord has set before us. The chief difficulties that have sprung up among us, and that still threaten somewhat our peace and usefulness, are connected with our arrangements about theological education. There had grown up among many of our brethren, through the latent influence, I fear, of a class of motives of a somewhat low and unworthy description, a desire to multiply theological seminaries beyond what, as it seemed to me, our circumstances and means require or admit of, and to the manifest detriment of theological education. This has led to some very unpleasant and somewhat dangerous discussions, and is likely, I fear, to lead to more. I sometimes feel perplexed as to the course I ought to pursue in the matter. I have hitherto been able to prevent any actual step being taken in the way of college extension, as we call it, but I do not see very clearly how long and how far the opposition to it ought to be carried. One painful and dangerous feature of the case is that while many of the ministers are in favour of college extension, the eldership, except where mere local feelings come into operation, are generally opposed to it.

We had some fear that we should be called upon to preach, as Dr Erskine, who succeeded Dr Witherspoon as leader of the evangelical party of the Church of Scotland, did about eighty years ago, upon the question, 'Shall we go to war with our American brethren?' But it is to be hoped that all danger of a result so disastrous as a war between the United States and Britain is overpast. There are not a few amongst us who have serious apprehensions of a continental crusade against Protestantism and freedom. And if Britain should be compelled in self-defence to fight against Popery and arbitrary power, we would confidently expect the sympathy and assistance of the United States. It has been alleged that Lord Palmerston had resolved, if he had continued in office, that in the event of the foreign troops not being soon withdrawn from the States of the Church, he would have taken possession of Sicily and established a constitutional government there. And I do not regard it as a thing very unlikely, or very much to be deprecated, that we may see a combined British and American fleet sweeping the Mediterranean, protecting Sardinia and liberating all the rest of Italy.[1]

I made a tour, lately, of a month on the Continent, visiting the principal towns of Holland and Belgium, the Rhine as far as Strasburgh, and Paris. My colleague, Dr Buchanan, was with me, and we enjoyed it vastly. But on my return I found my youngest child – a girl of 18 months – dead, though not buried, and another child – a boy of 6 years – dying. The boy lived five days after my return, and his whole deportment was of a kind fitted to encourage the hope that the Lord was graciously dealing with his soul to prepare him for heaven. It has been a very painful trial, but I trust we have been enabled to say, 'The Lord gave, and the Lord hath taken away; blessed be the name of the Lord.'

I am glad to see that your vacation has been extended to sixteen weeks. Would you not think of visiting the Old World again, and giving a few weeks to Scotland? There are many here who would rejoice to see your face in the flesh. There are few things that would afford me more pleasure. I hope you will forgive my negligence and procrastination and write to me soon.

Present my kindest regards to the members of your family, to your colleagues in the Seminary and College, so far as I know them, and believe me to be, my dear Dr Hodge,

Your affectionate friend,
WM. CUNNINGHAM

In July, 1857, Dr Cunningham published in the *British and Foreign Evangelical Review* an elaborate review of the volume

---

[1] Many in Britain at this time favoured the unification of Italy and the ending of papal secular power in the 'states of the church' or Papal States. [Ed.]

entitled *Essays and Reviews*, by Charles Hodge, published that year by Robert Carter & Brothers. In connection with an analysis and estimate of the contents of the volume, Dr Cunningham says:

Our readers are well aware that Dr Hodge is the senior Professor at Princeton, the oldest and most important theological seminary of the Old-School Presbyterian Church in the United States – a Church which constitutes the most numerous and the most influential Presbyterian body in the world. He was chiefly known in this country by his Commentary on Paul's Epistle to the Romans, until some of his articles in the *Princeton Review* were republished among us. The recent publication of his Commentaries on the Epistle to the Ephesians and on the First Epistle to the Corinthians, and the collection into one volume of his leading *Essays and Reviews*, have made him well known in this country, and have done much to promote the diffusion of sound theology. He is now recognized by general consent as one of the very first theologians of the present day. He has a very fine combination of the different qualities that go to constitute a great theologian, both as to mental capacities and endowments, and as to acquired knowledge and habits. His talents and attainments seem to fit him equally for the critical and exact interpretation of Scriptural statements, and for the didactic and polemic exposition of leading doctrines. He seems to be about equally at home in the writings of the great systematic divines of the seventeenth century and in those of the most distinguished continental divines of the present day. While solid ability and extensive erudition are the most obvious and fundamental characteristics of his writings, he exhibits also a play of fancy and a power of sarcasm, which, though rarely indulged, and kept much under restraint, do contribute not a little to make them more interesting and more effective.

But it is more important to advert to the place which Dr Hodge occupies, and the services which he has rendered as an expounder and defender of theological doctrine. And here the substance of what we have to say is, that he has rendered invaluable services to the cause of sound Christian doctrine by the talent and erudition, the manliness and the effectiveness, the moderation and the firmness, with which he has maintained and defended the Calvinistic system of theology against the assaults of every description of opponents.

. . . We regret that we have not space to quote any portion of the article upon the question, 'Is the Church of Rome a part of the Visible Church?' About ten or twelve years ago, the General Assembly of the Old-School Presbyterian Church decided that the Church of Rome is not a part of the visible Church; that consequently Romish baptism is invalid, and that converts from the Church of Rome ought to be rebaptized. Dr Hodge and his colleagues at Princeton did not approve of this decision, but adhered to the opposite view, which had been held by the Reformers, and by the great body of Protestant divines ever since the Reformation. The grounds of their opposition to the deliverance of the General Assembly are set forth in this article. It is characterized by its author's usual ability and thorough knowledge of the subject, and, we are persuaded, fully establishes its leading position. It is to be regretted that the General Assembly of so respectable and influential a body should have ventured to give such a deliverance, in opposition to the whole Protestant Churches, and to their own most distinguished divines.

We have room now only to express our profound respect and admiration for Dr Hodge as a theologian, our deep sense of the magnitude of the services he has rendered to the Church of Christ and the cause of sound doctrine, and our earnest desire and hope that he may be long spared to discharge the important public duties to which in providence he has been called, and for the efficient performance of which he has been so richly furnished by the Head of the Church.

Dr William Walker, of Dysart, Scotland, sends me the following through my good friend. Dr Robert Watts, of Belfast:

By the way, I can give you an anecdote, whose authenticity I can vouch for, because the man himself told me. One of our students, an accomplished fellow, took it into his head that he would like to go to Princeton. But he was anxious not on that account to lose a year. So he consulted Cunningham, putting to him the question, whether he thought a session there would count.

'COUNT!' said Cunningham, taking a snuff and speaking in that curious falsetto voice which he sometimes used when he wanted to be emphatic. 'Of course it would. My only difficulty is this: whether a session there under Hodge should not count TWO.'

DR HODGE TO DR CUNNINGHAM

PRINCETON, August 24, 1857

My Dear Sir:—I am very much in your debt for your letter, your address and your review. I have no means of payment, and must compound and pay only a shilling in the pound. I rejoice very much in the success with which you have opposed the course of the *North British Review*. Mr Isaac Taylor has evidently got out of his depth. It is often the case that a man of genius and general learning makes shipwreck when he enters on purely professional subjects, the logical relations of which he has never studied. He never could have written as he did had he seen how entirely subversive of the authority of the Bible his views on inspiration and other matters necessarily were. Dr Chalmers' fame is part of the heritage of Presbyterianism, and your vindication of his memory is a service for which all Presbyterians must feel grateful.

The degree of Doctor in Divinity was conferred in June last by the College of New Jersey on Professor Lorimer, and announced in our papers. I presume President Maclean communicated officially with Dr Lorimer on the subject. He promised to do so, and therefore I did not think it necessary to trouble either him or Dr McCrie with a separate letter. It was owing to an oversight on my part that the degree was not conferred at a previous meeting of the Board in December.

I do not know what to say, my dear sir, in reference to your friendly exaggeration of the merits of my essays. If your review shall have the effect of commending the views which they advocate to the favourable regard of our younger theologians, I shall rejoice. I have had but one object in my professional career and as a writer, and that is to state and to vindicate the doctrines of the Reformed Church. I have never advanced a new idea, and have never aimed to improve on the doctrines of our fathers. Having become satisfied that the system of doctrines taught in the symbols of the Reformed Churches is taught in the Bible, I have endeavoured to sustain it, and am willing to believe even where I cannot understand. I wish to express the special gratification I have derived from your approbation of the views expressed in the articles on the Church. I feel this the more because many of our brethren in this country have expressed great dissatisfaction with those articles. I am persuaded, however, that they contain nothing more than the common Protestant doctrine on the subject. I have a course of lectures in the rough on the nature, attributes, prerogatives and organization of the church, and it has been a favourite object with me to prepare them for the press. But I do not see any immediate prospect of my being able to do so, as they must be entirely rewritten and enlarged.

I am ashamed to send you a letter all about myself; but if you will pay me by writing me one equally egotistical I will forgive myself. My summer vacation, which I hoped to turn to good account in writing, has been broken up by my having to leave home repeatedly to attend a sick daughter-in-law, with whom Mrs Hodge has been obliged to spend the whole summer.

With great respect and affection, your friend,

Charles Hodge

CORRESPONDENCE WITH BISHOP JOHNS

Richmond, Jan. 23, 1849

Dear Charles:— . . . But that notice of the 'Apostolical Constitutions'![1] Part of it is too funny. Have you read it? I thought I would have shaken out of my chair as I ran my eyes over the writer's demonstration that of all others *Presbyterianism* comes nearest the platform

---

[1] An article entitled 'Apostolical Constitutions' – *Princeton Review*.

exhibited in said Constitutions! Well if the honest soul finds the model up there, it would be a pity to deprive him of the satisfaction, and indeed the process is so amusingly downright, that I could hardly help slapping the good fellow on the back, and exclaiming, 'Well done, my hearty! 'I hope for my sake 'he has a few more of the same sort left'.

I have not cut the leaves of the sixth article,[1] and don't think I shall. They say I am too favourably inclined toward that kind already, and I have no idea of coming under further suspicion. I shall read no more on that side till I get hold of your book,[2] which if the duration of pregnancy be any indication of the bulk of the thing to be born, will certainly be as much as I can stagger under for the rest of my days.

Yours truly,

J. Johns

DR HODGE TO BISHOP JOHNS

Princeton, Jan. 17, 1854

My Dear John:—I knew an excellent man, a pastor of a Presbyterian Church, who, whenever he was conscious of having neglected his duty and gone into the pulpit without preparation, took to scolding the people. You are one of the same sort. Your conscience has been upbraiding you all this time for your shameful neglect of me last fall, when you were weeks and months within two hours ride, and never came near me; and now you relieve yourself by a good scold. I hope you feel better; and as it is very unpleasant, as you know, to be mad at oneself, I trust you will behave better another time. I inquired of you when that sham trial was going on from every stray Episcopalian I could meet, sent messages to you, provided the messenger should fall in with you, but I did not know where to address you. I knew you did not stay in Camden, and I knew not where you stayed in New York. And when I heard you had at last gone home without stopping, I was so mad I could hardly have spoken to you in the street.

---

[1] Review of Dr Miller's *Manual of Presbytery*, January 1849.
[2] A book on *The Church*, which Dr Hodge began, but never completed.

I am glad you are going to resign the Presidency.[1] One office is enough. You will never find relief, however, until you get back to primitive episcopacy, when a diocese was no larger than a parish. An ancient province, half as large as Virginia, then had 300 bishops. I wish they could make you bishop of Alexandria, (Va.) and be done with it; and then you could stay at home like an honest man,

I am glad, too, to hear that your boys are settled to their own and your satisfaction. Give my love to Nancy and ask her to come and make us a visit, and try the effect of a northern winter. I do not believe in Williamsburg, and rejoice you are going to leave it.

What a dreadful scene of protracted suffering the wreck of the *San Francisco* must have exhibited.[2] The Doctor's (his brother) brother-in-law, Mr Woolsey Aspinwall, was one of the passengers. He is threatened with a pulmonary complaint and was going to Valparaiso for his health. He was one of those taken off by the *Kilby*, and was for two weeks aboard that vessel, crowded beyond measure, without a change of clothes, with scarcely anything to eat, and little water, and all the time in imminent peril. He is now in New York dreadfully exhausted, but likely to do well.

I sympathize with you in your building troubles. Get a good book (as I am told it is) written by a very foolish man, Prof. F—, the phrenologist, on octagon houses. I have seen some plans of his which were striking, not only from their effect, but for the wonderful facilities and roominess, which that form allows of, at a moderate expense. Nutman of Philadelphia furnished R. S., my next neighbour, a plan of a Gothic cottage, which cost some $14000, and has literally two parlours and two chambers, and no more, except a square room of eight by ten feet over the entry. This house, where I live, has four rooms on the first floor and five on the second, three finished rooms in the attic, besides three finished rooms in the basement, and cost

---

[1] Of William and Mary's College, Virginia.

[2] In late December 1853, the steamship *San Francisco* bound for Panama from New York was wrecked in a violent Atlantic storm, but some of her passengers were rescued by the sailing bark *Kilby* bound for Boston. [Ed.]

less than $5000 thirty years ago. Build either an octagon or a square house, and eschew anything pointed unless you mean to build a palace.

Mrs Hodge and myself will (D.V.) return your and Mrs Johns' visit right off when we get it. How can we do it before we get it? Answer that!

With much love to all about you, yours as young as ever while writing to you. God bless you, dear John.

CHARLES HODGE

BISHOP JOHNS TO DR HODGE

MALVERN, August 31st, 1855

Dear Charles:—I did not recognize the hand-writing on the envelope. Perhaps this was owing to the diminution of visual discernment which comes with the infirmities of *age*, or from want of practice arising from *lack of opportunity*, which I deprecate. When I stripped the pamphlet, Nannie was sitting by me, and as soon as she saw the title on its cover, 'What is Presbyterianism?'[1] she exclaimed, 'How uninteresting!' We both supposed it to be a new issue from the Protestant Episcopal Sunday School Union, and probably like the 'Presbyterian in search of the Church', the parthian[2] production from some deserter from your own ranks. Under this impression it was very near going unread, and unopened to add to the pile reserved for the fire. Happily it was rescued by the curling of the cover, as I held it in my hand disclosing the entry on the blank leaf, a line more precious to me than all the valuable publications of the Presbyterian Board, this pamphlet itself included. I cannot describe to you the sudden revulsion produced by this discovery. I will not say that I read the essay through without taking breath, but certainly I allowed nothing to interfere till I finished its perusal, for I was prepared to find that

---

[1] Delivered before the Presbyterian Historical Society, May 1855, and published by the Board of Publication. (See also p. 440. [Ed.])

[2] A parting shot, from the practice of the Parthians of ancient Persia who turned in the saddle to shoot arrows at pursuers. [Ed.]

under your skilful showing the subject of the treatise could present attractions not commonly apprehended. And now if we were only together, how I should like to hold the picture in my hand and answer you by my simple comments. As the great gratification of being with you is denied me, I must briefly report my impressions, just to indicate how far an honest Prelatist and a conscientious Presbyterian may agree. And to begin at the *end*:—

1. Your condemnation of Congregationalism is quite to our mind.

2. Your advocacy of the 'rights of the people with subjection to legitimate authority', is our doctrine out and out, though in the arrangements for the exercise of the popular element, we differ, yet that element pervades our ecclesiastical system from the appointment of parish officers and ministers, up to canonical enactments, and to the consecration of bishops. Nothing is done without the concurrence of the Laity. On this point we adopt your great principle, but cannot acquiesce in your exclusive claims.

3. In your opinion with regard to the limitations of the Apostolic office to the Apostles themselves, that *it* was not to be perpetual in the Church, this as you are aware was the view of the leading divines of the Church of England down to the days of Laud, and in the standards of that Church there is not a line to sustain what you controvert so ably. Those who maintain the contrary are alone responsible for their error.

4. I do not think you have distinguished as clearly as I wished you had done between the Church of England and the Anglican party in that Church. Common readers would be apt to regard them as one and the same, and to impute to the body, the sentiments of a faction. Have you made the *faction* the body, and the Church a scarcely observable caudal [tail-like] appendage?

5. With regard to exclusive claims you will not forget that as far as Protestants are concerned, Cartwright & Co., are entitled to the discovery. It was expressly combated by Hooker and others, see 'Goode's Vindication'.[1]

---

[1] William Goode, *A Vindication of the Doctrine of the Church of England,* 1853. [Ed.]

6. That the Apostolic office was not permanent does not prove that they did not appoint an order in the Church properly Episcopal. For although it would not be easy to prove that they did so from Scripture alone, yet connected with ancient authors, on whose testimony as to facts we all rely, and which it seems impossible to dispose of on any other theory, the fact was so, see 'Litton on the Church'.[1]

7. It strikes me that our Presbyterian brethren have fallen into the Romish error of suppressing what was an Apostolic order, then splitting another to supply its place; abolishing the Episcopate proper, and then dividing the office of Presbyter. On this point of the Ruling-Eldership, I was struck with the adroitness of the essay.

8. What have you done with the office usually styled the Deaconate?

But you are tired, and my paper only leaves room to say that my daughters join me in most affectionate regards to your family and self. With unchanged and unchangeable love, your brother,

J. JOHNS

THE DEATHS OF DR JAMES AND JOSEPH A. ALEXANDER

Dr Hodge suffered the great sorrow, in which a wide public sympathized, occasioned by the quickly succeeding deaths of his life-long and intimate friends, the illustrious brothers, Drs James W. and Joseph Addison Alexander. The elder brother died on the 31st of July, 1859, at the Red Sweet Springs in the mountains of his native Virginia. His biographical memorial is principally the two volumes of letters, the record of his correspondence of forty years with his bosom friend, the Rev. John Hall, D.D., of Trenton, N.J. With reference to the publication of these remarkable volumes the following letters of Dr Hodge to Dr John Hall remain.

PRINCETON, Sept. 28, 1859

My Dear Sir:—There is, I presume, no difference of opinion among the friends of our beloved friend, Dr J. W. Alexander, that some

[1] E. A. Litton, *The Church of Christ in Its Idea, Attributes and Ministry,* 1851. [Ed.]

work commemorative of the man and his character should be prepared. There is, I think, just as little difference in judgment that you
and you only are the proper person to perform this sacred duty. I
need not state the reasons of this judgment. Your life-long intimate
association with him, and your possession of the fullest record of his
thought and feelings, are enough to determine this point. His brother
Addison tells me that you have written to urge him to undertake
this task. I sincerely believe that he cannot do it. You know as well
as I do that what is painful to him in the way of mental or literary
effort, becomes impossible. His feelings are in such a state that I am
persuaded he could not turn his mind to this work. It would be like
busying himself for months about the funeral of his brother. It is
best for him and his usefulness to have his mind occupied with other
things. I do trust, therefore, that you will yield to the judgment and
wishes of those most interested and best qualified to judge, and consent to begin the work without delay. This is a point I think of much
importance. Whatever is done should be done at once. The interest,
the usefulness and success of any book which may be written would
be the greater the sooner it is in the hands of the public.

The only real question in this matter, is, what kind of work should
be prepared? As to this point Dr Addison Alexander and myself fully
agree. It ought not to be a memoir of his life; not a biography. The
materials for such a work are too few; and to make a biography in
name while the letters are relied upon to give interest and importance
to the work, is, I think, sure to fail; for it will be neither one thing nor
the other. What would be most interesting, most instructive, most
useful and most truly an exhibition of the man, would be a volume or
volumes containing your correspondence with him from beginning
to end, your letters and his. This would be a unique work. It would
be a literary, a theological, a religious and a conversational history
of the past forty years. Your letters are as important in such a work
as his, and needed for the explanation of his. You could give your
name or not. I would give it. But you might entitle the book 'The
correspondence of Dr J. W. A. and one of his Friends from 18— to

18—'. These letters are yours. You only can revise them. You only can say what should and what should not be published. Do give this suggestion a favourable hearing. It is entitled to serious consideration. No mere feeling of reluctance to bringing your own letters before the public should lead you to deprive the world of a work which would be of such peculiar interest and value.

Your affectionate friend,
Charles Hodge

TO THE SAME

Princeton, Jan. 17th, 1860

My Dear Sir:—I had entirely lost sight of the fact that Dr James Alexander was ever the Editor of the *Princeton Review*, or that after 1829 it ever had an Editor. It was conducted by an association of gentlemen in Princeton and its vicinity from 1829 until after the death of Dr Archibald Alexander. That imprint continued to be used until 1840, when, although the association continued, reference to it was not made on the title page. Dr Addison tells me he knows that his brother acted as editor in 1830, and thinks he continued to do so when he went to Philadelphia.

The sixty page article on Transcendentalism was written by Drs James and Dod – the former writing the first thirty pages, a survey of the German aspect of the case, and the latter the critique on Cousin. The article on the Modern Form of Infidelity, relating to the discussion between Ripley and Norton, was written by me. The whole of the Transcendental article and a good part of the other were printed in a pamphlet, under the auspices of Professor Norton. I have seen the pamphlet but have not now a copy of it.

Why do you strike out the playful parts of his letters ?

Your friend,
Charles Hodge

You are too free with your stamps. Does Uncle Sam supply you?

On Saturday afternoon, the 28th of January, 1860, his life-long friend and most eminent colleague. Dr Joseph Addison Alexander, died. In consideration of Dr Alexander's unparalleled learning and genius, of the fact that he was cut off in the flower of his days – in his 52nd year – at the very beginning of what promised to be a harvest proportionate to his extraordinary season of preparatory cultivation, and the fact that the event was, to the apprehension of his friends, very sudden, his death was the most disastrous blow the institutions of Princeton ever experienced. In a letter to the writer, Dr Hodge declared that, with the exception of the death of his wife, the death of Professor Alexander was the greatest sorrow of his life.

On the afternoon of the Sabbath which succeeded, he broke down from excess of emotion while attempting to read the words, 'Let not your heart be troubled', and transferred the reading to Dr Green. Afterwards he spoke at length of his friend, concluding thus:

> In all my intercourse with men, though it has been limited, both in this country and Europe, I never met with one having such a combination of wonderful gifts. The grace of God most to be admired was that, though of necessity perfectly familiar with all the forms of error held by the enemies of the truth, and especially the most insidious one of criticism, he had a most simple, child-like faith in the Scriptures, and the deepest reverence for the Word of God. Above all, his crowning glory was his spirituality and devoted piety. We cannot properly estimate our loss till we think of what he was, and what he would have been, for he was only fifty-two years old, and the next ten years is the best period of such a man's life.

He wrote to Dr John C. Backus, of Baltimore, January 30, 1860:

> The public papers will have informed you of the dreadful blow which has fallen on us, by which we are almost overwhelmed. You cannot tell how we feel. It is awful. All our treasure seems suddenly sunk in the bosom of the sea. Do pray for us, and for the Seminary. We have lost the greatest and one of the best men I ever knew.

DR THORNWELL TO DR HODGE.

THEOL. SEMINARY, Feb. 16, 1860

My Dear Brother:—I cannot describe to you the interest with which I have read your letter, nor the thoroughness of the sympathy with which I have entered into your case. My heart bled for you from the very beginning, for I knew precisely how you felt under the severe bereavement. My own mind was so greatly shocked that for successive days and nights I could think of nothing but the irreparable loss which the church had sustained. It was not my good fortune to be personally known to the deceased; but I admired his genius, his learning, his piety and eloquence. I was proud of him as a product of the Presbyterian Church in America, and he had not a friend on earth who felt a heartier satisfaction in the growing brilliancy of his name. His commentaries on Acts and Mark I regarded as models, as nearly perfection in their kind as human skill could make them, and I have been in the habit, not only of recommending them, but of insisting on my classes procuring and studying them. Then his modesty was equal to his worth. So free from vanity, from ostentation, from parade and pretensions.

But my dear brother, God reigns. Let us rejoice that we have this bright and beautiful light so long among us. It was given in grace, and it was removed not without wisdom and mercy. We must all soon follow. I feel the ties constantly snapping which bind me to earth. Many of the friends and companions of my youth are going; darling objects of domestic affection have been, one by one, removed; cherished schemes have been blasted, fond hopes crushed, the world has lost its charms, and I stand like a pilgrim with my staff in my hand ready to depart when the Master shall give the word. I feel that all is vanity but Christ and His Kingdom, The dead are the blessed ones. We are the ones to be pitied. My brother, pray for me that I may be faithful. To be found in Christ a loving, thriving member, that is all I ask, all that I desire.

I have written *currente calamo* [offhand, in an unpremeditated way] just as I feel. Excuse my freedom.

Make my kindest regards to Dr McGill. The Lord bless you all!

Most truly,

J. H. THORNWELL

CHOICE OF A NEW PROFESSOR

This supreme loss occasioned the necessity for a considerable change in the faculty. No one man could fill Dr Alexander's place. The different plans discussed by the Directors, and proposed for reference to the impending General Assembly, are stated in the following letter:

DR HODGE TO DR JOHN C. BACKUS

PRINCETON, March 5, 1860

My Dear Sir:—I have had it in mind to write to you respecting our affairs in the Seminary, but have been too much occupied. I ought to begin by stating that the transfer of the department of Ecclesiastical History from Dr Alexander to Dr McGill was submitted to most reluctantly by all concerned. It was necessary because the former had got into such a state of mind that he could no longer lecture on that subject. It was foreseen that it would overburden Dr McGill or necessitate neglect of some of his other duties. One of the conditions therefore to be answered in our future arrangements is to relieve him. He has now Pastoral Theology, Homiletics and Church Government and Ecclesiastical History. This is altogether too much especially considering two things, (1) That from disposition and necessity he is led to devote much time to our external affairs. In doing this he is of very great service to the institution. It, however, is a great burden. He tells me that often he has not two hours of the day to himself. (2) From the bent of his mind he devotes his strength very much to the students in preaching and writing sermons. Here again his services are of great value, but this leaves little time or effort comparatively for the other departments.

Another condition to be met in our plans, is to provide for the full development of the New Testament department. This Dr

Alexander had chosen for the field on which to bestow his immense talents and resources. It almost breaks my heart to think that he is lost to the Church just as he was beginning with new vigour to consecrate himself to that work. It cannot be left neglected. That department must be filled. Dr Green cannot touch it. He is fully occupied with the Old Testament, its language, literature, history, criticism, introduction and interpretation. Surely this is enough for any man. I cannot enter on that work. I have much in my own field which I am obliged to neglect.

The question is, how are these two great objects to be provided for?

(1.) The first plan proposed was to get a man of established reputation, capable of filling the New Testament chair, and at the same time of taking ecclesiastical history off of Dr McGill's hands. To this it was objected that no such man disengaged or available could be found.

(2.) The second plan was that proposed by Dr Murray, to let the New Testament department go and to allow Dr McGill to keep Ecclesiastical History and the Church, and to get an experienced pastor to take the practical department. To this there are two great objections. First of leaving [the] N.T. chair, one of the most important, unprovided for, and, secondly, it takes Dr McGill from that field in which he is evidently doing most good.

(3.) The third plan was to get a young man, not less than thirty, however, or at least old enough to have his character well tested, and put him in Dr Addison's place to grow up to it, as Dr Green was placed at 27 or 28 in the Old Testament department; and as I was taken still younger and brought along. To this Dr McGill decidedly objected; first, because we need 'a celebrity' at once to hold us up, and, secondly, because it would not afford him the desired relief.

(4.) The fourth plan is to try and get two men, one to fill the New Testament chair, who may be a young man, and the other a man of established reputation to take Ecclesiastical History and Ecclesiology. In this fourth plan all the Professors cordially acquiesce, and so do our friends as far as consulted.

The two objections to it are, (1), That other Seminaries have only four Professors. This I do not think will have any weight with the Assembly seeing our necessities demand the increase. (2). The great objection is the expense. This would be fatal unless it could be obviated. Our friends in New York assure us this shall not stand in the way of the plan. Now my dear sir, do you, one of our wisest and best friends, do you approve of this plan? And if so, who do you think would be the desirable man? The names of Dr Dabney and Dr Palmer have both been named for the chair of Church History, etc. I suppose the latter would not and perhaps ought not to leave New Orleans. The former may also be beyond our reach.

Perhaps I ought to mention that Wistar (his son) has been named for the N.T. chair as the young man, provided we can get a man of established notoriety for the other. This suggestion you will readily believe did not come from me. I do not know who first made it. It has received favour from several independent sources. I should greatly deprecate it, if he is not in fact, and in the estimation of those who have an opportunity of judging, the proper person. Wistar himself, I know, would greatly object, first because he regards himself as unfit, and, secondly because he would prefer to get along without being called upon to make so much exertion.

I hope you will write me soon on this subject, and aid us by your prayers and counsel.

Your affectionate friend,
Charles Hodge

DR HODGE TO HIS BROTHER

Princeton, April 4, 1860

My Dear Brother:—I am driven almost to death by demands on my pen; letters remain unanswered and correspondents neglected. The plan on which the friends of the Seminary have decided to propose to the Assembly, is to have two new professors, one a man of established reputation for the historical department, the other a younger man for the New Testament department. The Directors will probably recommend, either officially or indirectly (they doubt their right to nominate) Dr Dabney, of Virginia, for the former, and Wistar for the latter post. It is doubtful whether the Assembly will consent to our having five professors. It is feared that the friends of the other Seminaries will oppose it. Provision, however, is made for the salary of the fifth professor, so that no demand for the increased expense will be made on the churches. Should the plan be adopted, there is still, of course, the uncertainty of an election in a body of 200 members. The principle, however, is so generally recognized to allow the friends of the several Seminaries to select their own professors, that the probability is that anybody will be elected whom our Board of Directors recommend.

Wistar is dreadfully mad about it, and hates the whole thing. I have had nothing to do with the matter except to express the opinion when asked that he had the talents and learning which the post demanded to as promising a degree as any young man I know. Dr Leighton Wilson, Drs Boardman, Jones, Backus, McElroy, Mr Lenox, and others, had their minds turned to Wistar, and they have brought the matter to its present position. I have heard of no dissent among the Directors.

The bell is ringing. Love to all.

Your brother,
CHARLES HODGE

The eyes of all the friends of Princeton were now eagerly turned to Dr Robert L. Dabney, of Prince Edward, Virginia, who had already acquired the well-deserved reputation of being one of the very ablest teachers of theology which the American church had ever produced. It was the earnest desire of Dr Hodge that Princeton should be strengthened by so powerful a reinforcement, and he did his best to present the claims of the position before Dr Dabney in the most favourable light. The latter, however, after giving the proposition a candid and prayerful consideration, decided in the negative.

DR DABNEY TO DR HODGE

Union Sem., Va., April 10th, 1860.

Rev. and Dear Sir:—. . . Let me say, then, that I am led to it (his negative decision) by no affectionate clamour against my removal on the part of good brethren here . . . The true question you have correctly stated. It is: In which position shall I be likely to effect most for Christ and his church? And I cannot avoid the conviction, that so far as my fallible judgment can decide, the post of superior usefulness *for me* is here. My reasons for this conclusion are briefly summed up in this statement, that by going away I shall inflict an almost fatal injury upon a minor interest of the church, in order to render a very non-essential assistance to a major interest of the same church . . .

I would request you to communicate to your friends so much of the above as may be necessary to clear me from the appearance of inattention or discourtesy towards their request. That request I feel to be kind and flattering to me far above my deserts. I, therefore, beg that you will communicate to your friends and accept for yourself my gratitude for your favourable opinion, and for the generous manner of its expression. I remain, with affectionate respect,

Your friend and brother,
R. L. Dabney

Dr Dabney, therefore, being inaccessible, the Assembly of that year, at the instance of the Directors of Princeton Seminary, assigned Dr McGill to the chair of Ecclesiastical History, and elected Rev. Dr B. M. Palmer, of New Orleans, to the chair of Practical Theology, and Rev. Caspar Wistar Hodge to the chair of New Testament Literature and Exegesis. As Dr Palmer declined, the General Assembly of the next year assigned Dr McGill to the chair of Church Government and the Composition and Delivery of Sermons, and elected Dr James C. Moffat Professor of Church History. When the matter of granting Princeton a fifth professor was before the Assembly, Dr Hodge spoke as follows:

Mr Moderator, there is no indelicacy in my addressing the Assembly on this subject. We are seeking no personal object. We have full confidence in the members of this house. As this is a court of Jesus Christ, it must be assumed to be governed by His Spirit. Its members, I doubt not, will act not from personal or sectional motives, but from considerations they can present before the eyes of their Divine Master.

Princeton claims no superiority. We cheerfully admit that all our Seminaries stand on the same level, and should be treated on precisely the same principles. And, therefore, whenever any Seminary appears here by its authorized representatives, and says that it cannot discharge its duties to the church without additional aid, not a friend of Princeton will hesitate to vote that it should be granted.

There are two things, indeed, which give Princeton a special hold on the feelings of the Church. The one is that she is Alma Mater of some two thousand five hundred preachers of the gospel. That is her crown. As it is impossible that a son should fail to look with tenderness and respect on the face of his mother, so it is impossible that the Alumni of Princeton should not regard that institution with peculiar affection. A matron surrounded by her children grown to maturity, and filling stations of usefulness, must be the object of feelings which a blooming maiden cannot excite. The maiden may be more attractive and more promising, but she is not the mother of children. The other thing is that Princeton is on the frontier of our church. Our other Seminaries are safe in the interior. We stand on the borders in near proximity to the great institutions, Andover and Union Seminary in New York. Unless Princeton is able to stand erect by the side of these Seminaries, and present equal facilities for a thorough theological training, we shall lose our young men; our most promising students will be educated outside of our church. This would be a calamity not to Princeton only but to the church at large.

But, Mr Moderator, this is not the main ground on which we rest her application for a fifth professor. We are unable without additional assistance properly to cultivate the field assigned to us. Princeton has been prostrated in the dust. We come to you to beg you to raise us up. In the death of Joseph Addison Alexander we have lost our great glory and defence.

Permit me, Mr Moderator, to express my own individual convictions. I regard Dr Joseph Addison Alexander as incomparably the greatest man I ever knew – as incomparably the greatest man our church has ever produced. His intellect was majestic not only in its greatness but in its harmonious proportions. No faculty was in excess, and none was in defect. His understanding, imagination and memory were alike wonderful. Everything was equally easy to him. Nothing he ever did seemed to reveal half his power. His attainments in classical, oriental and modern languages and literature were almost unexampled. His stores of biblical, historical and antiquarian knowledge seemed inexhaustible. To all these talents and attainments were added great force of character, power over the minds of men, and a peculiar facility in imparting knowledge. His thorough orthodoxy, his fervent piety, humility, faithfulness in the discharge of his duties, and reverence for the Word of God, consecrated all his other gifts. His complete mastery of every form of modern infidelity enabled him to vindicate the Scriptures as with authority. He glorified the Word of God in the sight of his pupils beyond what any man I ever saw had the power of doing. Princeton is not what it was, and can never expect to be what it has been. You cannot fill his place. The only compensation for such a loss is the presence of the Spirit of God.

The department of N.T. Literature and Biblical Greek, to which this extraordinary man consecrated his life, and which he felt called for all his time and efforts, is vacant. You must put some one into it, to do what he can.

But when you have done that, Dr McGill remains burdened with the duties of two complete departments, the Pastoral and Historical. This is more than the most robust man can bear. Justice to him and to the Institution therefore requires that a fifth professor should be appointed to share his duties.

DR HODGE TO HIS BROTHER

Rochester, May 30, 1860

My Dear Brother:—We have a very pleasant meeting of the Assembly, and if we may believe all we hear the meeting has made a very salutary impression on this community. There has been no agitation. North and South have mingled without a jar. Southern men here say that they could not believe that in the heart of fanatical Western New York they should be so received and treated, and that the doings of the Assembly will do more to harmonize and quiet the country than anything which has occurred for five years. They say they intend to publish this sentiment in the papers when they get home. On the other hand, strong anti-slavery men residing here say they had purposely attended the preaching of the Southern members, and that they all preached one thing, and only one, Christ and him crucified. They say these Southern preachers are the best they ever heard.

Mary came with me. We have had a very pleasant time in this hotel – the Osburn House – with Dr Boardman and wife, Dr Thornwell, Dr Adger and family, Dr Spring, and several other members of the Assembly. The weather has been delightful, and the climate as good as it is in Princeton.

The election for Professors in Princeton was made yesterday afternoon. Dr Palmer was chosen Professor in the new chair (part of Dr McGill's), that of Pastoral Theology and Rhetoric, and Wistar Professor of the New Testament Literature and Biblical Greek. Each had all the votes cast. The most gratifying testimony was born to Wistar by his old classmates and co-presbyters and from other sources. The number of votes (244) cast show that the election was cordial; for had the members been indifferent or opposed they would not have voted as they did.

We are of course very thankful, and hope God means it all for good. Wistar is older than I was, and than Dr Addison was or than Dr Green was, at the time of our respective elections.

Love to Margaret and the boys.

Your brother, Charles Hodge

HIS GREAT DEBATE ON THE BOARDS OF THE CHURCH

This Debate on the subject of the Boards of the Church, and
virtually upon the fundamental question of the liberty of the
Church to adjust herself to providentially determined conditions,
in response to Dr Thornwell, was probably the most signal forensic
effort of his life. Though very prominent as a writer on ecclesiastical principles, he never could be regarded as a practical ecclesiastic.
His powers were those of the thinker, and writer, and speaker, not
those of executive tact and skill. Clear and far-seeing, as he was
in thought, he was not adroit in management, nor subtle in his
combinations. He produced whatever effects he did, simply by the
clearness of his views, the frankness of his statements, the earnestness of his appeals, and the weight of his character.

A writer styling himself 'a looker-on in Vienna', gives this
account of that debate in the *Presbyterian* for May 23rd, 1860:

MESSRS. EDITORS:—I write you not from the shadow of the Vatican, but from the bosom of the great, perhaps the greatest General
Assembly ever held in these United States . . . Here I see laymen
who have graced the Halls of your National Legislature . . . Here I
find Dr Thornwell, a representative man from the South, a person of
small stature, eagle-eyed – a John Randolph head in more senses than
one. He has a well-earned and distinguished reputation as a writer,
debater and preacher. He laid out his strength this morning in a
powerful exhibition of his theory for a change in the organization of
our Boards. He is clear, earnest, impassioned. He held his audience
enchained. His voice is deep and guttural, mellow and impressive,
– his gestures natural and forcible. The spirit he evinced was so kind,
so gentlemanly and Christian, that all his opponents praised him.

Dr Hodge appeared on the stage immediately after the conclusion of Dr Thornwell's speech. As he looked over the Assembly, he
saw perhaps more than half of the ministry of this great body who
once had sat at his feet as learners. Such heard, with an interest and

emotion, you may readily imagine, this one remaining representative of that cherished and honoured band of Professors in Princeton Seminary, whose names and praises too, are so widely known in all our churches. If any man is posted in the history of our church, in the nature of its polity, and in the teachings of the Holy Spirit in relation to its duties and prerogatives, it is Dr Charles Hodge, His speech of forty minutes told on the General Assembly with tremendous power – so much so that after Dr Krebs had gained the floor, Dr Spring moved that the question should then be taken. But Dr Adger and others protested.

The position assumed by Dr Thornwell is stated above, pp. 428–9. The argument of Dr Hodge, as stated by himself, *Princeton Review,* 1860, p. 566, concludes as follows:

The grand objection urged against this new theory, the one which showed it to be not only inconsistent and impracticable but intolerable, was, that it is, in plain English, nothing more than a device for clothing human opinions with divine authority. The law of God was made to forbid not only what it says, but what may be inferred from it. We grant that what a man infers from the words of God binds his own conscience. But the trouble is that he insists that it shall bind mine also. We begged to be excused. One man infers one thing, another a different thing from the Bible. The same man infers one thing to-day, and another thing to-morrow. Must the Church bow her neck to all these burdens? She would soon be more trammelled than the church in the wilderness, with this infinite difference, the church of old was measurably restricted by fetters which God himself imposed; the plan now is to bind with fetters which human logic forges. This she will never submit to.

Dr Thornwell told us that the Puritans rebelled against the doctrine that what is not forbidden in Scripture is allowable. It was against the theory of liberty of discretion, he said, our fathers raised their voices and their arms. We always had a different idea of the matter. We supposed that it was in resistance to this very doctrine of inferences they poured out their blood like water. In their time, men inferred from Romans 13:1 ('Let every soul be subject unto the higher powers. Whosoever resisteth the power resisteth the ordinance of God; and they that resist shall receive to themselves damnation'), the doctrine of passive submission. From the declaration and command of Christ, 'The Pharisees sit in Moses' seat; all therefore whatsoever they bid you observe, that obscrvc and do', thcy inferred the right of the Church to make laws to bind the conscience. On this ground tories and high-churchmen sought to impose on the church their trumpery vestments and their equally frivolous logical deductions. It was fetters forged from inferences our fathers broke, and we, their children, will never suffer them to be rewelded.

There is as much difference between the extreme doctrine of divine right, this idea that every thing is forbidden which is not commanded, and the doctrine of the Puritans, as there is between this free exultant Church of ours, and the mummied mediaeval forms of Christianity. We have no fear on this subject. The doctrine need only be clearly propounded to be rejected.

11

FROM 1861, AND THE COMMENCEMENT OF THE CIVIL WAR, TO 1872, AND THE CELEBRATION OF DR HODGE'S SEMI-CENTENNIAL

His Appearance and Health – His Occupations and Recreation – The Composition of His Systematic Theology – The Sabbath Afternoon Conferences – The Civil War: Correspondence with His Brother – The Assassination of Lincoln: Correspondence with His Brother – Letter to Dr Robert Watts on the Witness of the Spirit – The Relation of the Church to Political Questions, and the Merits of Decisions by the General Assembly (Old School) of Questions Growing out of the War – The Case of the Rev. S. B. McPheeters, D.D. – The Reunion of the Old and New School Presbyterians – The National Presbyterian Convention, Philadelphia, Nov. 1867

H E ENTERED UPON THIS PERIOD a hale and vigorous man, in the fulness of all his powers intellectual and physical, elderly, yet in perfect preservation, and he closed it an old man of seventy-four years, already showing the stealthy progress of decay. The light colour of his hair rendered less conspicuous the first sprinkling of frost, and his vigorous constitution and regular habits rendered his carriage, bearing and whole appearance unusually youthful. The peacefulness and sweetness of his disposition contributed to the same appearance of perpetual youth. His countenance, which had always been handsome, became beautiful as he grew older, radiant with the peace and love and hope which had now come to be the perpetual mood of his spirit. His health for the most part was excellent and uniform. He suffered from a decided though not dangerous attack of typhoid fever from February 26 to March 13, 1859; from inflammation of the bowels January and February, 1865, and from a very alarming attack of fever from January 28, to March 2, 1871. As he grew older his general nerve force grew less and less capable of resisting depressing influences. He wept easily, and often much against his will. He was easily exhausted by the effort involved in public speaking, and by all draughts upon his emotions. Although under ordinary conditions his health was apparently perfect, as a sound yet heavily laden boat floats well in smooth water, yet he sank easily and rapidly upon slight occasions of nervous shock or physical derangement, as the same boat fills and sinks when the water is agitated. Especially was he readily and often alarmingly exhausted by severe heat. Hence it came to pass that while he spent the month of May of each year (from 1866 to 1878) or a good part of it with his brother-in-law, General David Hunter, in the city of Washington, he spent the months of July and August always at some cool watering place. His journal shows that in the later summer of 1862 he was at Rhineland, on the upper coast of Long Island, and at Altoona, Pittsburg, Cresson, Lancaster and Saratoga. In 1863 he went to Rhineland in July and to Saratoga in August. In 1864 he spent August at Huntingdon, Long Island. In 1865 he spent July and the first of August at Saybrookpoint, Connecticut. From the summer of 1867 to the end of his life he spent with his wife, and often others of his family, the midsummer, generally all of July and August, at Narragansett Pier, Rhode Island. In all these places he carried with him the atmosphere of Christian love and devotion. He formed delightful acquaintanceships and some permanent friendships. He conducted religious services, and assisted in forming permanent religious institutions. And by these systematic refreshments he so preserved the tone of his physical system that he was enabled to bear his best fruit in old age.

HIS SYSTEMATIC THEOLOGY

During all these years he was working continuously and at least as hard as his health justified, for besides twenty-six of his most influential articles in the *Princeton Review* he wrote during this period his great work on *Systematic Theology*, of two thousand two hundred large octavo pages. The preparation of the first part of this vast work, treating on the foundations of Natural Theology, and its relation to materialism and other anti-theistic theories, scientific and philosophical and traditional, exacted of him a great amount of special reading and reflection. And the body of the work on the great common-places of Christian Theology are not copies of his past lectures, but are fresh compositions in which his views are recast and all the harvest of his past studies are gathered. The original manuscript, just as it passed from his hand, has been recovered from the printers, and bound in several volumes is preserved in the Seminary Library. It discovers for the most part that the composition was as free and easy as the style is clear, as it is remarkably free from all evidences of arrested or embarrassed thought in erasures and interlineations.

It was written entirely with one dilapidated gold pen, whose flexible side and divergent nibs long ago rendered it incapable of use in any other hand than his own. No one now knows certainly when the rewriting of this work commenced. It was probably projected and in some way commenced as early as 1864. But it was probably not grappled with very earnestly before 1867. The manuscript of the first volume was sent to Houghton & Co., the printers, December 27th, 1870, and the manuscript of the last volume was completed October 8th, 1872. Hence it was, with exceptions too small to be worthy of mention, all written since he past the end of his sixty-ninth year.

His correspondence continued, as it had been for many years, immense in volume and very burdensome. From his former pupils and others, ministers and laymen, in all parts of the country, questions were submitted to him and long and laborious answers were expected. Some of these required and frankly suggested wide special research, as he had the advantage, denied to the questioners, of access to large public libraries. The questions submitted covered the whole ground of doctrine, exegesis, experience, and ecclesiastical law. He conscientiously and laboriously responded to these appeals to the best of his ability, writing often answers covering several sheets. If these could now all be collected and classified, they would probably constitute a treasury of wisdom, equal both in value and in volume to all his other writings together. His letters to his brother, at this period, contain many such passages as the following, constantly recurring, 'I am driven almost to death by demands on my pen; letters remain unanswered and correspondents neglected', etc.

At the same time the requirements of advancing life led him more and more to seek refreshment of strength in relaxation. In December, 1856, he bought a beautifully situated farm on the Millstone river, three miles from his residence, and placed it for some years in the charge of one of his sons. He visited it in all possible weather during that son's occupancy, once a day, planning and superintending its draining and cultivation with the most unflagging interest. In summer weather during these years also he played croquet in the lawn before his front door; in the evenings of both summer and winter he played back-gammon. He entered into both these games with the most profound interest, contesting every inch, and debating every mooted point, with all the seriousness belonging of right to the most important matters, delighting to win, yet always submitting to the fates of war with the utmost sweetness of temper. From this time also we begin to have noticed that he was willing to rest his mind as well as his body by reading on due occasions the novels which the younger members of his family placed within his reach. He had always been an intensely interested observer of public events, and had entertained very positive opinions upon political questions. He was fundamentally an old Federalist, then a Whig, then a Republican of the Conservative wing. From the beginning of the war, this interest in public affairs was naturally very much intensified, and for many years he eagerly read every day all the newspapers he could conveniently reach.

THE SABBATH AFTERNOON CONFERENCE

After the death of Dr Archibald Alexander, Dr Hodge became, and continued to the end of his life, the great attraction and power in the Sunday afternoon religious conferences of the professors and students. The prominence and effectiveness of this weekly exercise was unquestionably for the last half century a grand special characteristic of Princeton Seminary. During these past years it was in many respects the most remarkable and memorable exercise in the entire Seminary course. They were held every Sabbath afternoon by the professors and students for the discussion and practical enforcement of questions relating to experimental religion and the duties of the Christian life. The members of all the successive classes will bear testimony to the unique character and singular preciousness of those Sabbath afternoon Conferences in that sacred old Oratory, whose walls are still eloquent to them with imperishable associations. Here the venerable professors appeared rather as friends and pastors than as instructors. The dry and cold attributes of scientific theology moving in the sphere of the intellect, gave place to the warmth of personal religious experience, and to the spiritual light of divinely illuminated intuition. Here in the most effective manner they sought to build up Christian men rather than form accomplished scholars and to instruct them in the wisest methods of conducting their future work of saving souls and edifying the Church of Christ.

The text or topic for consideration was announced at the preceding meeting. The professors presided in turn, and were called upon to speak in the inverse order of seniority, the professor presiding for the day coming last. For many years the discussion was opened by remarks volunteered by the students, but in later times, the entire hour has been occupied by the professors.

The historical character of this remarkable service is of course derived from the peerless endowments, intellectual and spiritual, of the first three professors in the institution. Men so different, yet together constituting such a singular completeness of excellence by the combination of their complementary graces.

Dr Miller, the model Christian gentleman, and typical divine, whose original, generous and genial nature had been transfigured by the long indwelling of the Holy Ghost, and whose outward manner had evidently been conformed by long self-training to the highest models, would have been the first to attract the eye and to impress the ear of the stranger. His long and active life had furnished him with rich stores of experience of men as well as a vast volume of learning derived from books. All this he poured forth with a deliberate and stately copiousness, in a manner serene and dignified, yet full of impressive force and tender unction. His adoring sense of the majesty of God, and of the seriousness of human life, of the reality and solemnity of divine things, and of the obligations attending the Christian profession, and above all attending the office of the Christian ministry, gave form and colour to all he said. His instructions were always wise and practical, and were characteristically illustrated from an inexhaustible fund of apt and often witty, but always dignified anecdote, drawn from all literature, sacred and profane, and from his own extensive intercourse with men as a pastor and as a citizen.

Dr Archibald Alexander, incomparably the greatest, as he was the first of that illustrious family, though neither more learned, nor more holy than his older colleague, was far more original. He was modelled upon nothing, but every thing in him and about him to the last detail of thought, or glance, or inflexion, or gesture was immediately determined by spontaneous forces working straight outward from within. It was this entire absence of self-consciousness, this absolute simplicity of thought, emotion and expression, and its spontaneous directness to its point, added to his other natural and gracious endowments, which gave this great teacher his singular pre-eminence. His intellect was intuitive rather than logical. Although he exhibited flashes of acute analysis, as sharp and rapid as a Damascus blade, yet he did not characteristically excel in broad views of truth in their relations, nor in lengthened processes of consecutive thought. He was eminently quick in his observation, and penetrating in his insight, accurately noting facts and reading characters in rapid glances. He held in his retentive memory the spoils of a vast and widely selected reading.

All the treasures of divine wisdom and grace, which the Holy Ghost communicates to life-long students of the Word, when to high intellect is added all the simplicity and docility of a little child, irradiated his soul and made it luminous to others. All the secrets of the human heart and its various experiences under the discipline of the natural conscience and of the Word and Spirit of God were known to him, and he possessed the finest skill in interpreting and in treating, with acute precision, the states and frames of all who sought his counsel or listened to his instructions. Dr Theodore D. Woolsey, ex-president of Yale College, at Dr Hodge's semi-centennial, said that 'Dr Alexander should be called the Shakespeare of the Christian heart, because of his wonderful knowledge of it in all its morbid and healthful exercises.' This utter simplicity, this all-penetrating insight, accompanied with a wonderful spontaneousness of thought, imagination and speech were personal attributes, inseparable from his presence and manner, and incapable of being transmitted to the printed page. During his later years, when urged to put the results of his studies and reflections in the permanent form of writing, he often said, 'No, if I have any talent, it is to talk sitting in my chair.' And however much he may have been mistaken in failing to recognise the value of his writings to the Church, there is no doubt that his gifts as a talker on the themes of Christian experience were without parallel among his contemporaries. He, more than any man of his generation, appeared to those who heard him to be endued with the knowledge, and clothed with the authority of a prophet sent immediately from God. He was to us the highest peak of the mountains, on whose pure head the heavens, beyond the common horizon, pour the wealth of their iridescent radiance.

In his early and middle life he had been an orator endowed with singular powers of dramatic representation. In his old age he was always calm and quiet, but such was his intense sense of the reality of the subjects on which he discoursed, that often, as he spoke of angels, of heaven, of the beatific vision of saints, of Christ and of his second coming and judgment, his hearers felt that their eyes also were opened to discern the presence of things unseen and eternal. Every Wednesday evening Dr Alexander presided at the public prayers in the Oratory. The instant the students were in their seats he came in rapidly, his cloak hanging often diagonally from his bent shoulders, his head inclined as in reverie, yet flashing sudden glances on either side with piercing eyes, which seemed to penetrate all the secrets of those upon whom they fell. He sat down with his back to the windows, and his right side to the students, sitting low – almost hidden by the desk. Drawing the large Bible down before him, he seemed to lose at once all sense of human audience, and to pass alone into the presence of God. As he read, and mused and ejaculated the utterances of all the holy exercises of his soul upon the Divine Word, a solemn hush fell upon us, and we felt not as those who listen to a teacher, but as those who are admitted to approach, with the shoes from off their feet, to gaze in and listen through an opened window to the mysterious workings of a sanctified soul under the immediate revelations of the Holy Ghost.

Dr Hodge was by a whole generation younger than these venerable fathers. Hence during the first years of his professorship his part in these Sabbath afternoon conferences, although regularly discharged, was less prominent than theirs. During the long period, however, from about 1848 to his death in 1878, he was recognized by all as the central sun which gave light and heat to the entire service. As all acquainted with his life-work know, Dr Hodge's distinguishing attributes were great tenderness and strength of emotion, and the power of exciting it in others; an habitual adoring love for Christ, and absolute submission of mind and will to his Word; a chivalrous disposition to maintain against all odds, and with unvarying self-consistency through all the years of a long life, the truth as he saw it – crystalline clearness of thought and expression, and an unsurpassed logical power of analysis and of grasping and exhibiting all truths in their relations. Dr Alexander once said to a friend that the mental constitution of Dr Hodge was, more than that of any man he knew, like that of John Calvin, without his severity. As he sat in the Conference he spoke freely, without paper, in language and with illustration spontaneously suggested at the moment. To the hearer the entire exercises appeared extemporaneous. The *matter* presented was a clear analysis of the scriptural passage, or theme, doctrinal or practical, chosen for the occasion. An exhaustive statement and clear illustration of the question. An exhibition of the evidence of the doctrine and of the grounds and reasons, methods, conditions and limits of the experience or duty. A development of each doctrine on the side of experience and practice; a demonstration of the practical character of all doctrine and of the doctrinal basis of all genuine religious experience and practice.

As to its *manner*, the entire discourse was in the highest degree earnest, fervent and tender to tears; full of conviction and full of love. While the temporary impression made upon most hearers was less remarkable than that produced by Dr Alexander in his happiest moods, all the students, and especially those who were diligent in taking notes, felt that they took away with them from Dr Hodge a far larger mass of coherent thought for permanent use than from any of the rest. The reason for this is abundantly evident when the drawers of his study are opened, and the large accumulation of careful preparations for this exercise are examined. He prepared and wrote out a careful analysis or skeleton of every Conference discourse. Although designed to meet no eye but his own, these analyses are fully written out, and are verbally complete in all their articulations. They cover every variety of subject relating to Christian doctrine and personal experience, and church life and work. And although his audience was completely changed every three years, it appears that he seldom used the same preparations twice, but prepared, even after he had passed his 80th year, a new paper for each Conference, often constructing analyses of the same theme several times. This was his method of mental preparation. He habitually thought with his pen in his hand. He prepared his analysis of his subject before he wrote his sermon, or lecture, or article, or chapter of his books. He also made written analyses of the important books he read.

Dr Prime wrote in the *Observer*, June 27, 1878:

Far above his fame as a champion of the truth, was and is his glory that he gloried in the Cross of Christ. He was a child-like, humble, praying, believing, hoping Christian. In the Oratory on Sunday afternoons his spiritual 'talks' to the students were like streams of the water of life flowing by the throne! The pathos of his voice, his words, his tears, his prayers were irresistibly affecting. Then he communed with God and his children. How the hearts of his disciples burned within them as he opened unto them the Scriptures! Beyond the lecture-room and the pulpit, the memory of those holy hours will remain with them who sat with him, in heavenly places.

One of his favourite pupils[1] has brought him before us at this service, in a sketch as beautiful as it is life-like:

No triumph of his with tongue or pen ever so thrilled and moved human hearts as did his utterances at the Sabbath afternoon conferences in the Seminary Oratory, which will live in the immortal memory of every Princeton student. A subject would be given out on the Sunday before, generally some one which involved practical, experimental, spiritual religion – such as Christian fidelity, love of God's Word, prayer, the Lord's Supper, the great commission. After brief opening services by the students, the Professors spoke in turn; but Dr Hodge's was the voice which all waited to hear. Sitting quietly in his chair, with a simple ease which seemed born of the moment, but was really the fruit of careful preparation, even with the pen, he would pour out a tide of thought and feeling which moved and melted all – solemn, searching, touching, tender – his eye sometimes kindling and his voice swelling or trembling with the force of sacred emotion, while thought and language at times rose to a grandeur which held us spellbound. Few went away from those consecrated meetings without feeling in their hearts that there was nothing good and pure and noble in Christian character which he who would be a worthy minister of Christ ought not to covet for his own.

His public work, during this most prominent and influential period of his life, related to three great questions: The civil war, and the duty of Christian citizens in relation to it. The relation of the Church to political questions, and the merits of the actual decisions of the General Assembly (O.S.) upon questions growing out of the

---

[1] William Irvin, D.D., of Troy, N.Y.

war. And third, the proposed reunion of the two branches of tlie Presbyterian Church.

THE CIVIL WAR

On this all-absorbing subject he wrote the following articles: 'The State of the Country', January 1861; 'The Church and the Country', April 1861; 'England and America', January 1862; 'The War', January 1862; 'President Lincoln', July 1865. Several of these were reprinted and widely circulated in pamphlet form, and were regarded as of great merit and practical value by prominent statesmen.

He has given his own account of these publications in a subsequent article reviewing the course of the *Princeton Review* in relation to 'The State of the Country', October 1865, and in his 'Retrospect of the History of the *Princeton Review*' in the Index Volume, 1871. In the latter he says:

> The *Princeton Review* has as freely as any other journal, and with the same right, neither more nor less, said what it felt bound to say on Secession, on the Rebellion, on the duty of loyalty and the support of the Government; on Slavery and Emancipation; on the power and authority of Church courts within the limits of the constitution, and on the principles which should govern our action in the great work of reconstruction, both in the Church and State.
>
> We have looked over the several articles in this journal published during the war, and we find in them nothing which we wish to retract. We are humbly thankful that our voice, however feeble, has throughout been on the side of the Union and the Government, and against the whole course of those who endeavoured to dissever the one and overthrow the other. There is no journal in the land can present a fairer record of patriotism and loyalty. It is true, as the *Presbyterian Banner*, of Pittsburgh, in an excellent editorial printed in December 1862, states (at least by implication) that among the supporters of the Union and the Government there are two parties,

a radical and a national party. On this subject it wisely taught 'that the people must be united. A platform broad enough for all loyal people to stand upon, must be adopted. The Radicals cannot carry their principles through. It is utter folly in them to think so. They have not the numbers. The people will not go with them. And the Republicans cannot, as a party, so wage the battle as to triumph. They have the reins of government, but only half the people, a power far too weak. Neither could the Democrats on party principles succeed. There must be union; and to have union we must adopt broad, noble, national principles.' This is the ground on which we have always stood. Party politics, as such, have had no place in this *Review*. Radical principles and measures are alien to its character and spirit. It has advocated the national cause on national principles, as a great moral and religious duty.

In his 'Retrospect', 1871, he says:

The first article having reference to our national difficulties was written before the secession of South Carolina, but did not appear in print until after that event, viz: January, 1861. The article is entitled 'The State of the Country'. It began by saying 'There are periods in the history of every nation when its destiny for ages may be determined by the events of an hour. There are occasions when political questions rise into the sphere of morals and religion; when the rule for political action is to be sought, not in considerations of state policy, but in the Word of God. On such occasions the distinction between secular and religious journals are obliterated.' It is on this ground that we, as conductors of a Theological Review, felt justified on entering upon the discussion of questions involving our national life. In taking this course we were sustained by the example of the whole religious press of the country, South as well as North.

The design of the article in question was, in the first place, to consider the complaints of the South against the North, which we endeavoured to show were either altogether unfounded, or did not furnish any justification for the dissolution of the national union;

and, in the second place, to prove that secession was not a constitutional mode of redressing evils, whether real or imaginary. That article was received at the South, to our surprise, with universal condemnation, expressed in terms of unmeasured severity. At the North it was pronounced 'moderate, fair and reasonable', except by the Abolitionists, who rivalled their Southern brethren in their denunciations.

DR HODGE TO THE EDITOR OF THE
SOUTHERN PRESBYTERIAN

PRINCETON, Jan. 3rd, 1861

My Dear Sir:—I received last evening a copy of the *Southern Presbyterian*, for Dec. 29th, 1860, containing a notice headed 'The *Princeton Review* on the State of the Country'. The article in the Review thus denominated, you characterize as 'an unfortunate, one-sided and lamentable attack upon the South'. I think, my dear sir, that it will promote the cause of truth and brotherly love which we both have at heart, if you will permit the Editor of the *Review* to state to your readers in few words the design of the article on which you pronounce so unfavourable a judgment.

It was intended to produce two effects within the limited range of its influence; first, to convince the South that the mass of Northern people are not abolitionists or hostile to the rights and interests of the South; and second, to convince the North that the course adopted by the abolitionists is unjust and unscriptural. You say that the writer of the article in question 'affirms that the aggressions or grievances of which the South complains have no real existence'. The article, however, says that the South has 'just grounds of complaint, and that the existing exasperation towards the North is neither unnatural nor unaccountable'. It says that 'the spirit, language and conduct of the abolitionists is an intolerable grievance'. It says that 'tampering with slaves is a great crime. That it is a grievance that would justify almost any available means of redress.' It admits that all opposition to the restoration of fugitive slaves, whether by individuals, by mobs or legislative enactments, is immoral, and that the South has a right to complain of all such opposition. It admits that the territories are the common property of the country, and that the South has the same rights to them that the North has, and it calls for an equal division of these territories on the plan of the Missouri compromise. The article does not deny the reality of the grievances complained of, but it denies that those grievances are justly chargeable on the people of the North. It endeavours to prove, by a simple process of arithmetic, that the abolitionists against whom these charges justly lie, are comparatively a mere handful of the people of the North. Southern men and ministers of the highest eminence pronounce the abolition party to be not only Antichristian but atheistic, to be perjured and instinct with the spirit of the French revolutionists, and then the North is pronounced to be thoroughly abolitionized. We know this to be untrue. We know this to be a false judgment pronounced upon thousands and hundreds of thousands of pious, God-fearing people. We hold it, therefore, to be a solemn duty to all concerned to show that such judgment is altogether unfounded, in fact. Such is the main design of the article in question. Whatever may be thought of its execution, the design must of necessity commend itself to every good man. If Southern men knew the North as we know it, they would no more think of secession than they would of suicide. We have done what we could out of a pure conscience to convince the South that we are not hostile to its rights and interests. If our Southern brethren take this in evil part we shall deeply regret it, but cannot repent of what has the full assent of our reason and conscience.

. . . It nowhere advocates coercion in the present crisis. It deprecates all appeal to force, and urges acquiescence in the recommendation of a convention of the States, that disunion, if it must come, may at least be peaceably effected.

Your friend and fellow-servant,
Editor of the *Princeton Review*

DR HODGE TO HIS BROTHER

Princeton, Dec. 13, 1860

I am thoroughly disgusted with the poltroonery of Northern men. If they would take moderate and just ground, and take it firmly, and not go down on their knees, and call themselves the sole wrongdoers, there would be some hope.

Your brother, C.H.

DR HODGE TO DR BOARDMAN

Princeton, Dec. 16, 1860

My Dear Sir:— . . . My own mind is decided for the publication of the article. If it is to do any good it is to be done now. I have no idea of producing the slightest effect on disunionists. But there are many conservative men at the South who wish to have their hands strengthened, to whom it will be a matter of importance to have it proved that the whole North is not abolitionized, and that the mass of the people are true friends to the constitutional rights of the South. Besides the Republicans need to be moderated. Mr—, a leading Republican of this State, expressed himself warmly against all concession, but after reading my article, wrote to me that he thought it took the true ground, and that it was right and best to conciliate.

I fully believe that the truth mildly spoken will always and everywhere do good, and I feel impelled to follow my own strong conviction of duty, and speak out what I solemnly believe to be the truth; the more especially, because, the country is about being plunged into unknown evils, mainly because the truth is not known.

Yours truly, C.H.

DR HODGE TO DR J. C. BACKUS

New York, Dec. 28, 1860

My Dear Sir:— . . . I greatly rejoice to hear that my article seems to you likely to do good. Since I came here I have heard a good deal about it, which confirms my own hopes.

There were two things in your letter which astonished me. *First,* That you supposed that I had changed my ground on the slavery question within the last ten or fourteen years. I cannot conceive how you got that impression. Within a few years past I re-printed the article on Slavery, (with my own name), printed first in 1836, which was circulated by southern men all over the South. And in the commentary on the Ephesians precisely the same doctrine is taught, which Southern men freely endorsed. I have not changed an inch, but I have not gone on with the extreme men of the Calhoun school. I utterly dissent from the doctrine of Dr Palmer's sermon.

The *second* thing that surprised me was that you should think that my article would render the Republicans more uncompromising and defiant. It condemns the principles and spirit of abolition; it calls for the faithful execution of the fugitive slave law; it represents all personal liberty laws designed to interfere with the restoration of fugitives immoral; it urges the restoration of the Missouri Compromise, which the conservative men North and South are calling for, and which the extreme Republicans resist. I know that it has induced some leading Republicans to be willing to take moderate ground and to meet the South half-way. Indeed my great hope of the pamphlet doing good is that it will correct public sentiment at the North.

Your friend,

CHARLES HODGE

DR HODGE TO DR BOARDMAN

PRINCETON, Jan. 17th, 1861

My Dear Sir:—I have already written to the *Southern Presbyterian,* Columbia, S.C, and to the *Central Presbyterian,* Va., letters which will appear in the next issues of those papers. In these letters I have said everything in the way of explanation that can be said. I have no doubt that good will come of it. I am not surprised at the reception my article has received at the South. The first impression will give way to serious consideration, except with those who will be satisfied with nothing but unmitigated abuse and condemnation of the North. I believe the article will do good at the South. A southern planter has, I understand, ordered a thousand copies of it. A letter received from Dr Smith of Danville Seminary says it is doing good there. A gentleman born at the South told me he knew there were thousands of men there who would heartily respond to its sentiments.

We must not, however, forget that there is a North as well as a South. If I am to believe a tenth of what I hear, I never wrote anything for the *Review* likely to do the Seminary and all concerned greater service. Letters have come from Democrats, (Douglas and Breckinridge) as well as Republicans giving that assurance in the strongest terms. I received last night a letter from Judge Elmer, a Democrat in Maine, thanking me for having written the article. Horace Binney and Daniel Lord are among the men who have expressed their approbation. Brethren at the West write that it has done more than they can well express to sustain the Old School cause and strengthen confidence in Princeton. Its influence against abolitionism and the *uncompromising* spirit of party leaders is everywhere recognized. I cannot, therefore, regret its publication.

You see that the secessionists everywhere resist submitting the question to the people. They can pack a convention, but they fear a vote direct from the polls. A gentleman from Alabama, himself a secessionist, told me to-day that had the question there been referred to the people it would be rejected by a great majority. He said not one man in a hundred in Alabama either expected or wished the State to remain out of the Union. They go out to compromise. The North, I am sure, would gladly accept the propositions of the border-states committee, which Mr Crittenden himself acceded to. Mr Crittenden's compromise which calls on the General Government to establish slavery everywhere south of 36.30 is what Henry Clay said no power on earth could force him to vote for. I still hope that God will deliver us.

Sincerely your friend,
Charles Hodge

DR HODGE TO HIS BROTHER

PRINCETON, Feb. 18, 1861

My Dear Brother:— . . . My article has been very extensively abused at the South, but there has been no attempt to answer it, except by 'a Pennsylvania elder' (Judge — or Judge —). Prof. Bledsoe's piece I have only looked at. He devotes his strength to the Missouri Compromise, which I have nothing to do with. I simply mentioned the fact of its abrogation as offending the conscience of the North, and as one of the political antecedents of our present troubles. No part of the argument turns on that point. The real question is, whether slavery is a municipal (or local) institution, or whether it is a national one founded on the common law of property, or on the constitution. This is the point to which the 'Elder' addresses himself. He censures me as a clergyman for writing on such subjects. I would venture anything that I could pick out blindfold 500 clergymen who could refute his argument to the satisfaction of any honest jury. The idea, however, which he insists upon has taken hold of the Southern mind. The people at the South have come to believe that the Constitution guarantees the protection of slavery in all the Territories, and, therefore, that any Congressional law forbidding its introduction is unconstitutional and a gross violation of their rights. This is the sole justification of secession as urged by Dr Thornwell in his article on the state of the country, reprinted in [the] last *New York Observer*. He says the adoption of the principle that Congress can prohibit slavery in the Territories is the abrogation of the Constitution, and even renders disunion a necessity. There never was a greater perversion of historical truth. The very opposite is true . . . (The remainder of this letter is lost),

Dr Hodge says in his article on the '*Princeton Review* on the State of the Country and of the Church', Oct. 1865, speaking of his article on the 'State of the Country', Jan. 1861,

No article ever printed in this journal from the pen of its editor ever excited greater attention. It was reprinted at length in several of the religious papers of the widest circulation in the country. It was published in pamphlet form and distributed in thousands, by the friends of the Union and of the North, and it was sent abroad as representing the views of the supporters of the government. It was bitterly condemned and stigmatized by three classes of men. First and principally at the South. The writer was there stigmatized as 'an Abolitionist' and 'Black Republican'. In the second place, it was severely criticized by men at the North who agreed with the South in principle and sympathized with it in feeling. Thirdly, as might be expected, we incurred anew the condemnation of men belonging to the radical party, of which Garrison and Wendell Phillips are the principal representatives.

He proceeds in his 'Retrospect' in 1871:

In April of the same year (1861) appeared another article on 'The Church and the Country'. Secession was then an accomplished fact, and the war with all its uncertainties was about to commence. The article was designed as a plea for the unity of the Church, even in the event of the dissolution of the national union. The two great sources of apprehension that the political troubles of the country would lead to a division of the Presbyterian Church, were the alienation of feeling on the part of our Southern brethren, and the new, unscriptural, and anti-Christian sentiment which leading men among them avowed on the subject of slavery. Instead of regarding it as merely allowable under certain circumstances, they had come to advocate it as a good; as the best organization of labour; as to be conserved, extended and perpetuated. They also maintained that slavery was founded on natural, and not on municipal law; that it did not depend on the *lex loci* [law of the place], and therefore that slaveholders had the right to carry their slaves and to retain them, as such, wherever they could carry any other kind of property, provided the holding of that kind of property was not specially forbidden by the sovereignty into which they went. On this ground it is claimed that slavery went of right into all the territories of the United States; that Congress had no authority to prohibit slavery in the territories, but was bound to protect property in slaves as well as any other kind of property. The assertion of the right of Congress to prohibit slavery in a territory in which it was the local legislature, was declared to be a 'thorough and radical revolution; it proposes new and extraordinary terms of union. The old Government is as completely abolished as if the people of the United States had met in convention and repealed the constitution.'[1] How new this astounding doctrine was is plain from the fact that the act of Congress prohibiting slavery north of latitude 36° 30′ was, as Mr Benton tells us, the wish of the South, sustained by the united voice of Mr Monroe's cabinet (including John C. Calhoun and William H. Crawford), the united voices of the Southern senators, and a majority of the Southern representatives.[2]

It is to the refutation of the extreme views just mentioned that the article in question is principally devoted.

In 1862 an article appeared entitled, 'England and America'. The Christian public in this country were very slow to believe that England sided with the South in our recent struggle.[3] This was so unexpected, so unreasonable, so contrary to the professed principles of both government and people, that Americans could not believe it until the conviction was forced upon them. The whole secular press of that country, whether metropolitan, provincial or colonial, with few exceptions, were as vituperative and denunciatory of the North, as the Southern papers themselves. The same is true, scarcely with the same number of exceptions, of the religious press, whether controlled by Episcopalians, Presbyterians, or Congregationalists. This is a fact for which we have never seen or heard any satisfactory explanation. The article in question was written as a protest against this unrighteous judgment. It was designed to show that the rebellion was made in the interest of slavery. This was proved by the fact that

---

[1] Dr Thornwell on 'State of the Country', p. 26.
[2] Thomas H. Benton, *Thirty Years in the Senate, 1820–50*, vol. 1, p. 8.
[3] Official British neutrality throughout the conflict perhaps suggests that British attitudes were not quite so clear cut as is here suggested. [Ed.]

the grievance complained of had almost exclusive reference to that institution. Those grievances were the denunciations of abolitionists; the obstructions thrown in the way of the restoration of fugitive slaves; the refusal to admit slaveholding in the free territories; the election of an anti-slavery president, and the like. It was proved by official declarations of public bodies; by the avowals of the leading politicians of the South; by the appeals of the Southern press to slaveholders to sustain a war made for their special interests. That English anti-slavery Christians should sustain a rebellion made to conserve, perpetuate, and extend slavery, was a moral phenomenon that astonished the Christian world.

In the second place, the article was designed to show that even with regard to slavery the South had no serious grounds for complaint: that the abolitionists, who denounced all slaveholders as criminal, were a small minority of the people of the North; that the general government, on which alone rested the obligation of executing the fugitive-slave law, so far from being remiss in the discharge of that duty, had erred in the opposite extreme; and that in refusing to sanction slavery in the free territories. Congress had acted on the principles not only of Jefferson, Madison, Monroe, Lowndes, and of all the great representative men of the South, but of the civilized world. Judge McLean, in the Supreme Court of the United States, said from the bench that the great principle decided by Lords Mansfield and Stowell, against which *there is no dissentmg authority*, was 'that a slave is not property beyond the operation of the territorial law which makes him such'. He further said, the Supreme Court of the United States has decided that 'slavery is a mere municipal regulation, founded on and limited to the range of territorial law.' Judge Curtis of the same Court said, ' Slavery being contrary to natural right is created only by municipal law. This is not only plain in itself, and agreed to by all writers on the subject, but it is inferable from the Constitution, and has been explicitly declared by this Court.' He further said, 'I am not acquainted with any case or any writer questioning the correctness of this doctrine.'

It was the practical assertion of this doctrine which men at the South said worked a repeal of the Constitution, and absolved them from all allegiance to the national government. That England should desire the success of a rebellion having such an object, and sustained by such reasons, was a grief and a marvel to the Christian world.

The article on 'The War,' January 7, 1863, was written during the gloomiest period of the struggle. The South, although inferior in point of numbers, had many advantages. They operated near their resources; they were united; their labouring population being slaves were not combatants, but carried on the work of production, while the population were at liberty to take the field. The North laboured under the disadvantage of operating at a great distance from their resources, and over a territory a thousand miles in extent, and the people were far from being united. A large party was opposed to the war from the beginning. A still larger portion of the people were opposed to the administration, and did all they could to prevent its success. Many who at the commencement of the struggle sided heartily with the national government, had become alienated and hostile on account of the measures which had been adopted. The design of the article was to promote harmony among the people of the North. There could be no hope of such harmonious action unless the conscience of the people was on the side of the government. 'There never was a time,' the writer said, 'when the public conscience was more disturbed, or when it was more necessary that moral principles in their bearing on national conduct should be clearly presented.' It was then urged that the great principle, that the moral law, or, the will of God, however revealed, binds nations as well as individuals, should be the rule of public action. The dictum of Coke, one of the greatest legal authorities, 'That any act of Parliament which conflicts with the law of God is null and void,' should be written in letters of gold in every legislative hall and in every court of justice in the country.

On this principle the article urged that the legitimate, the avowed object of the war, viz., the preservation of the union, should be religiously adhered to; and that the war itself should be conducted in strict observance of recognized military law. The two great subjects on which public sentiment was dangerously divided, were the right of the President to suspend the writ of *habeas corpus*, and his authority as commander-in-chief, and as a war measure, to decree the emancipation of the slaves. The article took the ground that both these rights belonged to the President during times of war, and for military ends, i.e. for the preservation of the country, and for the suppression of rebellion.

CORRESPONDENCE WITH HIS BROTHER

His letters to his brother during these memorable years contain many interesting expressions of opinions on passing events.

WASHINGTON, July 24, 1861

My Dear Brother:—As I am here at headquarters, you may think I ought to give you some definite information as to the disastrous battle of the 21st (the battle of Bull Run). Accounts of facts, however, and opinions as to the causes of those facts, are as discordant here as elsewhere. Some throw the blame on the volunteers; others on the original plan; others on the bad management of McDowell; others on the inefficiency and want of courage of the officers.

First, as to the plan and purpose of the expedition, Gen. Scott, as I hear from the best authority, endeavours to wash his hands of the whole business. He says that for the first time in his life he was a coward and yielded to the pressure of politicians in the Cabinet, in Congress, and to popular clamour; that he disapproved of the whole thing from beginning to end. This will be admitted by no one to be the slightest justification; besides, the object of the expedition was, even in the judgment of all concerned, a feasible and important one. That object, as Col. Hunter told me just before he started, was not to assail Manassas Junction, or to drive Beauregard from that position, but to threaten his rear and force him either to retreat or to come out and give battle on equal terms. Instead of this, however, either from a change of plan on the ground, or from error in its execution, there was a direct assault on the outworks of Manassas Junction, and an effort made to drive the enemy from that position. I heard it said beforehand that it would be as preposterous to assail Beauregard in a position which he had employed forty (?) days in strengthening as it would have been in him to assail our intrenchment on the other side of the Potomac. The force sent was sufficient to cope with Beauregard on the open field, but totally inadequate either to assail his intrenchments or to fight him and Johnston combined. The thing actually attempted was to do both. It was known before the battle that Johnston had arrived at the Junction, and yet the assault of the position was made. That it succeeded as far as it did is wonderful, and shows conclusively the superiority of our troops to their opponents. We fought from morning till night double our number, who had every advantage of position and covered batteries, driving the enemy in that time several miles. Until the panic seized our troops, every one thought the day was ours.

Now as to the question why we failed at last, the answer may be found in what has been said. More was attempted than could be accomplished with the resources at command. This may be a sufficient answer to the question. But it is openly said that there was great mismanagement in handling the troops. In the first place, they were exhausted by a long march before they came into action. The several divisions started from Centerville at 2 o'clock, A.M. Two of them had but three or four miles to go before getting into position. Col. Hunter's division, which was to make the principal attack, had twelve miles to march through the woods and over difficult ground. He was on the road from 2 A.M. to 11. His men were tired out. Some of the soldiers who have been here three months told me that that march was the hardest day's work they had performed since they came to Washington. In that state of exhaustion they came under fire, and were called upon to assail battery after battery, and charge regiment after regiment, and they did it successfully from 11 to near 5 P.M. Bringing his men into action in such a state of exhaustion was not Col. Hunter's fault. It was the service assigned to him in the programme of the battle.

In the *second* place, it is said that there was great delay on the part of Tyler's division. He had but two or three miles to go, and was expected to commence the fight by 6 o'clock in the morning, and draw attention to that part of the field, while in point of fact the real battle was begun by Hunter's division at 11 a.m. There were several shots fired from 6 o'clock onward by the large rifle gun in Tyler's division, to feel the position of the enemy, and wake them up; but there was no real fighting there until 11 o'clock. So I hear it said by men on the ground.

In the *third* place, what appears to me the greatest proof of mismanagement in the whole affair, is that not one-half our men were brought into action. The reserve, consisting of seven New Jersey regiments, under Gen. Runyan, were not called up until the stampede began and the day was lost. Mrs Howland tells me that her husband informed her that eight regiments of Miles' division, to which Mr Howland was attached, stood watching a ford, the whole day idle. They had a little skirmish of their own in the afternoon, but they received no order from morning until the order of retreat at the close of the day. Besides this, Blenker's brigade, including the German Turners, the Garibaldi, and other choice regiments, were not brought into action. And yet the retreat was covered by the regulars, cavalry and infantry. Miles was idiotically drunk the whole day, and was incapable of doing anything. But how McDowell could leave so many of his men unemployed, it is hard to understand. He may have thought the day was his own without the assistance of the idle troops, but those troops should have been in position to meet any emergency. The day was won to all appearance. This is the unanimous testimony of all on the ground, civilians as well as military men. The panic was probably on one part of the field where the battle had been actually fought out by the sudden appearance of large reinforcements to the enemy, and a successful charge of cavalry on one regiment, which was broken and put to flight, and thus created a panic in the exhausted troops around them. This did not extend to all the army. The division of Miles' to which Mr Howland belonged had nothing to do, retired in perfect order and got back to Alexandria without losing a gun or musket or soiling their hands.

I am very much pained to hear how the regular officers are disposed to speak of the volunteers. There were doubtless some regiments which behaved badly, but whatever fighting was done, was done by the artillery and the volunteers, and the loss fell principally upon them. That loss is very much less, however, than was at first supposed. The 71st New York, said to have been cut to pieces, lost only about 20 in killed; and so in many other cases the reports prove equally exaggerated.

Col. Hunter's wound is more serious than it at first appeared, but he is doing well, and will be about in a few days. He must have had his head turned to the right, and a fragment of a shell cut the muscle just under the right ear, and divided some small arteries. Dr Wood, the second medical officer in rank in the army, lives next door to us, and was here when the Colonel arrived. He told me afterwards that in all his experience he never saw a man so near death as the Colonel was when he fainted and sank on the floor of the entry. His pulse could not be felt for some time, his hands and feet were cold, and it was some hours before it was safe to raise his head. His wound bled the whole day. He lay in his carriage from 12 to near 5 P.M., and then when he started to return they got involved in the stream of soldiers, wagons and artillery, and had literally to fight their way through. This, of course, agitated him, and caused him to make more or less exertion. Mercifully he had a few friends around besides Sam, who gradually got a dozen troopers to surround the carriage and get it out of the press.

Col. Hunter is not responsible for anything said in this letter. The views are my own gathered from many different sources. You may tell Wistar that Sam says that Fanny is the greatest little fighting horse going. She wagged her tail when a shell burst over, or a cannon ball passed under her nose. He rode her all over the field in the midst of shot and shell for hours, the admiration of all beholders. The Col. says Sam took it as great fun, and seemed perfectly at home, exciting and encouraging the troops as though he had been used to it all his life. It is a great mercy the Col. was wounded so early in the day. He says he and Sam would certainly have been both killed had they continued all day in the advance, exposed as they were all the time before he was disabled. When the Col. was shot he sent Sam to tell Colonel Porter that the command of the division fell on him. Sam had to ride all over the field in every direction for an hour before he could find Col. Porter, and then was almost as long in finding the place to which his uncle had been taken.

God has been most merciful to us in this great trial.

PRINCETON, Jan. 9, 1862

My Dear Brother:—This letter is about myself. The pain in my chest, of which I spoke to you, instead of being occasional and shooting, has of late been constant, quiet and aching, (not severe). It is produced or increased by any prolonged exertion of any kind, mental, emotional or bodily. At times it is attended by increased action of the pulse both as to frequency and force, and then I feel queer, a little disposed to nausea, and a little to fainting. Twice I have had to give up and go to bed. All this is, I suppose, what you call nervous. Nevertheless it is dispiriting not to be able to work. Dr Alexander, although all his life dyspeptic and hypochondriac was as able to work at 80 as he was at 40.

RHINELAND, (north shore of Long Island,) July 15, 1862

My Dear Brother:—-Much to our regret we leave here to-morrow morning. If I was not obliged to be in Pittsburgh on the 22nd, we should much prefer remaining where we are until the close of the month. Here we have pure salt air, beautiful scenery, kind friends, abundance to eat and drink, delightful bathing, and a large library, and nothing to do. These are all the necessary conditions of recuperation. This house stands directly north and south on an eminence. To the north is the Sound with the Connecticut shore in the distance, on the west the broad inlet into Huntington harbour; and to the south the harbour itself and the village two miles distant, on the opposite shore. Mary says that I am better than I have been for a year. Certain it is that we are both getting awfully fat.

It is useless to speculate on our national affairs. Everything shows the great advantages of a military despotism in time of war over a republic, in the unity of plan and control, and in command over the resources of a country. It is clear that six millions of people by conscription can be made to furnish more men than twenty millions by volunteers. I fear we shall after all be out-numbered on every important battle-field, especially if our affairs are to be left in the hands of Mr Stanton. It was suggested that Gen. Halleck was to be made Secretary of War. This would be a grand move. But the radical Republicans, I fear, are too strong to allow Mr Lincoln to act according to his own judgment in this matter. I still have full confidence that God is on our side, and that He will bring us safe, and I trust purified, out of all our troubles.

We hope to be in Princeton before the first week of August is past, unless we are induced to linger longer at Altoona or Cresson.

May all good rest on you and yours, my dear brother.

Charles Hodge

Princeton, Dec. 7, 1862

My Dear Brother:— . . . Gen. Halleck labours hard but to little purpose to throw the responsibility of the disastrous Pope campaign on McClellan. This must ultimately recoil on himself. The disastrous results of his management are enough to appal him.

Your brother, C.H.

Princeton, Dec. 24, 1862

My Dear Brother:—When President Lincoln and Mr Stanton, by their mismanagement, had got everything into confusion, the country hoped that the appointment of Gen. Halleck to the chief command of the army would secure intelligent control of our vast resources and lead to a speedy and happy end of our great struggle.

He has proved an utter failure. Nothing but disaster has followed his measures, until at last the country is apparently on the brink of ruin. 'Oh that my enemy had written a book!' was the shrewd exclamation of an ancient patriarch. Halleck has written official letters and reports, and has thereby placed himself upon a pillory from which he will never be able to descend. He staked his own reputation and the interest and honour of thc country on the removal of McClellan from the Peninsula. All the disasters which McClellan predicted as the consequences of that movement have been realized. Thousands of lives have been sacrificed, millions of money have been squandered, the whole summer wasted, the prestige of our arms destroyed, the country disgraced, and foreign nations emboldened in their hostility. Burdened with the responsibility of these tremendous consequences of his mismanagement, he most ungenerously and unjustly endeavoured to throw the blame on McClellan, and finally succeeds in driving him from the command of an army which he had created and saved, and which was enthusiastically devoted to him. This was done in opposition to the judgment of two-thirds of the people in the country. It may be safely said that the whole Democratic party as represented in the recent elections, and at least one-half of the Republican party, regard McClellan (as Burnside does) as the only man competent to the command of that great army. This also is the judgment not only of the Prince de Joinville, but a Prussian officer of rank in the service of the Confederates has recently published in Germany an account of the battles before Richmond, in which he gives McClellan credit for consummate ability, and attributes his failure to take Richmond to the fact that McDowell did not co-operate with him.

It can hardly now be considered an open question that in the matters between Halleck and McClellan the former was fatally wrong. In the *first* place, common-sense would seem to teach that it was absurd to remove an army of eighty or ninety thousand men from a strong position within twenty miles of Richmond two hundred miles by water in order to march them back over a difficult route of 60 or

80 miles by land to the same place. In the *second* place, the reasons assigned for this strange movement show Halleck's incompetency. McClellan demanded 35,000 reinforcements. Halleck said the Government could only give him 20,000. For the sake of the difference of 15,000, he undertook to order the transfer of McClellan's whole command, although the country was raising 300,000 new troops at the rate of several thousands a day. His great reason, however, was the military principle that columns of attack should be within supporting distance, consequently it was a false position to have the enemy between McClellan's army and an army moving from Fredericksburgh. It is a sure mark of an ordinary mind to be governed by general maxims, without the power to see when and how their application is modified by circumstances. No one, I suppose, now doubts that if McClellan had been suitably reinforced at Harrison's Landing, Lee never would have dared to leave Richmond to attack Pope or McDowell.

It is not, however, so much the blunders of Halleck, disastrous as they have been, as the *animus* he displays, which have forfeited for him the respect and confidence of the people. His charges against McClellan are so evidently unjust and selfish in their motives that they reveal the character of the man. He complains of his delay to leave Harrison's Landing, and contrasts it with the promptness with which Burnside obeyed the order to evacuate New Port News. Burnside had no incumbrances. He had nothing to do but to strike his tents and embark. McClellan had immense siege artillery in position along miles of intrenchments, and vast accumulations of munitions and commissary stores, with innumerable wagons and horses. It required ten days of incessant labour night and day to get these things aboard the transports ready for a start. Besides, Lee did not move an inch from Richmond until McClellan was actually on march for Fortress Monroe. Had the delay been two weeks it could not have altered the matter the least. He censured McClellan for moving only six miles a day in Maryland, when he had the army to reorganize, everything to accumulate on his way, and when as it was

he kept so much in advance of his ammunition train that his artillery at Antietam had to fire blank cartridges for the last two hours
of the battle. He himself took fifty-four days to march a victorious
army from Pittsburgh Landing to Corinth, about 20 miles, and then
delayed an attack until Beauregard, and his whole army, and all he
had, had escaped. This may have been right, but it shows that Halleck
is not the man to sneer at delays. The *National Intelligencer* calls him
'the prince of *cunctators* [procrastinators] in the field, but a Prince
Rupert when sitting in the War Department'. Such was his anxiety to
vindicate himself and to injure McClellan that he published his plans
and principles to the world, and thereby informed Gen. Lee that
he had no reason to fear an assault on Richmond from Suffolk, but
might accumulate his whole force to resist the one attack from Fredericksburgh. This seemed incredible, and therefore many believed
that his report was designed as a blind, and that the movement on
Fredericksburgh was only a feint, while the real attack was to be made
by Banks on the south of the James River. No one can read the testimony given before the Senate's Committee without being painfully
impressed with the incompetency of all concerned in the movement
on Fredericksburgh. Halleck washes his hands of the whole thing, as
though he was not commander-in-chief. Burnside says he took it for
granted that Halleck, who gave the command about the pontoons,
would see it executed. Halleck says it was Burnside's business to see
that the order was carried into effect. Gens. Woodbury and Meigs say,
that as it would take only two days and a half for Burnside to reach
Fredericksburgh, it was impossible in that time to get the pontoons
on the ground. Woodbury swears that he begged Halleck to arrest
the transfer of the army to Fredericksburgh for five days, to give time
to execute the order about the pontoons, but he refused to delay the
movement an hour. The consequence was the delay of a fortnight,
giving Lee time to collect all his forces, and to render the position
impregnable. The greatest of all Halleck's sins against the country,
however, was the removal of McClellan from the command of such
an army in the midst of a march and the execution of a plan of

campaign, and appointing a man who says himself that he was not only incompetent, but that he knew less of the positive strength of the several corps than any division commander in the army. What the consequences of this step have been we now all see and deplore.

As to the deplorable affair at Fredericksburgh I think no one can read the testimony before the committee of the Senate without being further convinced that it was an inexcusable and criminal sacrifice of life. General Franklin testifies that the enemy could have prevented the passage of the river at either of the points proposed, had he chosen to do so, and that his own grand division was entirely at the mercy of Lee after he had crossed. He was, therefore, opposed to passing the river at all. Hooker says he was in favour of passing with his corps higher up, and with 40,000 men, taking, as he says he could have done, a position behind Fredericksburgh, from which the whole Confederate army could have been commanded. Sumner says he agreed to everything Burnside proposed, even to the passage of the river at least at that point. Then as to the attack on the enemy's position it was against all probability of success. To bring infantry to storm intrenchments well furnished with cannon, when the troops have to be any considerable time under fire, is a desperate affair. The rebels at Malvern Hills failed utterly, although they assailed an un-intrenched position, but one well defended by artillery. They failed notwithstanding their determined efforts at Corinth, though two to one to our troops; just as Packenham failed with his English veterans at New Orleans. The attempt proved that it was a foolhardy assault. After terrible slaughter and the most desperate efforts, continued from morning to night, not the slightest progress was made. Burnside said he failed because the thing attempted was 'impossible'! Sumner says that had we carried the first line we could not have held it, that the second was still stronger. Here then by the admission of the two Generals who approved the measure, the thing they attempted was an impossibility. Notwithstanding this, Burnside says he had all his troops all prepared to renew the assault on Sunday morning, and was only prevented by the remonstrance of all his division commanders.

Yet our President tells the army and the world that the attempt was not an error, that it failed only by accident. That is, they failed to accomplish an 'impossibility' by accident! It really seems as if God had given up our rulers to fatuity. It is this and not any doubt of the power of government, or of the resources of the country, which makes me so despondent. Stanton or Halleck, or whoever has the ordering of matters, cannot concentrate men enough to overcome Lee's army of 150,000 or 80,000 as some say. Banks is sent off to the ends of the earth; Foster is sent to make a raid and destroy a few bridges at the cost of 200 lives, and the whole resources of the country are frittered away.

You must think I have little to do when I write you such a letter. But my heart was so full I wanted to pour it out. Whether you agree with me or not I cannot say. I know I speak what hundreds and thousands of the best men of the country think.

Your affectionate brother,
CHARLES HODGE

PRINCETON, Jan. 27, 1863

My Dear Brother:—I enclose your check to my order. I cannot in conscience take your money. I have done too much of that already. As long as you were rich (at least in income), I did not care how much you gave me, but *tempora mutantur* [times change], and we must change with them. If I stick in the mud, which is not likely, I will call on you to help me out. If gold keeps going up we shall all be reduced to a common level.

PRINCETON, Sept. 16, 1864

My Dear Brother:— . . . Could I see you I would have a battle royal with you about McClellan. I think you do him great injustice. My view of the case is, (1) That McClellan is a gentleman, a Christian and a man of superior ability. (2) So far as his *public* acts or declarations go, he has been perfectly consistent. He has not only exhibited marvellous strength and self-control in submitting in silence to injuries, insults and misrepresentations, but he has uniformly adhered to his principles. Even in his letter advocating Judge Woodward's election, which was a great blunder, he said nothing which President Lincoln had not said over and over again. Into the blunder of writing that letter he was led not only by the importunity of friends, but I doubt not by false representations. Woodward was represented to him as holding [dis?]loyal opinions, which, according to common belief he did not hold.

(3) His letter of acceptance is, in the first place, consistent with all his antecedents, with his noble West Point oration, and with all his *published* and authorized declarations. And, in the second place, all its principles and statements are sound and good. They are identical, as to the necessity of the Union, the justice of the war, the suppression of the rebellion, the conditions of peace, with all of the declarations of Lincoln, with the unanimous vote of Congress, and with Secretary Seward's recent masterly speech at Auburn. The only exception as concerns Lincoln to the above remark, so far as I know, is his unfortunate proclamation of six lines, 'To whom it may concern', a proclamation which makes emancipation an indispensable condition of peace; a proclamation condemned by the *Evening Post*, the *Tribune* and the *N. Y. Times*, the three most influential republican papers in the country.

(4) In saying that he assumed that the resolutions adopted by the Convention at Chicago were consistent with the sentiments of his letter, he did not act *disingenuously!* It is notorious that the Democratic party is divided into unionists and disunionists, Peace and War Democrats, the war party being in the vast majority in the country and in the Chicago convention. That convention, or its managers, for the sake of carrying the election and getting the votes of both sections of the Democrats designedly framed a compromise platform, which, as the *Richmond Enquirer* says, and says truly, may be understood either in a war sense or a peace sense. McClellan knew that the great majority intended it in a war sense, and therefore said so in substance in his letter of acceptance. I agree with you

that that platform is mean, contemptible and treacherous, and had McClellan placed himself upon it, pure and simple, without explanation, he would have sunk to the bottom of the sea and stayed there. His letter I conceive has done the country as much good as national victory. It has given us a united North. It has placed the Democratic party distinctly on the ground that there is to be no peace except on the ground of Union. The insignificant faction of peace, or disunion Democrats has separated from the mass, and will only serve to weaken the party as a whole.

While I think thus highly of McClellan, I have no intention of voting for him. I agree with the *New York Times*, that this is no question of the relative merits of candidates. I regard Gen. McClellan as a first-rate Captain in a very bad ship, and with a horridly bad crew, and I have no notion of going to sea with him. I wish and pray for his defeat, because I do not wish to see the Democratic party, which has brought all these troubles and horrors upon us, restored to power.

These are my sentiments, and I believe them to be the sentiments of our best men and women.

The morning papers contain the sad intelligence of the death of the Rev. Dr Potts. He spent a week with us at the end of June and beginning of July, and I little thought it was to be his last visit. He has been for thirty years a director of the Seminary and one of my intimate friends. I feel his death very deeply. I expect to go to New York on Monday to attend his funeral.

Your affectionate brother,
CHARLES HODGE

THE ASSASSINATION OF LINCOLN

The assassination of President Lincoln, like an earthquake, convulsed his entire nature and broke up his deepest fountains of tears. The Rev. J. L. Russell contributed the following to the *Presbyterian* in April, 1879:

It was Saturday morning. Our class (the Junior) was to recite to Prof. Caspar W. Hodge, in New Testament Literature. The news of the horrible deed was spreading like wild-fire when the class assembled at nine o'clock. As Professor Hodge came into the class-room some one whispered the evil news to him, and after a short prayer he dismissed us. As I passed, in returning to my room, the old Seminary Hall, Dr Hodge stepped out on the stoop at the side-door of his study, and called to me. As I came near he said, 'My little grandson tells me that something has happened to President Lincoln.' I told him the facts of the case as reported. With quivering lips, and a face as pallid as death, he said, 'O, it cannot be, it cannot be!'

Just then 'extras' [special editions of newspapers] were cried on the street, and bringing one to him, I read Secretary Stanton's dispatch. Dr Hodge burst into a flood of tears and cried, 'My poor, poor country, what will become of thee!' and turning as one stunned and bewildered by a sudden stroke, he went into his study weeping as he went.

About an hour later the bell rang, and the professors and students of the Seminary and some others gathered in the Seminary. Dr George Junkin, who was to preach next day in the chapel, was present and made one of his intense soul-stirring speeches. Then Dr Hodge prayed, and such a prayer. Could any man forget it? Not the words, for we could not always follow them. The petitions began with a sob and ended with a sob, and the great heart seemed like to break with the weight that was upon it.

We saw the old time struggle at the ford of Jabbok reenacted in that quiet place, where we were wont to meet for prayer, morning and evening, and one whom we loved, one as mighty in soul, and purer in life than the Patriarchal Prince, wrestling with the same Angel of the Covenant, that he might learn the secret of God's mysterious dealing with us, and wring from Him the promise of peace for this stricken land.

That prayer came back to me a year ago, when I heard Dr Hodge pray for the first time, as he dismissed the class of 1878. But how different! Then it only seemed to me that he turned his face round from its heavenward onlook, that its light might fall upon us, his old students, in a blessed benediction before he went hence. Dr Hodge's face as I saw it in the recitation room, in the oratory, in the chapel, and his voice as I heard it in lectures, in those matchless conference talks and in sermons, I love to recall frequently; but his face as I saw it, his voice as I heard it that day we wept for Lincoln, come to me a thousand times unbidden. I saw deeper into his heart that day than ever before or since.

In the July number of the *Princeton Review*, he published an article on President Lincoln, which was a warm eulogy on his character and services, and a sincere lament for his death.

When Mr Lincoln died the nation felt herself widowed. She rent her garments, she sat in the dust, put ashes on her head, and refused to be comforted. Never in our history, seldom if ever in the history of the world, has the heart of a great people been so moved as when, on the 15th of April last, the intelligence flashed over the country that our President had been murdered. It was not merely sorrow for the loss of a great man when most needed, or of one who had rendered his country inestimable service, but grief for a man whom every one personally loved. It was this that gave its peculiar character to that day of lamentation. Still more remarkable in the annals of the country and of the world was the 19th of April – the day of the President's funeral. At 12 o'clock, noon, of that memorable day, the whole country was draped in mourning; our palaces and cottages, our public buildings and private residences, our cities and villages, and isolated dwellings. Wealth veiled herself in crape, and poverty sought some symbol of sorrow, however insignificant. All our churches at that hour were filled with weeping worshippers. Millions of people were on their knees before God. The sun never shone on such a spectacle. Where, moreover, can history point to a funeral progress of fifteen hundred miles through countless myriads of uncovered mourners? The fact cannot be recalled. It was truly said by the Rev. Dr Dix, of New York, 'Abraham Lincoln has been canonized and immortalized by the blow of an assassin.' No effect is without an adequate cause. Such an unparalleled movement of the heart of this great people; such an answering cry of indignation and sorrow from foreign and even unfriendly nations, prove beyond contradiction that Abraham Lincoln deserved to be reverenced, loved and lamented, as few rulers of men have ever merited the confidence and love of their fellowmen.

Dr Hodge took that occasion to plead the humanity and sagacious magnanimity of Lincoln against the natural but blindly passionate cry for the judicial punishment of rebels which prevailed in that dark day of national sorrow and anger.

DR HODGE TO HIS BROTHER

PRINCETON, Dec. 25, 1865

My Dear Brother:— . . . I trust the Radicals will not force us into a war either with England or Mexico. How wonderfully God has controlled and guided President Johnson. He has acted with consummate wisdom, and I think his annual message one of the best I ever read. Pennsylvania ought to be ashamed of such a representative as Thaddeus Stevens.

PRINCETON, Feb. 26, 1866

My Dear Brother:—I feel with you great anxiety about our public affairs. I think the President's (Johnson's) veto message conclusive, and that he ought to be sustained. I cannot understand the course of such men as Fessenden and Trumbull, whom I have been accustomed to regard as wise and moderate. Governor Olden and our ex-Congressman Mr Nixon, have both said to me that four-fifths of the party are with Johnson and against Congress. I fear sometimes that this may not turn out to be the case. The President's stump speech on the 22nd, although undignified in some things, was a very strong one and will tell on the people, Mr Seward's speech, the same night, at the Cooper Institute, I think was excellent.

PRINCETON, July 27, 1866.

My Dear Brother:—I am glad to hear that you and sister Margaret are enjoying yourselves so much in the delightful regions of the North River. The heat, I hope, has spared you. To us it has been very oppressive. For three days we took refuge in the Seminary, which, being a large stone building, and shut up for some months, we found comparatively cool.

The *Princeton Review* is at last out. I do not know whether it will satisfy either party. It sides with neither, but takes its own middle course, commonly the most unpopular, although the safest. I seldom see the *N. Y. Herald*, but its number for the 26th was terribly severe on Congress, and I believe for the most part justly. Any body led by Thaddeus Stevens must be led to evil.

The triumphant progress of the Prussians[1] strikes me as one of the most remarkable events of modern times. I do not believe the needle-gun had much to do with it. I know not which party has the right of it. But Prussia and Italy represent the Protestant interest, and Austria the Papal. Our sympathies are, therefore, with the Prussians. Great things will probably flow from this change in the dominant influence in Germany. Love to sister Margaret.

Your affectionate brother,

CHARLES HODGE

PRINCETON, Oct. 3, 1866

My Dear Brother:— . . . I am sad about the country. A distinguished Southerner, some time since, said the safety of the country depended upon the Democratic party. If they had patriotism enough to keep in the background, asking nothing for themselves or their party, but striving to sustain the moderate and conservative element in the Republican party, all would be well. But if they strove to make party capital out of the dissensions of their opponents, and to get the government into their own hands, the result would be only evil. This latter course the Democrats have taken. They force everybody

---

[1] In the Austro-Prussian War (Seven Weeks' War) of 1866. [Ed.]

to go with the Radicals or to turn Democrats, and give the power of the country into the hands of a party which, during the war, was to a large extent disloyal. This, I hope, will not be done. If I were in Pennsylvania nothing would induce me to vote for such a man as Clymer.

If the Republicans would be content with the constitutional amendments, I suppose the country will go with them. But the speeches of Stevens, Wade, Sumner, Wilson, and the declarations of the leading papers, show that the adoption of the amendments is, as Sumner says, only a drop in the bucket. What those men want is universal suffrage and the disfranchisement of the white population in the South – giving the whole power to the negroes and a few hundred renegade white men in every State. With such outrageously wicked men as Butler and Stevens to be their representatives and mouthpieces, I do not see what any party can expect. My hope is that the Copperhead Democrats and the Radical Republicans may both be consigned to political extinction, and all their leading men sent to Coventry.

Your brother,
CHARLES HODGE

WASHINGTON, May 12, 1868
My Dear Brother:— . . . Most persons whom I meet regard the impeachment[1] as altogether a party affair, and that judicially, or on the grounds of legal justice, there is no sufficient evidence to convict the President.

PRINCETON, December 20, 1867
My Dear Brother:—Should I live another week I shall be seventy years old. You have already passed that boundary. When we look back over this long period, how much cause for gratitude meets our view. What a Mother we had to watch over our infancy and train our youth, and secure for us, at such sacrifice to herself, a

[1] Of President Andrew Johnson. [Ed.]

liberal education. God has preserved us from wasting or disabling sickness. He has granted us a good measure of professional success and usefulness. We have children who are our joy and delight; all of them the professed and consistent disciples of our blessed Lord; all promising to be useful in their several vocations. Their mothers, after having been spared to us for many years, as inestimable blessings, are now safe in heaven. And we are still blessed with health and the use of all our faculties, surrounded and sustained by those who look upon us with respect and love. Above all, God has given us a good hope through grace of eternal life beyond the grave. Who of all our acquaintance can recount such a catalogue of blessings? Such thoughts, my dear brother, I am sure, fill your mind at this season of the year; a season connected with the commemoration of our Saviour's birth, the source of all good, and with the beatification of those we have so much reason to love.

We ourselves have nearly finished our course, and should strive to have our hearts filled with gratitude for the good in the past, and with joyful anticipation of blessedness in the future. Life for us is substantially over, and we have little to expect beyond the present, so far as this world is concerned. Our last days, however, may be our best, if we are only filled with the assurance of God's love, and with devotion to his service and submission to his will . . .

With much love and constant remembrance,

Your brother,
CHARLES HODGE

PRINCETON, April 19, 1869

My Dear Brother:— . . . I am glad to hear that you think Grant's administration still promises well. I do not. I am greatly disappointed. He promised to turn out no faithful, efficient officer, and to appoint no unworthy men for political reasons. He has not been able to keep either promise. He seems to have succumbed entirely to the politicians. He has swept the board, making some 1200 appointments in a few weeks, and displacing some of the very best officers of the revenue. Think of the appointment of such men as Ashley! proved to be guilty by his own confession of official corruption, to say nothing of his political course in Congress, which led to his rejection by his political party. The *N. Y. Times*, so uniform and devoted in its support of Grant, says it is clear that our hope of the promised reform must be indefinitely postponed. I am afraid this is true. What can be done with a Senate that refused to ratify a nomination because the nominee was offensive to a Senator, and that by a vote of 38 to 8? We are in a sad way. This is a good deal for me to say, for I am generally an optimist.

. . . Mary sends love, and I join, of course.

Your brother, CHARLES HODGE

PRINCETON, October 4th, 1869

My Dear Brother:—When I wrote to you that I had a cold, sore throat, pain in the chest, and a boil, you said you were sorry for the former, but intimated that you did not care much about the last. That anthrax *malitiosissimus, ferocissimus, execrabilissimus* [most malicious, ferocious and detestable], however, has kept me awake night after night, and tormented me day after day. That you call nothing! I presume the anthrax to be the *opprobrium medicorum* [hatred of doctors]. Shame on them! What could ever have put it into the head of Job to scrape himself with a potsherd when his body was covered with boils is more than I can understand. I could not touch mine with a feather. The old patriarch must have been in a desperate state of mind.

I do not believe that mine is a common boil. Dr Schank has seen it frequently, and said he will not call it names, but that it is not going to be any worse, and will not be much better for some days. I go about as usual, and hope to be able to attend Presbytery 9 miles from here to-morrow.

If as a doctor you think there is anything actionable in this letter, I shall be on hand prepared to put in a justification . . .

Your brother,
CHARLES HODGE

The following letter to his friend and former pupil, the Rev. Dr Robert Watts, Professor of Theology in the Presbyterian College of Belfast, Ireland, is a good specimen of a large part of his immense correspondence, with pupils and friends in all countries, in answer to questions relating to every department of the faith and work of the Church:

PRINCETON, October 5th, 1865

My Dear Sir:—Wistar has handed me your letter relating to the question raised among your brethren concerning the Witness of the Spirit. As you request an immediate answer, it is impossible for me to do more than state in a few words the view which I have been led to take on the subject, without any attempt to sustain that view either historically or exegetically. I write for you alone, as I have no idea that anything I say will be worthy of the attention of your Committee.

We must, of course, renounce all hope to understand the mode of the divine operation either in nature or in grace; as we have no idea how mind operates on matter, or matter on mind, we cannot understand how God produces the effects which in the Scriptures are attributed to his agency. The fact is all we can expect to know.

1. It seems to be plainly taught in the Bible, and to be the commonly received doctrine, that in the external world God operates constantly through, with, and without second causes. Whatever in the external world, as in plants and animals, is indicative of design is to be referred to the present agency of mind, i.e., to God. Matter cannot produce life, much less an immaterial, intelligent substance. Such substances, however, are constantly produced under the providential agency of God. The human soul operates in like manner through, with and independently of the functions of the body. Every time we speak or write, this threefold mode of exercise is evinced.

2. It is no less plain from Scripture and universally believed in the Church that the Spirit of God operates immediately on the soul. In the regeneration of infants this must be assumed.

3. It seems also clear that in the dealings of the Spirit with the souls of believers there is a constant exercise of His power in connection with and independent of the truth. We know not how one spirit operates on another; how evil spirits controlled the thoughts and feelings of the demoniacs, and of course we cannot pretend to know how the Holy Spirit controls the action of our minds, how He excites our affections or gives the truth a greater power over them at one time than at another. But He is more immediately present with our souls than the soul is with the body, and constantly controls them in a way consistent with the nature of mind and the laws of spiritual intercourse.

4. We are clearly taught that saving faith rests on the witness of the Spirit *by* and *with* the truth. This is represented in Scripture as something different from the evidence which the word itself contains of its own truth. It is 'an unction from the Holy One'. It is 'the demonstration of the Spirit'. The Spirit produces in our minds the infallible conviction that the Bible is true. This conviction is not the product of a process of reasoning, nor a conclusion from the facts of our own consciousness. If it were it would not be infallible, and our faith after all would rest in something human and not in the power of God.

5. In like manner the Spirit witnesses to the believer that he is a child of God. The assurance of his adoption the Apostle refers to two sources; *first*, the conscious filial exercises of the soul towards God, and, *secondly*, the witness of the Spirit, who bears witness together (συμμαρτυρεῖ) with our spirits that we are the sons of God. Although compound words are frequently used in the same sense with the simple forms, this is only to be assumed under the stress of the context. When the context admits of the full and proper force of the word it should be retained; much more when that force is required by the connection. The passage simply teaches that the Spirit produces in the mind of a believer the assurance of his adoption: as in *Rom.* 5:5, He is said to produce the assurance that we are the objects of God's love.

There is no real ground for the charge of enthusiasm or fanaticism against this view of the subject, (1). Because it attributes to the Spirit nothing out of analogy with the constant operations of God in the external world and on the minds of men in his providence.

(2). Because it is consistent with the constant representations of the Scriptures relating to the intercourse of the soul with God. We not only address Him and reveal or rather express to Him our thoughts and feelings, but He manifests Himself to us. We not only aver our love to Him, but He also reveals His love to us. The soul of the believer lives, or should live, in constant fellowship or intercourse with the Father of our spirits. He is at no loss for means and modes of communicating with his children.

(3). When our Confession attributes saving faith to the witness of God not only by or through but *with* the truth, it does not teach that God makes any new revelations. The word is true. It declares itself objectively to the reason, the conscience, and the affections to be true, and God by His Spirit affirms it to be true. There is no new revelation there. Neither is there in the witness of the Spirit to the believer's adoption. He is a child of God. He has all the filial affections of a child. The Spirit produces assurance that what is true is true. The soul is not left to deductions from its own imperfectly understood or partially interpreted consciousness. God gives it a peace which passes understanding.

The fanatics at the Reformation and in all times have abused the doctrine of the inward teaching of the Spirit. So they abuse the doctrine that He witnesses to the adoption of believers. But in neither case have they any just reason for their perversions. And the Reformers as you know gave up their doctrines on neither point from fear that the truth would be abused.

I fear these few remarks will not be of much service to you, but I am not able to write more.

Your friend, very truly,

CHARLES HODGE

THE RELATION OF THE CHURCH
TO POLITICAL QUESTIONS AND THE MERITS OF THE ACTUAL
DECISIONS OF THE GENERAL ASSEMBLY (O. S.), ON QUESTIONS
GROWING OUT OF THE WAR

It was inevitable that the Churches and ministers, both North and South, should be violently agitated by the passions which caused and sprang out of the tremendous political and military conflict between the hostile sections of the country. This excitement would also necessarily find expression alike in the writings and speeches of individual ministers and in the action of Church courts. Under these circumstances there came into existence also diversity of sentiment as to questions of principle and policy, and hence parties were formed within the Church, and violent struggles for predominance for a time disturbed her peace and dishonoured her dignity. Some action by our Church courts, under such circumstances, was necessary and wise, in accordance with all ecclesiastical precedent in the past, as well as with the obvious duty of the hour. There can, on the other hand, be no question that the character of much of the actual deliverances of our Church courts at that time, was determined by the political passions and prejudices existing in the bosoms of ministers and elders, and often by the pressure arising from the clamour and threats of the general populace without.

It was under circumstances such as these, when the political newspapers and mob in Philadelphia threatened the minority of the General Assembly, in May 1861, and when many members confessed that if they should vote according to their convictions they would be afraid to return to their constituents, that the conduct of Dr Hodge appears to his friends the most noble. He had unequivocally taken the side of the Country, and from the first advocated the war for the Union. But when many, who had at the beginning sympathized with secession, or at least favoured unworthy compromises, had become extreme radicals, and while the newspapers and other organs of public opinion severely denounced all dissent from the policy and spirit of the majority, he, for six years, without either fear or anger and with singular sagacity, sided with no party, maintained the attitude of an independent and incorruptible judge, criticized or commended the action of the Assembly, and laid down with clearness and force the principles which were involved in the burning questions, and the confused contentions of the hour.

He objected, as did also the Rev. Robert J. Breckinridge, D.D., in a paper presented by him and passed by the Synod of Kentucky in the fall of the same year, to the passage of the Spring resolutions of the General Assembly in May 1861, which decided in behalf of the Presbyterians of all the States, even of those already subject to the *de facto* government of the Confederacy, the political question as to whether their supreme allegiance was due to the States or to the Federal Government, and made consent to that decision a term of communion in the Presbyterian Church. He admitted all the principles involved in the paper of Dr R. J. Breckinridge, passed by the General Assembly of 1862, but lamented the passage on the ground of Christian expediency, and the testimony of eminently wise and loyal brethren from the Border States, that its passage at that time would only tend to distract the Churches in their section, and weaken the hands of loyal men. Against the action of the Assembly of 1865, in Pittsburgh, whose members came up from constituencies lately and naturally maddened by the assassination of President Lincoln, he protested and reasoned with all his force. The intention of the great majority of that assembly was to brand secession as an ecclesiastical crime, and all in any way compromised with it, as ecclesiastical sinners, and to make repentance and open confession the condition of the re-admission of all such sinners to the communion of the Presbyterian Church.

It is well known that these 'Pittsburgh orders', as they were called, remained a dead letter from the first, and were never enforced in the manner designed by their advocates in a single instance. It is also well known that they alone caused the action of the 'Declaration and Testimony' men of that autumn, and consequently the high-handed action of repression of the General Assemblies of 1866 and 7. They took off from the Northern Presbyterian Church the majority of the Presbyterians of the Border States, and they constitute the principal grievance in the sight of the members of the Southern Presbyterian Church which perpetuates and threatens to perpetuate indefinitely the unseemly divisions and jealousies, which so many good men have earnestly yet ineffectually laboured to allay.

In this regard Dr Ward of the *Independent* is certainly an impartial and competent witness. In an editorial on April 11th, 1872, he writes:

In May 1861, when the General Assembly adopted the 'Spring resolutions', introduced by the venerable Dr Spring of this city, in favour of sustaining the government against the rebellion, Dr Hodge led in a protest, on the ground that the Assembly assumed a position not warranted as an ecclesiastical body; but it is well known that from 1861 to the close of the war, no publication in the country, secular or religious, spoke out more boldly than did the Princeton Review, against the rebellion, and slavery as its cause, and none sustained the government more vigorously and heartily in all its measures to maintain itself and save the Union. The successive articles on these subjects are well known to come from the pen of Dr Hodge, and their tenor and influence were highly appreciated at the seat of government. When the war was over, the Old-School Assembly, meeting at Pittsburgh in May 1865, adopted by a very large majority what were deemed by many, extreme measures of ecclesiastical reconstruction bearing upon ministers and churches at the South. Dr Hodge was not a member of the body, but on reviewing these proceedings, he dissented from much of this action. Whatever may have been thought of their expediency at the time, these 'Pittsburgh Orders', as they have been termed, were never practically carried out, but have remained a dead letter ever since; and now as we look over our religious exchanges in the Presbyterian Church, there seems to be but one sentiment at the North on this subject, and that is in favour of uniting with the Presbyterians of the South on equal terms without any questions being raised growing out of the rebellion.

The principles for which Dr Hodge contended were the following:

1. Church courts are of divine appointment. The constitution is not a grant of powers, but an agreement between different Presbyteries and other church courts, as to the manner in which its inherent authority as a court of Christ shall be exercised. They have entered into various agreements by which they are united in the exercise of the powers derived from Christ. The same remark applies equally to our synods and general assemblies. The first General Assembly of the Church of Scotland met before there was any formal written constitution of the Scotch Church, but it met with all the powers that it ever subsequently possessed.

The limits assigned to the power of church courts are determined directly or indirectly by the word of God. As they are church courts their authority is confined to the church. It does not extend to those who 'are without'. It follows also from the same premises that being church courts they must be confined in their jurisdiction to church matters. They can only expound and apply the Word of God to matters of truth and duty, and to the reforming of abuses or to the discipline of offences.

As the Bible commands obedience to the powers that be, it is clearly within the province of the church to enjoin on all her members obedience, allegiance and loyalty . . . But as the Bible does not enable any man to decide whether these United States are a nation, or a voluntary confederacy of nations, the church has no voice in the decision of that question. Her members must determine it for themselves, and on their own responsibility. It was upon this ground that the editor of this *Review*, with many others, protested against the action of the Assembly of 1861, in adopting the Spring resolutions. In those resolutions it was declared the duty of Christians in the seceding states to support the national government. If the Northern (as we believe the true theory) of our Constitution be correct it was their duty. If the Calhoun (or Southern) theory is correct, it was not their duty. This is purely a political question, for the decision of which the Word of God gives no direction.

In the Assembly of 1859, it was urged by Dr Thornwell that the church is in such a sense a spiritual body, clothed only with spiritual powers for spiritual ends, that all intermeddling with anything not directly bearing on the spiritual and eternal interests of men was foreign to its office and derogatory to its dignity. All this is true, but it is very ambiguous. If by *spiritual* he meant what relates to the spirit, in the sense of moral and religious nature of man, then it is true that the church is restricted in her action to what is purely spiritual. But if the word be so restricted as to confine it to what pertains to the religious element of our nature, to what concerns the method of salvation, as distinguished from the law of God, then the above principle is most obviously false. It contradicts the great principle, universally admitted hitherto, that the church, as the witness of God, is bound to bear her testimony against all sin and error, and in favour of all truth and righteousness, agreeably to the Scriptures; that is, guided by the Word of God in her judgments and declarations . . . The Southern advocates of the new theory found it impossible to adhere to it. We find Dr Thornwell preaching from the sacred desk elaborate sermons on slavery, and writing articles in religious journals on the state of the country. Church papers were filled week after week with articles vindicating Southern principles, and synods pledged themselves to the support of the new confederacy. We do not blame these brethren for violating a false principle, and disregarding their own erroneous theory, but we protest against their condemning in others what they justify in themselves.

2. What is the authority due to the deliverances of our ecclesiastical judicatories? 1st. They are not infallible. 'All synods or councils,' says our Confession, 'since the Apostles' times, whether general or particular, may err; and many have erred. Therefore they are not to be made the rule of faith or practice; but to be used as a help to both.' If not a rule of faith or practice, acquiescence in their deliverances cannot be made a term either of Christian or of ministcrial communion. Acquiescence in their deliverances being a very different thing from submission to their judicial decisions.

2nd. If they are not infallible there must be a judge of their correctness, and a standard by which judgment is to be formed. The judge is every man who chooses to exercise the privilege. The standard of judgment is of course the Word of God. The censures which have been heaped upon this *Review* for the expression of its dissent from certain acts of the Assembly, as an act of presumption unbecoming in the members and servants of the Church, are to say the least undeserved.

3rd. It follows from what has been said that the deliverances of ecclesiastical courts, from the lowest to the highest, cease to have any binding force, *first*, when they transcend the sphere of the legitimate action of the Church ; *second*, when they contravene the compact contained in our Constitution; *third*, when they violate any principle revealed in the Word of God.

3. As to the relation of the Northern and Southern Churches he argued,

i. That it is Christ's will that his people should be one, and that it is the duty of all those who agree in matters of faith and order, and are so situated that they may act together, to be united in one organic body. All who are willing to unite with us on the terms of the cordial adoption of the standards of doctrine and order, we are bound to welcome with the right hand of fellowship. ii. That there are reasons which render the union of Presbyterians North and South, East and West imperative at the present day. Other bodies of Christians, as the Romanists and Episcopalians, are united and compact. These two Churches bid fair to be the only two national Churches in the land. Shall we remain divided? Must we forfeit our national character? iii. Considerations of patriotism are as urgent as those drawn from the interests of the Church. The great aim of the National Goverment, and the great aim of all good citizens is the reconstruction of the Union. We hear on almost every side the utterance of the self-evident truth that 'conciliation is essential to reconstruction'. The reunion of the Northern and Southern Churches is almost indispensable to this conciliation. The *New York Times*, the most influential Republican paper, the great advocate of the war (Sept. 29, 1865), says the action of the Assemblies of Presbyterians and Convention of Congregationalists months ago was not conciliatory. It commends in strong terms the amicable spirit of the late Episcopal Convention in New York.

In his review of the action of the General Assembly, July 1865, he argued against the demand that repentance and confession must be exacted of our Southern brethren as the condition of readmission to communion:

(1.) That such a deliverance of the General Assembly could bind no man's conscience and have no legal force. (2.) That secession was not an ecclesiastical sin. That, as all admit, revolution and rebellion are right on certain occasions, and no church has a right to decide upon those conditions. (3.) That such action was unprecedented, and (4.) It was unequal. Thousands of people at the North sympathized with the South, and in many ways gave aid and comfort to the rebels. No one calls for arraigning them before our church courts. It is plain that a principle that cannot be carried out is false; and that those who are strenuous in enforcing it in the one case, while they refuse to enforce it in another, are either mentally bewildered or insincere.

THE CASE OF DR SAMUEL B. McPHEETERS

He at great length and with great earnestness protested against the action of the General Assembly at Newark in 1864, in dismissing the complaint of that noble gentleman and Christ-like clergyman, the Rev. Dr Samuel B. McPheeters, against the body assuming to be the Presbytery of St Louis.

> Less than one-fifth of that Presbytery, knowing that the majority would not attend, came together the 3rd of June to dissolve the pastoral relation between the Pine Street Church and the Rev. S. B. McPheeters, D.D., without being requested to do so either by the pastor or the Church, and against the known wishes and judgment of the great majority of the Presbytery. The undeniable facts are these. 1. He was a man universally respected and beloved. 2. He had taken and faithfully kept a stringent oath of allegiance to the Government. 3. The highest authorities of the land, the President and the Attorney-General, pronounced themselves so satisfied with his loyalty that they forbade his being interfered with on the part of the authorities, either as a citizen or as a minister. 4. Whatever were his private feelings, he so conducted himself and so performed his ministerial duties, as to retain the affection and confidence of the community, of six out of seven of the elders of his church, of the vast majority of its members and attendants; and of four-fifths of the members of his Presbytery. That such a man should be dismissed from his church and forbidden to preach in its pulpit, by a mere fragment of the Presbytery to which he belongs, who knew him and all the circumstances of the case, seems to us an injustice which has few, if any, parallels in the history of our church.

There can be no doubt now that this action was not only unrighteous, but that it was also a great mistake for the supporters of the government, and of the true theory of the relation of the Church to the moral and religious relations of political questions, to give to the honest advocates of a mistaken view their martyr. And no human cause was ever crowned by one purer or more heroic.

Whatever may have been the prevalence and violent expression of unchristian prejudices and passions among the men of either side with whom he came in contact, Dr McPheeters at least always maintained Christian charity unwounded either by thought or word. His spirit was chastened with sorrow, and his physical health crushed, but he was never excited to bitterness. All his public and private utterances were full of love and grace. His letters all corroborate the testimony of his wife, that at no time during his years of trial did he, even in the privacy of home, speak a word which would have compromised him if known to the whole world.

For the last five years of his life he was the well-beloved pastor of the rural congregation of Mulberry, Kentucky. Here the beauty and glory of his life culminated and ripened fast for heaven as gently as the rich autumnal twilight melts into the perfect day. For more than three years he was confined to his couch, and preached and talked to his people always in a recumbent position. His house, the home of all his people, was thronged with constant visitors. From his couch the patient sufferer, at home and in the church, talked and preached with radiant countenance, and with matchless sweetness and spiritual power. A perennial dispensation of the gracious Spirit was kindly granted them. Many were converted, and the entire church walked with their angelic pastor on the heights of Beulah, in constant view of the celestial city, and under the perpetual inspiration of its hopes and joys. Thus one of the humblest, gentlest, loveliest of mankind exultantly bore testimony to the all-sufficiency of his Lord.

It was for thus standing in his place during a period of confusion and conflict, and for teaching these principles, that Dr Hodge was assailed, and his influence sought to be destroyed by angry and bewildered men. The Presbytery of Oxford, consisting of two pastors and four stated supplies, and an unusual proportion of men without charge, at its meeting, April 1866, overtured the General Assembly, that 'for the peace and purity of the Church', Dr Hodge should be directed to desist from teaching as he had done, and from thus 'corrupting the minds of the young men in the Seminary, in regard to their church and country.'

In his article, October 1865, he says:

It has been intimated in some quarters, with small indications of sorrow, that in pursuing the course above indicated, this *Review* has lost the support of the loyal States. We learn from the publisher that this is a mistake. The list of subscribers in those states is as large now as it was before the war. It is in the seceding states the falling off has occurred. Some kind friends, without our knowledge, brought the matter before the last Assembly, but the Editor has not lifted a finger to secure patronage for the *Review*. To him its discontinuance would be a great relief. He has carried it as a ball-and-chain for forty years, with scarcely any other compensation than the high privilege and honour of making it an organ for upholding sound Presbyterianism, the cause of the country, and the honour of our common Redeemer.

He had carried it for forty years, and in three years more he did finally lay it down. The reader of the past pages of these memoirs, will have some means of appreciating the pathos of the above sentences, coming as they do so near the closing scenes of such a period and character of service.

This is not recorded in the spirit of complaint. Dr Hodge's nearest representatives are gratefully sensible of the universality, sincerity and singular eminence of the honours awarded him in his closing life. But no picture can be drawn, if the shadows are left out, and these shadows of storm-drifted clouds are left where they fell, that the truth of history may be preserved in its integrity.

THE REUNION OF THE OLD AND NEW SCHOOL PRESBYTERIANS

As was shown in a previous chapter of this book the division of the Presbyterian Church was caused by the belief on the part of those, chiefly of Scotch and Scotch-Irish descent, who were strongly attached to the unmodified Presbyterian usages and doctrines inherited from a past age, that the Church as then situated, was in great danger of being disorganized by amalgamation with Congregationalism, and corrupted by the toleration of variations of the Calvinistic system of New England origin. These doctrinal variations were of different degrees, some of them classified under the general head of Hopkinsianism, which Dr Hodge thought did not occasion a ground of division, and others classified under the head of Taylorism, which he did regard as intolerable.

Immediately after the war, the two branches of the Church in the North approximated each other more nearly than ever before in size and condition, the Old School branch having been by that event separated from the large and intensely orthodox and conservative Southern section. They had moreover been drawn together by their intense sympathy in the great passions and sufferings of the immediately preceding years. The New School branch also, as Dr S. W. Fisher declared in his speech before the National Presbyterian Union Convention in Philadelphia, Nov. 1867, had become separate from its past Congregational alliances and thus 'God had eliminated discordant elements, which gave them (us) much trouble, and which gave the (our) brethren of the other branch great occasion for censure.' Both branches were now completely and equally (with slight and transient exceptions) Presbyterian in their organization, and the graver departures from the old Calvinistic system had ceased to prevail. Besides these facts justifying reunion, there existed, as generally prevalent conditions prompting to it: a disposition, upon the more politically radical party of the Old School to make up for the loss of the Southern Church, and an intense sympathy with that branch of the Church which was largely leavened with New England ideas; substitution on all sides of an interest in the history and comparison of theological doctrines and systems, for the interest in original speculation which had prevailed in the preceding generation; and last, though not least, the influence of the general spirit of the age, which deprecates the value of doctrinal distinctions, and emphasizes the value of character, and practical energy and work.

In 1837–8 Dr Hodge opposed, not the division of the Church, but the spirit, policy, and methods of some of the Old School leaders, in their attempts to effect that end. He did so because he was constitutionally a conservative, and spontaneously resisted all change; because he did not believe the evils prevalent to be as imminent nor as dangerous as represented by the ultra Old School men; and because he disapproved of many of the methods they pursued, as unconstitutional, and as impolitic, involving the danger of giving the opposite party the advantage of possessing the majority, and actual legal control of the organization and property. In 1867–70 he occupied precisely the same position. He had shared in none of the 'progress' of the times. He would not have divided the Church if reunited, but he saw no sufficient reason for uniting the actually and long-divided branches. For thirty years the Old School Presbyterian Church had been an established fact in the world. It had assumed its place, and discharged its functions in the family of Churches, as a witness-bearing body, as its special function maintaining intact by testimony and by discipline, the strict old Calvinism of our Fathers, and of the Westminster Confession, strictly interpreted. His life had been identified with this work; he loved it and believed it to be indispensable to the welfare of the sisterhood of Christian Denominations, which God had severally adorned with different graces, and to which he had severally assigned different functions. He did not believe that the reunited Presbyterian Church of the future would take the place of the Old School Church of the past. He was not insensible to the blessedness and the glories of Christian Union as he made plain by his speeches at the National Presbyterian Convention, Nov. 1867, and at the Evangelical Alliance, Oct. 1873. But he believed that under the present condition of the universal Church, each Denomination has its special gift and entrusted function, and that the gift and function of the Old School Presbyterian Church was one of the most precious and indispensable, and one which no other could fulfil. He never believed or said that his New School brethren were the holders or the teachers of heresy. He did not pretend to judge or to mistrust their orthodoxy. He simply maintained that as a historical fact those brethren had always, and did now, maintain and practice a principle and latitude of toleration different from that of the Old School. He held that if not for themselves, yet for others they interpreted the formula of subscription to our doctrinal standards in a different sense, or at least different spirit; that even if hereafter the Old School should produce all the heretics, the New School division of the New Church would provide their principal and most influential defenders, or excusers.

He therefore set himself once more to face and resist the current of the times, to oppose what he believed to be the rash course of the majority of his own church, and to call down upon himself the impatience and displeasure of many. He spoke and wrote in public and private, and voted against the movement on every occasion that was afforded him. He wrote in the *Princeton Review* the articles on the General Assembly for 1866 and 1867; on 'The Principles of Church Union and the Re-union of Old and New School Presbyterians' in 1865; and on 'Presbyterian Re-union', and on 'The Protests and Answer' in 1868. He spoke, voted, and wrote and signed the Protest against it in the General Assembly of 1868. And after the majority of his most thorough sympathizers, seeing the event inevitable, had capitulated in order to secure the most favourable conditions possible, he wavered not a hair's breadth, but rode nine miles to meet the Presbytery in Cranberry, on October 5th, 1869, with the '*anthrax malitiosissimus*' [see p. 522] on the back of his neck, for the purpose of casting his final vote against it.

THE NATIONAL PRESBYTERIAN CONVENTION, PHILADELPHIA, NOVEMBER 1867

On the 6th, 7th and 8th of November, 1867, on the invitation of the Synod of the Reformed Presbyterian Church, a National Presbyterian Union Convention met in the First Reformed Presbyterian Church, Philadelphia. Mr George H. Stuart was President. Besides many corresponding members allowed to speak but not to vote, the Convention consisted of 162 representatives of the Old School branch of the Presbyterian Church, 64 of the New School, of the United Presbyterians 12; of the Reformed Presbyterians 12; of Reformed Protestant Dutch 6; of the Cumberland Presbyterians 6. Dr Hodge was a member, and went to it under an 'entire misapprehension, supposing from the wording of the call that the object of the meeting was prayer and conference, for the promotion of Christian fellowship and harmonious action between the several bodies represented'. When, therefore, he found that the drift of all the speakers and resolutions was towards the establishment of a general organic union, he remained quiet, and made no address till the afternoon of the third day, when he expounded the sense in which he maintained the 'Standards' should be embraced as containing 'the system of doctrine taught in Holy Scripture'.

It came to the knowledge of this Convention that in the Annual Meeting of the Protestant Episcopal Evangelical Societies, consisting of about 450 members, bishops, clergy and laymen, held at that time in Philadelphia, prayer had been offered in behalf of the National Presbyterian body. Hence on Thursday a committee headed by Professor Henry B. Smith of New York, was deputed to carry the salutations of the representatives of all branches of the Presbyterian Church to their Episcopal brethren. On Friday morning, November 8th, a responding Episcopal delegation, consisting of Bishops McIlvaine of Ohio, and Lee of Delaware, and the Rev. Stephen H. Tyng, Jr., and the Hon. Judge Conyngham and Hon.

Felix B. Brunot, brought the salutations and blessings of the Episcopal body to the representatives of the National Presbyterianism. They addressed the Conference in warmly affectionate language, offered extemporaneous and eloquent prayers in their behalf, and pronounced upon them the Apostolic benediction. Such a scene has no parallel, considering the representative character of the bodies and persons concerned in the transaction, in the entire history of American Christianity.

Dr Hodge was brought forward by the President to respond to this deputation in the name of the Presbyterian Convention, and was greeted with great applause. He said:

> Gentlemen and brothers, honoured and beloved: I am called upon, as you hear, to present, in the name of this Convention, their hearty greeting and salutation. You here see around you, sirs, the representatives of six Presbyterian organizations of this country, comprising in the aggregate at least five thousand ministers of Jesus, an equal number of Christian churches, and at least one million of Christians, who have been baptized in the name of Jesus Christ. It is not only, therefore, as the organ of the Convention, but for the moment, as the mouth-piece of this vast body of ministers and public Christian men, that we, sirs, were commissioned to present to you our cordial and affectionate Christian salutations.
>
> We wish to assure you, sirs, that your names are just as familiar to our people as to your own! That we appreciate as highly your services in the cause of our common Master, as the people of your own honoured Church. And, sirs, we rejoice with them in all that God has accomplished through your instrumentality.
>
> I hope this audience will pardon a reference that might seem too personal under any other circumstances than the present. The honoured President of this Convention might easily have selected some more suitable person to be the mouth-piece of this body, but on the ground of one consideration, perhaps the choice of myself to be that organ is not altogether inappropriate.

You, Bishop McIlvaine, and Bishop Johns, whom I had hoped to see with you here to day, – you and I, sir, were boys together in Princeton College, fifty odd years ago. Often at evening have we knelt together in prayer. We passed through, sir, the baptism of that wonderful revival in that institution in 1815. We sat together, year after year, side by side, in the same class-room. We were instructed through our theological course by the same venerable teachers. You, sir, have gone your way, and I have gone mine; and I will venture to say in the presence of this audience, that I do not believe you have preached one sermon on any point of doctrine or Christian experience, which I would not have rejoiced to have uttered. And I feel fully confident that I never preached a sermon, the sentiments of which, you would not have publicly and cordially endorsed.

And now, sir, after these fifty odd years, here we stand, grey-headed, side by side, for the moment representatives of these two great bodies of organized Christians. Feeling for each other the same intimate cordial love, and mutual confidence; looking not backward, – not downward to the grave beneath our very feet, – but onward to the coming glory. Brethren, pardon this personal allusion, but is there not something that may be regarded as symbolical in this? Has not your Church and our Church been rocked in the same cradle? Did they not pass through the same Red Sea, receiving the same baptism of the Spirit, and of fire? Have they not uttered from those days of the Reformation to the present time, the same great testimony for Christ and his Gospel? What difference, sir, is there between your Thirty-nine Articles, and our Confession of Faith, other than the difference between one part and another of the same great Cathedral anthem rising to the skies? Does it not seem to indicate, sir, that these Churches are coming together? We stand here, sir, to say to the whole world, that we are one in faith, one in baptism, one in life, and one in our allegiance to your Lord and to our Lord.

The reporter says, 'During the delivery of this speech there was scarcely a dry eye in the house, and the speaker was frequently interrupted by the cries of "Amen", from the delegates.'

In an editorial of the next week, the *Presbyterian*, alluding to the irritation which Dr Hodge's course in opposing his Church on the matter of its war-deliverances and the project of Reunion had occasioned, said:

If any one has ever imagined that the influence of Dr Charles Hodge, of Princeton, was waning, either in the Church, of which he is the ornament, and in which he is ever held in honour, or in other Presbyterian communions, it was only necessary for him to be present in the late Convention, and witness the reception given to the venerable Professor, to assure him that his imaginings were vain. Dr Hodge chose to remain quiet during the most of the sessions of the body, but when he appeared upon the platform, it was to be greeted as no other man was received in that church. Spontaneously, and ere he had opened his lips to speak, applause started from all parts of the house, and was long continued and hearty. It was the ready homage of Christian men to one who had kept the faith, and taught it, and had ever been foremost in its defence, and so had won his way to the highest confidence and respect of the Church. It showed to all how good it is to work for one's generation, and for the Church of God, and receive, as the end of life draws near, the precious tokens of the Church's love and the Master's approbation. It added to the interest of the occasion that his early and life-long friend was there to witness these expressions of esteem and confidence from the gathered Church; and we are very sure that no one in the assembly would have acknowledged more fully the justice of the tribute paid to Dr Hodge than the beloved bishop of Ohio. We thank God for such men; for their lives and works, and for the honour and affection which are gathering about their names as passing years are bringing them nearer to the blessed home of the saints of God.

12

HIS SEMI-CENTENNIAL

APRIL 24, 1872

A S WE HAVE SEEN FROM Dr Hodge's journal given in chapter 6, in which he records the celebration of the jubilee of Professor Niemeyer in Halle, it has been customary in Germany to celebrate the fiftieth anniversary of veteran professors. The jubilee of his old friend, Professor Tholuck, was celebrated in 1874, two years after his own. But this, as far as known, is the first instance in which such an event has crowned the life of an American professor. As he had become a teacher in this seminary in 1820, and had been elected professor by the General Assembly in May 1822, the fiftieth year of his professorship terminated with the end of the academic year ending April 23rd, 1872. The suggestion of this great honour originated with and its execution for the most part devolved on his loving and filial pupil and colleague, Prof. William Henry Green, D.D. Nothing could be more beautiful than the affectionate attention with which for more than twenty-five years he honoured his senior and friend. Our father, just before his death, very solemnly laid upon his children the inheritance of obligation incurred by this long and singular kindness of his friend and theirs.

In anticipation of this event, the Board of Directors of the Seminary at their annual meeting in 1871, invited the alumni and friends of the Seminary to assemble in Princeton on the day subsequent to the completion of this half century, with a view to its glad and grateful commemoration. They also suggested the creation at that time of 'some memorial of the long, faithful and useful professorial labours' of Dr Hodge, and proposed further that an alumni association should be formed; and appointed a committee of seven, to devise and carry into effect such measures as might be requisite for the end contemplated.

This committee of the Directors forthwith named a committee of seventy alumni residing in various parts of the country, whose counsel and co-operation were solicited, and who were invited to meet in Princeton, June 28th, 1871, the day of the commencement of the College of New Jersey, in order to deliberate upon the best method of accomplishing what had been proposed and adopting such measures as might seem advisable for the purpose.

Encouraged by cordial responses to letters of inquiry and by the general interest manifested, the committee of seventy, with such others of the alumni of the Seminary as were then gathered in Princeton, met in the chapel of the College on Commencement day, and with great unanimity and cordiality endorsed the project in the following resolutions:

Resolved, 1. That the proposed celebration of the semicentennial of Dr Hodge meets our hearty concurrence, and we cordially unite with the Directors in inviting the friends and former students of the Seminary to meet for this purpose in Princeton, on Wednesday, April 24th, 1872; and that this invitation be very particularly extended to all our brethren in different Christian denominations, and in every section of our country, as well as in foreign lands, who have received their education here in whole or in part. And we express the earnest hope that the hallowed memories of the past, personal attachments, and local and literary associations with this cherished spot, may be permitted to overcome the long and wide separation of time and place, and ecclesiastical organization, so that we may all upon this glad occasion gather around the instructor whom we all love and revere, a band of brethren, cemented in Christian love, renewing and pledging a mutual confidence and affection which nothing in the past shall be suffered to dim or to obliterate, and nothing in the future shall be permitted to disturb.

Resolved, 2. That an Alumni association be then formed, consisting of all who have been for any length of time connected with the Seminary as theological students.

Resolved, 3. That, in our judgment, the most fitting memorial of this half century of faithful and distinguished service will be the permanent endowment of the chair which Dr Hodge has filled with such pre-eminent ability.

Resolved, 4. That this endowment be immediately undertaken, and, if possible, completed by the 24th day of April next.

Bishop Johns having found as the time approached that it was impossible for him to attend, intimated that fact to Dr Green by letter. To this Dr Hodge sent the following response:

PRINCETON, April 24, 1872

Dear John, my Twin-brother Friend:—Dr Green sent me over your letter to him, and I am so disappointed and grieved at its contents, I do not know what to do. I dread the 24th, and hoped for your support. Why can't you visit some of your churches before the 22nd, so as to be free a few days after that date? A bishop is not worth the mentioning if he cannot do what he pleases.

Another thing troubles me very much: your letter is not in your hand-writing. Why is this? Do let some one tell me that it is a lame finger or something of that kind. I am over head and ears in getting the third volume of my big book through the press and ready for it. It is really awful. Even worse to write than it is to read. Love to all your children within hearing.

You have only one such life-long friend as I am out of your own family.   CHARLES HODGE

'The appointed day of the celebration brought together a large con-course of friends of the Seminary, including four hundred former students. The first class upon its roll is now starred throughout [to indicate those deceased]; the second shows but a single survivor, and the third but two. From the next class, which entered in 1815, the year preceding Dr Hodge's own matriculation as a student, four of its five surviving members were present; and every subsequent class was represented with possibly three or four exceptions. They came from Texas and Colorado and California, as well as from places less remote. The leading theological and literary institutions of the coun-try deputed one or more of their Professors to indicate their interest in the occasion. The church in which the exercises were held was densely thronged, and by an assemblage remarkable for the number of venerable heads and thoughtful faces. Every available standing place was occupied. The enthusiasm, which was great throughout, reached its climax at that point in the proceedings when Dr Hodge himself, almost overcome by emotion, advanced to greet his gathered pupils and to respond to the address made to him by Dr Board-man. The exercises were admirably conducted throughout, and in harmony with the character of the day. And nothing occurred to mar the general gratification, which was heightened by the fact that notwithstanding the brevity of the time since the suggestion had first been made the projected endowment was brought to the verge of completion, $45,000 of the proposed $50,000 being already raised, and a purse of $15,350 having besides been made up as a present to Dr Hodge. One gentleman has also given $50 towards a fund, whose income shall be expended in the purchase of copies of Dr Hodge's *Theology* or of his *Commentary on the Epistle to the Romans* to be given to needy students of the Seminary.

'The amount thus far contributed to the endowment is from 575 separate donors, mostly former students of this Seminary, residing in twenty-five different States and Territories of this country, some of them missionaries in China, India, Siam and South America, a few in the Dominion of Canada, and one who is now Professor of

Theology in the Assembly's College in Ireland, and who has embraced this opportunity to renew his old allegiance. It may safely be said that few funds of like amount represent an equal measure of self-denial and devotion on the part of those who have contributed to them. Ministers, themselves receiving an inadequate support, have aided in this endowment with a generous enthusiasm, sending sums that they could not well afford to spare, but forward to testify their indebtedness to their honoured teacher, and eager to have a share in erecting this monument to bear his name.'

The 1st Presbyterian Church of Princeton was arranged with an extended platform as has been the custom on college commencements from time immemorial. Dr Hodge and Dr Boardman sat on the opposite sides of the President of the occasion, the Rev. Dr Snodgrass, President of the Board of Directors.

The first order, after prayer, was the delivery of an admirable Address on the appropriate theme, 'The Title of Theology to Rank as a Science', by the Rev. Joseph T. Duryea, D.D., of Brooklyn, N.Y.

Dr Snodgrass then introduced the Rev. Dr Henry A. Boardman, of Philadelphia, who, in the name of the Directors and Trustees of the Seminary, and of the Alumni, addressed Dr. Hodge, and spoke substantially as follows:

My Honoured Father, Brother, Friend:—I am commissioned by the Directors of our Seminary to present to you their cordial congratulations, and to assure you of the profound sense they entertain of the invaluable services you have rendered to the cause and kingdom of Christ. We this day bear our public testimony to the eminent ability, the ample and various learning, the practical wisdom, the thorough conscientiousness, the unswerving fidelity, and the humble, devout, earnest spirit which you have brought to the discharge of your high trust. We offer our thanksgivings to the Author of all good, that you have been spared to us so long, and in reviewing this half-century of your labours, we reverently glorify God in you.

The occasion takes our thoughts back irresistibly to the origin of this School of the Prophets. At this hour, hallowed by so many tender and sacred memories, there rise before us the venerable forms of those two patriarchal men, Drs Alexander and Miller, in whose arms the institution was cradled. We gratefully acknowledge the Divine goodness and mercy in sparing them for forty years to impress themselves upon its character, to define its theology, to determine its direction, and to infuse into it the animating tone and spirit by which it was to be controlled in after times. It was the universal feeling of our Church, that a mercy so signal was too great to be repeated. Yet what hath God wrought! The mantle of our Elijahs has certainly fallen upon our Elisha. Their associate first, and then, in the true line of the apostolical succession, their successor, he has taken up and carried forward their work, and we to-day commemorate a ministration, not of forty, but of fifty years, marked with every attribute which can command our homage, or win our gratitude. But I forget my errand. Assigned to a service to which I feel myself most unequal, and from which I sought in vain to escape, I am instructed to speak to you on behalf, not only of the Directors of our Seminary, but of the Alumni also. I have no words for this. *Here*, in the scene before us, is the only adequate expression that can be given to the feelings of your former pupils. From far and near, the aged and the young, moved by a common impulse, have hastened to this festal service. Commingled with them are the learned Faculties of other seminaries and colleges, distinguished laymen, and honoured legates of European Churches. No eye can look upon this sea of upturned faces without being impressed with the spectacle. As interpreted by its object, and by the free, generous inspiration which pervades the entire body, it bears an aspect of moral beauty – nay, of moral sublimity – beyond almost any convocation our Church, or even our country has witnessed. Who has ever seen a gathering like this? Ovations to heroes, and statesmen, and authors are no novelty, but here is the spontaneous homage paid to a simple teacher of God's Word, and defender of his truth, by a vast assemblage, worthily representing the highest culture, and the most exalted moral worth of our land. No man of our times has received a tribute comprising, in an equal degree, the choice elements that are blended here. And, my beloved friend and brother, there is but one name among the living that could have drawn this concourse together. Nor is this all. What we see, imposing as it is, is as nothing to what we do not see.

Of the twenty-seven hundred men who have sat at your feet, there are few in the field who are not here in spirit today. The wires are up, and there is a sweet tide of thought and sympathy flowing to us at this hour from our toiling brethren in Europe, in Africa, in Eastern Asia, in South America, and in the Isles of the Sea. It is not less for them I speak than for the hundreds of your students who are present, when I say we rejoice with you in this Jubilee; from our heart of hearts we thank you for the priceless benefits we have received at your hands; and we praise God for all that affluence of blessings which he has bestowed upon you, and through you upon his Church. Do not imagine, however, that we have come together merely to recognize in you the great expositor and defender of the faith once delivered to the saints. I appeal to you, Fathers and Brethren, that it is not this sentiment only, nor mainly, which throbs in our breasts to-day. Beheld from a distance, even friendly eyes see on this ancient hill simply a giant oak, with its grand old branches swaying to the winds of heaven. But to us, branches and trunk alike are so covered with vines, and flowers, and clustering fruits, that we scarcely wot of the massive props that are underneath. And so, whatever of honest admiration we may feel for our gifted master, it is not that which brings us here, but the affection rather which we cherish for him as an unselfish and sympathizing friend. If the homely phrase may be allowed, while we honour him for the great head which God has given him, we *love* him for his still greater heart.

Allusion has been made to the type of theology taught in this Seminary. It has two leading characteristics. In the first place, the principle upon which it rests, and which underlies every part and parcel of the lofty superstructure, is the absolute, universal, and exclusive supremacy of the Word of God as the rule of faith and practice. A censorious critic said the other day, derisively, in reviewing the volumes of Theology lately published: 'It is enough for Dr Hodge to believe a thing to be true that he finds it in the Bible!' We accept the token. Dr Hodge has never got beyond the Bible. It contains every jot and tittle of his theology. And woe be to this Seminary whenever any man shall be called to fill one of its chairs, who gets his theology from any other source. The second characteristic of this system is that it is a Christology. Christ is its central sun; its pervading element; the stem from which everything in dogma, in precept, in religious experience, radiates, and towards which every thing returns. Not as a mere anatomy does Christ dwell here – the crown of a speculative organism, symmetrical and complete, but without flesh and blood and vitality. Rather is He the living soul that animates, and guides, and hallows the whole. If a theology must needs take somewhat of its essential tone from the temper of its expounder, who can marvel that the theology of this institution should be instinct with a gentle, loving, humble Christ-like spirit ?

To be permitted to set forth and inculcate a system like this, even in the ordinary routine of personal labour, is no trivial privilege. But what honour, beloved Brother, has God put upon you! For fifty years you have been training men to preach the glorious gospel of the grace of God to their fellow-sinners. The teacher of teachers, your pupils have become professors in numerous Colleges and Seminaries at home and abroad. Not to speak of one or two thousand pastors, who are exerting an ameliorating influence upon this nation more potent than that of an equal number of men belonging to any other calling, you are helping, through your students, to educate a great body of Christian ministers, not a few of whom are to be employed in laying the foundations of Christianity in pagan lands. And now there is superadded that which all your friends regard as the crowning mercy of your life, viz.: that health and strength have been given you to complete and publish the only comprehensive work of *Systematic Theology* in our own or any other language, which

comprises the latest results of sound scriptural exegesis, discusses
the great themes of the Augustinian system from an evangelical
standpoint, and deals satisfactorily with the sceptical speculations
of modern philosophy and science. In thus supplying what was
confessedly, in the way of authorship, the most urgent want of
Protestant Christendom, you have extended indefinitely the range
of your beneficent power.

Your *Theology* must soon become the Hand-Book of all students
of the Reformed faith who speak the English tongue. Where you
have taught scores, you will now teach hundreds; and where you
have taught hundreds, you will teach thousands. Thus, through your
pupils, dispersed over the four quarters of the globe, and through this
great work, comprising your mature views in the noblest of all sciences, is your influence extending in ever-multiplying, ever-widening,
concentric circles, until the mind is awed in attempting to conceive,
not of its possible, but of its certain results, as the ages come and go.
That you should live to see this mighty mechanism in motion – to
guide into so many of its countless channels this broad stream from
the Fountain of living waters, is a distinction so rare and so exalted
that we cannot but look upon you as a man greatly beloved of God,
and honoured as He has honoured scarcely any other individual of
our age. When He has thus spoken, we have no right to be silent.
We render the praise to Him whose providence and grace have made
you what you are, and given you to us and to His Church. Again
we do offer our thanksgivings for all that He has done and is doing
for our Seminary, for the Church, and for the world through your
instrumentality. Again with one heart and voice do we, the Directors,
Trustees, and Alumni of the Seminary, the Faculties and graduates of
sister institutions, the representatives of the other liberal professions,
and your friends of every name and calling here assembled, congratulate you on this auspicious anniversary, and pay you the tribute of
our grateful love. 'The Lord bless you and keep you. The Lord make
His face to shine upon you, and be gracious unto you. The Lord lift
up His countenance upon you, and give you peace !' "

As Dr Hodge rose to reply, the audience spontaneously rose, and a large portion remained standing until he had finished his response, which was as follows:

Gentlemen of the Board of Directors and of the Board of Trustees, Friends from abroad who have honoured this occasion by your presence, and dear Brethren of the Alumni, I greet you.

A man is to be commiserated who is called upon to attempt the impossible. The certainty of failure does not free him from the necessity of the effort. It is impossible that I should make you understand the feelings which swell my heart almost to bursting. Language is an imperfect vehicle of thought; as an expression of emotion it is utterly inadequate. We say, 'I thank you', to a servant who hands us a glass of water; and we thank God for our salvation. The same word must answer these widely different purposes; yet there is no other. When I say I thank you for all your respect, confidence, and love, I say nothing, I am powerless. I can only bow down before you with tearful gratitude, and call on God to bless you, and to reward you a hundredfold for all your goodness.

Allow me to say one word. I have been fifty years connected with this Seminary as professor. During all those years no student has ever hurt my feelings by any unkind word or act. You are disposed to cover – to overwhelm me with your commendations. It is you who should be commended and blessed.

But I am not here to speak of myself. Let me speak of the Seminary. Brethren, I too am an Alumnus; I share your feelings. We love our Alma Mater, not because she is fairer, richer, or better than other mothers, but because she is our Mother.

Dr Boardman has anticipated in part what I wished to say. Princeton Seminary is what it is, and what, I trust it will ever continue to be, because Archibald Alexander and Samuel Miller were what they were.

The law of the fixedness and transmissibility of types pervades all the works of God. The wheat we now grow, grew on the banks of the

Nile before the pyramids were built. Every nation of the earth is now what it is, because of the character of its ancestors. Every State of our Union owes its present character to that of its original settlers. This holds good even of counties. Before the middle of the last century a whole church with its pastor emigrated from Massachusetts to Liberty County, Georgia; and that county is the Eden of Georgia to this day. It is a proverb that the child is father of the man. The same law controls the life of institutions. What they are during their forming period, they continue to be. This is the reason why this Institution owes its character to Dr Alexander and Dr Miller. Their controlling influence is not to be referred so much to their learning, or to their superior abilities, as to their character and principles.

It was of course not peculiar to them that they were sincere, spiritual, Christian men. This may be said of the founders of all our Theological Seminaries. But there are different types of religion even among true believers. The religion of St Bernard and of John Wesley, of Jeremy Taylor, and of Jonathan Edwards, although essentially the same, had in each case its peculiar character. Every great historical Church has its own type of piety. As there are three persons in the Trinity, the Father, the Son, and the Holy Spirit, so there appear to be three general forms of religion among evangelical Christians. There are some whose religious experience is determined mainly by what is taught in the Scriptures concerning the Holy Spirit. They dwell upon his inward work on the heart, on his indwelling, his illumination, on his life-giving power; they yield themselves passively to his influence to exalt them into fellowship with God. Such men are disposed more or less to mysticism.

There are others whose religious life is determined more by their relation to the Father, to God as God; who look upon Him as a sovereign, or law-giver; who dwell upon the grounds of obligation, upon responsibility and ability, and upon the subjective change by which the sinner passes from a state of rebellion to that of obedience.

Then there are those in whom the form of religion, as Dr Boardman has said, is distinctly Christological. I see around me Alumni whose heads are as grey as my own. They will unite with me in testifying that this is the form of religion in which we were trained. While our teachers did not dissuade us from looking within and searching for evidences of the Spirit's work in the heart, they constantly directed us to look only unto Jesus – Jehovah Jesus – Him in whom are united all that is infinite and awful indicated by the name Jehovah; and all that is human, and tender, and sympathetic, forbearing and loving, implied in the name Jesus. If any student went to Dr Alexander, in a state of despondence, the venerable man was sure to tell him, 'Look not so much within. Look to Christ. Dwell on his person, on his work, on his promises, and devote yourself to his service, and you will soon find peace.'

When I was about leaving Berlin on my return to America, the friends whom God had given me in that city were kind enough to send me an Album, in which they had severally written their names, and a few lines as remarks. What Neander wrote was in Greek, and included these words: 'Nothing in ourselves, all things in the Lord; whom alone to serve is a glory and a joy.' These words our old professors would have inscribed in letters of gold over the portals of this Seminary, there to remain in undiminished brightness as long as the name of Princeton lingers in the memory of man.

Again, Drs Alexander and Miller were not speculative men. They were not given to new methods or new theories. They were content with the faith once delivered to the saints. I am not afraid to say that a new idea never originated in this Seminary. Their theological method was very simple. The Bible is the Word of God. That is to be assumed or proved. If granted; then it follows, that what the Bible says, God says. That ends the matter.

There recently resided in this village a venerable lady, as distinguished for her strength of character as for her piety. A sceptical friend once said to her, 'My dear madam, it is impossible that a woman of your sense can believe that story in the Bible, about the whale swallowing Jonah.' She replied with emphasis, 'Judge, if the Bible said that Jonah swallowed the whale, I would believe it.' That may have been said by others ; I know it was said by her. I am not authorized to affirm that Dr Alexander would say the same thing. But he would come pretty near it. And he is no true Princetonian who will not come as near to it as he can.

But admitting that the Bible is the Word of God, there are different principles of interpretation which may be applied to it. Instead of understanding it in its plain historical sense, there are those who say that the letter killeth, the spirit maketh alive; that the literal sense amounts to nothing; that it is the hidden mystical sense which alone is of value. Others adopt what may be called the philosophical method. They admit that there are doctrines in the Bible, which are the objects of faith in the common people; but these are only the forms under which lie abstract truths, which it is the business of the philosopher to elicit. He throws the doctrinal formulas of Christianity into his retort and transmutes them into gas; thus losing the substance with the form. Thus the doctrine of Providence, or the control of all events by an extramundane, personal God, who governs by his voluntary agency the operations of second causes, working with them or without them, so that it rains at one time and not at another, according to his good pleasure; all this is evaporated into cosmical arrangements, leaving us no other God to pray to than the forces of nature. The same principle is applied to the doctrines of redemption. We were taught by our venerable fathers to take the Bible in the sense in which it was plainly intended to be understood.

The principles above stated are those on which those who founded this Institution acted. These are the principles which have determined its character, and give it its hold on the hearts of its Alumni.

Brethren, I said I am an Alumnus. I know the feelings with which you revisit your Alma Mater. Those feelings are very complex, including those with which children return to the home of their childhood, and those with which a man, with uncovered head and unsandalled feet, enters the cemetery of his fathers. Here are the tombs of Dickinson and Burr, of Edwards, of Davies and of their illustrious successors in the presidency of our sister-institution. Here lie the ashes of Archibald Alexander and of Samuel Miller. The memory of these men constitutes the aureola which surrounds the brows of Princeton, a glory which excites no envy, and yet attracts all eyes.

After the benediction had been pronounced by the Rev. Dr Musgrave, of Philadelphia, the meeting of the Alumni was called to order, a constitution adopted, and the Rev. John C. Backus, D.D., of Baltimore, was chosen President, and the Rev. Dr. Wm. E. Schenck, Secretary. After a public dinner, the Alumni Association met again at 3.30 p.m., in the Church, for the purpose of hearing congratulatory speeches from representative delegations, and receiving written addresses from friends not present.

Speeches were made by Rev. J. L. Porter, D.D., LL.D., of Belfast, Ireland, as a special representative of the Assembly's College in that city; by the Rev. James McCosh, D.D., LL.D., President of the College of New Jersey, as the appointed representative of the theological faculties of the Free Church, United Presbyterian and Reformed Presbyterian Churches of Scotland; by the Rev. Hugh Smyth, of Whitehouse, near Belfast, Ireland, as the appointed representative of Magee College, Londonderry, Ireland; by the Rev. Henry B. Smith, D.D., LL.D., as the representative of Union Theological Seminary, N.Y. City; by the Rev. Melanchthon W. Jacobus, D.D., LL.D., as representative of the faculty of the Western Theological Seminary, Allegheny City, Pennsylvania; by Professor Egbert C. Smyth, D.D., of the Theological Seminary of Andover, Massachusetts; by Rev. Theodore D. Woolsey, D.D., LL.D., Ex-President of Yale College; by the Rev. R. S. Vermilye, D.D., of Hartford, Professor in the Theological Institute of Connecticut; by the Rev. Joseph T. Cooper, D.D., Professor of the United Presbyterian Theological Seminary, Allegheny City, Penna.; by the Rev. Charles P. Krauth, D. D., of Philadelphia, Professor in the Theological Seminary of the Evangelical Lutheran Church; by the Rev. Francis L. Patton, Professor in the Presbyterian Seminary of the North-west; by the Rev. Joseph Packard, D.D., Professor in the Protestant Episcopal Theological Seminary of Virginia; by the Rev. E. P. Rodgers, as representative of the Reformed (Dutch) Church, and the faculty of the Rutger's Theological Seminary, New Brunswick, N.J.; by Rev. S. H. Kellogg, D.D., Professor in the Presbyterian Theological Training School, Allahabad, Northern India; and by his classmate Doctor Ravaud K. Rodgers, and by Doctor Irenaeus Prime of the *New York Observer*, and the Rev. Alfred Nevin, D.D., as the representative of the Alumni of the Allegheny Theological Seminary.

Deputations were also present from the Baptist Theological Seminary, Newton, Mass.; from the Reformed Theological Seminary at New Brunswick; from the United Presbyterian Seminary at Newburgh, N.Y.; from the Drew Theological Seminary at Madison, N.J., and the Crozer Theological Seminary at Upland, Pa. The Universities of the City of New York and of Pennsylvania, Union, Lafayette, Rutger's, and Bowdoin Colleges also were represented by their Presidents, or other members of their Faculties.

Letters were presented from the Faculties of Belfast Presbyterian College, signed in their behalf by W. D. Killen, D.D., President of the Faculty; from the Theological Professors of the Reformed Presbyterian Church, Scotland, signed by Wm. H. Goold, D.D., Wm. Binny, D.D., and Wm. Symington; from the United Presbyterian Presbytery of Edinburgh, signed by Wm. Reid, Moderator, and Wm. Bruce, Clerk. Also the following, (given as a specimen):

To the Rev. Charles Hodge, D.D., *Princeton, New Jersey*

Reverend Sir,—We, the Principals and Professors of the Theological Faculties of the Free Church of Scotland at Edinburgh, Glasgow and Aberdeen, desire to offer our most cordial congratulations to you on your entrance on the fiftieth year of your Professorship in the Theological Seminary at Princeton.

We only express to yourself what, on occasions without number, we have expressed to others, when we say that we regard your services in the cause of revealed truth, extending over half a century, as of inestimable value, and that we look on you as one of the chief instruments raised up by the Head of the Church, in these times of doubt and contention, for maintaining in its purity the faith once delivered to the saints.

While the *Princeton Review*, under your management, has continued from year to year to bear testimony fearlessly, yet firmly, for the truths of God's Word, and to commend them alike to the understanding and the conscience, and while your Commentaries have placed these truths in a similar light before the mass of readers, your *Systematic Theology*, the crown of your labours, has brought together the invaluable information and reasoning of your Articles and Lectures, and forms a Treasury of Evangelical truth expressed in a spirit eminently calm and Christian, which will extend still more widely the wholesome influence of your life and labours.

We congratulate you further on the honourable and distinguished place which you hold in the esteem of the whole Presbyterian Church, and of all churches that prize Evangelical truth, – on the affectionate regard so warmly cherished for you by your students both past and present, – and on the happy domestic influence which through God's blessing, has given to the Church sons like-minded with yourself, following in your footsteps, and aiding in your work.

It is our earnest prayer, and that of the whole church with which we are connected, that you may yet long be spared to your family, to the Seminary, and the Church universal, and eminently blessed in such further labours as your strength may enable you to undertake, and that in God's good time an entrance may be ministered to you abundantly into the everlasting kingdom of our Lord and Saviour Jesus Christ.

(*Edinburgh*)
ROBERT S. CANDLISH, D.D.,
Principal of the New College, Edinburgh

ALEXANDER DUFF, D.D., LL.D.,
Professor of Evangelistic Theology

GEORGE SMEATON, D.D.,
Professor of Exegetical Theology

ROBERT RAINY, D.D.,
Professor of Church History

A. B. DAVIDSON, LL.D., D.D.,
Professor of Hebrew, etc.

JAMES MacGREGOR, D.D.
Professor of Systematic Theology

WILLIAM G. BLAIKIE, D.D. LL.D.
Professor of Apologetic and Pastoral Theology

JOHN DUNS. D.D., F.R.S.E..
Professor of Natural Science

(*Glasgow and Aberdeen*)
PATRICK FAIRBAIRN, D.D.,
Principal of Free Church College, Glasgow

GEORGE C. M. DOUGLAS, D.D.,
Professor of Hebrew in the F. C. College, Glasgow

ISLAY BURNS, D.D.,
Professor of Divinity, F. C. College, Glasgow

JAMES LUMSDUN, D.D..
Principal and Senior Professor of Theology, F. C. College, Aberdeen

DAVID BROWN, D.D.
(*Princeton and Aberdeen*)
Professor of Theology and Church History, Aberdeen

WM. ROBERTSON SMITH,
Professor of Hebrew, etc., F. C. College

(This address was elegantly engrossed on vellum and forwarded in a purple morocco case.)

Also from the Faculty of Magee Presbyterian College, Londonderry, Ireland, signed by Thomas Witherow, Richard Smyth, James G. Shaw, John J. Given, J. T. McGaw, Henry Shell McKee and J. R. Leebody.

From the Theological Faculty of the University of Edinburgh, signed in their behalf by the Dean, Thomas J. Crawford, D.D. From the Professors of Theology in the United Presbyterian Church of Scotland, signed by James Harper, D.D., N. McMichael, D.D., John Eadie, D.D., LL.D.. and John Cairns, D.D.

Also from the Theological Seminaries at Bangor, Boston, New Haven, Auburn, the Divinity School of the Protestant Episcopal Church at Philadelphia, the Lutheran Theological Seminary at Gettysburg, the United Presbyterian Seminary of the Northwest, the Union Theological Seminary of Virginia, from the Faculty and from a Committee of the Students of the Seminary at Columbia, S.C, the Southern Baptist Theological Seminary at Greenville, S. C, the Theological Department of Cumberland University at Lebanon, Tenn., Danville Theological Seminary, Ohio, and the youngest born of all our Seminaries, the Presbyterian Seminary at San Francisco, Cal. From Williams and Amherst Colleges, Mass., and from Dartmouth, New Hampshire, from Hampden Sidney College, Virginia, and Westminster College, Missouri, and from the University of Mississippi, from the venerable Gardiner Spring, New York City, from many Alumni of Princeton in the Northwest, and from Chiengmai, North Laos, Farther India.

The letter from his life-long friend, Bishop McIlvaine, was as follows:

CINCINNATI, March 8, 1872

. . . As one of the associates and friends of Dr Hodge, than whom there can be but very few living whose loving associations began so early, or under circumstances so calculated to make it abiding, I cannot withhold an expression of lively interest in the contemplated celebration, as a rendering of honour to whom it is most justly due, and of praise and thanksgiving to the fountain of all wisdom and grace for having given to His Church on earth for so many years a light so bright and shining.

It is now some fifty-eight years since, while students together in the College of my native State, our friendship began; and nearly as many years since, by the grace of God making us new creatures in Christ Jesus, we became brethren one of another, in a very near and affectionate association. We were then, as now, of different churches in the one ever-living Church of Christ; but I am thankful to be able to say, that no dividing lines have ever touched our oneness of heart, or hindered the consciousness and manifestation of that confiding Christian attachment with which our religious life began.

It is under these circumstances that I regard with great pleasure the intended meeting and its object. It is very meet and right thus to acknowledge the goodness of God in having given and preserved to the work of His truth in the earth, during so many years of exacting study and labour, a teacher so efficient and beloved, and an author so enlightened and wise ; at whose lips so many have learned how to make known and defend the doctrine of Christ, and for whose writings of eminent learning and power, the whole Church is deeply indebted to the grace which made him sufficient for such valuable service.

Desiring my respectful and fraternal regards to those who shall meet together on the 24th of April, and hoping to meet them in that blessed Assembly and Communion of which it will be the universal joy to ascribe all honour and glory 'to Him that sitteth on the throne and to the Lamb forever and ever', I remain,

Your friend and brother,

Chas. P. McIlvaine

All the addresses and letters were dignified as well as full of kindness and respect. The testimony of Dr Charles P. Krauth, as the most active as well as earnest champion of Lutheranism in America, 'to the candour, love of truth, and perfect fairness which characterized all Dr Hodge's dealings' with the doctrines of Churches differing from his own, was the one particular personal vindication to which Dr Hodge referred afterwards with the most emphatic satisfaction.

During the afternoon, while these congratulatory addresses were being made Dr Hodge remained for the most part out of sight, sitting or reclining on the sofa in the pulpit behind the stage. Ex-President, Theodore D. Woolsey, LL.D., stood on the stage close by the side of the pulpit where Dr Hodge lay. When the former spoke tenderly of the affection he had cherished for his friend ever since 1828 when the latter had ministered words of Christian 'cheer, comfort and of strength' to his heart, then in darkness, Dr Hodge suddenly rose and interrupted him with a kiss.

Dr Boardman said to him, while he was lying there, as the long series of laudatory addresses closed, 'How did you stand all that?' 'Why,' said he, with a pleasant smile, 'very quietly. It didn't seem at all to be me they were talking about. I heard it all as of some other man.'

The editor of the *New York Observer* wrote:

It was a day of rare and memorable interest to the graduates who returned to the arms of their old mother, meeting their surviving teacher and one another, standing again by the graves of their departed and venerated professors. Of the first class, that of 1812–13, only one survives, James Hill Parmelee of Ohio; of the class of 1813–14 only one, John Ross of Indiana; of 1814–15, only one, Thomas Alexander of Indiana. None of these were present. Of the class of 1815–16 two live, Salmon Strong and Gilbert Morgan; the latter was present in a cheerful, bright old age. In the next class was Charles Hodge, who entered the Seminary in 1816, fifty-six years ago. Of his class George S. Boardman, Benjamin Gildersleeve, Samuel S. Hatch, John Johns, Aaron D. Lane, Constant Southworth, William B. Sprague, and Thomas S. Wickes are among the living. Of those who are now above the stars, and who are well known in the Church, from that class, were Artemas Boies, William Chester, Sylvester Easton, John Goldsmith, William James, William Nevins, Absalom Peters, William C. Woodbridge and Henry Woodward. Taking the dead and the living it was certainly a remarkable class. In the next was Bishop

McIlvaine, Caruthers, Coe, Crane, Austin, Dickinson, David Magie, S. S. Smucker and Thomas M. Strong.

Princeton Theological Seminary has given instructions in her halls to 2969 men, and of these 2700 (before his death in 1878 it amounted to over 3000), have sat at the feet of Dr Hodge!!! Among them are men who have been the shining lights of the Church, and yet they are not the brightest stars in his crown. Multitudes of men unknown to fame; of whom some have taken their lives in their hands and gone far hence to the heathen, and others in retired parishes who have kept the faith and fed the hopes of the Church, turning many sinners to righteousness and guiding them to heaven, will in the day when the jewellery of God is gathered, be as brilliant crowns of Dr Hodge's rejoicing, as those who have stood in what is called the bright places of Israel. Then who can estimate the extent of that one man's power over the human mind? And as that power has been in moral influence mainly, what estimate can be put on its effect on the destiny of the country and of individual souls? His eye is not yet dim, nor his natural force abated. He still discharges every duty with ability and regularity. He is cheerful, fond of that humour that good men always enjoy, and which tends to longevity, usefulness here and hereafter. In the midst of his family and friends he is playful, bright and genial, and takes the way of life as comfortably as any other intellectual and laborious man. His form is portly, his face ruddy, his eye lighted with love, and his voice as sweet as in youth.

The evening was set apart to a reception of the friends of Dr Hodge from all parts of the land, and from abroad, at his own residence. Over the doors were significant figures 1822–1872. The Seminary building was illuminated, and in every becoming way the affection and admiration of the Alumni for their venerated preceptor was gracefully manifested, and gratefully accepted.

In his private journal, under date, he notices the fact that his aged brother, now blind, and all his children, and all his own children and grandchildren were gathered around him at the time:

April 24th. The apex of my life. The Semi-centenary Anniversary of my connection with the Seminary as Professor. The day, by the blessing of God, was fine, and the celebration a wonderful success. The attendance of Alumni very large; delegations of other institutions numerous, and of the highest character; the congratulations from all at home and abroad of the most gratifying kind, altogether affording an imposing and most affecting testimony of the unity of the faith, and of common love to the same gospel, and to our common God and Saviour Jesus Christ.

13

HIS LAST YEARS, FROM 1872 TO
HIS DEATH, JUNE 19TH, 1878

*His Appearance and Habit of Mind – The Object of General Love,
in the Family, the Seminary and among His Students – The Death of
His Brother, Dr H. L. Hodge of Philadelphia – Biographical Sketch
– Visit of the General Assembly of 1872 to Washington – The Evangelical Alliance, New York, 1873 – Historical Sermon Delivered at
the Re-opening of the Chapel of the Theological Seminary, Sept. 27th,
1874 – Latest Correspondence and Interviews with His Friend,
Bishop Johns – The Appointment of His Assistant and Successor –
His Eightieth Birthday –His Writings during These Last Years*

FROM THIS TIME TO THE END, he was an old man visibly ripening
for another life. Compared with most men, and considering his
sedentary life and the amount of intellectual work he had accomplished, he was, with good reason, regarded as having survived his
years in a condition of excellent preservation. With the exception of
a few attacks of acute disease, his general health was very good. His
complexion, always fair, was beautiful in its perfect clearness and
soft roseate brightness. His blue eyes became more and more sweet
in their expression, and together with his strong yet gentle and flexible mouth overflowed with benevolence and humour, or at times
with reverence and melting devotion and love. As his old friend,
ex-president Woolsey, had wished for him at his semi-centennial,
he had 'a sweet old age'. No phrase could express it more perfectly.
The controversies were all past. The old warrior hung his arms upon

Charles Hodge in later years.

Charles Hodge's study. See 'The Gatherings in the Study', p. 257.

Charles Hodge's house, built in 1824. See pp. 49, 103.

the wall, as he rested under the clear skies of universal peace. He still followed and took interest in the conflict of opinion. But his own part was done. Although delayed for a time, the complete and universal victory of the cause, for which he had so long contended, was absolutely sure. His faith was the substance of things hoped for, and for him the triumph was virtually come.

All who loved Christ were heartily loved and cherished by him. He believed in the Holy Catholic Church, and in the Communion of Saints. He wrote in pencil with trembling lines on one of his 'Conference Papers', not long before his end, that he believed that the vast majority of the human race were to share the beatitudes and glories of his Lord's redemption. He was conscious of past sins and of present imperfections, but where sin had abounded grace did much more abound. More and more habitually he looked upward instead of inward. His heart was filled with hope and joy, as his face was made to shine by Him who was 'the health of his countenance, and his God'. He had no disappointments, no vain regrets; the past with all its contents he offered through Christ to God. He had no fears for the future, for there is no fear in love; perfect love had cast out all fear. He had no jealousies; he retained the uneasy sense of no old wounds nor injuries. He loved all in the sense of benevolence, and in the higher sense he loved all the brethren, admiring and rejoicing in their graces and sympathizing in their conflicts and their joys. And all parties, as far as he was known, came to love him. As he once said of his friend, Dr John Maclean, he also became the best beloved man in any circle in which he was embraced. The *odium theologicum* [theological hatred], with which he had been credited, both as subject and occasion, met with a strange transfiguration. The storms of the day made the peace and beauty of the setting sun more rich and wonderful. Supreme devotion to truth was once again proven to be a genuine form of supreme love to God and man.

There is always something essentially pathetic even in the brightest and balmiest late autumnal day. To the eye of faith it is the season which prepares after the interval of a short sleep in winter, for a new and more glorious spring. But to the eye of sense, it is, nevertheless, the end of the year. So was it with the autumn of this life. Though he was generally well, he was weak, and often very weary. Though he was beautiful, it was the wasting beauty of the fading leaf. And this was in perfect accord with the spirit of his own mind. Though he reclined with unwavering confidence upon a supernatural hope, his spirit and life were eminently natural. Though he had no fear, yet he had no desire to die. He looked beyond the world rather than rose entirely above it. His interest in all human things was genuine and strong, and his cheerfulness was never failing, yet often tinged with a pathetic wistfulness, arising from an habitual sense of the imminence of his own departure.

He delighted more and more in reminiscences of past events and persons. The friends of his early years were all gone, but their memory was very precious. The improvements which, during these last years were so extensively made in the buildings of the College and Seminary interested him exceedingly, and he was glad that he was privileged to see them before the final closing of his eyes on all earthly scenes. But his great delight was in his grand-children. Two families of them lived in the same village with him, and made as free of his study and of the arms of his great chair as his own children had done a generation earlier. All their smart sayings were reported to him, and repeated by him with the greatest zest. He knew and maintained all of their respective points of excellence and superiority with the zeal of a partisan. He was always on the alert in providing presents for them on all their anniversaries of birthdays and Christmas, and in selecting and dispatching appropriate St Valentines with a gleeful delight equal and like to that of the young recipients themselves. His love was faithfully returned by them all, and none, except the youngest, will ever forget the frequent and delightful occasions when all the resident family gathered with loving reverence around grandfather's chair.

Before he died he was for some years the oldest survivor of his entire family clan. Children and grand-children, nephews, grand-nephews and cousins in various degrees looked up to him with affection and pride, and constantly cheered his last days by their visits, and testimonials of sympathy and reverence.

This singular love and reverence was not confined to the circles of his kindred or of his private friends. It extended to his colleagues in the faculty, to the younger ministry, to all his old students, and beyond his own denomination to all Christian people to whom either his person or his reputation was known.

An old pupil under the pseudonym of 'Augustin', wrote in the *Presbyterian*, May 6th, 1876:

The late meeting of the Princeton Theological Seminary was a time of refreshing to all who participated in it. The face of our dear old Professor Hodge, broke out constantly into smiles of holy joy, as he sat like a father in the midst of his sons. And when his voice faltered and the tears came into his eyes, as he gave his reminiscences of his classmate and life-long friend, Bishop Johns (recently dead) or undertook to express his love for us, and his interest in the Seminary with which his life had been identified, what he called his weakness was stronger than his words, even as the showers of heaven fall no less potently on the flowers in the earth than the clear shining of the sun. It is a precious and glorious sight to behold an old age so green and graceful, to see one so eminent in intellect, so abundant in labours, so honoured in the world, as simple and tender and affectionate as a little child prepared for our Father's house in heaven. If this should meet his eye and offend him, he will forgive it, when he knows the pen that writes it is dipped in a heart that is melted in his love.

From about 1868 to the year of his death, each graduating class at the very last took a special, personal farewell of Dr Hodge. After receiving their diplomas, and the valedictory charge, and benediction of the representative of the Board of Directors, the class formed a circle with Dr Hodge at the centre, in the middle of the front campus.

> They sang (at least in April, 1869) several verses of the hymn, 'All hail the power of Jesus' name', and the verse of the missionary hymn beginning, 'Shall we whose souls are lighted', etc. Then making a close ring, each one crossing his arms, they held hand by hand, and sang 'Blest be the tie that binds', and then the Long-Metre Doxology. After that. Dr Hodge pronounced the Benediction. He then shook hands with each student, and each student shook hands with all the others, and they separated.

THE DEATH OF HIS BROTHER, DR HUGH L. HODGE OF PHILADELPHIA

The winter of 1872–3 was characterized by numerous waves of intense cold, recurring after intervals of about ten days or two weeks. On Monday, the twenty-fourth of February, one of these periods occurred. Dr H. L. Hodge, then in his ordinary health, and vigorous beyond most men of his age, was exposed to the cold while visiting patients up to ten o'clock that night. Upon his return to his home a letter was read to him from a widow of a physician in Virginia, whose husband had been a pupil of his in the long-past, in her poverty appealing to him for aid. Late as the hour was he called for his checkbook, and signed a check for her relief. This was the last time he ever used his pen. Fit ending to a life of unceasing charity. After conversing pleasantly with his son and daughter for a while, and sitting alone in his office as his custom was, he retired to bed about midnight. He was immediately seized with *angina pectoris* [a heart attack], and was found by his son, also a physician, in an unconscious condition. He was revived, and kept alive for twenty-six hours, until all his children had been gathered to his bedside, by frequent resort to artificial respiration. When awake he was perfectly conscious, full of humility, and love, faith, and peace. 'Let there be no eulogy', was the only injunction he laid upon his pastor. But innumerable patients, and pupils, witnesses and beneficiaries of his bounty in all parts of the land, and the Second Presbyterian Church, of which he was the preserver and second founder, bear witness alike to his wisdom and his goodness, to his self-denial and his munificence. When the despatch arrived in Princeton, on Tuesday, announcing his probably fatal illness, his brother Charles was forced to go to his own bed instead of to the bedside of his brother. And soon after his return, on the 3rd of March, from the funeral, he was attacked in his nervously prostrated condition, with a severe congestion of the chest, which came near being fatal, and which confined him to the house until the first week of April.

DR HODGE TO BISHOP JOHNS

PRINCETON, March 4th, 1872

Dear John:—We are left like two old trees standing almost alone. The fewer the dearer. My brother's death was entirely unexpected. He was perfectly well, and far stronger than I am. He was out attending his patients all Monday morning, and what of late was unusual with him, went out again in the afternoon, and remained out until it was so dark some one had to bring him home. That day was one of the severest of the season. It was that exposure in the opinion of his physicians, killed him, although its effects were not immediately manifest. He went to bed apparently in his usual health, but at midnight was heard to fall. His son, on reaching the room, found him lying on the floor unconscious. It was not apoplexy, but *angina pectoris*. His heart had ceased to act, and breathing was entirely suspended.

By artificial respiration he was gradually restored, and was entirely himself; his mind was clear as ever, and so continued until the end. But through the day at irregular intervals his heart would cease to act and his breathing ceased. By a renewal of artificial inflation of the lungs he would revive again. This occurred thirty or forty times, he gradually getting weaker, and at last, twenty-six hours after the attack, hc finally cxpircd.

The dear man was greatly blessed. No one touched his body after his death but his sons.[1] They prepared him for his coffin, laid him in it; carried him down stairs, carried him in the church, and carried him to his grave and lowered his body to its last resting-place. So that a lovely glory surrounded him to the last.

Dear John, let us pray for each other.

Yours as ever,
CHARLES HODGE

The following account of the life and character of Dr Charles Hodge's only brother and life-long friend and benefactor, is extracted from a *Memoir of H. L. Hodge, M.D., LL.D.*, prepared for Philadelphia County Medical Society, by William Goodell, M.D.

In 1820, Dr Hodge returned from India, but with means too limited to carry out the long cherished prosecution of his studies in Europe. The voyage had proved a commercial failure, but, nothing daunted, he opened an office in Walnut Street, opposite Washington Square. Soon after he was elected to the Southern Dispensary, and, a few months later, to the Philadelphia Dispensary. In these rich fields of practice he gained much experience, and acquired those habits of close observation and original research which ever after characterized him. He soon became a man of mark, for in the summer of 1821, he was selected to teach the anatomical class of Prof Horner, who was then absent in Europe. So acceptably did he fill this position, that in 1823 he was appointed to the Lectureship on Surgery in Dr

---

[1] Three Presbyterian ministers, one Presbyterian elder, and one Episcopal minister. Five beautiful and holy sons.

Chapman's Summer School, which, in 1837, became a chartered institution, under the name of the 'Medical Institute'. Of these lectures he was justly proud, for on them he was then able to spend all his time and strength. Old practitioners still refer to them in terms of high praise.

In September of the same year he gained a long-coveted position on the staff of the Philadelphia Hospital, and his practice began now steadily to increase. In 1828, at the age of thirty-two, he married Margaret E. Aspinwall, the daughter of John Aspinwall, a well-known merchant of New York city. From this union seven sons were born, of whom five are living. One is the well-known surgeon who bears his father's name; the rest are clergymen. After a happy married life of thirty-eight years, in 1866, this good wife and good mother died.

Thus far, Dr Hodge had concentrated all his energy on anatomy and surgery. His tastes lay in these directions; both these branches he had taught with great acceptance; as a surgeon, he was fast winning his way to fame. But a complete and very unexpected turn now took place in all his plans. The dim oil-lamps of his college days, his habits of late study, had greatly injured his eyesight, and compelled him to wear glasses of very high power. Year by year his vision so surely failed that he was at last warned to direct his ambition into new channels. Other circumstances confirmed him in making this change. The health of Dr Thomas C. James, the Professor of Midwifery in the University of Pennsylvania, was beginning to fail. Dr William P. Dewees, the heir-apparent to his chair, and the most brilliant of American obstetricians, had long passed the noontide of life. For many years the brothers Joseph and Harvey Klapp had enjoyed the pick of the midwifery practice of a rapidly-growing city. But, at this juncture, the one died, and the other retired to his secluded country-seat in the wilds of West Philadelphia. These accidents and opportunities at once determined Dr Hodge to give up, but with a bitter heart, his long-cherished specialty of surgery for that of obstetrics. Shortly after making this decision, he was enabled to exchange his lectureship of surgery for that of obstetrics, which the resignation of

Dr Dewees had left vacant. He was also the winning candidate in an excited canvass for a position on the staff of the Lying-in Department of the Pennsylvania Hospital.

For the possession of the empty chair, left vacant by the resignation of Dr Wm. P. Dewees, November 1835, a battle royal, one of giants, now took place. The struggle lay between two such men as Hugh L. Hodge and Charles D. Meigs, and was, therefore, a very hotly contested one. The strong claims of the rival candidates, and the very equally balanced influence of their respective friends, made the issue doubtful. Dr Hodge, who was a very modest man, could not be prevailed upon to visit any of the trustees. At last his friends refused to work for him unless he did so. He, therefore, provided himself with a list of their names and residences, and nerved himself up to this imposed and distasteful mission. As luck would have it, the first gentleman on whom he called was an upright but very eccentric Friend [Quaker], who, upon learning his errand, at once said, 'Young man, I should have thought better of thee, hadst thou not come.' In great confusion the modest candidate took his leave, tore up his list, and at once returned home. That trustee was the only one on whom he called. No persuasions, no entreaties, could thereafter move him to solicit another vote. But his friends, despite their threats, worked manfully for him. Perhaps this very modesty stood him in good stead. At any rate, he proved the successful candidate.

From the time of his election to the chair of obstetrics until his resignation in 1863, no teacher ever gave a more thorough or a more conscientious course of lectures. The strong feature of his teaching was not to display his knowledge, but to impart it. He possessed, in an eminent degree, those essentials of a good teacher – the *subtilitas explicandi* [precision of explanation], as well as the *subtilitas intelligendi* [precision of understanding]. Dependent, as he was, on account of imperfect vision, exclusively upon his memory, he yet delivered new lectures with the utmost neatness and precision. There was no faltering over a demonstration, no omission of a diagram. Although gifted with a fluent delivery, he used no trope or figure, and made no effort at oratorical display. So pure-minded was he, and so far removed from making 'points' – as they are technically called – that, when some madcap student distorted an accidental juxtaposition of words into a *double entendre*, his face flushed up with vexation. Over the young men who flocked to hear him, his influence was great and good. At the beginning and the end of each curriculum, they listened, with respectful and often tearful attention, to his happy words of greeting and tender words of parting. What graduate of those days can ever efface from his memory that gracious manner which seemed to convey a benediction, and that halo of goodness which floated about him? Men will come, and men will go, but we shall never see his like again.

During a large portion of Dr Hodge's life, the pressure of his professional engagements was so great as to prevent him from writing anything besides his early lectures on surgery and those on obstetrics. But during his early professional career he was one of the editors of the *North American Medical and Surgical Journal*, to which he contributed many reviews and original papers. Later in life imperfect vision hindered Dr Hodge from becoming a prolific writer. Besides several articles written for various medical journals, he published a memoir of Dr James, a eulogium on Dr Dewees, and a number of introductory lectures. One of these on criminal abortion, after being reprinted several times, was published with some additions under the title of *Foeticide*. In 1860 he published his work on *Diseases Peculiar to Women*, and in 1863 his great work on *Obstetrics*. In editing the latter, few of my hearers are aware of the difficulties he had to encounter; difficulties from which most men would have shrunk. From title-page to colophon this large work was written by an amanuensis at his dictation. The beautiful and original lithographs which enrich its pages gave him a world of trouble and anxiety. He knew that to a student a work on obstetrics without illustrations is practically valueless. But how were illustrations to be made whose accuracy a blind man could verify! This was a problem of difficult solution, one to which he devoted many anxious thoughts and sleepless nights. At last his son, Dr

H. Lenox Hodge, suggested the use of photography. Here, indeed, was the means presented, by which nature could be faithfully copied; here the prospect of making stepping-stones of the very obstacles which lay in his way. With a thrill of pleasure, he jumped at the idea, and fairly laughed aloud with joy. From the noble collection which he afterwards gave to the unrivalled museum of the University, a typical pelvis and foetal head were selected. The former was placed upon an appropriate stand, the latter he held in the proper position within the pelvic cavity to illustrate the various positions and presentations. In this manner they were photographed, but in the lithographic plates copied from these originals, the sustaining fingers and hand of the author were of course left out. In graceful recognition of this and other literary labours, and of his distinguished reputation, he was in 1871 honoured by his Alma Mater with the degree of LL.D.

As an author, the writings of Dr Hodge are characterized by clearness, by conscientious accuracy, and by great originality. He contemplated the soul of a subject, and not its mere habiliments. In proof of this, witness his remarkable papers on 'Synclitism,' and his careful study of the 'Mechanism of Labour'. Although aggressive when needful, his mind was strongly constructive, and not destructive. He pulled down to build up, but never for the mere sake of pulling down. Of too rugged an individuality to fashion himself to the modes and opinions of others, he thought out for himself with intense convictions of truth. These convictions he defended with rigid and drastic logic. To them he was always true; from them he never swerved. Like the builders of Jerusalem, he worked with a spear in one hand and a trowel in the other. But while clinging tenaciously to what he had elaborated, he dissented from the opinions of others with a courteous hospitality of thought, with perfect fair play. Such encounters never kindled into angry controversy, for it was not his system that he defended, but the truth, the truth as he interpreted it. In this respect he satisfied Schiller's definition of a true philosopher. By his loss a great gap is left in medical literature – a gap that is felt in other lands as well.

Thus far I have spoken of Dr Hodge as a physician, but great injustice would be done to his memory were this memoir to take note simply of the services he rendered to our common profession. In the sacred relations of kindred and of friendship, his love never chilled. By his kindness he won the affection of all who knew him; by his inflexible integrity he gained the respect of those who came in contact with him. In 1830 he became a member of the Second Presbyterian Church, a Church born of the fervour of his ancestors. His after life proved the sincerity of this step. He ever after walked as if he felt that 'the Christian was the world's Bible'. The calamity of his blindness, and that more grievous one of the death of his beloved wife, took sunlight from his eyes and sunshine from his heart, but he bore each with Christian fortitude. As a church member no one showed a greater consistency, a broader philanthropy, a more unstinted liberality, or set a brighter example of loyal Christian faith. Never once did this faith waver before the rude assaults and aggressive ventures of human thought. Two years before his death, when the congregation of his church decided to move further up town, he was unanimously chosen the Chairman of the Building Committee. On this new work he now bent all his strength. To it he subscribed munificently, and was active in raising contributions. Since he could not see, the various plans of the new church were carefully explained to him by the architect. None of them pleased him, and yet he found himself unable to make his criticisms in technical and therefore in intelligible language. With characteristic ingenuity, he took the books lying on the desk, and with them built up a structure which conveyed the idea of the plan ultimately adopted.

The last years of this strong-headed and strong-hearted man were not spent in idleness. His sight grew more and more dim, but his natural force did not abate, his brain did not grow weary, his hand lost not its cunning. Apart from giving much of his time and strength to Church matters, he continued to visit some old patients, and to keep up a lively interest in everything pertaining to his profession. All papers bearing on the branches which he had taught were read to him by some member of his family, or by some person regularly employed for this purpose. He dictated several papers for the *American Journal of the Medical Sciences*. Two of them on 'Synclitism' attracted much attention. Deeply impressed with the conviction that a lack of proper clinical instruction is the crying evil of our medical schools, he subscribed liberally towards the endowment of the noble Hospital of the University of Pennsylvania, which is soon to inaugurate a new and important departure in the medical education of this country.

My first acquaintance with Dr Hodge was made at this time of his life. We met in the library of the College of Physicians, where he was collecting material for some essay. I shall never forget his warm grasp and hearty shake as he took my hand in both of his. His kind words of encouragement are indelibly fixed in my memory; and so is the playful manner in which he took me to task – 'scolded' me, as he termed it – for some of my published writings which did not accord with his views. His noble but sightless face lighted up with pleasure when I told him that I had twice read his work on *Obstetrics* from beginning to end, and that it was the means of first awakening in me a love for his chosen branch of medicine. Other very pleasant interviews I had with him, for like pursuits and congenial tastes drew us together. On these occasions obstetric matters were always discussed. On this favourite topic he spoke so fluently, and was so much at home that, in order to follow him intelligently, the closest attention on my part was needed.

A happier man I never saw; his face beamed with smiles; his days seemed hymns of thanksgiving. Some natures, like vitreous bodies, become iridescent with age. But why, I often asked myself, why should he be otherwise? Why should he repine? Surrounded by devoted friends and loving children; with much grain stored away in the garner of his brain; with the consciousness of never having wasted the prerogatives of life; with a noble history behind him, and a glorious immortality before him, could earthly estate be more princely?

DEATH OF FRIENDS

Dr Charles Hodge writes in his journal: 'Came downstairs Friday, the 14th of March (1873), and heard within an hour of the death of two life-long friends, both College and Seminary fellow-students – the Rev, James V. Henry, who died at Jersey City, aged 75, and Charles P. McIlvaine, Bishop of Ohio, whose death in Florence had just been announced. I am almost alone.'

The wife of his colleague, Rev. A. T. McGill, D.D., had also died a few days previously. On that occasion he wrote to Dr McGill:

My afflicted friend and brother:—God has brought upon you the greatest of all bereavements, but you have the greatest of all consolations. You know that the companion of your life is now happy and glorious, forever free from all pain and sorrow, and forever blessed in the presence of the Lord. You cannot grieve, therefore, as those who have no hope. You know too that you will soon be reunited to be no more separated forever. And while you remain here still to labour and suffer in the service of the Lord, He will not leave you comfortless; he will send the Comforter, the Spirit of truth, to be with you and to dwell in you, and to give you the peace that passes all understanding. You can look backward as well as forward, and feed upon the recollection of all the excellence and goodness of her who was so long your own, and who now awaits you in heaven.

You have the consolation, which is a very great one, to know she was admired and loved, and is now lamented by all who knew her. No lady in this community was the subject of higher regard or more sincere affection. You are not alone. Your sons and daughters are about you to share your grief and to alleviate it by their devotion and tenderness.

I write not that I may comfort you, but that I may share with you in your sorrow, and mingle my thanksgiving with yours for the wonders of redeeming grace, which are never felt to be so precious as when the desire of our eyes is taken from us.

Praying that God may fill your heart with the assurance of his love, and with the consolations of his Holy Spirit, I am, my dear brother.

Yours in sincere affection,
CHARLES HODGE

THE VISIT OF THE GENERAL ASSEMBLY OF 1873 TO WASHINGTON

This General Assembly contained many of his old students, and also many strangers from a distance, especially of the late New-school branch of the Church, who had heard of his fame, and yet had never seen his face. Among many of both classes a strong desire to see him gradually gathered force. This led ultimately to the adjournment of the Assembly during the day-time of Wednesday, the 28th of May, and their visit as a body to Washington, in order to meet him as their guest at Willard's Hotel. An account of the whole matter is given in the following letter from Dr Joseph T. Smith, of Baltimore, who was on that occasion chairman of the Assembly's Committee of Arrangements.

BALTIMORE, April 8, 1880

REV. A. A. HODGE,—

Dear Doctor:—I have just returned from Washington, where I used all diligence to get the facts connected with your father's visit to the Assembly. I was able to get very little beyond what I already knew. During the session of the Assembly of 1873 in Baltimore there was a very general and very earnest desire expressed on the part of the members of the Assembly, and particularly those from a distance, to meet with your father. As Chairman of the Committee of Arrangements this was brought to me from many quarters, and the committee was anxious in some way to gratify it. Your father was then on a visit to his brother-in-law, General Hunter, in Washington. The first movement was to invite him to Baltimore, but to this he replied that his health would not permit, as he was then convalescent from a severe attack of acute bronchitis.

It was then proposed that the Assembly should visit Washington, and have an interview with him there. After some correspondence a delegation came on from Washington and invited the Assembly to spend a day there, assuring them that proper arrangements would be made for an interview with Dr Hodge. On the evening of the 27th of May the Assembly adjourned to meet at half-past 7 o'clock, p.m. on the 28th. The Moderator, Dr Crosby, was not able to go, but the greater portion of the Assembly went, with Dr Niccolls, the last Moderator present, acting in Dr Crosby's place.

They first repaired to the Capitol, and after a short address of welcome from the Washington Brethren, and a response from the Moderator, they united in singing the Long-Metre Doxology, in the Rotunda. Hence they repaired to the White House, where in the absence of the President, they were received by Secretary Fish and the ladies present. They then moved in a body to the grand dining-room in Willard's Hotel, where a rich collation had been provided by the Churches of Washington.

Dr Hodge, very feeble, and showing signs of great emotion, entered on the arm of Dr Niccolls, and took his seat by his side at the head of the table. The room, spacious as it is, was crowded, and the greatest interest was manifested in the proceedings. After quiet was secured an Address of Welcome was made by Dr Niccolls to the honoured guest of the occasion. Dr Hodge rose under great emotion, and replied, after which the brethren crowded around him with the greatest heartiness and unanimity with their congratulations. This action of the Assembly touched him very deeply. When first told of the desire thus to honour him he was almost overcome, and the cordial greeting he received on every side, he said, was among the most cherished recollections of his life. I am sorry that I cannot give you more than the above, but these are the main facts.

Yours in Christ,

J. T. SMITH

THE EVANGELICAL ALLIANCE

In the early days of October 1873, the Sixth General Conference of the Evangelical Alliance, was held in the city of New York. Taken all together, as to its object, the character of its members, the value of their discussions, the vastness and enthusiasm of the attendant audiences, and the impression made upon the entire Christian community, this Conference was one of the memorable events in the history of American Christianity.

In an article entitled 'American Lights of the Evangelical Alliance, by Camera Obscura', printed in the *Sunday-school Times* for October 18th, 1873, the subject of this memoir is photographed thus:

> There is the Rev. Charles Hodge, D.D., LL.D., of Princeton Theological Seminary, the most impressive personality of the Alliance. Who ever saw a face more radiant, more serene, more suggestive? Strength lying in repose, sweetness and an indescribable innocence beam from his countenance. Dressed in a dress-coat and snowy cravat of the olden pattern, carrying a gold-headed ebony cane, upon the top of which he is wont to recline, he is growing old far too fast. When he addresses the audience, only those who are half-way toward the platform can have any pleasure in the hearing. Those beyond are only conscious of their loss by seeing how such as sit hard by are being fed.

The chief end of the Alliance is to promote and to exemplify the essential unity of evangelical Christendom, however widely distinguished by denominational differences, or separated by national or geographical barriers. The part assigned to Dr Hodge, therefore, struck the key-note for the whole Conference and the exercises of all its divisions. His subject was 'THE UNITY OF THE CHURCH BASED ON PERSONAL UNION WITH CHRIST'. His points were, 1st. 'The Unity of Individual Believers', first with Christ and then with each other, which has its ground in the indwelling of the Spirit and in faith. This is manifested (1) In their agreement in faith. They all essentially embrace the same system of truth. (2) In the sameness of their spiritual life or religious experience, and (3) In their mutual love, the bond of perfectness, which is founded first, on congeniality and second on relationship, and is manifested first in mutual recognition, and second, in a disposition to bear each other's burdens and to bear each other's wants. Secondly, 'The Unity of Individual Churches or Congregations'.

> The idea of the Church, therefore, as presented in the Bible, is that believers scattered over the world are a band of brethren, children of the same Father, subjects of the same Lord, forming one body by the indwelling of the Holy Ghost, uniting all to Christ as their living head. This indwelling of the Spirit makes all believers one in faith, one in their religious life, one in love. Hence they acknowledge each other as brethren and are ready to bear each other's burdens. This is the communion of saints. The Church, in this view, is the mystical body of Christ.
>
> But by a law of the Spirit, believers living in the same neighbourhood unite as Churches for public worship, and for mutual watch and care. These local Churches constitute one body, first, spiritually, because they are all subject to the same Lord, are animated by the same Holy Spirit, and are bound together by the bond of Christian love. Secondly, they are externally one body, because they acknowledge each other as Churches of Christ, and recognize each other's members, ordinances, ministers, and acts of discipline; and also because they are all subject to the same tribunal. That tribunal in the beginning was the apostles; now it is the Bible, and the mind of the Church, expressed sometimes in one way and sometimes in another.
>
> That this normal state of the Church has never been fully realized is to be referred partly to unavoidable circumstances, and partly to the imperfections of believers . . . In the present state of the world denominational Churches are, therefore, relatively a good. The

practical question is, What is their relation to each other? What are their relative duties? How may their real unity be manifested in the midst of these diversities.

3rd. 'Denominational Churches'. (1) Their first duty to each other is mutual recognition. (2) Their second duty is intercommunion. They owe then (3) recognition of each other's sacraments and orders, (4) non-interference, and (5) the duty of co-operation.

If the principles above stated be correct it is of the last importance that they should be practically recognized. If all Christians really believed that they constitute the mystical body of Christ on earth, they would sympathize with each other as readily as the hands sympathize with the feet, or the feet with the hands. If all churches, whether local or denominational, believed that they too are one body in Christ Jesus, then instead of conflict we should have concord; instead of mutual criminations we should have mutual respect and confidence; instead of rivalry and opposition we should have cordial co-operation. The whole visible Church would then present an undivided front against infidelity and every form of anti-Christian error, and the sacramental host of God, though divided into different corps, would constitute one army glorious and invincible.

Dr Hodge also took part in the extemporaneous discussion on Darwinism and the doctrine of Development in the Philosophical Section, held Oct. 6.

Under the title of 'Noticeable Things at the Alliance', in the *Presbyterian*, Oct. 18, 1873, Dr Cuyler of Brooklyn says:

The 'corns' of sectarianism have suffered occasionally, to be sure, when some hard logic set its boot heavily on them. This was the case when Dr Hodge trod squarely on the sore spot in 'close communionism' in his superb address; and some of our good Baptist brethren winced a little. This was inevitable. What does the Alliance signify but the free and open communion of all the faithful in Christ Jesus? Dr Hodge spoke with intense emotion, and was heard with intense interest.

One eminent foreign delegate said to me, 'It paid me for crossing the ocean just to see Dr Hodge during that glorious speech.'

The *Examiner and Chronicle* (Baptist), in an editorial on Oct. 9th, 1873, affirmed that Dr Hodge in that address had 'overlooked the claims of courtesy, propriety and justice'. In the *Presbyterian* of Nov. 1, 1873, Dr Hodge's answer is given. He says:

I was distinctly informed that no one was expected to speak in the name of the body which he addressed. He was to express his own views, for which no one was to be held responsible but himself. I find that every other member of the Alliance acted on the same principle that I did – expressing his own sentiments without intending to commit anybody else. Some of our scientific brethren expressed views on the Mosaic account of the creation, and of the modern theory of 'development' from which others dissented. No one took offence at this. Others again advocated the propriety of the Union of Church and State. We Americans were not thereby offended.

An Evangelical Alliance conducted on the principle that every member must agree with what every other member says, it seems to me must be a failure.

If you agree with me as to the design of the great convocation of Evangelical Christians which has been such a blessing and such an honour to the age in which we live, I am sure you will exonerate me from the charge of having violated the claims of 'courtesy, propriety and justice'.

Your brother in the bonds which no difference between Baptists and Pedo-baptists can sunder.

CHARLES HODGE

HISTORICAL SERMON DELIVERED AT THE
RE-OPENING OF THE CHAPEL, SEPT. 27, 1874

During the summer of 1874, by the generous provision of the munificent benefactor of the Seminary, Mr John C. Green, of New York city, the Chapel was thoroughly repaired, improved and beautified. On the occasion of its being re-opened for worship, on the 27th of September, the sermon was delivered by Dr Hodge as senior professor. This sermon is so delightful and valuable in its historical and biographical contents, that I feel it proper to insert a large portion of the text uncondensed:

> The first signal manifestation of the divine favour to this Institution was the selection of Dr Archibald Alexander and Dr Samuel Miller as its professors, and their being spared for nearly forty years to devote themselves to its service. It is admitted that the most important part of a man's life is the formative period of youth. The same is true of communities and institutions. If a college be dependent on the State, its character may vary with the change of parties in the State; but if it be independent, it bids fair to retain its original character from generation to generation. If a father commit his child to incompetent and wicked tutors and governors, the fate of the child is sealed; but if it be confided to faithful guardians, as a rule, it will grow up to be an ornament and a blessing. The favour of God to this infant Seminary was manifested in its being intrusted to the hands of men pre-eminently qualified for the sacred trust.
>
> They were in the first place eminently holy men. They exerted that indescribable but powerful influence which always emanates from those who live near to God. Their piety was uniform and serene; without any taint of enthusiasm or fanaticism. It was also Biblical. Christ was as prominent in their religious experience, in their preaching, and in their writings, as he is in the Bible. Christ's person, his glory, his righteousness, his love, his presence, his power, filled the whole sphere of their religious life. When men enter a Roman Catholic Church, they see before them a wooden image of Christ extended upon a cross. To this lifeless image they bow. When students entered this Seminary, when its first professors were alive, they had held up before them the image of Christ, not graven by art or man's device, but as portrayed by the Spirit on the pages of God's Word; and it is by beholding that image that men are transformed into its likeness

from glory to glory. It is, in large measure, to this constant holding up of Christ, in the glory of his person and the all-sufficiency of his work, that the hallowed influence of the fathers of this Seminary is to be attributed.

It often happens, however, that men are very pious without being very good. Their religion expends itself in devotional feelings and services, while the evil passions of their nature remain unsubdued. It was not so with our fathers. They were as good as they were pious. I was intimately associated with them, as pupil and colleague, between thirty and forty years. In all that time I never saw in either of them any indication of vanity, of pride, of envy, of jealousy, of insincerity, of uncharitableness, or of disingenuousness. I know that what I say is incredible. Nevertheless it is true. And it is my right and my duty to scatter these withered flowers upon their graves. Most men have reason to rejoice that their bosoms are opaque, but these holy men, as it always seemed to me, might let the sun shine through them.

Another characteristic of the men of whom I speak was their firm and simple faith in the Scriptures, and in the system of doctrine contained in the standards of our Church. Their faith was founded on the demonstration of the Spirit, and therefore could not be shaken. No Sunday-School scholar, no mother in Israel, could be more entirely submissive to the teachings of the Scriptures than were these venerable men. There was something sublime and beautiful in the humility of old Doctor Alexander, when he found himself at the feet of Jesus. There was no questionings of the reason, no opposition of the heart. The words of Scripture were received as the revelation of what is true and right from the highest source of truth and goodness. No one can estimate the influence of this trait of the character of our first professors operating through forty years on successive generations of their pupils.

There are theologians who exhort men to think for themselves, and to receive nothing on authority . . . And others who crave after novelty and aspire after originality . . . And others who have a philosophical disposition.

It pleased God that the first professors in this Seminary should belong to neither of these classes. They exhorted their students to be humble rather than high-minded. They had no fondness for new doctrines, or for new ways of presenting old ones; and they dreaded the thought of transferring the ground of faith from the rock of God's Word to metaphysical quicksands. For this reason Princeton Theological Seminary was regarded by the illuminati in every part of the land as very umbrageous, impenetrable to any ray of new light. This did not move the men of whom we speak. They had heard Christ say of certain men that the light that is in them is darkness. And knowing that man is blind as to the things of God, they thought it safer to submit to be guided by a divine hand, rather than, with darkness within and darkness without, to stumble on they knew not whither.

As to the method of instruction adopted by our first professors little need be said. They both used text-books where they could be had. Dr Alexander's text-book in theology was Turretin's *Theologia Elenchtica*, one of the most perspicuous books ever written. In the discussion of every subject it begins with the *Status Quæstionis* [state of the question], stating that the question is not this or that; neither this nor that, until every foreign element is eliminated, and then the precise point in hand is laid down with unmistakable precision. Then follow in distinct paragraphs, numbered one, two, three, and so on, the arguments in its support. Then come the *Fontes Solutionum*, or answers to objections. The first objection is stated with the answer; then the second, and so on to the end. Dr Alexander was accustomed to give us from twenty to forty quarto pages, in Latin, to read for a recitation. And we did read them. When we came to recite, the professor would place the book before him and ask, What is the State of the Question? What is the first argument? What is the second, etc.? Then what is the first objection and its answer? What the second, etc.? There were some of my classmates. Dr Johns, the present bishop of the Episcopal Church in Virginia, for example, who would day after day be able to give the State of the Question, all the arguments in its support in their order, all the objections and the answers to them, through the whole thirty or forty pages, without the professor saying a word to him. This is what in the College of New Jersey used to be called 'rowling'. Whatever may be thought of this method of instruction, it was certainly effective. A man who had passed through that drill never got over it. Some years ago I heard the late Bishop McIlvaine preach a very orthodox sermon in the Episcopal Church in this place. When we got home, it being a very warm day, he threw himself on the bed to rest. In the course of conversation he happened to remark that a certain professor failed to make any marks on the minds of his students. I said to him, 'Old Turretin, it seems, has left his mark on your mind.' He sprang from the bed, exclaiming, 'That indeed he has, and I would give anything to see his theology translated and made the text-book in all our Seminaries.' The Jesuits are wise in their generation, and they have adopted this method of instruction in their institutions.

Dr Alexander, however, did not confine himself to his text-book. He lectured from time to time on those doctrines which were exciting general attention. These lectures from year to year became more numerous, until they constituted an important part of his course. He was accustomed also to give out lists of theological questions, which the students were expected to answer in writing. On the departments of mental and moral philosophy, polemic and pastoral theology, his instructions were by lectures, so that his mind was constantly brought into contact with those of his students. His lectures on Pastoral Theology were devotional exercises, which we attended as we would attend church.

Dr Miller also had a text-book on Ecclesiastical History which he supplemented and corrected by a running commentary at each recitation. He, too, gave out lists of questions covering the whole course of biblical and church history. His instructions on Church Government and Discipline, and on the Composition and Delivery of Sermons, were by lectures. These venerable men were remarkably punctual and faithful in attending on all their official duties.

Their influence on the students was after all mainly religious, arising from the doctrines which they taught, the character which they exhibited, and the principles which they inculcated. To this must be added the power of calling the religious feelings into exercise, which Dr Alexander possessed beyond any man whom I have ever known. He had the gift of searching the heart; of probing the conscience; of revealing a man to himself; of telling him his thoughts, feelings, doubts and conflicts. As with a lighted torch he would lead a man through the labyrinth of his heart, into places which his intelligent consciousness had never entered. He would thus humble him, instruct him, comfort or strengthen him. He could melt his hearers to penitence, make their hearts burn within them, inspire them with zeal, and give them a foretaste of the joy that is unspeakable. This power he exerted not only in the pulpit, but in our Sabbath afternoon conferences, and in his addresses to the students at evening prayers. There are three of his sermons which I specially remember; one on Abraham's offering up Isaac; one on the transfiguration of Christ; and one on our Lord's passion. The only way in which I can give an idea of the impression produced by these discourses, is by saying that his hearers felt, in a measure, as they would have done had they been present at the scenes described. We left this Chapel after his sermon on the transfiguration, feeling that we had seen the Lord in his glory, at least as through a glass darkly. His sermon on the passion of Christ was delivered in the Church on a communion Sunday. The impression which it made was profound. The students became clamorous; they would take no denial of their request for its possession. I do not think that it was printed; but the manuscript came into our hands; and when I read it, there was nothing there but what is in the Gospels. So that the mystery of its power remained unsolved.

There was another peculiarity in Dr Alexander's preaching. He would sometimes pause and give utterance to a thought which had no connection with his subject, and then resume the thread of his discourse. He seemed to think that these thoughts were given to him for a purpose, and he sent them forth as arrows shot at a venture.

When a boy I attended a service which he conducted in the old school-house, which stood on the ground now occupied by the First Presbyterian Church. I sat in the back part of the room, on a shelf with my feet dangling half-way to the floor. The Doctor suddenly paused in his address, and stretching out his arm to attract attention, deliberately uttered this sentence, 'I don't believe a praying soul ever enters hell.' That bolt, I suspect, pierced more hearts than one. It may well be believed that more than one poor sinner in that little assembly, said to himself, ' If that be so, I will keep on praying while I keep on breathing.'

We all know that the man who is instrumental in bringing us near to God, who enables us to see the glory of Christ, who stirs up our hearts to penitence and love, becomes sacred in our eyes, and that the place in which we have enjoyed these experiences can never be forgotten. Hence the feeling which our old alumni cherish for this Seminary, is not pride, but a tender, sacred, love, as for the place in which they passed some of the holiest, happiest, and most profitable hours of their lives.

Owing to the peculiar power of Dr Alexander over the feelings, the students were more demonstrative of their regard for him than for Dr Miller. But in their heart of hearts, in the place where reverence dwells, in the inner temple of the soul, neither of these holy men stood higher than the other.

Dr Addison Alexander was appointed teacher of Hebrew in this Seminary in 1833. In 1836 he was elected professor of Biblical and Oriental Literature. He did not consent, however, to be inaugurated until two years later, although he discharged the duties of the chair to which he had been appointed. He continued connected with the Seminary as one of its professors until his death, February 1860.

I believe that I was rash enough to say on the floor of the General Assembly of 1860, that I thought Dr Addison Alexander the greatest man whom I had ever seen. This was unwise: both because there are so many different kinds of greatness; and because I was no competent judge. I feel free to say now, however, that I never saw a man who so constantly impressed me with a sense of his mental superiority – with his power to acquire knowledge and his power to communicate it. He seemed able to learn anything and to teach anything he pleased. And whatever he did, was done with such apparent ease as to make the impression that there was in him a reserve of strength, which was never called into exercise. The rapidity with which he accomplished his work was marvellous. The second volume of his Commentary on Isaiah, a closely printed octavo volume of five hundred pages, with all its erudition, was written, as I understand, during one summer vacation, which he passed in the city of New York. Few literary achievements can be compared to that.

He had two marked peculiarities. One was that although he had apparently the power to master any subject, he could not do what he did not like. Being in his youth very precocious and very much devoted to intellectual pursuits, he needed neither excitement nor guidance. He was, therefore, allowed to pass from one subject to another at pleasure. A habit of mind was thus induced which rendered it almost impossible for him to fix his attention on subjects which were disagreeable to him. There were consequently some departments of knowledge of which he was purposely ignorant. This was true of psychology, or mental philosophy. I never knew him to read a book on that subject. He never would converse about it. If when reading a book, he came across any philosophical discussion, he would turn over the leaves until he found more congenial matter. When Dr Schaff's work on *The Apostolic Age* came out, he was greatly delighted with it. The theory of historical development which it broached, he took no notice of. He did not even know it was there. When, therefore, he reviewed the book, he never adverted to one of its most marked characteristics. The same thing was true, in good measure, of natural science, to which he devoted very little attention. It was specially true of physiology and hygiene. It would be hard to find an educated man more profoundly ignorant of the structure of the human body or of the functions of its organs. Hence he was constantly violating the laws of health. He was a whole year seriously ill without knowing it : and only two or three days before his death, he said to me, 'Don't look so sad, I'm as well as you are.'

The other peculiarity referred to was his impatience of routine. He could not bear to go over the same ground, or to attend long to any one subject. Hence he was constantly changing his subjects of study and methods of instruction. He would begin to write a book, get it half done, and then throw it aside. Or, he would begin to write on one plan, and then change it for another. He occupied three different chairs in this Seminary. He first had the Old Testament department; then the Language and Literature of the New Testament. The friends of the Seminary cared little what he did, for whatever he undertook, he was sure to do so grandly that every one would be more than satisfied. As he advanced in life these peculiarities became less apparent. He was constantly getting his powers more under his own control. At the time of his death we flattered ourselves that he had before him twenty or thirty years for steady work. Then suddenly our great treasure ship went down – disappearing under the waves – a dead loss – leaving us, as we then felt, utterly bankrupt.

The departments in which he took the most interest were languages, literature, history, and above all, the Bible. His earliest reputation was as a linguist. It was known that he had without any instruction made himself so familiar with the Arabic that he had read the Koran through before he was fourteen. In the same way he learned Persic, and while but a lad delighted in reading the Persian poets. He then learned Hebrew, Chaldee and Syriac. He kept up his familiarity with the Greek and Latin classics through life. He read all the modern languages of Europe, unless the Slavonic dialects be excepted. His object in these studies was not simply the vocabulary and grammar of these languages, but their mutual relations, and specially the literary treasures which they contained. He was specially master of his own tongue. He had read all the leading English authors of every age. His style was a model of precision, perspicuity, felicity of expression, purity and force. His command of language did not seem to have any limit. He could speak in correct and polished English as easily as he could breathe. Extemporary speaking is an every-day matter. But I have known Dr Addison to come into this chapel, without having committed or written his sermon, and read it off from blank paper from beginning to end without hesitation or correction. He was constantly doing such things, which made those around him think he could do whatever he pleased.

As to his qualifications as a theological professor, the first in importance was his sincere and humble piety. Religion, however, even when genuine, assumes different forms in different persons. Some men it impels to live before the public as well as for the public. In others it leads rather to self-culture and intercourse with God. Dr Addison's life was in a great measure hidden. He never appeared in church-courts or in religious conventions. But although he lived very much by himself, he did not live for himself. All his powers were devoted to the service of Christ, as writer, teacher, and minister of the gospel. His temper was naturally irritable; but if it ever got the better of him in the class-room, the next prayer he offered in the oratory was sure to manifest how sincerely he repented. The students, on leaving the prayer-room, would sometimes ask each other, 'What has Dr Addison been doing for which he is so sorry?'

The second great qualification for his office was his firm faith in the Bible and his reverence for it as the Word of God. He believed in it just as he believed in the solar system. He could not help believing. He saw so clearly its grandeur as a whole, and the harmonious relation of its several parts, that he could no more believe the Bible to be a human production than he could believe that man made the planets. He never seemed to have any doubts or difficulty on the subject. Although perfectly familiar with the writings of the German rationalists and sceptics from Ernesti to Baur and Strauss, they affected him no more than the eagle is affected by the dew on his plumage as he soars near the sun. The man who studies the Bible as he studied it, in the organic relation of its several parts, comes to see that it can no more be a collection of the independent writings of uninspired men, than the human body is a haphazard combination of limbs and organs. It was in this light that he presented it to his students, who were accustomed to say that he glorified the Bible to them, that is – he enabled them to see its glory, and thus confirmed their faith and increased their reverence.

Another of his distinguishing gifts as a professor was his ability as a teacher. The clearness, rapidity, and force with which he communicated his ideas aroused and sustained attention; and the precision and variety of his questions, in the subsequent catechetical exercise on the subject of the lecture, drew out from the student every thing he knew, and made him understand himself and the matter in hand. Students from all the classes, often crowded his lecture-room, which they left drawing a long breath as a relief from overstrained attention, but with their minds expanded and invigorated.

As a preacher his sermons were always instructive and often magnificent. He would draw from a passage of Scripture more than you ever imagined it contained; show how many rays concentrated at that point; and how the truth there presented was related to the other great truths of the Bible. This was not so much an exhibition of the philosophical or logical relation of the doctrine in hand with other doctrines, as showing the place which the truth or fact in hand held in the great scheme of Scripture revelation. Thus in his sermon on the words of Paul to the Jews at Rome, 'Be it known to you, that the salvation of God is sent unto the Gentiles, and that they will hear it', he showed that everything Moses and the Prophets had taught culminated in the proclamation of the religion of the Bible as the religion of the world. At times he gave his imagination full play; and then he would rise in spiral curves, higher and higher, till lost to sight; leaving his hearers gazing up into heaven, of which they felt they then saw more than they had ever seen before. These three men, Dr Archibald Alexander, Dr Samuel Miller, and Dr Addison Alexander are our galaxy. They are like the three stars in the belt of Orion, still shining upon us from on high. Their lustre can now never be dimmed by the exhalations of the earth.

I have not forgotten two others of our professors, now we doubt not in heaven, Dr John Breckinridge and Dr James W. Alexander. These men, however, were never given to the Seminary; they were only lent to it for a short time. Dr Breckinridge was elected in 1836 and resigned in 1838; Dr James Alexander was elected in 1849 and resigned in 1851. God had fitted and designed them for other fields of action. They were both eminent, each in his own way; but we cannot claim them specially as our own. Dr Breckinridge was one of the leaders of the Church in its conflicts. Dr Alexander was a man of varied scholarship and accomplishments. The former was proud of calling himself a Kentuckian. His State, however, had as much reason to be proud of him, as he had of his State. He was tall, handsome, spirited and courteous. He made a friend of almost every man he met. Being a natural orator, his appropriate place was the pulpit and platform. Dr James Alexander, as you all know, was one of the most eminent and useful preachers of his day.

The second signal manifestation of God's favour to this institution is to be seen in the munificent patrons which he has raised up for its support. Mr James Lenox, to whom we are indebted for our library building and the extensive grounds on which it is erected; for one of our professor's houses, and for liberal contributions to our general funds. Messrs. Robert L. and Alexander Stuart, who have contributed sixty thousand dollars to our scholarship, library and miscellaneous funds, a professor's house, and who have recently purchased land for the erection of a handsome building for our recitation-rooms. Mrs George Brown, of Baltimore, to whom we are indebted for Brown Hall; Mr Levi P. Stone, who founded the Stone Lectureship; Mr John C. Green, who endowed the Helena Professorship of Ecclesiastical History, purchased a house for a professor, contributing generously to our permanent funds, and at whose expense this Chapel has been transformed from what it was to what it is; so that we can never enter this room without being reminded of his kindness.[1]

---

[1] Since the date of this sermon these munificent benefactions have been greatly increased. Mr Lenox has added another and most admirable Library building, and

There is another class of benefactors, who not having gold or silver to bestow, gave their prayers, their counsels, and their disinterested labours. Dr Ashbel Green, Dr John McDowell, Dr William Philips, head a long list of friends who should always be held in grateful remembrance.[1]

A mother's pride, however, is in her children. Much as she may love and reverence her parents, she turns her fondest gaze on those whom she has nurtured at her bosom and fondled on her knees. So our Alma Mater, while she cherishes with reverence the memory of her fathers, turns her streaming eyes with gratitude to heaven, and says, ' Here, Lord, am I and the children whom thou hast given me.' More than three thousand ministers of the gospel have been trained within these walls. With rare exceptions they have been faithful men. They have laboured in every part of our own land and in almost every missionary field. This goodly company of ministers, confessors, and even martyrs, is God's best gift and our crown.

The preaching of this sermon was the occasion of the following pleasing letter from Rev. Samuel Miller, D.D., of Mt. Holly, N.J., the son and biographer of the second professor in this Seminary.

DR S. MILLER, JR. TO DR HODGE

MOUNT HOLLY, 30th Oct., 1874

My Dear Doctor Hodge:—I received last evening a copy of your discourse at the re-opening of the Seminary Chapel, for which I most heartily thank you, and which I cannot acknowledge without taking the opportunity of going a little beyond mere formal thanks. However partial and unreliable a judge I may be of the fitness of what you have so kindly said of my dear Father, I can make no mistake in

---

two professors' houses. The Messrs Stuart have erected the finest hall for recitations possessed by any educational institution in the land, and, as also the representatives of Mr Green's estate, have added large sums to the endowment of the Seminary.

[1] To these should now be added the beloved name of the Rev. H. A. Boardman, recently deceased.

assuring you, that it is all very grateful to my own feelings, and so must be to the feelings of every one of his children. Pardon me for adding that I never heard him mention your name, which of course was a most familiar household word with us, excepting in terms of respect and affection. From his example alone I imbibed sentiments of sincere regard to you, which all our intercourse has constantly strengthened and which must, I believe, continue to increase as the years – many yet I trust to you on earth – roll by. What I owe to you as a preceptor and a friend, I shall never forget.

My sincere compliments to Mrs Hodge and all the members of your household. I am

Truly and affectionately yours,

S. MILLER

LATEST CORRESPONDENCE AND INTERVIEWS WITH HIS FRIEND, BISHOP JOHNS

Dr Hodge was necessarily separated from his friend, the Bishop of Virginia, during all the years of the civil war between the States. They did not meet until the latter part of May 1866. Dr Hodge was then staying with his brother-in-law, General Hunter, when Bishop Johns came over to meet him from his own residence at Malvern, near Alexandria, Virginia. The scene of reunion is thus described by Dr A. A. E. Taylor, now President of Wooster University, Ohio:

As we talked, suddenly without any announcement the parlour door was opened, and there entered a man of slight build and medium stature, whose hair was long and grey, and who was clad from head to foot in what seemed to be Virginia homespun. He modestly paused inside the threshold, for the moment not being observed by Dr Hodge, who was walking towards the front window. I rose to my feet, when Dr Hodge, whose attention was thus attracted, turned, quickly glanced up through his glasses at the visitor, and took a few hasty steps towards him, as if but half recognizing the face in the shadow of the room. Then as he advanced with outstretched arms, the two venerable men were clasped in a long and affectionate embrace, the only exclamation heard being, 'My brother, my dear brother!' Bishop Johns did say, with that humorous vivacity so characteristic of him, 'Charley, you have been a bad boy, but I'll forgive you.'

The embrace ended, they clasped hands, silently looking each other in the eye, for a few moments, and then interchanged words of tender joy at being permitted once more to meet. Then Dr Hodge, with one arm round his friend, and still clasping his hand, turned towards me and cordially introduced Bishop Johns, of Virginia. I saw that these men were deeply moved, and that their eyes were full of tears, and immediately withdrew.

DR HODGE TO BISHOP JOHNS

PRINCETON, October 30th, 1872

Dear John:—Hail Columbia![1] Tell me what train you are coming in that I may meet you. I can't afford to lose a minute.

Yours of 1812,

CHARLES HODGE

What on earth has a Bishop to do at a Bible House?

PRINCETON, November 13th, 1874

Dear, blessed, old John:—I did not know you were 79; though I might have known it, as, if I live to December 27th, I shall be 77, so that you have not much to brag of.

I lived in hopes, during the meeting of your Convention, that you would stop in Princeton on your way home. I can sympathize with you in your lameness. On the first day of September, walking in the dark, I stepped into a newly made trench, nearly two feet deep, which caused such a concussion in the hip-joint of my weak limb, that I have not since been able to walk further than into the Seminary. I am gradually improving, but I fear I shall not get over it for months to come.

---

[1] A humorous exclamation. *Hail Columbia!* was the unofficial anthem of the United States till the official adoption of *The Star-spangled Banner* in 1931. [Ed.]

I am glad you sympathize with what I say of our dear old Professors,[1] for you must think it sober-minded; which I fear those who did not know them as we did might be inclined to doubt.

I am not inclined to be a *laudator temporis acti* [one who praises past times], for I really believe that the world, on the whole, is getting better, and that the cause of Christ is on the advance. Yet at times I am somewhat startled at the decay of faith, or the prevalence of broad-churchism among all denominations, and of scepticism among men of the world. Among the masses speculative faith seemed, a few years ago, to be the rule. I fear the reverse is true now. Evangelical truth appears to be confined very much to true believers, of whom, I hope, the number is now greater than during any former period of the history of the world. As long as piety lasts, the truth will last, and not much longer.

Ravaud Rodgers, you and I, so far as I know, are all who remain of the class of 1815. God has been very good to us, and one of his great blessings has been sparing us so long to love and pray for each other. God bless you, dear brother.

Mrs Hodge joins me in love to you and yours. All you feel for me I feel toward you, only a little more so.

As ever and forever yours in the bonds that cannot be broken.

CHARLES HODGE

In 1873 Dr Hodge sent to the Bishop a copy of the little volume containing the 'Proceedings of the Semi-Centennial Commemoration', etc., with a photographic likeness of himself attached. He inscribed it thus: 'Charles Hodge to John Johns, friends from November 1812 to 1872'. When they met on the next occasion Johns opened the book, and pointing to the inscription, said, 'Charles, I'll not take it so.' Dr Hodge took up a pen instantly and added the words, 'καὶ εἰς τὸν αἰῶνα' (and forever).

Then came the last interview, 'An occasion', said Bishop Johns, 'probably never to be repeated, but certainly never to be

---

[1] In the sermon noted above on the re-opening of the chapel.

forgotten.' Dr Hodge records it as 'a lingering and solemn farewell of each other, feeling that it was probably the last for this world'. Dr Hodge sought the interview by the following note:

WASHINGTON, May 22, 1875

Dear, Dearest John:—It is mighty hard for a man as old as I am to shoot flying. I do not know where you are. The newspaper said you were in Richmond on the 20th inst. But where are you now? If I could know what day next week you would be at home, I would (D.V.) come to see you. I am lame, and use a crutch out of doors, so that I want to know beforehand whether at the depot I can get a cab to take me out to your mountain residence. On the 1st of September last, walking in the dark, I stepped into a newly made trench, two feet deep, which so jarred my weak limb that I have not been able to walk more than a square since. I am improving, and as there is no injury except to the nerve, I hope during the warm weather to get over the trouble.

Yours as ever,
CHARLES HODGE

P.S.—My wife says that if it is hot I shall not go a step.

The next week Bishop Johns called for him in Washington, and insisted upon the visit to Malvern. The Bishop had already had a slight attack of paralysis, and was shaken in his physical system; but his mind was as clear and his heart as fresh and tender as ever. They took dinner together, no one being present but their wives. At the table Johns suddenly turned to his friend, and regarding him very seriously, said, 'Charley, you have had more influence on my life than any other person I have ever known.' After dinner the two walked out together to a seat under a maple tree in front of the house, commanding a lovely view over the Potomac and surrounding country, and there they talked for the last time over the past and the future. When he left, the Bishop threw his arms over his neck and said, 'It is the last time. Let me have a good look at your face, Charley, for we shall never see each other again until we meet in heaven.'

On his return to Washington, Dr Hodge sent his friend a print he happened to pick up, of two old soldiers sitting together on a bench, entitled the 'Last Muster', to which he appended the interrogative clause, 'In the future?' To this the bishop alludes in his next note.

MALVERN, June 30, 1875

Dear Charles:—Since we parted I have been over the hills and far away, returning to a week of examinations, ordinations, etc.; hot and exhausting almost beyond endurance.

But I steal time daily to go from the step where we parted to the rustic bench where we sat together, and keep the covenant for refreshment and comfort.

Thank you for the 'Muster'. No! not the last; that will be everlasting.

Love to your wife and children and children's children. Mrs J. and my daughter say so too. Bless you every way and always.

Truly your brother,

J. JOHNS

The venerated and beloved Bishop went to heaven on the opening of the next spring. My father kept hanging within sight on the wall of his study, neatly framed, the last note he ever received from the Bishop – a postal card, on which the Bishop had written in pencil, with a strong, clear hand:

January 1st, 1876.

To dear Charles and his family, greeting—

From all at Malvern, with a specialty from his loving friend and brother of 1812, and since with increase, and so forever. J.

To which my father appended in ink: 'The last communication received from my friend, Bishop Johns, of Virginia. He died April 5th, 1876.'

DR HODGE TO THE REV. PROF. JOSEPH PACKARD, D.D.

In the great day of penitential sorrow predicted by the prophet, it is said, 'Every family shall mourn apart.' So when such a man as Bishop Johns is taken away, the whole land mourneth, his own household, his church, the community, each apart. So I mourn alone. He was an honour and blessing to his church; but he was to me what he was to no one else. With the single exception of my own and only brother, I never had such a friend. For nearly sixty-four years we were as intimate and confidential as though we had been born at one birth. In all this time, to the best of my recollection, there was never an angry word passed between us. I feel like the last tree of a forest. Two of our college vacations of six weeks I spent with him in his home at Newcastle. We prayed together and, in each social religious meeting, told the people the little we knew of Christ, helping each other out. He was only eighteen months my senior, and yet his feeling towards me was somewhat paternal. Alas! alas! he has gone, I cannot speak of him except as to what he was to me – so good, so kind, so loving, without a shadow of change for sixty-four years! My last visit to him, in May last, was the most loving of our whole lives. The recollections and love of sixty years were gathered into those few hours. Our parting was solemn, tender and lingering. We looked steadily at each other with tearful eyes, knowing that possibly, and even probably, it was for the last time, but in the calm hope that in any event the separation could not be for long. I have no such friend on earth. I mourn apart.

THE APPOINTMENT OF HIS ASSISTANT AND SUCCESSOR

About the time of his semi-centennial some of the friends of the Seminary began to consider what steps should be taken to provide him with assistance during his declining years, and to secure for the Seminary a successor in his chair after his departure. In 1873 a committee, consisting of four or five of the oldest and most experienced Directors, were appointed by the Board to consider this matter, and to ascertain by correspondence the wishes of Dr Hodge. Their first proposition was to appoint his eldest son, who had been for some time Professor of Systematic Theology in the Western Theological Seminary, Allegheny City, Pennsylvania, temporarily to the chair of the History of Doctrine, in Princeton, with the intention that he should render his father any desired assistance in the labour of teaching while he lived, and succeed him afterward. Having received from the committee, in the summer of 1874, some intimation of their design, Dr Hodge wrote to Dr H, A. Boardman as follows:

NARRAGANSETT PIER, July 13, 1874.

Dear Doctor:—I do not know what other people think, but so far as *I* know I *need* an assistant no more now than I did twenty years ago. Bringing Alexander to Princeton was not designed, as I understood the matter, to relieve me, but as a rather cumbrous device to secure the fidelity of the Seminary to the type of doctrine taught in it from the beginning. It was never the intention, so far as I was informed, of those who started this plan, that there were to be two permanent professorships of theology, one Didactic, and the other Polemic or Historical Theology. This would be out of proportion. The students would not have time to attend two such courses and do justice to the other departments. The permanent professorship should be for the relief of Dr Green. He is invaluable to the institution, and he has been overworked ever since he was connected with it, until the appointment of Mr McCurdy.

The fidelity of the Seminary to our Standards is the great object which the Directors, I doubt not, feel conscience-bound to secure. If that end can be obtained as well without Alexander as with him, I have always thought it would be better to let him remain where he is. According to all accounts he is doing good there. We do not know that he would be equally successful in Princeton.

I see no harm in allowing things for the present to remain as they are. At my age, life or fitness for service hangs by a thread. Providence may soon make the path of duty plain.

Yours truly,
CHARLES HODGE

This letter naturally brought the committee to a full stop, and nothing more was done in the matter until it was again opened by the Professor himself.

DR HODGE TO DR H. A. BOARDMAN

PRINCETON, Feb. 3rd, 1877

My Dear Doctor:—Last winter, to the best of my recollection, I did not miss a single exercise, whether of lecture-room or conference, during the whole term of eight months. This term I caught cold the latter part of October, was confined to the house about a fortnight, and although I have attended my classes regularly since that first fortnight, I have not attended the chapel or conference.

There is, I believe, nothing wrong about any of my organs, but my chest and vocal organs are very weak. There is every reason to hope that when the warm weather returns I shall be as well as usual. I had a similar attack of bronchitis in the spring of 1873. The old alumni, who heard me attempt to speak at the alumni meeting, said they never expected to hear my voice again. Nevertheless, some of them were astonished when, at the Evangelical Alliance, a few months after, they heard me speak like the old Homeric Stentor. I had a similar attack last spring which prevented our going to Washington as we usually do during the month of May. I did not get over that attack till I went to the sea-shore in July.

Under these circumstances I think the time has come when I should give up, either in whole or in part, my duties in the Seminary. I honestly believe that, in my usual health, I am as well able to discharge those duties as I ever was. But I am liable to be disqualified in the middle of a session, and this winter have been constrained to meet my class when my physician thought I ought to remain at home.

Some two or three years ago the Directors kindly appointed a committee, of which Dr Musgrave and yourself were members, to consider the best means for making provision for aiding me, or for supplying my place in the Seminary. I do not know whether that committee is regarded as still in existence. I wish this note to be considered as a formal intimation to you, either as a member of that committee or as a Director, that it is my purpose to apply to the Board of Directors to be relieved in whole or in part from my duties in the Seminary.

You can understand the feelings with which I look forward to severing, or loosening my connection with this sacred Institution which has been uninterrupted for fifty-five years.

Your affectionate and grateful friend,

CHARLES HODGE

DR HODGE TO DRS MUSGRAVE AND PAXTON

PRINCETON, Feb. 8, 1877

REV. DRS MUSGRAVE AND PAXTON

Dear Brethren:—I understand that you are members of a Committee appointed by the Directors of the Theological Seminary, in reference to the instruction in the Theological Department.

The facts in the case are:

1. That last winter (1875 and '76) I did not, to the best of my recollection, miss a single exercise the whole term, whether in the classroom, chapel or conference.

2. This term I caught cold the last week in October, and for ten days or a fortnight I was unable to attend any classes. Since then I have regularly met the classes, but have not attended chapel or conference, since the end of October. My general health is good, and I am free, as far as I know, from any organic complaints, but I am very soon exhausted; I have great weakness and a good deal of dull pain in the chest. My voice fails me if I attempt to read aloud a chapter from the Bible. My physician thinks there is every reason to expect that I shall be as well as usual when the warm weather comes.

3. Under these circumstances I do not think it wise that the whole responsibility of the Department of Didactic Theology should continue to rest on me. There are two plans for meeting the emergency, which I would respectfully submit to the decision of the Committee and of the Board.

First. That I should resign my professorship. In this case I should be entirely disconnected with the Seminary, and have neither the responsibility nor the right to take any part in its instruction or government.

Second. That provision should be made to carry on the instruction in the department, in case of entire or partial failure on my part. This would leave me still a member of the Faculty and give me the right to do what I could, and yet relieve me from the obligation of working when I did not feel fit for it.

I would, of course, cheerfully acquiesce in either of these plans the Board may prefer. So far as my personal feelings are concerned it is natural I should prefer to have the right to work while I can work. I might give up to a colleague Dogmatic Theology and retain what is called Exegetical Theology; or the division of duties might be left to be privately determined. All which is respectfully submitted.

CHARLES HODGE

DR HODGE TO DR BOARDMAN

SUNDAY EVENING, Feb, 18, 1877

My Dear Doctor:—I understood Dr Musgrave to say that the Committee of the Directors were to meet in Philadelphia on Tuesday next. From the few words which passed between us at the meeting of the Trustees of the College, I gathered that he had the impression that I was adverse to my son Alexander being chosen for a professor in this Seminary. I have neither the right nor the wish to be consulted on the subject, but to prevent any embarrassment arising from any kind regard to my views or wishes, I think it well to let you know exactly how I feel about the matter. I cannot do this better than by sending a copy of the letter which I wrote Alexander a few days ago.

Praying that God may over-rule all things for the good of the Seminary and the Church, I am very sincerely yours as ever,

Charles Hodge

DR HODGE TO HIS SON

Princeton, Feb. 16, 1877

My Dear Alexander:—You say I told you to go to Allegheny; your memory may be better than mine, but I have no recollection of having been so unwise. At any rate, in the event of your being called to Princeton, I shall not assume the responsibility of deciding whether you ought to come. You ought to decide the question before the election is made by the Board, if the Committee determine to recommend your appointment. The view I take of the matter is simply this:

1. Our Board is bound to take that course which it thinks will best promote the interests of this Seminary and the general interests of this Church.

2. If our Directors think there is any other man available, as well qualified to fill the position as you, they ought to leave you where you are.

3. But if they are satisfied that you are the best man to keep up the character of this Institution for fidelity to our doctrinal standards, I, if a Director, although your Father, would vote for your election.

4. I would do this, because I think that this Seminary, not because of any superiority of its faculty, but simply because of providential circumstances, is at present at least, of special importance. It, therefore, should be specially considered.

5. All such considerations, as delicacy, your personal wishes, cheapness of living here or there, are not of any serious weight.

6. The question whether you are the best available man to fill the place here, is for our Directors to decide. Their decision, however, is subject to a veto from your 'inner consciousness', if your conscience constrains you to exercise it. 'Commit your way unto the Lord, and He will direct your steps.'

Your Father

The result was that his son was elected Associate Professor of Didactic Theology, with the understanding that he should undertake whatever work his father desired to be relieved of. During the session of 1877–78 Dr Hodge taught the senior class Didactic Theology, and lectured to the junior class as usual on the Exegesis of the Epistles, while his son simply taught the middle class theology. At the end of that year Dr Hodge handed over to his son the entire department of Didactic Theology, intending to retain to the end of his life the exegesis of the doctrinal epistles. His death immediately after necessitated the transference of that department to his other son, Professor C. W. Hodge.

When his eldest son was inaugurated in the old First Presbyterian Church of Princeton, November 8, 1877, the *Presbyterian* says, 'During all the services we noticed that many eyes were turned to a corner of the church in which a venerable man sat apart communing with himself, with his heart doubtless filled with varying emotions.' His mind must have gone back to August 12th, 1812, when he, a stripling, lying on the rail of the gallery of the same church, looked down on the inauguration of Dr A. Alexander to the same office. For from August 12, 1812, to November 8, 1877, for more than sixty-five years there had been only two professors of Systematic Theology in Princeton, and Dr Hodge received the office from a man he delighted to call father, and now transmitted it to his son.

HIS EIGHTIETH BIRTHDAY

On the occasion of his eightieth birthday a number of his dear friends united in making him a present as a testimonial of affection. This was transmitted to him by Dr H. A. Boardman, who also published a graceful notice of the anniversary of the beloved patriarch in the *Presbyterian*.

Hence arose the occasion of the following letters.

DR HODGE TO DR BOARDMAN

PRINCETON, December 27, 1877

My Dear Friend:—I need not say that your letter and its inclosures were a surprise. Much less is it necessary to assure you that I am very grateful to all the friends named in your letter for their kindness and kind feeling. Least of all need I say that you, as the alpha and omega of the whole, claim my warmest thanks. You are not yet old enough to know how friends increase in value as they decrease in number. So large a proportion of those to whom I was most attached, and on whom I most depended, has gone before, that I cling like a tottering man to those who are left. Out of mere selfishness I pray that they may be spared, and be allowed to diffuse happiness around them to the end.

I must beg you to express my thanks to the friends who have joined you in placing this chaplet on my hoary head.

Your landlady (Mrs Hodge) returns her acknowledgments for your New Year's card; it occupies a conspicuous place in the study.

With entire confidence and warm affection, your friend,

CHARLES HODGE

TO THE SAME

PRINCETON, January 15, 1878

My Dear Doctor:—If you were in one room and Angelina Patti singing in another, the doors being opened, you would not need ask who it was. So when I read the article in the last *Presbyterian*, I was at no loss as to its author. I knew only one man who has the goodness, the skill, the delicacy and refinement which it manifests. I should be a churl if I were not grateful for such a tribute. Nevertheless I cannot absorb it. It is a delusion. It is not what I am, but what God's providence has done with me, that you have in the eye of your imagination. Had I been settled in a retired parish, no body would have ever heard my name. Besides, I believe that every man, unless partially demented, whatever men may say of him, knows in his own heart that he is 'a poor shote'.

I don't believe that the rod with which Moses smote the rock in the wilderness, was any great thing of a stick after all. Nevertheless, although I see through your delusion, I am not less grateful for your goodness and love.

We are looking forward to the pleasure of seeing you before the close of the week.

Your affectionate friend,
CHARLES HODGE

HIS WRITING DURING THESE LAST YEARS

He published in the *Repertory*, January 1871, 'Preaching the Gospel to the Poor', and April 1876, 'Christianity without Christ.' These are his last articles in that *Review*, so long connected with his name, and worthily close his long and consistent warfare for the truth, as it is in Jesus, and for the interests of his people. In 1872 he wrote the latter part of his *Systematic Theology*. In 1874 he published a small book entitled *Darwinism*, in opposition to the prevailing doctrine of Atheistic Evolutionism. In December 1877, he wrote at the request of a member of the Free Church Presbytery of Glasgow, a letter defining and maintaining the old doctrine of the plenary inspiration of the Scriptures. And the *Independent* of May 9th, 1878, published his very last contribution to the press.

The *Independent* and its correspondent had insisted that the 'first question' (in regard to the eternity of sin and misery) 'is not the exegetical but the ethical one. We want to know what God says; but it is impossible to believe that God says anything which our moral sense tells us he ought not to say.' In a long and, as was on all hands admitted, a clear and forcible argument, worthy of his prime, Dr Hodge argued that this is no new question, and the dangers of the present moment are not beyond precedent; that the difficulty grows out of the decline of piety, and that a clearing of the horizon was more to be expected through a revival of religion than from the speculations of those who had rendered such a confused account of the matter in hand. He shows that the word 'intuition' is taken in two senses. 1st. In the proper sense, it signifies those immediate judgments of the mind, whether intellectual or moral, which are *necessary* and universal in all times. 'Such primary truths are part of the primary law written by the finger of God on the hearts of men. They are the barrier against utter scepticism. The man who breaks through them plunges into the abyss of outer darkness.' 2. In the popular sense of the word, it means 'the immediate judgment, whether a thing is true or false, right or wrong. They are as variable as the wind, and as unstable as water. To make them the rule by which to interpret the Word of God is simply to annihilate it as a rule of faith and practice. It is to substitute our reason for God's reason, our moral judgments for his moral judgments. Whatever euphuistic phraseology may be adopted, this is the soul and essence of infidelity.' He shows, then, that the *Independent* and its correspondent had used the phrase in the popular sense, and hence that their argument was built upon false premises and led to dangerous consequences.

It was claimed that we must interpret the Bible by what our moral sense teaches.

> By moral sense here must be meant the moral sense of the individual reader. It cannot by possibility mean those moral judgments which are necessary and universal. It is a contradiction to say that the Christian Church has for ages believed what no man can by possibility believe . . . What the Bible teaches is a matter of fact. It is a philosophical axiom that what all men believe, in virtue of the constitution of their nature, must be true. It is scarcely less certain that what all Christians believe that the Bible teaches, in point of fact it does teach.

14

HIS LAST DAYS

T<small>HE END CAME</small>, not from positive disease, but from exhaustion of nature. During the entire session he had met his four appointments a week with his classes with perfect regularity, only two exceptions being remembered. Yet his strength was gradually, though almost imperceptibly failing. He took his nourishment very regularly, but with almost no appetite and in diminishing quantities. In the early spring he once fainted at the table. Then his weak resources were very severely tried by the sudden deaths of two of his best-beloved nieces on successive Saturdays in April. His record is: 'April 6th – Our dear niece, Harriet Woolsey, wife of Dr H. Lenox Hodge, died suddenly. She apparently fainted, and never revived. One of the loveliest and best of women.' Then, alas! again: 'April 13 – Died suddenly, Alice Van Rensselaer, wife of Rev. Edward B. Hodge. The joy and pride of her whole family connection.'

On April 14th he discoursed for the last time at the 'Conference' in the old Oratory, in which he had delivered the first student's speech a few months more than sixty years before. His subject was, 'Fight the Good Fight of Faith', and on the afternoon of April 21st he administered and partook with the professors and students in the Seminary Chapel of his last communion.

It had been his custom for years to spend the month of May with his brother-in-law, General David Hunter, in the city of Washington, and the months of July and August at Narragansett Pier, Rhode Island. From these changes he had hitherto uniformly experienced very decided advantage. But at the close of the Seminary term, on this last year, his physician and friends were in great doubt whether his strength was sufficient for either of these journeys. Suggestions were made with regard to his seeking relief from the midsummer heats at some nearer and more readily accessible point on the New Jersey coast. But after much hesitation he went to Washington at the usual time, the 2nd of May.

Then came the death of his life-long friend, Prof. Joseph Henry of the Smithsonian Institute. For this noble man of science and truly Christian Philosopher, Dr Hodge had a long-cherished and warm personal affection, as well as intellectual sympathy and sincere admiration. Professor Henry had said of Dr Hodge that 'he had made the best use of his talents his life through of any man he ever knew.' When visited, May 1873, at the Smithsonian by a large part of the General Assembly, just retiring from their sessions in Baltimore, he declared, in response to their salutations, that 'by birth, by education, and by preference he was a Presbyterian'. The last letter, except a few brief business notes, he ever wrote, contains a statement of his conviction that physical science demonstrates the existence of an omnipotent, omniscient, omnipresent and absolutely good God. And further than this, that the facts of experience prove the necessity of such a mediator between God and man as Christians believe Christ to be. And that Christ he lived and died trusting and loving.

Thursday afternoon, May 16th, Dr Hodge attended the funeral of Professor Henry in the New York Avenue Presbyterian Church. He made a long prayer, emphasizing in climacteric order the great fundamental principles of the plan of salvation, with such an effort of voice that he was fairly well heard by that vast audience. Yet this was simply the result of an exhaustive excitement. It was the last occasion in which he was ever in a church. His decline, which had been marked ever since he came to Washington, became now more rapid. He suffered from indigestion, weakness, weariness, and from acute neuralgic pains. On the next Thursday his son-in-law, Colonel S. W. Stockton, brought him to Baltimore, where they spent the night with the beloved family of the Rev. Andrew B. Cross. On Thursday, by the kindness of Wolcot Jackson, General Superintendent of the New Jersey division of the Pennsylvania Railroad Co., the limited express stopped for his accommodation at the Princeton Junction. He came in a horizontal position, and as he affirmed, with more comfort than ever before.

His pulse indicated vital exhaustion, and he gradually grew weaker. He rode out every day up to the 29th of May. He spent the days in his old chair in the study and his nights in his bedroom, in the second storey, up to the 2nd Sabbath of June. Then his absent children were summoned, and then a bed was erected for him in the back parlour, next adjacent his study, and where, a generation before, he had lectured to his classes during his lameness. He strove to spend the day-time in the study, on the old chair, to the last. On one of those very last days he said: 'This old chair and I have been growing to fit each other for forty years.' When at last, on Monday, two days before he died, late in the afternoon, he fainted almost for his bed; it was indeed a touching sight to see him delay his needed movement to the other room to the last possible moment, as he was as conscious as we were that he was leaving that chair and study for the last time. He suffered frequent pain, and almost constant uneasiness and distress. Yet he reclined and waited in beautiful patience and peace, his face always overflowing with love. 'Even through the last hours of his illness, when freedom from pain and from torpor was gained for a little, he was alert and inquisitive, with his usual interest in events around him, and events of the day: the Presbyterian Assembly, the Congress at Washington, the Congress at Berlin, the College at Princeton, and the minutest concerns of his own children and grand-children here and elsewhere. This rapid and wide synoptical vision was that of a consciously dying man. For he had been busy in setting his house in order, and wisely making the most exact arrangements in view of his final demise. He knew that death was at hand, and though it did come sooner than he looked for, he repeatedly spoke of its approach being "slow".'[1]

He did not wish to die, yet he was evidently without the shadow of fear or of painful reluctance. He maintained to the last his characteristic aversion to being read to, and his shyness as to the expression of his intimate, personal feelings. To a loving inquiry of his wife he once said, 'Yes, my love, my Saviour is with me every step of the way, but I am too weak to talk about it.' Once she asked him if it would comfort him if she should repeat aloud his favourite hymn; he answered, 'No, dearest, I am repeating it over and over again to myself all the while.'

That his dying thoughts may be known the hymn is given:

HYMN OF THE LATE MRS WEISS
Daughter of the late Archbishop of Dublin; composed on her death-bed.

I.

Jesus, I am never weary,
    When upon this bed of pain ;
If Thy presence only cheer me,
    All my loss I count but gain, –
        Ever near me, –
    Ever near me, Lord, remain!

---

[1] Dr A. T. McGill's letter to the *New York Observer*.

2.

Dear ones come with fruit and flowers,
   Thus to cheer my heart the while,
In these deeply anxious hours;
   Oh! if Jesus only smile! –
     Only Jesus
Can these trembling fears beguile.

3.

All my sins were laid upon Thee,
   All my griefs were on Thee laid;
For the blood of Thine atonement,
   All my utmost debt has paid;
     Dearest Saviour!
I believe, for Thou hast said.

4.

Dearest Saviour! go not from me;
   Let Thy presence still abide ;
Look in tenderest love upon me, –
   I am sheltering at Thy side.
     Dearest Saviour!
Who for suffering sinners died.

5.

Both mine arms are clasped around Thee;
   And my head is on Thy breast;
For my weary soul has found Thee
   Such a perfect, perfect rest.
     Dearest Saviour!
Now I know that I am blessed.

Seeing his widowed daughter weeping while she watched him, he stretched his hand towards her and said: 'Why should you grieve, daughter? To be absent from the body is to be with the

Lord, to be with the Lord is to see the Lord, to see the Lord is to be like Him.'

On the Wednesday previous to his death his dear friend, Dr H. A. Boardman called, and with great tenderness set upon his forehead a farewell kiss. On the last day of conscious life he saw Dr William Adams, who gave the following account of the interview to the *New York Observer*:

Being in Princeton, as a trustee of the College, last Tuesday, and having heard through the papers of the illness of Dr Hodge, I called at his home to inquire how he was. Hearing that I was in the library with his sons, Dr H. requested to see me. Such a request was to me at once a surprise and a gratification. I found him in extreme debility, so that I immediately cautioned him against making any effort to speak. He had taken my hand as I came to his bedside, and held it through the whole interview; his conversation with me being chiefly by its responsive pressure and the intelligent expression of the eye. My words were very few, assuring him how many there were who held him in their thoughts and hearts; and, most of all, how certain it was, amid all his discomforts, that he was not forgotten by Him who, knowing our frame, '*pitieth* those who love Him even as a father *pitieth* his children.' Both hand and eye responded that he felt the beauty and force of that one inspired word – which taken out from the Bible would leave an irremediable vacancy – '*pitieth*'. Entirely conscious was he as he lay calmly waiting for the lifting of that curtain which alone separated him from the vision of his Lord.

I have since been informed that I was the last person out of his own family who saw Dr Hodge before his death. A few hours later he passed into a sleep from which there was to be no waking.

Thus he slept until, in the presence of his wife and children and elder grand-children, life ebbed away entirely at six o'clock, p.m., on Wednesday, the 19th of June, on the middle day of Commencement Week of the College.

At one o'clock on Saturday, the 22nd, an informal meeting of the Presbytery of New Brunswick was held in the lecture-room of the First Presbyterian Church, Princeton, where resolutions were passed, expressive of their sense of the Christian elevation of his character, and of the value of his services, and of the loss involved in his death. Then the Presbytery, with many other clergymen, alumni of the Seminary, and others, met in the chapel, where the remains of the venerable Professor were borne, and for a short time presented to the view of his pupils and friends. At this meeting Dr Atwater presented another set of appropriate resolutions, at the request of several members of the Boards of Directors and Trustees of the Institution, which were unanimously passed. The procession was formed in the grounds of the Seminary, the body being borne and deposited in the grave only by the sons and nephews of the deceased. The Presbytery of New Brunswick, the Directors and Trustees and other officers of the Seminary and College and other institutions, and other clergy and friends, forming in line, proceeded to the First Presbyterian Church. All the stores in the town were closed, and all business suspended in token of respect.

In the church the Rev. President McCosh read the Scriptures; the Rev. Dr Paxton, of N.Y., delivered a funeral address with admirable taste and effect; the Rev. Dr Adams, President of Union Theological Seminary, and the Rev. Dr Henry A. Boardman, of Philadelphia, offered prayers. The procession then reformed, and the body was carried to its resting place in the lot next to that of the Alexanders, in Princeton Cemetery. Here, as he was lowered into the grave, his pastor, the Rev. Horace G. Hinsdale, repeated the fifteenth chapter of First Corinthians, and after prayer, pronounced the benediction.

Resolutions expressive of the reverence and love with which he was regarded, and the sorrow which his death occasioned, were passed by the Trustees of the College, by the Alumni of the

Seminary at their next annual meeting, and by the various Boards and Societies of which he was a member. Cordial and appreciative notices of his death appeared as editorials in all the papers of all evangelical denominations. Especially it is proper to notice three eminently intelligent and discriminating, as well as affectionate notices of his character and achievements: (1) An article on 'The late Dr Hodge', in the *British and Foreign Evangelical Review*, October 1878, by his loved and trusted pupil, Rev. Robert Watts, D.D., Professor of Systematic Theology in the Assembly's Theological College, Belfast, Ireland. (2) An address delivered before the First Presbyterian Church, of which Dr Hodge was a member and life-long communicant, by the Rev. Prof. Lyman H. Atwater, D.D., for some years his colleague in the editorship of the *Princeton Review*. (3) An address by his friend. Dr H. A. Boardman, before the Directors and Alumni of the Seminary, in the First Presbyterian Church, Sunday morning, April 23rd, 1879. These addresses were printed and widely circulated. A tablet was also erected to his memory in the chapel of the Seminary, and unveiled with an address by Dr Boardman, Tuesday, April 25th, of the same year.

I append the following selections from the contemporary notices of his death, because of their character, and because they furnish the testimony of Christian scholars of other denominations.

The editor of the *National Repository*, a Methodist magazine, wrote:

Timothy Dwight, Nathaniel Emmons, Samuel Hopkins, Edwards A. Park, Moses Stuart, Nathaniel W. Taylor, Albert Barnes, the Alexanders, Francis Wayland, Tayler Lewis, Bishop McIlvaine, Bangs, Fisk, McClintock, Whedon, Bledsoe, Dr True, whose loss we have just been called on to mourn also, and a hundred others have shed lustre on the American name since the era of independence opened; but none of these can, in grandeur of achievement, compare with Charles Hodge, who recently died at Princeton, an octogenarian. He was not only *par excellence* the Calvinistic theologian of America, but the Nestor of all American theology, and though we differ widely with him in many things, we yet accept this master mind and beautifully adorned life as the grandest result of our Christian intellectual development. He produced many valuable writings, but above all stands his *Systematic Theology*, a work which has only begun its influence in moulding the religious thought of the English-speaking world. We could wish that its fallacy of dependence on the Calvinistic theology were not one of its faults. But what is this slight failing compared to the masterful leading of a thousand, lost in speculation, from the labyrinth of doubt and despair to the haven of heavenly faith and angelic security? We may say of this now sainted man, 'With all thy faults we love thee still.' Princeton has lost its greatest ornament, the Presbyterian Church its most precious gem, the American Church her greatest earth-born luminary.

The Congregational paper, the *Christian at Work*, for June 27th, 1878, edited by Dr Wm. M. Taylor, contained an editorial written by Dr Doolittle, a Professor in the Reformed (Dutch) Church, and a former pupil of Dr Hodge. He closes thus:

It is not, however, as the erudite Professor, nor as the masterly reviewer, nor as the impressive pulpit orator, nor as the gifted author of commentaries and theologies, that the venerated Princetonian will be most remembered by former pupils. It was rather on those fondly memorable Sabbath afternoons when he used to unfold before the hearts of rapt listeners the meaning of Scripture passages. Oh, with what sweet evidences of love, born not of earth but of heaven; of unaffected grace burning in his heart and beaming, like the glory of Moses, from his countenance – that he appeared at his greatest and best. Can any one that ever saw this good man while in the endeavour to portray the entrance of a divine life into our human life, opening unconsciously the door of his own heart, and exhibiting Jesus enthroned there on a believing, yearning, loving, rejoicing disposition, ever forget how he realized at that supreme moment that Jesus is greater than the greatest of great men, that the Redeemer who could thus irradiate and transform his worshipper is worthy of universal adoration and love. Oh, profound earthly teacher, thou wast yet infinitely less than the Heavenly Teacher whose words thou didst live to exemplify in thine own character and utterances; for showing us this we bless thee more than for all thine other works.

CHARLES HODGE, OF PRINCETON

A Prince, wise, valiant, just, and yet benign;
His own will free, and still by law controlled:
No King, with armaments and fleets untold,
Such mastery had with purpose so divine,
O'er unseen forces active and malign.
He fought th' invisible spirits of the air,
Nor for himself alone, but for his race.
And men grew wiser, better, unaware
That he in silence, by his faith and prayer
Saved their beleaguered souls. Spirit of Grace
Who in him wrought, and held him in the strife.
We give Thee thanks that Thou didst him ordain
Unto a work wherein no act is vain.
And death but longer makes the service and the life.

A. D. F. R.

15

DR HODGE CONSIDERED AS A TEACHER, PREACHER, THEOLOGIAN, AND CHRISTIAN MAN

I HAVE IN THE PRECEDING CHAPTERS, given the facts which constitute what remain to us in memory of the earthly life of the subject of this memoir. In this chapter will be presented a reflection of the image he cast in the several offices he filled on the minds of some of the most competent of his pupils and friends.

1. DR HODGE AS A TEACHER OF EXEGESIS

By the Rev. Benjamin B. Warfield, Professor of the Western Theological Seminary, Allegheny City, PA

Rev. A. A. Hodge:—Remembering your request, I shall endeavour to write absolutely impartially the impressions made upon me as a student of your father's exegetical teaching. This is no easy matter, the danger being that like the sceptics I shall lean over backwards from the very effort not to lean forwards.

He taught exegesis only to the juniors, and although five years have elapsed, the impressions made at that time remain as vivid as though it were yesterday. His very mode of entering the room was characteristic. Infirm as he was, he was not bent by extreme age or infirmity; his carriage was erect and graceful, and his step always firm. The mantle that hung from his shoulders during the cooler months heightened the effect of graceful movement. I well remember that when he stepped into the aisle of the first church to welcome Drs Dorner and Christlieb on their visit to Princeton, in the autumn of 1873, I thought I had never witnessed a finer spectacle of strength and grace combined. And yet it was but an example of his ordinary bearing; he gave me the same impression every time he entered the recitation room. After his always strikingly appropriate opening prayer had been offered, and we had been settled back into our seats, he would open his well thumbed Greek Testament – on which it was plain that there was not a single marginal note – look at the passage for a second, and then throwing his head back, and closing his eyes, begin his exposition. He scarcely again glanced at the Testament during the hour, the text was evidently before his mind, verbally, and the matter of his exposition thoroughly at his command. In an unbroken stream it flowed from subject to subject, simple, clear, cogent, unfailingly reverent. Now and then he would pause a moment to insert an illustrative anecdote – now and then lean forward suddenly with tearful, wide-open eyes, to press home a quick-risen inference of the love of God to lost sinners. But the web of his discourse – for a discourse it really was – was calm, critical and argumentative. We were expected to take notes upon it and recite on them at our next meeting. This recitation was, however, brief, covering not often more than a quarter of an hour; and we consequently felt that lecturing was the main thing.

This, then, was how he taught us exegesis. The material of the lectures resembled very much his printed commentaries. I thought then, and I think now, that Dr Hodge's sense of the general meaning of a passage was unsurpassed. He had all of Calvin's sense of the flow and connection of thought. Consequently the analysis of passages was superb. Nothing could surpass the clearness with which he set forth the general argument and the main connections of thought. Neither could anything surpass the analytical subtlety with which he extracted the doctrinal contents of passages. I can never forget how bitingly clear his sentences often were, in which he set forth in few words the gist of a chapter. He seemed to look through a passage, catch its main drift and all its theological bearings, and state the result in crisp sentences, which would have been worthy of Bacon; all at a single movement of mind.

He had, however, no taste for the technicalities of Exegesis. He did not shrink from them in his lectures, indeed; but on such points he was seldom wholly satisfactory. His discussion of disputed grammatical or lexical points had a flavour of second-handedness about them. He appeared not to care to have a personal opinion upon such matters, but was content to accept another's without having made it really his own. He would state, in such cases, several views from various critical commentators, and then make choice between them; but I could not always feel that his choice was determined by sound linguistic principles. He sometimes seemed to be quite as apt to choose an indefensible as a plausible one – guided, apparently, sometimes by weight of name, sometimes by dislike to what seemed to him over-subtlety, and sometimes, it seemed, by theological predilection.

He made no claim, again, to critical acumen; and in questions of textual criticism he constantly went astray. Hence it was that often texts were quoted to support doctrines of which they did not treat; and a meaning was sometimes extracted from a passage which it was far from bearing. But this affected details only, the general flow of thought in a passage he never failed to grasp, and few men could equal him in stating it.

From what I have written you will see that Dr Hodge commanded my respect and admiration as an exegete, while at the same time I could not fail to recognize that this was not his forte. Even here he was the clear, analytical thinker, rather than a patient collector and weigher of detailed evidence. He was great here, but not at his greatest. Theology was his first love.

I would like to say one word before the closing of my impressions of your father as a teacher, because I fear that in writing to you of other things most of your correspondents may neglect this. I have sat under many noted teachers, and yet am free to say that as an educator I consider Dr Hodge superior to them all. He was in fact my ideal of a teacher. Best of all men I have ever known, he knew how to make a young man think. All the rote-learning that could be done could not secure a good recitation to him. One must have so learned a chapter of his theology, for instance, as to be able to apply all the principles laid down in it on need, in order to be able to recite to him at all. He had a way too of commencing his questioning away back of these principles, and by skilful interrogation gradually making the student evolve them for himself, so finely managing it that at last they would burst upon him as new and self-discovered facts; educed from his own thoughts. Thus they were made part of the permanent furniture of his mind – they were no longer acquired things borrowed for occasional use, but his own, 'bone of his bone, and flesh of his flesh'. After that he could as soon part with life as give them up.

I cannot hope either to describe this mode of teaching or express my profound admiration of it. I can only say that in that room of Systematic Theology, I think I had daily before me examples of perfect teaching. The way he managed his own accumulations of learning too – constantly drawing on them for illustration and enforcement, constantly the master of them, and of every detail of them, was marvellous. We think that though learning is fuel to the mental fire, yet there is such a thing as smothering the flames with a superabundance of fuel. But 'so intense and ardent was the fire of his mind that it was not only not suffocated beneath this weight of fuel, but penetrated the whole superabundant mass with its own heat and radiance'. Every jot of that learning, consecrated to the Master's cause, was ready to be utilized in the recitation room. Every jot of it was Christianized by its passage through his mind from whatever source it was drawn. Had I never gained another thing at Princeton, I would bless God for permitting me to see this! *O si sic omnes* [If only all teachers were like this]!

Believe me as ever, yours, etc.

BENJAMIN B. WARFIELD

2. DR HODGE AS A TEACHER OF DIDACTIC THEOLOGY AND AS A PREACHER

By Dr Wiliam Paxton of New York

As a Teacher of Theology.

It gives me great pleasure to think of Dr Charles Hodge, as I remember him when I was a student; and to mingle those early impressions with my riper judgment of his gifts and character, when in after life we were brought into more intimate relations.

I entered the Seminary at the time when he was recovering from a painful illness which confined him to his couch for a long period – during which the grace of God had wrought in him such a matured and happy Christian experience, that his face shone in brightness and beauty as if it had been the 'face of an angel'. This was noticed by all the students, and was the frequent occasion of remark. When he came into the class-room, still lame, leaning on a staff, and blushing like a bashful boy, our sympathy was excited – but when he took his seat upon the chair, the glance which he cast upon the class was one of such beaming benevolence mingled with such quiet peace that we all felt he had come in the spirit of the Apostle John, to teach us out of his own deep spiritual intuitions the mystery of the kingdom of God.

His characteristics as a teacher of theology were distinctly marked.

The *first* impression which he made upon the student was, his deep sincerity. It was his custom to introduce each lecture with a short prayer, which was so simple, so humble, and so manifestly the expression of a heart in close fellowship with God, as to impress upon our minds the conviction – This is not a perfunctory professor, but a man of deep experience, who comes to 'testify what he knows'. The whole spirit and tone of the lecture was such as to deepen this impression. He did not teach a system which he had wrought out, but truths the power of which he had felt in his own soul.

A *second* characteristic of his teaching was the perfect clearness with which he presented every subject. His mind was both analytical and synthetical. Sometimes he combined thought with singular power. His resources of knowledge were large, and he often drew together truths and facts from various quarters and built up massive, cumulative arguments that we could see increasing in force and power until they reached an irresistible demonstration. But his chief power was analysis. A subject, as if by magic, seemed to fall in pieces in his hands, in its most lucid, logical, and striking form. The student often looked on with astonishment to see how the light penetrated a subject, and how the most abstruse things seemed reduced to perfect simplicity. This clearness of thought which was one of his great elements of power as an educator arose partly from his comprehensiveness of mind, and his peculiar capacity to balance points of thought and to exhibit them in all their relations and adjustments. We take it to be the attribute of a great mind to make difficult subjects simple and clear. It is just here that Dr Hodge shows his superiority to other men. His intellect penetrated so far down into the deep well of truth, that the water which he brought up was as clear as crystal.

Connected with his lucid thinking was his unusual capacity for putting questions. He had no vague generalities, he left nothing ambiguous, his questions went directly to the heart of the subject. He had the faculty of putting and of following up his questions with such skill as to stimulate the mind of the pupil in the highest degree and to make him detect and correct his own fallacies. In his examination of the class he was always kind and genial, and sometimes his vein of humour came to the surface. On one occasion he asked a student what the Apostle Paul meant by the expression, 'I am sold under sin.' 'He meant,' replied the student, 'that he was taken in, or deceived by sin.' 'Oh no,' exclaimed the Doctor, his eyes sparkling with fun, 'Paul was not a Yankee.'

Third. Another marked feature of Dr Hodge's teaching was its Scripturalness. He taught, not *what he thought*, but *what God said*, not what a *certain system required*, but what the *Scriptures reveal;* not what the learning or piety of past ages has formulated, but what the sure Word of truth has enunciated. With him, the simple question was. What do the Scriptures teach? And when this was ascertained by the light which the study of the original languages and exegetical investigation threw upon it, he did not think that it was our province to stop and inquire whether this was in harmony with our own reason, but to accept it with an humble and trustful spirit. When God speaks, and we understand his meaning, there is nothing left for us but to bow and adore.

From the earliest ages there has been a strong tendency upon the part of theological teachers to strain after novelties. There has been an impression that even in this sense, Theology is a progressive science, and that things old must be constantly giving place to things new. Hence the teacher must show his superiority to all who have ever preceded him by discovering in the Scriptures what no one had ever found before; or if he fails in this, he must exert his own ingenuity to invent a new system, and then show his power to twist the interpretation of the Scriptures to its support. Hence the whole track of the Church's history is strewn with novelties. From all such tendencies Dr Hodge was absolutely exempt. From originalities in this sense he shrank with alarm. On the day of his semi-centennial celebration, he turned with a beautiful simplicity to his brethren and said that 'Princeton had never been charged with originating a new idea'. To his mind this was a high distinction. It is mind that has made Princeton a synonym for greatness, but it was mind that feared God and never dared to originate what He had not taught.

Another tendency in the history of the Church is to mingle God's truth with the world's philosophy, and the admixture is sometimes proudly called a Philosophic Theology. We occasionally hear certain teachers styled Philosophic Theologians. The appellation is designed to be complimentary, but it has always seemed to me that if such men do not stand directly within sweep, their hair at least will be ruffled with the wind of Paul's tremendous denunciation. 'Though I or an angel from heaven preach any other gospel unto you, let him be accursed.' *Bible* ✓

This peril Dr Hodge avoided with a conscientious honesty, and with the most entire success. He did not teach a philosophy, but a theology. Neither his system, as a whole, or any part of it, was based upon philosophical principles apart from the Word of God. We do not mean to undervalue philosophy, nor do we mean to intimate that Dr Hodge had any light estimation of its worth. He was a philosopher as well as a theologian. In all his teachings he was abreast of the times. There was nothing in science or philosophy which he did not strive to master, and when such points came up in the course of theological discussion he showed how capable he was of pointing out every line of agreement, and every point of contrast, and of exhibiting the hollow pretences of every philosophy, falsely so called. It was just because of this mastery that he was able to keep philosophy in its proper place. He never sought to ally it with Gospel truth. Every student remembers, and his public works now show, with what a simple confidence he rested upon the Word of God for every proof, and that he never asked us to accept any one point of doctrine simply on the ground of a rational demonstration. He was not a rationalist in any sense of the word. His sole authority for everything was the teaching of the Scriptures.

Fourthly. Still another feature of Dr Hodge's teaching was its spirituality.

The teaching of some great and good Professors is purely intellectual; they develop splendid systems, reason with interest and force, and communicate abundance of instruction, but the impression which they make is purely intellectual. The students listen with a profound attention, just as students in other schools listen to lectures upon law and medicine – and go away, instructed, indeed, but without any spiritual or moral impression upon their minds or hearts. The reverse of all this was true of Dr Hodge. His was not a dead theology. It was instinct with life. What he gave us was bread from our Father's table. It was life to his soul, and he dispensed it to us under the deep conviction that it would be life to us, and that we could make it the Word of life to others. His great intellect shone in every discussion, but it was accompanied with spiritual power, and it made upon us a deep practical impression. He created an interest in the study of scientific theology, but his impression on us did not stop there; he made us feel that we were dealing with sacred things, and that these truths were to be to us and to others 'savours of life unto life or death unto death'.

A *Fifth* distinguished feature of Dr Hodge's teaching was what may be called its Christocentric character. Christ was the centre of his whole system. What he taught was 'The truth as it is in Jesus'. In this view all truth has its relations to Jesus, and nothing is truth in its highest sense, until it is seen and understood in this relation. There is truth in astronomy and geology, but these truths only attain their full significance when they are seen in their relation to Christ, and it is understood that the planets and stars and solid granite were made by Him, and that the end of their existence is to subserve his purpose. Separate what are called the truths of science from Christ, and they either lose their significance or become false lights that lure us into error. As in nature all things are luminous by reflecting the light of the sun, so in his theology, all things shine in the light of Christ and his cross. There was no point in his whole system of theology that did not derive its chief meaning from its relation to Christ. Did he speak of God? – it was God in Christ. 'He is the revelation of the invisible God.' When Professor Albert Dod died at Princeton, he left this message for the students of the College: 'Tell them that Jesus Christ is the God whom I worship.' When Dr Hodge in the funeral address delivered this message to the students which crowded the galleries, he threw into it a meaning that thrilled and penetrated every heart. Did he treat of creation? – it was the act of Christ. 'All things were created by Him, and without Him was not anything made that was made.' He knew nothing of a God who identified himself with nature, his God was extra-mundane, and creation was not part of himself but the effect of his fiat. He made this world for a purpose, and how grand it now is as the arena of redemption. Did he treat of Providence? – it is the moral government of Christ over this world, 'sustaining all things by the word of his power', and directing all things in the interests of his Church. Did he treat of the Fall? – it was in the light of the cross. The first Adam is best interpreted by the second Adam. Our ruin is best understood by our recovery, the greatness of our loss is demonstrated by the greatness of the price of our redemption. In the same manner, he taught us to look upon every subject as related to Christ. Man is nothing, Christ is everything. We have no worthiness, Christ is altogether worthy: He was so identified with us that he stood for us, we are so united to him that we stand in him; our acceptance with God from beginning to end is 'in the beloved'. He is the ground of our Election, the foundation of our Justification, the fontal head of our Regeneration, the means and medium of our Sanctification and the efficient cause and model of our glorification. He is all in all, and we are complete in Him.

I remember that as students under Dr Hodge we were deeply impressed with the conviction that the thought most in his mind was Christ, the being nearest his heart was Christ, the centre of all his theology was Christ. Now that many years have passed, and I have heard other teachers and read other authors, the impression grows upon me as I remember my early instructor, that no teacher, no author, so centralizes all things in Christ, or so uses all things to glorify Christ.

What I have thus far said of Dr Hodge embodies my estimate of him as he rises upon my memory, sitting in the class-room, and instructing us as students. Since that time, however, his great work upon *Theology*, in three volumes, has appeared, embodying the matured results of his life of thought and study. The estimate which the Church and the world will form of him as a theologian will be determined by this work. We are willing that he shall be so judged. Our own estimate is deepened and strengthened as we read these wonderful pages. We recognize familiar features in the book, but it is essentially a new work. I took elaborate notes of his lectures, and have them still, in three bound volumes; but there is not a single subject which is not changed both as to matter and treatment. The thought is wholly recast, new accumulations of learning are added, and the discussion adapted to the most recent phases of thought and opinion. The impression which it makes upon me is that of massive learning, of profound original investigation, of close, accurate, irresistible logic, and of a comprehensiveness which takes in the vast reach of thought in all its biblical and philosophical connections, and exhibits each point of truth in its relations to the whole.

The spirit of charity which reigns in this book will reflect honour upon its author in all time. Theology and controversy are inseparable, but here is controversy in its most beautiful and attractive form. He has no word of bitterness to utter, every sentence is kind, every difference of opinion is stated with fairness, and every argument is distinguished by candour and courtesy. Such volumes as these will do much to redeem theology from the discredit which the asperities of controversy have thrown upon it.

The system of theology which Dr Hodge leaves us is the old system which has been precious to the hearts of saints in all ages, and yet in an important sense it is his own system. Many recognize originality in nothing but novelty, but in a far higher sense Dr Hodge's system is original – it may be called Augustinian. Upon the day of his semi-centennial, he was called the greatest living Augustinian theologian. The leading features of these systems are alike. The great doctrines of grace which Augustine developed from the Scriptures with so much power, are no less characteristic features of Dr Hodge's theology. They both had the unction from the Holy One which teaches all things. They both speak from the depths of a profound spiritual experience. They were both natural logicians, and were prone to formulate their thought in a systematic expression; but the system of Dr Hodge is far more learned, far more intelligent and complete than that of Augustine. It is founded upon original investigation, and contains points of thought and methods of proof of which Augustine never dreamed. It may also be called Calvinistic, and yet the idea which arises in the popular mind at the word Calvinism is not realized in the system of Dr Hodge. There are two ways of presenting the same truth or doctrine; the one is in its hard, severe, repulsive form, and the other in its no less true but attractive garb. The shield of our faith has two sides; the one is a dark iron side, the other is its bright brazen side. To look on either side alone, will convey a false idea. It is only when we see them both in their unity and harmony that we get the true impression. This harmony Dr Hodge realized with great success. There is not one point of the Calvinistic system that he obscures, but he lets in upon it the full light of God's love and mercy until the heart melts into submission to His sovereignty.

The system of Dr Hodge may also be said to be that of the Westminster Confession and Catechisms, but he fills out those statements of doctrine in a much more complete and rounded form. The statements of the Confession are so accurate that we could never consent to the alteration of a single formula, but there can be no doubt that they need to be supplemented by those views of God's love and mercy and grace under which every doctrine of God's Word should be made to shine in its practical presentation. To the expounding of these doctrines in this light Dr Hodge was eminently fitted. His heart was filled with the love of God, and this light he shed over every doctrine, whilst at the same time his logical perception was so clear that he never sacrificed a point of truth out of the mere gush of emotion.

But whilst it is true that in all these respects the theology of Dr Hodge is the old system that is rendered sacred to us by the faith and experience of ages, it is, nevertheless, in an important sense his own. It is his own conception of what the Scriptures teach. He has reached these same conclusions by his own independent line of thought. It is the result of his own original investigation, and of his exegetical examination of the divine record. He has formulated the statement in his own way, articulated the system in his own logical sequences, and established it by his own proofs and modes of reasoning. His book remains to the Church as a precious treasure. As a living theologian he exerted a formative influence upon the theology of this country in the times of controversy and change, and now when he is gone this book will impress itself with great power upon the thought of ages to come.

As a Preacher.

As a preacher, Dr Hodge was distinguished by the same characteristics which marked him as a theologian. He was not an orator in the common sense of the term. He was too able to be popular. His train of thought was usually above the comprehension of the majority of hearers in an ordinary congregation. It was his habit to use a manuscript, and his reading was not animated. It is true, however, upon the other hand, that he was listened to by people of thought and education with the greatest interest. He always treated great subjects, and his clear thought, to those who would appreciate him, was like water from a crystal spring. I have frequently heard professional men speak with great satisfaction of the way in which their minds had been cleared upon certain subjects by hearing Dr Hodge preach. Others have quoted sayings which he uttered, and passages from his sermons which had made an impression upon their whole lives. His sermons upon public occasions were always great, because he selected important themes, and bestowed such thought and care upon their preparation. His sermon, for example, upon 'the teaching office of the Church', delivered before the Board of Foreign Missions, will remain as a treatise of permanent value, to instruct all those who wish to understand the principles which underlie the work of Missions.

The students who heard his preaching in the chapel will also remember a tender and devotional strain which often mingled with his great lines of thought, and produced a deep and lasting influence upon our hearts. Of this character I remember particularly a sermon upon our Lord's invitation to the 'labouring and heavy laden', which stirred the hearts of the students profoundly. It was just such a sermon as would stimulate a great revival of religion.

As a public speaker, Dr Hodge was most effective when he did not use a manuscript. On a few occasions, before smaller audiences, he spoke in this way, and always with much impression. This left him free to be influenced by his strong emotional nature, which sometimes rose into ascendancy, and invested him with the power of a great orator. No one who was present will ever forget an impromptu address which he delivered in the First Church, in Princeton, about the time his son sailed as a missionary to India. His fatherly affection working in unison with his religious feeling, awoke him to a power of pathos which thrilled the whole assembly with a wonderful impulse. Another instance of a similar kind occurred at the funeral of Professor Dod. They had been intimate friends. They were both great thinkers, and had often talked together upon the greatest themes. Dr Hodge had been with Professor Dod in his last hours, when his heart had been opened to speak of Christ, and his dying confidence. With these powerful impressions upon his mind, he arose to deliver his funeral address. Professor Dod had left with him a message for the College students. When he came to that point in his discourse, his heart swelled, and lifting his head from the manuscript, he stood erect, and waving his hand to the students who sat in the gallery, whilst the tears poured down his face, he delivered the message with a gust of emotion that went through that audience like the sweep of a storm through the forest. All hearts were broken, and for a moment were held and swayed by a mighty power. The scene stands before my mind this moment as the most powerful effect of oratory which I have ever witnessed.

3. HIS SOCIAL QUALITIES AND THE MAIN TRAITS OF HIS RELIGIOUS CHARACTER

By his life-long friend, Rev. Dr Henry A Boardman of Philadelphia

His social qualities.

A retired student, in close and habitual communion with the masterminds, ancient and modern, in the realms of Biblical criticism and theology, he was no pent-up recluse who saw nothing and cared for nothing beyond the sphere of his own professional engagements. His sympathies were as broad as our common humanity. And so vigilant an observer was he of events, that nothing of importance escaped his notice as he looked out through the loop-holes of his retreat upon the great Babel.

His visitors were sure to find him as much at home with the questions of the day, scientific or literary, political or financial, domestic, foreign or international, as though these had been his special study. Deep thinkers are apt to be poor talkers. It was pleasant to sit down with a man who, without being like Madame de Staël, simply 'admirable in monologue', could interest and instruct you upon any topic you might propose.

His home was in the empire of the affections. Never did a more kindly, loving heart throb in a human bosom. There were those of old who said to the Master, 'Thou hast a devil.' What wonder that some of their successors should charge the disciple with bigotry, intolerance, malignity? All they knew or cared to know was, that he was the accredited defender of a theology they hated. Accustomed as they are to associate with its avowed creed ideas of narrow-mindedness, virulence, and the like, they must needs take it for granted that the Pontifex Maximus of this creed was the very incarnation of these amiable qualities. Had they charged simply that he was resolute in maintaining his opinions; that he would make no compromise with what he believed to be error; that no adverse array of numbers, talent, official station, or personal vituperation, could repress the frankest expression of his sentiments on all fitting occasions; that, in a word, truth was dearer to him than life, and he would have stood for it like Luther at Worms, with an empire or a world in arms against it; had this been the indictment, no one could have traversed it. But when it comes to be a question of tone and temper, it is a different matter. Here he was a very child. Not one of his various eulogists has failed to advert to this feature of his character. Addicted as he was to laborious study in the grandest fields open to our research, and capable, beyond most men, of scaling the heights and sounding the depths which define the limits of human thought, he entered with a lively zest into the current talk of the hour, the amusements of children, the petty news-gatherings of his visitors – nothing, indeed, was too trivial to interest him.

In society, he was no monopolist like Coleridge and Macaulay, but, as already hinted, he was certainly one of the most fascinating of talkers. A very noticeable thing about him was the facility with which he would pass from the lightest to the gravest themes. Abounding as he did in anecdote, no boy enjoyed a good story more. Grim Calvinist as he was said to be, his airy spirit revealed itself in a tide of humour as inexhaustible as it was refreshing. Wit he had, no less; as many a remembered pleasantry, and many a sentence in his polemical essays will attest. But this keener weapon was kept more in reserve. It was wit as refined and sweetened into humour by sympathy, tenderness and affection, that set off to such advantage his massive intellectual powers, and sparkled through his conversation like the shimmer of the moonbeams upon the rippling lake. This beautiful gift – for such it surely is – never degenerated with him into irreverence, coarseness, or buffoonery. It never carried him so far away from the cross and its sublime verities that he could not pass at once, and without violence to his own feelings or those of others, from the sprightliest to the gravest topics; from the commerce of small talk, bristling with amusing reminiscences and brilliant repartee, to the discussion of some subtle question of metaphysics or theology, or the luminous exposition of some controverted scripture. Whatever the company or the theme, he was always natural. He never paraded his learning; never introduced a topic for the sake of 'showing off' upon it; never assumed, in his intercourse with his students or others, an air of superiority. His world-wide fame brought to his hospitable door numerous visitors from remote States and foreign countries ; and nothing surprised and charmed them more than the perfect simplicity and the quiet, unostentatious manners of the man whom they had been accustomed to look at from a distance with a sort of awe. With that inborn refinement and courtesy which came of his gentle blood, he aimed at drawing out his guests, while he listened; and, it must be said, he added to his many other graces the rare accomplishment of being a good listener, even where there was not much to listen to. If they thwarted his purpose and constrained him to do the talking, it was certain to be in a strain that would run out the hour glass very swiftly, but without one word designed for self-laudation. All the more surely did it win their homage. For it is a law written as well upon the heart as upon the inspired page, 'He that humbleth himself shall be exalted'; and when we meet with a person of rare powers or of signal usefulness, who loses sight of himself in his concern for the welfare of others, we instinctively pay him the tribute of our loving admiration. How could Dr Hodge's visitors help carrying away this feeling with them?

He was formed for friendship. His nature craved it. He could not do without it, and happily he was not put to the trial. I do not now refer to that home which was blessed and brightened with his presence, and where his loving heart found full scope and verge, and was in turn enriched by the reciprocal in-flow of a love as tender as his own. There was a circle outside of this upon which he lavished his warm affection. No niggard in his generous sympathies, his kindly wishes went out towards all whom he knew; and there were many who shared his love. But with him, as with us all, there were a chosen few whose place came next after his own household. Among the names which were oftenest on his lips were those of Johns and McIlvaine, Nevins and B. B. Wisner, Dod and James Alexander, and Van Rensselaer. All these preceded him to the better country. The first two were his fellow-students at Nassau Hall, and the first four were his companions in the Seminary. A brilliant constellation in the moral firmament – collectively, with the addition of him who was *facile princeps* [easily first] among them, they represented as much of mental power and brilliant imagination, of keen dialectic and exquisite taste, of racy humour and quick sensibility, of liberal letters and commanding eloquence, of Christian activity and usefulness, and, above all, in all, and through all, of humble, earnest piety, as could be found among any similar group selected from the entire rolls of our Seminaries and Colleges.

The ties which linked Dr Hodge with these kindred spirits were never severed nor weakened, except as, one by one, they were sundered by death.

The principal traits of his religious character.

'If a man love me, he will keep my words: and my Father will love him, and we will come unto him, and make our abode with him.' The remarkable phraseology here employed by the Saviour, which has no parallel in His other recorded utterances, clothes the promise with a significance beyond our grasp. But here, if anywhere, was one to whom it was given to enjoy the priceless distinction it conferred. Manifest it was to all eyes that the Father and the Son had come to him, not as a wayfaring man, to tarry for a night, but to *abide* with him; or, translating this unusual language into familiar phrase, that the Holy Spirit was given to him in a very unwonted measure. Rarely, if ever, did any one hear him speak of his own religious exercises; but this were as superfluous as to ask the harvest-moon where she gets her splendour. His daily walk betrayed the secret; and the Oratory, beyond all other spheres, showed that the 'hiding of his power' lay in that indwelling of the Spirit which made his life an habitual communion with God.

In these exercises, as in his prayers – above all, his prayers at the family-altar – the Christological type of his piety constantly appeared. Not Rutherford himself was more absorbed with the love of Christ. Around this central sun, and so near to it as to be always aglow with its beams, his whole being revolved. Christ was not only the ground of his hope, but the acknowledged sovereign of his intellect, the soul of his theology, the unfailing spring of his joy, the one all-pervading, all glorifying theme and end of his life. His very presence was felt by his students as a benediction – a means of grace, carrying with it a silent rebuke, an encouragement, a stimulus to watchfulness and fidelity – according to their individual needs. A

personality like this has a power all its own. It is something different from talent, learning, eloquence, dialectic skill, affable manners,
or all these combined. You cannot see it. You cannot define it. But
you can and must feel it. No one could sit down with Dr Hodge
without feeling it – perhaps more sensibly than with almost any
one they will have known. And these young men felt it, not only in
'his opening prayers, which seemed to constitute his class-room a
Bethel, and the savour of which was as the incense of morn to the
soul, wooing it upward to communion with God',[1] but through the
entire routine of the daily lecture or recitation, and, no less, in their
familiar visits to his study.

If one were called upon to specify the most conspicuous feature
of Dr Hodge's religious character, next to that pure love with which
his whole nature was transfused, it would be his *humility* – perhaps
the most distinctively Christian grace in the whole garniture of
the believer. Here was a man clothed with brilliant intellectual
gifts, an accomplished scholar, laden with generous stores of the
choicest learning, his utterances on all ecclesiastical and dogmatic
questions listened to by a great church with a deference accorded to
no other living teacher, lauded by eminent theologians in Europe
and America as 'the theologian of the age', and the constant object
of undisguised and loving reverence to all around him, yet modest
and unassuming as a child – never asserting his consequence; never
obtruding his opinions; never courting a compliment; never saying
or doing anything for effect; never challenging attention to himself
in any way. Of course he could not be blind to the homage which
was paid him from every quarter; but his own estimate of himself
was framed by quite another standard. His vast learning taught him
that he had barely crossed the border of that boundless domain of
truth which stretches off in every direction into the infinite; and his
habitual feeling was that of La Place, who, being complimented,
when near his end, on the splendour of his attainments, replied:

---

[1] Article in the *British and Foreign Evangelical Review*, by his distinguished pupil,
Professor Robert Watts, D.D., of Assembly's College, Belfast.

'What we know is very little; what we do not know is immense.' So in respect to his personal piety. To all eyes but his own he had approached as near to 'the stature of a perfect man in Christ Jesus' as any, the most favoured, of those saints whose names the church has embalmed. But so clear was his apprehension of the spotless holiness of God, so transcendent his views of the love of Christ and the debt we owe Him, and so inwrought his sense of the turpitude of sin, that he could only think of himself as a poor, miserable sinner saved by grace ineffable, whose best services were utterly unfit to be presented to God, whose purest aspirations were too impure to be accepted save through the ever-prevalent intercession of our great High Priest. Here, indeed, was a clear intimation that the path he was treading lay close along the suburbs of the heavenly city. For the inevitable effect of a near discovery of the divine glory must always be what it was with Isaiah and the beloved apostle – to overwhelm the soul with a sense of its own vileness. Therefore it was that our dear Professor was ever 'clothed with humility' – *clothed* with it: it covered him like 'a raiment of needlework' – covered all the powers of his mind, all the treasures of his learning, all the wealth of his affections, all that made him great and good, loving and beloved, all that moved us to look upon him as one given to the church (may it be allowed me to say) to show how much a Christian may, even in this world, become like Christ.[1]

The topics with which we have now been engaged have brought into view the gentler side of Dr Hodge's character. There are those who will regard the qualities indicated as revealing a certain sort of weakness – pardonable indeed, but still a weakness; and an impeach-

---

[1] May I illustrate this point by an incident not related at the delivery of the discourse. I was saying, 'You ought to be a very happy man. Consider what you have accomplished, and the universal feeling towards you –' 'Now, stop!' said he, with a wave of the hand. 'All that can be said is, that God has been pleased to take up a poor little stick and do something with it. What I have done is as nothing compared with what is done by a man who goes to Africa, and labours among a heathen tribe, and reduces their language to writing. I am not worthy to stoop down and unloose the shoes of such a man.'

ment, so far, of the title asserted for him by his friends to have his place assigned him among the really 'great' men of this age. It is simply a question as to what constitutes true greatness. In the common judgment of the learned world, this distinction belongs by preeminence to pure intellect in its loftiest manifestations, as, e.g., in the case of Thomas Aquinas or Kant. Others would enthrone in their Pantheon the men who combine with rare intellectual gifts, rich stores of knowledge, a wide range of literary accomplishment, and a voice or pen that can instruct and fascinate whole nations – like Cicero or Goethe. Others still, taught in a better school, would have an intellectual Colossus, not only decorated with the triumphs and trophies of genius, but animated by a spirit of genuine piety – devout and conscientious – 'walking uprightly, working righteousness, and speaking the truth', meeting all the claims of justice and equity, and really kind at heart, albeit stern, phlegmatic, unsympathizing. No one would refuse to accord the epithet 'great' to the choice spirits who make up any one of these classes; but do they, singly or united, supply all the attributes essential to constitute the *highest type* of greatness? Can it be necessary to answer this question, with the New Testament open before us? This world has seen, since the Fall, but one perfect man. If you deify intellectual force, vast erudition, philosophic penetration, here is one upon all whose faculties is the stamp of infinitude; whose mind holds in its grasp all time and all space; who guides alike the stars in their orbits, and the pollen that floats through the summer air; and in comparison with whom the magnates of your eulogy are but nursery-striplings. Yet where will you find such meekness, such humility, such affectionateness? What language have you to describe His ineffable tenderness, His gentle bearing towards the erring, His ready sympathy with every form of sorrow and suffering, His overflowing love towards friends and foes. His delight in little children – in a word, that whole life which was in truth a child-life? No one, standing in the presence of Jesus of Nazareth, will have the presumption to deny that we have here the very highest style of humanity; and that these milder graces are just as indispensable to its completeness as that array of grand intellectual endowments to which the world pays willing homage.

Now why do I introduce our blessed Saviour upon this scene? Is it that we may challenge for our friend whom we today commemorate, the first place among the great men of our race? Is it that we may exalt him above this or that illustrious philosopher or theologian in or out of the church? Far from it. It is simply to show that his true position is among the very foremost of a class never large, and augmented by only a few names in the course of a century, who illustrate the supreme type of greatness – a type which demands the union of the rarest mental power, with self-abnegation, patience, kindliness, and a feminine tenderness of disposition. The combination of strength and gentleness in his character was not merely conspicuous; it was transcendent: as among the men whom we may, any of us, have known, it was unequalled – unapproached. It was the admiration of all who met him. It was the charm that captivated his friends. It was the secret of that magnetic power which he exerted over so many hearts. It was at once the fruit and the evidence of his close assimilation to that loving Saviour in whose love he rejoiced with a joy unspeakable and full of glory. The mind struggles in vain to conceive what must be the rapture of such a soul on being received into a world whose very atmosphere is love – into the immediate presence of that adored Redeemer, whose nature is the same as when He *wept* with the sisters of Bethany, at the very moment He was about to command the grave to give back its dead.

Here, then, we have the true criterion of Dr Hodge's greatness. It is not questioned that there have been men of still loftier intellectual culture, nor that there are names still more suggestive of universal knowledge. But no example is recalled in which an imperial intellect, mature scholarship, a creative imagination, acute sensibility, taste, affectionateness, sterling humour, a soldier's courage and a woman's gentleness, the freshness of youthful feeling unimpaired at fourscore, and all the graces of the Spirit, were more exquisitely blended. In the perfect harmony of his mental and moral powers, the purity and benevolence of his life, the wisdom and felicity of his doctrine, and the charm of his conversation, we recognize the completeness of a character, the like of which we do not expect to see this side of heaven. From our heart of hearts we render thanks to that God who made him what he was, and blessed the church with his presence for eighty years.

4. GENERAL ESTIMATE OF DR HODGE'S *SYSTEMATIC THEOLOGY*

BY CHARLES P. KRAUTH, D.D.,
Professor of Theology in the Lutheran Theological Seminary, Philadelphia

The work opens with an Introduction, which treats of Method; Theology; Rationalism; Mysticism; the Rule of Faith in the Roman Catholic and Protestant view.

The *First Part* embraces Theology proper; under which are treated: Origin of the Idea of God; Theism; Antitheistic Theories; Knowledge of God; His Nature and Attributes; the Trinity; Divinity of Christ; the Holy Spirit; the Decree of God; Creation; Providence; Miracles; Angels.

The *Second Part* is occupied with Anthropology; Man, his Origin and Nature; Origin of the Soul; Unity of the Human Race; Original State of Man; Covenant of Works; the Fall; Sin; Free Agency.

The *Third Part* presents Soteriology: the Plan of Salvation; Covenant of Grace; the Person of Christ; His Mediatorial Work; Prophetic and Priestly Offices; Satisfaction; for Whom did Christ Die? Theories of the Atonement; Christ's Intercession; Kingly Offce; Humiliation; Exaltation; Vocation; Regeneration; Faith; Justification; Sanctification; the Law, with a Particular Commentary on each Commandment; the Means of Grace; the Word of God; the Sacraments; Baptism; the Lord's Supper; Prayer.

The *Fourth Part* is Eschatology: the State of the Soul after Death; Resurrection; Second Advent; Concomitants of the Second Advent.

Of the general fullness and logical order of this arrangement there can be no question. The discussion of the Divinity of Christ as distinct from the Trinity might perhaps better have been given under Soteriology, so as not to separate the 'Divinity of Christ' from the 'Person of Christ'. The most important defect in the plan is that it does not embrace a distinct and full treatment of the doctrine concerning the Church. The omission has been made for some reason which satisfies Dr Hodge. We hope that it means that he proposes to give to the Church a monograph on this subject, one of the most vitally important and interesting doctrines of all times, but especially in our own day. We know of no man more competent than Dr Hodge to rebuke, with the effectual weapons of fact and logic, the insane pretences of the rampant pseudo-ecclesiasticism of our time, and the yet insaner radicalism, which frightens many into the ecclesiasticism.

The first thing which strikes us in reading Dr Hodge's book is the style. Whether we shall accept or reject what he maintains may sometimes involve a question, or a pause; but his simple, luminous mode of statement rarely leaves us in any embarrassment as to *what* it is on which we are to decide. The sentences are never involved. The language is a model of clearness. There is a plain solid sense, the result of a sound judgment thoroughly matured, which is delightful beyond expression in this day and land of fine writing. This, of course, will expose Dr Hodge to the charge of shallowness, from those who think that nothing is deep but what is unintelligible, and that the art of good writing is the art of putting words to things in the proportion of Falstaff's sack to Falstaff's bread,[1] and that the measure of words is like the measure of Falstaff in the girth.

Another great feature of Dr Hodge's book is, its value to our common Christianity – nay, in a wide sense, to religion on that broader definition in which the believing Jew has a common interest with the Christian. To the gratitude of Jew and Christian, Dr Hodge is

[1] 'One half-penny-worth of bread to this intolerable deal of sack' (sweet wine); Shakespeare's *Henry IV, Part 1*, Act 2, Scene 4. [Ed.]

entitled by the able vindication of Revelation against the assaults
which would bring the faith of Jew and Christian alike to the dust.
To Roman Catholic and Protestant, Dr Hodge comes with a defence
of the common creeds of Christendom; to Calvinist and Lutheran,
with the able argument on the distinctive elements of Protestantism
and the precious truths reasserted by the original Churches of the
Reformation. Even in its relative isolation as distinctively Calvinistic, Dr Hodge's book is invaluable. It is the gauge of the type of
Calvinism which is considered by its ablest living representatives
as tenable; a Calvinism so gentle in its spirit toward other forms of
evangelical Christianity, and so full of the disposition to mitigate
its own harder points, as to furnish irenical elements of the most
hopeful kind.

The general mildness, fairness, and clearness of the book are far
beyond dispute. It treats Polemics in the spirit of Irenics, for the
most part, but with here and there a delightful little dash of merited
sarcasm, a suspicion of irony, a playful contempt for small presumption, and a quiet smile at the absurd, which humanize the argument,
and, with those touches which make the whole world kin, bring
the author nearer to the reader. Nor are there wanting earnest and
eloquent passages, which deal with sin in a manner in keeping with
its exceeding sinfulness, and with conscious perversions after their
evil deserts. There is no amiable inanity in the book. It is not done
in water-colours, as some people would think it must be, because it
is not executed with a red-hot poker on an oak-board. Yet its prevailing character is mild, quiet, firm, judicial. If it is often pleading, it is
still more frequently the decision of a judge, who sums up evidence,
interprets the law, and pronounces the sentence.

The evidences of enormous, yet reflective reading, everywhere
present themselves, reading of the most varied kind, among the
best books and the worst books. There is a gathering of honey for
stores, and of poisons for the study of antidotes. The range stretches
over the ages, takes in largely the German theology, and reaches
apparently almost to the days in which the volumes have come from

the press. The result of this anxiety to bring things down to the hour has necessarily been that some of the latest reading has been hasty and has involved Dr Hodge in mistakes. But the Doctor's greatest weakness, in this immensity of reading, is where it might least have been suspected – it is in Calvinistic theology. He seems to have neglected a part of the Calvinistic theologians of no inconsiderable number and bulk. On his own confession, so far as his memory can recall, he has failed to have seen a single one of a very large and influential portion of those divines, so large in fact that for some two centuries it is hard to find one who does not belong to it. But we account for this on the principles of a latent elective affinity. Like seeks only its like and holds it. There rise up in history the grim and grisly features of those old divines who liked election but who loved reprobation; who conceived of the human race as created chiefly as fuel for Tophet, – divines who would have thought nothing of the perdition of a universe or two, and, if necessary, of throwing themselves in, if their logic proved that it was all for God's greater glory – those inexorable Jonahs on whom a wilderness of gourds would have been lost in the attempt to reconcile them to the sparing of Nineveh. If Dr Hodge long ago encountered these divines, he quietly turned away into his own brighter path, with other visions of the divine glory. He did not plunge into the Sahara, in the possibility of finding an oasis. Penetrated, as all his works show, with the completest recognition which is possible to Calvinism, that God is love, Calvinism itself is hardly in sharper contrast with Lutheranism than, within Calvinism, Dr Hodge himself is with Gomarus and his pitiless school. The only apology which can be made for that school is that which they constantly make for themselves – that the logic of the system is with them, and that they are with the logic of the system. They did not create the horrors, they only told of them.

The general tone of the book is profoundly devout. Though Dr Hodge has moved largely and freely in the living world, his most marked affinities are yet with the old. He saith 'the old is better'.

He has not put enough of the new wine into the old bottles to rend them – except perhaps in a spot or two. In spite of recent reading, and of the space devoted to the callow heresies of the hour, the conception and organism of the book is prevailingly scholastic, of the old Protestant type. It is old-fashioned theology in the main; and, like the best old-fashioned theology, it has the heart of living piety beating through it. It is not satisfied with teaching *about* theology: it teaches theology, it is theology – a true *'theologia regenitorum'* [theology of the regenerate]. Its solid judgment and learning will mark it to scholars as one of the classics of Calvinistic Dogmatics, the ablest work in its specific department in English literature. But it is more than this, better than this. The graces of Christian life are not repressed in it, as they have often been in the arid formulating of systems. Molière's Mock Doctor[1] claimed no more than that the medical profession had changed the place of the heart from the left side to the right; some of the doctors in theology have left the heart out altogether. But in Dr Hodge's Body of Divinity there is a heart whose beat is that of the fullest health – and you can touch the system nowhere without feeling a pulse. It is a book for the affections. No man could obtrude himself less in his books than Dr Hodge does; yet all the more for this very reason do we see the man himself in his books. His life has been shaped upon the advice of old Sir John Davies:[2]

> Study the best and highest things that are,
> But of thyself, an humble thought retain.

Dr Hodge's system furnishes a general landmark for Christian thinking in one of its most influential shapes; it also furnishes a revelation of the spirit of Christian science, a picture of the Christian scholar, a miniature of the Christian life. Dr Hodge constitutes in himself a distinct evidence of Christianity, and alike in what he writes and what he is, vindicates the supremacy of Protestant culture.

[1] In Molière's comedy, *Le Medecin malgré Lui* (1666). [Ed.]
[2] English poet, 1569–1626. [Ed.]

It is a marked feature in Dr Hodge's book that it does unusual justice to the relative importance of Lutheran theology. There are but two developed systems in the world that claim with any show of probability to be purely Biblical. These systems are the Lutheran and the Calvinistic. They possess a common basis in their recognition of the same rule of faith; their profession of the Old Catholic faith as set forth in the three General Creeds; in their acknowledgment of the doctrine of justification by faith and of its great associated doctrines; and they have vast interests, great stakes, mighty bonds of sympathy in common. No two bodies of Christians have more reason for thoroughly understanding each other than Calvinists and Lutherans have, and no two parts of Christendom are closer together in some vital respects than consistent Calvinism and consistent Lutheranism. It is well worth their while to compare views.

But Dr Hodge is not only full in his notices of Lutheran theology – he is also fair. Mistakes he has made, and very important ones; but designed misrepresentations he has never made. Next to having Dr Hodge on one's side is the pleasure of having him as an antagonist; for where conscientious men must discuss a subject, who can express the comfort of honourable, magnanimous dealing on both sides – the feeling that in battling with each other they are also battling for each other, in that grand warfare whose final issue will be what all good men desire, the establishment of truth?

INDEX

651

Where is Happiness to be found?

Jay Gould : worth $72 million dollars said :–
' I suppose I am the most miserable man on earth."

George Eastman (Photographic Industry!) worth
$75 million – Suicide March 1932 (60 yrs old).

Lord Byron – indulged earthly pleasures :– wrote.
' My days are in yellow leaf – The flowers and fruits
of love are gone – The Canker, and grief are
mine alone.'

Alexander the Great : Wept in his tent: 'Oh there's no more
worlds to conquer!"

Voltaire " I wish I'd never been born!" "I am
abandoned by God and man.'

— · — · — · —

— The Lord Jesus Christ said:" <u>I am the Way, the
Truth and the Life.</u>"

— God So Loved the World, that HE GAVE His only
begotten Son, that whosoever believeth in HIM should
— not perish, but have everlasting life John 3:16.

— <u>By grace are ye saved</u> through Faith : and that not
of yourselves: it is the Gift of God. Eph. 2.v8.

— <u>Jesus Said</u>:" <u>Come unto me</u>, all the ends of the earth
and be saved :

— The wages of Sin is death : But the Gift of God
is (Forgiveness of Sins) and eternal life through
        Jesus Christ of our Lord Romans 6:23.

Jesus Said :–
" Seek Ye first the Kingdom of God
            Matthew 6:33.